CULTURE
AND
PSYCHOPATHOLOGY

CULTURE AND PSYCHOPATHOLOGY

Edited by
Ihsan Al-Issa, Ph.D.
Professor
Department of Psychology
University of Calgary
Calgary, Alberta, Canada

University Park Press
Baltimore

UNIVERSITY PARK PRESS
International Publishers in Science, Medicine, and Education
300 North Charles Street
Baltimore, Maryland 21201

Copyright © 1982 by University Park Press

Typeset by Oberlin Printing Company
Manufactured in the United States of America by The Maple Press Company

Library of Congress Cataloging in Publication Data

Main entry under title:

Culture and psychopathology.

Includes index.
1. Psychology, Pathological—Cross-cultural studies. I. Al-Issa, Ihsan.
[DNLM: 1. Cross-cultural comparisons. 2. Psychopathology. 3. Research.
4. Mental disorders. WM 31 C968]
RC455.4.E8C83   616.89'07   81-11508
ISBN 0-8391-1679-9   AACR2

CONTENTS

CONTRIBUTORS

Ihsan Al-Issa, Ph.D.
Department of Psychology
University of Calgary
2500 University Drive N.W.
Calgary, Alberta T2N 2A4
Canada

Herbert Barry, III, Ph.D.
Department of Pharmacology
School of Pharmacy
University of Pittsburgh
1100 Salk Hall
Pittsburgh, Pennsylvania 15261

George W. Brown, Ph.D.
Department of Sociology
Bedford College
University of London
Inner Circle, Regents Park
London NW1 4NS
England

Juris G. Draguns, Ph.D.
Department of Psychology
The Pennsylvania State University
417 Bruce V. Moore Bldg.
University Park,
Pennsylvania 16802

Frank Engelsmann, Ph.D.
Allan Memorial Institute
1025 Pine Avenue West
Montreal, Quebec H3A 1A1
Canada

H. J. Eysenck, Ph.D., D.Sc.
Department of Psychology
Institute of Psychiatry
DeCrespigny Park
Denmark Hill
London SE5 8AF
England

S. B. G. Eysenck, Ph.D.
Department of Psychology
Institute of Psychiatry
DeCrespigny Park
Denmark Hill
London SE5 8AF
England

Horacio Fabrega, Jr., M.D.
Western Psychiatric Institute
University of Pittsburgh
3811 O'Hara Street
Pittsburgh, Pennsylvania 15261

Tirril Harris, M.A.
Department of Sociology
Bedford College
University of London
Inner Circle, Regents Park
London NW1 4NS
England

Joseph B. Juhasz, Ph.D.
Environmental Design College
University of Colorado
Boulder, Colorado 80302

Stewart Meikle, Ph.D.
Department of Psychology
University of Calgary
2500 University Drive N.W.
Calgary, Alberta T2N 1N4
Canada

H. B. M. Murphy, M.D., Ph.D.
Department of Psychiatry
Section of Transcultural
Psychiatric Studies
McGill University
1266 Pine Avenue West
Montreal, Quebec H3G 1A8
Canada

Wolfgang M. Pfeiffer, M.D.
Institut für Medizinische
Psychologie
Westfälische Wilhelms-Universität
Hüfferstrasse 75
Münster 44
West Germany

David Rosenthal, Ph.D.
Laboratory of Psychology &
Psychopathology
National Institute of Mental
Health
NIH Bldg. 31, Room 4C33
Bethesda, Maryland 20014

Victor D. Sanua, Ph.D.
Department of Psychology
St. John's University
Grand Central and Utopia
Parkways
Jamaica, New York 11439

Theodore R. Sarbin, Ph.D.
Adlai E. Stevenson College
University of California
Santa Cruz, California 95064

Hector Warnes, M.D.
Department of Psychiatry
Faculty of Medicine
University of Ottawa
Ottawa General Hospital
501 Smyth Road, Room 4420
Ottawa, Ontario K1H 8L6
Canada

Matisyohu Weisenberg, Ph.D.
Department of Psychology
Bar Ilan University
Ramat Gan
Israel

Eric D. Wittkower, M.D.
Department of Psychiatry
Section of Transcultural
Psychiatric Studies
McGill University
1266 Pine Avenue West
Montreal, Quebec H3G 1A8
Canada

PREFACE

During the last two decades, there has been increasing interest in the effects of culture on psychopathology. Reports of cross-cultural research in psychopathology from both individual and collaborative research teams have become more common in journals and at national and international meetings. This volume brings together those achievements that have increased our understanding of the relationship between culture and psychopathology. The book covers almost the whole spectrum of psychopathology, including functional, personality, and psychosomatic and other organic disorders. The contents of the book reflect the interdisciplinary nature of research in psychopathology, involving psychiatry, psychology, sociology, anthropology, and genetics. The book also reflects the belief that the effects of culture on behavior cannot be isolated from basic psychological processes and from the biological makeup of the organism.

Research presented in this volume, not unlike research in psychopathology within and across cultures in general, is dominated by assumptions and concepts derived from the medical model. However, other alternatives to the medical model, such as the dimensional model and the cultural relativity approach to psychopathology, which have been gaining strength and popularity among researchers, are also represented. Many research areas that as yet have not been systematically investigated cross-culturally, such as genetics, social class, the family, and sex roles, are discussed in separate chapters to emphasize their potential for future research. Readers may note that there is no separate chapter on culture and psychotherapy or on other types of treatment. We believe that psychiatric treatment is still a controversial area, containing much speculation but little cross-cultural data. However, research on treatment has been incorporated into Chapters 1, 8, and 9.

The research presented here should demonstrate convincingly that the study of culture and psychopathology has passed from an era of speculation on, and description of, the exotic habits of foreign countries to the objective collection of data and the use of sophisticated methodology. This volume should also be a useful source of information and a stimulus for further research to students interested in the effects of culture on behavior. Because of its interdisciplinary approach, this publication is of particular interest to social scientists in the areas of anthropology, psychiatry, psychology, sociology, social work, and social medicine.

Many of the distinguished contributors to this volume have influenced my own research and thinking, and I am pleased that readers also are now able to share these ideas. In particular, I am indebted to Professor Hans J. Eysenck for his influence on me inside and outside the Institute of Psychiatry and for his encouragement to proceed with this book. I am also grateful to Professor E. D. Wittkower and Professor H. B. M. Murphy of the Section of Transcultural Psychiatric Studies at McGill University, Montreal, for their helpful suggestions during my organization of the volume. Since my arrival in Canada in 1966, I have found a continuous source of stimulation through direct contact with Professor Wittkower and with Professor Murphy as well as through reading the *Transcultural Psychiatric Research Review,* which is edited by them. Thanks also to Professor William H. Davenport and to Professor Albert C. Heinrich for their comments on individual chapters of this book.

Ihsan Al-Issa

CULTURE
AND
PSYCHOPATHOLOGY

I

INTRODUCTION

Chapter 1

Does Culture Make a Difference in Psychopathology?

Ihsan Al-Issa

THE STUDY OF CULTURE AND PSYCHOPATHOLOGY

Many definitions have been suggested for the concept of culture (Kroeber and Kluckhohn, 1952). Most definitions regard culture as those aspects of the environment that are man-made, including the subjective environment, which consists of the beliefs, values, norms, and myths that are shared by the group and symbolically transmitted to its members, as well as the physical environment, which is comprised of artifacts like roads, bridges, and buildings that are handed down from one generation to another. The concept of psychopathology, on the other hand, is most often used as an equivalent of mental illness.

In the area of cross-cultural psychology in general and culture and psychopathology in particular, cultural variables are usually differentiated from psychological variables (such as learning, motivation, and perception) and from genetic-biological variables. In contrast to cultural variables, which are considered to be dependent on specific cultural settings, psychological and genetic-biological variables are supposed to represent those basic human processes that are the same wherever they are encountered. For example, processes involved in learning (e.g., acquisition, extinction, and discrimination) are thought to be the same all over the world, although the rates of learning may vary from one individual to

This work was completed during a Killam Resident Fellowship at the University of Calgary.

another or from one situation to another. Similarly, the process of genetic transmission is assumed to be universally the same, although genetic endowment may vary between individuals and groups. A major objective in the investigation of psychopathology across cultures is the evaluation of the relative influence of psychological and genetic-biological variables within the context of different cultures. This objective is clearly reflected in the major questions put forward by researchers in the area of culture and psychopathology: Are concepts of mental illness and the Western system of psychiatric diagnosis universal and applicable to other cultures? Are the incidence of mental illness and its symptomatology the same across cultures? Are there culture-bound syndromes? If culture-bound syndromes do exist, are they the same types of syndromes familiar to Western psychiatrists, but merely expressed differently, or do they represent different psychiatric entities?

Early in this century, Emil Kraepelin traveled to Southeast Asia and to other parts of the world to find answers to some of these questions (Lauter, 1965). He reported that mental illness as known in the West (such as dementia praecox and manic-depressive syndrome) does exist in non-Western countries, but it differs in incidence and symptomatology from its Western counterpart. Kraepelin also observed culture-bound syndromes (such as amok and latah) in Southeast Asia, but he believed them to be similar to diseases common in the West (hysteria, catatonic episodes, epileptic twilight, for example). With the orientation of a biologist, he concluded that Western disease entities are universal (Lauter, 1965), and his initiative later inspired epidemiological research in different cultures. Many of his findings on variations in the incidence and symptomatology of psychopathology have been confirmed by more recent epidemiological research. [See H.B.M. Murphy (Chapter 9) on schizophrenia and Engelsmann (Chapter 10) on depression, this volume.]

The finding that psychopathology is a universal phenomenon supports the view that it is part of human nature, and that, although they do not eliminate it completely, some cultural contexts may influence only the threshold of its manifestations. This is particularly true of those universal abnormalities that are demonstrated to have a biological basis. On the other hand, finding psychopathology in some cultures but not in others suggests that it is culture-bound rather than the inevitable destiny of human existence. Similarly, attempts by cross-cultural psychopathologists to differentiate between the pathoplastic and the pathogenic aspects of symptomatology imply that psychopathology may be expressed in culture-bound symptoms, which bear the marks of culture and are closely associated with the cultural context, as well as in universal symptoms, which are considered to be an inherent part of the disease.

A general trend in the early development of the study of culture and psychopathology was to dichotomize the world into Western and non-Western cultures. This strategy, which is described by Sarbin and Juhasz as "a cognitive separation between *Us* and *Them,*" took two opposite and extreme forms. One approach is characteristically expressed by the "nature cult" of the eighteenth century, which attributed the increase of insanity in Europe to a degeneration from "a golden age of natural virtue" (Rosen, 1968, p. 182). The Freudian conflict model of psychopathology seems to be compatible with this view. In *Civilization and Its Discontents,* Freud (1961) conceptualized neurosis as the result of a conflict between instinctual drives and the repressive processes of civilization. A major cross-cultural hypothesis derived from this approach is that non-Western life-style provides an immunity against mental illness, but research data in support of this idea are disappointingly negative (Eaton and Weil, 1955). The second approach is very closely associated with the historical development of the concept of mental illness. [See Sarbin and Juhasz (Chapter 3), this volume, for details.] Psychopathology, according to this view, represents a regression to a childish and rather primitive level of development. Western civilization, which is symbolized by industrial supremacy and Christian morality, constitutes an ultimate stage of human evolution and mental health. In accord with this view, high rates of mental illness would be predicted in non-Western cultures.

A division between Western and non-Western cultures has not proven to be a viable method of examining research data. The relationship between culture and psychopathology seems to be mediated by more specific factors than simply a variation in the degree of westernization. When only westernization is taken into consideration, epidemiological data on psychopathology are inconsistent. For example, there have been reports that schizophrenia (Torrey, 1973) and depression (Kiev, 1972) are very rare in non-Western cultures. In contrast, Field (1960) and Orley and Wing (1979) reported excessive rates of depression among African women. Similarly, Murphy (Chapter 9, this volume) reported high rates of schizophrenia, not only among the Irish (a Western group), but also among the Singapore Indians and among some tribes in Ghana and Liberia. Thus, westernization alone seems to be a poor predictor of rates of psychopathology.

Cross-cultural differences in psychopathology and its symptoms may be expected on the basis of the diathesis-stress hypothesis. It is accepted by the majority of Western researchers that variation in the rates of psychopathology among individuals within the same culture reflects the interaction between genetic predisposition and environmental factors. Moving from the intracultural to the cross-cultural level, one finds that peoples of the world vary so much in their environment, and perhaps in their genetic predisposition, that it seems almost impossible to expect the same rates of psychopathology across cultures.[1]

Although the mode of genetic transmission of psychopathology is still a controversial issue, the degree of biological relation that is used to estimate the genetic component of psychopathology or other behavior is an invariant criterion across cultures; that is, the biological family (brothers, sisters, and parents) can be objectively defined regardless of the cultural background of, or the family system adopted by, the group. However, the definition of cross-cultural variables, including that of psychopathology itself, may raise many rather complex problems that may be even more intractable than those encountered in research carried out within one culture. In the testing of a hypothesis, or in the study of empirical relationship within and across cultures, variables must be precisely defined through reference to direct operations in which each single variable is represented by a single operation (Sears, 1970). In the area of psychopathology, an operational definition for symptoms may be easier to achieve than one for syndromes. Auditory hallucinations, for example, may be defined as the reported hearing of voices from nonexisting stimuli. However, in dealing with psychiatric syndromes, the variables under investigation are removed from a perceptually unique measurement operation. Schizophrenia, depression, and other psychiatric syndromes are concepts that subsume several kinds of behavior or actions, and therefore they cannot be measured by a single operation. Whether or not these actions and behaviors underlying psychiatric syndromes are the same in different cultures raises the problem of conceptual nonequivalence (or equivalence); that is, whether or not psychiatric syndromes represent a unitary kind of behavior that exists in the behavioral repertoires of all peoples, regardless of the cultures in which they are brought up. Conceptual nonequivalence is, of course, the major issue in the etic-emic approaches to cross-cultural psychology (Triandis, 1980). Draguns (Chapter 2, this volume) has pointed out that cross-cultural psychopathology tends to be etic in orientation, because researchers have assumed that concepts and measures of mental illness are universal.

Basic to the issue of transcultural variables and their conceptual nonequivalence is the view that culture is a complex system of signs and symbols that provides the context and meaning without which concepts and behavior cannot be intelligently described (Geertz, 1973). Thus, cultural variables may resist measurement and comparison across cultures

---

[1]In her discussion of the rates of mental illness among Canadian (18%), Eskimo (19%), and Yoruba (15%) groups, Jane M. Murphy (1976) presented the opposite view. She pointed out that the rates of mental illness are so similar from one culture to another that its causes, whether genetic or experiential, are ubiquitous in human groups. Data reported in many chapters of this volume do not support the view that rates of mental illness are similar across cultures.

because it is difficult to isolate them from the context and meaning in which they are embedded (Edgerton, 1980; Price-Williams, 1980). Consider, for example, recent results from the International Pilot Study of Schizophrenia (WHO, 1973, 1979). It has been shown that it is possible to develop an equivalent transcultural diagnosis of schizophrenia based on common symptomatology; similar groups of schizophrenic patients can be identified by indigenous psychiatrists in countries with different cultures and different socioeconomic systems. However, it has been found that prognosis and rates of recovery are not equivalent among the various centers of investigation. Cultural beliefs and expectations about the nature of illness (for example, short-term versus chronic illness) as well as other variables reported by Murphy (Chapter 9, this volume) may explain these cultural differences. However, these variables, which may bear a possible relationship to the rates of prognosis and recovery, cannot be compared across cultures before a holistic study is made of individual sociocultural contexts, in order to unravel the world of meaning in which the patients and their compatriots live (Edgerton, 1980). Indeed, as Fabrega has convincingly argued, (Chapter 14, this volume) understanding of the semantic aspects of culture (its context and meaning) is important not only in the study of variables related to psychopathology, such as schizophrenia and depression, but also in the study of those variables related to physical illness. Conceptual nonequivalence, cultural context, and other methodological problems in cross-cultural psychopathology (such as measurement, sampling, and setting) are extensively discussed in the next chapter (2) by Draguns. His critical evaluation of methodology serves as an excellent background for understanding both the limitations and the achievements of research in cross-cultural psychopathology that are reported in this volume.

CULTURE AND PSYCHOPATHOLOGY IN PERSPECTIVE

This book shows how the understanding of psychopathology can be furthered by viewing it within a sociocultural context. In addition to cross-cultural methodology, a book dealing with the influence of culture on psychopathology should discuss the role of genetic factors. Although Chapter 4, entitled "The Genetic-Environmental Perspective in Psychopathology," is not intended to offer an extensive review of genetic-biological factors in mental illness, it reports impressive evidence on genetic factors derived from adoption studies carried out by Rosenthal and his colleagues, and should serve as a reminder that culture does not work in a vacuum, but always interacts with the biology of the organism. Just as culture is not a static entity but is in a state of a continuous flux and change, psychopathology is also expected to vary not only cross-culturally but also cross-temporally within the same culture. The historical analysis of the concept of mental illness by Sarbin and Juhasz suggests that cross-temporal studies may serve as a useful data source that would complement cross-cultural findings. [See examples in Murphy on schizophrenia (Chapter 9), Barry on alcohol (Chapter 12), and Meikle on sexual behavior (Chapter 13), this volume.]

The remainder of this chapter introduces some of the major findings and issues discussed in this volume. First, culture-bound syndromes, schizophrenia and depression, which have attracted the attention of researchers more than any other psychiatric syndromes, are considered. This topic is followed by psychosomatic disorders, brain and behavior, reaction to pain, alcoholism, and sexual behavior, which seem to be related to organic factors, such as tissue damage, physiological reaction, and biological drive. Intracultural factors, such as sex, family, and socioeconomic status, which are usually excluded from the definition of culture, but which often interact with and are modified by it, are also discussed. Next follow general issues of cultural relativity and the dimensional approach, which have presented a recent challenge to the medical interpretation of psychopathology. Finally, the general issues of culture, stress, and psychopathology are examined.

Culture-Bound Syndromes

Culture-bound syndromes are often considered atypical forms of psychopathology (for example, schizophrenia, severe functional psychosis, or neurosis) rather than specific cultural entities (Kiev, 1972; Opler, 1967). However, Pfeiffer has argued that many of these syndromes are so different from psychiatric syndromes in their onset, manifestations, and course, and so specific to certain ecological and social settings, that it is difficult to integrate them into Western nosological systems. The very existence of these syndromes, according to Pfeiffer, cannot be separated from culture-specific areas of stress (such as nuptial psychosis in North Africa) and culture-specific situations (such as kayak-angst among the Eskimos). Yet Pfeiffer considers the possibility that some culture-bound syndromes involve experiences shared by peoples from different cultures, although the events occur in diverse situations. For example, both kayak-angst and highway trance involve a disturbance in alertness brought about by sustained concentration and monotonous stimulation. Indeed, the same human experience may be differently emphasized, depending on the availability of a label in one culture but not in another. [See Draguns (Chapter 2), this volume, for further details.] Fabrega (this volume) draws attention to the neurological basis of culture-bound syndromes by noting the similarity of their features to those of toxic and confusional psychosis (e.g., impairment in the level of consciousness, confusion, and amnesia). A final decision about whether culture-bound syndromes are the same as, or are different from, traditional psychiatric syndromes must await better understanding of etiology.

Culture and Schizophrenia

In the study of cognitive functioning in schizophrenia, a consistent finding is that patients experience difficulty in information processing, particularly in situations that involve complex stimuli. Evidence revealing that the relatives (parents and siblings) of schizophrenic patients are also predisposed to cognitive difficulties suggests that environmental factors within the family may be involved (however, this evidence can also be adequately explained in genetic terms). Murphy suggests that certain cultural contexts beyond the family may hinder information-processing and thereby may raise the risk of schizophrenic breakdown. This disorder could occur through the process of training individuals or through exposing them to complex information without helping them to make decisions. Murphy notes that the Hutterite study and his own data from the South Pacific (which both indicate low risk of schizophrenia) seem to be consistent with a cultural framework that provides communal decisions and clear-cut paths of action for individuals who are predisposed to schizophrenia. On the other hand, the Irish have a complex style of communication that makes it difficult for the individual to separate reality from fantasy; this situation is a suggested explanation for the high risk of schizophrenia among Irish people. An intriguing question for future cross-cultural research is whether cultural characteristics, such as verbal communication and cultural emphasis on fantasy, not only are associated with a risk of schizophrenic breakdown, but also are related to thinking disorders as assessed by psychometric tests in both schizophrenic and normal samples. [See Draguns (Chapter 2), this volume, for discussion of research problems involved in implementing such a research strategy.]

Murphy reports wide cultural differences in schizophrenic symptoms, but such differences could be caused either by differences among psychiatrists in the perception of, and the relative emphasis on, certain symptoms or by differences in the sociocultural background of patients. Cooper et al. (1972) found differences between the United States and the United Kingdom in the perception of the presence and severity of symptoms. Schizophrenic symptoms may be (to some extent) related to the norms for social deviance that vary from one culture to another. Murphy observed that the schizophrenic symptoms that represent an exaggeration of personality characteristics already common in the general population often reflect the pathoplastic features of schizophrenia. Others, however, may be part of the "disease" process. Murphy proposes several hypotheses to explain the association between sociocultural background and symptomatology or types of schizophrenia, but the validity of these hypotheses must await the confirmation of future cross-cultural research. There is still little understanding of the processes mediating many of these associations. Consider, for example, the relationship between Western education and the development of certain kinds of hallucinations (auditory) and delusions (paranoid). These schizophrenic symptoms could reflect the effects of Western schooling on normal processes of perception, thinking, and categorization (Rogoff, 1980).

Finally, Murphy documents the available data on cultural differences in the course of schizophrenia and its response to treatment. These differences in prognosis seem to be independent of cultural differences in diagnostic practices or cultural variations in the types of illness (for instance, acute psychosis, borderline schizophrenia, and chronic schizophrenia). Summing up the evidence, Murphy hypothesizes seven factors (social rejection, rigidity of role ideals, assignment of responsibility, reality testing, sick-role typing, acceptance of dependency, and social networks) that might hinder or facilitate recovery. Whether these factors influence prognosis singly or through interacting with each other within the sociocultural context is still poorly understood (Edgerton, 1980).

Culture and Depression

Culture can be expected to contribute to the risk of depression as well as to its symptoms, prognosis, and response to treatment. However, unlike the research reported by Murphy on schizophrenia, data reported by Engelsmann (Chapter 10, this volume) have been confounded by basic methodological problems that include the definition of the concept of depression itself. As Engelsmann points out, the term *depression* describes a normal feeling, a syndrome, and a pathological state. However, researchers often fail to make such a distinction, although they assume that they are dealing with depression as a pathological condition. It is therefore noteworthy that Engelsmann's chapter starts with a discussion of the classification of depressive states. Several attempts have been made to dichotomize depressive states (primary versus secondary, bipolar versus unipolar, endogenous versus neurotic) in order to relate them to prognosis and response to treatment, but this effort has not yet been successful.

Cross-cultural data reveal significant variations in both the incidence and symptoms of depression. Early reports have indicated that depression is rare or absent in many African countries, but later studies seem to confirm the universality of depressive illness. Similarly, early reports suggested the absence of cognitive symptoms (such as guilt and self-depreciation) in some cultures, although these findings have not been supported by more recent data. Engelsmann discusses many sociocultural factors that might explain these contradictory findings. He points out that terms referring to depressive illness may be absent in some cultures, and that the depressive state itself may be considered normal and may be integrated into other practices (such as grief, mourning, and religion). Cultural differences in evaluating the dimensions of the depressive experience, such as intensity, frequency, and duration, may differentially determine the threshold of depressive illness across cultures and may in turn influence epidemiological data (Marsella, 1980). [See also Brown and Harris (Chapter 5), this volume, for the definition of "caseness" in depression.] In contrast to older data, more recent findings (for example, in Africa) of high rates of depression with cognitive symptoms may emphasize the importance of cultural change and variations in psychopathology across time (H.B.M. Murphy, 1978).

Not unlike data on schizophrenia, data reported by Engelsmann represent a shift of emphasis from a preliminary stage of data collection to hypothesis formation in an attempt to integrate and explain cross-cultural findings. Engelsmann's discussion of general theories of depression suggests several cross-cultural hypotheses: Is loss related to depression across cultures? Are family structures like multiple mothering protective against depression? Does social cohesiveness provide an antidote to depression? However, empirical cross-cultural data in support of or against these hypotheses are rare. Many of these hypotheses have been investigated and discussed by Brown and Harris in their London and Scotland research, but Engelsmann's chapter prepares for the extension of their methodology and theory to the cross-cultural arena.

Cultural Variations in Alcohol Abuse

Barry's survey (Chapter 12, this volume) reveals a wide spectrum of alcohol use and abuse among peoples of the world. He reports that cultural variation in the rates of drinking and alcoholism is related to three factors: motivation, social control (degree of permissiveness), and availability of alcohol. The interaction between these three factors may explain the disparity in the rates of alcoholism all over the world. A predominant cross-cultural hypothesis to explain cross-cultural differences in motivation for drinking is that alcohol may serve as a reinforcer that reduces anxiety, tension, and depression. The adaptive functions of drinking and alcoholism both for the individual and for society as described by Barry may explain the almost universally high motivation for drinking, and may counteract the physical hazards inherent in alcoholism. Work with animals indicates that indulgence in drinking seems to represent a uniquely human experience. Animals tend to drink only in order to compensate for caloric deficiencies, and not enough nor so fast that they exceed the rate of metabolism and become intoxicated (Keehn, 1979).

Barry observed that, in all societies, chronic excessive drinking seems to be limited to a minority of drinkers. He points out that a culture could not survive for long if heavy drinking were the typical behavior of its members. However, if a small number of individuals in a specific group are vulnerable to alcoholism, it may reflect their high sensitivity to alcohol. On the cross-cultural level, evidence of racial differences in sensitivity to alcohol reported by Barry may also account for variations in the rates of drinking and alcoholism. Furthermore, many drinking customs (e.g., the amount of alcohol allowed to various individuals within a culture) may be influenced by the relative physiological effects of alcohol on different groups within the culture. For example, sex differences in drinking, and the tendency of women in most societies to drink little or not at all, may be related to the observation that the same amount of alcohol intake results in higher blood concentration in women than in men. Thus, physiological factors may subtly interact with cultural factors to encourage or to inhibit drinking and alcoholism.

Culture and Sexual Behavior

Cultural variation in sexual behavior reported by Meikle (Chapter 13, this volume) illustrates the plasticity of a human behavior that is biological in origin. Although the sexual drive is biologically determined, sexual behavior depends not only on the (sexual) drive but also on the availability of the opposite sex and the cultural control of sexual relations. Selection of the sexual object may depend, to a large extent, on permissiveness in the culture. Meikle emphasizes the meaning of sexual behavior in different cultural contexts. For example, homosexuality may be only a precursory activity to full heterosexuality, it may be situational (when there is nonavailability of the opposite sex), or it may be practiced simply for economic gain (male prostitution). Similarly, exhibitionism may be practiced not only as a method of sexual excitement, but also as an expression of contempt, hostility, elation, and surprise, or as a response to fearful stimuli. There are many reports on transsexualism, transvestism, and other gender disorders in different cultures. However, there is a need for systematic cross-cultural studies of the role of socialization in the development of gender disorders.

It must, however, be noted that the biological basis of sexual behavior may account for many universal human sexual experiences. For example, regardless of cultural differences in attitudes toward various sexual behaviors, heterosexuality appears to be the most dominant and preferred behavior in all societies (Ford and Beach, 1951). Similarity of sexual behavior in different cultures, such as the promiscuity of the male or the difficulty of the female in experiencing orgasm (Davenport, 1977), may reflect biologically determined behavior that might unwittingly lend itself to cultural interpretation. For example, the elusiveness of the female orgasm may be attributed to male clumsiness or to male disregard of female sexual needs. [See Eysenck and Wilson (1979) for a sociobiological interpretation of cross-cultural data.]

Culture and Psychosomatics

The interaction between the biology of the organism and the sociocultural context is demonstrated by Warnes and Wittkower (Chapter 15, this volume). The authors use various interacting factors to explain cultural differences in the incidence or prevalence of, and the mortality rates from, psychosomatic disorders. These factors may be related to personality, to cultural adaptation (social and economic development, westernization, cultural change, and urban-rural settings), or to general life-style (diet, salt use, eating habits, work habits, alcohol consumption, and weight gain). The evidence reported by Warnes and Wittkower strongly supports cultural rather than racial factors to explain cultural differences in psychosomatic disorders. For example, they found that subjects who live in cohesive societies that are isolated from social change tend to show low blood pressures, with no relation between age and blood pressure found in most of the studies carried out with Western groups. However, individuals who left these societies through migration and had prolonged contact with Western culture tended to show a higher blood pressure, and the usual Western pattern of increased blood pressure with age. Warnes and Wittkower note that, in general, the longer the duration of residence in the host country, the higher the rate of psychosomatic disorders. They urge follow-up studies of immigrants to disentangle the sociocultural factors in psychosomatic disorders from the selective factors (which imply that high-risk individuals tend to leave their own countries). In conclusion, the authors discuss the implications of the sociocultural data on psychosomatics (hypertension, heart disease, ulcer, and asthma) for preventive medicine. Overall, the data presented by Warnes and Wittkower forms an essential basic repository of knowledge for both researcher and practitioner.

Cultural Effects on the Brain

Fabrega (Chapter 14, this volume) deals with the important but rather neglected issue of how culture is encoded in the brain and how it consequently influences reaction to environmental stimulation as well as the development of other brain capacities (taste, emotion, and pain). He suggests that cultural differences are to be expected more in the organization and function of the cortical structures of the brain, which are responsible for language, thought, and other social behavior, than in subcortical areas, which are responsible for "reflexive" and "unmotivated" behavior. For example, he distinguishes between personality changes in temporal lobe epilepsy (religiosity, hypermoralism, and changes in sexual interest and activity), which bear the stamp of cultural influences, and ictal behavior (automatisms of the face and mouth, confused and dazed wanderings, and unformed hallucinations), which is invariant across cultures. He also suggests that depression involves psychological symptoms (cognitive symptoms, such as guilt and self-depreciation) whose presence may vary across cultures, as well as uniform vegetative changes (somatization), which are detected in patients regardless of cultural background. Similarly, many of the major schizophrenic symptoms may reflect basic Western assumptions about human behavior, concepts of the self, and social reality.

Culture influences not only the expression of symptoms through its impact on the organization and function of the brain, but also the reaction of the individual and his social environment to these symptoms. Fabrega makes a distinction between the concept of disease, which refers only to damage of bodily tissues, and the concept of illness, which represents cultural conventions about bodily experience, emotions, and thinking. The concept of illness emphasizes the meaning and the cultural context of symptoms and their relation to the labeling process, to prognosis, and to recovery.

The relationship between culture and illness or illness behavior is well demonstrated by ethnic and cultural differences in the reaction to pain. Weisenberg (Chapter 16, this volume) demonstrates that, although socio-cultural factors are not related to discrimination of pain sensations caused by tissue damage, they tend to be involved in reaction to, and tolerance of, pain. Perception and tolerance of pain seem to result from sociocultural differences in modeling experiences, in which some stimuli are labeled as painful, while others are not. Weisenberg emphasizes that ethnic and cultural differences in reaction to pain are relevant both to diagnosis and to treatment in medical practice. Thus, although disease may be initiated by physical factors, the illness behavior described in the chapters by Fabrega and Weisenberg reflects sociocultural background.

The Role of Family Relations in Psychopathology

Sanua's review of the role of family relations and family interaction styles in psychopathology (Chapter 6, this volume) reveals no definitive evidence. Data indicating disturbed relations among families of patients are not clear about whether the family as a whole causes psychopathology or whether the psychopathology of one member of the family affects the behavior of other family members. Sanua also shows that family relations and interactions cannot be isolated from the wider framework of society; they vary according to religious affiliation, social class, ethnicity, and rural-urban settings. Research presented by Rosenthal (Chapter 4, this volume) indicates that, for biologically normal children, the risk of having schizophrenia does not increase if they are adopted by schizophrenic parents. This finding argues strongly against the family as a major causal factor in the development of schizophrenia. However, the relationship between psychopathology and the structural characteristics and the emotional environment of the family is noteworthy (Brown, 1967). Parental loss, for example, is associated with vulnerability to depression. [See Brown and Harris (Chapter 5) and Engelsmann (Chapter 10), this volume.] Schizophrenic patients may also have better prognosis and less chronicity in the extended family (El-Islam, 1979). Brown, Birley, and Wing (1972) found more disturbed behavior and relapse among schizophrenic patients from families with high emotional expression (criticism, hostility, and overinvolvement). Depressed patients are also affected by the quality of emotional relationship with relatives, but they tend to be more sensitive to the critical remarks of these relatives than are their schizophrenic couterparts (Vaughn and Leff, 1976). More recently, Leff and Vaughn (1980) found that depressive patients living with highly critical relatives had a high rate of events compared to those living with less critical relatives, but such an association was not found in schizophrenic patients. The family may, of course, play a major role in the labeling process and in the use of treatment facilities. Thus, although the family seems to be a doubtful cause in the development of psychopathology (Sanua, Chapter 6, this volume), it may provide some clues regarding the cultural factors that could initiate a disorder or could facilitate or hinder recovery. Many of these factors (such as the degree of expressed emotions and family overinvolvement) are still not being investigated across cultures, but they should provide the cross-cultural psychopathologist with a rich source for hypothesis formation.

Socioeconomic Status and Psychopathology

The strong association that is often detected between socioeconomic status and psychopathology is usually explained in terms of the drift hypothesis and/or the stress hypothesis. For example, the high rate of schizophrenia in the lower socioeconomic strata may be explained by the finding that these patients tend to show downward mobility and greater concentration than their fathers, brothers, or grandparents in Classes IV and V (lower class) (Goldberg and Morrison, 1963). In support of the drift hypothesis, Wender et al. (1974) also found that the socioeconomic status of schizophrenic patients who were adopted as children was lower than that of their biological fathers or of their adopted fathers. However, studies in the United States indicate that the absolute downward mobility of schizophrenic patients is almost nil (Turner and Wagenfeld, 1967), which suggests that the stress hypothesis may explain the excess of schizophrenia among lower classes (Kohn, 1972). Recognizing the tendency of psychiatrists in the United States to give the diagnosis of schizophrenia to many cases of depression, Brown and Harris (Chapter 5, this volume) observe that the relationship between social class and schizophrenia may have been inflated by the inclusion of depressive patients. Unlike data for schizophrenia, data on depression presented by Brown and Harris give strong support to the stress hypothesis rather than to the drift hypothesis.

Brown and Harris, in a detailed analysis of social class and depression, unravel a host of complex and interacting factors related to depression in two contrasting social settings, London and the Hebrides (Chapter 5, this volume). An important implication of their data for cross-cultural researchers in psychopathology is that vulnerability and provoking factors found in an urban setting may not be generalizable to other sociocultural backgrounds. There is a need for research on the cross-cultural generality of the impact of life events, as well as on other factors (emphasized by Brown and Harris), such as intimacy, number of children, employment, and loss. Prospective research may reveal the particular underlying processes mediating these factors within and across cultures. [See section on culture, stress, and psychopathology, p. 21.] Researchers interested in social stratification and social differentiation across cultures should take note of Brown and Harris's findings, which suggest that the indices of socioeconomic status used in industrialized urban centers may not be applicable to another sociocultural setting. The two researchers found that indices of social integration rather than those of socioeconomic status are related to psychopathology in a rural population. An intimate knowledge of the culture under investigation is required in order to construct specific indices of social stratification (which may not be applicable to other sociocultural groups).

Sex Differences in Psychopathology

Data on sex differences reviewed by Al-Issa (Chapter 7, this volume) reveal vast variations in symptoms and syndromes between males and females. Clinical descriptions of symptomatology among the sexes seem to emphasize characteristics that are common in the general population, but that are considered deviant because they represent an exaggeration of, or breaking away from, sex role prescriptions. Thus, adaptation to sex roles seems to be considered an index of mental health. For example, it is implicit in the description of schizophrenia that the withdrawn and passive behavior of the male and the aggression and overt sexuality of the female are part of the schizophrenic process rather than a simple deviation from sex role expectations.

Sex differences in the symptoms and/or the rates of psychopathology raise the question whether risk factors for the sexes are also different. Mednick et al. (1978) found that factors associated with schizophrenic breakdown in high-risk females are different from those in high-risk males. For example, breakdown in females is negatively associated with the age of onset of the mother's illness. Other factors, such as early parental separation, rate of recovery, responsiveness of the autonomic nervous system, and perinatal complications are significantly related to the development of schizophrenia in the male but not in the female. Sex differences on the process-reactive dimension and the premorbid adjustment scales also have differential prognostic implications for male and female schizophrenic patients. In depression, there is a need for replication of the Brown and Harris study to discover whether vulnerability and provoking factors apply to males as well as to females. However, Radloff (1980, in press) found that socioeconomic status is inversely related to depression in both sexes. Moreover, Radloff and Rae (1979) found that depression is related to most of the risk factors in the same direction for both sexes. When risk factors are taken into account, Radloff and Rae (1980) found that sex differences in depression are substantially reduced, with no indication of a higher level of depression for women independent of these factors.

Finally, it should be noted that sex is a biological fact; cross-cultural data can only provide an estimate of the extent to which culture can interact with the biology of sex and consequently modify behavior. For example, the universally higher rates of personality disorders (and aggression) in males than in females may indicate the effect of biological factors. Such findings also raise the possibility that cross-cultural similarities in the socialization of males or females may result in universal patterns of psychopathology among members of the same sex.

CULTURAL RELATIVITY AND THE DIMENSIONAL APPROACH TO PSYCHOPATHOLOGY

Implicit in the previous discussion is the acceptance of the medical model that considers psychopathology an absolute entity that is qualitatively different from a healthy state. However, the approaches discussed in this section offer an alternative to the medical model, namely the cultural relativity approach of Sarbin and Juhasz and the dimensional approach of Eysenck and Eysenck. These two approaches question the concept of psychopathology itself, particularly the dichotomy between states of health and disease.

Cultural relativity implies that normality and abnormality are defined within a social and cultural context. In light of the historical and contemporary evidence, Sarbin and Juhasz (Chapter 3, this volume) conclude that mental illness is not a medical or a scientific concept but rather a moral or a political one. Although Sarbin and Juhasz are firmly committed to science for the study and explanation of behavior, they have argued strongly that the classification of behavior as "unwanted" could be explained on the basis of moral, theological, mystical, and astrological criteria. Many recent trends have established the concept of cultural relativity as an accepted and integral part of the mental health service. For example, the treatment of the "insane" is no longer carried out exclusively by medical practitioners. Similarly, there has been a proliferation of several brands of nonmedical therapies to compete with psychiatric treatment (behavior therapy, lay analysis, client-centered therapy, encounter groups, yoga, meditation, biofeedback, and a variety of psychotherapies and counseling). Although the influence of the theological model has been diminishing in favor of the medical model since the nineteenth century, the clergy have continued to play a major role in mental health; there have been as many "patients" counseled for mental health problems by clergymen as by psychiatrists (Ryan, 1969). The finding that the practices and therapeutic achievements of native healers and witchdoctors are similar to those of psychiatrists has increased the prestige of these practitioners and has somehow reduced the "scientific" authority of psychiatrists as the sole guardians of the insane (Torrey, 1972).

The epidemiological surveys that have revealed that a large number of the population is "psychiatrically impaired" have narrowed the gap between the sane and the insane. Thus, the distinction between hospitalized patients and "normal" members of the community has become rather vague and somehow arbitrary and confusing. Consider the following two statements made in the sixties. Opler (1967) writes: "In New York City, we found people who had never been known to psychiatry or psychological medicine who were as utterly incapacitated as any I have seen in chronic wards" (pp. 266–267). In contrast, Braginsky, Braginsky, and Ring (1969) observed that schizophrenic patients on chronic wards are very normal: "They did not appear to us to be the disoriented, dependent, and socially inept creatures that the textbooks described" (p. 29). This type of situation has given credence to the argument against institutionalization and may have speeded up the movement toward disalienation described by Sarbin and Juhasz.

The medical model is weakened by the notoriously unreliable psychiatric diagnosis and by its lack of an external criterion independent of the social context. Attempts by the World Health Organization to formulate an acceptable diagnostic system that can be applied across nations regardless of social factors did not fulfill that aim. As Draguns aptly noted, "These efforts, however, have taken the form of reconciling differences among diagnosticians and coming up with generally acceptable compromises, often with political overtones rather than a more thorough revision of the classificatory scheme on an empirical and/or conceptual basis" (1980, p. 110).

The dimensional approach that is presented by Eysenck and Eysenck (Chapter 11, this volume) considers "pathological" states as an extension of the same processes involved in normal behavior.[2] Subjects are given a score on a continuum rather than an absolute label on a discrete point. In this

---

[2]The following discussion is consistent with the movement toward disalienation during the cultural revolution of the sixties. In particular, the ideas of Goffman, Kesey, Foucault, Szasz, Laing, and Sarbin that madness is potentially applicable to everyone and the attempts of these authors to abolish the gap between the sane and the insane are compatible with a dimensional approach to psychopathology (see Sarbin and Juhasz, Chapter 3, this volume).

view, psychopathology exists only as the end points of a continuum that is assessed by rating scales and questionnaires. This approach may be contrasted with the traditional anthropological research on culture and personality that has attempted to differentiate between cultures or nations on the basis of personality types and national character, ignoring individual differences within the same culture. Both the methods used in personality assessment and the theoretical base of the culture and personality movement have been discredited in recent years. The use of projective techniques, accounts of dreams, and the interpretation of artistic production to assess national character or personality types has proven to be of little reliability and validity (Al-Issa and Dennis, 1970; Barnouw, 1979; Draguns, 1979). Personality types and national character are also based on psychoanalytical theory, which assumes universal principles of behavior that are actually culture specific. In contrast, the dimensional approach discussed by Eysenck and Eysenck uses objective and relatively reliable instruments: for example, questionnaires for psychoticism, neuroticism, anxiety, and depression. One advantage of the Eysenck research strategy is the selection of a representative sample of the population that is not subject to the effects of institutionalization. Subject selection by questionnaires may also avoid social evaluation and social labeling (for example, a subject may be included in a high anxiety or a high psychoticism group regardless of whether he or she is labeled crazy, a saint, or a witchdoctor). Furthermore, questionnaires and personality inventories may eliminate cultural and training differences among psychiatrists during diagnosis and clinical interviews. Methods of personality assessment used by the Eysencks are derived from a theory with an experimental basis. The transcultural equivalence of concepts like psychoticism, neuroticism, extraversion, and anxiety could be empirically assessed by the factor patterns that emerge in factor analysis across cultures.

Neurosis in general, and anxiety and depression in particular, have long been accepted by psychopathologists as an exaggeration of normal behavior; they are different from normal responses only in intensity, frequency, and duration. For example, pathological depression is considered similar to normal grief and mourning. Because of the overlap between "normal" behavior and symptoms of patients, it has been suggested that the disorders may serve an adaptive function. Averill (1968) suggested that grief (and depression) may have the biological function of ensuring the cohesiveness of the group, which is in turn necessary for survival. (Grief provides a strong motive for the care and protection of group members.) Anxiety is also believed to serve the useful biological purpose of stimulating efficient psychological performance (Claridge, 1972).

However, it is the psychotic, and particularly the schizophrenic, who is regarded as the prototype of "the crazy" and who is isolated in a mental institution. Recently, however, there have been changes in attitudes toward these patients, as is evident in the movement toward disalienation, which has reduced the number of hospitalized patients. [See Sarbin and Juhasz (Chapter 3), this volume.] Contrary to the medical model, which dichoto- mizes human experience, research data tend to support quantitative rather than qualitative differences between normal and psychotic behavior. Psychometric measures of thinking disorder suggest that a single dimen- sion exists, with psychotic thinking found in the general population, but in less severe or less debilitating forms (Prentley, 1979). The evidence suggests that a genetic component is involved in the cognitive style of both schizophrenics and normals. It has been demonstrated that both siblings and parents of schizophrenics who are considered genetically predisposed to the disease obtain abnormal scores on measures of thinking disorders. Moreover, normal subjects in the general population are similar to their parents on tests of thinking disorders. Those high on overinclusive thinking have parents who are also high on these measures (Claridge, 1972).

The biological advantages of anxiety and depression mentioned earlier are also suggested for the schizophrenic genotype (Huxley et al., 1964). In support of this view, it has been shown that the relatives of schizophrenics have a lower incidence of accidents and viral infections (Carter and Watts, 1971). Similarly, it was revealed that the average childhood IQ of the siblings of a group of schizophrenics was higher than that of a group of their peers (Schaffner, Lane, and Albee, 1967). Heston (1966) also found an exceptional degree of creativity among nonschizo- phrenic persons whose mothers were schizophrenics, as compared with another group whose mothers were normal. High scores of creative persons and schizophrenic patients on measures of overinclusive thinking (Dykes and McGie, 1976; Prentley, 1979) suggest that an overinclusive cognitive style may faciltate both creativity and psychosis, characteristics that may arise from a common genetic predisposition.

More evidence in support of a dimensional approach to schizophrenia and psychosis may be derived from the general characteristics of hallucina- tions and delusions. These symptoms do not seem to be dichotomous, but tend to form a continuum ranging from concept to percept, with delusions and auditory hallucinations involving the contact receptors (gustatory, olfactory, and tactile) located near the perceptual end of the continuum (Al-Issa, 1977). Hebb (1968) argued that processes underlying hallucina- tions are the same as those underlying normal imagery. He describes a continuum of normal imagery that includes the vivid imagery of hallucina- tions, the less vivid memory image, and the completely abstract conceptual activity that has nothing representational about it (auditory or verbal imagery, which may include delusions, belong to the last kind of imagery). It has been found that hallucinations are not independent of delusions in schizophrenia; the majority of hallucinating patients (88%) tend also to be deluded (Lewinsohn, 1963). Moreover, hallucinations are not exclusively a schizophrenic phenomenon, but occur in a relatively large number of the normal population (Schwab, 1977), which suggests an overlap between schizophrenic and normal experience. Like normal imagery, hallucinatory experience seems to be one of the basic potentials of the human nervous system: "If one were to design an electronic brain which behaves in all respects like a normal brain, one would have to include in its specifications both a capacity for hallucination and a capacity to distinguish hallucination from sensory perception" (Wallace, 1959, p. 61).

Consistent with a dimensional approach to delusions, Maher (1974) argued that the process of inference underlying a delusion is not different from that underlying normal belief. The normal-paranoid difference is only in the kind of perceptual experience that provides the evidence from which inference is to be drawn. Both individual and sociocultural factors may affect perceptual experience, which may in turn increase the tendency to delusion. Consider, for example, the high rate of delusions among the elderly. When they become hard-of-hearing, the gradual decrease in the loudness of the speech of people around them can very easily lead to the interpretation that these people are whispering. Once elderly people believe this, it seems reasonable for them to conclude that the speakers are attempting to conceal something from them, which is an ideal situation for the development of delusions of conspiracy. Changes in perception that may result in delusions can be experienced by normal subjects during the chronic use of drugs, such as amphetamines (Snyder et al., 1974). Similarly, the degree to which persons have access to relevant social information may affect the perception of social events and could result in delusions; for example, those who are subjected to social exclusion from meaningful communication with others as a result of changes in values and norms, displacement, strange environments, isolation, and linguistic separation may become prone to the development of paranoid delusions (Lemert, 1962). Cultures that either provide explanations of social experiences to their members or do not demand them tend to discourage the development of delusions (Murphy, 1967). These individual and sociocultural factors that influence the processing of information from the environment seem to be common factors in the development of both normal beliefs and delusions, which again emphasizes a dimensional interpretation of the symptoms of psychopathology.

CULTURE, STRESS, AND PSYCHOPATHOLOGY

One general assumption in cross-cultural psychopathology is that some cultures are more stressful than others, and that the more stressful the culture, the higher the rates of psychopathology. There is also the belief that the presumed absence of stresses and strains in "primitive" societies gives its members an immunity to mental illness, but this belief has received little support. Cultural differences in stress are implied in the concepts of "easy" and "tough" cultures (Arsenian and Arsenian, 1948; Draguns, Chapter 2, this volume). Concepts of cultural stress, such as those suggested by the Arsenians, are difficult to define and quantify. However, an objective rating of stressful life events that has recently been developed by researchers may have implications for cross-cultural research in psychopathology (Brown and Harris, 1978; Dohrenwend and Dohrenwend, 1978; Rabkin, 1980; Van Praag, 1979).

It is believed that the impact of life events depends on their perception and evaluation by the subject rather than on the objective characteristics of these events. If an event is evaluated by the subject as threatening or uncertain, this would result in high activation. If, however, the subject evaluates the event as safe and able to be effectively handled, the resulting reaction would diminish (Levine, Weinberg, and Ursin, 1978). Thus, sociocultural factors can be expected to influence both the perception and the evaluation of events. Cross-national studies have, in fact, demonstrated differences in the rating of stressful life events between the United States and Sweden (Rahe, 1969), and between the United States and Japan (Masuda and Holmes, 1967). Miller et al. (1974) also found rural-urban differences in the rating of events.

Examples of life events given by Pfeiffer (Chapter 8, this volume) amply demonstrate that they tend to be culture specific. Yet these events may be mediated by universal factors. Studies reveal that certain factors, such as whether the event is a novel experience or a repetition of a previous experience, the ability of the individual to anticipate and control the stressful stimulus, and the presence of social bonds, all seem to mediate the impact of stress (Dohrenwend and Dohrenwend, 1978). Some cultures protect individuals against novel stresses, provide them with social bonds (satisfactory and intimate relations), and influence their choice of a coping mechanism that would enable them to escape or avoid stressful situations. However, the cross-cultural generality of the relationship between factors that mediate the impact of stress and psychopathology must be determined by future research.

SUMMARY AND CONCLUSIONS

The research reported in this volume illustrates that reaction patterns labeled psychopathological are universal. All over the world, there are people who hallucinate, who express improbable beliefs and delusions, who become fearful, anxious, and depressed, and who reveal excesses or deficits in behavior. These common experiences and behavior reflect, to a large extent, the universality of biological factors and human potential. Yet the incidence and the contents of psychopathology, as well as the course it takes, vary from one culture to another. Traditionally, the medical approach to psychopathology follows a monogenic model, which suggests an organic or biochemical explanation of psychopathology. In contrast, the diathesis-stress hypothesis accepted by most researchers indicates a polygenic or multifactorial model, which allows for both biological-genetic predisposition and environmental influences. Although there has been sophisticated and rather influential genetic research in many Western populations, the polygenic approach has been neglected in non-Western cultures. Replication of genetic research in different cultures is needed, not only because the criterion used for the selection of subjects is invariant across cultures and does not pose severe methodological problems, but also because it is important to establish whether or not the relative genetic-environmental influences on psychopathology are constant within different cultural contexts.

In recent years there has been an increasing interest in the study of culture and psychopathology, but researchers in this area have to deal with complex and somewhat intractable methodological problems. Two general problems deserve note here. The first concerns the elusive nature of the concept of culture. Although researchers have now accumulated substantial data that indicates an association between cultural background and psychopathology, there is still very little known about the nature of the cultural processes underlying these associations. The nature of culture needs an extensive analysis before anyone can confidently describe how culture makes a difference in psychopathology (Geertz, 1973). The second problem is related to the transcultural validity of psychiatric diagnosis. The unreliability of psychiatric diagnosis and its dependence on social evaluation has, in part, hindered generalization of research data within and across cultures, because patient samples selected for research are not comparable from one study to another. More recently, however, serious attempts have been made to objectify diagnosis in cross-national and cross-cultural studies, as in the U.S.-U.K. project and the World Health Organization study of schizophrenia. Nevertheless, the concept of psychopathology used across cultures still is affected by Western ideas about emotions, thinking, behavior, and social reality. Medical theories of health and disease, which form the basis of psychiatric classification, are also culture bound. What is needed is a classification system that could integrate knowledge of psychology, psychiatry, anthropology, sociology, and neurobiology. Such systems should be based on a holistic view of health and illness that takes into account the sociocultural, psychological, and physical factors involved in psychopathology. Indeed, theories of disease in other cultures that take a holistic view may serve as a better model for the cross-cultural psychopathologist than the present medical model (Fabrega and Manning, 1973). A holistic approach to medicine and psychiatry is implicit in the discussion presented in this volume by Fabrega (Chapter 14) and by Warnes and Wittkower (Chapter 15).

Data on the influence of culture on normal cognitive, affective, somatic, and motor (behavioral) reaction patterns should form the basis for understanding and even defining psychopathology across cultures. The study of normal reaction patterns may lead to the understanding of cultural variation in the expression of distress. For example, cultural differences in the expression of cognitive and somatic symptoms may simply reflect a normal cultural bias and the exaggeration of reaction patterns that are common in the normal population. Similarly, the form in which hostile feelings are normally expressed in different cultures may give clues to the expression of delusions. For example, cultures in which hostile feelings are normally expressed in action (hitting and killing somebody) rather than in thought may make it difficult for the psychiatrist to elicit paranoid delusions during the clinical interview (Al-Issa, 1967). Cultural influences on "normal" fantasy and imagination may also throw light on hallucinatory experiences and delusions. A dimensional approach to psychopathology requires that cross-cultural psychopathologists be aware of normal reaction patterns across cultures. Recent cross-cultural studies of the frequency, intensity, and duration of dysphoric affects in "normal" populations are attempts to integrate the investigation of normal behavior with that of pathological states.

A major aim of cross-cultural research is the study of the etiology of psychopathology. Culture not only determines the amount of stress experienced by the individual, but also plays a part in the person's perception and evaluation of the stress and the mechanisms used to cope with it. Research on how culture modifies the impact of universal stressors is also useful. Circumstances involving change and loss (people dying, loved ones changing, life becoming less meaningful and pleasant, and aging) are related to depression and seem to be universal. However, cultural differences in the way the individual perceives and handles these circumstances may be crucial in the development of psychopathology. Another useful research area is the generality of risk factors across cultures. There is evidence that the family plays a major role in the labeling process and in the initiation of individuals, particularly females, into the patient role. In some cultures, however, the family may be protective of some of its members (often the females) against outside stressors, including institutionalization (this would explain the large number of hospitalized male patients in some countries). Also, in some family structures (such as the extended family) stress related to interpersonal conflicts (such as those between husband and wife) may become diffused and somehow alleviated by the social support of other family members. Furthermore, the family and other social networks may provide a situation conducive to learning illness behavior (for example, somatic complaints and cognitive symptoms), which in turn might determine cross-cultural differences in the form and function of symptomatology. Overall, many risk factors associated with the family (parental loss, emotional expression, marital status and its interaction with sex, number of children, and intimacy) require investigation in different cultures. Surprisingly little research is carried out within and across cultures that deals with the effects of peers on psychopathology. Peers may expose the individual to values that are either compatible or in conflict with those of adults (the so-called generation gap), resulting in adaptive behavior and delinquency or psychopathology.

Culture may protect some of its members from, or expose them to, stress, depending on sex, position in the social hierarchy, and age. There are cultural differences in sex role differentiation and the extent to which deviation from sex role expectations is considered psychopathological. Sex roles may be so stressful (because of their rigidity or because of the low tolerance of the individual who must carry them out) that the culture may consider sex role deviation as an acceptable coping mechanism. There are also cultural differences in the relative protection of children and the elderly from stressors. In some cultures the oldest child is usually given more responsibility and therefore becomes more exposed to stress than other children. Boys may be more protected against stress than girls in certain cultures but the opposite may be true in others. Aging may either enhance or lower the status of a person, depending on cultural background. Similarity between age patterns of psychopathology across cultures (for example, the earlier onset of schizophrenia in the male than in the female) may reflect ubiquitous stressors during the life cycle (WHO, 1973). Finally, social stratification based on socioeconomic position may be a potent factor in depriving some individuals of various resources and may increase their helplessness and their vulnerability to psychopathology.

Coping behavior and help seeking are also related to cultural background. In many cultures, the whole social network, including the family, is mobilized to help the distressed individual. The incarceration of the individual away from his group may be considered a form of rejection. As Prince (1980) has pointed out, many cultures provide for the individual through training with what are called "endogenous healing mechanisms," which appear spontaneously in the face of stress. Many altered states of consciousness and other experiences akin to psychosis are used in the alleviation of individual suffering. Behavior that may be considered pathological in some contexts (sex role reversal, drinking, sexual license) is used by some cultures to preserve the emotional stability of its members (Prince, 1980; Pfeiffer, Chapter 8, this volume).

Illness behavior and reaction to, or tolerance of, pain are distress reactions, but they also involve the relations of the individual with the group. Illness may be used to manipulate and change these relations; it may be perpetuated, suppressed, or completely eliminated, depending on its social consequences (escape from responsibility, attention and love, dismissal from job, and so on). After bereavement, for example, the depressive sick role may be reinforced as the only alternative available to the individual or it may serve as a temporary stepping stone that paves the way for a new role. In general, cultural differences in labeling and the assignment of the sick role to individuals, as well as the role of culture in prognosis and outcome of treatment, provide virgin and fertile areas for future research.

REFERENCES

Al-Issa, I. 1967. Literacy and symptomatology in chronic schizophrenia. Br. J. Soc. Psychiatry 1:313–315.

Al-Issa, I. 1977. Social and cultural aspects of hallucinations. Psychol. Bull. 84:570–587.

Al-Issa, I. and Dennis, W. 1970. Cross-Cultural Studies of Behavior. Holt, Rinehart & Winston, Inc., New York.

Arsenian, J., and Arsenian, J. 1948. Tough and easy cultures: A conceptual analysis. Psychiatry 11:377–385.

Averill, G. R. 1968. Grief: Its nature and significance. Psychol. Bull. 70:721–748.

Barnouw, V. 1979. Culture and personality. 3rd Ed. The Dorsey Press, Homewood, Illinois.

Braginsky, B. M., Braginsky, D. D., and Ring, K. 1969. Methods of Madness: The Mental Hospital as a Last Resort. Holt, Rinehart & Winston, Inc. New York.

Brown, G. W. 1967. The family of the schizophrenic patient. In:A. Coppen and A. Walk (eds.), Recent developments in schizophrenia. Br. J. Psychiatry, Special Publication no. 1. Headley, Ashford Kent.

Brown, G. W., and Harris, T. 1978. Social Origins of Depression: A Study of Psychiatric Disorders in Women. Tavistock Publication, London.

Brown, G. W., Birley, J. L. T., and Wing, J. K. 1972. Influence of family life on the course of schizophrenic disorders: A replication. Br. J. Psychiatry 121:241–258.

Carter, M. and Watts, C. A. H. 1971. Possible biological advantages among schizophrenics' relatives. Br. J. Psychiatry 118:453–460.

Claridge, G. S. 1972. The schizophrenics as nervous types. Br. J. Psychiatry 121:1–17.

Cooper, J. E., Kendell, R. E., Gurland, B. J., Sharpe, L., Copeland, J. R. M., and Simon, R. 1972. Psychiatric Diagnosis in New York and London. Oxford University Press, London.

Davenport, W. H. 1977. Sex in cross-cultural perspectives. In: F. Beach (ed.), Human Sexuality in Four Perspectives. Johns Hopkins University Press, Baltimore.

Dohrenwend, B. S., and Dohrenwend, B. P. 1978. Some issues in research on stressful life events. J. Nerv. Ment. Dis. 166:7–15.

Draguns, J. G. 1979. Culture and personality. In: A. J. Marsella, R. G. Tharp, and

T. J. Ciborowski (eds.), Perspectives on Cross-Cultural Psychology. Academic Press, Inc., New York.

Draguns, J. G. 1980. Psychological disorders of clinical severity. In: H. C. Triandis and J. G. Draguns (eds.), Handbook of Cross-Cultural Psychopathology. Vol. 6. Psychopathology. Allyn & Bacon, Inc., Boston.

Dykes, M., and McGie, A. 1976. A comparative study of attentional strategies of schizophrenics and highly creative normal subjects. Br. J. Psychiatry 128:50–56.

Eaton, J. W., and Weil, R. J. 1955. Culture and Mental Disorders. Free Press, New York.

Edgerton, R. B. 1980. Traditional treatment for mental illness in Africa: A review. Cult. Med. Psychiatry 4:167–189.

El-Islam, M. F. 1979. A better outlook for schizophrenics living in extended families. Br. J. Psychiatry 135:343–347.

Eysenck, H. J., and Wilson, G. 1979. The Psychology of Sex. J. M. Dent and Sons Ltd., London.

Fabrega, H., and Manning, P. K. 1973. An integrated theory of disease: Ladino-Mestizo views of disease in the Chiapas highlands. Psychosom. Med. 35:225–239.

Field, M. J. 1960. Search for Security: An Ethnopsychiatric Study of Rural Ghana. Northwestern University Press, Evanston, Ill.

Ford, C. S., and Beach, F. A. 1951. Patterns of Sexual Behavior. Harper & Row Pubs., Inc., New York.

Freud, S. 1961. Civilization and Its Discontents. W. W. Norton & Company, Inc., New York. (Originally published in 1930.)

Geertz, C. 1973. The Interpretation of Cultures. Basic Books, Inc., New York.

Goldberg, E. M., and Morrison, S. L. 1963. Schizophrenia and social class. Br. J. Psychiatry 109:785–802.

Hebb, D. O. 1968. Concerning imagery. Psychol. Rev. 75:466–477.

Heston, L. L. 1966. Psychiatric disorders in foster home reared children of schizophrenic mothers. Br. J. Psychiatry 112: 819–825.

Huxley, J., Mayr, E., Osmond, H., and Hoffer, A. 1964. Schizophrenia as a genetic morphism. Nature 204:220–221.

Keehn, J. D. 1979. Psychopathology in animal and man. In: J. D. Keehn (ed.), Psychopathology in Animals. Academic Press, Inc., New York.

Kiev, A. 1972. Transcultural Psychiatry. Free Press, New York.

Kohn, M. 1972. Class, family, and schizophrenia: A reformulation. Soc. Forces 50:295–313.

Kroeber, A. L., and Kluckhohn, C. 1952. Culture: A Critical Review of Concepts and Definitions. Vol. 47, no. 1. Peabody Museum, Cambridge, Mass.

Lauter, H. 1965. Kraepelin's importance for cultural psychiatry. Transcult. Psychiatr. Res. Rev. 2:9–12.

Leff, J., and Vaughn, C. 1980. The interaction of life events and relatives' expressed emotion in schizophrenia and depressive neurosis. Br. J. Psychiatry 136:146–153.

Lemert, E. M. 1962. Paranois and the dynamics of exclusion. Sociometry 25:2–20.

Levine, S., Weinberg, J., and Ursin, H. 1978. Definition of the coping process and statement of the problem. In: H. Ursin, E. Baade, and S. Levine (eds.), Psychobiology of Stress: A Study of Coping Men. Academic Press, Inc., New York.

Lewinsohn, P. M. 1963. An empirical test of several popular notions about hallucinations in schizophrenic patients. In: W. Keup (ed.), Origin and Mechanisms of Hallucinations. Plenum Publishing Corp., New York.

Maher, B. A. 1974. Delusional thinking and perceptual disorder. J. Individ. Psychol. Pp. 98–113.

Marsella, A. G. 1980. Depressive experience and disorder across cultures. In: H. C. Triandis and J. G. Draguns (eds.), Handbook of Cross-Cultural Psychology. Vol. 6. Psychopathology. Allyn & Bacon, Inc., Boston.

Masuda, M., and Holmes, T. H. 1967. The social readjustment rating scale: A cross-cultural study of Japanese and Americans. J. Psychosom. Res. 11:227–237.

Mednick, S. A., Schulsinger, F., Teasdale, X. W., Schulsinger, H., Venables, P. H., and Rock, D. R. 1978. Schizophrenia in high-risk children: Sex differences in predisposing factors. In: G. Serban (ed.), Cognitive Defects in the Development of Mental Illness. Brunner/Mazel, Inc., New York.

Miller, F. T., Bentz, W. K., Aponte, J. R., and Brogan, D. R. 1974. Perception of life crisis events. In: B. S. Dohrenwend and B. Dohrenwend (eds.), Stressful Life Events: Their Nature and Effects. John Wiley & Sons, Inc., New York.

Murphy, H. B. M. 1967. Cultural aspects of the delusion. Studium Generale 20:684–692.

Murphy, H. B. M. 1978. The advent of guilt feelings as a common depressive symptom: A historical comparison of two continents. Psychiatry 41:229–242.

Murphy, J. M. 1976. Psychiatric labeling in cross-cultural perspective. Science 191:1019–1028.

Opler, M. K. 1967. Culture and Social Psychiatry. Atherton Press, New York.

Orley, J., and Wing, J. K. 1979. Psychiatric disorders in two African villages. Arch. Gen. Psychiatry 36:513–520.

Prentley, R. A. 1979. Creativity and psychopathology: A neurocognitive perspective. In: B. Maher (ed.), Progress in Experimental Personality Research. Academic Press, Inc., New York.

Price-Williams, D. 1980. Toward the idea of a cultural psychology. J. Crosscult. Psychol. 11:75–88.

Prince, R. 1980. Variations in psychotherapeutic procedures. In: H. C. Triandis and J. G. Draguns (eds.), Handbook of Cross-Cultural Psychology. Vol. 6. Psychopathology. Allyn & Bacon, Inc., Boston.

Rabkin, J. G. 1980. Stressful life events and schizophrenia: A review of the research literature. Psychol. Bull. 87:400–425.

Radloff, L. S. 1980. Risk factors for depression: What do we learn from them? In: D. Belle and S. Salasin (eds.), Mental Health of Women: Fact and Fiction. Academic Press, Inc., New York.

Radloff, L. S., and Rae, D. S. 1979. Susceptibility and precipitating factors in depression: Sex differences and similarities. J. Abnorm. Psychol. 88:174–181.

Radloff, L. S., and Rae, D. S. 1980. Components of the sex differences in depression. In: R. G. Simmons (ed.), Research in Community and Mental Health. Vol. 3. JAI Press, Greenwich, Conn.

Rahe, R. H. 1969. Multi-cultural correlations of life change scaling: America, Japan, Denmark, and Sweden. J. Psychosom. Res. 13:191–195.

Rogoff, B. 1980. Schooling and the development of cognitive skills. In: H. C. Triandis, and A. Heron (eds.), Handbook of Cross-Cultural Psychology. Vol. 4. Developmental Psychology. Allyn & Bacon, Inc., Boston.

Rosen, G. 1968. Madness in Society. The University of Chicago Press, Chicago.

Ryan, W. (ed.), 1969. Distress in the City. Case Western Reserve University Press, Cleveland.

Schaffner, A., Lane, E. A., and Albee, G. W. 1967. Intellectual differences between suburban preschizophrenic children and their siblings. J. Consult. Psychol. 31:326–327.

Schwab, M. E. 1977. A study of reported hallucinations in a southeastern county. Ment. Health Soc. 4:344–354.

Sears, R. R. 1970. Transcultural variables and conceptual equivalence. In: I. Al-Issa and W. Dennis (eds.), Cross-Cultural Studies of Behavior. Holt, Rinehart & Winston, Inc., New York.

Snyder, S., Banerjee, S., Yamamura, H., and Greenberg, D. 1974. Drugs, neurotransmitters, and schizophrenia. Science 184:1243–1253.

Torrey, E. F. 1972. The Mind Game: Witchdoctors and Psychiatrists. Emerson Hall Publishers, New York.

Torrey, E. F. 1973. Is schizophrenia universal? An open question. Schizophr. Bull. 7:53–59.

Triandis, H. C. 1980. Introduction to handbook of cross-cultural psychology. In: H. C. Triandis and W. W. Lambert (eds.), Handbook of Cross-Cultural Psychology. Vol. 1. Perspectives. Allyn & Bacon, Inc., Boston.

Turner, R. J., and Wagenfeld, M. O. 1967. Occupational mobility and schizophrenia: An assessment of the social causation and social selection hypotheses. Am. Sociol. Rev. 32:104–113.

Van Praag, H. M. 1979. Psychopsychiatry: Can psychosocial factors cause psychiatric disorders? Compr. Psychiatry 20:215–224.

Vaughn, C. E., and Leff, J. P. 1976. The influence of family and social factors on the course of psychiatric illness: A comparison of schizophrenic and depressed neurotic patients. Br. J. Psychiatry 129:125–137.

Wallace, A. F. C. 1959. Cultural determinants of response to hallucinatory experience. Arch. Gen. Psychiatry 1:58–69.

Wender, P. H., Rosenthal, D., Kety, S. S., Schulsinger, F., and Welner, J. 1974. Cross-fostering: A research strategy for clarifying the role of genetic and experimental factors in the etiology of schizophrenia. Arch. Gen. Psychiatry 30:121–128.

World Health Organization. 1973. Report of the International Pilot Study of Schizophrenia. World Health Organization, Geneva.

World Health Organization. 1979. Schizophrenia: An International Follow-up Study. John Wiley & Sons, Inc., New York.

II

GENERAL ISSUES

Chapter 2

Methodology in Cross-Cultural Psychopathology

Juris G. Draguns

Cross-cultural psychology aspires to two standards: worldwide comparability and cultural sensitivity. The ideal of all cross-cultural psychological research is to compare units of behavior, yet to do so without distoring their function or meaning in the milieus in which they occur (Lonner, 1979).

In pursuit of these two ambitious goals, cross-cultural investigators in psychology have often discovered that they operate at cross-purposes. The differential pull toward worldwide equivalence on the one hand, and cultural sensitivity on the other, is the source of the two contrasting perspectives in cross-cultural psychology: the emic, or the culturally indigenous, and the etic, or the humanly universal (cf. Berry, 1969; Jahoda, 1977; Malpass, 1977; Price-Williams, 1974; Triandis, Malpass, and Davidson, 1973). In comparing behaviors across different cultures that are also geographically removed from one another, there is risk of carelessly neglecting sensitivity to, and awareness of, the setting in which these behaviors take place. What may come about as a result is the comparison of behaviors that differ widely in both context and meaning—there may be tabulation of discrete instances of behavior that seem to be similar, but that are far from being equivalent. However, it must be kept in mind that cultural sensitivity and the desire to describe behaviors in relation to their unique social, man-made context are eminently conducive to description, but are refractory, perhaps even inimical, to comparison of cultures. At its logical endpoint, cultural sensitivity makes any and all generalization beyond culture lines impossible. How can one transcend the charmed cycle of a unique culture? How, conversely, can one maintain awareness of the unique culture while persisting in a comparative orientation? Combining and integrating these two perspectives in the conduct of cross-cultural investigation has become the subject of an extensive and growing theoretical literature (Berry, 1969; Davidson et al., 1976; Malpass, 1977).

Generally, there is a proliferation of contemporary and recent writing in cross-cultural psychology that is characterized by a high degree of methodological self-consciousness (Boesch and Eckensberger, 1969; Brislin, Lonner, and Thorndike, 1973; Triandis and Berry, 1980). This body of writing is germane to the two objectives of comparing behavior across culture and maintaining sensitivity to the meaning and function of this behavior within the culture in which it occurs.

In contrast to the abundant harvest of methodological writing on cross-cultural psychology in general, the yield of explicit methodological concern in the cross-cultural study of abnormal behavior has been rather slim (Brody, 1973; Draguns, 1977a; H. B. M. Murphy, 1969), although several recent reviews have raised and dealt with methodological issues (Draguns, 1973, 1977b, 1977c, 1980; King, 1978; Kleinman, 1977; Marsella, 1979). The goal of this chapter is to contribute to this growing, but as yet meager, body of literature. The chapter examines a number of important features of cross-cultural investigation of disturbed and abnormal behavior in light of the two broad basic issues of worldwide comparability and cultural sensitivity. History of cross-cultural methodology of investigation can be described as a series of ever more sophisticated attempts to steer clear of modern versions of Scylla and Charybdis (i.e., avoiding equally hazardous alternatives). The focus of this chapter is comparative; that is, it is concerned with the simultaneous and planned observation of abnormal behavior at two or more sites of investigation. [See reviews by Draguns (1973, 1980) and Marsella (1979).] A large body of reports pertains to observations of disturbed behavior in only one culture, but is written with a cultural orientation in mind. These monocultural studies are not systematically recapitulated here because they are reviewed elsewhere (see Dohrenwend and Dohrenwend, 1974; Draguns, 1980; Dunham, 1976; Favazza and Oman, 1978; King, 1978; Marsella, 1979; Wittkower, 1969). However, such studies are selectively brought to bear upon the various methodological issues discussed in this chapter.

CONCEPTS

Variability of Diagnostic Terms

Psychiatrists around the world use the same vocabulary to describe and classify disturbed behavior. This shared nomenclature is traceable to the late nineteenth-century pioneers of descriptive psychiatry, notably Kraepelin. The use of the same descriptive terms around the world does not necessarily imply that these terms are applied identically. The various national diagnostic classification systems, as exemplified by the *Diagnostic and Statistical Manual* (DSM) of the American Psychiatric Association (in three editions) in the United States, and by the *Glossary of Mental Disorders* in Great Britain, are subtly divergent and discrepant, both in the categories included and in the criteria for their individual application. As a result, there exists in the world a number of interrelated, overlapping, but nonidentical systems of diagnostic classification, derived from a common lineage but differing in their features. Moreover, by virtue of reliance upon key terms, such as *psychosis, schizophrenia, depression, mania, hysteria,* and others, these systems create the appearance of greater similarity than exists in reality. It is well known that even culturally related countries like the United States and the Netherlands (Saenger, 1968) or the United States and Great Britain (Kramer, 1969) differ dramatically in the recorded incidence of diagnostic categories, such as schizophrenia and depression. It would be rash to attribute these differences in categorization exclusively or even largely to the condition of the psychologically disturbed individuals of the countries in question. Instead of providing the answer, these data offer only a basis for exploring the question about the source of these major diagnostic discrepancies. In the case of United States–United Kingdom distribution of affective psychosis and schizophrenia, research designed to resolve differences in these diagnostic categories has traced these discrepancies primarily to diagnosticians and not to patients (Cooper et al., 1972). The differences were resolved by instituting uniform and explicit criteria of diagnostic assignment at both sites of investigation.

Another major step toward resolving diagnostic variability has been taken by the international research teams coordinated by Engelsmann et al. (1971). As a result of these efforts, empirical, established patterns of equivalence between categories of several national diagnostic systems in Europe and America have been produced. In the optimal case, it is now possible, on a factual basis, to "translate" a diagnosis made in Great Britain into its closest approximation in Germany or France. The intermediate step in this process is the identification of the symptoms on which such a category rests. Of course, not all categories possess an exact counterpart across national frontiers. There are, moreover, entities similarly named, but based on different symptoms. *Schizophrenie paranoïde* in France is not equivalent to paranoid schizophrenia in the United States. In fact, it carries a greater resemblance to hebephrenic schizophrenia, as diagnosed in the United States.

One also wonders whether the availability of officially sanctioned labels facilitates the identification of cases that conform to the category in question. The abundant French literature in Africa and elsewhere (Collomb, 1965) on *bouffée délirante aigüe,* a short-term psychotic state that has points of similarity with acute undifferentiated schizophrenia in DSM-

II, may have been sparked by the presence of this category in the official French diagnostic manual. In Japan, the syndrome of *Taijin-kyofushu* (loosely translated as "interpersonal anxiety," "anthropophobia," or, simply, "fear of people") looms large in the psychiatric literature (Ojino, Kuba, and Suzuki, 1977; Tanaka-Matsumi, 1979). Two prominent Japanese cultural themes, the concern with fastidious cleanliness and the prevalence and positive valuation of shyness (Zimbardo, 1977), seem to have coalesced to produce the symptoms of this disorder. Again, in the absence of systematic comparative data, the proportions in which the frequency of the syndrome and the psychiatric preoccupation with it respectively contribute to its perceived prominence in Japan are open to question.

Culture-Bound Syndromes

The broad topic of culture-bound psychiatric syndromes has accumulated a substantial literature (H. B. M. Murphy, 1972; Tan and Carr, 1977; Weidman and Sussex, 1971; Yap, 1974). These patterns of maladaptive behavior are usually reported at remote and exotic sites and described by names like *koro, latah, amok,* and *windigo.* The possibility that such syndromes may also occur closer to the home base of Western psychiatric investigators has been recognized, notably by Ellenberger (1960) in the case of *Putzwut,* the compulsive cleaning behavior of some German and Swiss housewives, and also by Yap (1974) in the case of the formerly widespread "masturbatory disturbance" of many Western adolescents and adults.

The description and investigation of culture-bound syndromes represent an emic intrusion into what is, by common agreement, the etically dominated field of psychiatric disorders. Researchers in culture-bound syndromes consider concepts and categories from within the culture seriously. Beyond the description of specifically local patterns of disturbance, two possibilities exist: either these syndromes represent disorders *sui generis,* found only at a circumscribed geographic site, or they are instances of a more widely diffused disorder, but are more readily noticed, coded, and communicated because of the availability of the special term and the concept. Yap (1974), on the basis of his searching analysis of such disorders around the world, leans toward the latter possibility. Similarly, Doi (1973), the expert on the Japanese personality dynamic of *amae,* or the lifelong quest for dependent gratification, maintains in his more recent writings that, although amae is an experience for which the Japanese have a unique word, many more people of different cultures share the same impulse.

Even when an identical word is used and understood in different cultures, there are divergences. There is no denotative difference between *depression* in English and *dépression* in French. However, work with English and French speakers in Montreal has demonstrated that the connotations of these two dictionary equivalents diverge in the two languages. Essentially, French-Canadians regard depression as the result of the accumulation of external stress; Anglo-Canadians trace it to the individual's internal states (Benoist, 1964). Tanaka-Matsumi and Marsella (1976) investigated the subjective meaning of depression by means of word associations and semantic differential ratings in Japanese and Japanese-American participants. The researchers found different clusters of meaning associated with the terms, depending largely on the individual's native language. Similarly, small but detectable differences were established in the self-reported psychiatric symptoms of bilingual Mexican-American individuals, depending on the language in which they were tested (Edgerton and Karno, 1971).

Certain symptoms appear frequently in the psychiatric literature of one nation, but are absent from the analogous body of writing in another country. A case in point is the symptom of *Gedankenentzug* (translated with some difficulty as "thought withdrawal"), which is included among Schneider's (1958) well-known first-rank symptoms in schizophrenia. Despite its importance in German psychiatric writings, Gedankenentzug is neither frequently observed nor accorded a great diagnostic significance in the English-language psychiatric literature (Marsella, 1979; Stengel, 1961).

Psychiatric Classification and Diagnosis

On the most general plane, psychiatric classification and diagnosis are based on the concept of abnormality, or mental illness. These methods are, in turn, anchored in more concrete and specific criteria that, to an unknown degree, may be subject to cultural shaping. During the twentieth century, concepts of psychological disturbance, mental illness, and abnormality have been considerably broadened in the United States; it is not yet clear to what extent, if any, the assimilation of social deviance into a psychiatric frame of reference is a worldwide phenomenon.

In any case, acceptable limits are implicit in ideas of social behavior; these limits are intertwined with standards of conduct and views of what constitutes a "good life." Both of these attitudes are, of course, patterned and shaped by culture. The problem of diverging definitions is magnified as the concept of positive mental health is introduced, because it inevitably reflects culturally shared values. Thus, M. Jahoda's (1958) well-known criteria of positive mental health, which include self-acceptance; an ability for growth, development, and self-actualization; a capacity for integration; a sense of autonomy; a perception of reality; and environmental mastery, are not automatically applicable across time and culture. Static traditional cultures, for example, may place a lesser value on sense of autonomy and environmental mastery, and a greater emphasis on fitting into a supraordinate social unit (family, community, society) and accommodating to the unchanging and perhaps immutable aspects of the environment. Perhaps this cultural variability is the reason why positive and comprehensive ideas of mental health have so far played a limited role in cross-cultural investigation of psychopathology. If conceptions of mental health are utilized in future research, it is mandatory that their cultural and philosophical sources be made explicit, and that such ideas be investigated on the several cultural levels at which the study is being conducted, prior to their being incorporated into research operations. Conceptions of optimal social and personal functioning are likely to be divergent; therefore, a means for blending these distinct criteria into uniform and standardized research procedures must be determined. Can a hybrid set of universally applicable criteria of ideal or optimal performance be constructed? Such a task has not yet been attempted, but it constitutes a worthy, although uncertain, research objective.

Until uniform criteria have been established, empirical investigators have turned to concrete, minimal standards of acceptable behavior. In culturally uniform settings, basic definitions of mental health prominently rest on the criteria of psychiatric hospitalization or treatment (Scott, 1958). Such minimal yardsticks of mental health have also been largely utilized in cross-cultural studies of psychopathology resulting in "comparisons of cultures proceeding from their most disturbed members" (Draguns et al., 1971). There are undoubtedly fewer problems when the minimal standards of normal behavior implicit in such definitions are applied. This is especially so if the cultures compared differ little in their psychiatric hospitalization rates, in their availability of mental health services, and in their general acceptance by the populations in question. Even across widely different cultures, as J. M. Murphy's (1976) naturalistic research demonstrates, there is convergence in the identification and labeling of the most extreme instances of disturbed behavior. Moreover, Lorr and Klett (1968, 1969a, 1969b) identified the same factors of disturbed inpatient behavior in a variety of cultures. Similarly, the staff of the Transcultural Psychiatric Research Center in Montreal (H. B. M. Murphy, Wittkower, and Chance, 1967; H. B. M. Murphy et al., 1963) discovered sets of culturally invariant symptoms of depression and schizophrenia, respectively. More recently, the International Pilot Study of Schizophrenia, coordinated by the World Health Organization in nine countries of Europe, Asia, Africa, and the Americas, led to the identification of a core syndrome of schizophrenia, observed at all sites of this multinational investigation (World Health Organization, 1973, 1979).

All of these results, obtained by a variety of research approaches, powerfully support the case for a universal set of criteria for abnormality, provided that abnormal behavior is conservatively conceived. Elsewhere (Draguns, 1980) the conclusion was reached that all abnormal behavior can be placed at the extremes of one of the four following axes: 1) affective experience, from high to low; 2) perceptual-cognitive functioning, from consensually validated to arbitrary and idiosyncratic; 3) organismic expression, from tense to relaxed; and 4) social behavior, from that which is reliable and appropriate to that which is unreliable and inappropriate. In different combinations and with different cut-off points, these four axes of evaluation seem to be used extensively to define and to separate the abnormal part of the continuum from the normal.

There is no denying the possibility, however, that specific behaviors may be differently evaluated, depending on culture (Benedict, 1934). Hallucinations, for example, do not have a culturally universal psychopathological meaning, as demonstrated in Al-Issa's (1977, 1978) worldwide review and conceptual analysis. Moreover, the concrete application of criteria of hospitalization and treatment is greatly complicated by the imported and culturally alien character of modern mental health institutions in many non-Western countries of the world (Higginbotham, 1979a, 1979b), and by the frequent coexistence of scientific and traditional-indigenous avenues of mental health treatment. In the extreme case, the culturally extraneous mental hospital becomes the institution of last resort, reserved for those individuals with whom local ministrations have failed. On a more specific level, the more modernized, Westernized segment of the population may selectively turn to such services (Higginbotham, 1979a, 1979b), resulting in only partial and biased representation of the total segment of the psychologically disturbed population.

In response to this dilemma, a consensus seems to be developing that the standards of abnormal behavior should be strict and circumscribed, but should not be applied exclusively to treatment settings of either the modern or the traditional type (Dohrenwend and Dohrenwend, 1974; Draguns, 1977b). Wherever possible, the local standards of minimally acceptable behavior should be incorporated into the research definitions of normality and abnormality. This course of action has rarely been followed in actual cross-cultural investigations. More typically, in some of the more flexible and culturally sensitive epidemiological investigations, the judgment of local informants on the nature and quality of functioning in particular cases (Bash and Bash-Liechti, 1969; A. H. Leighton et al., 1963) has been incorporated into the studies as an additional check upon the appropriateness of extraneous experts' judgment and diagnosis.

MEASURES

Psychiatric Rating Scales

As has been pointed out elsewhere (Draguns, 1977a), methodological progress in the investigation of abnormal behavior across cultures has been characterized by two trends: 1) the shift from diagnostic category to symptom as a basic unit of observation, recording, and comparison; and 2) the application of modern standardized symptom scales in lieu of the traditional clinical procedures of appraisal and diagnosis. Several such measures have been incorporated into a number of important cross-cultural investigations of abnormal behavior: the Present State Examination by Wing (1970) in the International Pilot Study of Schizophrenia (World Health Organization, 1973) and in the U.S.-U.K. Project (Cooper et al., 1972); the Inpatient Multidimensional Psychiatric Scale (Lorr and Klett, 1968), in a series of multicultural investigations of its factorial structure; the Katz Adjustment Scale, in a continuing series of multiethnic studies in Hawaii (Katz et al., 1978), and many more. These instruments have, for the most part, been developed to help objectify and standardize the operations of psychiatric observers. A few of the measures, such as the Katz Adjustment Scale, have been constructed so that they are usable by professional personnel, by the lay public, and by the patients themselves. The Katz Adjustment Scale has been applied in comparing the findings of different kinds of observers, both in hospital and in community settings.

Closely related to these rating scales are a variety of self-report measures that inquire into the patient's subjective state. These measures concentrate upon a specific psychological experience, such as depression (Hamilton, 1967; Marsella and Sanborn, 1973; Zung, 1969) or anxiety (Spielberger, Gorsuch, and Lushene, 1970), or they extend over the entire gamut of maladaptive and adaptive behavior, as do some of the prominent self-report inventories, such as the MMPI (Butcher and Tellegen, 1978).

All of these tools have typically been developed in the West, most frequently in one of the English-speaking countries of the world. More recently, they have experienced extensive application beyond the cultures of their origin. In the process, these measures have been translated, edited, transformed, and adapted to their new locales.

Perhaps the most basic problem with the application of these tools is cultural variations in the readiness to share subjective experiences and to do so in a standardized and, to some respondents, artificial and impersonal manner. Local preferences affect both the direct self-report and its indirect variants, in which the informant is asked standardized questions. Variability constitutes less of a problem when the rater's or recorder's operations are standardized, but the manner of eliciting the requested information is left to the interviewer's discretion, which is the case in various semistructured interviewing procedures that may be combined with psychiatric rating scales. Under more flexible circumstances, there is a greater opportunity to adapt the procedure to the individual and his or her culture. At the same time, however, the risk of introducing error into recorded behaviors is increased across individuals and across cultures.

As Boesch (1971) has observed, the ability to communicate one's subjective experiences is a universal human quality; the willingness, however, to produce such information on demand is a cultural variable. Breaking up personal experience into question-size units and reducing answers to binary true/false or yes/no choices, or to a limited number of graduations of agreement, are Western practices that are by this time widely accepted and deeply ingrained, especially in the United States culture. In other settings, people have less experience with, and may to different degrees be "put off" by, inquiries into their experience that are couched in the objective, limited-option inventory format. Variations in readiness of response to standardized testing are often observed, although so far they have rarely been systematically studied.

As paper-and-pencil inventories and rating scales are exported beyond the confines of their culture of origin, they must be translated. The consensus of cross-cultural investigators is that individuals should be tested in their native language, i.e., their idiom of subjective experience. This requirement applies even in the case of bilingual or multilingual individuals who possess the language skills for responding to the scale in its original version. Nevertheless, their response to the instrument may, to an unknown degree, be affected not only by the content of the instrument but also by the language in which it is presented. There are some studies (Edgerton and Karno, 1971) of bilingual persons that demonstrate a subtle shift in response, depending on the language in which the questions are administered.

Translation of Psychological Instruments

A substantial body of writing has developed on the methodology of translation of psychological instruments (Brislin, 1970, 1976; Prince and Mombour, 1967; Sechrest, Fay, and Zaidi, 1972; Wagatsuma, 1977). The most important safeguard repeatedly recommended involves back-translation. The translated scale or inventory must be independently rendered back into its original language in order to test its accuracy. In the case of perfect correspondence between the translation and the original language version of the test, the adequacy of the translation is verified. If, however, discrepancies result, they are reconciled in conference by the translator and back-translator. In this manner, major errors as well as subtle slippages of meaning are detected and eliminated. Once a linguistically accurate translation has been prepared, further checks on its appropriateness are recommended. The translation may be field-tested and reactions of the participants in relation to the intelligibility of the items, their linguistic and social appropriateness, and other features of the instrument may be observed, recorded, and incorporated into any further revisions of the instrument. Empirical studies of bilingual individuals (Spielberger and Diaz Guerrero, 1976) are especially valuable to ensure the equivalence of the translated and original versions of the measure. Although certain discrepancies may remain because of the different subjective valences of items in the two languages, the convergence of response patterns across language is another important indication that the original and translated versions uniformly measure the characteristics in question.

A particular problem in the cross-cultural investigation of abnormal behavior involves the translation of terms that describe subjective emotional states. It is these affectively laden terms that are especially difficult to translate realistically and effectively, because they often differ in intensity, commonality, and range of usage even when their denotative, dictionary usage may be identical. Wagatsuma (1977, p. 143) provides a number of significant examples of subtle shifts in connotative and associative meaning with words like *relaxed, outgoing,* and *changeable,* from three interrelated European languages: English, French, and German. Even with the best resources of judgment and expertise, some distortion remains evident in the use of specific words and phrases.

How can language limitations be transcended? One expedient, recommended by Brislin (1972), is to write maximally translatable prose. Specifically, Brislin recommends using short, simple sentences consisting of fewer than sixteen words, employing the active rather than the passive voice, repeating nouns instead of substituting pronouns for them, avoiding metaphors and colloquialisms, employing specific rather than general terms, and avoiding the subjective mode, the possessive form, and adverbs pertaining to space and time.

These suggestions are highly useful for the development of new tests. The tests in wide current use, however, have antedated the formulation of these recommendations. As a consequence, an array of measures exist that pose a number of translation problems. By and large, it is easier to translate a term in context than by itself; redundancy is a great help in increasing intelligibility and reducing ambiguity (Brislin et al., 1973).

An accurate translation is indispensable for the cross-cultural equivalence of measures. By itself, however, an adequate translation does not ensure such accuracy. Test items may be identical in linguistic meaning and yet evoke very different reactions, depending upon the culture in question. As Butcher and Clark (1979) point out, the term *shyness* is readily and identically understood in the United States and Japan. Yet, the item "I wish I were not so shy" is incomprehensible to the Japanese because shyness is more widespread in Japan (Zimbardo, 1977) and, moreover, is positively valued. The experience of several major projects involving adaptation of tests introduced to new cultures (Butcher and Pancheri, 1975; Spielberger and Diaz Guerrero, 1976) suggests that items inevitably have to be added, subtracted, and reworded to yield meaningful and equivalent responses in a different culture and language. The standards of equivalence in this context are subjective and intuitive. No clear and specific rules have been established to determine whether an item on one test that is different in content and wording from the same item on a translated test is identical in psychological meaning. In contrast to the more concrete and specific rules that have been devised for translating, investigators concerned with the cultural readaptation of an instrument must make their own decisions about what to add, drop, substitute, or reword in developing a new and culturally fitting version of the test.

The less similar the cultures, the greater the change that the original test undergoes in being adapted to a new setting. Zeldine et al. (1975), in their attempts to translate and readapt the Hamilton Depression Scale in Senegal in West Africa, had to drop one-third of the original items as irrelevant to the African experience of depression. Upon consultation with local informants, the researchers added several new items that reflected the locally prevalent complaints and manifestations. Their report is notable because it is concerned with the process of translating and adapting a psychological scale and not just with the result or product of such adaptation. Such a procedure is in keeping with the recommendations of Butcher and Clark (1979), who encourage authors to share with their readership any unanticipated problems and difficulties encountered in culturally adapting a test as well as any solutions attempted or implemented in the course of their research. In this way, there remains room for creative improvisation and trial-and-error in cultural adaptation of tests.

The final product of changing a test for a new setting is a set of items or questions that is not identical to the original. Tests are translated and culturally adapted for two reasons: 1) to perform in a new cultural setting the same tasks for which they were originally designed, and 2) to remain as close to the original as possible in content, format, and rationale. In the context of this chapter, it is the second objective that is paramount. The authors of a new test adaptation are most interested in the practical usefulness of a translated and culturally redesigned measure. These two goals of translating and adapting a test ideally should be complementary; however, in practice they all too often exercise a pull in opposite directions. By the process of culturally editing and revising a paper-and-pencil instrument, the operation of decentering (Werner and Campbell, 1970) a measure from its cultural foundation is accomplished. As a result, a detectably different, although similar, test comes into being. For the purpose of cross-cultural comparison, this operation should be followed by recentering the test and making it comparable to the original from which it was derived. How can this objective be fulfilled? In the cross-cultural research literature, such recentering has not received the attention it deserves. Methodological writings in this area are replete with cautionary statements on difficulties in cross-cultural comparison, but are much less explicit on how these difficulties are to be overcome. Elsewhere (Draguns, 1977a), three solutions to this problem have been proposed: 1) restricting cross-cultural comparison to those items that have survived readaptation in a linguistically and semantically identical state; 2) bilaterally transforming items in both the original and translated versions, so that a new test usable at both sites of investigation is created; 3) assuming or demonstrating the equivalence of items in both versions of the test. None of these solutions is perfect and, with the exception of the first, they are not easy to carry out.

Finally, the revised and adapted version of the test must be empirically demonstrated to possess reliability and validity in its milieu. Consequently, norms on the test must be collected, performance on it must be related to a variety of relevant external criteria, and the factorial composition of the test must be determined anew. Once all of this information is collected, the test may be used in its new location. Whether or not it is comparable to the original remains to be ascertained.

Paper-and-pencil measures have been discussed at considerable length because they currently constitute the major tools of cross-cultural investigation. They are not, however, the only possible set of instruments for comparing abnormal behavior across cultures and should not be regarded as such. What other options are open to the cross-cultural investigator?

INSTRUMENTS OF PERSONALITY APPRAISAL

Projective Techniques   The cross-cultural researcher of abnormal behavior may turn to indirect, rather than direct, tools of personality appraisal. The projective techniques, for instance, hold a historically prominent place in the study of personality and culture (Holtzman, 1980; Lindzey, 1961; Spain, 1972), although they have been used remarkably little in the cross-cultural study of abnormal behavior, and their current place in the total armamentarium of the contemporary cross-cultural investigator remains minor. When projective techniques are conceived of broadly as "interviews by other means" (Zubin, Eron, and Schumer, 1965), and when the complex question of their validity is momentarily dismissed, they are valuable for increasing the variety of data collected and for transcending the limitations of self-report. Of course, a number of cautions must be observed in applying projective techniques cross-culturally, and Lindzey (1961) identified a number of pitfalls. In particular, he warned against the practice, prevalent at one time, of diagnosing individuals or whole cultures on the basis of signs and norms extraneous to that culture. However, such activity is not significant in the investigation of psychopathology in relation to culture. Instead, projective techniques, in the few instances in which they are employed for that purpose, are simply considered to be additional measures, beyond subject self-report or objective observation. Holtzman's (1980) review reveals a moderate amount of cross-cultural projective research, but only a small share of this activity is relevant to the cross-cultural comparison of psychopathology.

Projective stimuli may differ in demand characteristics across cultures. Although inkblots are presumably equally ambiguous in Seattle and in Samoa, cultures differ in the extent to which they foster and inhibit the kind of conditional suspension of disbelief that the task of responding to such projective stimuli requires. Thus, records collected in one culture may be elaborate and expressive, while in another culture they are sparse and impoverished. To echo Lindzey's warnings, it would be rash to interpret these characteristics in the same manner that one would interpret the performance of two individuals within the same cultural setting. The meaning of a confrontation with projective stimuli can be ascertained empirically; semantic differential ratings, interview data, and psychophysiological recordings lend themselves to that end. However, such explorations of personal meaning, beyond the customary responses to projective stimuli, have not yet been pursued cross-culturally.

Experimental Laboratory Research   The direct methods of the experimental psychology laboratory provide another set of techniques of potential applicability for cross-cultural investigators. Al-Issa (1968) suggested extending experimental laboratory research on schizophrenia across cultures, but these proposals remain unimplemented. Very likely, it is mainly the practical difficulties in the application of the complex, expensive, and bulky experimental apparatus that have prevented the realization of these suggestions. However, the experimental methods, as such, may evoke widely different personal reactions, depending on the person's familiarity with them and with their subjective meaning. With normal subjects, Lazarus et al. (1966) demonstrated such differing reactions in a comparison of Americans and Japanese. The diffuse effects of the experiment upon the Japanese subjects were so intense that they overshadowed the consequences of the specific stressor that was experimentally inflicted. Such instances should cause potential experimental investigators to proceed cautiously, but not to cease experimentation completely. It should not be overlooked that an impressive body of experimental literature on abnormal behavior now exists in a number of countries, including France, Germany, Great Britain, Italy, Japan, and the Soviet Union. If, in all of these countries and many others, it has been possible to study psychopathological behavior in the experimental laboratory, then it should be possible to compare such studies cross-culturally, subject to a number of cautions. So far, this type of comparison has not been made, but divergences in the results of national investigators may, to an unknown degree, be traceable to cultural differences.

Phenomenological Investigation   The naturalistic phenomenological methods of exploring the subjective world of the person are exemplified in cross-cultural psychiatric research by the Japanese psychiatrist Kimura (1965, 1967, 1972), and are grounded in the procedures of European pioneers of phenomenological psychiatry (Minkowski, 1966; Tellenbach, 1972). By systematically delving into the implicit assumptions of perceiving the personal and objective worlds, subtle differences between Japanese and German depressive patients were uncovered. Beyond these differences, Kimura (1972) was able to demonstrate culturally and linguistically based constants in the perception of self in Western countries and in Japan. Such systematic explorations of the subjective world of phenomena are qualitative; they may serve as stepping stones to more conventional quantitative research studies of the same phenomena. Kimura's pioneer formulations have led to studies of Japanese and American experiences of depression by means of word associations and semantic differential ratings, with both language and culture varied (Tanaka-Matsumi and Marsella, 1976). From another perspective, Parin and Parin-Matthey (1976) discovered subtle differences between the members of two cultures as closely related as the Swiss and Southern Germans in the process of psychoanalysis. These findings were reported qualitatively, but are potentially amenable to quantification.

Observation over Time   Current trends in objective observation and recording of psychopathological states have resulted in an unfortunate emphasis upon psychopathology at a given moment, as opposed to over a period of time. There are weighty conceptual and empirical reasons for expecting that the course of psychological disorder is subject to cultural influence, and that this influence may operate independently of cultural factors that shape the manifestation of disorder (H. B. M. Murphy, 1977; Waxler, 1979). For these reasons, it is highly desirable that systematic study of abnormal behavior across cultures be extended to careers of mental patients in their treatment settings and communities. To some extent, this is already being done. [H. B. M. Murphy (Chapter 9, this volume) reports on the details of the procedures and results of this research.]

The objectification of both psychiatric ratings and self-reports has been, unquestionably, a positive development. Its value, however, should not blind us to the potential of other approaches, used independently or complementarily. Contemporary investigators of abnormal behavior and culture have a number of options open to them; they should not concentrate on one to the exclusion of all others.

POPULATIONS

To what groups of people does the study of cross-cultural psychopathology pertain? Three problems arise in response to this question:

1. As already indicated, standards of normality and abnormality differ across cultures. Although there is mounting evidence that the most serious manifestations of disturbance are recognized, regardless of site and culture (A. H. Leighton et al., 1963; J. M. Murphy, 1976; WHO, 1973), there is a vast "gray area" within which cultures may draw the line between normality and abnormality at different points.
2. The populations recognized as disturbed differ across cultures in a variety of social characteristics and dimensions. Thus, they may be typically literate in one culture and predominantly illiterate in another.
3. The psychologically disturbed individuals may differ in their access to available therapeutic or healing facilities, whether the facilities are modern or traditional, indigenous or imported.

In reference to the first of these points, lines designating the category of psychological disturbance may be drawn with either narrow or wide boundaries. Historically, the bulk of cross-cultural psychopathological research has been concentrated upon manifestations of abnormal behavior narrowly or restrictively defined, i.e., at the disturbed end of the continuum. It is widely agreed, however, that these kinds of comparisons are subject to contamination by differences in cultural meaning of hospitalization or psychiatric treatment. (Higginbotham, 1979a). It is therefore incumbent upon the investigator to demonstrate that mental health facilities in the countries in question are equally accessible and are used by the population in the same proportion, a procedure that has rarely been followed.

At the other extreme, the comparison may be extended to include broad populations. There is a growing number of studies concerned with aversive affective states, such as anxiety or depression, as they are experienced at two or more points around the world, not within predefined samples of psychiatric clients or cases, but in the population at large. [See Engelsmann (Chapter 10, this volume), Marsella (1980), and Sharma (1977) for reviews.] Significant strides have also been made in the development of cross-cultural measurement and comparison of these states in clinically diagnosed samples (Spielberger and Diaz Guerrero, 1976).

Epidemiological Studies

Another ambitious and inclusive approach to the cross-cultural comparison of psychopathology is the psychiatric census or the epidemiological study in which all cases of mental illness, within its entire range, are identified, diagnosed, and recorded. The history of this type of investigation extends over almost the last fifty years. Comprehensive and inclusive searches for psychiatric cases have been conducted in all regions and continents of the globe. Potentially, then, they represent a valuable source of comparative cross-cultural information on incidence and prevalence of psychiatric disorders. In actuality, however, very few of these studies have been conducted with an explicit comparative intent. Extracting meaningful trends from a host of independent studies has proved to be an uncertain and complex enterprise. Several recent reviewers (Adis Castro, 1970; Dohrenwend and Dohrenwend, 1974; Marsella, 1979) have earnestly attempted to integrate the evidence from this literature. At this point, however, only a few conclusions can be safely drawn, and these, for the most part, pertain to worldwide trends in relating variables like experience of stress to major categories of psychopathological manifestation. It is much more difficult to identify established findings on cross-cultural variations in incidence of psychopathology from epidemiological sources.

However, it is possible to coordinate the planning and conduct of epidemiological studies at several sites. With the exception of the projects coordinated by the Leightons in Nigeria (A. H. Leighton et al., 1963), Canada (D. C. Leighton et al., 1963), and Sweden (D. C. Leighton et al., 1971), such an effort has as yet not been undertaken. The realization of such a study is rendered less likely by the necessity for generous funding. A psychiatric census, even at one site, is an ambitious and costly undertaking; its requirements are multiplied as it is extended to several cultures and locations.

Samples of Convenience

Until epidemiological studies become more widespread, cross-cultural investigators of psychopathology are left with groups of individuals that can best be designated "samples of convenience," i.e., collections of clients or cases to which they have access in two or more cultures. These cases are likely to be incomparable in a number of social respects, and these sources of social differences are likely to distort, and probably to exaggerate, the more purely cultural contrasts between groups. An expedient that has been widely practiced to help remedy this problem has been individual matching, i.e., trying to find a close counterpart in one culture for a member of a sample in another, in such pertinent social variables as education, occupation, sex, age, psychiatric diagnosis, and marital status. However, this procedure has been severely criticized on methodological and conceptual grounds.

Brislin (1977) has provided a persuasive and articulate critique of this approach toward equalizing disparities in samples of convenience drawn from different cultures. Whenever individuals from two samples with unequal means are matched, the resulting artificially equated pairs of subjects are susceptible to regression effects upon replication. Suppose that an investigator has succeeded in matching subjects from a nearby universally literate culture with subjects from a culture in which literacy is the exception rather than the rule. This feat has been accomplished by matching illiterate (but, in their own milieu, entirely typical) subjects in one case with highly deviant and atypical subjects in another. Apart from all the other problems that such a procedure entails, this "success" would be unlikely to be repeated upon replication. Unusual arrays of subjects do not usually turn up twice; therefore, the repetition of the study pushes the subjects of the study closer to their population mean—they are no longer unable to read or write, although they are still sparsely educated. Such an outcome is almost inevitable in a comparison of two groups when one is at an extreme and the other is typical.

Other defects of matched-group comparisons are perhaps even more obvious. By definition, the matched subjects in one group, and perhaps in both groups, are atypical of the populations from which they were drawn. To whom, then, do we generalize any differences obtained between these two artificially constructed groups of subjects? Furthermore, as the Brazilian psychologist Angelini (1967) has reminded us, it is misleading to eliminate differences that may very much be a part of the two cultures in question. A comparison of those psychiatric patients from Canada and India who have been equated in annual income might, at first glance, seem to be methodologically "clean" and elegant. On closer scrutiny, however, the comparison illustrates one of the most obvious differences between Canada and India: most Indians, by Canadian standards, are poor, while most Canadians, from the Indian viewpoint, are affluent, and even wealthy. Finally, matching subjects when discrepancies in means of social variables (and probably in cultural characteristics as well) are major can be almost guaranteed to shrink a large group to a small one or, at best, to one of a moderate size. As a result, the power of whatever statistical techniques are applied is lost. The likely consequence is that differences that truly exist between the two groups will go undetected and unrecognized.

If matching is laden with these multiple and serious defects, what procedures can be recommended to take their place? Brislin and Baumgardner's (1971) proposal is both simple and far-reaching. These researchers suggest that unmatched samples of convenience be left as they are, but their characteristics should be described in scrupulous detail. Once this is done, subsequent investigators can refer the discrepancies in their findings to the specifics of their sample characteristics, and to the data of their predecessors. In the case of abnormal behavior across cultures, such a description should mandatorily include the basis on which the persons' behavior was judged to be abnormal, and the circumstances under which their responses were observed, elicited, or recorded. It is gratuitous to assume that the range of behavior defined as abnormal is constant across cultures or that cultures are identical in their thresholds of acceptability for a variety of acts.

The solution proposed by Brislin and Baumgardner (1971) is, of course, arguable. The point can be made that the cost of forgoing any attempt at equating samples from two or more cultures is extremely high.

Alternatives to this "radical surgery" are either partialing out or covarying noncultural but social sources of difference. However, the range of application of these procedures continues to be subject to controversy, and it is not clear whether requirements for the implementation of these techniques would be met in many cases of cross-cultural comparison of abnormal behavior. Another possible method is restricting the comparison to similar or identical groups of patients; for example, only those who are depressed, or suicidal, or who have developed symptoms and complaints while studying for their final examinations in their senior year of college. Conversely, it is possible to start with people in the same social situation, like being a junior executive or the oldest brother, and to inquire into the personal problems and difficulties that people in that situation are likely to develop in several cultures. Finally, it may even be permissible to match, provided this is done with the awareness of the very severe limitations of the procedure. Fabrega, Swartz, and Wallace (1968), for example, performed two kinds of comparisons of Mexican-Americans and "Anglos" in Texas, one matched and the other unmatched. There is some merit in comparing empirically the results of these two operations.

A preferable method is the comparison of representative or random samples of psychiatric patients in several cultures. So far such a step has rarely been taken (Engelsmann et al., 1972). Moreover, a large share of psychopathological research within culture, in the United States and elsewhere, is not based on either representative or random samples.

OBSERVERS

Psychiatrists and other mental health professionals are commonly re-garded as objective evaluators of disturbance and as experts in its classifi-cation, diagnosis, and treatments. Their knowledge base, however, rests on the implicit recognition of the cultural baselines for modal and for acceptable behavior. Thus, mental health professionals also function as cultural agents concerned with the standards of permissible and appropriate behavior. The role of psychiatrists and members of related professions as gatekeepers of social deviance has been emphasized in the iconoclastic writings of the critics of the medical model (Laing, 1967; Sarbin, 1967; Szasz, 1969). The questionable tenet of these writers is that the cultural judgment of deviance encompasses the psychiatrist's entire role. Neverthe-less, the fact that psychiatrists function on the basis of this specialized knowledge and also on behalf of their culture complicates the comparison of the results of psychiatric observation across cultural lines. Moreover, the effects of personal training and of the modeling of psychiatrists' behavior must be considered. In the case of the well-known U.S.–U.K. comparison (Cooper et al., 1972), some of the differences between the diagnostic habits of British and American psychiatrists may be traceable to the personal influence of respected, admired, and powerful leaders of the psychiatric profession in their respective two countries. Thus, a research practice based on personal judgment and idiosyncrasy may be enshrined as an implicit, but nonetheless widely followed, model of professional activity, including the method of diagnostic modeling.

Relatively haphazard personal influences are, however, only one source of cultural divergence in the use and assignment of diagnostic categories. The results of the U.S.–U.K. project (Cooper et al., 1972) as well as those of a number of other Anglo-American comparisons indicate that psychiatric diagnosticians in these two English-speaking countries differ in the range of conditions subsumed under a disorder and in the threshold of recognition for its features. In the case of British psychiatrists, the range of the symptoms diagnosed as schizophrenia was narrow, and the threshold for its recognition was high. The opposite obtained for depression; British specialists diagnosed depression liberally and did so on the basis of clues that might have been overlooked by their United States counterparts.

Observer effects also operate in a number of other spheres of activity. Mexican and United States psychiatrists have been shown to differ in their ratings of the seriousness of various psychiatric symptoms (Fabrega and Wallace, 1967). A host of stylistic differences have been identified in Anglo-American comparisons of psychiatrists (Edwards, 1973; Katz, Cole, and Lowery, 1969; Sandifer et al., 1968) in the number of symptoms observed, in the reliability of these observations, and in the rank ordering of symptoms for different diagnoses.

A German-American comparison (Townsend, 1975a, 1975b, 1978) indicates that mental health professionals share the conceptions of mental health with the lay public and the patient population of their respective culture. Information on the effect of the cultural setting upon the feelings and perceptions of the mental health professional has been provided by Wintrob and Harvey (1981, in press). Collomb (1973), a French psychiatrist with extensive research and clinical experience in West Africa, has identified three recurring attitudes among expatriate mental health professionals: rejection of their own culture, idealization of the host culture, and a medical orientation emphasizing the uniformity of mental illness, regardless of site. Each of these biases can conceivably affect the recording and reporting of cross-cultural observations. As yet, however, no objective data are available on the translation of these personal attitudes into any cross-cultural equivalents of the Rosenthal (1966) effect, i. e., a subtle influence by the experimenter upon the subject's behavior. In fact, the interaction of the observer's personal beliefs, values, and attitudes with his/her orientation toward the culture in which research is being done has not yet received the research attention that it deserves.

Several steps can be taken to make observer effects explicit and to include them systematically in research designs. Generally, these attempts aim at restricting and specifying the role of the observer. In the U.S.–U.K. study (Cooper et al., 1972), and in other recent research projects (WHO 1973, 1979), this objective was accomplished by relying upon uniform schedules of symptom recording and by deriving diagnoses from them in an objective manner. This method results in a substantial reduction of, although not the elimination of, observer errors. The initial duty of the observer is the detection of symptoms; the selective sensitivities and biases associated with detection appear early in the process. These biases might be counteracted by a greater explicitness in the operational definition of symptoms, as exemplified by DSM-III (American Psychiatric Association, 1980). In the cross-cultural field, Sechrest's (1969) exploratory study of Filipino and United States patients is notable for its attention to detailed and specific criteria for the recording of symptoms.

A more ambitious step, proposed (Draguns, 1973) but not yet implemented, would involve a systematic and counterbalanced exchange of psychiatric observers at several sites of the investigation. The practical problems of executing this ambitious step remain prodigious, involving cost above all, but also including issues of cultural sensitivity and language skill. Nonetheless, such an exchange of observers seems to be the only decisive way of establishing objectively the observer's contribution to the diagnostic process across cultures.

SETTING

The proponents of the social learning point of view have reminded us (Higginbotham and Tanaka-Matsumi, 1981; Higginbotham, 1979b) that no behavior automatically constitutes a symptom, and that it only becomes an indicator of experienced distress or of perceived disturbance in the course of transaction with the environment. Al-Issa (1977, 1978) demonstrated that hallucinations differ in the social response that they provoke across space and time. Cultural factors facilitate the expression of hallucinations through a sense modality, visual or auditory, and determine their acceptance as normal behavior or even as a supernormal gift, or their rejection as a manifestation of disturbance.

It is therefore important to specify where and how the allegedly symptomatic behavior occurs and how it is conceived, labeled, and responded to, both by the person most immediately concerned and by his or her peers. Equally essential is the specification of behaviors and events that have preceded and followed the alleged symptom. Finally, the setting in which the symptomatic behavior occurred must be indicated. The specification of the context of psychopathological manifestations in cross-cultural research is still in its infancy. It constitutes an important adjunct to description, especially in cultures very much different from that of the United States.

A widely accepted conclusion is that symptomatic behavior is responsive to the setting in which it occurs. Institutional atmosphere is subject to cultural variation (Draguns, 1974; Townsend, 1978; Yamamoto, 1972); thus, the institution may reflect the culture at large. However, the institution may also possess unique features of its own and may foster or impede behaviors in a variety of ways. It is therefore hazardous to generalize to the entire culture from one institution within it, yet a sampling of institutions within a culture has rarely been attempted.

What has been said of therapeutic or custodial institutions applies to other social units, such as the family. Even autistic children have been shown to behave differently within highly sociable and crowded Hong Kong families than they have traditionally been reported to behave in the West. Thus, even the least social category of psychological disturbance is not altogether immune to the effects of social context (Ney et al., 1979).

Chinese patients experience a lifetime of social attention to their physical complaints (Kleinman, 1977; Tseng, 1975; Tseng and Hsu, 1969). In contrast, they show repeated indications of lack of social response to expression of their psychological distress. As a consequence, the former type of behavior is perpetuated and the latter extinguished. Somatic expressions, under these circumstances, become the favored modes of expression for a variety of emotions, such as frustration, disappointment, and loss. Examples like that of the Chinese, then, show that the symptom constitutes only a link in the chain between its antecedents and consequents. Cross-cultural research, however, is very much concentrated upon the symptom as an isolated occurrence at a frozen moment. The use of standardized symptom scales unfortunately brings about the perpetuation of this isolating approach by plucking the symptom out of its context.

Furthermore, contexts of observation across cultures need not only to be specified, but also to be compared. So far, this has been done infrequently and atypically. Usually, the spotlight is on the disturbed individual rather than on the system or setting in which he or she functions. The question may be asked: Given a particular set of circumstances, how do individuals respond to them in cultures A, B, and C? Of particular interest in relation to psychopathology is the role of stress and its effect upon the social unit and its members. Comparisons of the behavior of disturbed individuals in various cultures are numerous, yet cross-cultural studies of the impact of psychological disturbance on the other members of the family are entirely lacking. The closest available approximation of this type of research was coordinated in three countries of Latin America by Seguin (1961). His study compared family responses to an identical stressful event: the child's physical illness. Apparently, this project was not completed.

Important advances in understanding the setting for the observation of psychopathology have come from the research program by Katz et al.

(1978). These researchers systematically recorded observations in family and hospital environments of their patients in Hawaii belonging to three ethnic groups. Noteworthy interactions emerged between ethnicity and setting of observation. It is worth emphasizing, however, that not only the milieus but also the observers were varied in this series of investigations.

Therefore, it can be concluded that patient behavior varies to some degree as a function of the setting in which it is observed. The settings, in turn, interact with the culture in which they are located to mold and to shape patients' reactions in somewhat different ways. The picture is complicated and all of its components are not evident. What is clear, however, is that settings deserve to be incorporated systematically into cross-cultural psychiatric research.

CULTURE

Defining Cultural Characteristics

As a concept, culture intuitively seems to have a self-evident meaning. At the same time, one has to agree with Triandis' (1980, p. 52) statement that "after a century of serious work there is not a widely accepted definition of this term, or a clear specification of the best procedures for its study. Nor do we have very good ways of specifying the interaction of other variables such as sex, age, social class, race, nationality, religion, ideology, and the like with culture." Triandis (1980) emphasized the need, in Whiting's (1976) words, to "unpackage" culture. Culture is a global and complex variable of a high order of abstraction. Identifying the operation of a cultural influence upon a domain of behavior is but the first step. Once it has been taken, the questions must be asked: What about the culture makes the behavior difference? What feature or characteristic of the culture is the active ingredient of the effect demonstrated?

In cross-cultural psychological investigation, culture typically consti- tutes the independent variable or the quasi-independent treatment (Brown and Sechrest, 1980; Sechrest, 1977). The objective is to disentangle the multiple threads of this global influence.

Forfeiting for the moment a rigorous and comprehensive definition of culture, one could say that culture pertains to the concrete and symbolic man-made parts of the environment (Herskovits, 1948). Culture, then, is that legacy of human experience that we share with some, but not all, members of the human species. Although all people are members of a culture, their cultures are different in language, historical sources, institu- tions, and artifacts. Comparing individuals in different cultures in their maladaptive manifestations is the goal of cross-cultural research in psychopathology. Operationally, culture is used in one of the three following senses in this body of investigation; national, tribal-traditional, and ethnic:

1. *National.* In its most frequent usage in cross-cultural investigation of abnormal behavior, culture is equated with nation. Two assumptions are implicit in this definition of culture. First, it is assumed that each of the almost 170 nations of the world, existing as sovereign entities in 1980, possesses its own distinct culture; for example, the culture of Canada is identifiably different from that of the United States, that of Norway is different from Sweden's and that of Zimbabwe is different from Zambia's. The second assumption in the definition of culture as nation is that cultural variations existing within a nation are lesser in scope and in degree than those that exist between nations. This second assumption underlies, implicitly at least, the prevailing use of nonrandom samples of convenience in cross-cultural comparison. It is believed, whether it be for realistic or for convenient reasons, that variations within the culture will not distort or obliterate differences across cultures. Comparing individuals across national lines poses no inherent problems when the cultural gulf is wide and the physical distance great, as, for example, between the United States and Japan. There is at least the potential for creating subtle and intractable difficulties, however, when nations as closely related as Germany and Austria or Argentina and Uruguay are compared. Empirically, few such comparisons have been attempted to date.

2. *Tribal-traditional.* The national sense of the concept of culture stands in contrast to a more restricted usage in anthropological literature, that of the tribal-traditional. Naroll (1971) defined the cult unit on the basis of a mutually intelligible dialect and went on to differentiate four types of cult units: 1) the Hopi type—a society in the absence of a state, based on language and community contact; 2) the Flathead type—a group sharing a state and a language; 3) the Aymara type—a politically subjugated people defined on the basis of a shared language; and 4) the Inca type—a politically dominant and linguistically homogeneous group in a linguistically heterogeneous state (Naroll, Michik, and Naroll, 1980). The same tribal-traditional principles implicitly underlie the definition and differentiation of cultures in anthropology. These cultures are, for the most part, small-scale, traditional, and not isomorphic to any of the modern states. Such groups are exemplified by the Ojibwa Indians of Canada, the Luo of Kenya, the Yoruba of Nigeria, the Hmong of Laos, and the Lapps of Finland. Some work has been done on the psychopathology of such people, although the evidence extant tends to be, with some exceptions, descriptive rather than comparative. In contrast to cultural anthropologists, psychia-

trists and psychologists have devoted a much larger share of their energies to the study of members of more complex modern cultures.

3. *Ethnic.* In pluralistic, multicultural nations, the concept of culture has been applied to yet another principle of division of these societies: the so-called ethnic groups defined on the basis of racial physical characteristics, shared language, common historic origins, and shared contemporary customs. On this basis, some people are designated Italian-Americans, Mexican-Americans, blacks, Japanese-Americans, and Irish-Americans in the United States; there are Chinese, Indians, and Malays in Singapore; Koreans in Japan; and many more groups similarly identified in a wide variety of nations. What constitutes the defining properties of an ethnic group is difficult to determine. Probably no single criterion, such as the possession of a unique language, is adequate to encompass all such groupings. This problem has, in any case, occupied a number of writers from several social science disciplines (Berry, 1979; Isajiw, 1974; Singh, 1977; Schermerhorn, 1970). Without dwelling on the subtleties and complexities of these conceptual and definitional problems, one can propose three basic criteria of individual determination of ethnic group membership. The first of these is ascriptive and concrete—ethnic membership is decided on the basis of specific and nonpsychological indicators, such as birthplace, parentage, family name, skin color, and other physical characteristics. The assumption of this criterion is that membership in an ethnic group is conferred at birth and that it remains immutable throughout the life span. The second approach is based upon self-identification, as it is expressed through interest in, and association with, various ethnic activities; this involves ancestral language, dress, food, customs, values, historical heritage, and leisure activities. On this basis, it is possible to regard ethnic involvement and identity on a continuous and quantitative rather than on a categorical, all-or-none basis. The third principle of determining ethnic group membership involves group consensus. From the perspective of the in-group and the out-group, who is regarded as a Sioux Indian or a Polish American, and who is not? In the typical case, the given three criteria for determining ethnic membership lead to convergent results; in a sufficient number of instances, however, they do not. Cross-cultural investigators of abnormal behavior have, for the most part, relied upon external ascriptive criteria of ethnicity and have placed less importance on the subjective and consensual ones.

The existence of multiple ethnic groupings in the modern pluralistic or multicultural societies of East and West provides the opportunity to execute cross-cultural research projects close to investigators' home bases. At the same time, such undertakings are fraught with methodological complications, specifically of two kinds. One problem is that, in a setting in which several groups interact and share the same locale, mutual influence and interpenetration occur. Two questions are sparked by this phenomenon: 1) To what extent are the members of a group typical of its cultural characteristics? 2) Where is the "outward boundary" of an ethnic group, or, at what point does a familial or historical association with an ethnic group cease to be a significant influence? The second problem concerns the inequality of status of the various ethnic groups in many, although not necessarily all, pluralistic societies. In such a case, differences in symptom patterns and incidence of, and severity of, psychopathological responses may well be the direct results of externally imposed stress rather than characteristics of the ethnic culture itself (DeVos, 1980; King, 1978).

Determining Cultural Influence

However cultural variables are distinguished or defined, the basic problem with which the interpreter of cultural data in relation to psychopathology must contend is the diffuse and global nature of cultural influence. Culture is an abstraction several steps removed from the observable. Few investigators are, at this point, content with tracing a psychopathological manifestation to a cultural influence. A number of techniques have been evolved through attempts to pinpoint the exact nature of cultural influence. Sechrest (1977) proposed preselecting cultures on the basis of the knowledge of their relevant antecedent variables (such as a particularly harsh or lenient socialization style), in order to investigate the effects of these experiences. Unquestionably, choosing cultures on the basis of their known and pertinent features would go a long way toward making cross-cultural comparisons of psychopathology closer approximations of "experiments of nature." Throughout the world, cultural variations constitute quasi-experimental "independent variables" that are much more powerful than those that the experimenter is capable of imposing and manipulating. Sechrest's (1977) recommendation of such preselection as a feature of *all* future cross-cultural research is, however, probably unrealistic. Just as in individual projects the actual participants all too often constitute samples of convenience, the cultures compared will probably continue to be, for the most part, targets of opportunity, chosen because of practical considerations of access and availability. Although opportunistic, poorly conceptualized cross-cultural research is to be decried, there is enough chance of serendipitous discovery in comparing the psychopathology across cultures without an explicit, *a priori* reason for doing so. The prerequisite for research in several cultures to be worthwhile is that the cultural characteristics be knowingly and sophisticatedly evaluated.

Because cultures may differ in a host of dimensions, it may be difficult to assign a specific cultural source to a difference in psychopathological manifestation. This problem is especially likely to be encountered if two highly dissimilar cultures are compared, such as Arctic Eskimos and the inhabitants of midtown Manhattan. The difficulty is so intractable that it has caused a number of productive cross-cultural investigators, for example, Collomb (1966) in Senegal in West Africa and H. B. M. Murphy (1978) in Canada, to concentrate entirely or exclusively on differences between cultural groups high in overall similarity, either geographically adjacent or sharing a territory. In such a case, the chances are increased of at least approximating the ideal of experimental research: holding all variables constant except one.

Whatever differences are obtained, however, the problem of the generic cultural influence upon behavior cannot be resolved. For this purpose, as Campbell and Naroll (1972) have noted, the comparison of two cultures is inadequate. Such comparison may be of some descriptive value in shedding light on the nature of the differences between the two cultures in question, but in order to resolve the general issue of cultural influence, a sufficient number of cultures is needed to provide instances of graduations and linear, curvilinear, or other types of influence. In the body of pertinent research extant, bicultural studies are legion, and multicultural investigations few.

Sources of Multicultural Data

For practical reasons of cost, few investigators have been able to conduct major multicultural investigations involving representation of the major regions of the world and the collection of original data. The World Health Organization's International Pilot Study of Schizophrenia and the projects that have followed it are notable for the accomplishment of these objectives. At least in the reported stages of this ongoing series of projects, the orientation of this team of investigators has been remarkably universalistic. They have refrained from drawing generalizations from the observed psychopathological manifestations to the political, regional, economic, or other cultural features in the nine settings compared.

In the absence of opportunities for the collection of pertinent data in various regions of the world, cross-cultural investigators of abnormal behavior may turn to the examination of already available archival materials. The most prominent and comprehensive repository of such information is contained in the Human Relations Area Files (HRAF) at Yale University in New Haven, Connecticut (Barry, 1980; Naroll et al., 1980). This collection is based on uniformly coded ethnographic accounts from all regions of the world, spanning several historical periods. HRAF materials have been utilized in a modest number of projects of psychopathological interest, such as Denko's (1964, 1966) studies of emic explanations of psychological disorder in "primitive" cultures and of the taxonomy of culture-bound disorders, and projects by Palmer (1965) and Lester

(1967) on suicide. Two factors prevent a more extensive use of this unique collection of data in psychopathological research. One obstacle is the paucity of information on psychopathology in most of the original ethnographic accounts on which HRAF are based. The gamut of observed human maladaptation is not a topic routinely or traditionally included in anthropological field reports. Another problem is that the slant of HRAF construction has been explicitly to maximize human diversity, even at the expense of human representativeness. As a consequence, small-scale traditional-tribal cultures from all the regions of the world, of the kind that traditionally have been studied by anthropologists, are overrepresented in the HRAF quality sample and in other samples. By the same token, HRAF samples so far only sparingly include the major historical civilizations of East and West.

To a limited degree, two additional sources of multicultural indirect data have been used in psychopathological research. National statistics on various social phenomena of psychopathological interest constitute one repository of such data. Indeed, the cross-cultural use of suicide statistics goes back to Durkheim (1951; original edition, 1897) and Masaryk (1970; original edition, 1884), with their classical contributions. More recent work by Lynn (1971) represents an attempt to use a much wider range of data from publicly available statistics of a number of nations, such as caloric intake, rate of alcohol consumption, and automobile accident rates, to indirectly study national differences in manifestations of anxiety. Many obstacles and complications make it difficult to derive conclusive results from these indices. Because it is difficult to study psychopathology multiculturally by other means, further judicious use and refinement of such indicators is worth pursuing.

In three multicultural projects (H. B. M. Murphy et. al., 1963; H. B. M. Murphy et al., 1967; Rogan, Dunham, and Sullivan, 1973) another expedient was tested; psychiatrists were used as informants on the characteristic manifestations of psychopathology in their cultures. This approach is open to criticism because it confounds observer effects with the psychopathological phenomena investigated. Each step that is interposed between data and their recording increases chances of error. Nevertheless, the technique of a worldwide psychiatric poll provides the opportunity for the quick and relatively inexpensive collection of worthwhile preliminary data. Thus, the results by H. B. M. Murphy et al. (1963, 1967) on the universal features of schizophrenia and depression have been corroborated and extended in more intensive recent investigations like the WHO (1973) study.

Relating Culture to Psychopathology

A final problem remains: How can cultural characteristics be linked with psychopathological manifestations? To contrast cultures on such obvious characteristics as those of technologically advanced versus those of developing nations seems to be an easy task, but contemporary investigators of psychopathology across cultures have been reticent about formulating principles on this plane of generality. A number of other, more subtle cultural dichotomies have received attention in the recent literature; for example, complex versus simple (Murdock and Provost, 1973), tight versus loose (Pelto, 1968), and tough versus easy (Arsenian and Arsenian, 1948; Marsella, 1979). None of these contrasts has so far been conclusively related to psychopathological manifestations.

An alternative to the global characterization of culture is the inclusion of normal samples of individuals in investigations of cultural influences upon psychopathology. This approach has been repeatedly recommended (Draguns, 1973; Draguns and Phillips, 1972) and is beginning to be implemented in studies like that of Katz et al. (1978) among the various ethnic groups in Hawaii. It is essential to continue and extend the use of normal samples in order to answer one of the basic questions about the relationship of psychopathology to modal or normal behaviors: Does psychopathology stand in a relationship of contrast to, or exaggeration of, the normal baseline (Draguns, 1973, 1977c, 1980)?

Another area of concern is the transformation of implicit cultural assumptions, such as ideas of space and time, into psychopathological symptoms. The German phenomenological psychiatrist, Tellenbach (1972), first raised this issue. More recently (Draguns, 1980), seven specfic links between culture and psychopathology were identified, but, as of the time of this writing, none has been conclusively and exhaustively investigated.

In contrast to these theoretical concerns, H. B. M. Murphy's work (1974, 1975, 1977; Chapter 9, this volume) exemplifies an orientation based on common sense. Murphy has been involved in a search for cultural groups and settings with a reputation for high or low rates of schizophrenia. His objective, as presented at greater length in Chapter 9, has been twofold: 1) to verify or refute reports of increased or decreased incidence, on the basis of the aggregate of available data; and 2) to trace the validated reports, if any, to the familial and more broadly social features of the cultural milieu in question.

Thus, a variety of approaches are available to cross-cultural investigators in their attempt to bridge the gap between the features of the culture and its characteristic patterns of maladaptation. The continued pursuit of all of these approaches is necessary if the field is to move from the repeated identification of cultural effects upon psychopathology to their description and specification. As Jahoda (1975) has pointed out, cross-cultural psychology represents an intermediate step toward a complete, explanatory account of all the sources of human diversity. Once these sources are pinpointed, the need for a semiautonomous cross-cultural psychology will disappear, and it will merge with a general psychology.

CONCLUSIONS

This chapter gives a somewhat rapid review of the field, but a few general trends emerge from this survey:

1. Research on psychopathology across cultures has been marked by a pronounced etic slant. Typically, both concepts and measures have been transferred across culture lines; often, they have simply been assumed to be universal. A mounting body of evidence points to the pancultural nature of some of the major varieties of psychopathology, especially in the most serious manifestations of abnormal behavior. Although the importance of these results should be recognized, it must be reiterated that the emic approach to psychopathology and culture has been largely bypassed and has not been given a serious chance. This neglect has been independently recognized by a number of recent reviewers and evaluators of the field (Draguns, 1977a; Kleinman, 1977; Marsella, 1979). The application of the emic orientation in psychopathological research across cultures entails incorporating and taking seriously the local concepts of abnormal behavior. Marsella (1978) proposed a sequence of four steps in the cross-cultural study of depression, but his scheme is equally applicable to other diagnostic entities. The process involves: 1) the emic determination of categories of disorder within cultures; 2) the establishment of symptom frequencies, intensities, and durations; 3) objective determination of symptom patterns by means of multivariate data processing techniques; and 4) comparative studies using similar methodologies with culturally defined categories of disorder. These operations should be supplemented by the simultaneous and independent development of measures of psychopathology at the several sites of a cross-cultural investigation.

2. As yet, no methodologies of appropriate power and complexity have been developed that would give the emergence of both cross-cultural differences and similarities an equal chance and that would provide the specific weights of pancultural universals and cultural particulars in the total picture of a group's psychopathology. There is no project extant that provides objective indications of the proportions of worldwide constancy and variation in psychopathological manifestations of populations across cultures.

    Finifter (1977) identified two contrasting types of cross-cultural research: universalist, slanted toward the demonstration of similarities, and specifist, geared toward an emphasis on differences. Much rarer is the third type, the agnostic one, which allows the emergence of both differences and similarities. Both similarities and differences across culture in psychopathological manifestation must be related to each other, and not just recorded in an absolute fashion.

3. The consideration of the several available approaches to cross-cultural investigation of psychopathology amply demonstrates that no research method is ideal, and that each provides but a partial and potentially distorted view of the phenomena in question. Recognizing this, the admonition toward diversification by H. B. M. Murphy (1969) is well worth reiterating. In the last two decades, the development of objective, face-valid, paper-and-pencil scales and their application to the problems of cross-cultural comparison of abnormal behavior (Draguns, 1977a) have particularly advanced. However, this positive development presents the danger of crowding out other approaches and producing one mode of modern streamlined cross-cultural research on psychopathology. Such a trend is to be regretted; it should be counteracted by an equally vigorous development of other measures that go beyond paper-and-pencil symptom checklists and scales, however useful and valuable these kinds of instruments may be. For example, Opler and Singer (1959), in their pioneering study of Italian and Irish schizophrenics, relied upon a variety of methods, from self-report to projective techniques. Therefore, patterns of findings, rather than discrete results, must be produced as an indispensable condition for further growth and progress in this rapidly developing and changing field.

4. It has been said that cross-cultural psychology does not have any methodological problems peculiar to itself (Guthrie, 1979). However, it cannot be denied that the problems encountered in cross-cultural research often represent magnifications of dilemmas and difficulties in better-established fields of investigation. Similarly, there are no solutions unique to cross-cultural research. Such research, at its best, involves sensitive and realistic resolution of complications that hinder systematic and objective observation as well as the derivation of clear and compelling inferences therefrom. Good cross-cultural research is simply good research that has been performed in relation to cultural variables.

5. Methodological writings in cross-cultural psychology (including this chapter) are usually directed at the most difficult and problematic situation: how to deal with a host of potential contaminants of collected data, many of which are interpenetrated with cultural variables. In the real world, the problem may be much less consequential. Although all of the considerations in this chapter apply to cross-cultural research in principle, only some of them are applicable to an actual given research project. Students and young investigators, in

particular, may be overwhelmed, or even immobilized, by the forbidding complexities of investigation of abnormal behavior cross-culturally. A relatively neglected, but potentially fruitful avenue of study involves performing comparisons and studies of cultural variations close at hand. As seems evident, it is easier to compare and to study individuals in depth in similar cultures than in very different ones. Thus, cross-cultural research is relevant to social phenomena both far away and close at hand.

REFERENCES

Adis Castro, G. 1970. Salud mental, investigación y contexto sociocultural. In: J. Mariategui and G. Adis Castro (eds.), Epidemiología Psiquiátrica en América Latina. Fondo para la salud mental, Buenos Aires.

Al-Issa, I. 1968. Problems in the cross-cultural study of schizophrenia. J. Psychol. 71:143–151.

Al-Issa, I. 1977. Social and cultural aspects of hallucinations. Psychol. Bull. 84:570–587.

Al-Issa, I. 1978. Sociocultural factors in hallucinations. Int. J. Soc. Psychiatry 24:167–176.

American Psychiatric Association. 1980. Diagnostic and Statistical Manual of Mental Disorders (DSM-III). 3rd Ed. American Psychiatric Association, Washington, D.C.

Angelini, A. 1967. Alguns problemas methodologicos na pesquisa transcultural. In: C. F. Hereford and L. Natalicio (eds.), Aportaciones de la Psicología la Investigación Transcultural. Trillas, Mexico City.

Arsenian, J., and Arsenian, J. M. 1948. Tough and easy cultures: A conceptual analysis. Psychiatry 11:377–385.

Barry, H. III. 1980. Description and uses of the Human Relations Area Files. In: H. C. Triandis and J. W. Berry (eds.), Handbook of Cross-Cultural Psychology. Vol. 2. Methodology. Allyn & Bacon, Inc., Boston.

Bash, K. W., and Bash-Liechti, J. 1969. Studies of the epidemiology of neuropsychiatric disorders among the rival population of the province of Khuzestan, Iran. Soc. Psychiatry 4:137–143.

Benedict, R. 1934. Culture and the abnormal. J. Genet. Psychol. 1:60–64.

Benoist, A. 1964. Valeurs culturelles et dépression des canadiens français de Montréal. Paper presented at the First International Congress of Psychiatry, August, London.

Berry, J. W. 1969. On cross-cultural comparability. Int. J. Psychol. 4:119–128.

Berry, J. W. 1979. Research in multicultural societies: Implications of cross-cultural methods. J. Cross-Cult. Psychol. 10:415–434.

Boesch, E. E. 1971. Zwischen zwei Wirklichkeiten: Prolegomena einer ökologischen Psychologie. Huber, Berne.

Boesch, E. E., and Eckensberger, L. H. 1969. Methodische Probleme des interkulturellen Vergleichs. In: C. F. Graumann, L. Kruse, and B. Kröner (eds.), Sozialpsychologie: I. Halbband: Theorien und Methoden: Handbuch der Psychologie. Band 7/1. Verlag für Psychologie, Göttingen.

Brislin, R. W. 1970. Back-translation for cross-cultural research. J. Cross-Cult. Psychol. 1:185–216.

Brislin, R. W. 1972. Translation issues: Multi-language versions and writing translatable English. Proceedings of the 80th Annual Convention of the American Psychological Association, pp. 299–300.

Brislin, R. W. (ed.) 1976. Translation: Aplications and Research. Wiley/Halstead, New York.

Brislin, R. W. 1977. Methodology of cognitive studies. In: G. Kearney and D. McElwain (eds.), Aboriginal Cognition. Australian Institute for Aboriginal Studies, Canberra, Australia.

Brislin, R. W., and Baumgardner, S. 1971. Non-random sampling of individuals in cross-cultural research. J. Cross-Cult. Psychol. 2:397–400.

Brislin, R. W., Lonner, W. J., and Thorndike, R. M. 1973. Cross-Cultural Research Methods. John Wiley & Sons, Inc., New York.

Brody, E. B. 1973. The Lost Ones: Social Forces and Mental Illness in Rio de Janeiro. International Universities Press, New York.

Brown, E. D., and Sechrest, L. 1980. Experiments in cross-cultural research. In: H. C. Triandis, and J. W. Berry (eds.), Handbook of Cross-Cultural Psychology. Vol. 2: Methodology. Allyn & Bacon, Inc., Boston.

Butcher, J. N., and Clarke, L. A. 1979. Recent trends in cross-cultural MMPI research and application. In: J. N. Butcher (ed.), New Developments in the Use of the MMPI. University of Minnesota Press, Minneapolis.

Butcher, J. N., and Pancheri, P. 1975. A Handbook of Cross-Cultural MMPI Research. University of Minnesota Press, Minneapolis.

Butcher, J. N. and Tellegen, A. 1978. Common methodological problems of MMPI research. J. Consult. Clin. Psychol. 46:620–628.

Campbell, D. T., and Naroll, R. 1972. The mutual methodological relevance of anthropology and psychology. In: F. L. K. Hsu (ed.), Psychological Anthropology. New Ed. Schenkman, Cambridge, Mass.

Collomb, H. 1965. Bouffées délirantes en psychiatrie africaine. Psychopathologie Africaine 1:167–239.

Collomb, H. 1966. Psychiatrie et cultures. Psychopathologie Africaine 2:259–273.

Collomb, H. 1973. L'avenir de la psychiatrie en Afrique. Psychopathologie Africaine 9:343–370.

Cooper, J. E., Kendell, R. E., Gurland, B. J., Sharpe, L., Copeland, J. R. M., and Simon, R. 1972. Psychiatric Diagnosis in New York and London. Oxford University Press, Oxford.

Davidson, A. R., Jaccard, J. J., Triandis, H. C., Morales, M., and Diaz Guerrero, R. 1976. Cross-cultural model testing: Toward a solution of the emic-etic dilemma. Int. J. Psychol. 11:1–13.

Denko, J. D. 1964. The role of culture in mental illness of non-Western peoples. J. Am. Wom. Med. Assoc. 19:1029–1044.

Denko, J. D. 1966. How preliterate peoples explain disturbed behavior. Arch. Gen. Psychiatry 15:398–409.

DeVos, G. A. 1980. Ethnic adaptation and minority status. J. Cross-Cult. Psychol. 11:101–124.

Dohrenwend, B. P., and Dohrenwend, B. S. 1974. Social and cultural influences upon psychopathology. Annu. Rev. Psychol. 25:419–452.

Doi, T. 1973. The Anatomy of Dependence. Kodansha International, Tokyo.

Draguns, J. G. 1973. Comparisons of psychopathology across cultures: Issues, findings, directions. J. Cross-Cult. Psychol. 4:9–47.

Draguns, J. G. 1974. Values reflected in psychopathology: The case of the Protestant ethic. Ethos 2:115–136.

Draguns, J. G. 1977a. Advances in methodology of cross-cultural psychiatric assessment. Transcult. Psychiatr. Res. Rev. 14:125–143.

Draguns, J. G. 1977b. Problems of defining and comparing abnormal behavior across cultures. Ann. New York Acad. Sci. 285:664–675.

Draguns, J. G. 1977c. Mental health and culture. In: D. S. Hoopes, P. B. Pedersen, and G. W. Renwick (eds.), Overview of Intercultural Education, Training, and Research. Vol. 1. Theory. Society for Intercultural Education, Training, and Research, Washington, D.C.

Draguns, J. G. 1980. Psychological disorders of clinical severity. In: H. C. Triandis, and G. Draguns (eds.), Handbook of Cross-Cultural Psychology. Vol. 6: Psychopathology. Allyn & Bacon, Inc., Boston.

Draguns, J. G., and Phillips, L. 1972. Culture and Psychopathology: The Quest for a Relationship. General Learning Press, Morristown, N. J.

Draguns, J. G., Phillips, L., Broverman, I. K., Caudill, W., and Nishimae, S. 1971. The symptomatology of hospitalized psychiatric patients in Japan and in the United States: A study of cultural differences. J. Nerv. Ment. Dis. 152:3–16.

Dunham, H. W. 1976. Society, culture, and mental disorder. Arch. Gen. Psychiatry 33:147–156.

Durkheim, E. 1951. (J. A. Spaulding and G. Simpson, trans). Suicide. Free Press, Glencoe, Ill. (Originally published in 1897.)

Edgerton, R. B., and Karno, M. 1971. Mexican-American bilingualism and the perception of mental illness. Arch. Gen. Psychiatry 24:286–290.

Edwards, G. 1973. Diagnosis of schizophrenia: An Anglo-American comparison. Int. J. Psychiatry 11:442–452.

Ellenberger, H. 1960. Cultural aspects of mental illness. Am. J. Psychother. 14:158–173.

Engelsmann, F., Murphy, H. B. M., Prince, R., Leduc, M., and Demers, H. 1972. Variations in responses to a symptom check-list by age, sex, income, residence, and ethnicity. Soc. Psychiatry 7:150–156.

Engelsmann, F., Vinar, P., Pichot, P., Hippius, H., Giberti, F., Rossi, L., and Overall, J. E. 1971. International comparison of diagnostic patterns. Transcult. Psychiatr. Res. Rev. 7:130–137.

Fabrega, H. J., and Wallace, C. A. 1967. How physicians judge symptoms: A cross-cultural study. J. Nerv. Ment. Dis. 142:486–491.

Fabrega, H. J., Swartz, J. D., and Wallace, C. A. 1968. Ethnic differences in psychopathology: Clinical correlates under varying conditions. Arch. Gen. Psychiatry 19:218–226.

Favazza, A. R. and Oman, M. 1978. Overview: Foundations of cultural psychiatry. Am. J. Psychiatry 135:293–303.

Finifter, B. M. 1977. The robustness of cross-cultural findings. Ann. New York Acad. Sci. 285:151–184.

Guthrie, G. M. 1979. A cross-cultural odyssey: Some personal reflections. In: A. J. Marsella, R. G. Tharp, and T. J. Ciborowski (eds.), Perspectives on Cross-Cultural Psychology. Academic Press, Inc., New York.

Hamilton, M. 1967. Development of a rating scale for primary depressive illness. Br. J. Soc. Clin. Psychol. 6:278–296.

Herskovits, M. J. 1948. Man and His Works. Alfred A. Knopf, Inc., New York.

Higginbotham, H. N. 1979a. Culture in the delivery of psychological services in developing nations. Transcult. Psychiatr. Res. Rev. 16:1–27.

Higginbotham, H. N. 1979b. Culture and mental health services in developing countries. In: A. J. Marsella, R. G. Tharp, and T. J. Ciborowski (eds.), Perspectives on Cross-Cultural Psychology. Academic Press, Inc., New York.

Higginbotham, H. N., and Tanaka-Matsumi, J. 1981. Social learning theory applied to counseling across cultures. In: P. B. Pedersen, J. G. Draguns, W. J. Lonner, and J. A. Trimble (eds.), Counseling Across Cultures (Revised Ed.). University Press of Hawaii, Honolulu.

Holtzman, W. H. 1980. Projective techniques. In: H. C. Triandis and J. W. Berry (eds.), Handbook of Cross-cultural Psychology. Vol. 2: Methodology. Allyn & Bacon, Inc., Boston.

Isajiw, W. W. 1974. Definitions of ethnicity. Ethnicity, 1:111–124.

Jahoda, G. 1975. Presidential address. In: J. W. Berry, and W. J. Lonner (eds.), Applied Cross-Cultural Psychology: Selected Papers from the Second International Conference of the International Association of Cross-Cultural Psychology. Swets & Zeitlinger, Amsterdam.

Jahoda, G. 1977. In pursuit of the emic-etic distinction: Can we ever capture it? In: Y. H. Poortinga (ed.), Basic Problems in Cross-Cultural Psychology. Swets & Zeitlinger, Amsterdam.

Jahoda, M. 1958. Current Concepts of Positive Mental Health. Basic Books, Inc., New York.

Katz, M. M., Cole, O. J., and Lowery, H. A. 1969. Studies of the diagnostic process: The influence of symptom perception, past experience, and ethnic background on diagnostic decisions. Am. J. Psychiatry 125:937–947.

Katz, M. M., Sanborn, K. O., Lowery, H. A., and Ching, J. 1978. Ethnic studies in Hawaii: On psychopathology and social deviance. In: L. C. Wynne, R. L. Cromwell, and S. Mathysse (eds.), The Nature of Schizophrenia: New Approaches to Research and Treatment. John Wiley & Sons, Inc., New York.

Kimura, B. 1965. Vergleichende Untersuchungen über depressive Erkrankungen in Japan and Deutschland. Fortschr. Psychiatr. Neurol. 33:202–215.

Kimura, B. 1967. Phänomenologie des Schulderlebnisses in einer vergleichenden psychiatrischen Sicht. Aktuel. Fragen Psychiatr. Neurol. 6:54–65.

Kimura, B. 1972. Mitmenschlichkeit in der Psychiatrie. Zeitschrift für Klinische Psychologie 20:3–13.

King, L. M. 1978. Social and cultural influences upon psychopathology. Ann. Rev. Psychol. 29:405–434.

Kleinman, A. 1977. Depression, somatization, and the "new cross-cultural psychiatry." Soc. Sci. Med. 11:3–9.

Kramer, M. 1969. Applications of Mental Health Statistics. World Health Organization, Geneva.

Laing, R. D. 1967. The Politics of Experience. Pantheon Books, New York.

Lazarus, R. S., Tomita, M., Opton, E. Jr., and Kodama, M. 1966. A cross-cultural study of stress-reaction patterns in Japan. J. Pers. Soc. Psychol. 4:622–633.

Leighton, A. H., Lambo, T. A., Hughes, C. C., Leighton, D. C., Murphy, J. M., and Macklin, D. B. 1963. Psychiatric Disorders among the Yoruba. Cornell University Press, Ithaca, N. Y.

Leighton, D. C., Harding, J. S., Macklin, D. B., Macmillan, A. M., and Leighton, A. H. 1963. The Character of Danger: Psychiatric Symptoms in Selected Communities. Basic Books, Inc., New York.

Leighton, D. C., Hagnell, O., Kellert, S. R., Leighton, A. H., Harding, J. S., and Danley, R. A. 1971. Psychiatric disorder in a Swedish and a Canadian community: An exploratory study. Soc. Sci. Med. 5:189–209.

Lester, D. 1967. Suicide, homicide, and the effects of socialization. J. Pers. Soc. Psychol. 5:466–468.

Lindzey, G. 1961. Projective Techniques and Cross-Cultural Research. Appleton-Century-Crofts, New York.

Lonner, W. J. 1979. Issues in cross-cultural psychology. In: A. J. Marsella, R. J.

Tharp, and C. J. Ciborowski (eds.), Perspectives on Cross-Cultural Psychology. Academic Press, Inc., New York.

Lorr, M., and Klett, J. C. 1968. Major psychiatric disorders: A cross-cultural study. Arch. Gen. Psychiatry 19:652–658.

Lorr, M., and Klett, C. J. 1969a. Cross-cultural comparison of psychotic syndromes. J. Abnorm. Psychol. 74:531–545.

Lorr, M., and Klett, J. C. 1969b. Psychotic behavior types: A cross-cultural comparison. Arch. Gen. Psychiatry 20:592–598.

Lynn, R. 1971. Personality and National Character. Pergamon Press, Inc., New York.

Malpass, R. 1977. Theory and method in cross-cultural psychology. Am. Psychol. 32:1069–1079.

Marsella, A. J. 1978. Thoughts on cross-cultural studies on the epidemiology of depression. Cult. Med. Psychiatry 2:343–357.

Marsella, A. J. 1979. Cross-cultural studies of mental disorders. In: A. J. Marsella, R. G. Tharp, and T. J. Ciborowski (eds.), Perspectives on Cross-Cultural Psychology. Academic Press, Inc., New York.

Marsella, A. J. 1980. Depressive experience and disorder across cultures. In: H. C. Triandis, and J. G. Draguns (eds.), Handbook of Cross-Cultural Psychology. Vol. 6: Psychopathology. Allyn & Bacon, Inc., Boston.

Marsella, A. J., and Sanborn, K. 1973. The Comprehensive Depressive Symptom Checklist. Institute of Behavioral Sciences, Honolulu.

Masaryk, T. G. 1970. Suicide and the Meaning of Civilization. University of Chicago Press. Chicago. (Originally published in 1884.)

Minkowski, E. 1966. Traité de Psychopathologie. Presses Universitaires de France, Paris.

Murdock, G. P., & Provost, C. 1973. Measurement of cultural complexity. Ethnology 12:379–392.

Murphy, H. B. M. 1969. Handling the culture dimension in psychiatric research. Soc. Psychiatry 4:11–15.

Murphy, H. B. M. 1972. History and the evolution of syndromes: The striking case of latah and amok. In: M. Hammer, K. Salzinger, and S. Sutton (eds.), Psychopathology. John Wiley & Sons, Inc., New York.

Murphy, H. B. M. 1974. Differences between the mental disorders of French Canadians and British Canadians. Can. Psychiatr. Assoc. J. 19:247–258.

Murphy, H. B. M. 1975. Alcoholism and schizophrenia in the Irish: A review. Transcult. Psychiatr. Res. Rev. 12:116–139.

Murphy, H. B. M. 1977. Chronicity, community, and culture. In: C. Chiland and P. Bequart (eds.), Long-term Treatments of Psychotic States. Human Sciences Press, New York.

Murphy, H. B. M. 1978. European cultural offshoots in the New World: Differences in their mental hospitalization patterns. Part I: British, French, and Italian influences. Soc. Psychiatry 13:1–19.

Murphy, H. B. M., Wittkower, E. W., and Chance, N. A. 1967. Cross-cultural inquiry into the symptomatology of depression: A preliminary report. Int. J. Psychiatry 3:6–15.

Murphy, H. B. M., Wittkower, E. W., Fried, J., and Ellenberger, H. 1963. A cross-cultural survey of schizophrenic symptomatology. Int. J. Soc. Psychiatry 3:6–15.

Murphy, J. M. 1976. Psychiatric labeling in cross-cultural perspective. Science 191:1019–1028.

Naroll, R. 1971. The double language boundary in cross-cultural surveys. Behav. Sci. Notes 6:95–102.

Naroll, R., Michik, G. L., and Naroll, F. 1980. Holocultural research methods. In:

H. C. Triandis and J. W. Berry (eds.), Handbook of Cross-Cultural Psychology. Vol. 2: Methodology. Allyn & Bacon, Inc., Boston.

Ney, P., Lieh-Mak, F., Cheng, R., and Collins, W. 1979. Chinese autistic children. Soc. Psychiatry 1977. 14:147–150.

Ogino, K., Kuba, M., and Suzuki, J. 1977. A review of transcultural psychiatric research in Japan. Transcult. Psychiatr. Res. Rev. 14:7–22.

Opler, M. K., and Singer, J. L. 1959. Ethnic differences in behavior and psychopathology: Italian and Irish. Int. J. Soc. Psychiatry 2:11–23.

Palmer, S. 1965. Murder and suicide in forty non-literate societies. J. Crim. Law Criminol. Police Sci. 56:320–324.

Parin, P., and Parin-Matthey, G. 1976. Typische Unterschiede zwischen Schweizern and Süddeutschen aus dem gebildeten Kleinbürgertum. Psyche 30:1028—1048.

Pelto, P. J. 1968. The difference between "tight" and "loose" societies. Transaction April, pp. 37–40.

Price-Williams, D. 1974. Psychological experiment and anthropology: The problem of categories. Ethos 2:95–114.

Prince, R. and Mombour, W. 1967. A technique for improving linguistic equivalence in cross-cultural surveys. Int. J. Soc. Psychiatry 13:229–327.

Rogan, E. N., Dunham, H. W., and Sullivan, T. M. 1973. A worldwide transcultural survey of diagnostic, treatment, and etiological approaches to schizophrenia. Transcult. Psychiatr. Res. Rev. 10:107–110.

Rosenthal, R. 1966. Experimenter Effects in Behavioral Research. Appleton-Century-Crofts, New York.

Saenger, G. 1968. Psychiatric patients in America and the Netherlands: A transcultural comparison. Soc. Psychiatry 3:149–164.

Sandifer, M. G., Horden, A., Timbury, G. C., and Green, L. M. 1968. Psychiatric diagnosis: A comparative study of North Carolina and Glasgow. Br. J. Psychiatry 126:206–212.

Sarbin, T. R. 1967. On the futility of the proposition that some people be labeled "mentally ill." J. Consult. Psychol. 31:447–453.

Schermerhorn, R. A. 1970. Comparative Ethnic Relations: A Framework for Theory and Research. Random House, New York.

Schneider, K. 1958. Clinical Psychopathology. Grune & Stratton, New York.

Scott, W. A. 1958. Research definitions of mental health and mental illness. Psychol. Bull. 55:29–45.

Sechrest, L. 1969. Philippine culture, stress, and psychopathology. In: W. Caudill and T. Lin (eds.), Mental Health Research in Asia and the Pacific. East-West Center Press, Honolulu.

Sechrest, L. 1977. On the need for experimentation in cross-cultural research. Ann. New York Acad. Sci. 285:104–118.

Sechrest, L., Fay, T., and Zaidi, S. 1972. Problems of translation in cross-cultural research. J. Cross-Cult. Psychol. 3:41–56.

Seguin, C. A. 1961. La actitud de la familia frente al niño enfermo. Proceedings of the Third World Congress of Psychiatry. McGill University Press, Montreal.

Sharma, S. 1977. Cross-cultural comparisons of anxiety: Methodological problems. Topics Cult. Learn. 5:166–173.

Singh, V. P. 1977. Some theoretical and methodological problems in the study of ethnic identity: A cross-cultural perspective. Ann. New York Acad. Sci. 285:32–45.

Spain, D. H. 1972. On the use of projective techniques in psychological anthropology. In: F. L. K. Hsu (ed.), Psychological Anthropology. New Ed. Schenkman, Cambridge, Mass.

Spielberger, C. and Diaz Guerrero, R. (eds.) 1976. Cross-Cultural Anxiety. Hemisphere Press, Washington, D.C.

Spielberger, C. D., Gorsuch, R. L., and Lushene, R. E. 1970. Manual for the State-Trait Anxiety Inventory. Consulting Psychologists Press, Palo Alto, Calif.

Stengel, E. 1961. Problems of nosology and nomenclature in the mental disorders. In: J. Zubin (ed.), Field Studies in the Mental Disorders. Grune & Stratton, New York.

Szasz, T. S. 1969. Psychiatric classification as a strategy of social constraint. In: T. S. Szasz (ed.), Ideology and Insanity. Doubleday & Company, Inc., New York.

Tan, E. K., and Carr, J. E. 1977. Psychiatric sequelae of amok. Cult. Med. Psychiatry 1:59–67.

Tanaka-Matsumi, J. 1979. Taijin-kyofusho: Diagnostic and cultural issues in Japanese psychiatry. Cult. Med. Psychiatry 3:231–245.

Tanaka-Matsumi, J., and Marsella, A. J. 1976. Cross-cultural variations in the phenomenological experience of depression. J. Cross-Cult. Psychol. 7:379–396.

Tellenbach, H. 1972. Das Problem des Massstabs in der transkulturellen Psychiatrie. Nervenarzt 43:424–426.

Townsend, J. M. 1975a. Cultural conceptions, mental disorders, and social roles: A comparison of Germany and America. Am. Sociol. Rev. 40:739–752.

Townsend, J. M. 1975b. Cultural conceptions and mental illness: A controlled comparison of Germany and America. J. Nerv. Ment. Dis. 160:409–421.

Townsend, J. M. 1978. Cultural Conceptions of Mental Illness. University of Chicago Press, Chicago.

Triandis, H. C. 1980. Reflections on trends in cross-cultural research. J. Cross-Cult. Psychol. 11:35–58.

Triandis, H. C. and Berry, J. W. (eds.) 1980. Handbook of Cross-Cultural Psychology. Vol. 2: Methodology. Allyn & Bacon, Inc., Boston.

Triandis, H. C., Malpass, R. S., and Davidson, A. H. 1973. Psychology and culture. Ann. Rev. Psychol. 24:355–378.

Tseng, W. S. 1975. The nature of somatic complaints among psychiatric patients: The Chinese case. Compr. Psychiatry 16:237–245.

Tseng, W. S., and Hsu, J. 1969. Chinese culture, personality formation, and mental illness. Int. J. Soc. Psychiatry 16:5–14.

Wagatsuma, H. 1977. Problems of language in cross-cultural research. Ann. New York Acad. Sci. 285:141–150.

Waxler, N. E. 1979. Is outcome of schizophrenia better in nonindustrial societies? The case of Sri Lanka. J. Nerv. Ment. Dis. 167:144–158.

Weidman, H. H., and Sussex, J. H. 1971. Culture values and ego functioning in relation to the atypical culture-bound reactive syndromes. Int. J. Soc. Psychiatry 17:83–100.

Werner, O., and Campbell, D. 1970. Translating, working through interpreters, and the problem of decentering. In: R. Naroll and R. Cohen (eds.), A Handbook of Method in Cultural Anthropology. American Museum of Natural History, New York.

Whiting, B. 1976. The problem of the packaged variable. In: K. Riegel and J. Meacham (eds.), The Developing Individual in a Changing World. Vol. 1. Mouton Publishers, The Hague.

Wing, J. K. 1970. A standard form of psychiatric present schedule examination (PSE) and a method for standardizing the classification of symptoms. In: E. H. Hare and J. H. Wing (eds.), Psychiatric Epidemiology. Oxford University Press, London.

Wintrob, R. M. and Harvey, Y. K. 1981. The self-awareness factor in intercultural psychotherapy: Some personal reflections. In: P. B. Pedersen, J. G. Draguns, W.

J. Lonner and J. A. Trimble (eds.), Counseling Across Cultures. Revised ed. University Press of Hawaii, Honolulu.

Wittkower, E. D. 1969. Perspectives of transcultural psychiatry. Int. J. Psychiatry 8:811–824.

World Health Organization. 1973. Report of the International Pilot Study of Schizophrenia. World Health Organization, Geneva.

World Health Organization. 1979. Schizophrenia: An International Follow-up Study. John Wiley & Sons, Inc., New York.

Yamamoto, K. 1972. A comparative study of "patienthood" in the Japanese and American mental hospital. In: W. P. Lebra (ed.), Transcultural Research in Mental Health. Vol. 2. University Press of Hawaii, Honolulu.

Yap, P. M. 1974. Comparative Psychiatry: A Theoretical Framework. University of Toronto Press, Toronto.

Zeldine, G., Ahvi, R., Leuckx, R., Boussat, M., Saibou, A., Hanck, C., Collignon, R., Tourame, G., and Collomb, H. 1975. A propos de l'utilisation d'une échelle d'evaluation en psychiatrie transculturelle. L'Encéphale 1:133—145.

Zimbardo, P. G. 1977. Shyness: What It Is and What To Do About It. Addison-Wesley, Publishing Company, Inc., Reading, Mass.

Zubin, J., Eron, L. D., and Schumer, F. 1965. An Experimental Approach to Projective Techniques. John Wiley & Sons, Inc., New York.

Zung, W. W. K. 1969. A cross-cultural survey of symptoms in depression. Arch. Gen. Psychiatry 126:115—121.

Chapter 3

The Concept
of Mental Illness
A Historical Perspective

Theodore R. Sarbin and Joseph B. Juhasz

No historical account can be written without including the element of interpretation. Even the reportage of a chronology of events is influenced by the historian's selection of what events to include. Most important, the interweaving of the happenings of the period and their concurrent interpretation are not always available. To make a historical narrative convincing, then, requires some speculative "filling in," that is, interweaving of the "facts" and the concurrent matrix of stated and unstated ideological premises (Mannheim, 1929, White, 1973). The history of the concept of mental illness (and of cognate concepts, such as psychopathology and behavior pathology) is no exception to this rule of historiography.

Chronologies must be organized according to some guiding theme in order to be of interest to anyone. An example of such a theme is "milestones on the road to freedom." With this theme, a number of recorded events may be selected and perceived as central features in a complex narrative; among them the Magna Carta (1215), the Declaration of Independence (1776), the Emancipation Proclamation (1863), the Women's Suffrage Amendment (1920), and the *Brown* v. *Board of Education* decision (1954). Implicit in such a chronology is the selection of meaningful events according to the individual historian's lens through which they are viewed.

The historian tries to explain events by referring to the antecedent and concurrent conditions that are presumed to be causal. In twentieth-century histories of medical psychology and psychiatry, the guiding theme is not difficult to discern. The theme is the gradual displacement of superstitious belief by scientific truth, and might be called "milestones in the scientific care and management of people with disordered or diseased minds." The lens through which most historians examine the chronology of madness is the lens of nineteenth- and twentieth-century science. Such historians do not see the need to justify the use of the "science-on-the-march" lens instead of, for example, a moral, theological, mystical, or astrological lens. The idea that science is the road to truth has become so entrenched that the historian is often blind to the possibility of using other lenses.

This view is well represented by Coleman in his best-selling *Abnormal Psychology and Modern Life.* In the Fifth Edition (1976), he states: "Throughout most of history . . . beliefs about mental disorders have been generally characterized by superstition, ignorance, and fear. Although successive advances in the scientific understanding of abnormal behavior have dispelled many false ideas, there remain a number of popular misconceptions . . . " (p. 10). Similarly, in the 1975 edition of *Fundamentals of Behavior Pathology,* Suinn states: "In one period of modern man's history, the abnormal person was viewed with suspicion, superstition, and horror. Although much of the superstitious fear has been swept away by modern science, some misconceptions still persist . . . " (p. 38).

Traditional histories, such as those of Ackerknecht (1959), Alexander and Selesnick (1966), or Zilboorg and Henry (1941), present the concept of mental illness as an achievement of science in its efforts to displace superstition. Such historians begin their work from the unexamined assumption that the mental illness concept is on firm ontological grounds. The vocabulary of mental illness contains implicit assumptions that attribute certain kinds of causality to the conduct of a person whose actions are identified by certain others as nonconforming, silly, outlandish, unpredictable, bizarre, dangerous, or embarrassing; in sum, it is unwanted conduct, but not clearly criminal. These historians typically fail to ask the initial question: What are the criteria for classifying conduct as unwanted, conduct that is explicable in the causal language of mechanistic science? There are other ways of conceptualizing unwanted conduct. Furthermore, these alternate constructions are also influenced by historical events and by the construals of these events. This chapter sorts out the ideological, metaphorical, and mythic elements that have sustained the employment of the scientific model, especially that variant of the scientific model that has served the medical and mental health professions for the past hundred years or more.

In broad perspective, this chapter considers the following stages in the history of the concept of mental illness: 1) the early nineteenth-century "moral treatment" and its implications for a scientific theory of deviant conduct; 2) the consolidation and elaboration of the "illness" model in the latter half of the nineteenth and the early part of the twentieth centuries; 3) early challenges to the biomechanical explanations offered by social scientists and reformers; 4) the major attack on the medical model mounted in the 1960s, and 5) the current status of competing paradigms.

THE FORMATION OF THE CONCEPT OF MENTAL ILLNESS

This chapter is not intended to be a complete history of madness. However, there are some stipulations that can be made. In the Middle Ages, theological models were in ascendency and generated theories of demonology, possession, witchcraft, and miraculous intrusions to account for at least some contranormative conduct. Furthermore, during that same period, some conduct that would now be contranormative was acceptable, and vice versa. This chapter identifies some of the historical conditions that facilitated the shift from theological to naturalistic models (Sarbin and Juhasz, 1967). An example of this shift in the sixteenth century was the felicitous metaphor employed by Teresa of Avila, an outstanding figure of the counter-reformation. A cloister of nuns was exhibiting conduct that later diagnosticians would have labeled "hysterical reaction." By defining the conduct of these women as "sickness" (*como enfermas*), Teresa foiled the agents of the Inquisition. She changed a moral verdict of possession to a diagnosis of illness invoking natural causation, including melancholia (as described in the recently resurrected writings of Galen), a weak imagination, and drowsiness. The acceptance of sickness as a metaphor had implications for public policy: practitioners of *physick*, rather than priests, were to be the responsible agents for dealing with certain violating performances.

The extraordinary success of the analogy between physical disease and unwanted conduct can, in retrospect, be associated with the special authority of the physician. As theological models were fading and naturalistic models were gaining ascendancy in the sixteenth and seventeenth centuries, the status of physician began its meteoric career, which culminated in its present Aesculapian authority.

The physician, unlike other professionals, possesses a unique kind of authority. Paterson (1966) has shown that conventional categories of authority (or power) fail to describe the special features of the authority of the physician. He makes clear that the medical doctor, unique among professionals, exhibits a combination of expert, moral, and charismatic authority. Paterson adopted the label "Aesculapian" (after the Greek god of healing) for this combination.

Siegler and Osmund (1974) have provided a useful elaboration of the institutional basis of Aesculapian authority. The medical doctor's unique authority resides first in his claim to knowledge or expertise. The physician possesses expert power because he is assumed to have knowledge of the workings of the body in health and in illness. The second aspect of Aesculapian authority is moral authority. It is based on the belief shared by both physician and patient that the physician intends to do good, to alleviate suffering, and to prolong life. The third element is charismatic authority; this kind of authority entitles the doctor to order and control others. It is a remnant of the priestly role, and is perceived to have some God-given features. Charisma is a quality that sets the physician apart from others, but the quality is lost if the individual is perceived as *not* having special features or powers. Charismatic authority depends upon the doctor conducting himself in ways that are consistent with the priestly attributions that others assign to him. He makes use of his Greco-Latin vocabulary, his technical skills, and his rituals to confirm his charisma. Siegler and Osmund regard the Aesculapian authority as necessary in order to confer the sick role. They go on to say that without Aesculapian authority, "one cannot function as a doctor, and indeed cannot even be a successful medical imposter."

As Illich (1978) has pointed out, the emergence of the special authority of the physician at the beginning of the age of reason grew out of a fragmenting of the priestly role: the role of a person who knows what is good for you more than you know yourself. This fragmentation is part and parcel of the specialization of labor and multiplication of "expert" roles typical of post-agricultural systems of production and distribution.

The seventeenth and eighteenth centuries saw the continued displacement of theological explanations by natural science explanations. In the area of human relationships, the secularization of the causes of conduct reflected increasing acceptance of natural science doctrine, as was the case in the early nineteenth century, where we begin our more detailed analysis of the history of the concept of mental illness.

The Early Nineteenth Century: Moral Treatment

In the early nineteenth century, concurrent historical events influenced beliefs about the actions that should be taken toward persons who violated propriety norms. The chronicle is unambiguous, because deviant conduct was interpreted with metaphors drawn from theological *and* naturalistic sources. The creation of asylums and colonies for the care of persons who could not care for themselves, and who were rejected by their families and communities, was a reaction against the draconian measures of the preceding historical period as well as an adjustment to urbanization, specialization, and the fragmentation of role systems. Moral treatment— kindness, wholesome food, sanitary lodging, prayer, moderate work, and recreation—did not arise simply as an alternate to the unsuccessful treatment procedures of the past. By the end of the eighteenth century, medical doctors had repudiated the idea that unwanted conduct, labeled madness or insanity, had supernatural origins. They subscribed to the view that human beings were subject to the same laws of natural science as were other objects in the universe. For this reason, the medical doctor qua scientist was the professional best equipped for diagnosing and treating persons regarded as insane. Despite their scientific outlook, eighteenth

century physicians were pessimistic about "curing" insanity. Their prescribed treatments were not different from those of the jailers, almshouse
keepers, and madhouse proprietors; these treatments included physical
restraint, bleeding, induced vomiting, cathartics, punishment, control by
fear, and, in especially refractory cases, flogging. To be sure, some
physicians advised the jailers and keepers to avoid violence, but in practice
the draconian measures were continuous with concurrent medical and
penological practice (Dain, 1964).

The shift from "medical" to moral treatment is usually dated from the
actions of Pinel in France and Tuke in England. The obvious humanitarian
approach had to come from persons who had a more optimistic outlook
about the human condition than their predecessors. Publication of Pinel's
work in 1802 and of Tuke's detailed account of the York Retreat in 1813
helped to give form and structure to moral treatment. It is important to
note that medical theories were based on Cartesian assumptions. Madness
was believed to be caused by a deranged mind, mind being the immaterial
aspect of the body, localized in the brain (Griesinger, 1845). A sick brain (or
bad blood) was the ultimate target of the treatment. The theories were
strangely compounded, joining concepts borrowed from theology and concepts derived from, and evolving toward, natural science, with mind serving as a secularized version of the immortal soul. From the descriptions of
moral treatment, it is clear that the natural science concept of "brain" was
not the object of therapeutic attention, rather the *person* seemed to be the
focus of moral treatment.

The Paradox of Natural Science Approaches to Moral Problems

From the perspective of the modern historian, medical practitioners in the
nineteenth century were faced with a paradox: on the one hand, they
argued that insanity was caused by physical entities; on the other, they
subscribed to moral treatment methods. Various attempts to resolve this
paradox account for many of the twists and turns in the history of the
concept of mental illness. The inchoate paradigm of medicine was derived
from the empirical methods of natural science. It was to become firmly
entrenched as the mechanistic conception of life before the end of the
century. In America, at least two conceptions helped resolve the apparent
paradox created by the advocacy of moral treatment for supposedly
physiologically initiated disorders. Among the ideological origins of the
American Revolution were resolute stances on freedom of religion and on
the priority of civil liberty. Bailyn (1967) has argued that the first of these
stances carried with it a belief in the dignity of the person. The development
of nationhood during the first quarter of the nineteenth century, along with
the extending frontiers and the general prosperity, also created a climate of
optimism. It is probable, then, that the prevailing optimism influenced a

choice of treatment that more clearly resembled the Christian ideal. The second ideological premise is described by Bailyn as the "contagion of liberty." The dehumanized practices of the eighteenth century and before—justified by then prevailing medical theories—were only secularized extensions of practices consistent with the older theologically based demonic theories. These older attitudes toward nonconforming conduct were set aside in the "unleashing of democracy."

As Skultans (1975) has pointed out, nineteenth century physicians took pride in these recently acquired moral management procedures. They evaluated these procedures as an improvement over the "repressiveness of the eighteenth century." Although it is certainly the case that moral treatment was more humane than its predecessors, it is also the case that it continued to be a form of social control. What changed was the mode of control. As Skultans explains: "In abandoning the methods of the eighteenth century, nineteenth century physicians were not abandoning their roles as guardians of the moral order and agents of social control. Physical restraint, coercion, and exile are replaced by the philosophy of the self which emphasizes the dual nature of man, the power of the will to prevent and control insanity, and which elaborated the arts of self government" (1975, p. 9).

The ideological climate in England and the rest of the industrializing nation-states bore certain similarities to that of America. Agriculture and trade, the development of a middle class, and the philosophy of individualism promoted moral management, thus creating conditions fostering an ideal of self-control.

In fact, there is some confusion about the usage of the word *moral* in the terms "moral treatment" and "moral management." *Moral* was used by many writers as roughly equivalent to *psychological.* However, the ethical and religious connotations were not deleted from the semantic structure, given the strong adherence to individualism and the associated positive valuation of self-reliance.

The Biological Conception of the Mind and the Great Chain of Being

By the mid-nineteenth century the medical view had become consolidated into a set of assumptions that bears close resemblance to contemporary medical viewpoints. In his "Treatise on Insanity" (1845), Esquirol describes the asylum: ". . . we see man, fallen from the high rank which places him at the head of creation, despoiled of his privileges, deprived of his most noble character, and reduced to the condition of the most stupid and vilest creature. He thinks not. Not only is he destitute of ideas and passions, but has not even the determinations of instinct" (pp. 20–21).

Three elements are readily identified in this synopsis of insanity: 1) the three-way disjunction—instinct, passion, and intellect; 2) the notion that instinct should be controlled by passion, and passion by intellect; and 3) the notion that lack of self-control and insanity are identical, because these control mechanisms have failed. An implication of Esquirol's remarks is that individual human development (ontogeny) produces control of instinct by passion, and passion by intellect. The core of the mental illness concept, then, as it reached development in the mid-nineteenth century, was that a person was ill if that person thought like a child. If a grown person was controlled by preinstinctual forces, he or she had regressed to the status of newborn infant; if ruled by instinct, the person was equivalent to a young child; if ruled by passion, he or she was like a pubescent child or a prehistoric, aboriginal human. From this viewpoint, the etiology of mental illness could be related either to improper biological development or to regression to a previous state of development. The educational philosophy of the mid-nineteenth century could accommodate the relatively humane practices of moral treatment, as well as the theory of biological maldevelopment. If the nonconforming person were regarded as a child or as a partially developed human, then it was the responsibility of his betters to firmly guide that person toward maturity. This was the period during which flogging was outlawed in British schools through the efforts of reformers like Thomas Hughes (1857). It was also the period of maximum European expansionism and open imperialism which was supported by the theory of the white man's burden—the idea that firm, consistent, and moral treatment would lead to the advancement of inferior races from the darkness of superstition and animism to the enlightenment of modern science and self-governance.

The conception of human beings as the lords of creation is deep-seated in the history of biology. This conception assimilates into mechanistic science the ancient conception of the *scala naturae,* or the great chain of being (Lovejoy, 1936; White, Juhasz, and Wilson, 1973). The former notion of the moral excellence of humans, attributed to the freedom of the will, was assimilated with the contemporary notion of intellectual excellence because of the unique ability of humans to control passion by reason. The person who engaged in unwanted conduct, and who was assigned the status "mentally ill," was a person who had fallen, whose intellect had failed to control passions and instincts—a weak-willed person.

However, if there was a fall, there is also an implicit redemption, and this was education. A passage from Esquirol illustrates this belief:

> In this assemblage of enemies, who know only how to shun, or injure each other; what application, what devotion to duty, what zeal are necessary, to unfold the cause, and seat of so many disorders; to restore to reason its perverted powers; to control so many diverse passions, to conciliate so many opposing interests; in fine, to restore man to himself! We must correct and restrain one; animate and sustain another; attract the attention of a third, touch the feelings of a fourth. One may be controlled by fear, another by

mildness; all by hope. For this untiring devotion, an approving conscience may be our chief reward. For what can a physician hope, who is always considered wrong when he does not succeed, who rarely secured confidence when successful; and who is followed by prejudices, even in the good which has been obtained. [1845, p. 21]

In this paragraph are embedded the fundamental creeds of bourgeois liberalism as they existed since the time of the maximum colonial expansion of European power in the mid-nineteenth century. There was an underlying belief in the power of education and upbringing to overcome differences between people, whether caused by age, culture, genetics, or any other factor. The tactics had to suit the status of the person being educated, but the power of education itself could not be disputed. Equally important was the idea of the self-concept of the educated European adult male as a man of reason, as the norm for all other creatures to follow: he was at the head of the *scala naturae* (because of his superior education and biological endowment) and it was his duty (the white man's burden) to bring those less fortunate up to his level of intellectual development and self-governance. The missionary zeal for the fallen soul of the savage or the unrepentant sinner was then replaced (during the mid-nineteenth century, at any rate) with a similar zeal for the fallen mentality of the child, the colonial, the woman (at the time of the introduction of educational opportunities for women), the peasant, the immigrant, the proletarian, and even the insane. In effect, as eloquently expressed by Esquirol, the asylum became one of the many philanthropies of the bourgeoisie.

The Growth of Self-regulation and
the Asylum: Ordering the Wild Man Within

It is important to emphasize that the growth of the asylum was not solely in the interest of satisfying philanthropic motives. In fact, in the overarching political ideology of the nineteenth century, maintaining order was probably the more important consideration (Rothman, 1971). Even the moral treatment of the early part of the century was heavily suffused with order, regularity, and predictability—characteristics that were considered necessary for the smooth functioning of a rapidly growing economic and political system. Furthermore, social order was (and is) required to contain "dangerous individuals" or "dangerous classes." The etymology of the word *danger* provides clues to its use in the phrases "dangerous person" and "dangerous classes." *Danger* came to mean the potential for inverting the *dominium,* the relationship of controller and controllee (Sarbin, 1967c). The labels "dangerous to self" and "dangerous to others" remain part and parcel of the semantics of deviant or perplexing conduct. The phrases are used abundantly in legislative acts that support deprivation of liberty for potential harmdoers. Dershowitz (1973), Morse (1978), Kittrie

(1971), Sarbin and Mancuso (1980), Szasz (1963), and others have argued that such preventive detention is contrary to the traditions of due process, which demands proof of the performance of some criminal act before a person is confined. In the case of the so-called dangerous person, instead of the constitutional guarantees of due process, the courts act on the assumption that the adjudged "mentally incompetent" person *might* in the future engage in offensive conduct.

In the nineteenth century, however, not every nonconforming person was perceived as potentially dangerous, and, in the strict sense, denied due process of law. How were candidates for confinement selected? The answer is to be found in the development of the asylum as an institution dominated by the idea of order. Rothman (1971) carefully points out that a definite social class bias existed. Persons who were aliens (immigrants), paupers, or otherwise regarded as social failures were the candidates for the educational and moral practices of the asylum. These were the people for whom the abstraction "dangerous classes" was employed in political tracts and in arguments for social legislation. To claim that dangerousness was associated with being foreign-born or poverty-stricken, or with other stigmata of failure, required a cognitive transformation supported by a firm ideological premise. The concept of the "wild man within" was such a premise. White (1972) has shown that the "wild man within" is a common feature of Western implicit personality theories. The remote origins of the connection between the diagnosed mentally ill and dangerousness is obscure. The brutality inflicted on seventeenth and eighteenth century inmates of Bedlam, La Bicêtre, and Salpêtrière shaped creatures that could hardly be identified as human. They were caged and chained and treated as if they were wild beasts or untamed savages, and they responded in kind.

In his account of the origins of the myth of the "wild man within," White (1973) has shown how Europeans nurtured the belief. When large areas of the world were still unexplored, Europeans thought the inhabitants of the unknown lands had no civilization, and that, therefore, they had to be unsocialized, wild, uncontrolled savages.

The beliefs followed from naive assumptions of how humans would appear if they had had no opportunity to receive the benefits of civilization. Although little of the earth remains unexplored, no wild man of Borneo or of anywhere else has yet been discovered. However, the myth lingers on—implicitly in the ideological premises of Western elites, and only partially concealed in the coinage of Lombroso's atavistic man and Freud's impulse-ridden id.

The myth continues to receive support from extensions of the "wild beast" theory of insanity drawn from early English law (Platt and Diamond, 1965). The widespread acceptance of Freudian theory in modern psychiatry and psychology also contributes to the persistence of the myth.

To the agents of society charged with helping to maintain order, the image of the "wild man within" can be a powerful support for declaring an alienated person dangerous.

From his detailed review of the founding and maintaining of the asylum in the nineteenth century, Rothman concluded that middle-class deviants seldom found their way to the asylum. To have employed the asylum for *all* persons would have required a repudiation of the premise that only some people (such as inferiors and aliens) are potentially dangerous and in need of control. In short, to identify dangerousness, wildness, uncontrollability, and disorder required first a cognitive separation between *Us* and *Them*. Doctors became the arbiters of morality because they were proper agents of the middle class, as well as the carriers of Aesculapian authority.

By fiat, the superintendents of the asylums became medical superintendents of mental hospitals, but the underlying guides to action persisted. Observations have been documented over and over again that the diagnosis of insanity, madness, psychosis, and schizophrenia is usually declared on poor, powerless, alienated people and not on middle-class peers (Dohrenwend and Dohrenwend, 1969; Hollingshead and Redlich, 1958).

THE CREATION OF THE SCIENCE OF PSYCHOPATHOLOGY

Two ideological constructions were prominent in the development of the new science of psychopathology, which grew out of the resolution of the paradox of moral treatment being used for disorders of physical origin. The resolution of the paradox had begun with the biological conception of mind as formulated by Esquirol. In this new version, the residue of the world view of formism produced the conception of mind, the first of the two ideological constructions. The second construction was the root metaphor of mechanism: objects in the world could be perceived as parts of a giant mechanical apparatus that was able to transmit forces from one place to another. These two conceptions brought together two unjoinable concepts: mind, an abstraction derived from linguistic sources, and mechanism, derived from empirical observation of physical objects.

Even a casual acquaintance with the history of Western thought would lead to the inference that the concept of soul had firm ontological footings. Western thought patterns included such elements as psyche, nous, phrenes, and consciousness, which were derived from post-Homeric Greeks (Jaynes, 1976). Soul, in the context of theological explanation, was a concept that prepared the way for the belief in propositions about the actions of an inner form. Credibility was assigned to such inner activity through the authority of theologians and also through the attribution of causality to emotional reactions evoked during religious worship.

In Western languages, *mind,* derived from an old Indo-European root, overlapped with *soul.* The latter term seemed to be employed primarily in theological and cosmological contexts. *Mind,* being a word of the common language, stood for silent and private components of ordinary human actions. Jaynes (1976) has suggested that *mind* as a substantive was probably created by the cognitive imperative that led to the uncritical acceptance of the notion of a mind-space. *Consciousness,* Jaynes' general term for all mental state words, was invented relatively late in the development of human language. The mind-space metaphor served the need to locate ordinary events that were not localizable in geographical space. Jaynes argues that the mind-space was the analogue for geographical space. Time was determined by locating events in a narrative plot structure that included past, present, and future. The analogue for the narrative was the sequential action of invented mental objects in the mind-space. 'Consciousness,' 'mind,' 'psyche', and similar terms have been transformed from poetic metaphors to myths—to belief systems that guide human action (Sarbin, 1964, 1968).

To understand the invention of psychopathology, it is necessary to accept the fact that mind is without empirical reference. It is a Platonic form. It simply *is.* No empirical tests can assess or confirm its existence because it is an abstraction: its status as a substantive is the result of assigning credibility to a figure of speech.

When we review the writings of the nineteenth century psychopathologists, it is clear that they had acquired the idea of mind as a cognitive imperative. To them, the mind was as credible as the soul had been for true believers. Concurrently, a second cognitive imperative asserted its influence: the world view of mechanism and its corollary of linear causality.

In the same way that the formist worldview cleared the way for the credibility of mind and psyche, the mechanistic metaphor provided the scientist with an easily understood model for discovering how forces were transmitted into and out of the mind-space. Employing more than one metaphysical system must result in paradox: however, the paradox was too subtle to obstruct the view that the source of contranormative conduct was an abstraction, a Platonic form, and at the same time a transmutable force subject to the laws of mechanics. Such illicit and hidden eclecticism was not recognized by the psychopathologists.

The nineteenth century witnessed the development of biology as a scientific discipline. From the recorded casual observations of naturalists, biology evolved into a collection of refined observations and controlled experiments. The evolution of the science of biology was dependent upon the successful application of the world view of mechanism to questions raised by natural science. Singer (1959) describes the "mechanization of biology," which reached its apex in the latter half of the nineteenth century. The root metaphor of the machine, implying the transmittal of force, had worked extremely well for the development of the sciences of astronomy, physics, and chemistry. It was now providing the paradigm for the developing science of biology. The mechanistic conception of life took on programmatic characteristics. It was taken seriously and had a quasi-religious coloring. For example, responding to the scientists and theologians who continued to advocate the doctrines of vitalism, four young soon-to-become-famous physiologists—Brücke, DuBois Reymond, Helmholz, and Ludwig—swore the now famous mutual oath: "to account for all bodily processes in physio-chemical terms" (Fleming, 1964). Under the influence of the mechanistic metaphysic, experimental biology moved by leaps and bounds, the study of the nervous system and neuropathology being no exception. It was in this period that the interest of physicians in explaining and controlling contranormative conduct was renewed.

With a mechanistic conception of brain, and with support from laboratory science and clinical observation, biologists could locate the causes of abnormal behavior in damage to, and disease of, the brain. It was in this context that physicians like Charcot and Freud became involved in patient *conduct* in addition to the traditional activity of medical science — diagnosing and treating *sickness.* They noted resemblances between various odd behaviors that could be accounted for as a result of neurological trauma and contranormative conduct without neuropathological antecedents. These superficial resemblances were sufficient to assimilate all unwanted conduct into the category of disease.

A reading of the psychopathologists of the late nineteenth century indicates that "hysteria" was the overriding concept for classifying conduct, the symptoms of which resembled nervous system pathology. The context that influenced the construction of hysteria as illness can be exemplified in Charcot's clinics and consulting rooms. Because he was regarded as one of the giants of neuropathology, his theoretical pronouncements were taken seriously. He offered a theory of hysteria that was based on his assigning the same nervous system causality to patients with hysterical symptoms and to patients with demonstrable neuropathology. The diagnosis of hysteria in the nineteenth century was assigned to women (and occasionally to men) who exhibited contranormative conduct in the absence of lesions of the nervous system and who were brought to the attention of physicians. Szasz (1961) suggests that hysteria became a wastebasket category and was used synonymously with *functional disease* or *psychogenic disorders,* diagnostic terms that are still employed in medical circles to exclude "organic" disease.

The word *psychopathology,* even to readers ignorant of Greek, shows its medical roots. The term *pathology* came into use as early as the seventeenth century to denote the study of disease, but it was not applied to conditions other than physical illness until the mid-nineteenth century.

Combining *pathology* with *psycho,* the word *psychopathology* stimulates imagery that is consistent with its medical context. Toxins, tumors, and traumata are imagined when the word *pathology* is uttered. To find equivalent causal terms for psychopathology required the invention of abstractions that were seen as parts of the grand abstraction—'mind'.

Physicians of the nineteenth century did not label contranormative conduct with transparent terms from the popular lexicon. Greek labels provided an opaque cover, and a technical vocabulary could conceal metaphysical abstractions as well as plain ignorance. Written a hundred years before the development of psychopathology, Moliére's humorous recognition of the opacity of medical language is still applicable. In *The Physician in Spite of Himself* (1667), Moliére records an interchange between a man pressed into service as a phony physician and the father of a young woman who has lost her speech. The impostor knows in advance that the woman cannot speak.

DOCTOR (to the patient and the father):   Give me your arm, I can tell by the pulse that your daughter is dumb.

FATHER: Yes, Monsieur, that is her affliction. You have discovered it at once.

•   •   •   •   •

FATHER: But I want you to tell me the cause.

DOCTOR: The cause of her dumbness is the loss of her powers of speech.

FATHER: Quite so. But why has she lost her powers of speech?

DOCTOR: All our best authors will tell you that it is an impediment in the action of her tongue.

FATHER: Yes, but what in your opinion has caused this impediment in the action of her tongue?

DOCTOR: Ah, on that point Aristotle says (pause) . . . some very fine things indeed.

FATHER: I'm sure he does.

DOCTOR: A very great man (pause) . . . But to return to what we were saying. In my opinion (pause) . . . is caused by certain humours (pause) . . . unhealthy humours formed by the exhalation of the influences that take rise in the seat of the maladies, coming, so to speak . . . from . . . er . . . Do you understand Latin?

FATHER: No.

DOCTOR: You don't know a word of Latin?

FATHER: Not a word.

DOCTOR (with enthusiasm):   Cabricias arci thuram, catalamus, singulariter, nominative, haec musa, then muse, bonus, bona, bonum . . . .

FATHER: A clearer explanation would be impossible. There is only one thing that surprises me. That is the position of the liver and the heart. You seemed to place them the wrong way around. I always thought the heart was on the left side and liver on the right.

DOCTOR: Yes, that used to be the case. But we have changed all that now. The whole science of medicine is run on an entirely new system.

FATHER: Oh, I didn't know that. Please excuse my ignorance.

DOCTOR: It's quite understandable. You can't be expected to be as clever as we are.

Theories of psychopathology mirrored theories of physical pathology. Nineteenth-century medicine, as a whole, focused more and more on internal cause-and-effect sequences, the understanding of which was conditioned by the overarching premise that the human body was a biological machine.

The Mechanistic Conception of Hysteria

Contemporary controversies about the ontological status of such entities as schizophrenia, neurosis, psychosis, and psychopathy can hardly be appreciated without examining the historical context that encouraged the creation of psychopathology as a special field of study. Prominent in this context is the mechanistic formulation of hysteria.

From antiquity on, observations of strange conduct led to explanations that were influenced by the state of knowledge and metaphysical assumptions of the time. The theory of hysteria as the outcome of a floating uterus was no better and no worse than any other theory in the absence of a science of semiotics and of an understanding of the effects of conflicting interpersonal relations.

Szasz (1961) documents the observation that persons who had received the medical diagnosis of hysteria were given short shrift by physicians. Most physicians regarded hysterics as dissimulators, malingerers, or frauds. Veith (1977) quotes Falret, a French physician who, in a paper written in 1866, accused hysterical women of being unlikable and difficult in their domestic relations: . . ."These patients are veritable actresses: they do not know of a greater pleasure than to deceive . . . all those with whom they come in touch . . . [The] life of the hysteric is nothing but one perpetual falsehood. . . ." The subtle diagnostic signs, now claimed but not confirmed by twentieth-century psychopathologists, which might differentiate between "genuine" hysterical illness and malingering, had not then been invented. Whether a set of performances was ascribed to hysteria or to malingering followed upon the unconfirmable inferences from answers to the question: Is the dissimulation conscious or unconscious?

Charcot redefined hysteria as illness (Szasz, 1961). As a result, contra-normative conduct could come under the purview of a science committed to the mechanistic world view. "Counterfeit" illness was assimilated to genuine illness, the assimilation being facilitated by the surface resemblance of hysterical patients to patients with demonstrable neuropathological disorders. Charcot's pronouncements were taken seriously by other physicians; he had already established himself as a leader in the field of neuropathology. His investigations between 1862 and 1870 of multiple sclerosis, tabetic arthropathies, amyotropathic lateral sclerosis, and localization of spinal chord lesions made him famous. These studies were conducted within a mechanistic framework. It is worth emphasizing that Charcot, and later Freud, approached the subject matter of hysteria with the same mechanistic paradigm that had served so well in diagnosing nervous system disorders. The contranormative conduct of patients with trauma or disease of the central nervous system could be convincingly explained as the interference of energy transmission in circumscribed nerve trunks. The explanations were couched in mechanistic language—the patients' symptoms were the inevitable consequence of the excitation and inhibition of the flow of impulses through a complex network of nerves.

The Great Neuropathologists and the Height of Scientism

The mechanization of biology paved the way for theories of nervous action, the transmission of energy along neuronal channels. Imagery of the anatomy and physiology of the nervous system was influenced by the contemporary development of telephonic technology and also helped to construct a model for the mechanistic construal of mind. The writings of the great neuropathologists, Charcot (1872), Freud (1910, 1959b), Janet (1911), and Prince (1891), supply ample evidence that the pathology of the nervous system served as a source of metaphors for describing the psychic components of behavior. The anatomy and physiology of the nervous system served as the fount for metaphors to account for performances, some of which superficially resembled symptoms of neurological disease, shock, or lesion.

When Freud joined Breuer in the study of hysteria (Breuer and Freud, 1895), he brought with him interest and competence in neuropathology. The reclassification of hysteria as a disease had already been accomplished. Medical practitioners, however, had not yet established any reliable treatment. Freud's theoretical and clinical writings can be traced to the ideas developed at the juncture of his career when he shifted from the search for causality in the nervous system to the search for causality in the psyche. To carry out his objective of understanding hysteria, he had to reinvent the unconscious. The nineteenth century witnessed a number of attempts to explain puzzling behavior by hypothesizing processes identified by such metaphors as unconscious cerebration, unconscious inference, instantaneous ratiocination, and others. Freud's invention of the tripartite structure of mind—id, ego, superego—was undoubtedly influenced by his knowledge of the morphology and supposed phylogenesis of the brain.

Mention should be made of at least two other authorities in the growing field of psychopathology: Pierre Janet and Morton Prince, who made their contributions during the same period in which Freud developed his seminal ideas. Their theories were consonant with those of Freud in their belief that the causality for hysteria and other functional disorders had to be sought in the intricate patterns of mind. All three of these thinkers came to their work on hysteria through medicine and neurology, a condition that helped mold their conceptions. As a neurologist, Freud had been interested in the blocking of sensation through the injection of cocaine. Menninger (1963) noted that when Freud began his clinical career, "the phenomena of blocked sensations were of particular interest to him as they appeared in 'hysterical' patients and in experiments with hypnosis."

Departing from strict medical models, Morton Prince employed the vague concept of "personality." In his studies of hysteria, hypnosis, and multiple personalities, Prince believed the personality to be an organized psychophysiological system. As a psychophysical interactionist, he saw the mind as influencing the body and vice versa. The mechanism that account-ed for contranormative conduct was dissociation, a concept elaborated by Janet (1911). Prince reported on a series of hysterical cases in 1891, arguing for the interactional mind-brain model:

> The explanation of such groups of symptoms is properly to be found, not in the peripheral nerves, not in spinal or cerebral centres, but rather in associations established by previous acute processes between such centres, or to diffusion of stimuli along physiological channels. It may be regarded as hyper-excitability of the association systems of fibres, or a species of pathological physiology . . . [In] a large class of neuroses, we are to look for their causes, not in diseased nerves or centres, but rather in a pathological association of normal anatomi-cal elements, and the treatment is to be directed to the breaking up of this association, and the regrouping of the nervous centres. [p. 82]

In the *Mental State of Hystericals* (1911), Janet, the successor to Charcot at the Salpêtrière, introduced the concept of dissociation. Origi-nally termed *disaggregation*, dissociation referred to the proposal that one system of ideas could be split off from another system, the patient being unable to account for the splitting. Dissociation was clearly a metaphor based on the idea of neuronal blocking or lesion.

The psychopathologists looked for etiology in the hypothesized mind-space, and the neurologists examined the condition of the nervous system. In the late nineteenth century, and even in the early twentieth century, neurology and psychiatry were undifferentiated. When Kraepelin (1883) set out to construct a nosology, he was guided by his mechanistic physiological orientation. The concerns of the psychopathologists were assimilated into his system. It would not be difficult to trace the origins of Kraepelin's nosology to Griesinger or even to Esquirol. Some aspects of Kraepelin's nosology were modified by Bleuler (1911), especially the concept of dementia praecox. Bleuler worked in the tradition of the psychopathologists, taking seriously the reified conception of mind. From the turn of the century to the present, nosological systems in psychiatry have been, for the most part, variations on the themes set by Kraepelin and Bleuler. This conclusion applies to the 1952, 1968, and 1980 versions of the *Diagnostic and Statistical Manual* of the American Psychiatric Association.

The psychopathologist was cast in the role of microbe hunter or medical research scientist who could advance the state of knowledge by unearthing pathologies of which the neurological causes were not yet clearly understood. Rather than acting as an enforcer of public morals, then, the psychopathologist could convincingly present himself as the disinterested scientist studying abnormal neural functioning through the comparison of obviously diseased persons with intact normals. This was, of course, no sham; the convincing enactment of the role of disinterested scientist demanded a congruent self-concept. However, that very disinterest held the seeds of the major challenge to the medical model, a challenge that continued into the late 1960s: the challenge of cultural relativism.

CULTURAL RELATIVISM

The disinterested scientist does not make value judgments; he records, observes, makes theories, and leaves matters of morals and ethics to others better qualified to deal with them. In short, nineteenth- and early twentieth-century science, as a consequence of its own liberalism, became wedded to the concept of itself as "value free," as dealing with the 'is' rather than the 'ought'. From this perspective, the description of the mental functioning of savages, women, children, and ultimately even of madmen as *inferior*, rather than merely as *different*, became highly questionable. This situation is an example of cultural relativism, that is, the definition of "normal" behavior can vary within and between cultures.

The public role or social type who first challenged the prevailing view of the sober scientist as the acme of perfection was that of the "mad artist," embodied by a few turn-of-the-century characters like Wilde, Baudelaire, Yeats, DeQuincey, and, above all, Van Gogh. Particularly in later paintings from his overtly "mad" period, Van Gogh offers the world a lesson: everyone has the ability to see the world through the eyes of the insane. The artist drives home the point that the child, the savage, indeed, the creature whom we have pursued around the globe and have suppressed, colonized, educated, and confined, is ourselves. In art, as adults we see the primitivism

of young children who misperceive and haven't "learned," and we thereby
find a common ground of experience with them. As soon as we can see the
value of the child's vision on its own terms, it becomes intrinsically
treasured in and of itself. Only when it is taken outside its own system of
representation can the child's vision be considered reprehensible; then, in
terms of the conventional adult, it is crazy, primitive, and disordered.

The final expression of this dilemma is presented in Freud's famous
introduction to *The Brothers Karamazov*:

> Four facets may be distinguished in the rich personality of Dostoevsky:
> the creative artist, the neurotic, the moralist, and the sinner. How best to find
> one's way in this bewildering complexity?
>   . . . The creative artist is the least doubtful: Dostoevsky's place is not far
> behind Shakespeare, *The Brothers Karamazov* is the most magnificent novel
> ever written, the episode of the Grand Inquisitor, one of the peaks in the
> literature of the world, can hardly be valued too highly. Before the problem of
> the creative artist analysis must, alas, lay down its arms. [1959a, p. 222]

Freud's capitulation to the superior forces of creativity comes neither
from shyness nor from lack of ability as a theorist, but rather from the
simple fact that the criterial attributes of neurosis and psychosis are
remarkably close to the criterial attributes of creative genius: both require
the exhibition of deviant and troubling conduct, which, however, does not
fall within the region of criminal activity (Becker, 1978). Specifically,
creative people are said to be troubling because of their loose association,
sloppy and slovenly appearance, disregard for bourgeois convention, and
apparent desire to shock conventional sensibility—but more than anything
else, because of their childish, impish, and playful conduct.

THE RISE OF RELATIVISM

The dispassionate scientist, in formulating a theory of behavior, is proscribed from making moral judgments on his subject matter. On the one
hand, this difficulty for persons like mental health practitioners, who are
specifically charged with the monitoring and rectification of public and
private morals, has led to the development of an extraordinarily large and
abstruse technical vocabulary (Sarbin and Juhasz, 1978) which attempts to
hide its pejorative character under the guise of Greco-Latin descriptive
terms (Sarbin and Juhasz, 1975). On the other hand, this dilemma gave rise
to an ever increasing desire to describe the behavior and activity of spoiled
identities in objective language, and particularly in terms of social context
rather than internal motivation.

With this orientation, from the beginning of the twentieth century the
study of deviance moved away from exclusive concentration on the
identified norm violator as an abstract individual. Instead, the accent was
on the social system; the identified norm violator was but one actor in an

ongoing drama, and those who passed judgment on him or her were other actors. If this kind of analysis is extended to its logical limits, there is a simultaneous study of the target person and of the other persons who make the value judgments, as well as a study of the codified and uncodified rules that the valuing person employs to construct his judgments about the target person.

To twentieth-century social scientists, it was an exercise in futility to search for disturbance originating *within* the individual, or within an abstraction called 'mind' or 'psyche' or 'personality'. Their emphasis was on the social system and its institutions which support beliefs about unwanted conduct.

The development of sociology and social work (Addams, 1910; Boas, 1909; Durkheim, 1897) and the popularity of reformist writings and novels that depicted the oppressiveness of social institutions and the degrading effects of colonialism (Conrad, 1902; Dickens, 1850; Sinclair, 1905; Steffens, 1904; Zola, 1885) introduced an alternate paradigm for conceptualizing unwanted conduct.

The scientific study of culture was well underway by the end of World War I and is historically equivalent to the beginning of the decline of European colonial power, both in the crass military-economic sense and in the more subtle sense which gave moral justification for the acts and practices of colonialism. In this context, the scientific study of people shifted from the ethnocentrism of the colonial era to a relativism based on a functional approach to the social sciences. Friedman and Juhasz discuss the functional approach:

> From the pioneering researches of Malinowski among the Trobriand Islanders to the present, a dominant theme among anthropologists has been a comprehensive functionalism that attempts to show how various features of a culture and the environment "fit together" and "make sense." In Malinowski's *Argonauts of the Western Pacific* (1922), for example, a convincing argument is presented to show that a people's economic activity cannot be looked at in isolation—the economic activity is embedded in religion, kinship systems, and features of the physical environment. The function of the economic activity is to support this intricately interconnected order.
>
> Malinowski's functionalism can be seen as flowing from his dramatically innovative notion that methodology in anthropology should be different from objective study of artifacts and customs by a European who divorces himself from the stresses and strains of daily life among "savages." Malinowski pitched his tent right in the midst of Trobriand villages; by living with the natives, he discovered that their quaint beliefs and practices were quite sensible from the point of view of the culture. Each queer belief or practice had a function in a self-maintaining system, the culture. [1974, p. 204]

In "taking the role of the other," European culture was decentering from its ethnocentrism and discovering that what looks like nonsense, savagery, or infantilism from the outside can be sensible from the inside—

that which is considered meaningless out of context can be meaningful within a particular system of the culture. Whether Ruth Benedict's *Patterns of Culture* (1934) or Reo Fortune's *The Sorcerers of Dobu* (1932) or Margaret Mead's *Coming of Age in Samoa* (1928) or Malinowski's *Sex and Repression in Savage Society* (1927), the message was the same: what is highly regarded in one society may not be highly regarded in another, but each society, whatever it rewards or punishes, works reasonably well as a coherent system. The generalization to "abnormal" behavior was not long in coming. Ruth Benedict (a student of the most influential anthropologist of his generation, Franz Boas) wrote significantly:

> It is clear that culture may value and make socially available even highly unstable human types. If it chooses to treat their peculiarities as the most valued variants of human behaviour, the individuals in question will rise to the occasion and perform their social roles without reference to our usual ideas of the types who can make social adjustments and those who cannot. Those who function inadequately in any society are not those with certain fixed "abnormal" traits, but may well be those whose responses have received no support in the institutions of their culture. The weakness of these aberrants is in great measure illusory. It springs not from the fact that they are lacking in necessary vigour, but that they are individuals whose native responses are not reaffirmed by society. They are as Sapir phrases it, "alienated from an impossible world."
>
> The person unsupported by the standards of his time and place and left naked to the winds of ridicule has been unforgettably drawn in European literature in the figure of Don Quixote. Cervantes turned upon a tradition still honoured in the abstract the limelight of a changed set of practical standards, and his poor old man, the orthodox upholder of the romantic chivalry of another generation, became a simpleton. The windmills with which he tilted were the serious antagonists of a hardly vanished world, but to tilt with them when the world no longer called them serious was to rave. He loved his Dulcinea in the best traditional manner of chivalry, but another version of love was fashionable for the moment, and his fervour was counted to him for madness. [1934, pp. 270–271]

We quote Benedict at length because her challenge is so clear, and because so many who were college students in the 1930s finally applied her analysis to deviance within our society upon reaching positions of power and responsibility in the 1960s. Nor were Benedict and the other anthropologists alone in preaching cultural relativism as the only "value free," or scientific method and theory in the study of culture. They had their counterparts in the Chicago School of Sociology (Park and Burgess, 1921; Wirth, 1928) and its outgrowths into urban sociology and the study of the ecology of social pathology in the thirties and forties. Similarly, in psychology, the social psychology of G. H. Mead (1918; 1934) stressed a form of cultural relativism applied to the individual's interactions with his or her immediate neighbors.

There was no subtle change; what occurred in the 1920s and 1930s was the emergence of competing versions of deviant conduct. The traditional version, which stems from the search for implicit or undiscovered neuropathology, is challenged by the theory of social stigmatization, or behavior judged as unwanted on the basis of some arbitrary set of mutable social rules/roles. The history of the concept of mental illness from the 1920s to the late 1960s involves a struggle between these two competing and irreconcilable viewpoints.

CULTURAL RELATIVISTS AND PSYCHOPATHOLOGISTS

Theories of deviant conduct flowed from two radically different root metaphors (Pepper, 1942), formism and mechanism. The proponents of these perspectives were the psychopathologists and related personality theorists, who were supported by a growing army of bureaucrats and the popular mental hygiene movement. Textbooks of psychiatry and abnormal psychology through the 1940s continued to focus on symptoms and the derivatives of Kraepelinian nosology. Beginning in the late 1930s and the early 1940s, the corpus of Freudian writing was employed to augment the standard descriptions. Hardly anyone within psychology or psychiatry paid attention to the claims of the social scientists whose theories were guided by an entirely different root metaphor: the historical event. Rather than seeking causality in the transmission of force or in the immanence of Platonic forms, the contextualists saw deviant performances as the outcome of institutional and social forces and of the application of values by one person on the public conduct of another. Because the categories of each root metaphor are not transferable, no logical debate can establish which root metaphor is better. A future historian could point to the final outcomes of theories guided by one or another root metaphor.

The methodology of social science developed slowly. The classic study of Faris and Dunham (1939) on the social ecology of deviance gave some support to the claim that deviant conduct was influenced by neighborhood of residence. That is, there was a higher rate of mental hospital admissions from the transitional neighborhoods in Chicago than from established middle-class neighborhoods that were removed from the industrial center of the city. From our present perspective, the study was flawed because it used mental hospital admissions as a measure. The mental hospital admissions were, in part, a reflection of the formist/mechanist model because a psychiatric diagnosis was prerequisite to being admitted. From a contextualist viewpoint, psychiatric diagnosis is a fallible guide to a person's psychological competence, as witnessed by a large number of systematic studies, including the exciting study of Rosenhan (1973).

In 1946, the Veterans' Administration mounted a colossal attack on mental illness among veterans of World War II. Extensive training programs were initiated that were designed to prepare psychiatrists, clinical psychologists, and social workers to deliver mental health services to veterans and their families. The training programs were dominated by physicians. The prevailing methods of diagnosis and treatment were organized around the conceptions of psychopathologists, with a strong loading of psychoanalytic theory. The impact of social science theories was minimal. The doctrine of individualism with its emphasis on the acquisition of self-governance had persisted as the guiding motif. In 1947, a textbook appeared that attempted to bring together a social learning approach and the clinical observations of people identified with traditional psychiatric labels (Cameron, 1947). It is interesting that Cameron's biosocial view of behavior disorders was not widely accepted, in spite of the convincing clinical descriptions.

This is not to say that no efforts were made to locate the origins of deviant conduct in a contextual matrix. Although basically oriented to mechanical categories, Adolf Meyer (1866—1950) taught several generations of psychiatric residents to take into account contextual features. The influential writings of Henry Stack Sullivan (1953) were also in the same tradition.

Working with people diagnosed as schizophrenic, Bateson et al. (1956) took a contextual approach and focused on communication patterns with special attention to communication within the identified patient's family. They introduced the double-bind as a condition that promoted the development of a special form of communication called schizophrenic. These studies were influenced by, and laden with, the relics of the formist/mechanist approach, yet their communication approach paved the way for later studies of family communication patterns as significant features of the context for conduct, both normal and abnormal (Singer, 1967).

The struggle between the arguments of the social scientists and the manifest power of the mental health professions could not be resolved. By the end of the 1950s, numerous attempts were made to establish a culture-free definition of abnormality, usually by defining its obverse—mental health. The most quoted effort was that of Marie Jahoda (1958). She attempted a pancultural definition of positive mental health stating six criteria: balance of psychic forces, self-actualization, resistance to stress, autonomy, competence, and perception of reality. Other authors, among them Kubie (1954), Redlich (1957), Scott (1958), Shoben (1957), and Wishner (1955), all struggled with the same problem of establishing criteria that would stand up to the arguments of the relativistic social scientists. Looking at Jahoda's criteria, we can see that they are intended to displace the traditional psychiatric nosology with criteria that reflected the arguments of such observers as Ruth Benedict and other relativists. The Jahoda criteria are a strange admixture reflecting unrecognized ideological biases.

Autonomy, for example, is a conception clearly relevant to some, but not all, political systems. Perception of reality cannot be a criterion without defining the cosmology of the person or group under study. Balance of psychic forces and resistance to stress, on the other hand, are clearly mechanistic concepts tied to psychopathology and psychoanalysis, by no means culture-free systems of thought. Self-actualization must be understood in the context of Western theology—the self being an abstraction located in the transcendental ecology, the actualization of which might be of little interest to a Zen Buddhist practitioner. Competence is the most clearly contextual of Jahoda's terms, for it clearly suggests the question: Competence at what? The judgment must be based on what is valued in a given set of circumstances.

Attempts to give scientific status to mental illness by answering the implied criticism and challenge of the cultural relativists were brought about in part by the proliferation of professions. It was becoming increasingly commonplace for sociologists, anthropologists, and psychologists to invade the territory that for so long had been occupied exclusively by the medical profession. The rapid expansion of the mental health world had an unintended outcome: fragmentation, according to the professional competences and biases of its increasingly manifold practitioners. The formist/mechanist hegemony of the thirties and forties had depended on the Aesculapian authority of the physicians, supported by powerful bureaucratic, legislative, and magisterial sanctions. The cultural relativists uncloaked the charismatic authority of the physician and challenged not only the practice of psychiatry but also the metaphysical foundations and ideological grounds of its theories.

Paradox Redivivus

The early 1960s witnessed a series of reports that attempted to resolve the old contradictions latent in mechanist/formist theories of psychopathology since their inception. The paradox in the early nineteenth century centered on the incompatibility of notions of moral treatment with physiological causality. Later the psychopathologists had to struggle with the same paradox recast as immaterial mind and its relation to a biomechanical brain. The paradox was finally expressed in the "positive mental health" definitions of the 1950s that attempted to unite criteria derived from mechanistic sources (forces, stresses, etc.) with criteria of theological and cosmological origin (such as actualization, autonomy, and competence).

In works of the 1960s, cultural relativism makes its strongest claim on the study of person, normal and abnormal. In a direct challenge to the validity of absolutist psychopathological definitions and of "culture-free" definitions, Foucault (1961), Goffman (1961), Kesey (1962), Laing (1960),

Sarbin (1962), Scheff (1964), and Szasz (1961), among others, examined and reported on the contradictions inherent in the practice and theory of mental illness.

Goffman and the Tragicomedy of the Asylum

Goffman (1961) pointed out with ironic clarity that even the inhabitants of back wards demonstrate conduct that, given the context, is appropriate and rule-following. He also showed how institutional practices can result in the systematic degradation of the inmates, and how the normal identity of the patients is removed step-by-step until there is a total loss of dignity. The remaining identity is that of the child, the unaccultured savage, the mental patient—in short, the nonperson. Goffman suggests that the industrial concept of division of labor could be employed as a poetic metaphor to emphasize the degradation practices of the mental hospital at mid-century. With sharp irony, he shows that each professional worker in the asylum has a specific function, the outcome of which is a reduction of the individual patient's autonomy and claims to identity. The metaphor of the factory and its assembly line (Rothman, 1971) is burlesqued in Goffman's account of the degradation of the inmate, whose claims to humanity are systematically disassembled, one step at a time. Goffman observes in the workings of the medical bureaucracy of the madhouse the diffusion of responsibility and the practice of sanctioned madness. Goffman describes how the patient is treated as if he were a broken-down radio. He explores the irony of the myth that the demeaning treatment of the patient by doctors, nurses, and attendants is only "for his own good." The collusion of the patient in the degradation ceremonials is sometimes written in the idiom of comedy and sometimes in the idiom of high tragedy.

Kesey, (1962), in preparing his novel *One Flew Over the Cuckoo's Nest*, took note of the repressive and oppressive features of the mental hospital. In the mythoclastic tradition of the turn-of-the-century muck-rakers, Kesey does not conceal the irony that the mental health profession-als' degradation rituals are presented as being performed for the betterment of the patient. Unlike Goffman and other academic critics, Kesey has no professional ax to grind. The thrust of his novel is that the general human condition can be characterized by madness, whether one focuses on the inmate, the doctor, the nurse, or the author.

What was new about criticism of mental illness in the 1960s was the application of the methods and ideas of Benedict, Malinowski, and Wirth et al. to the back ward of a mental hospital. What is particularly important is the receptivity of the public and of the profession to the disclosures of writers like Goffman (for which the ground had been prepared for 30 years). Not less important is the oblique, but nevertheless clear, sense of moral outrage that permeates Goffman's writing.

Public receptivity was related to the increasing clarity of people's dissatisfaction with the facade of philanthropy and egalitarianism that hid the rather dreary and irresponsible behavior of systems of authority— whether government bureacracies or the economic system. Higher education had been perceived as a way of liberating the children of industrial workers into white-collar jobs. Rather than a liberating process, it had become a trap. The lack of fit between educational goals and employment opportunities set the stage for frustration and alienation. The educated reader of Goffman's work could see the similarity in form between the nonperson identity of the inmate and his own alienated self. "The mentally ill are like you and me" could become a rallying cry of dramatic proportions.

Goffman's readers were ready to respond to his disclosures with moral indignation. Although he wrote in a style that resembled objective scientific, or at least journalistic reportage, the selection of events was guided by the liberal tradition. Both the author and the reader saw in the actions of the asylum personnel the perpetration of injustice. It was not necessary to be an extreme liberal to recognize injustice and to express moral outrage. Once the reader experienced the outrage, he affiliated with the degraded and disenfranchised and alienated. Having weakened the metaphysical barriers that separated *Us* from *Them,* the ground was being prepared for new and radical definitions of unwanted behavior and for the recognition of the disutility of mental illness doctrines.

Goffman contained his moral outrage at the treatment of asylum inmates by fully implementing his role as scientist and by exposing the hypocritical system from within by working within the rules of scientific method. His commitment to liberalism was hidden behind the mask of objectivity in the same way that the psychiatrists' moral stance for enforcing societal conventions was concealed by their Greco-Latin vocabulary and Aesculapian authority.

Goffman's and Kesey's tragicomedies are indeed in the tradition of Moliére's iconoclasm. They expose the "expert" as a witting, unwitting, or witless supporter of a social system. Goffman, working from within, and Kesey, working from without, went far beyond the social relativism of the 1930s by attacking the very foundations of "objective social science" itself. They prepared for work in the 1970s that explictly labeled social scientific endeavor as moral, fictive, and influential in the very definition of human nature itself.

Foucault and the Internalization of the Asylum

The work of Foucault (1961) is relevant to our analysis of the effect of Goffman's writings. Goffman presented the premises to the reader with the expectation that the reader would construct the inference, but Foucault was more direct. He described the process of confinement as the exercise of those with power in disowning their own irrationality. Foucault believed that we all share the dark side of life with Van Gogh, Artaud, and the legions of schizophrenics, manic-depressives, social failures, and moral cripples. To maintain our power structure, the face of insanity, the face of unreason, had to be denied. To be effectively functioning citizens, we had to deny any similarity between ourselves and the insane. *We* and *They* were separated by an unbridgeable gulf.

Foucault shows a moral revulsion against the encapsulation of cultures, subcultures, neighborhoods, and even individuals in the functionalist models of social science. His arguments for disalienation are based on the belief that all human beings share the same characteristics of rationality/irrationality. In a sense, this is a formist metaphysic with a strong moral base. If all human beings are basically the same, then the separation of a special class of persons—the mentally ill—from the normal is controverted. Although Foucault's work received little attention in America when first published, it became influential after the trails had been blazed by Goffman, Szasz, and others.

Thus, Foucault, like Goffman, in embracing cultural relativism takes it beyond itself. Unlike Goffman, he does not point to the need for moral commitment, but rather to the need for finding true, underlying cultural universals that can take the social sciences out of the encapsulation of cultural relativism. In this sense, Foucault, his critics notwithstanding, is in the emerging structuralist tradition.

Szasz and the Paradoxes of Self-regulation

Beginning with his influential book, *The Myth of Mental Illness* (1961), Szasz has continued to mount a polemic against the mental health industry, particularly psychiatry. He challenged the validity of the underlying metaphor that had sustained the various psychopathological models: namely, mental illness. In his historical essay on the origin of mental illness, he makes clear that illness was a metaphor that had become transformed into a myth. The word *myth* is not a transparent term. In Szasz's writings, myth stands for falsity and error in some places, but in other places, myth is a belief system uncritically accepted by the power structure as a heuristic. He argues against involuntary hospitalization; very few if any sick people require coercion to undergo medical treatment. It is illegitimate, says Szasz, to label unwanted conduct as illness if people must be coerced to accept treatment for mental illness but not for somatic illness. Involuntary hospitalization, or incarceration, is properly administered by the criminal justice system following the requirements of due process of law. Voluntary help can take any form: pastoral counseling, education, psychotherapy, and so on. Szasz, along with sociologically oriented writers like Scheff

(1964), separates deviance into two categories: criminal behavior, where codified laws are violated, and problems in living. He argues convincingly that no intermediary mental health system is needed to deal with deviant conduct, that voluntary help seeking is appropriate for those with problems in living, and that involuntary incarceration should be reserved for law violators.

In this application and extension of relativism, law violation is considered an absolute, while other forms of deviance are treated only at the request of the deviant person. Szasz points out that only a part of the imprisoned and confined population require disalienation. All of us have problems in living; not all of us are criminals. Like Goffman and Foucault, Szasz is outraged by the use of psychiatry for micro- or macro-political purposes. Like Foucault, he is reaching for an absolute with which to temper his relativism.

Szasz's substantive contribution to understanding the conduct that has traditionally been labeled "hysteria" is noteworthy. He rejected the official doctrine that the hysterical symptom was a happening in the unconscious mind. He described the development and persistence of symptoms as forms of intentional behavior employed to communicate in nondiscursive ways. The implication of this formulation takes perplexing deviant conduct out of the realm of the mysterious and arcane and encourages a semiotic view (Sarbin and Coe, 1979).

Laing's Anti-psychiatry

Laing's (1960) work has had a tremendous impact on the cultural revolution of the mid-1960s. His writings have given birth to a movement called "anti-psychiatry" (Ruitenbeek, 1972) and to radical innovations in the diagnosis and treatment of role violators. What gives Laing his distinctiveness is the claim that the deviant response is anything but a sick response. Instead, it is a response to the sick society. Laing confronts us directly with our own forms of irrationality: war, rape, urban violence, eroticized sexuality, consumer culture, and so on, and contrasts our irrationality with the relative meekness and helplessness of the human beings who are confined to asylums. The inmates are more victims of a corrupt society than carriers of undesirable psychological traits. Insofar as insanity itself is concerned, Laing suggests that the movement toward the private, irrational, and dark side of life is a normal and desirable characteristic of human development, and that it only becomes psychologically harmful if the individual is restrained from returning to the public world. (The same arguments had been advanced in the 1940s by Anton T. Boisen (1947), a clergyman working with mental hospital patients.)

Laing has formulated a new definition of madness: The person who needs the attention of psychological and moral healers is the person who is unable to move back and forth between the rational and the irrational, between the public and private worlds, between the dark side of passion and the bright side of reason. In effect, Laing articulates the romanticization of the noble savage, implicit in much of Western thought, from Rousseau (Vaughan, 1939) to Foucault (1961) to Rachael Carson (1962). The mentally ill are promoted to the status of anti-hero, and each inmate of the asylum is seen as another Van Gogh or Artaud. For Laing, then, psychotic behavior is a healthy phenomenon—everyone needs it on a temporary basis. It provides us with a means of viewing ourselves and others from alternative metaphysical perspectives. Laing dissolves the old paradox by unashamedly and wholeheartedly assimilating the conduct of human beings into a theological model. He goes behind the concept of mind to its predecessor, soul; but more than that, he sees no virtue in separating classes of people in terms of their choice of language and ritual in order to resolve their existential problems. The continuity of Laing's philosophy with the social rebellions of the sixties is evident. In this new perspective, a person can announce with pride that his imaginings have a quality that is undifferentiated from the perception of sensible objects. Hallucination need no longer be seen as a pejorative, but rather as a sign of transcendent vision (Sarbin and Juhasz, 1978).

Laing begins from the position of relativism, but of the four "scientists" so far discussed, he extends it furthest. In effect, he turns the psychopathologists' position upside down by offering his own definition of "mental health"—one that excludes the narrow-minded and overrational mental health professionals. The tragicomedy of Goffman is turned into historical drama, in which the dramaturgist (Laing) himself influences the outcome of history by rewriting it.

Sarbin's Contextualism

In 1962, Sarbin presented his cognitive strain model as an alternative to the prevailing medical model. A part of the model had been developed earlier in his work with Taft and Bailey (1960). The special feature of the model was its inclusion of the conduct of others in assigning value to the actions employed to solve problems inherent in making sense of an imperfect, probabilistic, and changing world.

Adaptive conduct, that is, actions taken by an individual to resolve the strains of ecological uncertainty, is classified according to the intentions of the actor. Was the action directed toward changing the spatial relationship of the actor to potential perils? Was the action directed toward modifying the actor's beliefs or values that provided the meaning of particular sensory inputs? Was the action directed toward the physiological arousal associated with strain-in-knowing? Sarbin classified adaptive actions in terms of the intention of the actor. He identified five antecedent stages in the development of strain-in-knowing. The person could focus on one rather than another of these antecedents as targets for actions to resolve the strain. The adaptive actions were classified according to which antecedent phase was the target of the action: instrumental acts, attention redeployment, changing beliefs and values, tranquilizing and releasing acts, and no action. Self-valuation of success or failure could be explicitly and/or implicitly assigned to the adaptive act. Successful adaptive acts were likely to be repeated, given similar problems and settings (a process reminiscent of Hull's drive reduction theory of learning). Most important, adaptive acts that were under public scrutiny were subject to sanctions by others who had the power—coercive, legitimate, or charismatic—to declare moral verdicts on the adaptive actions. That is, an adaptive act that was successful in resolving the strain-in-knowing from the actor's viewpoint could be declared a norm violation by significant and powerful others. A simplistic example would be the drinking of whiskey to reduce the physiological arousal associated with strain. The drinker could explicitly and/or implicitly act as if the strain had been reduced or eliminated. If the drinking came under public scrutiny in a society that proscribed the imbibing of alcohol, then a negative moral judgment might be made. Any of the actions described by psychopathologists as "symptoms of mental illness" could be seen instead as the performance of actions in order to deal with existential problems in ways that were judged contranormative by relatives, neighbors, and, most importantly, by doctors and/or priests.

Appealing to everyday conduct as well as to ethnographic reports in the tradition of Benedict, Boas, Sapir, Malinowski, and others, Sarbin argued that all people engage in adaptive actions to solve problems of living. Whether the conduct is judged good or bad, sane or insane, mad or rational is not inherent in the action itself, but is determined by powerful and relevant others—the social reinforcers, so to speak. Thus, the attribution of madness follows not exclusively from the actions of the suspected madman, but also from the combination of the actions *and* the judgments of appropriateness and propriety made by others who have been assigned the role of moral judge.

This formulation, elaborated in other papers (Sarbin, 1962; 1964; 1967a, 1967b; 1968; 1969), unites the *We* and the *They* in the recognition that existential problem solving is universal. The forms of problem solving are multiple and subject to cultural and individual variation. Also posited as a universal is the possibility that any adaptive act can, in principle, be the subject of moral valuation by others. In modern times, in the industrialized world, if an action is judged against encoded norms, the person will be judged as criminal; if the action is judged against unencoded norms (in Scheff's term, *residual deviance),* madness is the likely verdict.

Sarbin argued seriously that the diagnosis of mental illness is not a diagnosis at all, but a moral judgment expressed in ill-concealed moralistic language. He traced the origin of the medical model to its metaphorical beginnings and showed how the original metaphor had become transformed to a myth. In the course of his analysis, he elaborated the notion of the universality of strain-in-knowing when a person has difficulty in locating himself in various ecologies. It is true of all human beings that to survive, a person must locate self in the self-maintenance ecology; he or she must locate self with reference to food and shelter and to the world of physical perils. To use a semiotic shorthand, every person must find answers to the constantly asked question: What am I in relation to this or that potential peril? Similarly, to survive as a member of a human society, the individual must locate self with reference to others, such location being guided by knowledge about, and participation in, systems of social roles. In other words, the person is perpetually confronted with challenges to social identity, the challenges being contained in the symbolic performances of other social beings who ask the question *Who are you?* reflexively phrased as *Who am I?* In addition, because the maintenance of any social organization depends upon rules of conduct, the human being must locate self in the ecology of norms, standards, and moral codes. Finally, what makes the human being different from other social creatures is a dependency on symbolic abstractions—beliefs, premises, and meanings that arise from the unique talent for treating symbols as if they were things and things as if they were symbols. Placement in the world of abstractions—the transcendental ecology—is mediated by the implicit (sometimes explicit) query: What am I in relation to the Deity, my nation, departed ancestors, the universe? The reply to the query is constrained by one's lexicon of abstract terms.

Beginning with the cultural relativism of the ethnologists, Sarbin extended his model to include the pancultural universals of ecological placement. The forms of adaptive conduct to resolve the cognitive effects of nonplacement in a particular ecology are, to be sure, culture bound and subject to individual variation. Similarly, sanctions imposed on a person who has been subject to the moral valuation of his social group are characterized by great diversity from time to time and from culture to culture.

Such a formulation is vastly different from the models that had been employed in Western societies for at least 200 years—models that attributed norm-violating conduct to deformed minds or diseased brains or both. Along with Szasz, Goffman, and the cultural relativists of an earlier generation, Sarbin argued that no theory of norm-violating conduct can be complete without considering the person who declares the moral valuation as well as the person who may have tried to dissolve his strain-in-knowing in atypical ways. Furthermore, the recognition that madness is an attribution that is potentially applicable to everyone leads to the adoption of a contextual world view as a guide to understanding human action (Sarbin, 1977; Sarbin and Mancuso, 1980).

The foregoing theses of deviant conduct did not arise sui generis. They were part of, and perhaps contributed to, the cultural revolution of the 1960s. The antinomianism (Adler, 1972) that spawned new life-styles, student upheavals, urban riots, challenges to constituted authority, removal of gender qualifications, and more, challenged existing beliefs about human potential and social organization. From our present perspective, it seems that the ideological theme of the cultural revolution was disalienation, which required the removal of the tradition-supported barriers that separated one person from another, barriers that had for so long facilitated the separation of *Us* from *Them,* so that *We* could pass moral verdicts on *Their* conduct.

BEYOND RELATIVISM

The cultural revolution, which had its spokespersons in people like Goffman, Szasz, Foucault, Laing, and Sarbin, popularized and (to some extent) legitimized the cultural relativist view of mental illness. However, each of these theorists found the traditional relativist view inadequate. Schooled in the tradition of "value-free" science and political liberalism, they could accept neither the full burden of moral and political choice nor the amorality of acquiescing to exploitation under the guise of being scientists. Thus, they searched for ways out of their own dilemma, and their search forms the history that is sketched out in this chapter. With the cultural revolution of the mid–1960s, this history of the concept of mental illness ends. Other researchers in the present volume are collectively writing the denouement.

Throughout the history of mental illness appears a persisting paradox, and the attempts to resolve the paradox have structured this account. The fundamental paradox is that, on the one hand, mental illness entails the invocation of causal features of unacceptable conduct that have to do with morality, custom, power relations, and a transcendental commitment; on the other hand, it entails the concurrent claim that such moral causality operates according to "scientific," i.e., mechanistic principles. This chapter exposes the face of this paradox in the attempts to fit moral treatment into the medical vocabulary of the early nineteenth century, and shows that the paradox persisted during the heyday of the mechanization of biology and medicine in the second half of the nineteenth century. The implicit question was: How does the mind, an abstraction, not a thing, influence the actions of the body, an actual material object, and vice versa?

One resolution of the paradox was radical materialism: denying that moral elements entered into the diagnosis of insanity. This resolution was simply the annexation by somatic medicine, especially neuropathology, of the province of declaring valuation on human actions. This resolution was of the same form, but opposite in content to that taken by Mary Baker Eddy (Glover, 1875), the founder of Christian Science. Her metaphysical assumption was that matter was an illusion and that the immaterial mind was the only reality. In short, if there is no body, there is no paradox.

To most physicians, the fact that they were at least implicitly espousing an illegitimate eclecticism was not bothersome. They equated mind with brain, or saw mind or mental activity as the function of the brain, in much the same way that they saw circulation as the function of the heart. Such a tour de force avoided the necessity for grappling with moral issues, cultural relativism, and so forth.

Contained in the primary mind/body paradox was another, more subtle contradiction. If conduct, or human performance, was the object of study and diagnosis, then one had to deal with the problem of determining what conduct should be isolated for attention. The concern of the physicians was not with any conduct, but with performances that violated proprietary norms. The actions that came to the attention of the diagnosers and healers were actions that, in general, violated concurrent normative expectations. The preceding statement stimulated the question: Whose expectations? This question turned the inquiry toward statements about who judged whom, and about what actions stimulated persons to render moral declarations. This chapter discusses how these questions were raised and answered, primarily in the twentieth century, by social reformers, sociologists, anthropologists, and novelists who espoused the theme of cultural relativity.

When systematic studies of mental illness attributions were made, it became clear that the insane were drawn from some, but not all, classes of people and strata of society, and that the procedures for making the attribution of madness or insanity or mental illness were special ceremonials of institutions that were concerned with political control and social order. Historical, semantic, political, and sociological analyses all converged to support the proposition that the use of the mental illness concept was not a medical, but a moral and political enterprise. Thus, the stage was set for the next phase in the cultural revolution.

The cultural revolution of the 1960s, with its theme of disalienation, has had a profound influence on our institutions for the identification and control of deviant conduct, including the mental illness establishment. Disalienation was the goal of the social minorities, who were aliens without power. They used the streets, the press, the campuses, the legislative halls and courts, and even the findings of social scientists to make their nonperson status a matter of public record. They pressured governmental and legislative bodies to enact and enforce ordinances to implement the theme of disalienation. Applying and extending the arguments of cultural relativists fostered a breakdown in the arbitrarily imposed *We–They* barriers that made it possible for one class of persons to declare a member of another class as alien and unwanted. The recognition of the cultural revolution is central to understanding recent developments in theory, research, and practice in the field of social deviance.

RECENT DEVELOPMENTS: MOVES TOWARD DISALIENATION

The following recent developments require scrutiny from the critical orientation advocated in the present chapter.

1. *The mass reduction of mental hospital populations.* Milazzo-Sayre (1978) has shown that resident patient populations of state and county mental hospitals in the U.S. have declined by 60% in the decade 1965–1975. That this is not simply a result of the discovery and/or use of psychotropic drugs just prior to the cultural revolution is attested to by at least two facts. First, at least since the 1850s (Esquirol, 1845; Hamilton, 1886; Hammond, 1883), it has been known how to control unwanted human behaviors through the use of opiates and other morphia. Second, Witkin (1978) has convincingly shown that the reduction in state and county hospital beds for mental illness indicates complex regional and statewide patterns from dramatic decrease to actual increase. These patterns and the preknowledge of effective psychotropics show that these changes must be, at least in part, attitudinal, political, ideological, and economic.

    Thus, the consequence of a diagnosis of mental illness is no longer typically lifetime incarceration, but rather short periods of restraint alternating with periods of release (Ozarin, Redick, and Taube, 1976). It is not as if people were ready to admit that the concept of mental illness itself was mistaken—rather it is being somewhat redefined. At least in poorer neighborhoods, the *We–They* differences have become more neutralized.

2. *Communication patterns.* Some researchers believe that communication patterns in the family provide the context for unwanted conduct from some family members (Bateson, 1961; Berger, 1978; Bowen, 1959; Sluzki and Ransom, 1976; Wynne and Singer, 1963a, 1963b). This theory is fundamentally contextualist and social, and is ill-adapted to traditional conceptions of health and illness.

3. *Documentation of the political implications of the mental health/illness enterprise.* (See Braginsky and Braginsky, 1974; Fisher et al., 1973; Halleck, 1971; Rotenberg, 1978; Wing, 1978.)

4. *Problems in the mental illness system.* Continuing disclosures have been presented of the failure of the mental illness system to deal with moral matters from a cognitive foundation that depends on the

mechanistic actions of toxins, traumata, and tumors (Rosenhan, 1973; Scheff, 1975; Torrey, 1974).

5. *Independent organizations.* There has been a rise of self-help and mutual-help groups and a proliferation of community resources not under the control of medicine and psychiatry (Fisher et al., 1973; Levy, 1979; Morrison, 1979).

The ultimate resolution of the paradoxes that have influenced the history of the concept of mental illness from antiquity is not likely to be found. The resolution of the problems generated by the human condition is never suitable to all times and places. It is true that every social group defines some conduct as inappropriate or improper and worthy of change. Some of the conduct will have its origins in somatic conditions, such as general paresis. Most of the conduct that stimulates the value judgment of peers and others can be seen as episodes in an historical event. There is a multiplicity of influences both on the person of interest and on the person who acts as his or her judge. Most significantly, both parties in a normative situation are intending creatures: they make use of a wide variety of instrumental and symbolic actions to realize their intentions.

Each person, each group, each society, must begin anew to recognize what limits, if any, should be placed on conduct, and what sanctions, if any, should be imposed on norm violators. In the context of cultural relativism, and its aftermath, it is vital that we look neither toward "normlessness" nor toward a new moral absolutism as salvation. The personal recognition that each of us operates from a moral system should embrace even our work as social scientists and/or historians. This recognition should lead to the acceptance of pluralistic perspectives and value systems. A pluralism that does not eschew moral commitment must flow from our understanding of ourselves and our social systems as they are, and not as our scientific or other fictions would have them be (Juhasz, 1976).

ACKNOWLEDGMENTS

We gratefully acknowledge the assistance of the University of Colorado's Council on Research and Creative Work in the preparation of this manuscript. The library research and other help of John Gates and Jesus Salazar is also gratefully acknowledged.

REFERENCES

Ackerknecht, E. H. 1959. A Short History of Psychiatry. S. Wolf, (trans.). Hafner Publishing Co., New York.
Addams, J. 1910. Twenty Years at Hull House. Macmillan Publishing Company, Inc., New York.

Adler, N. 1972. The Underground Stream. Harper & Row Pubs., Inc., New York.

Alexander, F., and Selesnick, S. T. 1966. The History of Psychiatry. Harper & Row, Pubs., Inc., New York.

American Psychiatric Association. 1952, 1968, 1980. Diagnostic and Statistical Manual: Mental Disorders. American Psychiatric Association, Washington, D.C.

Bailyn, B. 1967. The Ideological Origins of the American Revolution. Harvard University Press, Cambridge, Mass.

Bateson, G. 1961. The biosocial integration of behavior in the schizophrenic family. In: N. Ackerman et al. (eds.), Exploring the Base for Family Therapy. Family Services Association of America, New York.

Bateson, G., Jackson, D., Haley, J., and Weakland, J. 1956. Toward a theory of schizophrenia. Behav. Sci. 1:251–264.

Becker, G. 1978. The Mad Genius Controversy. Sage Pubns., Inc., Beverly Hills, Calif.

Benedict, R. 1934. Patterns of Culture. Houghton Mifflin Company, Boston.

Berger, M. M. (ed.). 1978. Beyond the Double Bind. Brunner/Mazel, Inc., New York.

Bleuler, E. 1911. Dementia Praecox. F. Deuticke, Leipzig.

Boas, F. 1909. The Kwakiutil of Vancouver Island. G. E. Stechert & Co., New York.

Boisen, A. T. 1947. Onset in acute schizophrenia. Psychiatry 10:159–165.

Bowen, M. 1959. Family relationships in schizophrenia. In: A. Auerback (ed.), Schizophrenia: An Integrated Approach. Ronald Press, New York.

Braginsky, B. M., and Braginsky, D. 1974. Mainstream Psychology. Holt, Rinehart & Winston, Inc., New York.

Breuer, J., and Freud, S. 1895. Studien über Hysterie. Deuticke, Leipzig.

Cameron, N. 1947. The Psychology of Behavior Disorders. Houghton Mifflin Company, Boston.

Carson, R. L. 1962. Silent Spring. Houghton Mifflin Company, Boston.

Charcot, J. M. Lecons sur les maladies du système nerveux fuites à la Salpêtrière. A. Delahaye, Paris.

Coleman, J. C. 1976. Abnormal Psychology and Modern Life. 5th Ed. Scott, Foresman & Company, Chicago.

Conrad, J. 1902. Typhoon. G. P. Putnam's Sons, New York.

Dain, N. 1964. Concepts of Insanity in the United States, 1789–1865. Rutgers University Press, New Brunswick, N. J.

Dershowitz, A. M. 1973. Preventive confinement: A suggested framework for constitutional analysis. Texas Law Rev. 51:1277–1324.

Dickens, C. 1850. The Personal History of David Copperfield. Bradbury & Evans, London.

Dohrenwend, B. P., and Dohrenwend, B. S. 1969. Social Status and Psychological Disorder: A Causal Inquiry. John Wiley & Sons, Inc., New York.

Durkheim, E. 1897. Le Suicide. F. Alcan, Paris.

Esquirol, E. 1845. Mental Maladies: A Treatise on Insanity. Lee & Blanchard, Philadelphia.

Faris, R. E. L., and Dunham, W. 1939. Mental Disorders in Urban Areas. University of Chicago Press, Chicago.

Fisher, W., Mehr, J., and Tuckenbrod, P. 1973. Power, Greed and Stupidity in the Mental Health Racket. Westminster Press, Philadelphia.

Fortune, R. F. 1932. The Sorcerers of Dobu. G. Routledge & Sons, Ltd., London.

Foucault, M. 1961. Histoire de la folie à l'âge classique. Librairie Plon, Paris.

Freud, S. 1959a. Dostoevsky and parricide. In: Collected Papers. Vol. 1, pp. 222–242. Basic Books, Inc., New York. (Originally published in 1928.)

Freud, S. 1959b. The neuropsychoses of defense—1894. In: Collected Papers. Vol. 1, pp. 59–75. Basic Books, Inc., New York.

Freud, S. 1910. Über Psychoanalyse. F. Deuticke, Vienna.

Friedman, S., and Juhasz, J. B. 1974. Environments. Brooks/Cole, Monterey, Calif.

Glover, M. B. (later, M. B. Eddy) 1875. Science and Health. W. F. Brown & Co., Boston.

Goffman, E. 1961. Asylums. Aldine Publishing Company, Chicago.

Griesinger, W. 1845. Die Pathologie und Therapie der psychischen Krankheiten. Stuttgart.

Halleck, S. 1971. The Politics of Therapy. Science House, New York.

Hamilton, A. M. 1886. Insanity and its Treatment. William Wood & Co., New York.

Hammond, W. A. 1883. A Treatise on Insanity. D. Appleton & Co., New York.

Hollingshead, A. B., and Redlich, F. C. 1958. Social Class and Mental Illness: A Community Study. John Wiley & Sons, Inc., New York.

Hughes, T. 1857. Tom Brown's Schooldays. Macmillan & Co., Cambridge, Mass.

Illich, I. 1978. Toward a History of Needs. Pantheon Books, New York.

Jahoda, M. 1958. Current Concepts of Positive Mental Health. Basic Books, Inc., New York.

Janet, P. 1911. The Mental State of Hystericals: A Study of Mental Stigmata and Mental Accidents. Putnam, London.

Jaynes, J. 1976. The Origins of Consciousness in the Breakdown of the Bicameral Mind. Houghton Mifflin Company, Boston.

Juhasz, J. B. 1976. Psychology of paradox, and vice versa. Psychol. Rep. 39:911–914.

Kesey, K. 1962. One Flew Over the Cuckoo's Nest. Viking, New York.

Kittrie, N. N. 1971. The Right to be Different. Johns Hopkins Press, Baltimore.

Kraepelin, E. 1883. Compendium der Psychiatrie. Abel, Leipzig.

Kubie, L. S. 1954. The fundamental nature of the distinction between normality and neurosis. Psychoanal. Q. 23:187–188.

Laing, R. D. 1960. The Divided Self. Tavistock, London.

Levy, L. M. 1979. Processes and activities in groups. In: M. A. Lieberman and L. D. Borman (eds.), Self-help Groups for Coping with Crisis: Origins, Members, Processes, and Impact. Jossey-Bass, Inc., Pubs., San Francisco.

Loeb, J. 1964. D. Fleming (ed.). The Mechanistic Conception of Life. Harvard University Press, Cambridge. (Originally published in 1912.)

Lovejoy, A. O. 1936. The Great Chain of Being. Harvard University Press, Cambridge, Mass.

Malinowski, B. 1922. Argonauts of the Western Pacific. Routledge & Kegan Paul, London.

Malinowski, B. 1927. Sex and Repression in Savage Society. Routledge & Kegan Paul, London.

Mannheim, K. 1929. Ideologie and Utopie. F. Colen, Bonn.

Mead, G. H. 1918. The Conscientious Objector. National Security League, New York.

Mead, G. H. 1934. Mind, Self, and Society. University of Chicago Press, Chicago.

Mead, M. 1928. Coming of Age in Samoa. W. Morrow & Co., New York.

Menninger, K. A. 1963. The Vital Balance. Viking, New York.

Millazzo-Sayre, L. 1978. Changes in age, sex, and diagnostic composition of the resident population of state and county mental hospitals, United States, 1965 1975. Mental Health Statistical Note no. 146, March. U. S. Department of HEW, Washington, D.C.

Moliére, J. - B. P. 1667. Le Médicin malgré lui. J. Ribou, Paris.

Morrison, J. K. (ed.). 1979. The Consumer Approach to Community Psychology. Nelson-Hall, Chicago.

Morse, S. J. 1978. Crazy behavior, morals, and science: An analysis of mental health law. South. Calif. Law Rev. 51:524–654.

Ozarin, L. D., Redick, R. W., and Taube, C. A. 1976. A quarter century of psychiatric care, 1950–1974: A statistical review. Hosp. Community Psychiatry 27:515 519.

Park, R. E., and Burgess, E. W. 1921. Introduction to the Science of Society. Chicago University Press, Chicago.

Paterson, T. T. 1966. Management Theory. Business Publications, London.

Pepper, S. C. 1942 World Hypotheses. Universiy of California Press, Berkeley.

Pinel, P. 1802. La Médicine cliniqiue rendue plus précise et plus exacte par l'application de l'analyse. Brosson, Gabon et. Cie., Paris.

Platt, A. M., and Diamond, B. L. 1965. The origins and development of the "Wild Beast" concept of mental illness and its relations to theories of responsibility. J. Hist. Behav. Sci. 1:355 367.

Prince, M. 1891. Association neuroses: A study of the pathology of hysterical joint affections, neurasthenia, and allied forms of neuromionesis. J. Nerv. Ment. Dis. 18:257 282.

Redlich, F. D. 1957. The concept of health in psychiatry. In: A. M. Leighton, J. A. Clausen, and R. N. Wilson (eds.), Explorations in Social Psychiatry, pp. 138—164. Basic Books, Inc., New York.

Rosenhan, D. C. 1973. On being sane in insane places. Science 179:250–258.

Rotenberg, M. 1978. Damnation and Deviance: The Protestant Ethic and the Spirit of Failure. Free Press, New York.

Rothman, D. J. 1971. The Discovery of the Asylum. Little Brown & Company, Boston.

Ruitenbeek, H. M. (ed.) 1972. Going Crazy: The Radical Therapy of R. D. Laing and Others. Bantam Books, Inc., New York.

Sarbin, T. R. 1962. A new model of the behavior disorders. Gawein, Tigdschrift voor Psychologie 10:315–323.

Sarbin, T. R. 1964. Anxiety: The reification of a metaphor. Arch. Gen. Psychiatry 10:630 638.

Sarbin, T. R. 1967a. On the futility of the proposition that some people be labelled "mentally ill." J. Consult. Psychol. 31:447–453.

Sarbin, T. R. 1967b. The concept of hallucination. J. Pers. 35:359–380.

Sarbin, T. R. 1967c. The dangerous individual: An outcome of social identity transformations. Br. J. Criminol. 7:285—295.

Sarbin, T. R. 1968. Ontology recapitulates philology: The mythic nature of anxiety. Am. Psychol. 23:411 418.

Sarbin, T. R. 1969. The present status of the mental illness metaphor. In: A. Plog and W. Edgerton (eds.), Changing Perspectives in Mental Illness. Holt, Rinehart & Winston, Inc., New York.

Sarbin, T. R. 1977. Contextualism: A world view for modern psychology. In: A. Landfield (ed.), 1976 Nebraska Symposium on Motivation. University of Nebraska Press, Lincoln.

Sarbin, T. R., and Coe, W. C. 1979. Hypnosis and psychopathology: Replacing old myths with fresh metaphors. J. Abnorm. Psychol. 88:506–526.

Sarbin, T. R., and Juhasz, J. B. 1967. The historical background of the concept of hallucination. J. Hist. Behav. Sci. 3:339–358.

Sarbin, T. R., and Juhasz, J. B., 1975. The social context of hallucinations. In: R. K. Siegel and L. J. West (eds.), Hallucinations: Behavior, Experience, and Theory, pp. 241–256. John Wiley & Sons, Inc., New York.

Sarbin, T. R., and Juhasz, J. B. 1978. The social psychology hallucination. J. Ment. Imagery 2:117–144.

Sarbin, T. R., and Mancuso, J. C. 1980. Schizophrenia: Medical Diagnosis or Moral Verdict. Pergamon Press, Inc., New York.

Sarbin, T. R., Taft, R., and Bailey, D. E. 1960. Clinical Inference and Cognitive Theory. Holt, Rinehart & Winston, Inc., New York.

Scheff, T. J. 1964. The societal reaction to deviance: Ascriptive elements in the psychiatric screening of mental patients in a midwestern state. Soc. Problems 11:401–413.

Scheff, T. J. (ed.). 1975. Labelling Madness. Prentice Hall, Inc., Englewood Cliffs, N. J.

Scott, W. A. 1958. Research definitions of mental health and mental illness. Psychol. Bull. 55:29–45.

Shoben, E. J., Jr. 1957. Toward a concept of the normal personality. Am. Psychol. 12:183–189.

Siegler, M., and Osmund, H. 1974. Models of Madness, Models of Medicine. Macmillan Publishing Company, Inc., New York.

Sinclair, U. B. 1905. The Jungle. Wayland Co., Girard, Kansas.

Singer, C. 1959. A Short History of Scientific Ideas to 1900. Oxford University Press, New York.

Singer, M. 1967. Family transactions and schizophrenia. Vol. 1. Recent research findings. In: J. Romano (ed.), The Origins of Schizophrenia. Excerpta Medica, Amsterdam.

Skultans, V. 1975. Madness and Morals. Routledge & Kegan Paul, London.

Sluzki, C. E., and Ransom, D. C. (eds.). 1976. Double Bind: The Foundation of the Communication Approach to the Family. Grune & Stratton, New York.

Steffens, J. L. 1904. The Shame of the Cities. McClure's, Phillips & Co., New York.

Suinn, R. M. 1975. Fundamentals of Behavior Pathology. 2nd Ed. John Wiley & Sons, Inc., New York.

Sullivan, H. S. 1953. The Interpersonal Theory of Psychiatry. W. W. Norton & Company, Inc., New York.

Szasz, T. S. 1961. The Myth of Mental Illness. Paul B. Hoeber, New York.

Szasz, T. S. 1963. Law, Liberty, and Psychiatry. Macmillan Publishing Company, Inc., New York.

Torrey, E. F. 1974. The Death of Psychiatry. Chilton Book Co., Radnor, Pa.

Tuke, S. 1964. Description of the Retreat, an Institution near York for the Insane Persons of the Society of Friends. Dawson's of Pall Mall, London. (Originally published in 1813.)

Vaughan, C. E. 1939. Studies in the History of Political Philosophy Before and After Rousseau. Vols. 1 and 2. University of Manchester Press, Manchester.

Veith, I. 1977. Four thousand years of hysteria. In: M. J. Horowitz (ed.), Hysterical Personality. Jason Aronson, New York.

White, H. 1972. The forms of wildness: Archeology of an idea. In: E. Dudley and M. E. Novak. (eds.), The Wild Man Within. University of Pittsburgh Press, Pittsburgh.

White, H. V. 1973. Metahistory. Johns Hopkins Press, Baltimore.

White, K. G., Juhasz, J. B., and Wilson, P. 1973. Is man no more than this?: Evaluative bias in interspecies comparison. J. Hist. Behav. Sci. 9:203–212.

Wing, J. K. 1978. Reasoning About Madness. Oxford University Press, Oxford.

Wirth, L. 1928. The Ghetto. University of Chicago Press, Chicago.

Wishner, J. 1955. The concept of efficiency in psychological health and in psychopathology. Psychol. Rev. 62:69–80.

Witkin, M. J. 1978. State and regional distribution of psychiatric beds. Mental health statisical note no. 144, February. U. S. Department of HEW, Washington, D.C.

Wynne, L. C., and Singer, M. T. 1963a. Thought disorder and family relations of schizophrenics: I. A research strategy. Arch. Gen. Psychiatry 9:191–198.

Wynne, L. C., and Singer, M. T. 1963b. Thought disorder and family relations of schizophrenics: II. A classification of forms of thinking. Arch. Gen. Psychiatry 9:199 206.

Zilboorg, G., and Henry, G. W. 1941. A History of Medical Psychology. W. W. Norton & Company, Inc., New York.

Zola, E. 1885. Gérminal. Dunod, Paris.

Chapter 4

The Genetic-Environmental Perspective in Psychopathology

David Rosenthal

Culture, environment, and psychopathology may be regarded as a triad in which each element constantly interacts with the others in some way. Culture is always in flux, and is never fully understood. Environments can also be unstable and subject to change. Either by choice or by chance, psychopathology is part of the day-to-day life-style of every person. How the interaction of these three elements affects human development and behavior is a major concern of researchers.

Human genetics is another important factor in the study of behavior. Genetics is primarily concerned with similarities regarding body build, facial features, and behavioral patterns of various kinds, both in the nuclear family and in the extended family. Geneticists seek to determine how these features may bear on behavioral patterns, in regard to both acceptable and unacceptable behavior. The genetic-environmental perspective in psychopathology is complex, with genetic factors playing crucial roles in the development of psychopathology. Many of these factors are now identified as components of biological psychiatry, a field in which new discoveries have helped to clarify some important factors regarding psychopathology. These new findings have helped to develop earlier theories in psychopathology that were pioneered largely by English and European scientists, and by American psychologists as well.

Much psychological and psychiatric research has also been directed toward environmental factors that presumably induce psychopathology in deviant subjects. There is no doubt that such factors often contribute to psychopathology in afflicted individuals, but it is also very difficult to determine with certainty exactly which environmental factors are causing the disorder. Many people assume that genetic factors in psychopathology are more complex than environmental factors, and thus less proven, but this is not necessarily the case; in fact, in many instances (perhaps most), genetic factors provide some of the most important and most reliable data regarding major mental illness, particularly schizophrenia and affective disorders.

Through careful genetic analyses, my colleagues and I were able to determine that, to a great extent, schizophrenia tends to be genetically transmitted in the family. Also, in identical twins and even monozygous quadruplets, the individuals manifest many behavioral patterns that are common to their siblings. Some patterns are probably induced and learned, but some groups have such similar and unique behavioral patterns that it does not seem likely that these patterns could be duplicated by trial and error, even if other individuals in the group tried their best to do so. Such similar patterns among relatives present strong evidence that the genetic perspective should be taken seriously. They also imply that important research regarding the family is still lacking. New approaches to study of the family in regard to psychopathology could be very helpful in understanding both the environmental and the genetic perspectives, as well as their respective interactions.

RESEARCH STUDIES

There has been much long-running controversy over schizophrenia, with one group holding that schizophrenia is not an illness but a life-style, and other groups holding that the condition is indeed an illness. Many studies have been made to determine which theory is correct. One of the more interesting studies was carried out by Rosenhan (1973). Normal subjects were sent to mental hospitals, where they feigned symptoms of mental illness, most often by claiming that they were hearing voices. These subjects were then admitted by the hospital personnel, and remained in the institutions for various periods of time in the guise of patients. Most of them were given a diagnosis of schizophrenia. Rosenhan concluded: ". . . We cannot distinguish insanity from sanity." By contrast, the research study by Kety et al. (1975) provided strong evidence that schizophrenia is indeed a form of what many call mental illness (a term that is not acceptable to others, such as Szasz and Menninger and Laing). How can we compare the respective validity of the Rosenhan and Kety studies? In the Rosenhan study (1973), the subjects gained secret admission to 12 different hospitals. Their diagnostic experiences constitute the data of the first part of Rosenhan's article. The eight pseudopatients were a varied group. One was a psychology graduate student in his twenties. The other seven were older and "established"; three were women, four were men. By contrast, the Kety et al. (1975) study was carefully constructed, with index and control subjects totaling more than 100 altogether. In his study, Rosenhan knew at the outset that the hospital staffs may not have been competent in some ways: hospital psychiatrists may have been overworked, caught up in a routine, not fully trained, and so forth. There were no controls in the study, only the possibility that hospital personnel could be lax, which would demonstrate that the diagnosis of schizophrenia could be invalid under certain conditions. The outcome of the Kety et al. study, on the other hand, was verified statistically.

The meaning of Rosenhan's study could be debated at length, probably without an acceptable conclusion. His findings do not provide us with any new discoveries regarding psychopathology or schizophrenia itself. They do indicate that normal persons can simulate some of the behavioral patterns that one finds in individuals who are placed in mental institutions. The pseudopatients of Rosenhan left the institutions without manifesting the behavioral patterns that the real patients manifested in the hospital. If both the real patients and the pseudopatients were left free, would they both manifest the same behaviors in the street? It is not likely. It is not institutions for the insane that are our great concern, although we hope to improve them. The primary problem is the unfortunate individuals whose behavioral patterns deviate so much from those of most other persons that both the individual himself and the people around him are affected, especially if the individual is schizophrenic. In the case of schizophrenia, and in the affective disorders as well, we find that genetic factors play an important role in the development of these disorders.

The pseudopatients of Rosenhan raise the crucial issue of psychiatric diagnosis. Were they properly examined? Would they have been able to fake the data on such tests as the Spitzer-Endicott Schedule for Affective Disorders and Schizophrenia—Lifetime Version (SADS-L) and other similar inventories? In the Rosenhan study, there is no indication of what the psychiatrists at the hospitals thought about the pseudopatients, or if they examined them at all. Psychiatric diagnosis, which has become much more sophisticated in the past several years, is very important in such studies. Although it is probably not possible to construct a perfect diagnostic system, the guidelines that are in current use have been accepted by most psychiatrists and psychologists, although some diagnoses, such as schizoaffective disorder, have been criticized.

ADOPTION STUDIES

Our own major research strategy in studying schizophrenia involved naturally occurring adoptions, with the stipulation that the adoptees were not adopted by a biological relative. In this way, we could examine the relative merits of the genetic and environmentalist positions in regard to schizophrenic disorders. We could determine whether these disorders had a genetic basis or were caused by idiosyncratic, noxious rearing practices of the parents, such as double-binding the child, creating a chaotic home climate, fragmenting the child's attention, or other related child-rearing phenomena postulated to be of etiological signifcance in schizophrenia.

Three of the several research designs that we employed are presented here. In the first design, Kety et al. (1971) identified adult adoptees who had a schizophrenic disorder. These were our index cases. We then selected other nonschizophrenic adoptees who were matched to the index cases for age, sex, age at transfer to the adopting family, socioeconomic class of the rearing family, and time spent in homes with biological relatives, in child care institutions, or in foster homes before their transfer to the adopting family. These nonschizophrenic adoptees served as controls. We then examined the biological and adoptive parents, sibs, and half sibs of the index and control groups, and found that the highest concentration of relatives with schizophrenic disorders occurred in the biological relatives of the index cases. This finding reached high statistical significance, whereas the other three groups of adoptive relatives did not differ in the relative frequency of schizophrenic disorders.

In the second study (Rosenthal et al., 1971), we scrutinized hospital records of the biological parents of adoptees and identified those parents who had a schizophrenic disorder. The adopted-away child of each such parent became an index case. Control adoptees were selected by matching criteria, as before, and differed from the index adoptees primarily in that neither parent of the control subject had a known psychiatric record. We then examined the adoptees and found a higher concentration of schizophrenic disorder among the index cases than among the control group.

In the third study (Wender et al., 1974), we examined the hospital records of the *adoptive* parents of the adoptees and selected those adoptive parents who had a known schizophrenic disorder. We wanted to know how the adoptees who were reared by these parents, but whose biological parents did not have any schizophrenic disorder, would develop. We call this group of adoptees the cross-foster subjects. We did not find significantly more schizophrenic disorder among the cross-foster subjects than among a group of control adoptees.

Thus, our findings in the three studies are consistent, and they provide strong evidence that schizophrenic disorders are heritable.

THE SCHIZOPHRENIA SPECTRUM

In discussing these cases, I have not referred to schizophrenia as such, but instead have used the term *schizophrenic disorders*. It is important to discuss what these disorders are, because they bear directly on the topic of schizophrenia.

In conducting genetic research on schizophrenia, investigators in the past have examined the frequency of schizophrenia in relatives of index cases, and have found that the frequencies were always greater than the population incidence, but were always *less* than a theory of simple dominance or recessiveness would predict. One possible explanation of this consistent finding might be that not all affected relatives were being counted. Usually the investigators included only those relatives who manifested clear symptoms of schizophrenia, although some noted *doubtful schizophrenia* among the relatives as well. It is possible that not all affected relatives show the major primary and secondary signs of schizophrenia, but, for some reason, they may manifest less flagrant but somewhat related symptoms. Predictably, good nosologists would properly refuse to diagnose such cases as schizophrenia. From the standpoint of genetic analysis, however, it may be desirable to include these cases, which we may temporarily designate *subschizophrenic*, as affected. In the possible extreme case, the investigator may find that when these cases are counted, the distribution of affected cases might prove to be compatible with that of a simple dominant or recessive mode of transmission, or at least more compatible with one of these transmission patterns than when such cases are not counted. In such an instance, the investigator would probably be inclined to acknowledge the possibility that the subschizophrenic disorders found in the relatives were schizophrenia equivalents.

For this reason, we decided to include in our research not only counts of schizophrenia as generally diagnosed, but also counts of disorders that resembled some of the major features of schizophrenia. To select such disorders, we relied mainly on the classification of psychiatric disorders listed in DSM-II, the second edition of the American Psychiatric Association's *Diagnostic and Statistical Manual of Mental Disorders* (1968).

We accepted the major subtypes of schizophrenia as described in the manual. For entirely fortuitous reasons, we referred to cases of chronic or process schizophrenia as B1 (see Table 1). Because our B1 concept referred to chronic illness, whereas Acute Schizophrenic Episode, as referred to in DSM-II, did not meet the chronicity criterion, we referred to this latter category as B2. The manual also listed a category called Schizophrenia, Latent Type, "for patients having clear symptoms of schizophrenia but no history of a psychotic schizophrenic episode." We elaborated this category somewhat beyond the manual description, and referred to it as Borderline Schizophrenia, or B3. In this way, we reduced the fifteen subcategories of schizophrenia listed in DSM-II to three categories, for purposes of genetic analysis.

Table 1.   Summary of symbols used in the adoption studies on
the schizophrenia spectrum

Symbol	Disorder
	Hard spectrum (B)
B1	Chronic (process) schizophrenia
D1	Doubtful (or uncertain) chronic schizophrenia
B2	Acute schizophrenic episode
D2	Doubtful (or uncertain) acute schizophrenic episode
B3	Borderline schizophrenia
D3	Doubtful (or uncertain) borderline schizophrenia
	Soft spectrum (C)
C	Paranoid state
C	Paranoid personality
C	Schizoid personality
C	Inadequate personality

The manual also included categories like Paranoid States, In-
volutional Paranoid State, Acute Paranoid Reaction, Paranoid Personality, and Alcoholic Paranoia. These could be thought of as possible lesser
manifestations of paranoid schizophrenia. Other categories that suggested
a possible relatedness to schizophrenia included Reactive Psychosis, unspecified; Schizoid Personality; and Inadequate Personality, characterized
by " . . . ineffectual responses to emotional, social, intellectual, and
physical demands . . . inadaptability, ineptness, poor judgment, social
instability, and lack of physical and emotional stamina."

These paranoid, schizoid, and severely inadequate personality disorders were also included for genetic analysis. Because they were less likely
to have a genetic association with schizophrenia, they were excluded from
the B categories, and identified simply as a C group. We did not assume
that these diagnostic groups were all related genetically to schizophrenia,
but we attempted to determine empirically which ones might be related to
classically defined chronic schizophrenia and which ones might not.
Primarily, we did not want to lose possible affected cases by oversight.
Other diagnostic categories might have been added, such as depersonalization neurosis, but some restrictions were necessary, and we agreed to
include only the B and C groups. We tentatively referred to all these
diagnoses combined as the *schizophrenia spectrum*. We also referred to the
B group as the *hard* spectrum, and the C group as the *soft* spectrum. The
term *spectrum* seemed appropriate because the diagnostic categories
included in it seemed to manifest a gradation of severity of symptoms that
shaded off as one moved from B1 to C. For example, uncertainty might
occur in deciding whether a given case should be classified as B1 or as a

lesser category. In such instances, the diagnosis might be Doubtful B1, which indicates that the case is B1 or somewhere between B1 and B3. We also established Doubtful B2, Doubtful B3, and Doubtful C categories to accommodate the shading of diagnostic nuances in the spectrum. Such doubtful cases of B1, B2, and B3 were designated as D1, D2, and D3, respectively.

Benefits of Diagnostic Classification

The concept of a schizophrenia spectrum may help us to obtain a clearer picture regarding the mode of genetic transmission in schizophrenia. The spectrum concept also benefits our system of diagnostic classification. Historically, many psychiatric nosologies have been proposed (Zilboorg and Henry, 1941), but attempts to define the principles underlying such nosologies have never been convincing. In ancient times, Asclepiades maintained the principle that all illnesses were based on patterns of tension and relaxation of body tissues. In more modern times, the trend has been to increase the number of mental disease categories. In the nineteenth century, however, Thomas Beddoes asked "whether it be not necessary either to confine insanity to one species, or to divide it into almost as many as there are cases . . . ." In addition, Heinrich Neumann stated that there was only one kind of mental disorder. Thus, a trend was developing to reduce the number of psychiatric diagnoses, which were getting too cumbersome.

Toward the end of that century, Kraepelin (1896) grouped a number of diagnostic categories into two separate major diseases, dementia praecox and manic-depressive psychosis, thus achieving a goal his predecessors had strived for and, in the process, revolutionizing psychiatric nosology. The virtue of any classification system is not primarily the accurate portrayal of special features or symptoms, but the heuristic value inherent in the classification itself. If the spectrum concept can reduce an appreciable number of diagnostic categories to one or two, and if it can be shown that at least some categories are related, in the sense that they share certain genotypes in common, then it offers a more meaningful nosology. To some extent, such a nosology would simulate the Kraepelinian strategy and at the same time meet the demands for a more heuristic classification.

Practical Application of the Spectrum Concept

In our most recent project, the Interview Study (Kety et al., 1975), the research design was the same as that in our First Study, in which we began with index adoptees who had a diagnosis of B1 (chronic schizophrenia), B2 (acute schizophrenic reaction), or B3 (borderline schizophrenia). Control adoptees were again matched to the index adoptees. The difference between the two studies is that in the original study, the assessment of biological and adoptive relatives was based primarily on records obtained from hospitals. In the Interview Study, the relatives were interviewed personally by a psychiatrist who went to the homes of these relatives to obtain the interview, and who succeeded in interviewing 90% of the available relatives, both biological and adoptive. In the original study, based on hospital records, 21 relatives had a spectrum diagnosis, 13 of whom were biological relatives. In the Interview Study, 67 relatives had a spectrum diagnosis, 41 of whom were biological relatives. Thus, many relatives who had been missed in the original hospital record study proved to be spectrum cases upon personal interview.

For the spectrum concept to be meaningful, it is necessary to show that all spectrum disorders occur more frequently in the biological relatives of index cases than in those of controls. In the First Study (Kety et al., 1971), based on hospital records, we did find a higher prevalence of spectrum disorders in the biological families of index cases as compared to controls, the difference reaching statistical significance beyond the 0.01 level. However, it is important to note the distribution of these disorders according to the three subgroups of index cases, as shown in Table 2. The frequency and distribution of spectrum disorders are highly similar in the relatives of the B1 and B3 probands, and the range of disorders is from B1 to C, thus spanning the complete spectrum. However, the B2 relatives had no spectrum disorders at all. This finding suggests that acute schizophrenic reaction may be genetically different from the B1 and B3 forms of schizophrenia.

The findings of the Interview Study indicate that psychoneurotic and personality disorders are distributed randomly across the biological relatives of both the index and control groups. Such a finding is essential if the spectrum concept is to be meaningful and relatively specific. The frequency of spectrum disorders is about twice as great in the biological relatives of index cases as compared to control relatives. The difference is again statistically significant beyond the 0.01 level. An analysis can also be made in terms of families rather than in terms of affected individuals. Of the 33 index biological families, 17 had at least one member with a diagnosis of B1 or D1, as compared to 5 of 34 control biological families

Table 2. First Study results, based on hospital records, of the type and frequency of spectrum disorders in the biological relatives of schizophrenic index cases

Index cases	Number of biological relatives	Type of spectrum disorder (frequency)
B1 ($N = 16$)	82	B1(1), B3(3), D3(2), C(1)
B2 ($N = 7$)	30	0
B3 ($N = 10$)	38	B3(3), D1(1), D3(1), C(1)

having a member with such a diagnosis. The difference is significant at well beyond the 0.005 level. There were significantly more B1 and B3 diagnoses in the relatives of index cases as compared to control relatives. However, the frequency of C diagnoses did not differ between index and control relatives.

Table 3 shows the type and frequency of spectrum disorders in the biological relatives of index cases, this time based on interviews. Whereas the First Study turned up only one B1, in the Interview Study we found five, all related to B1 probands. Among relatives of B1 probands, we also found eight D1 and six B3 cases. There were also seven C cases, but because the C group did not discriminate the index and control relatives, we were uncertain about the appropriateness of including such cases in the spectrum. A slight increase of hard and soft spectrum diagnoses is also found in the relatives of B3 probands. However, most surprising was our finding that four biological relatives of B2 probands were diagnosed D3, Doubtful Borderline. In the light of such data, we must now reexamine the possibility that acute schizophrenic reaction (B2) may indeed belong in the spectrum (although it did not appear in relatives in the First Study) and that the soft group might not belong to the schizophrenia spectrum, because it fails to differentiate index and control cases.

It may be that acute schizophrenic reactions are not entirely homogeneous, and that at least some will eventually show signs of more chronic forms of the illness. Such a possibility of fluctuating disorders is consistent with observations made as far back as Kraepelin, who noted that some first admission praecox cases did not go on to chronic dementia, but recovered satisfactorily. This problem still exists. Included in our B2 category were cases of acute undifferentiated schizophrenic reaction, schizoaffective psychosis, possible schizophreniform psychosis, acute paranoid reaction, and homosexual panic. Criteria for inclusion as a B2 were similar to those applied to reactive schizophrenia: 1) relatively good premorbid adjustment, 2) relatively rapid onset of illness with clear-cut psychological precipitant, 3) presenting picture including secondary symptoms and comparatively lesser evidence of primary ones, 4) good posthospital course, 5) tendency to relatively brief episode, and 6) good response to drugs or other treatment. Thus, it seems likely that a fair

Table 3.   Interview Study results of the type and frequency of spectrum disorders in the biological relatives of schizophrenic index cases

Index cases	Number of biological relatives	Type of spectrum disorder (frequency)
B1 ($N = 16$)	104	B1(5), B3(6), D1(8), C(7)
B2 ($N = 17$)	31	D3(4), C(1)
B3 ($N = 10$)	38	B3(3), D1(2), C(5)

amount of symptomatic heterogeneity may occur in B2 diagnoses, and that a few types of B2 cases may, in fact, have some genetic relatedness to the more continuous forms of the schizophrenic disorders.

Our collaborating Danish psychiatrists most frequently use the terms *schizophreniform psychosis* or *psychogenic psychosis* in cases that meet the criteria for our B2 diagnosis. These terms clearly indicate that Danish psychiatrists do not believe that such conditions are genetically related to schizophrenia.

Our current problem regarding the B2 diagnoses is largely a methodological one. When the research procedure was based on hospital records, we found no spectrum cases among relatives of B2 probands, but when the procedure was based on personal interviews of subjects, four relatives of B2 probands were diagnosed as Uncertain Borderline, a diagnosis that we had included in the hard spectrum. Had these relatives been hospitalized, we would have identified them in the First Study. Clearly, in studies based on hospital records only, much important information is lost. It is highly desirable that all relatives be examined personally and in fair depth. Of course, a 100% sample of relatives can never be achieved, for such reasons as death, migration, and refusal to submit to psychiatric interviews.

In any case, we cannot at the present time rule out the possibility that at least some types of acute schizophrenic reaction may be genetically related to process schizophrenia. If the four relatives of B2 probands were all related to only one or two B2 probands, we might be able to determine which B2 types are genetically associated with schizophrenia and which ones are not. Unfortunately, we have not yet been able to carry out such an analysis. It will also be worthwhile to compare the D3 diagnoses among the B2 relatives with the D3 cases who were related to B1 and B3 probands to see whether the features in the two groups differ in any appreciable way. If they do, we will have to evaluate this issue anew. However, finding such differences is difficult, because we are dealing with small numbers and diagnoses that shade into one another.

The second most troublesome issue involves the C group, or soft spectrum, which did not discriminate the index and control relatives. On this basis alone, we would ordinarily rule the C group out of the spectrum. There are, however, several findings that suggest that the C group may belong to the spectrum. For example, the diagnoses of the relatives of index and control probands in the Interview Study were made independently by three "blind" judges: Dr. Kety, Dr. Wender, and myself. One of the three judges made soft spectrum diagnoses that *did* discriminate the index and control relatives at the 0.05 level, and it is unlikely that such a finding would occur by chance. This raises the possibility that some clinicians may possess the appropriate skills for making such distinctions that others would miss.

In another one of our studies (Rosenthal, 1975), we compared two groups of matings. In each group, one spouse of the B1 patient had a spectrum diagnosis, which was almost always in the soft spectrum. In the second group, the spouse of the B1 patient did not have a spectrum diagnosis. We found that in the matings in which the spouses of the B1 patients had a spectrum diagnosis, the frequency of spectrum disorders in the offspring was significantly greater ($p = 0.024$) than in the offspring in which the second parent did not have a spectrum diagnosis.

Finally, in a study of the schizophrenic spectrum carried out in England, Stephens et al. (1975) found that among the relatives of schizophrenics, there was an elevated frequency of sociopathic personality, paranoid personality, and schizoid personality combined; this finding reached a statistical significance greater than 0.01.

Thus, there is ample reason to keep the C group in the schizophrenia spectrum at the present time. Our problem is to determine why the soft spectrum does not discriminate index and control relatives consistently. Part of the problem may reflect the distinct possibility that we are not able to diagnose soft spectrum cases as reliably as other spectrum diagnoses. In this respect, we still have much work to do.

CONCLUSION

Classification systems are always complicated, and perhaps never perfect. Charles Darwin, during his Beagle voyage, was struck by the sharp distinctions between species of groundfinches, but he noted that all were connected by gradations and intermediates. In 1931, Swarth, after classifying the groundfinches into 5 genera and 35 species and subspecies, confessed that it would have been as logical to put them all into one single species. In this connection, Huxley (1939) quotes Darwin, stating:

> Certainly no clear line of demarcation has as yet been drawn between species and sub-species . . . or again between sub-species and well-marked varieties, or between lesser varieties and individual differences. These differences blend into each other by an insensible series; and a series impresses the mind with the idea of an actual passage. . . I look at the term *species* as one arbitrarily given, for the sake of convenience, to a set of individuals closely resembling each other, and that it does not essentially differ from the term *variety*, which is given to less distinct and more fluctuating forms.

Darwin might also have been talking about our own classifications regarding the schizophrenia spectrum. What he terms *species* is analogous to our chronic or process schizophrenia. His *varieties* are analogous to the lower categories in the spectrum; they are less distinct and more fluctuating forms that resemble one another and process schizophrenia as well. Whether we should refer to them as varieties of schizophrenia is another matter; I think we should not. For research purposes, however, we can legitimately continue to apply the term *schizophrenia spectrum disorder* to the various categories that prove to be genetically associated. It is this association that makes the concept meaningful.

REFERENCES

American Psychiatric Association. 1968. DSM-II: Diagnostic and Statistical Manual. Second Ed. American Psychiatric Association, Washington, D. C.

Huxley, J. 1939. The Living Thoughts of Darwin. Fawcett, Greenwich, Conn.

Kety, S. S., Rosenthal, D., Wender, P. H., and Schulsinger, F. 1971. Mental illness in the biological and adoptive families of adopted schizophrenics. Am. J. Psychiatry 128:302–306.

Kety, S. S., Rosenthal, D., Wender, P. H., Schulsinger, F., and Jacobsen, B. 1975. Mental illness in the biological and adoptive families of adopted individuals who have become schizophrenic: A preliminary report based on psychiatric interviews. In: R. R. Fieve, D. Rosenthal, and H. Brill (eds.), Genetic Research in Psychiatry. Johns Hopkins Press, Baltimore.

Kraepelin, E. 1976. Psychiatrie. Arno Press, New York, (Originally published in 1896.)

Rosenhan, D. L. 1973. On being sane in insane places. Science 179:250–258.

Rosenthal, D. 1975. Discussion: The concept of subschizophrenic disorders. In: R. R. Fieve, D. Rosenthal, and H. Brill (eds.), Genetic Research in Psychiatry. Johns Hopkins Press, Baltimore.

Rosenthal, D., Wender, P. H., Kety, S. S., Welner, J., and Schulsinger, F. 1971. The adopted-away offspring of schizophrenics. Am. J. Psychiatry 128:307–316.

Stephens, D. A., Atkinson, M. W., Kay, D. W. K., Roth, M. and Garside, R. F. 1975. Psychiatric morbidity in parents and sibs of schizophrenics and non-schizophrenics. Br. J. Psychiatry 127:97—108.

Wender, P. H., Rosenthal, D., Kety, S. S., Schulsinger, F., and Welner, J. 1974. Cross-fostering: A research strategy for clarifying the role of genetic and experiential factors in the etiology of schizophrenia. Arch. Gen. Psychiatry 30:121 128.

Zilboorg, G., and Henry, W. G. 1941. A History of Medical Psychology. W. W. Norton & Co., Inc., New York.

III

INTRACULTURAL ISSUES

Chapter 5

Social Class and Affective Disorder

George W. Brown and Tirril Harris

THE RELATIONSHIP OF SOCIAL CLASS AND MENTAL DISORDER

There are a number of excellent reviews of the relationship of social class and mental disorder. Particularly notable are those done by the Dohrenwends at Columbia University, who conclude that the majority of studies show a greater prevalence of psychiatric disorder in the lower social classes (Dohrenwend, 1975; Dohrenwend and Dohrenwend, 1969, 1974).

The results of the Dohrenwends' thorough review can be contrasted with a much more selective one done by Bagley (1973), which was based largely on studies of disorder treated by psychiatrists. The Bagley study concludes that depression, the most frequent of psychiatric disorders, tends to be more common in higher class groups. There is, in fact, a fairly widespread belief that depression is more common among middle-class women. For example, in a recent review a sociologist states that "middle-aged, middle-class, married, never divorced housewives, those women who assumed the traditional roles of wife and mother, have a higher rate of depression than working women or women who have been divorced" (Bart, 1974, p. 144). Similar statements by psychiatrists (Becker, 1964) and psychologists (Costello, 1976) can be found. However, none are based on population surveys. The conclusion reached by the Dohrenwends concerning all psychiatric disorders is based on population surveys and shows the reverse—that working-class women are more likely to suffer from depression.

Research has been consistent on one point: only a minority of persons suffering from psychiatric disorder receive psychiatric care. [Certain relatively rare conditions, such as schizophrenia, might be exceptions (see Odegaard, 1952).] Moreover, because background factors like social class almost certainly have a powerful influence on who receives such care, the inescapable conclusion is that for common conditions, such as depression, studies of patient series alone are useless if we wish to investigate the role of social class either in terms of etiology or in terms of who receives psychiatric care. With rarer conditions the issue is less clear. Because the prevalence of schizophrenia among adults in the general population probably does not exceed more than 1 in 100, and because those suffering from schizophrenia are often reluctant to be interviewed, a population survey is not a practical way to study the condition. Furthermore, if, as some have argued, the majority of sufferers will turn up at *some* point in psychiatric care in places where psychiatric services are well developed, those contacting psychiatric services may provide a viable basis for epidemiological research. Whatever view is held on this question, there can be no doubt that research concerning social class and schizophrenia differs fundamentally from that which has been concerned with the more common affective disorders. There have been many recent reviews concerning social class and schizophrenia. In North America this diagnosis is widespread, whereas in Europe a diagnosis of affective disorder more often would be made. However, there is little to suggest that there is a significant social class involvement in the etiology of schizophrenia. It is likely that the excess of cases in the lower status groups were of the diagnostically ambiguous variety and would have been classed as affective disorder by a European investigator (Cooper et al., 1972). One of the key pieces of research carried out in London twenty years ago concluded that the correlation between schizophrenia and unskilled and semiskilled occupations is largely the result of patients falling in occupational status after the onset of the disorder or failing to achieve an occupational status congruent with educational achievements (Goldberg and Morrison, 1963). Subsequent research has, we believe, failed to shake this conclusion in any important respect, although there is a persistent and widespread belief that lower class status does increase risk of the condition. In many ways such results are surprising: it is possible that future research will reveal significant social class correlates that have etiological implications, but, given these essentially negative results, we do not think it justified to attempt yet another systematic review of the research on social class and schizophrenia. [An interesting introduction to the issues can be found in the twin papers by Kohn (1972) and Mechanic (1972).] Our concern in this chapter is with the etiological role of social class in the onset of affective disorders and particularly of depression, the most common of such disorders.

RESEARCH INSTRUMENTS

The Dohrenwends' review concluded that affective disorders are more common in lower social class groups, and a more recent review has reached the same conclusion about depression (Bebbington, 1978). Such studies in

North America have largely used questionnaire-type instruments. These instruments give results that agree in broad terms with those of standardized clinical-type interview instruments, such as the Present State Examination (PSE) and the Schedule for Affective Disorders and Schizophrenia–Research Diagnostic Criteria (SADS-RDC) (Spitzer et al., 1975, 1977; Wing et al., 1974). However, such questionnaires probably overestimate the prevalence of disorder, because a number of individuals who report high scores do not suffer from psychiatric disorder (Finlay-Jones and Murphy, 1979). These instruments also are unable to establish the date of onset of a condition, an essential requirement for fully effective etiological research. In addition, they probably cannot be used to *distinguish* conditions, such as depression, anxiety and phobia, and obsessional conditions. However, because depressive phenomena seem to be the most common of psychiatric disorders, at least in urban settings, these questionnaires can provide a rough index of the distribution of depression. Two recent studies in the United States using such questionnaires have shown sizable class differences (Warheit, Holzer, and Schwab, 1973; Comstock and Helsing, 1976). The earlier survey, for example, used an eighteen-item depression questionnaire on a random sample of adults in a city of 75,000 in the southeastern United States. The instrument was not validated but had grown out of research with psychiatric patients. Twenty-one percent of the white women were considered to have a high score (this percentage is double that of white men, the same as black men, and one third less than black women). Using a fivefold measure of social class, there was a sevenfold difference between the top and bottom categories; the higher the social class, the lower the rate of depression (Warheit et al., 1973).

The first population survey in North America using a clinical-type interview (SADS-RDC) has also shown large social class differences in minor depression (Weissman and Myers, 1978). Unfortunately, because it was part of a long-term prospective study with some fall-out over the years, and because the SADS-RDC was only employed on the last wave of interviews, the percentage of the original sample actually interviewed was low (511 of 938, or 54%). However, the biases stemming from this probably have resulted in relatively more *lower* class individuals with psychiatric disturbance dropping out. It seems safe to conclude that there were higher rates of unipolar depression among working-class groups, although not necessarily of the much rarer bipolar depression.

The clinical-type interviews have been more commonly employed in Great Britain, and they also show much higher working-class rates (Richman, 1974, 1976; Rutter and Quinton, 1977; Rutter et al., 1975). Our own survey, using the Present State Examination (PSE) on a random sample of 458 women living in Camberwell in southeast London, showed that affective disorder (depression in particular) was much more common among working-class women: 23% were considered to be cases in the three months before the interview, compared to only 6% of middle-class women.

Stating results in this way immediately raises important questions. What is meant by "caseness" of depression? How is social class measured? Do the results reflect a social class gradient, or is it simply a matter of a higher rate among the low-class group? Although we deal with these questions in this chapter, our main argument is that knowledge has reached a point at which it is no longer sufficient to establish an association between class and psychiatric disorder. In order to progress, it is essential to put effort into the task of establishing a credible etiological model for conditions like depression and anxiety. Only after this is done should researchers try to explain social class differences. In this way, we may be able to break from the stultifying path that so much epidemiological research dealing with social class follows: that of finding correlations between rates of disorder and measures of social class and then speculating on what may be the process involved. Speculation has been necessary because, by and large, data about the individual's environment have not been collected in sufficient detail or with enough knowledge about time order for etiological hypotheses to be developed and tested. Therefore, we urge a strategy that begins with the lives of individuals. Only when an adequate etiological model has been developed at this level should the investigator move into the wider social structure and attempt to understand the impact of social class position.

The usual correlations of class and psychiatric disorder should not be asked to do too much; their job is to tell us that there is a question worth pursuing. If we are not careful, too much concern with *measurement* of social class will impede us; we may be tempted to believe that we can progress by simply improving these measures. Such demographic-type measures are inevitably flawed. At best they can point to the presence of problems to be tackled; in themselves they cannot provide explanations of anything. Because the underlying social processes linked to class are inevitably extremely complex, it is impossible for simple measures based on, for example, education and occupation, to do more than pallidly reflect what is really going on. Indeed, efforts at improvements tend eventually to be self-defeating; a change in measurement that increases the correlation of psychiatric disorder with class for some groups of individuals will, in all likelihood, do the reverse for others, and the net result is little change in the size of the overall correlation. Our main goal is to develop ideas and measures that will enable us to fill in what happens between the independent measure, social class, and the dependent measure, psychiatric disorder. Progress depends on reaching a certain minimal level of sophistication in the measurement of class and psychiatric disorder. In this chapter, we deal with measurement before turning to the more fundamental issue of the etiological model itself, which is needed to explain any link between social class and psychiatric disorders. Different models are almost certainly required for different diagnostic conditions.

THE MEASUREMENT OF PSYCHIATRIC DISORDERS

Our study deals with the measurement of psychiatric disorder in terms of onset, severity, and diagnosis. Depression is our primary concern, although exactly the same points can be made about other conditions. The basic measure we used, the Present State Examination (PSE), is typical of the recently developed semistructured, clinical-type interviews that are capable of being used in general population surveys. It has at its core a glossary of terms and definitions about specific symptoms, with which it is essential to be familiar. The glossary provides standards in terms of frequency or duration for the interviewer to note (for example, when brooding is marked enough to be included as a symptom) and can be used reliably by nonmedical interviewers (Cooper et al., 1977; Wing et al., 1977). The shortened version that has been used in general population surveys covers a possible fifty-five symptoms.

There is common agreement that far more is meant by "clinical depression" than a depressed mood, however severe. When women in the general population are asked in detail about symptoms often found to form part of a depressive syndrome, a heterogenous and varying number of symptoms are revealed. At the lower end of the scale a woman may report crying, sadness, loss of interest, and tiredness; at the other extreme a woman might add feelings of guilt, various forms of sleep disturbance, appetite loss, social withdrawal, irritability, ideas of suicide, various symptoms of anxiety, and so on. In our Camberwell survey just over 33% of the 458 women had at least one such (PSE) symptom, with an average of seven symptoms and a range between one and twenty-six. Eight percent of these women had only one symptom, after which there was a steady reduction in the percentage having two, three, four symptoms, and so forth, with no sharp discontinuity between adjacent proportions. Therefore, if a symptom count is employed, any judgment about who suffers from psychiatric disorder must clearly be an arbitrary one. We have treated the problem in two stages. We first developed a method of judging whether someone was suffering from a definite psychiatric syndrome, classifying him or her as a *borderline case* if the symptoms were not sufficiently frequent or intense enough to be classified as a *case*. There were also women in the general population with psychiatric symptoms, such as fatigue, sleep disorder, or nervous tension, who were not impaired enough to warrant even a borderline case rating. In order to establish a minimal level for caseness, we used a number of anchoring examples of women whose psychiatric symptoms were at a level of severity that would justify psychiatric outpatient care, and who, at least if seen in a London outpatient clinic, would undoubtedly be treated as psychiatrically ill. Similar anchoring examples were used for borderline cases. Almost all conditions we have defined in this way in a series of population studies have been of a depressive, anxiety, or phobic nature.

A further stage was then added. In addition to a rating of severity, a diagnostic judgment was made. If necessary, joint diagnoses were made, either at the case or at the borderline case level—for example, case depression/borderline anxiety or borderline anxiety/borderline obsessional neurosis. However, if etiological research is to be pursued, it is equally essential to take a third step, one that is not usually taken. The onset of any disorder in the year before interview must be carefully dated. (In practice, we find that it is possible to go back even further than one year.) Conditions beginning within the year are termed *onset* and all others are termed *chronic*, because many of them have lasted at least one year. This third stage can be integrated with the other two—for example, onset case depression/chronic borderline case anxiety. The overall scheme has been used in a number of studies, and it has proved possible to develop explicit and reliable criteria for such severity-diagnostic judgments (Finlay-Jones et al., 1980).

THE MEASUREMENT OF SOCIAL CLASS

The concept of social class has played a prominent role in social theory. When viewed in terms of the experience of the individual, most social scientists would probably emphasize the relation of social class to socially valued resources, both in terms of access (such as owning a house) and in terms of motivation (such as wanting advanced schooling for one's children). Social class can determine what people desire as well as what access they have to what they want. Social class also has innumerable correlates with experiences having little or no direct link with access to resources or desire for them—for example, the risk of a burglary or of serious accident to a child is probably much greater for a working-class woman (Brown and Davidson, 1978). In short, class is an extremely complex stratifying factor correlated with a multitude of different experiences. More formal accounts have emphasized social status and prestige, power, economic position, and culture. These elements can in turn be further analyzed, for instance, in terms of share of material rewards, nature of work, security of employment, and respect associated with the various roles. Actual measurement of social class, however, has largely relied on the use of some index, such as type of occupation, or on a self-assignment to a class. Occasionally, workers have utilized a more ethnographic approach, collecting detailed descriptive material about each person and then making an overall judgment of class position, relying particularly on accounts of "style of life." Hollingshead employed this method in New Haven, Connecticut, in the United States to classify families into five social levels. He also showed that such ratings were very highly correlated with more formal criteria, such as educational level and type of occupation. The correlation of occupation classified into socioeconomic groups used by the United States Bureau of the Census with the judged class positions was 0.88 (Hollingshead and Redlich, 1958).

Particularly in the context of health, it is usual to emphasize the link of social class with inequality. Although its measurement is based on attributes of the individual and his family, there is a general agreement in sociology that there is a need to emphasize the importance of structural inequality; in this sense, class position is largely the result of historical processes that are external to, and independent of, the particular person or family. We note this because we wish to emphasize that the use of individual characteristics like occupation does not (and need not) represent any position taken on our part about this distinction between personal and structural "responsibility" for one's class position. Although we believe that the greatest emphasis should be given to structural sources of inequality, we recognize that the role of personal responsibility can be extremely important when tackling issues concerning the etiology of *particular* medical and psychiatric conditions. The research on schizophrenia has been dominated by the possibility that the schizophrenic illness itself has played an important part in determining the patient's class position.

Given the great complexity of experiences of inequality and other correlates of class position, what justification is there for the general use of the crude and arbitrary methods of measurement of class based on indicators like occupation? First, and most obvious, is the decision about which indicator, or combination of indicators, to use. Should occupation be the sole measure of class, or should it be combined with or displaced by income, educational attainment, possession of car and telephone, subscription to certain attitudes, or even by a subjective definition of class by the interviewee himself?

Even if it is agreed that occupation should play a major role in classification, it is still necessary to decide which of the many occupational measures of social class to use. After the particular index has been selected, there are still crucial decisions involved in how to use it with any particular set of data. Should every one of the Registrar General's six status groups (OPCS, 1970) be used, for example, or should more opportunity be given for the data to produce significant correlations if certain groups are combined in, for instance, only a two- or threefold grouping.

If occupation is to be used, whose occupation is to be taken? Should it be that of the respondent, or would the occupation of the head of the respondent's household give a truer picture of his or her place in the social structure? Certainly in a study of women, use of the latter has distinct practical advantages when the difficulty of categorizing the many women who are currently housewives is taken into account. Even if former occupations are taken for these women, there will still be a proportion who have never worked at any time in their lives, and who thus defy classification. This raises yet another question: Should the time at which the defining occupation is held be strictly current? If so, how should unemployed and retired respondents be classified? If occupation *is* allowed to be based on an earlier time period, how far back should it be permitted to extend? The respondent who insists that he is *really* an orchestral conductor, but who has not done anything but clerical work for the past fifteen years, is not just a Thurberesque fantasy where surveys of psychiatric disorder are concerned. The downward occupational drift consequent upon schizophrenic onset raises the probability of finding such respondents in one's sample, making it vital to have a clear decision about the time period over which one can include an occupation as the index of a person's class.

In our own research, we did classify a woman by the current occupation of her husband or her father, if she was living with either of them, and only by her own when she was not. This raises further problems: What if the woman was widowed, separated, or divorced? The decision about how to categorize widows and separated or divorced women can often be an important one in the presentation of results when the dependent variable to which social class is to be related is, like psychiatric disorder, often associated with marital status. Because the rate of depression, for example, is much higher among widows and the separated or divorced, and because women whose husbands have skilled manual jobs often take semi- or unskilled jobs themselves when they take up work again after the loss of their husbands, there may well be a curious phenomenon that differences between the intermediate skilled group, on the one hand, and the lower semi- and unskilled group, on the other, will vary according to the person whose occupational level is chosen to be the indicator of social class. If it is the woman's own occupation, the higher rate of depression among widows and the separated or divorced will mean that the rate in the lowest status group will seem to be higher than if the husband's usual occupation is chosen. We decided to take the husband's usual occupation if the woman's economic circumstances had apparently not changed a great deal since he died or left. If circumstances had clearly changed, we took her current occupation, or, if she was not working, her last occupation no matter how long ago. As a rule, we used the husband's occupation if his death or the separation had occurred within *five years*, unless there was very clear evidence for change in economic circumstances. A similar set of conditions was developed to deal with a father who was retired and perhaps infirm.

The use of a husband's or father's occupation to study women can be criticized on the grounds that it merely repeats the mistakes of current male-dominated prejudice and that only when women are examined as beings in themselves rather than as appendages to men will they be fully understood. Although we are sympathetic to the outlook that underlies these criticisms, we did not feel that our choice of measure had the ideological importance ascribed to it by possible critics. Instead, we saw it as having the practical advantage of providing a means of locating those women who had nearly always been housewives somewhere in the social class structure. Because we had also examined the same distributions for women who had worked, at least briefly, using the woman's own occupation, and had found much the same order of difference between these and the distributions using the husband or father's occupation, we were not blindly choosing to ignore the woman's own occupational achievement. We were merely maximizing the number of women who could be included in the tabulations. There was also a further advantage. The use of the husband's occupation helped to rule out the possibility that any social class association was caused by drift. For example, many chronically depressed women may have taken unskilled part-time jobs outside the home in an effort to deal with their condition, although before they were married they had held more responsible jobs. (Aside from the issue of depression, such change in occupational level is a common occurrence in London.)

Classification Schemes

In terms of the measures of occupation, our subjects were first rated on the Registrar General's sixfold classification, which claims to be based on the general standing in the community of the occupations concerned (OPCS, 1970). A more sophisticated occupational classification has recently been produced by Hope and Goldthorpe to put the Registar General's use of occupation on a firmer basis. One hundred and twenty-four occupations were ranked in terms of criteria like standard of living by people in a random sample of the general population (Goldthorpe and Hope, 1974). A number of the resulting occupational positions make more intuitive sense than those of the Registrar General. For instance, lorry (truck) drivers are no longer placed with other skilled workers. We have based our own use of the scheme on thirty-six occupational groupings provided by the authors. Some representative occupations and their rating are: doctor (1), university lecturer (2), managing director (3), nurse (10), manager of shop (14), car mechanic (15), builder's foreman (17), maintenance engineer (18), self-employed carpenter (19), accounts clerk and assayer for silversmith (21), printer's compositor (22), bricklayer, carpenter, gas fitter, and plumber

(23), hairdresser and chef (25), latheturner and welder (26), train driver and crane driver (27), shop assistant and cinema projectionist (28), self-employed taxi-driver (29), butcher and machine operator (30), scaffolder (32), driver and bus conductor (33), barman (34), laborer (35), self-employed street vendor (36).

In our research, we used two versions of the Hope-Goldthorpe scheme. The first version of the scheme simply divides the women into approximately equal numbers, according to the thirty-six categories ranked in terms of "prestige" (1–19, 20–31, 32–36). In the second version, the categories are brought together in terms of whether the members share in broadly similar market and work situations. Categories were combined by the original investigators if the occupation of their members seemed to be broadly comparable in terms of their levels of income, degree of economic security, and chances of economic advancement, and also in terms of the system of authority and control governing the processes of production in which they were engaged (Goldthorpe et al., 1980). The resulting sevenfold scheme departs markedly from a simple ranking, as can be seen from the following listing:

Rank 1 includes categories 1, 2, 3, 4, and 7.
Rank 2 includes categories 5, 6, 8, 9, 10, 12, 14, and 16.
Rank 3 includes categories 21, 25, 28, and 34.
Rank 4 includes categories 11, 13, 19, 24, 29, and 36.
Rank 5 includes categories 15, 17, and 20.
Rank 6 includes categories 18, 22, 23, 27, and 30.
Rank 7 includes categories 26, 31, 32, 33, and 35.

This sevenfold ranking can be further simplified so that rankings 1–3 are combined in a high group, rankings 4–6 are in an intermediate group, and ranking 7 forms the lowest group.

Education provides a straightforward index, but we also developed a more complex measure of class, taking into account skill of job, education reached, and whether or not the household unit had a car or telephone. We called this the Social Status Index (Brown, Ní Bhrolcháin, and Harris, 1975, p. 241).

Such measures are highly correlated, but at the same time, women are often ranked differently. This can be seen by comparing the details of the 36 Hope-Goldthorpe rankings with those of their sevenfold scheme. The correlation between the rankings of the 458 Camberwell women on two different schemes based on occupation (the 36-fold scheme and that of the RGO) is 0.80 ($r^2 = 0.64$).

In Table 1 we have, for simplicity of presentation, reduced the various measures to threefold classifications; essentially the same conclusions are reached if the full range of categories is used. The table shows that generally the choice of measure makes remarkably little difference to the overall conclusions. [Goldthorpe and Llewellyn suggest a different threefold classification: 1 and 2 equal service or high; 3, 4, and 5 equal intermediate;

Table 1. Prevalence of caseness in Camberwell during year of enquiry by various measures of social class, presented in terms of threefold schemes of high, intermediate, and low status

	High status	Intermediate status	Low status
	— Expressed as percent (cases/sample)		
Household head, H-G[a]	9 (13/143)	H-G 20 to 31[b] 14 (23/163)	26 (40/152)
Household head, H-G, 7 classes amalgamated to 3	8 (14/178)	H-G 4 to 6 16 (22/138)	28 (40/142)
Household head, RGO[c] sixfold scheme	10 (18/173)	Skilled manual 19 (30/162)	23 (28/123)
Household head, Social Status Index	10 (10/104)	Intermediate[d] 11 (15/135)	23 (51/219)
Woman's current or last occupation, RGO	5 (3/59)	Skilled manual 17 (22/130)	19 (48/259)
Woman's highest ever occupation, H-G[e]	9 (7/77)	H-G 20 to 31 15 (40/265)	25 (26/106)
Woman's education	10 (13/136)	15 years 19 (29/169)	23 (34/151)
Husband's education (Including married women only)	9 (5/59)	15 to 16 years 16 (27/171)	22 (34/156)

[a] H-G denotes Hope-Goldthrope category ratings.

[b] Only the intermediate status group is defined in each instance, e.g., here the full three categories are: 1-19 (high), 20-31 (intermediate), and 32-36 (low).

[c] RGO denotes the Registrar General's sixfold classification scheme.

[d] Routine nonmanual; only manual if subject or husband had 16 years or more education or if household possesses a car *and* telephone.

[e] Ten women who had never worked, etc., are omitted from the grouping.

and 6 and 7 equal working class. This gives a similar result: 7% (7/98), 11% (15/141), and 25% (54/219).] The term *interchangeability of indicators* was coined a number of years ago by Lazarsfeld to describe the way in which lowly correlated indicators like those listed in Table 1 can give much the same results in terms of a dependent variable—in our case, psychiatric disorder (Lazarsfeld and Barton, 1951). There is reason to believe that much the same conclusions would be reached for many other factors, such as poverty (see Townsend, 1979; Table 10.23). This issue on the whole has been avoided by arguing for the importance of a particular indicator in *theoretical* terms and then using only this indicator.

However, the argument must not be taken too far. Our results apply only to women. For other questions, such as the study of social mobility, distinctions not apparently important in the study of psychiatric disorder may be more useful. It is possible that some *combinations* of different indicators of class may prove successful. However, experience has shown that consideration of more than one indicator may add extremely little. For example, the combination of five of the indicators of social class shown in Table 1 in a multiple regression analysis failed to improve on the size of the relationship of occupation alone, based on the 36 Hope-Goldthorpe categories. Furthermore, for certain questions it may be essential not to combine indicators into a common index, as, for example, with the Social Status Index. Hollingshead's three-factor index of class based on education, place of residence, and occupation was highly related to a general rating of class based on extensive ethnographic-type data about families (Hollingshead and Redlich, 1958). Nevertheless, its use in the study of schizophrenia created confusion because the patient's illness (and probably his pre-illness personality) almost certainly related differently to the various components of the index. Education and place of residence are probably much less influenced by the illness itself (particularly among first admitted patients) and are therefore a much better basis for a social class index than is occupation. Finally, there are *some* differences in rates of caseness shown in Table 1. The sevenfold scheme of Hope and Goldthorpe is marginally superior to the other schemes as a discriminator. This is probably (at least in part) because of its more realistic allocation of occupations in terms of "life-chances." However, the difference is a modest one at best.

THE DEVELOPMENT OF A SPECIFIC RESEARCH SCHEME

There can be compelling practical reasons for the use of a particular scheme. Throughout our analysis of the Camberwell material, we sought to divide the women in Camberwell into class groups of roughly equal numbers. (This is why we developed the Social Status Index to reflect a simple twofold relationship with prevalence of caseness.) We did this in order to facilitate analysis; using such a simple division made it easier to cross-tabulate results concerning caseness, remembering that only relatively few women in Camberwell were *cases.* When numbers are small in the target group, it is clearly helpful not to distribute them widely over a large number of groups representing a demographic variable, such as social class, because this leaves even fewer in each cell when the demographic variable is further subdivided in other cross-tabulations. [Although statistical methods, such as multiple regression, offer a potential solution to this problem, in practice they tend to have significant shortcomings, and we believe that there is still a great deal to be said in favor of more traditional tabular forms of analysis (Gordon, 1967).]

Table 1 shows that, in order to obtain two roughly equal status groups, the intermediate category needs to be divided more or less into two halves to be allocated up into the high group and down into the low group. With the Hope-Goldthorpe (H-G) measure, this task of reallocation is relatively simple because there are ten separate categories ranked in prestige order in the intermediate section. For the RGO scheme there is only one skilled manual grade, and because this has been used by us to represent the intermediate category, there is no rationale for reallocating one-half of the group in the opposite direction from the other half. If the whole skilled group is shifted from the intermediate category, the distribution between the classes in the new twofold class division will become highly skewed (173 in high and 285 in low).

There can, therefore, be an important pragmatic element in the choice of an indicator of social class. What we need even more than measures of class is better theory to account for the results obtained by the use of the measures we have. Only after developing such theory can we hope to be confident about what we have measured. A crude index is almost certainly enough to tell whether there are important differences to explain. We need then to generate and test theoretical ideas about underlying etiological processes. It is necessary to emphasize that in taking this pragmatic position, we are distinguishing the *measurement* of social class from *theoretical* conceptions of it. If traditional measures of class based on occupation and the like fail to reveal significant differences in the rate of psychiatric disorder (or anything else), it is still possible that class may be important if conceived in an alternative manner, especially in rural populations. *One* possible source of ideas about the role of social class when traditional measures of class have *failed* to reveal significant correlations with rates of psychiatric disorder is the detailed study of the immediate social environment in terms of etiological processes. Since we have already argued that it is necessary to do this when positive correlations between class and disorder have been established, it is to this we now turn.

Findings

Consider the results shown in Table 2 concerning prevalence of caseness for 458 women between the ages of 18 and 65, living in Camberwell, and for 355 comparable women selected at random from two small rural communities, North Uist and Lewis, in the Outer Hebrides off the northwest coast of Scotland. This survey was carried out after the Camberwell study in

Table 2.   Prevalence of caseness (in the year of enquiry) in an urban (Camberwell) and a rural (Outer Hebrides) population[a]

	Middle class H-G 1–22	Working class H-G 23–36	Total
	Expressed as percent (cases/sample)		
Camberwell	8 (18/218)	24 (58/240)	17 (76/458)
Outer Hebrides	15 (18/125)	13 (30/230)	14 (48/355)
Outer Hebrides, excluding full-time crofters	16 (18/110)	16 (27/174)	16 (45/284)
Outer Hebrides, island upbringing	10 (9/89)	13 (28/213)	12 (37/302)
Outer Hebrides, mainland upbringing	25 (9/36)	12 (2/17)	22 (11/53)

[a] H-G denotes Hope-Goldthorpe category ratings.

collaboration with our psychiatric colleague, Ray Prudo. A threefold social class difference in an urban setting totally disappears in the rural population. The result is reminiscent of surveys by Leighton in Nova Scotia and Hagnell in Sweden that failed to find important class differences in psychiatric disorder in rural populations (Leighton et al., 1971).[1] However, certain difficulties in using occupation as a social class index in the Hebrides should be noted. Sixty-four percent of the women lived on a small farm known locally as a *croft*, although few of the families supported themselves by farming alone. Most crofters held (or had held) other jobs as well. Only 20% of the crofts were run on a full-time basis, i.e., the household head did not have another job and the croft was worked on more than a half-time basis. However, a number of these 71 men were either retired or infirm. Therefore, an occupational classification of 24 on the Hope-Goldthorpe scale, "small-holders without employees," would be somewhat misleading. We dealt with these problems by classifying the head of household of a croft in terms of the usual occupation, even if the individual was unemployed or retired; otherwise we employed the same classificatory procedures as in Camberwell. However, even if the 71 full-time crofters are excluded from the table altogether, results remain

---

[1] If there is a social class association in the Hebrides, it is a curious curvilinear one, with high-class groups (H-G 1–17) having a 9% rate of caseness, the intermediate group (H-G 18–30) having a rate of 19%, and the low group (H-G 31–36) having a rate of 10%. We have been unable to make any theoretical sense of this result, and because the rate of caseness in the low-class group does not differ from that of the high-class group, it would seem safer to conclude that social class in the Hebrides does not relate to prevalence of caseness, at least when measured in terms of occupation.

essentially unchanged: 16% of middle-class and 16% of working-class women are cases.

A further complication concerns 51 women not brought up in the Hebrides. Some had married islanders and were currently living lives much like other women, but others had come to the islands because of the "professional-type" occupation of their husband or themselves—that of district nurse, veterinary or dental surgeon, and so forth. They had a higher overall rate of caseness than other women (22% versus 12%), although this does not reach statistical significance. Because the rate of disorder among women brought up off the islands remains high whatever their social class level, their exclusion slightly decreases the rate of caseness among middle-class women. However, the difference that emerges between middle- and working-class women when they are excluded falls far short of statistical significance (Table 2).

An Etiological Model

The etiological model developed for Camberwell women was later found to be broadly applicable for women in the Hebrides. In both populations, approximately 50% of the women who were considered cases had had an onset during the year before interview, and 50% were chronic conditions, their onset also occurring before the year of interview. All but one of the onset cases were depression. This particular woman's disorder had important depressive factors. Chronic conditions included other diagnoses, especially of anxiety, although depression was still much the most common syndrome.

Women in Camberwell have been grouped according to three life stages: 1) younger women aged between 18 and 35, no child at home; 2) older women between 36 and 65, no child at home; and 3) women with a child at home (age of child unimportant). Although most of the women were married, the group also included single, widowed, and divorced or separated women. Particularly notable is the fact that the risk of developing depression in the year before interview was higher only among working-class women with a child living at home. Among chronic cases, prevalence of caseness was greater for working-class women in all three life stages (see Figure 1). Therefore, although social class in Camberwell relates very highly to overall caseness, it has different implications for onset and chronic conditions. Another anomaly concerns borderline conditions. Caseness in Camberwell is far more common among working-class women, but the frequency of borderline caseness shows no social class differences. The causal model of depression developed in Camberwell helps to explain these two anomalies.

A major component of the model is the power of a particular type of life event to provoke onset of depression. All types of event to be included

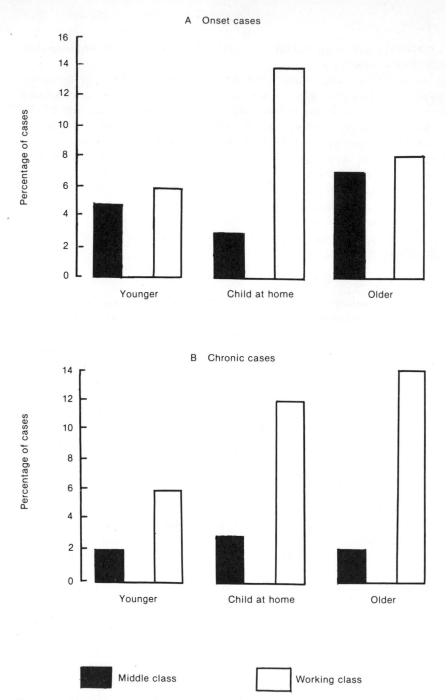

Figure 1.   Proportion of women in Camberwell who were cases in the three months before interview—by social class, life stage, and whether onset or chronic.

in the study were defined in detail before the research began and were all likely to arouse significant positive or negative emotion. For instance, the admission of a husband or child to a hospital was included only if it was urgent or if the stay was for more than seven days.

On the basis of substantial background information about individual women, an event was characterized in terms of two contextual scales: short-term threat, based on its likely threat on the day it occurred or in the next few days, and long-term threat, based on the situation resulting approximately one week later. The raters were allowed to take account of everything known about a particular woman except her psychiatric condition and her personal reaction to the event. Both types of scale rated the degree of threat an average woman would have been judged likely to feel, given her particular biography and current situation. One of the most remarkable results of the entire program is that it was only the most threatening events on the *long-term* scale, what we term *severe events,* that were capable of provoking onset of depression. They formed only 16% of the total events occurring in women in Camberwell (and about the same proportion in the Hebrides). Events severely threatening only in the short-term showed not the slightest association with onset, however threatening they were on the day they occurred. An example of such a short-term threat would be the emergency hospital admission of a child with an extremely high temperature, who was discharged as perfectly fit five days later.

Figure 2 shows the frequency of events in the two populations. (This data for the Hebrides was not collected for the entire population, but only for the 201 women surveyed on Lewis.) Two main points are illustrated. First, although there is a major fall with life stage in both populations in the frequency of all types of life events, positive and negative, there is little or no falloff in severely threatening events, which we have discovered are the only type of event capable of provoking onset. Second, the figure makes clear that the frequency of all types of event, including severe events, is much lower in the rural population (Brown and Prudo, 1981).

Provoking Agents   Severe events were the major component of the first factor in our model—the provoking agents. The results are comparable to those of Paykel and his colleagues in New Haven (Paykel, 1974). Using their concept of *exit event,* the size of the effect is smaller than in the London study. At the same time, their categorization is a less sensitive indicator of long-term threat, that is, the type of event that seems to be critically involved in the etiology of depression. We do not usually include as severe events the exit events of a child marrying an unexceptional partner or a son drafted to peacetime military service. Paykel apparently would.

However, there is a second type of provoking agent. We recorded ongoing difficulties (such as poor housing) that might or might not have

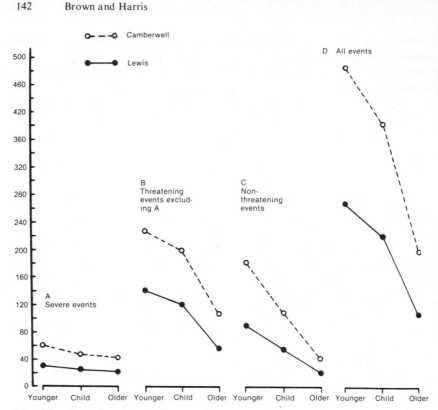

Figure 2.   Rate of events per 100 women in Camberwell and Lewis by severity of threat and life stage.

been associated with an event. We found that certain difficulties were capable of producing depression, but not with the same frequency as severe events. Such difficulties were all markedly unpleasant, had lasted at least two years, and did not involve health problems. However, as with severe events, these difficulties were less common in the Hebrides than in Camberwell.

When such severe events and major difficulties are considered together, our search for provoking agents both in Camberwell and the Outer Hebrides was as successful as we reasonably could have hoped. Almost all instances of onset of caseness of depression in the year were preceded by one or another of the provoking agents. However, just as a well-established carcinogen does not always lead to cancer, so a provoking agent does not always bring about depression. Both in Camberwell and in the Hebrides, only about one in five women with a provoking agent developed clinical depression. Therefore, although provoking agents largely determine whether a woman will develop depression, they do not tell who will break down among those with a severe event or major difficulty. This is the function of the second factor of the model, which deals with ongoing vulnerability.

We first needed to explain why only one in five of the Camberwell women broke down. Lack of an intimate, confiding relationship with a husband or boyfriend seemed to make women more vulnerable to the effects of provoking agents. For the women who had had a provoking agent and who were not already depressed, lack of such a tie greatly increased risk. Furthermore, as predicted, for those without a provoking agent, lack of intimacy was not associated with an increased risk of depression (see Table 3).

Intimacy, unfortunately, is a soft measure, at least in a cross-sectional survey, and we cannot altogether rule out the possibility of bias. We therefore looked for harder indicators of vulnerability. When considered together, three indicators that gave much the same result as intimacy were: having 3 or more children under 14 years of age living at home, lacking employment away from home, and loss of a mother before the age of 11. The four vulnerability factors provide the main reasons why particular women get depressed following a provoking agent. However, it should be noted that employment had an influence only when at least one other vulnerability factor was present (Brown and Harris, 1978).

Effects of Provoking Agents   The model as a whole explains most of the social class differences in Camberwell in risk of developing caseness of depression in the year of our enquiry. The rate of severe events remains much the same in all life stages, but when social class is considered, it is only *severe events* that show a clear difference and then only among women with children. The most straightforward way to present results is to deal with the population of women experiencing at least one severe event. Thirty-four percent of working-class women, both with and without a child at home, and 34% of middle-class women without a child at home had at least one such event, but only 22% of middle-class women with a child have such an event. These results are in several ways remarkable. Not only were class

Table 3.   Percentage of women in Camberwell who experienced onset of depression within year of interview, classed according to intimacy context and experience of severe event or major difficulty

	Intimate relationship with husband or boyfriend	Intimate relationship with someone seen regularly, other than husband or boyfriend	No intimate relationship
	Expressed as percent (cases/sample)		
Severe event or major difficulty	10 (9/88)	26 (12/47)	41 (12/29)
No severe event or major difficulty	1 (2/193)	3 (1/39)	4 (1/23)

differences in experience of events restricted to severe events (the only type capable of provoking depression), but the class difference also was confined to women with a child at home. Such women with a child at home showed a class difference in risk of developing depression (Figure 1A). Also important was the finding that only a subset of severe events shared clear differences: crises involving finance, housing, husband, and child (excluding crises concerning health). A few examples of such *household* events, omitting details of the context that gives them significance, are enough to suggest their class-linked nature: a woman being given a month's notice at a job she had had in a laundry for many years, a husband losing his job, a son getting into trouble with the police, a son being killed while at play, a husband being sent to prison, a husband from whom the woman had been estranged coming home to live after being away for many years at sea, moving to escape from difficult neighbors, leaving a job in order to look after an invalid son, having an arrangement for a new flat (apartment) fall through, receiving notice to quit a flat, being threatened with an eviction by the landlord, having a husband released from prison, being summoned for a court appearance for not paying rent (with the husband out of work), and being forced to have an unwanted abortion because of housing conditions.

Analysis of major difficulties broadly paralleled these results for severe events. Surprisingly, although severe events and major difficulties were more common among working-class women, this explained only a small part of the class difference in risk. If we consider only those women who experienced a severe event or major difficulty in the year before we saw them, thus controlling for class differences in the incidence of the provoking agents, there was still a large difference in risk. For example, 8% (3/36) of middle-class women who had experienced a provoking agent and who had a child developed depression, compared to 31% (21/67) of working-class women—a fourfold difference in vulnerability. For those without a provoking agent, risk was only 1% in both groups, (1/80) and (1/68), respectively.

Vulnerability Factors   Why is it that class differences in frequency of provoking agents do not explain social class differences in risk of depression? The answer is that they are overshadowed by the greater likelihood of working-class women experiencing one or more of the four vulnerability factors. This largely explains the social class differences in Camberwell among women with children at home. Working-class women without children at home did not show a greater risk of developing depression because they were little different from their middle-class counterparts in their experience of either provoking agents or vulnerability factors. Vulnerability factors also help to explain another of the anomalies discussed earlier. There is no social class difference in the prevalence of borderline case conditions. The reason for this seems to be that the more protected middle-class women tend to develop a borderline rather than a case condition after a provoking agent. This result underlines the theoretical importance of distinguishing affective disorders by severity: without this distinction, the class differences would have been attenuated, and we might have missed the significance of vulnerability in influencing severity of disturbance as well as onset.

The other anomaly noted in Figure 1 is that, although risk of *onset* showed a class difference in Camberwell only among women with children, all working-class women had a much greater chance of developing a chronic condition. There is some evidence to suggest that this is caused in part by the major long-term difficulties that serve to perpetuate caseness of depression. Working-class women find it less easy to resolve such difficulties, particularly once they have developed a psychiatric disorder.

Past Social Status

So far we have implicitly assumed that it is the current social environment that is of importance in bringing about or perpetuating psychiatric disorder, although the importance of loss of mother before the age of 11 is an instance that suggests that past experience cannot be ignored. Difficult conceptual and measurement problems arise in cases like early loss of mother. Does this effect arise through early and fundamental changes in a woman's personality, leaving her more at risk of depression, or does it arise in some way via the impact of such losses on her present environment? For example, perhaps educational and household changes stemming from the loss are important influences that tend to lead women to have a greater number of children under less than optimal conditions. Early personality changes may also lead to a greater number of children—this possibility offers a major research challenge. Lee Robins has done important research on problems of the long-term course of sociopathic conditions arising in childhood, and has provided incisive discussions of some of the methodological problems of studying such long-term effects (Robins, 1966; Robins and Wish, 1977).

One possible source of long-term impact is past social status, represented by the father's usual occupational level. Langner and Michael (1963) have emphasized the methodological importance of such measures as a way of dealing with the questions of drift and selection already noted in relation to research on schizophrenia. If the association between psychiatric disorder and social class holds for father's social class, it is difficult to argue that the results are caused by the psychiatric disorder itself leading to occupational decline or to failure to rise.

The Camberwell research obtained the usual occupation of the father of each woman, and, although the information was not always as complete as we had wished, it was sufficient to be rated in terms of the Registrar

General's sixfold categories. Because there was not a great deal of differentiation in terms of caseness *within* the manual occupations of the RGO (Table 1), we have compared the current occupational level of the household head with that of the level of the usual occupation of the father in terms of a twofold manual and nonmanual differentiation. The results are clear-cut and are shown in Table 4. As would be expected from the major increase in the proportion of nonmanual occupations in the general economy over the last twenty-five years, the woman's household head is more likely than her father to have a current nonmanual status. It is an important point that the result for rate of caseness in the year of interview was almost identical in terms of the manual or nonmanual categories, whether the occupation of the current household head or of the father is taken. The result confirms information implied by the educational level of the woman: indicators of social class from the woman's past give results similar to those based on the current situation of her household. However, this tells nothing about the relative influence of the past or present on psychiatric disorder; it merely helps to rule out the possibility of biased results because of some form of selection. The result as such does not directly indicate anything about the past because there is such a high association between current and past status: 72% of the women in Camberwell had the same classification as their father in terms of the nonmanual-/manual distinction. This finding makes particularly interesting the rates of caseness among women where the status is discrepant (the 42 subjects whose fathers were of nonmanual status, but are currently manual, and of the 85 whose fathers were manual, and are currently nonmanual). We will refer to these women as nonmanual-manual and manual-nonmanual, respectively, and to the other two categories as nonmanual and manual. The rate of caseness for these two discrepant groups is the same and is close to the nonmanual group and much lower than the manual group (Table 4).

Table 4.   Comparison of occupation of current household head of woman and that of her father in terms of the Registrar General's classification of nonmanual and manual occupations by prevalence of caseness in Camberwell in year of survey

Current occupation of woman's household head	Father's occupation[a]		
	Nonmanual[b]	Manual[b]	Total[b]
Nonmanual	9 (7/79)	12 (10/85)	10 (17/164)
Manual	12 (5/42)	22 (51/232)	20 (56/274)
Total	10 (12/121)	19 (61/317)	17 (73/438)

[a] Occupation of father for 20 women was not known.

[b] Expressed as percent (cases/sample).

This suggests that the nonmanual-manual women have much the same rate of current experience as other currently nonmanual women. Why should their rate be lower than that of the currently manual women with manual fathers?

A straightforward explanation is provided by the two components of the causal model. Both discrepant groups follow fairly closely the experiences of the current nonmanual women; that is, they have much the same rate of provoking agents and vulnerability factors as the current nonmanual group. The proportion of the women experiencing at least one provoking agent in the nonmanual, nonmanual-manual, manual-nonmanual, and manual groups is 25%, 33%, 33%, and 51%, respectively, and having at least one vulnerability factor (excluding lack of employment, which was not related to class) is 32%, 29%, 39%, and 56% respectively. The result for the 42 women currently in the manual group, but whose fathers were nonmanual, is of particular interest. However, their lower rate of caseness when compared with the rest of the manual group is not statistically significant, and the result therefore does no more than suggest interesting possibilities for future research. Why is it that such women are apparently able to take with them some of the advantages of a nonmanual environment?

It is possible to carry out more sophisticated measures of past status, although to our knowledge these have not been used successfully in the study of defined psychiatric disorders. For example, status inconsistency in terms of father's and mother's background is a widely recognized instance (Jackson, 1962). To take one example, women with rheumatoid arthritis were found to be much more likely to come from families in which the mother's educational level was discrepant with the educational or occupational level of the father, or where the father's occupation was either of higher or lower status than would be expected from his education (Kasl and Cobb, 1969). Kasl and his colleagues (1979), in a recent study of infectious mononucleosis among military cadets, have tentatively interpreted such a measure of father's "overachieving" as reflecting the imparting of stronger values about achievement to the son, with the result that he is more strongly committed to achieve in his chosen career. The measure is related to risk of developing clinical mononucleosis, and this interpretation agrees with the total set of results. It is highly desirable for such complex measures to be given a particular theoretical interpretation and to be integrated, if possible, into a much broader analysis concerning etiology of the condition—what we have termed a *causal model.*

Theory

We have also attempted a theoretical interpretation of the etiological model, but this is much less secure than the model itself. We have speculated that low self-esteem is the common feature behind all vulnerability factors and it is this that makes sense of our results. It is not loss itself that is important but the capacity of a woman to hope for better things once an important loss has occurred. In response to a provoking agent, relatively specific feelings of hopelessness are likely to occur: the person has usually lost an important source of value, something that may have been derived from a person, a role, or an idea. If this hopelessness develops into a general feeling of hopelessness, it may form the central feature of the depressive disorder itself.

We have come to see clinical depression as an affliction of a person's sense of values that leads, in Aaron Beck's terms, to a condition in which there is no meaning in the world, where the future is hopeless and the self worthless (Beck, 1967). It is after such generalization of hopelessness that the well-known affective and somatic symptoms of depression develop. Essential in any such generalization of hopelessness is a woman's ongoing self-esteem, her sense of her ability to control her world, and her confidence that alternative sources of value will, at some time, be available. If the woman's self-esteem is low before the onset of depression, she will be less likely to be able to see herself as emerging from her privation. Once depression has occurred, feelings of confidence and self-worth can sink even lower.

Such an interpretation can easily be related to class position. It reminds us that an appraisal of general hopelessness may be entirely realistic: the future for many women *is* bleak. Here our ideas probably depart most decisively from current opinion. We do not emphasize an inherent "personality weakness." Although we do not rule out influence from the past (indeed, we have demonstrated that it has some importance), it is the link with the present that needs emphasis. Nor is it adversity or unhappiness or even loss that is central. They, doubtless, will always be present. Clinical depression is much less inevitable. What happens depends on the resources that allow a person to seek alternative sources of value and that allow her to hope that they can be found.

This interpretation is clearly relevant to factors of the model involving the current situation, but it also seems possible that loss in childhood and adolescence can work through similar cognitive factors. For instance, the effect of loss of mother before age 11 may be linked to the development of a sense of mastery. The earlier a mother is lost, the more impeded is the growth of mastery, and this may permanently lower a woman's feelings of control and self-esteem.

SOCIAL CLASS IN A RURAL POPULATION

We are confident of the validity of our model, recognizing that it is compatible with a number of theoretical interpretations. We must then consider how the model helps to explain the *lack* of social class differences in the Outer Hebrides. Although provoking agents are less frequent in the rural population, they play much the same etiological role in the onset of depression as in urban Camberwell. There is also evidence that in the Hebrides vulnerability factors play a comparable role in increasing risk of caseness of depression in the presence of a provoking agent.

There is also some similarity with Camberwell in the factors of importance. In the Hebrides, lack of employment of the woman outside the home did not increase risk, nor did loss of mother before age 11.[2] However, lack of an intimate tie, and having 3 or more children under age 14 at home, increased risk in much the same way as in Camberwell. Furthermore, lack of regular churchgoing in this still highly religious population also increased risk of depression in the presence of a provoking agent. A threefold vulnerability index, omitting lack of employment in Camberwell and early loss of mother in the Hebrides, and adding irregular churchgoing in the Hebrides, gives strikingly similar results in the two populations.

Table 5 provides the basic data, which show that, when class is defined in terms of the Hope-Goldthorpe scheme, provoking agents occur more frequently to working-class women in *both* Camberwell and the Hebrides. Although the difference does not reach statistical significance on Lewis, it clearly is a result that is incongruous with the lack of social class differences in depression in the Hebrides. The answer seems to be provided by the second component of the etiological model: although in Camberwell all three vulnerability factors are more common among working-class women, they are, if anything, *less* common among working-class women on Lewis. (The result is unchanged if full-time crofters are excluded altogether from the analysis.)

One final result completes this account of class in a rural population. There are other simple indices of social differentiation in the Hebrides that produce the same order of differences in prevalence of caseness as social class in Camberwell. We call them indices of integration as they relate to the traditional way of life of the islands. We describe here one dealing with type of dwelling. Sixty-four percent of the women live on a croft, and these women have been classified in terms of the degree of involvement of the head of household in the croft. *Subsidiary* crofting is defined by minimal involvement of a few hours a week, *full-time* by a major commitment, and *part-time* by at least 10 hours a week. Women not living on a croft are divided into those in *private* housing and those in *council* (i.e., public) housing. Households closest to the traditional living arrangements had the lowest rate of caseness: 7% (9/137) full- or part-time crofting, 16% (28/173) in subsidiary crofting or private housing, and 24% (11/45) in council

<hr>

[2]The numbers with such a loss were small. However, if chronic cases, which must always be excluded in any consideration of *risk* of onset, are taken into account, there is a relationship on Lewis between such loss and caseness: 31% (5/16) for those with a loss and 14% (25/185) for the remaining women ($p=0.06$).

Table 5.   Proportion of women by social class with at least one provoking agent and one of three types of vulnerability factor in Camberwell and on Lewis[a]

	Camberwell		Lewis	
	Middle class, H-G 1–22 (N = 218)	Working class, H-G 23–35 (N = 240)	Middle class, H-G 1–22 (N = 65)	Working class, H-G 23–35 (N = 136)
Caseness	8 (18)	24 (58)	15 (10)	14 (19)
Provoking agent	33 (71)	48 (116)	25 (16)	35 (47)
Nonintimacy	26 (57)	46 (111)	40 (26)	34 (46)
Three children under age 14	7 (15)	13 (32)	22 (14)	13 (17)
Early loss of mother (before age 11)	6 (14)	11 (26)		
Irregular churchgoing			37 (240)	38 (52)

[a] H-G denotes Hope-Goldthorpe category ratings.

housing ($p < 0.001$). Furthermore, type of dwelling was related to both frequency of provoking agent and the vulnerability index. The difference in frequency of provoking agents was far more marked than that obtained by the social class measure—20%, 34%, and 44%, respectively ($p < 0.001$). Most important of all, differences in the experience of the vulnerability factors emerged. For example, 49% (67/137) of those women associated with full- and part-time crofting did not experience one of the three factors compared with only 27% (68/218) of the remaining women ($p < 0.001$).

Women without an island upbringing had a higher rate of psychiatric disorder, although the difference does not reach statistical significance. The women do not show obvious differences in the frequency of provoking agents and vulnerability factors, although they did have significantly more with three or more children under age 14 living at home. Their higher rate of psychiatric disorder may be related to their greater isolation from supporting kin ties, i.e., their lack of integration. However, larger numbers are necessary to settle the matter. Meanwhile it should be noted that the main findings in the Hebrides are influenced very little if women without an island upbringing are excluded.

Why is it that in the Hebrides, integration relates so much more successfully to the two components of our causal model than social class based on occupation and produces differences just as great as those in Camberwell found between working-class and middle-class women? There is a tradition in sociological theory that rural smallholders should be classified separately from other small proprietors and not amalgamated with gradings of occupations based on an urban experience—in other words, the peasantry itself forms a separate class. Although we do not wish to equate the modern Scottish crofters with peasantry, the use of the measure of crofting involvement, far from representing a move away from a social class analysis, might be considered by some as a further refinement of it.

We have linked integration with two other factors besides crofting involvement: churchgoing and a childhood upbringing on one of the Hebridean islands. Both factors are related to caseness, and serve to support the interpretation we have given to crofting involvement: the more integrated persons (those closest to the traditional way of life of the islands) have a lower rate of caseness (Brown et al., 1977). There is, however, the possibility of social class implications of crofting.

It might appear that the degree of crofting involvement could obscure the effects of social class as measured by occupation, because almost 50% of the lower occupational groups (106/230) belong to a full- or part-time crofting household, compared with only 25% (32/125) of the higher occupational groups ($p < 0.01$). However, Table 6 shows that the rate of

Table 6.   Percentage of women with a psychiatric disorder in the Outer Hebrides by occupation of household head and type of dwelling[a]

	High ranking (H-G 1–22)	Low ranking (H-G 23–36)	Total
	Expressed as percent (cases/sample)		
Full-time crofting	(0/15)	(3/56)	(3/71)
Part-time crofting	(0/16) 0	(6/50) 8	(6/66) 7
	N.S.		
Subsidiary crofting	(6/34)	(11/56)	(17/90)
Private housing	(6/41) 16	(5/42) 16	(11/83) 16
Council housing	(6/19) 32	(5/26) 19	(11/45)24
	N.S.		
Total	(18/125) 14	(30/230) 13	(48/355)14

[a] H-G denotes Hope-Goldthorpe category ratings. N.S. = not significant.

caseness is still not significantly different for the two occupational groups *within* each type of dwelling, indicating that the latter is unlikely to explain why traditional measures of occupation fail to relate to prevalence of psychiatric disorder in the Hebrides.

Nonetheless, the differences in rates of psychiatric disorder within the Hebrides revealed by the integration measure are just as marked as those revealed by the use of a traditional social class measure in Camberwell. Furthermore, women in public housing in the Hebrides have a particularly high rate of psychiatric disorder. In this sense, social class, in terms of deprivation, is certainly involved in the Hebrides. Elucidation of its exact role will require more detailed analyses, for instance how "failures" of the traditional crofting system gravitate to council housing. For example, a single woman in her fifties, no longer able to run the family croft after the death of her parents and siblings, could be forced to give up the croft and take up council housing. Another topic for analysis is the apparently higher risk of disorder in women not born on the island, and the possibility that this may be greatest in the higher occupational groups (Prudo et al., 1981). Until this kind of detailed analysis has been done, we can only claim that social class as usually measured fails to reveal the marked internal differences within this particular rural population in the prevalence of psychiatric disorder.

CONCLUSION

The surveys in Camberwell and the Outer Hebrides have shown just how well crude, demographic-type measures of social differentiation can perform their main scientific task—indicating whether or not there is something important to explain about the distribution of psychiatric disorder within a given population. Traditional social class measures perform this role in Camberwell, an urban population, but fail to do so in the Hebrides, a rural population where it is more illuminating to employ measures of social integration.

However, it is necessary to emphasize that in claiming that social class is not of importance in explaining rates of psychiatric disorder in the Outer Hebrides, we mean that traditional occupational measures of such class do not play this directive role. We do not claim that social class viewed in more fundamental terms is unimportant. Indeed, the high rate of psychiatric disorder among women living in council housing in the Hebrides suggests that there is an important social class component in the etiology and course of psychiatric disorders there as well. Such council house women tend not only to be the least integrated into the traditional culture, but also to be the most likely of all the women on the island to have undergone the kind of crises and difficulties experienced by working-class women in Camberwell (Brown and Prudo, 1981).

Whether the introduction of type of dwelling and crofting measure is considered a part of, or a contrast to, full social class analysis, we believe that, in order to understand the implications of such findings, and indeed the correlates of demographic-type measures in general with rates of psychiatric disorder, the investigator must develop an effective causal model that will help interpret such epidemiological findings. Beyond this, theory must be developed and tested in the context of the model. Only with the development of a causal model can we hope to have the beginnings of an adequate understanding of what is going on. When a model was established in Camberwell, the basic social class results turned out to be a great deal more complex than might at first have seemed likely. The unraveling of such complexity required us to go beyond straightforward epidemiological correlates. Data of a caliber capable of developing the necessary etiological models has not, until recently, been collected in population surveys. To our knowledge, only one other survey, that by Hagnell in Sweden, has paid any attention to the essential requirement of etiological research in dating onset of the disorder. [This was done in a longitudinal study that did not collect data about social factors of possible etiological significance (Hagnell, 1966).] It is probably because such data cannot be satisfactorily collected by questionnaire-type instruments that this extraordinary situation has arisen. In Camberwell, differences in *risk* of developing caseness of psychiatric disorder only occurred among working-class women with children living at home, although there was a much greater chance of a *chronic* disorder occurring among working-class than among middle-class women, whether or not they had children at home. By contrast, borderline conditions showed no difference, and so on. Similar complex patterns emerged in the Hebrides, but with social integration and not social class as an index of social differentiation. (It is of interest that the Camberwell result concerning social class, onset and chronic caseness, and whether or not a woman had a child at home were almost exactly repeated in the Hebrides when the integration factor and not social class was employed.)

Clearly, we cannot claim entirely to have resolved the various anomalies surrounding the question of psychiatric disorder and social class in the two populations, but we do believe that the causal model provides the basis for satisfactory understanding. In time it is reasonable to hope that such insights will be translated into effective theory; however, this will be unlikely to occur without far more attention to questions of measurement than is generally given. Present demographic-type measures of social class and similar social differences, although crude, are probably adequate; they are good enough to reveal differences in prevalence of psychiatric disorder if these exist. There is a need for more subtle measures of provoking agents and vulnerability factors that can contribute to the establishment of the components of causal models; and for measures of psychiatric disorder that take account of severity, date of onset and course, and diagnosis. (Anxiety states, for instance, need a slightly different etiological model to explain them, and may well be related to social class in a manner different from depression.) The final challenge is perhaps the most difficult of all: to return to the original epidemiological findings in the context of the etiological model and theory and see them in a new light. We must take into account much wider considerations of social structure and must ground our findings in the light of historical development and current social change. Camberwell is part of an inner city area with many social problems, including decline in economic base, and physical fabric. Major social change is often brought about by immigration of new social groups. Our results do not necessarily apply to all urban working-class populations, and, under certain circumstances, middle-class groups might also have high rates of disorder. Questions of the representativeness of findings such as our own can be settled only by a series of comparative enquiries, which, in turn, will almost certainly lead to the development of the etiological model itself and its associated theory. Such developments are likely to return us to the need to consider the social system as a whole. It is hoped that in time they will lead to effective programs of intervention, and even of prevention.

ACKNOWLEDGMENTS

Our colleague, Ray Prudo, now at McMaster University Medical Centre, Hamilton, Ontario, played a major role in the survey on Lewis in the Outer Hebrides. We would like to acknowledge our considerable debt to him and also to thank James Greenley for helpful comments on the chapter.

REFERENCES

Bagley, C. 1973. Occupational class and symptoms of depression. Soc. Sci. Med. 7:327–339.

Bart, P.E. 1974. The sociology of depression. In: P. M. Roman and H. M. Trice (eds.), Explorations in Psychiatric Sociology. F.A.Davis Co., Philadelphia.

Bebbington, P.E. 1978. The epidemiology of depressive disorder. Cult. Med. Psychiatry 2:297–341.

Beck, A.T. 1967. Depression: Clinical, Experimental, and Theoretical Aspects. Staples Press, London.

Becker, E. 1964. The Revolution in Psychiatry. Free Press, New York.

Brown, G.W., and Davidson, S. 1978. Social class, psychiatric disorders of mothers, and accidents to children. Lancet I: 378–381.

Brown, G.W., and Harris, T.O. 1978. Social Origins of Depression: A Study of Psychiatric Disorder in Women. Tavistock Publications, London, and Free Press, New York.

Brown, G.W., and Prudo, R. 1981. Psychiatric disorder in a rural and an urban population. I. Aetiology of depression. Psychol. Med. 11:581–599.

Brown, G.W., and Ní Bhrolcháin, M., and Harris, T.O. 1975. Social class and psychiatric disturbance among women in an urban population. Sociology 9:225–54.

Brown, G.W., Davidson, S. Harris, T., Maclean, U., Pollock, S., and Prudo, R. 1977. Psychiatric disorder in London and North Uist. Soc. Sci. Med. 2:367–377.

Comstock, G.W., and Helsing, K.J. 1976. Symptoms of depression in two communities. Psychol. Med. 6:551–63.

Cooper, J.E., Copeland, J.R.M., Brown, G.W., Harris, T. and Gourley, A.J. 1977. Further studies on interviewer training and inter-rater reliability of the Present State Examination (PSE). Psychol. Med. 7:517–23.

Cooper, J.E., Kendall, R.E., Gurland, B.J., Sharpe, L., Copeland, J.R.M., and Simon, R. 1972. Psychiatric Diagnosis in New York and London. Institute of Psychiatry, Maudsley Monograph no. 20. Oxford University Press, London.

Costello, C.G. 1976. Anxiety and Depression: The Adaptive Emotions. McGill-Queen's University Press, Montreal.

Dohrenwend, B.P. 1975. Sociocultural and social-psychological factors in the genesis of mental disorders. J. Health Soc. Behav. 16:365–92.

Dohrenwend, B.P., and Dohrenwend, B.S. 1969. Social Status and Psychological Disorder: A Causal Inquiry. John Wiley & Sons, Inc., New York.

Dohrenwend, B.P., and Dohrenwend, B.S. 1974. Psychiatric disorders in urban settings. In: G. Caplan (ed.), American Handbook of Psychiatry. Vol. 2. Child and Adolescent Psychiatry, Sociocultural and Community Psychiatry. Basic Books, Inc., New York.

Finlay-Jones, R.A., and Murphy, E. 1979. Severity of psychiatric disorder and the 30-item general health questionnaire. Br. J. Psychiatry 134:609–16.

Finlay-Jones, R.A., Brown, G.W. Duncan-Jones,P., Harris, T., Murphy, E., and Prudo,R. 1980. Depression and anxiety in the community: Replicating the diagnosis of a case. Psychol. Med. 10:445–454.

Goldberg, E.M., and Morrison, S.L. 1963. Schizophrenia and social class. Br. J. Psychiatry 109:785–802.

Goldthorpe, J.H., and Hope, K. 1974. The Social Grading of Occupations: A New Approach and Scale. Oxford University Press, London.

Goldthorpe, J.H., Llewellyn, C., and Payne, C. 1980. Social Mobility and Class Structure in Modern Britain. Clarendon Press, Oxford.

Gordon, R.A. 1967. Issues in multiple regression. Am. J. Sociol. 73:592–616.

Hagnell, O. 1966. A Prospective Study of the Incidence of Mental Illness. Norstedts-Bonniers, Svenska Bokforlaget.

Hollingshead, A.G., and Redlich, F.C. 1958. Social Class and Mental Illness. John Wiley & Sons, Inc., New York.

Jackson, E.F. 1962. Status Consistency and Symptoms of Stress. Am. Sociol. Rev. 27:469–479.

Kasl, S.V., and Cobb, S. 1969. The intrafamilial transmission of rheumatoid arthritis— 6. Associaion of rheumatoid arthritis with several forms of status inconsistency. J. Chronic Dis. 22:259–78.

Kasl, S.V., Evans, A.S., and Niederman, J.C. 1979. Psychosocial risk factors in the development of infectious mononucleosis. Psychosom. Med. 41:445–466.

Kohn, M.L. 1972. Class, family, and schizophrenia: A reformulation. Soc. Forces 50:295–304 and 310–313.

Langner, T.S., and Michael, S.T. 1963. Life Stress and Mental Health. Collier-MacMillan, London.

Lazarsfeld, P.F., and Barton, A.H. 1951. Qualitative measurement in the social sciences: Classification, typologies, and indices. In: D. Lerner and H.D. Lasswell (eds.), The Policy Sciences. Stanford University Press, California.

Leighton, D.C., Hagnell, O., Leighton, A.H., Harding, J.S., Kellert, S.R., and Danley, R.A. 1971. Psychiatric disorders in a Swedish and a Canadian community : An exploratory study. Soc. Sci. Med. 5:189–209.

Mechanic, D. 1972. Social class and schizophrenia : Some requirements for a plausible theory of social influence. Soc. Forces 50:305–309.

Odegaard, O. 1952. The incidence of mental disease as measured by census investigations versus admission statistics. Psychiatr. Q. 26:212–218.

Office Of Population Censuses and Surveys (OPCS). 1970. Classification of Occupations. Her Majesty's Stationery Office, London.

Paykel, E.S. 1974. Recent life events and clinical depression. In: E.K.E. Gunderson and R.D. Rahe (eds.), Life Stress and Illness. Charles C Thomas, Publisher, Springfield, Ill.

Prudo, R., Brown, G.W., Harris, T., and Dowland, J. 1981. Psychiatric disorder in a rural and an urban population. 2. Sensitivity to loss. Psychol. Med. 11:601–616.

Richman, N. 1974. The effects of housing on pre-school children and their mothers. Dev. Med. Child Neurol. 16:53–58.

Richman, N. 1976. Depression of mothers of pre-school children. J. Child Psychol. Psychiatry 17:75–78.

Robins, L.N. 1966. Deviant Children Grown Up. Williams & Wilkins Company, Baltimore.

Robins, L.N., and Wish, E. 1977. Childhood deviance as a developmental process : A study of 223 urban black men from birth to 18. Soc. Forces 56:448–473.

Rutter, M., and Quinton, D. 1977. Psychiatric disorder — Ecological factors and concepts of causation. In: H. McGurk (ed.), Ecological Factors in Human Development. North Holland, Amsterdam.

Rutter, M., Yule, B., Quinton, D., Rowlands, O., Yule, W., and Berger, M. 1975. Attainment and adjustment in two geographical areas: III. Some factors accounting for area differences. Br. J. Psychiatry 126:520–33.

Spitzer, R.L., Endicott, J., and Robins, E. 1975. Clinical criteria for psychiatric diagnosis and the DSM-III. Am. J. Psychiatry 132:1187–1192.

Spitzer, R.L., Endicott, J., and Robins, E. 1977. Research diagnostic criteria: Rationale and reliability. Paper presented at the Annual Meeting of the American Psychiatric Association, May, Toronto, Canada.

Townsend, P. 1979. Poverty in the United Kingdom: A Survey of Household Resources and Standards of Living. Penguin Books and Allen Love, Harmondsworth, Middlesex, England.

Warheit, G., Holzer, C., III, and Schwab, J. 1973. An analysis of social class and racial differences in depressive symptom-aetiology: A community study. J. Health Soc. Behav. 4:921–99.

Weissman, M.M., and Myers, J.K. 1978. Affective disorders in a United States urban community : The use of research diagnostic criteria in an epidemiological survey. Arch. Gen. Psychiatry 35:1304–1311.

Wing, J.K., Cooper, J.E., and Satorius, N. 1974. The Measurement and Classification of Psychiatric Symptoms: An Instruction Manual for the Present State Examination and CATEGO Programme. Cambridge University Press, London.

Wing, J.K., Nixon, J.M., Mann, S.A., and Leff, J.P. 1977. Reliability of the PSE (ninth edition) used in a population study. Psychol. Med. 7:505–16.

Chapter 6

Family Studies in Psychopathology

Victor D. Sanua

This chapter reviews research studies that have tried to relate familial deviance and psychopathology in the offspring. These studies are reviewed critically from the sociocultural perspective. Very few authors of family studies have included references to sociocultural variables. Sanua (1961) reviewed the literature on the sociocultural factors in families of schizophrenics and found little agreement about which type of family is conducive to schizophrenia in the offspring.

Sociocultural forces may be the forces that shape the individual through the family. Bott (1971) pointed out that although there is an enormous amount of literature on the family in Western society, little is known about the relationship between the family and society. There are few attempts to combine anthropological studies of the family with the psychological examination of the personalities of husband and wife and the relationship between them. After studying a sample of families in London, Bott concluded that performance of familial roles depends on the personal needs and preferences of the members of the family in relation to the tasks they must perform, the immediate social environment in which they live, and the norms to which they adhere (p. 23). In a provocative book, Keniston (1977) insists that to blame the family for all the ills of today's children is a myth, because the family cannot be separated from the society at large. Keniston feels that the entire social ecology defines and limits what parents can do.

This review of the family in psychopathology is divided into four major parts, each one dealing with related research efforts. The first part deals with clinical studies of family communication and interaction that are therapeutically oriented. These studies were initiated by the work of Bateson and his group at Stanford on the double-bind hypothesis, the work of Lidz and his group at Yale, and the investigations of the Wynne group.

(The Wynne studies were originally started in the Adult Psychiatry Branch at the National Institute for Mental Health and continue today in the Department of Psychiatry at Rochester University Medical School, where Dr. Wynne moved a few years ago.) The second part deals with studies that were more sophisticated in approach, used objective measures, and tended to be experimental in nature. In this approach, the sex of the patient, the patient's poor or good premorbid condition prior to the illness, and the patient's nonschizophrenic siblings were considered. [A classic example of this type of research is illustrated by the work of Mishler and Waxler (1968) from the Department of Psychiatry, Harvard Medical School.] The third type of research (Waring and Ricks, 1965) located schizophrenics and nonschizophrenics who had been seen in child guidance clinics. Their case records were thoroughly examined for early parental interaction. Such retrospective studies are more objective because the workers on the cases did not know which patients would become schizophrenic in later years. Because only limited results were obtained with these approaches, a fourth model using high risk studies was initiated by Mednick early in the 1960s. Garmezy (1974, 1978) has provided extensive reports on the development of this approach and has pointed out that such studies could be classified under three categories, depending upon which factors are emphasized by the researcher (the genetic, psychological, or sociological model). Fisher and Jones (1978) reviewed about seventy such studies and provided suggestions for planning a new series of high risk studies. The advocates of each of these approaches tend to reflect their biases by the weight they assign to specific causes of disorder.

STUDIES IN FAMILY COMMUNICATION
AND INTERACTION AS ETIOLOGICAL FACTORS

Pre-World War II studies on the family concentrated on parental pathology, which was thought to determine pathology in the offspring. Most notably, Frieda Fromm-Reichman (1948) introduced the concept of the "schizophrenogenic mother," and Kanner (1943) introduced the concept of the "refrigerated mother." These notions have been highly criticized, because they attribute the onus of the illness primarily to the mother. The father's attributes that contributed to illness were much less well defined. Reviews of this work have been done by Sanua (1961, 1967) and by Spiegel and Bell (1959); Sanua's reviews particularly emphasize the sociocultural variables in pathology. Among the later major reviews are Fontana (1966), Frank (1965), and Heilbrun (1973).

During the latter part of the 1950s and early part of the 1960s, a shift occurred in the etiology of mental illness from the focus on the parents to focus on the whole family. This shift developed jointly with the trend toward family therapy and the development of social systems theory. Instead of concentrating on the mother, investigators turned their attention toward the entire family and interested themselves in communication between the sick person and the other members of the family. Different approaches were tested in these studies.

The Double-Bind Theory

Family-centered investigation has produced a voluminous literature, and its major organ is the journal *Family Process*. The development of family-based explanations possibly stems from the double-bind theory, formulated by Bateson. Within the perspective of this theory, the child is subjected to incongruous messages and is then expected to select one of two equally undesirable choices under the threat of punishment. Ultimately the child loses the ability to discriminate the true meanings of messages, and as a result manifests schizophrenic behavior.

Bateson et al. (1956) provided the following classic example to illustrate the concept of double-bind:

> A young man who had fairly well recovered from an acute schizophrenic episode was visited in the hospital by his mother. He was glad to see her and impulsively put his arm around her shoulders, whereupon she stiffened. He withdrew his arm, and she asked, "Don't you love me anymore?" He then blushed, and she said, "Dear, you must not be so easily embarassed and afraid of your feelings." [p. 477]

Thus, the mother was giving the son two conflicting messages.

Besides the double-bind, other concepts that have been introduced include three-party interaction (Weakland, 1960), overadequate-inadequate reciprocal functioning, emotional divorce (Bowen, 1960), and complementary functioning (Jackson, 1960), all of which have been used to describe intrafamily relationships. More recent concepts include fragmentation, amorphous relations (Wynne and Singer, 1963b), pseudo-mutuality (Wynne et al., 1958), skewed family, and marital schism (Lidz et al., 1957). Most of these studies concentrate primarily on families with a schizophrenic member and do not seem to be concerned with other mental deviancies.

Bateson (1959), as an anthropologist, seems to be aware of sociocultural differences when, in a later article, he writes:

> Work of this kind is a necessary preliminary to a study of the family homeostasis in different cultural settings. Only after this can we meaningfully ask about the specific roles of father, mother, spouse, grandparents, and so forth, in the pathogenic families in the particular culture. [p. 143]

However, there is no evidence in the literature that his suggestion was seriously followed.

Using the same principle, Haley (1963) directed his attention toward the whole family rather than toward a dyad. According to him, in psychogenic families no member of the family is willing to define clearly the nature of his responsibility toward the other members of the family. Searles (1959) also dealt with the etiology of schizophrenia. He described six modes of "driving the other person crazy," all variations on giving a pair of conflicting messages. However, Searles focused on the mutual satisfaction needs provided by the binding, rather than on the formal structure of the exchanges.

Hoekstra (1971) argued that the double-bind interaction applies to neurotic as well as to psychopathic disorders, raising the question of why the double-bind leads to schizophrenia in certain instances, while in others it leads to other deviancies.

Schuham (1967), in looking at the research evidence, concluded that no study has shown that the double-bind has an etiological connection with schizophrenia. "The very existence of a double-bind phenomena," he states, "is open to serious question, and it is axiomatic that assertions concerning its differential association with schizophrenia and normal communication processes and its etiological connection with the schizophrenic thought disorders are extremely tenuous" (p. 409). Stark and Von der Haar (1977) were also critical of the double-bind hypothesis. They wrote that, although the theory is a fruitful starting point, it fails to explain the mother's contradictory behavior. Furthermore, they questioned whether this schizophrenic-producing communication style is valid for all social classes.

The double-bind hypothesis has suggested some research that does not tend to support it (Ciotola, 1961; Loeff, 1966; and Potash, 1965). However, the double-bind situation in these studies was simulated, bringing into question the adequacy of the investigations. Ringuette and Kennedy (1966) submitted letters of mothers of schizophrenics and of controls to five judges to test the presence of double-bind communication. The letters of the two groups could not be differentiated. However, the double-bind communication may not manifest itself in letters because of the extra time for thought they afford. Olsen (1972) also reviewed the empirical evidence available to support the double-bind hypothesis, and wrote that "until more creative and valid measures are obtained, it will be impossible to empirically unbind the 'double-bind'" (p. 91). Olsen feels that the double-bind concept remains an elusive abstract. He concludes, ". . . to retreat in a humorous note to the psychologizing of Charlie Brown, one might not too inappropriately respond to the double-bind concept the same way that Lucy does to Charlie Brown: 'You are a good concept, Double-Bind, if only you weren't so wishy-washy'" (p. 80).

Studies in Family Interaction

A well-known study of family interaction was conducted at the Yale University Psychiatric Institute by Lidz and his group (1957, 1965). In spite of the exploratory nature of the project, there has been a profusion of writing on it; never has so much been written on so few cases. Parent-child relationships play a key role in the theory of Lidz and his colleagues about the development of schizophrenia. Only those patients who could afford private hospitalization and who were willing to cooperate were included in the research. The goal of the research was to reconstruct the complete histories of those families with one schizophrenic member. Fourteen of these families were upper class and upper-middle class, and three families were lower-middle class. Only two fathers were absent. After years of research, it was found that 60% of the parents were ambulatory schizophrenics.

On the basis of these few cases and using no controls, Lidz and his group (1957) developed two concepts: marital schism, in which the family is in a constant state of discord with recurrent threats of separation by the parents, who seem held together by some kind of masochistic dependency, and marital skew, in which one parent, who is dominant, is invariably pathological and is often a nonhospitalized schizophrenic. The Lidz group indicated that the child of such parents has little exposure to the normal world. Being exposed to irrationality of all kinds within the family, the child develops a tendency to give up reality, and this ends in schizophrenia. In the skewed family, the schizophrenic child tends to be a boy, while in the marital schism family, the schizophrenic child tends to be a girl.

Lidz and his colleagues, primarily interested in the intrapsychic familial relationship, neglected the larger social network. A weakness in their approach is that in their model the family seems to be solely responsible for the socialization of the child. There is very little attention to outside influences. The family is considered a total institution that is hermetically closed. A second problem is that the conclusions derived from observations of patients by any group of investigators cannot be authenticated solely by the communications of the patients. Furthermore, there is no way of determining whether disturbance results from schizophrenia or whether disturbance causes schizophrenia.

Evidence of the highly selective factors involved in studying those families willing to cooperate was revealed by Wild, Shapiro, and Abelin (1974). They compared families of schizophrenics who were willing to collaborate with those who refused to collaborate. In their study, 29% of a schizophrenic group was considered on the basis of intactness and availability. Of those selected, 30% volunteered to participate in the study; finally, only 9% of the original group was selected. The members of the final group were of higher socioeconomic status, were more likely to be first born, were younger when interviewed and when admitted to the hospital, and were more likely to be diagnosed as acute rather than as paranoid or chronic schizophrenics. The most apparent inference is that all studies on schizophrenia that depend on volunteers clearly deal with a very specific group of schizophrenics. An adequate theory regarding the role of the family in schizophrenia should be concerned with disrupted as well as with intact families.

Seifer (1971) tried to use two measurement methods to analyze Lidz's theory of interaction in families with a schizophrenic member. He used these scales with schizophrenic and nonschizophrenic families. Contrary to his prediction, he was not able to differentiate parental roles within or between families.

Arieti (1974) has criticized studies of family interaction in general, pointing out that none of the studies has illustrated how the family's irrationality has passed through and been transformed by intrapsychic forces. What is transmitted, he says, is not schizophrenia per se. Instead, Arieti suggests that perhaps only 25% of the parents of schizophrenics act in the same manner described by Lidz and, furthermore, that a number of parents of nonschizophrenics act similarly. Clearly Lidz's group presented their findings as being more certain than the results would vouchsafe.

Communication in Families with Schizophrenic Children

A third major development in the study of the family and schizophrenia was instituted at the National Institute of Mental Health by Wynne and Singer (1963a, 1963b) and Singer and Wynne (1963, 1965a, 1965b), and recently pursued in Rochester by Wynne, Singer, and Toohey (1976), Wynne et al. (1977), Singer, Wynne, and Toohey (1978), and Wynne, Toohey, and Doane (1980). This group of researchers draws its ideas primarily from social-psychological theories of socialization as developed by Heinz Werner, who used the differentiation-integration principle. They give special attention to ego disturbances and thought disorders emanating from deficient communication patterns in families with schizophrenic children. Observation of families in therapy provided them with the major source of family interaction. Their initial research included 35 families: 26 Protestant, 8 Jewish, and 1 Catholic. Nineteen were upper class, 11 were middle class, and 5 were from the lower class, a breakdown that does not well reflect the general population. Later in their research they added more objective forms of data collection, such as projective techniques.

In summary, the investigators of the Wynne group found that the diagnosis, the form of thinking, and the severity of the disorganization of young schizophrenics were successfully identified from projective test data provided by other members of the family, and, further, that when test results from patients were matched blindly with the families to which they belonged, both findings were statistically significant. Thus, parents of depressed and neurotic children were clearly differentiated from parents of schizophrenics. The authors (Singer and Wynne, 1965b) added a note of caution regarding the universality of their findings:

Thus, the important issue here is whether our criteria for dealing with family patterns are in fact universally relevant to schizophrenic illness, wherever such illness may occur, or are merely idiosyncratically within the cultural and class setting of this study. [p. 207]

Singer and Wynne (1963b) developed two variants in the disturbed relationship. They argued that the fragmented style is more often found in parents of a schizophrenic with a good premorbid history, while parents of poor premorbids exhibit amorphousness more often.

The amorphous state is attributed to the schizophrenic who has not been able to differentiate the self from the nonself, which includes the capacity to recognize and distinguish different kinds of feeling states, impulses, and wishes. Failure of hierarchic integration after some degree of clear differentiation results in the fragmented state. In this analysis, Wynne and Singer relate stylistic features of family relations to the structure of schizophrenic thought and affective disorders. The family social subsystem is internalized in the ego functioning and forms of illness of the offspring. Parents who reinforce each other's deviant style increase the danger of schizophrenia in the offspring. However, if one parent tends to become a corrective agent to the deviant communication style, the chances of schizophrenia are reduced (Singer, 1968).

Wynne, Singer, and Toohey (1976), in a more recent development in their research, concluded that biological and adoptive parents of schizophrenics were indistinguishably deviant on communication scales. All parental pairs with a schizophrenic child, regardless of biological or adoptive parental status, were perfectly separated, on the basis of their communication, from members of the control group with a nonschizophrenic child. This finding seems to be a strong argument against a purely genetic explanation of schizophrenia. However, according to these researchers, communication deviance may be a necessary cause, but not a sufficient one.

Singer and Wynne (1965b), unlike the contributors to the field of family studies mentioned previously, are also aware of other variables, such as the social class and the cultural background of the family. They state:

We regard these problems of the links of nuclear family with extended family community, and broader cultures as of great importance in a comprehensive transactional approach to schizophrenics and their families, but outside the scope of the empirical research which is reported in this paper. [p. 207]

Wynne (1969) illustrates his interest in applying his principles of deviant communication to other cultures by citing unpublished papers on Japan and Lebanon, where Rorschach was used. He notes: "In our NIMH work, we are greatly interested in considering modifications of theory that may be necessary for families of different kinds in studying families of schizophrenics using a cross-cultural and cross-class frame of reference." However, information on the NIMH work is not immediately available in the literature.

Hirsch and Leff (1975) tried to replicate Wynne and Singer's studies in England, but reported far fewer differences between the parents of schizophrenics and the parents of nonschizophrenics. However, Wynne et al. (1977), in a rebuttal, pointed out that the study failed to be a replication. Besides the gross differences in methods in administering the tests, Hirsch and Leff studied only parents of acute schizophrenics and patients whom Wynne would diagnose as borderline. There are a number of problems involved in comparing the two studies, as Hirsch (1971) has revealed; but primarily there exists the possibility of diagnostic differences between the United Kingdom and the United States. Cooper et al. (1972) have shown that American psychiatrists tend to diagnose schizophrenia twice as often as British psychiatrists. Furthermore, because patients selected by the Wynne group had to undergo family psychotherapy, it is believed that some bias of selection was created in the process.

Reviews of Research in Family Interaction

An early review on the interactional studies was prepared by Meissner (1964). He summarized the findings, and, like others who have dealt with the antecedents of psychopathology, found that the pattern of interaction within the family was not characteristic of any specific pathology. In a forty-page review, Meissner devoted ten lines to what he called extra-familial influences, which may be at work in establishing such interactional patterns within the family structure. After referring to the 1961 article by Sanua, he stated: "This is not surprising, since the family is the mediating agency of cultural influence."

Mishler and Waxler (1966) also wrote a critical review of the family interaction processes and schizophrenia, in which they examined the theories of Bateson, Lidz, and Wynne. They pointed out that there is an unnecessarily high level of ambiguity and imprecision in these studies. Nevertheless, they thought that the theories were important because they focused on the family, and because they developed certain specific concepts. In Mishler and Waxler's article (1966), Bateson, Lidz, and Wynne were given an opportunity to provide critical evaluation of the review.

Riskin and Faunce (1972) presented an extensive review of quantifiable family interaction research. They found that researchers, often seemingly unaware of related work, continued to use outdated, inadequate techniques and methods and were repeating exploratory work from previous years.

EXPERIMENTAL STUDIES ON PARENTAL
INTERACTION WITH SCHIZOPHRENIC OFFSPRING

Research that followed these pioneer efforts focused less on clinical observations of family interactions than on systematic observations in single sessions and included the use of objective measures. Jacob (1975) classified direct observation studies into four categories, which concentrate on dominance, conflict, affect, and clarity of communication. The purpose in the dominance-submission studies was to determine whether there was either insufficient parental authority or a reversal in the authority relationship between fathers and mothers in a laboratory situation. Dominance was measured by verbal fluency, and the judgment of dominance was made by the investigators. Sometimes common tasks were given both individually and jointly, including the administration of the Thematic Apperception Test and Rorschach.

Mishler and Waxler (1968) reported rather extensive research on the communication process in the families of schizophrenics. They controlled for variables not carefully documented in the previous studies, such as the sex of the patient and good and poor premorbid families. All sessions were taped and analyzed. The study included 32 schizophrenics and 17 normal families. All schizophrenics were patients at the Massachusetts Mental Health Center, English-speaking, white, and had intact families. Controls were selected from two Catholic colleges and three Protestant churches. It is to be noted that 30% of the schizophrenic families and 88% of the control familes refused to volunteer. Members of the families were given a number of items to answer, and later, if there was disagreement, they were asked to reach consensus. They found different family norms for expressiveness (feelings and emotions) for the males only. Normal families with sons have higher rates of expressiveness, and good premorbid families have particularly low rates of this behavior. This norm is manifested most clearly in a situation in which the schizophrenic son is present, but not when his well sibling is present. There was little difference between poor premorbid families and families of normals. With daughters, significant differences were found to be sparse and scattered. When Mishler and Waxler tried to determine who was influencing whom, they received only ambiguous answers. The authors took five years to complete the study, and they do not seem to be enthusiastic with their findings. They state: "The results of the study provide further evidence that hard knowledge does not come easy in this area, no more so than in any area of scientific work" (p. 296).

Becker and Finkel (1969) analyzed verbal communication of good and poor premorbid schizophrenic and nonpsychotic controls. They found that poor premorbid schizophrenics, although showing the least anxiety in speech, had the highest predictability in seriousness of illness. Normal controls tended to have the highest speech anxiety and lowest predictability, which are somewhat different findings from those of Mishler and Waxler (1968).

The investigative approach using premorbid factors was initiated by Garmezy and Rodnick (1959). It was found that poor premorbid schizophrenic cases (process schizophrenics) have had dominating mothers, while good premorbid schizophrenics had dominating fathers. Information about the dominance of parents of schizophrenics was derived from verbal reports provided by the patients, from patients' reactions to parental stimuli, and from observed patterns of parental dominance. Cicchetti (1969), however, after reviewing the literature and conducting a number of studies with his colleagues, was not able to replicate the findings. He concluded:

> Unfortunately, the literature in schizophrenia research abounds with statements in support of the Rodnick-Garmezy theory, due to an uncritical analysis of the data these authors present. It is hoped that this paper demonstrates that the theory rests more upon misinterpretation of the research than upon empirical fact. [p. 557]

Social Class Studies

Wild et al. (1975) used a 20-question schedule of tasks in studying a group of families with a schizophrenic member and a group of normals who volunteered, 40% of whom were recruited through newspaper ads. All their subjects were English-speaking and white with intact families. The interviewers compared what they called the amorphous attention difficulties and problem-solving efficiency of middle- and lower-class subjects. Family members were instructed to work together on tasks they had previously solved individually and then were asked to agree on the same tasks as a joint venture. The data show class comparisions that are significant. Lower-class families had more amorphous attention difficulties than upper-class families and were less efficient at problem solving than upper-class families. Also, lower-class fathers were less dominant than upper-class fathers. The upper-class mothers of schizophrenics had more amorphous attention difficulties than upper-class mothers of normals. Such differences were not found among the lower classes. Fathers of schizophrenics were significantly more dominant than fathers of normal controls within the lower class, but not within the upper class. This is a clear indication that the results of studies of normal and sick families will be confounded by the researchers unless they control for social class. Wright (1973) found that, within families of poor premorbid schizophrenics, conceptual inadequacy of the same-sexed parent was an important determinant in the severity of the disorder.

Both of the above studies support the sex concordance theory of schizophrenia. However, as indicated by Keith et al. (1976), it would be premature to combine the results in view of the sample differences. Wright dealt with poor premorbid patients whose parents were matched in IQ and education. Wild, Shapiro, and Goldenberg (1975) included good and poor premorbid patients and husbands who were more educated than their wives. The following represent other examples of research in family interactions with objective measures: Cheek (1966), Friedman and Friedman (1970), Hassan (1974), Jones (1973), and Straker and Jacobson (1979).

As an example of the possibility of confounding results between sick families and controls, we can refer to the study by Lennard, Beaulieu, and Embrey (1965). The families with a sick member selected for their research were all Jewish and belonged to the working class. The controls included volunteers from a state-sponsored project near Kings County Hospital who made $7,000 a year and who accepted $10 to participate. Some investigators studied family interaction among normals and controlled for sociocultural variables. In every instance important differences were found between social classes and cultures in the analysis of the data.

Jacob (1975) controlled for social class and the age of the child when trying to study the nature of the family relationship. He found that initial disagreement among all family members was greater in lower-class than in middle-class families. In middle-class families, the son gained influence clearly at the expense of the mother, whereas the relative influence of middle-class fathers remained the same regardless of the child's age. In contrast, the son's gain in influence in lower-class families was often associated with the father's loss of influence.

Moos and Moos (1976) conducted a cluster anaylsis on 100 normal families with the Family Environmental Scale Profile. They found that 18 of the families represented in the cluster analysis were ethnic minority families (black and Mexican-American). The ethnic families were somewhat overrepresented in the Structure-Oriented and Achievement-Oriented clusters and somewhat underrepresented in the Expression-Oriented and Moral/Religious-Oriented clusters.

Strauss (1968) studied communication, creativity, and the problem-solving abilities of middle-class and working-class families in three societies: India, the United States, and Puerto Rico. The measurements used are similar to those used by interactionists. Tests of communication block, cognitive style, problem solving, and creativity revealed large social class differences in the three societies. However, the more urbanized and industrialized the society was, the smaller the social class differences.

An interesting study by Liem (1974) tried to use an experimental procedure to measure the influence of parents on their schizophrenic offspring and the influence of the schizophrenic sons on their parents. His findings offered no support for the etiological position that parents' disordered communication contributes to disorder in the offspring. Liem discusses the alternate position that parents of schizophrenics may learn peculiar ways of communicating in response to their schizophrenic sons.

Further Studies on Sociocultural Variables

More specific studies of mental patients, which are not necessarily of family interaction, but which clearly show the role of the sociocultural variables in the analysis of research data, have also been conducted. Query (1961) pointed out differences in urban and rural families, which may have some bearing on the currently inconclusive results. In rural areas, families tend to follow a puritanical, religious creed, described as familistic or patriarchical, whereas families in cities tend to be nuclear. Query believed that the father figure in urban areas provides inadequate role identification, while at the same time the mother figure tends to be overprotective or dominant. The premorbid adjustment of the rural subject was found to be significantly better than that of the urban subject, as measured by the Phillips Check List (Phillips, 1953), which distinguishes the poor premorbid from the good premorbid subject. Strict fathers tend to be more frequently found in rural families than in urban families.

Because female dominance is unusual in some cultures, it is worthwhile to replicate such studies in order to determine if there is a correlation between mother-father dominance and good or poor premorbid history. On the basis of this hypothesis, one could state that in most cultures where the father is dominant, a large percentage of the schizophrenic cases would have a good premorbid history. Recent research (World Health Organization, 1979) has shown that chronicity in schizophrenia tends to be much lower in developing countries than in Western countries. Murphy and Raman (1971), as a result of a twelve-year follow-up of schizophrenics in Mauritius, found that a high percentage of discharged schizophrenics were functioning normally and symptom-free in comparison to British samples. This is somewhat difficult to explain in view of the poor psychiatric facilities in these countries. One explanation is that the kind of interaction that these patients have with their families and friends, which is probably encouraged by the culture, tends to prevent chronicity (see Murphy, Chapter 9, this volume).

Baxter and Arthur (1964) showed that interpersonal conflicts are highest among schizophrenics of good premorbid adjustment and middle-class status and schizophrenics of poor premorbid adjustment and lower-class standing. Thus, these authors suggest that in future studies of family transaction patterns, the social standing of the family needs careful control.

Heilbrun (1973), in a book devoted to the aversive control of the mother, reviews the literature on family interaction studies. He does not feel that maternal communication as an etiologic factor in schizophrenia should be a major contribution. He writes:

> It is most difficult to generate enthusiasm over the importance of maternal communication as an etiologic factor in schizophrenia based on this survey of relevant research. The impressive amount of work that went into the small sample study (32 schizophrenic families and 17 normal families) of Mishler and Waxler (1968) makes it clear why better communication research is out of reach, except for those who have substantial research funding. While there may be technical barriers to human communication in research, the paucity of positive findings relevant to mother—or parent—schizophrenic child interactions certainly make this the sector of maternal behavior in which we can invest the least confidence as a source of influence in schizophrenic development. [p. 25]

Heilbrun (1961) provides an excellent illustration of how important the sociocultural factors are, and how the neglect of such variables could confound the results of researchers. In his research he found that the mothers of schizophrenics who had completed formal schooling were more controlling in their child-rearing attitudes than educated mothers of normals. On the other hand, the less-educated mothers of schizophrenics were less controlling than their counterparts with normal daughters.

Chapman and Baxter (1963) tested the process-reactive distinction with schizophrenic subjects, controlling for social class. The Phillips Symptom Check List was used to examine whether the schizophrenic person was of the process or reactive type. The correlation between the total Phillips score and the fathers' social position was found to be minus 0.57. Chapman and Baxter suggest that those research workers who use the Phillips Scale to study behavioral correlates of good and poor premorbid adjustment should compare the parental families as to social class, ethnic origin, rural-urban background, and other sources of subcultural differences, in order to rule these out as artifacts. The Phillips Scale includes two major premorbid characteristics to identify process and reactive schizophrenics—premorbid sexual behavior and premorbid affiliative behavior. Because both of these vary widely among subcultures, the use of the Phillips Scale is limited. As pointed out by Kinsey et al. (1948), lower-class individuals have sexual experiences at an earlier age and are very active sexually. Also, it has been found that lower-class persons are less isolated from their peers than middle-class persons. The scale would show validity in a hospital that receives middle-class patients who are sent as a last resort after previous treatment. They would be chronic cases, because the two major indicators of the scale, little sex experience and little affiliative tendency, would be characteristic of this group. On the other hand, the Phillips Scale would show low validity in a hospital that receives middle-class patients with no previous treatment.

Two research studies illustrate the importance of the ethnic-nationality backgrounds of the patients studied. Opler (1957) found that Irish families with a schizophrenic son were dominated by the mother, and that the father was a weak and shadowy figure. The opposite pattern was found in the parents of schizophrenics of Italian origin. Sanua (1963a), in comparing Jewish and Protestant families with a schizophrenic of the lower class, found that there was excessive pathology and high emotional temper in the Protestant father. Many were passive or seemed to have had normal relationships with their sons. There was also excessive pathology among the Jewish mothers of the lower class with excessive emotional temper, while there was much overprotectiveness on the part of the Protestant lower-class mother. Thus, the picture of the weak, passive father is likely to be found in Jewish families of schizophrenics and not in the Protestant families of the lower class. If an investigator's sample includes rural and urban patients and lower- and middle-class patients (persons of different cultural background), he encounters difficulties trying to interpret his data meaningfully.

STUDIES USING THE RETROSPECTIVE APPROACH

Considering the bias that enters into the present evaluation of schizophrenic families and controls, a more valid approach would be to study the records of children who had been treated in child guidance clinics and who ultimately became schizophrenics. Then there would be less chance of contamination, because the data would be collected from records written by individuals who could not possibly have known who would turn out to be schizophrenic. However, there still exists the problem that the examiner of the records would be aware of the ultimate diagnosis of the individual being studied. In a little-known study, Frazee (1953) examined the records of those children who had been seen at the Institute of Juvenile Research in Chicago, and found that the fathers of those who became schizophrenic were severely cruel and rejecting, contrary to the ". . . passive ineffectual father generally assumed in the literature" (p. 148).

A more systematic approach to this type of study was conducted by Ricks and Berry (1970), and by Waring and Ricks (1965). Using 18,000 client records of the Judge Baker Child Guidance Clinic, the researchers were able to locate 200 children who had been hospitalized for mental illness, half of them for schizophrenia. The schizophrenic group was divided into two groups—those who were still in mental institutions and those who had been released. Forty percent of the patients belonged to Classes I–III (middle and upper), and the remainder belonged to Classes IV and V (lower class). A control group of persons who did not become schizophrenic was selected from the same clinic matched for IQ, socioeconomic status, and ethnic background. The investigators found that more of the mothers of schizophrenics who were still hospitalized were themselves psychotic, schizoid or borderline, or had character disorders. There was little information about the fathers except what was reported by the mothers. In a large percentage of the marriages, emotional divorce was evident in the parents of schizophrenics. There seemed to be a long symbiosis between the sick child and the disturbed parent. Cold, demanding, compulsive mothers, the schizophrenogenic stereotype of the usual clinical picture, occurred more frequently in the released group and control groups than in the chronic schizophrenics. Released schizophrenics tended also to come from depressed families. In this study, although these groups were matched for economic status, the data would probably be confounded by combining the lower and upper classes into one group. It is possible that because 60% of the families belonged to the lower social class, the mothers did not manifest the usual schizophrenogenic behavior found in previous studies conducted primarily with upper-class mothers. Gardner (1967), using the same material, found that the mothers of schizophrenics were described as shy, inadequate, vague, and fearful. This finding, which is at variance with other research studies, should be noted in reference to the studies reviewed in this chapter where ethnicity and social class were controlled.

Another well-known research study in this area was conducted by Robins (1966). She found that those who became schizophrenics as children had somatic symptoms and were depressed, overdependent, and ruminative. The schizophrenic children also demonstrated more truancy and running away from home. In addition, there was a higher rate of separation, divorce, and unemployment among the parents of the boys who became schizophrenics.

STUDIES OF HIGH RISK

In the early sixties, a different type of study was initiated, probably because of the discouraging results of retrospective studies and studies in communication. The new approach was known as studies of high risk. In such investigations, studies were carried out on populations with a higher than normal risk of developing schizophrenia. These studies tended to be longitudinal in nature, and therefore required a greater investment of time on the part of the researcher because they had to follow and compare the psychological adjustment of children with low risk and high risk. Garmezy (1974, 1978) has written an extensive evaluation and critique of this type of research.

A classic effort in studies of populaton at high risk was made by Mednick (1978) and Schulsinger (1976, 1980), who followed the development of 207 children of schizophrenic mothers and compared their autonomic instability with that of the children of 104 normals. In an early evaluation, they found that the disturbed group among the offspring of schizophrenics had significantly longer periods of separation from their mothers during early development than those offspring of schizophrenic mothers who showed no deviance. The disturbed individuals suffered more birth complications that were related to deviant psychophysiological reactions. In addition, they had more problems in school. Thus, the picture is complex, and the sequence and importance of each factor is difficult to disentangle.

At the Second Rochester International Conference on Schizophrenia, Mednick (1978) presented a paper that pointed out the hazards involved when other researchers asserted failure in their replications of his findings. A variety of factors must be considered, such as the severity of parental illness, the intactness of the family, the age of the subjects studied, and the personality of the nonschizophrenic parent. Mednick found in his research that a high proportion of schizophrenic mothers married fathers with criminal tendencies.

A study by Erlenmeyer-Kimling and Cornblatt (1978) did not reveal important psychophysiological differences between the high risk and the low risk groups. Mednick (1978) stated appropriately that the intactness of the family in Copenhagen in 1962 may not be the same thing as the intactness of the family in New York in 1972. He further added that there may be changing patterns of psychiatric treatment over a ten-year period. What seems most important is Mednick's statement that there might be "cultural differences" (p. 450) between the two countries. This is an interesting observation that so far has played no part in any of the studies reviewed.

Anthony (1974) evaluated 138 grade school-age children from 46 families with a psychotic parent on four clinically derived variables, such as logical thinking, reality testing, identity, and organizational competence. Anthony showed that, on the basis of these measures, these children could be distinguished from a matched group of children whose parents were normal. Four intervention approaches were used: a compensatory program, individual and group therapy, a cathartic program emphasizing family interviews during the time of the psychotic illness, and a corrective program, or reality-testing sessions. There are some indications that vulnerability was lessened. However, only tentative conclusions can be drawn, because the study does not have an untreated control group.

In a recent statement, Anthony (1978), commenting on a number of high risk studies presented at the Second Rochester International Conference on Schizophrenia, noted: "It is fair to say that only now are researchers growing more aware of methodologic uncertainties and marked logistical difficulties that characterize studies of vulnerable children" (p. 480). The Rochester group of Singer, Wynne, and Toohey (1978) at the

University of Rochester Child and Family Study has shifted its attention to studying families with younger children (as reported by Romano, 1978). These high risk children could develop personality aberration. The Rochester group is testing a number of hypotheses that emerged from their earlier studies of families with adult children.

Bleuler (1978) has studied the life course of 184 children of 206 schizophrenic parents whom he had treated, and has followed them systematically since 1938. He found a higher rate of normality among those children than other investigators have found. This may be attributed to two factors: differential diagnosis and Bleuler's familiarity with his subjects. He felt that a long-term exposure to a parent who is schizophrenic is insufficient to explain the subsequent development of schizophrenia in the offspring. However, the early suffering of children because of the illness of the parents made an indelible mark on their personality. They could not enjoy life fully.

Other studies of high risk include the following: Garmezy (1975), Grunebaum et al. (1974), Neil and Weintraub (1972), and Roff (1976). Garmezy (1974) provided an extensive evaluation of this type of research, which seems to have replaced the large number of interaction studies that were started about two decades ago. Garmezy is extremely cautious about relying on this approach to provide the answers to the etiology of schizophrenia. However, he feels that "current investigations and the ones to follow should enhance our understanding of the disorder and provide data that will eventually have to be incorporated into the complex etiological equation this extraordinary, complex disorder will require" (p. 116).

Fisher and Jones (1978), on the basis of a review of 70 longitudinal studies conducted over the past three decades, have emphasized the methodological problems in such research, particularly in the clarification of the objectives and in the selection of the sample. They feel that unless action is concerted in this field, investigators are likely to continue indefinitely producing research marred by the same limitations.

SUMMARY AND CONCLUSIONS

In this chapter the evolution of family studies with particular reference to schizophrenia is discussed. Large numbers of such studies started immediately after World War II and evolved in a systematic manner. The researchers started with retrospective studies. Next, they conducted interaction studies of families, which tended to be psychoanalytically inspired. When interaction studies showed weaknesses, family studies using experimental procedures and measurements were developed. Until now, another method of study was used that has produced little research—the analysis of clinic records of children who became schizophrenic at a later age. At the present time, numerous studies on vulnerable children or children of high risk are being conducted.

The slim findings and lack of replications of these studies force a reevaluation of research on mental illness in order to decide what methodology would be the most fruitful in the coming decade. In spite of the tremendous expenditure of effort in family studies, as Reiss (1975) indicates, the overall findings "have done something less than set the world afire" (p. 9). With very few exceptions, these studies have not dealt with the social and cultural system in general, or with the early socialization processes, partly because the researchers have themselves been blind to their own prejudicial sampling tendencies.

Many years ago, Schaffer and Meyers (1954) analyzed the process of selecting patients in a psychiatric outpatient clinic for psychotherapy in New Haven, Connecticut. They found that 65% of the patients belonging to the professional and executive class were assigned for therapy to senior psychiatric staff and residents, whereas only 2.5% of the lowest class and 33% of the next lowest class were seen by the same high-caliber staff. The majority of the lower-class patients received therapy from medical students. In the Lidz study, in the Wynne, Singer, and Toohey reports, and in others, subjects for research are similarly selected. In general, they are white, English-speaking, generally middle and upper class, with intact families. Romano (1978), commenting on the selection of the sample in the high risk research at the University of Rochester Child and Family Study, indicates that there is a need for those engaged in clinical research to define clearly and fully the population under study. The uneven selection of patients presents the obvious hazard of reaching biased conclusions.

The paucity of research on the family of the lower class and on blacks in particular stands out. In an unusual research project conducted by a group of social workers (Miller, Challas, and Gee, 1972), it was found in a follow-up study of children of schizophrenic, welfare, and convict mothers that all of them displayed many behavioral problems: inschool psychiatric referrals, antisocial behavior, arrests, high residential mobility, dropping out of school, failures on draft tests, and so forth. Miller et al. came to the surprising conclusion that the life experience of these subjects seemed to reflect the effects of growing up poor in an urban world; the children of black schizophrenic mothers do not differ markedly from other children of the black poor.

However, there are a number of researchers who have been interested in studying cultural differences among various ethnoreligious groups in the United States. These investigators include: Brody (1967)—blacks; Fantl and Schiro (1959) and Singer and Opler (1956)—Irish and Italians; Mintz and Schwartz (1964)—Italians; Piedmont (1966)—Germans and Poles;

Sanua (1962, 1963)—Irish, Italians, Jews, and Protestants; Stein (1973)—Slovak-American; and Sunshine (1971)—blacks and Puerto Ricans.

Sanua (1980) has provided an outline of a research study designed to answer some of the questions that have often been raised by the Wynne group regarding the universality of the interactions in families of schizophrenics. The study suggests that a group of investigators familiar with the language of two or even three cultures, and well versed in more than one discipline, should select groups of paranoid schizophrenics of different social classes in different countries (such as the United States, France, and Italy) and should replicate some of the research conducted in the past in the United States. Paranoids were suggested for study because they present fewer problems in diagnosis, and they tend to be of higher intelligence. The major question to be raised in this proposed study is whether paranoid schizophrenics from different sociocultural groups reflect familial communication and interactions common to their specific psychiatric illness, or whether the patterns found are more reflective of the differences in their cultural backgrounds.

Novack (1976) pointed out that the Jewish family is not like the Italian family, the family of the Scotch-Irish of Appalachia has emotional ties different from those of families from Eastern Europe, and the communal families of the South Slavs are not like those of the Japanese. Similarly, there is not just one family pattern in America, there are many. Thus, if there are differences in the behavior of families of normals of different cultural backgrounds, a justifiable assumption is that there are differences in the behavior of schizophrenics of different cultural backgrounds and differences in their communication patterns with their families.

Culture as it is manifested in the interactions of the family logically should be considered as an antecedent variable that may affect the findings of different investigators and that may possibly lead to contradictory conclusions.

REFERENCES

Anthony, E. J. 1974. The syndrome of the psychologically vulnerable child. In: E. J. Anthony and C. Koupernik (eds.), The Child in His Family: Children at Psychiatric Risk, pp. 3–10. John Wiley & Sons, Inc., New York.

Anthony, E. J. 1978. High risk and pre-morbid development. In: L. Wynne, R. L. Cromwell, and S. Matthysse (eds.), The Nature of Schizophrenia: New Approaches to Research and Treatment, pp. 397–400. John Wiley & Sons, Inc., New York.

Aricti, S. 1974. An overview of schizophrenia from a predominantly psychological approach. Am. J. Psychiatry 131:241–249.

Bateson, G. 1959. Cultural problems posed by a study of schizophrenic process. In: A. Auerback (ed.), Schizophrenia: An Integrated Approach. Ronald Press Co., New York.

Bateson, G., Jackson, D. D., Haley, J., and Weakland, J. 1956. Towards a theory of schizophrenia. Behav. Sci. 1:253–264.

Baxter, J. C., and Arthur, S. C. 1964. Conflict in families of schizophrenics as a function of premorbid adjustment and social class. Fam. Process 3:273–279.

Becker, J., and Finkel, P. 1969. Predictability and anxiety in speech by parents of female schizophrenics. J. Abnorm. Psychol. 74:517–523.

Bleuler, M. 1978. The Schizophrenic Disorders: Long Term Patient and Family Studies. Yale University Press, New Haven.

Bott, E. 1971. Family and Social Network: Roles, Norms, External Relationship in Ordinary Urban Families. Free Press, New York.

Bowen, M. 1960. A family concept of schizophrenia. In: D. Jackson (ed.), The Etiology of Schizophrenia, pp. 346–372. Basic Books, Inc., New York.

Brody, E. B. 1967. Socio-cultural influences on vulnerability to schizophrenic behavior. In: J. Romano (ed.), The Origins of Schizophrenia, pp. 228–238. Excerpta Medical Foundation, Amsterdam.

Chapman, L. J., and Baxter, J. C. 1963. The process-reactive distinction and patients' subculture. J. Nerv. Ment. Dis. 136:352–359.

Cheek, F. E. 1966. Parental role distortions in relation to schizophrenic deviancy. Psychiatr. Res. Rep. 20:54–64.

Cicchetti, D. V. 1969. Critical review of the research relating mother dominance to schizophrenia. Proceedings of the 77th annual convention of the American Psychological Association. 4:557–558.

Ciotola, P. V. 1961. The effect of two contradictory levels of reward and censure on schizophrenics. Doctoral dissertation, University of Missouri. University Microfilms, no. 61-2278, Ann Arbor.

Cooper, J. E., Kendall, E. E., Gurland, B. J., Sharpe, L., Copeland, J. R. M., and Simon, R. 1972. Psychiatric Diagnosis in New York and London. Oxford University Press, Oxford.

Erlenmeyer-Kimling, L., and Cornblatt, B. 1978. Attentional measures in a study of children at high risk for schizophrenia. In: L. Wynne, R. L. Cromwell, and S. Matthysse (eds.), The Nature of Schizophrenia: New Approaches to Research and Treatment, pp. 359–365. John Wiley & Sons, Inc., New York.

Fantl, B., and Schiro, J. 1959. Cross-cultural variables in the behavior patterns and symptom formation of 15 Irish and 15 Italian female schizophrenics. Int. J. Soc. Psychiatry 4:245–253.

Fisher, L., and Jones, F. H. 1978. Planning for the next generation of risk studies. Schizophr. Bull. 4:223–235.

Fontana, A. F. 1966. Familial etiology of schizophrenia: Is a scientific methodology possible? Psychol. Bull. 66:214–227.

Frank, G. H. 1965. The role of the family in the development of psychopathology. Psychol. Bull. 64: 191–205.

Frazee, H. E. 1953. Children who later became schizophrenic. Smith College Stud. Soc. Work 23:225–249.

Friedman, C., and Friedman, A. 1970. Characteristics of schizogenic families during a joint story-telling task. Fam. Process 9:333–354.

Fromm-Reichmann, F. 1948. Notes on the development of treatment of schizophrenics by psychoanalytic psychotherapy. Psychiatry 11:263–273.

Gardner, G. G. 1967. The role of maternal psychopathology in male and female schizophrenics. J. Consult. Psychol. 31:411–413.

Garmezy, N. 1974. Children at risk: The search for the antecedents of schizophrenia. Part II: Ongoing research programs, issues, and intervention. Schizophr. Bull. 9:55–125.

Garmezy, N. 1975. The experimental study of children vulnerable to psychopathology. In: A. Davids (ed.), Child Personality and Psychopathology: Current Topics. Vol. 2. John Wiley & Sons, Inc., Inter-Science Division, New York.

Garmezy, N. 1978. Observations on high-risk research and premorbid development in schizophrenia and current status of a sample of other high-risk research programs. In: L. Wynne, R. L. Cromwell, and S. Matthysse (eds.), The Nature of Schizophrenia: New Approaches to Research and Treatment, pp. 460–480. John Wiley & Sons, Inc., New York.

Garmezy, N., and Rodnick, E. H. 1959. Pre-morbid adjustment and performance in schizophrenia: Implications for interpreting heterogeneity in schizophrenia. J. Nerv. Ment. Dis. 129:450–466.

Garmezy, N. and Streitman, S. 1974a. Children at risk: The search for the antecedents of schizophrenia. Part I: Conceptual models and research methods. Schizophr. Bull. 8:14–90.

Grunebaum, H., Weiss, J. L., Gallant, D., and Cohler, B. 1974. Attention in young children of psychotic mothers. Am. J. Psychiatry 131:887–891.

Haley, J. 1963. Strategies of Psychotherapy. Grune & Stratton, New York.

Hassan, S. A. 1974. Transactional and contextual invalidation between the patients of disturbed families: A comparative study. Fam. Process 13:53–76.

Heilbrun, A. B. 1961. Maternal authoritarianism, social class, and filial schizophrenia. J. Gen. Psychol. 65:235–241.

Heilbrun, A. B. 1973. Aversive Maternal Control. A Theory of Schizophrenia Development. John Wiley & Sons, Inc., New York.

Hirsch, S. R. 1971. Abnormal communication and communication in the aetiology of schizophrenia, a double blind quantitative study. Paper presented at the Fifth World Congress of Psychiatry, Mexico City, December 30.

Hirsch, S. R., and Leff, J. P. 1975. Abnormalities in Parents of Schizophrenics. Oxford University Press, London.

Hoekstra, R. C. 1971. The "double-bind". That is to say a psychic stranglehold. Psychiatria, Neurologia, Neurochirurgia (Amsterdam) 74:391–400.

Jackson, D. (ed.). 1960. The Etiology of Schizophrenia. Basic Books, Inc., New York.

Jacob, T. 1975. Family interaction in disturbed and normal families: A methodological and substantive review. Psychol. Bull. 82:33–65.

Jones, F. J. 1973. Current methodologies for studying the development of schizophrenia: A critical review. J. Nerv. Ment. Dis. 157:154–178.

Kanner, L. 1943. Autistic disturbances of affective contact. Nervous Child. 2:217–250.

Keith, S. J., Gunderson, J. G., Reifman, A., Bucksbaum, S. and Mosher, L. R. 1976. Special report: Schizophrenia 1976. Schizophr. Bull. 2:509–565.

Keniston, K., and The Carnegie Council on Children. 1977. All Our Children: The American Family Under Pressure. Harcourt Brace Jovanovich, Inc., New York.

Kinsey, A. C., Pomeroy, W. B., and Martin, C. E. 1948. Sexual Behavior in the Human Male. W. B. Saunders Company, Philadelphia.

Lennard, H. L., Beaulieu, M. R., and Embrey, N. G. 1965. Interaction in families with a schizophrenic child. Arch. Gen. Psychiatry 12:163–183.

Lidz, T., Fleck, S., and Cornelison, A. R. 1965. Schizophrenia and the Family. N.Y. International Press, New York.

Lidz, T., Cornelison, A. R., Fleck, S., and Terry, D. 1957. The intrafamilial environment of schizophrenic patients: Marital schism and marital skew. Am. J. Psychiatry 114:241–248.

Liem, H. 1974. Effect of verbal communication of parents and children. A comparison of normal and schizophrenic families. J. Consult. Clin. Psychol. 42:438–450.

Loeff, R. G. 1966. Differential discrimination of conflicting emotional messages by normal, delinquent, and schizophrenic adolescents. Doctoral dissertation, Indiana University. University Microfilms, no. 66–1470, Ann Arbor.

Mednick, S. 1978. Berkson's fallacy and high risk research. In: L. Wynne, R. L. Cromwell, and S. Matthysse (eds.), The Nature of Schizophrenia: New Approaches to Research and Treatment, pp. 442–452. John Wiley & Sons, Inc., New York.

Meissner, W. W. 1964. Thinking about the family. Psychiatric aspects. Fam. Process 3:1–40.

Miller, D., Challas, G., and Gee, S. 1972. Children of deviants: A fifteen-year follow-up study of children of schizophrenic mothers, welfare mothers, matched controls, and random urban families. Unpublished report.

Mintz, N. L., and Schwartz, D. T. 1964. Urban ecology and psychosis: Community factors in the incidence of schizophrenia and manic depression among Italians of Greater Boston. Int. J. Soc. Psychiatry 10:101–117.

Mishler, E. G., and Waxler, N. E. 1966. Family interaction processes and schizophrenia: A review of current theories. Int. J. Psychiatry 2:375–430.

Mishler, E. G., and Waxler, N. E. 1968. Interaction in Families: An Experimental Study of Family Process and Schizophrenia. John Wiley & Sons, Inc., New York.

Moos, R., and Moos, D. 1976. A typology of family social environments. Fam. Process 15:357–372.

Murphy, H. B. M., and Raman, A. C. 1971. The chronicity of schizophrenia in indigenous tropical peoples: Results of a twelve-year follow-up survey in Mauritius. Br. J. Psychiatry 118:489–497.

Neil, J. M., and Weintraub, S. 1972. Selecting variables for high risk research. Paper presented at the Conference on High Risk, October, Dorado Beach, Puerto Rico.

Novack, M. 1976. The family out of favor. Harper's, April, pp. 37–40.

Olsen, D. N. 1972. Empirically unbinding the double-bind: Review of research and conceptual reformulations. Fam. Process 11:69–94.

Opler, M. K. 1957. Schizophrenia and culture. Sci. Am. 197:103–110.

Phillips, L. 1953. Case history data and prognosis in schizophrenia. J. Nerv. Ment. Dis. 117:515–525.

Piedmont, E. B. 1966. Ethnicity and schizophrenia: A pilot study. Ment. Hyg. 50:374–379.

Potash, H. M. 1965. Schizophrenic interaction and the concept of the double-bind. Doctoral dissertatiaon, Michigan State University. University Microfilms, no. 65–2052, Ann Arbor.

Query, J. M. 1961. Premorbid adjustment and family structure: A comparison of selected rural and urban schizophrenic men. J. Nerv. Ment. Dis. 133:333–338.

Reiss, D. 1975. Families and the etiology of schizophrenia. Schizo. Bull. 14:9–11.

Ricks, D. F., and Berry, J. C. 1970. Family and symptom patterns that precede schizophrenia. In: M. Roff and D. F. Ricks (eds.), Life History Research in Psychopathology, pp. 31–50. University of Minnesota, Minneapolis.

Ringuette, E. L., and Kennedy, T. 1966. An experimental study of the double-bind hypothesis. J. Abnorm. Psychol. 71:136–141.

Riskin, J., and Faunce, E. E. 1972. An evaluative review of family interaction research. Fam. Process 11:365–456.

Robins, L. N. 1966. Deviant Children Grown Up: A Sociological and Psychiatric Study of Sociopathic Personality. Williams & Wilkins Company, Baltimore.

Roff, J. E. 1976. Peer-status and the directionality of symptomatic behavior: Prime social competence predictors of outcome for vulnerable children. Am. J. Orthopsychiatry 46:74–88.

Romano, J. 1978. The central core of madness. In: L. Wynne, R. L. Cromwell, and S. Matthysse (eds.), The Nature of Schizophrenia: New Approaches to Research and Treatment, pp. [6. John Wiley & Sons, Inc., New York.

Sanua, V. 1961. The sociocultural factors of families of schizophrenics: A review of the literature. Psychiatry 24:246–265.

Sanua, V. 1962. Comparison of Jewish and Protestant paranoid and catatonic patients. Dis. Nerv. System. 23:320–325.

Sanua, V. 1963. The sociocultural aspects of schizophrenia: A comparison of Protestant and Jewish schizophrenics. Int. J. Soc. Psychiatry (London) 8:27–31.

Sanua, V. 1967. The sociocultural aspects of childhood schizophrenia: A discussion with special emphasis on methodology. In: G. H. Zuk and I. Boszormenyi-Nagy (eds.), Family Therapy and Disturbed Families, pp. 159–176. Science & Behavior Books, Inc. Palo Alto, Calif.

Sanua, V. 1969a. The sociocultural aspects of schizophrenia: A review of the literature. In: L. Bellak and L. Loeb (eds.), The Schizophrenic Syndrome, pp. 256–331. Grune & Stratton, New York.

Sanua, V. 1980. Sociocultural aspects of the family and psychopathology. Unpublished paper.

Schaffer, L., and Meyers, J. K. 1954. Psychotherapy and social stratification: An empirical study of practice in a psychiatric outpatient clinic. Psychiatry 17.83–93.

Schuham, A. I. 1967. The double-bind hypothesis a decade later. Psychol. Bull. 68:409–416.

Schulsinger, F. 1976. A ten-year follow-up of children of schizophrenic mothers: The clinical assessment. Acta Psychiatr. Scand. 53:371–376.

Schulsinger, R. 1980. Biological psychopathology. In: M. Rosenzweig and L. W. Porter (eds.), Annu. Rev. Psychol. 31:583–606.

Searles, H. 1959. The effort to drive the other person crazy: An element in the etiology and psychotherapy in schizophrenia. Br. J. Med. Psychol. 32(1):1–18.

Seifer, R. 1971. An analysis of Lidz's theory of interaction in families of normals, schizophrenics, and non-schizophrenic adolescents using two measured methods. Doctoral dissertation, University of Maine. Dissertat. Abstr. Int. 32(5B):3017–18.

Singer, J., and Opler, M. K. 1956. Contrasting patterns of fantasy and mobility in Irish and Italian schizophrenics. J. Abnorm. Soc. Psychol. 53:43–47.

Singer, M. T. 1968. The consensus Rorschach and family transaction. J. Project. Techn. Pers. Assess. 32:348–351.

Singer, M. T., and Wynne, L. C. 1963. Differentiating characteristics of parents of childhood schizophrenics, childhood neurotics and young adult schizophrenics. Am. J. Psychiatry 120:234–243.

Singer, M. T., and Wynne, L. C. 1965a. Thought disorders and family relations of schizophrenics: III. Methodology using projective techniques. Arch. Gen. Psychiatry 12:187–200.

Singer, M. T., and Wynne, L. C. 1965b. Thought disorders and family relations in schizophrenics: IV. Results and implications. Arch. Gen. Psychiatry 12:201–212.

Singer, M. T., Wynne, L. C., and Toohey, M. L. 1978. Communication disorders and the families of schizophrenics. In: L. Wynne, R. L. Cromwell, and S.

Matthysse (eds.), The Nature of Schizophrenia: New Approaches to Research and Treatment, pp. 499–511. John Wiley & Sons, Inc., New York.

Spiegel, J., and Bell, N. 1959. The family of the psychiatric patient. In: S. Arieti (ed.), American Handbook of Psychiatry. Vol. 1, pp. 114–149. Basic Books, Inc., New York.

Stark, E., and Von der Haar, H. 1977. Double-bind hypothesis in schizophrenia research. Psychol. Rundschau 28:31–44.

Stein, H. F. 1973. Cultural specificity in patterns of mental illness and health: A Slovak-American case study. Fam. Process 12:69–92.

Straker, G.,and Jacobson, R. 1979. A study of the relationship between family interaction and individual symptomatology over time. Fam. Process 18:443.

Strauss, M. A. 1968. Communication, creativity, and problem-solving ability of middle- and working-class families in three societies. Am. J. Sociol. 73:417–430.

Sunshine, N. C. 1971. Cultural differences in schizophrenia. Doctoral dissertation, City University of New York. Dissertat. Abstr. Int. 32:1197–1198.

Waring, M., and Ricks, D. 1965. Family patterns of children who become adult schizophrenics. J. Nerv. Ment. Dis. 140:351–364.

Weakland, J. H. 1960. The double-bind hypothesis of schizophrenia and three-party interaction. In: D. Jackson (ed.), Etiology of Schizophrenia. Basic Books, Inc., New York.

Wild, C., Shapiro, L. N., and Abelin, L. 1974. Sampling issues in family studies of schizophrenia. Arch. Gen. Psychiatry 30:211–215.

Wild, C., Shapiro, L. N. and Abelin, L. 1977. Communication patterns and role structures in families of male schizophrenics. A study using automated techniques. Arch. Gen. Psychiatry 34:58–70.

Wild, C., Shapiro, L. N., Abelin, L., and Goldenberg, L. 1975. Transactional communication disturbances in families of male schizophrenics. Fam. Process 14:131–160.

World Health Organization. 1979. Schizophrenia: An international follow-up study. John Wiley & Sons, Inc., New York.

Wright, D. M. 1973. Thought disorder in the parents of poor premorbid male schizophrenics. Arch. Gen. Psychiatry 2:472–475.

Wynne, L. C. 1969. The family as a strategic focus in cross-cultural psychiatric studies. In: W. Caudill and T. Lin (eds.), Mental Health Research in Asia and the Pacific, pp. 463–477. East West Center Press, Honolulu.

Wynne, L. C., and Singer, M. T. 1963a. Thought disorder and family relations of schizophrenics: I. A research strategy. Arch. Gen. Psychiatry 9:191–198.

Wynne, L. C., and Singer, M. T. 1963b. Thought disorder and family relations of schizophrenics: II. Classification of forms of thinking. Arch. Gen. Psychiatry 9:199–206.

Wynne, L., Singer, M. T., and Toohey, M. L. 1976. Communication of the adoptive parents of schizophrenics. In: J. Jorstad and E. Egelstad (eds.), Schizophrenia, 75: Psychotherapy, Family Studies, and Research, pp. 413–452. Universitats-Forlagets, University of Oslo, Norway.

Wynne, L. C., Toohey, M. L., and Doane, J. 1980. Family studies. In: L. Bellak (ed.), The Schizophrenic Syndrome. Grune & Stratton, New York.

Wynne, L. C., Ryckoff, I., Day, J., and Hirsch, S. 1958. Pseudomutuality in the family relations of schizophrenia. Psychiatry 21:205–220.

Wynne, L., Singer, M. T., Bartko, J. J., and Toohey, M. L. 1977. Schizophrenics and their families: Recent research on parental communication. In: J. E. Tanner (ed.), Developments in Psychiatric Research, pp. 254–256. Hodder and Stoughton, Ltd., London.

Chapter 7

Sex Differences in Psychopathology

Ihsan Al-Issa

Sex differences in behavior and role socialization are almost universal. One important question is to what extent these differences are reflected in the rates of mental illness within and across cultures. For example, two recent extensive studies by Chesler (1972) and by Gove and Tudor (1973) have concluded that the rates of mental illness are higher for women than for men, suggesting that, because the roles of females are more stressful than those of males, women tend to be more mentally ill. However, in their attempt to use role theories, both Chesler and Gove have ignored the interaction between sexual status and other factors, such as life stage, socioeconomic status, and racial and cultural background. Sociocultural factors may interact with sexual status to such an extent that psychiatric disturbance may increase in both males and females or in one sex but not in the other. Thus, it is difficult to draw general conclusions about sex differences in mental illness without first giving consideration to sociocultural background. The interaction between sexual status and sociocultural factors may also explain some inconsistent data in this research area.

The main objective of this chapter is to examine the relationship between sexual status and major adult psychopathology, with particular emphasis on sociocultural factors that might mediate this relationship. First considered are sex differences in mental illness, referring to the general categories of psychoses, neuroses, and personality disorders. The remaining sections deal with less general psychiatric entities, specifically schizophrenia, depression, phobias, anxiety, and conversion disorders. Although the main concern of this chapter is adult psychopathology, childhood disorders are also discussed in order to provide a point of departure for, and a focus for contrast with, disorders of adulthood.

SEX DIFFERENCES IN THE RATES OF MENTAL ILLNESS

Gove and Tudor (1973) examined statistics on rates of mental illness from 1956 to 1970 in different psychiatric facilities in the United States. They found that women have higher rates than men of psychoses and neuroses, but men have higher rates than women of brain syndromes and personality disorders. Gove and Herb (1974) compared boys and girls between ages 5 and 19 contacting treatment facilities and concluded that males tend to have higher rates than females of mental illness in childhood, but, for those aged 15–19, female rates tend to catch up with and exceed the male rates. In neuroses, there are more males than females between the ages of 5 and 9, but this tendency is reversed between ages 10 and 19. In the area of psychoses, however, males tend to have higher rates of the disorder than females from age 5 to age 19, although the difference between the sexes decreases with age. Similarly, personality disorders are consistently higher in males than in females among all age groups studied by Gove and Herb.

Among aged patients (65 and over) in the various types of psychiatric facilities, Busse and Pfeiffer (1973) reported that, in 1969 in the United States, females outnumbered males (in both admission and residency) except in admissions to state and county mental hospitals where the sexes were almost equally represented. The larger number of female patients among the elderly, especially in the hospital resident population, may be attributed in part to the longer life expectancy of females and the larger number of aged females in the population.

Community studies by Gove and Tudor (1973) after World War II reveal higher rates of mental illness for women than for men, supporting data from treatment facilities. However, in the pre–1950 investigations of sex differences, there was no consistent pattern (Dohrenwend and Dohrenwend, 1976).

Data from psychiatric facilities in Britain are similar to those in the United States, indicating higher rates for women than for men, both of psychoses and of neuroses (Smart, 1977). As is the case in the United States, personality disorders are more prevalent among men than among women in Britain.

Gove (1972) found that studies published after World War II consistently show that married women have higher rates of mental illness than married men. Comparing single women to single men, divorced women to divorced men, and widowed women to widowed men, the majority of studies found that men had higher rates of mental illness. Married women are more likely than married men to remain residents in mental institutions. Of the single and the divorced or widowed, men are more likely to be hospital residents. This is consistent with the findings that single, divorced, and widowed males have higher rates of mental illness than their female counterparts.

EXPLAINING SEX DIFFERENCES IN MENTAL ILLNESS

Four hypotheses have been put forward to explain the higher rate of mental illness among women than among men. First, women may report illness more often than men because it is culturally more acceptable for them to be ill. Second, the sick role is more compatible with female than with male role responsibilities. Third, social roles are imputed with differential power, and because the female role implies less power than the male role, women are more vulnerable to the ascription of madness and hospitalization than men (Al-Issa, 1980; Nathanson, 1975; Sarbin and Juhasz, 1978). Finally, the stress hypothesis suggests that because the female role is more stressful than the male role, women tend to have more illness. In contrast to the stress hypothesis, the first three hypotheses assume that the female rate of mental illness is comparable to that of the male, but because of their sex role, females become more involved with the psychiatric profession.

Sex Roles, Report of Symptoms, and Contact with Physicians

Phillips and Segal (1969) put forward the hypothesis that sexual status affects recognition and expression of illness as well as help-seeking behavior in response to illness. They found that women report significantly more psychological distress than men, even when the two groups are matched for physical symptoms. Phillips (1964) investigated the hypothesis that males are rejected more than females for the expression of psychiatric symptoms. He found that males are more strongly rejected than females when both sexes exhibit identical behavior and consult the same help course, such as a clergyman, physician, psychiatrist, or mental hospital. However, a later study did not support these data (Farina, Felner, and Boudreau, 1973).

Health service may be more accessible to women than to men because women's role obligations give them more time, and they incur less loss in attending health clinics (Nathanson, 1975). Studies indicate that the report of sickness is lower among married women than among those women who are single, widowed, or divorced. This finding supports the hypothesis that the more demanding situation of married women makes it difficult for them to contact clinics and to adopt the sick role (Nathanson, 1975). Women with young children or with a job outside the home tend to have a low rate of contact with physicians for psychiatric treatment (Brown, Bhrolchain, and Harris, 1975; Feld, 1963).

Sex Roles, Power, and Mental Illness

In an analysis of social roles, Sarbin (1969) differentiated between ascribed and achieved roles on the basis of the degree of choice the person exercises in entering them. Sarbin and Juhasz (1978) pointed out that, because the performance of the man is heavily weighed with occupational roles (achieved roles), and the behavior of the woman is biased toward the performance of family roles (ascribed roles), she is more vulnerable to be labeled "mad." The authors noted that, because of the male power that is associated with achieved roles, in a strained relationship between a male and a female over role enactment it is more likely that the female will be degraded to the status of a mental patient. This view is supported in a study by Linn (1961), demonstrating that female patients living with their spouses or parents are more likely to be hospitalized by these persons than are male patients in the same living situations. In their achieved roles husbands may be committed to a hospital if they get in trouble with the police (Linn, 1961), but the police are usually reluctant to initiate hospitalization because they do not regard committing a person to an institution as a proper law reinforcement. Strained relationships with employers may also lead to the hospitalization of men; however, Linn (1961) found that men are more likely to be dismissed from their jobs than to be sent to a mental hospital.

The Stress Hypothesis

Gove (1972) and Gove and Tudor (1973) suggested that marriage is more stressful for women than for men. Most women have only the one major role of housewife, whereas men occupy the roles of worker as well as family head. Even when a married woman works, her position is often less satisfactory than that of a man. This hypothesis, presented by Gove to explain the increase in mental illness in women after World War II, has been criticized by Dohrenwend and Dohrenwend (1974, 1976). The Dohrenwends noted that a broader definition of mental illness by American psychiatrists after World War II, as well as changes in research methods employed by investigators, may explain sex differences. Another argument against the stress hypothesis suggested by Gove is that it does not explain rural-urban incidence of psychoses and neuroses (Dohrenwend and Dohrenwend, 1974). The Dohrenwends pointed out that, according to the Gove hypothesis, there should be lower rates of mental illness in rural than in urban areas because the female role is more traditional and less stressful in rural areas. However, studies published after 1950 indicate higher rates of neurosis for women than for men in both rural and urban areas. In the area of psychosis, contrary to the Gove role hypothesis, women tend to have higher rates in rural areas, while men tend to show higher rates in urban areas. The Dohrenwends concluded that the tendency of women to have higher rates of neuroses and of men to have higher rates of personality disorders, irrespective of time and place, may require an explanation other than the amount of stress involved in sex roles.

SEX ROLES AND STANDARDS OF MENTAL HEALTH

One hypothesis used to explain sex differences in mental illness suggests that, because there are more desirable characteristics associated with masculinity than with femininity, the former may be conducive to better mental health. Desirable personality characteristics are more often ascribed by professionals and students to a healthy adult and to a healthy man than to a healthy woman (Broverman et al., 1970). In contrast, high femininity scores are associated with indices of maladjustment, such as high anxiety, low self-esteem, and low social acceptance (Cosentino and Heilbrun, 1964). Jones, Chernovetz, and Hansson (1978) found that the more adaptive, flexible, unconventional, and competent patterns of behavior were characteristic of masculine subjects, regardless of their gender. The scores of feminine males showed them to be more neurotic, lower in self-esteem, and more susceptible to alcoholic problems than masculine males. On the other hand, females who were high on masculinity were reported to be happier, more competent, and more adaptive than sex-typed females. La Torre (1978) also found that, for both sexes, high femininity scores are related to high neuroticism scores on the Eysenck Personality Inventory.

Rigid sex roles may affect mental health because they may not equip a person with the necessary skills to cope with situations arising from role discontinuity, in which role expectations at one stage of the life cycle are incompatible with those at another (Benedict, 1938). There is traditionally less role differentiation in childhood than in adulthood, with child rearing and training oriented more toward the male adult role than toward the female adult role. Therefore, many of the adjustment problems of women may be traced in part to inadequate childhood preparation for the female adult role (Barry, Bacon, and Child, 1957; Darley, 1976). However, with the recent de-differentiation of sex roles in adulthood, early school training for achievement and competition may create more adjustment problems for men in the face of tasks requiring "feminine" traits (Hoffman, 1977).

Role discontinuity is expected to become a major problem as changes are made in sex roles. Androgynous socialization may, in this case, equip persons with skills that enable them to handle changing role demands during the life cycle. Bem (1975) suggested that the androgynous person who acquires desirable masculine and feminine characteristics is more adaptive, more flexible, and less prone to psychopathology than a sex-typed person. Contrary to expectations, however, Jones et al. (1978) found that androgynous men have higher incidence of neurosis and problem drinking than do masculine men. Garnets and Pleck (1979) suggested that androgyny may indeed be associated with poor rather than with good adjustment because androgynous persons are still not accepted in society.

MASCULINITY-FEMININITY AND PATTERNS OF MENTAL ILLNESS

There have been many attempts, in both Western and non-Western contexts, to explain the symptoms of psychopathology in terms of an intensification of, or breaking away from, sex roles (Al-Issa, 1980; Pfeiffer, Chapter 8, this volume). Individuals may react to stress not only by exaggerating the negative characteristics of their own sex, but also by adopting the undesirable aspects of the opposite sex. This approach to psychopathology suggests two patterns; one is associated with masculine characteristics (a male pattern), and the other is associated with feminine characteristics (a female pattern).

There is a consistent tendency in both sexes to reveal the sexual pattern of their particular gender more than that of the opposite sex, thereby intensifying sex roles rather than breaking away from them. For example, statistics indicate higher rates of neuroses (a female pattern) among women and of personality disorders (a male pattern) among men. A study by Zigler and Phillips (1960) of hospitalized patients has shown that patterns of symptoms are related to sex. The researchers found more men than women in the categories of self-indulgence and turning against others (drinking, rape, robbery, and assault) but more women than men in the categories in self-deprivation, turning against the self (depression, suicidal attempts, bodily complaints, and tension), and avoidance of others (perplexity, apathy, and withdrawal). Childhood disorders reveal sex differences similar to those of adult psychopathology. Boys tend to show more disorders in which behavior is directed toward the environment (excessive approach behavior involving destructiveness, fighting, disruptiveness, and temper tantrums). Girls, on the other hand, tend to show disorders in which the behavior is directed toward the self (excessive avoidance involving anxiety, fear, physical complaints, and crying).

Sex role reversal of undesirable behavior seems to be less tolerated and to be considered more pathological than the intensification of an undesirable behavior that is compatible with one's own sex role. Costrich et al. (1975) found that college students considered men who revealed dependency on a therapist to have far more serious problems than women who expressed the same level of dependency. On the other hand, women who were aggressive in the therapy situation were considered more disturbed than men who showed the same behavior. Similarly, Coie, Pennington, and Buckley (1974) found that students perceived of aggressive females and males complaining of somatic symptoms (headache, nausea, shortness of breath, and heart pounding) as being more maladjusted than aggressive males and "sick" females.

SCHIZOPHRENIA

Sex Differences in the Rates of Schizophrenia

Overall rates of hospital admission for schizophrenia are the same for males as for females (Rosenthal, 1970). Community studies reveal inconsistent trends; some studies favor men, others favor women (Dohrenwend and Dohrenwend, 1969). There are, however, sex differences in the age pattern for hospital admission (Rosenthal, 1970). In childhood, adolescence, and early adulthood, males have higher admission rates than females. In middle age, however, this tendency is reversed (Rosenthal, 1970). This age pattern of admission, which is based on pre–World War II data in the United States, is evident in rates of admission to state and county mental hospitals in 1972 reported by Guttentag et al. (1977).

Community studies by H.B.M. Murphy (1977; Chapter 9, this volume) reveal that conflicts related to the fulfillment of sex role expectations and the achievement of the ideal prescribed by the culture are associated with sex differences in the age of schizophrenic breakdown. Cross-cultural and cross-temporal studies described by Murphy (Chapter 9, this volume) indicate that age of breakdown in women or men seems to coincide with stresses related to sex role enactment. Sexual status may also interact with ethnic background and educational level (Murphy, 1977). For example, among Canadians of British origin, males with a low level of education have a much higher rate of breakdown than their female counterparts; at a high level of education sex differences become small and almost diminish. Among Canadians of Dutch origin, a high level of education tends to increase the rate of disorder for females, but to decrease it for males.

Schizophrenic Symptoms, Sex Role, and Sex Identity

The available evidence does not reveal sex differences in hallucinations among hospitalized patients (Zigler and Phillips, 1960) or in the general population (Schwab, 1977). However, schizophrenic females tend to have more delusions than males (Lucas, Sainsbury, and Collins, 1962). The greatest sex differences in delusions occur between ages 40 and 50, when the incidence in the female is twice that in the male (Swanson, Bohmert, and Smith, 1970). Busse and Pfeiffer (1973) reported that paranoid psychoses in old age is markedly higher among females in all the studies reviewed, with males accounting for only 5%–25% of the patients with this diagnosis.

Lucas et al. (1962) found that schizophrenic women, particularly those who are married, tend to have significantly more sexual delusions, whereas schizophrenic men tend to exceed women in the frequency of delusions of inferiority. Weinstein (1962) found that sexual ideas are not very frequent in the delusions of native women in the Virgin Islands, in contrast to delusions of Western women. Weinstein thought that the low rate of sexual delusion among native women is related to social expectations; they do not expect to gain their objectives by playing the part of the helpless female or by acting in a seductive fashion.

Studies have suggested sex role reversal in schizophrenia. Cheek (1964) found that schizophrenic men tend to be more passive and withdrawn than normal men, whereas schizophrenic women seem to be more active and domineering than their normal counterparts. A community study of Puerto Rican families, conducted on the island by Rogler and Hollingshead (1965), revealed that schizophrenic husbands tend to withdraw and become dependent on their wives. The schizophrenic wives, on the other hand, tend to become belligerent and to defy their husbands.

Selective factors may explain sex differences in the behavior of hospitalized schizophrenic patients. The selective hypothesis is supported by Hafner, Quast, and Shea (1975), who found that externalizing males (i.e., antisocial, aggressive, and undercontrolled) are more often diagnosed for personality disorder, and that none had been given psychiatric treatment outside prison. However, the researchers also found the tendency to diagnose internalizing males (i.e., withdrawn, shy, and overcontrolled) as schizophrenic and to hospitalize them. In contrast, externalizing females are usually given the diagnosis of schizophrenia and are sent to a mental hospital rather than to a correctional institution. Internalizing females are also hospitalized, but are given the diagnosis of neurosis.

Rather than using clinical observations of reversal of sex roles, McClelland and Watt (1968) gave a role-preference test to normals and to schizophrenic patients of both sexes. The investigators found that schizophrenic males liked to play feminine roles more often than did normal males. As compared to normal females, schizophrenic females more often preferred to play masculine roles. A replication of this study by Ecker, Levine, and Zigler (1973) revealed no significant difference between normals and schizophrenics, throwing some doubt on the hypothesis of reversal of sex roles in schizophrenia.

McClelland and Watt (1968) used satisfaction with certain parts of the body as an index of the patient's sex identity. The researchers found that schizophrenic men, like normal women, were more concerned about how they looked than about their strength. Schizophrenic women simply showed less concern for all aspects of their bodies, whether masculine (strength) or feminine (appearance). Appearance is important for the female and it is understandable that long-term institutionalization may result in alienation from one's own body. That institutionalization (or the degree of chronicity) may be involved in sex identity is suggested in a study by Ecker et al. (1973), who did not find changes in body image among recently hospitalized schizophrenic males and females.

Kayton and Biller (1972) gave an Adjective Checklist and a Femininity Scale to male paranoid schizophrenics, neurotics, and normals. The diagnostic groups were significantly higher on femininity than the control group, suggesting a reversal of sex role, not only in schizophrenia but also in neurosis among male patients. Using the Bem Sex-Role Inventory, La Torre and Piper (1979) found that, as compared with normals, schizo-phrenic males obtained lower scores on femininity. Using the MMPI Mf (masculinity-femininity) scale, Petzel and Gynther (1969) found that both schizophrenic males and females obtained normal masculinity-femininity scores. Thus, the findings that schizophrenic patients show reversal of sex roles on masculinity-femininity measures are not consistent.

Studies of sex role and sex identity in schizophrenia are based on the conception of masculinity and femininity as bipolar rather than orthogonal. Bipolar-oriented studies ignore the category of persons who can be either high on both masculinity and femininity (androgynous) or low on both (undifferentiated) (Spence, Helmreich, and Stapp, 1975). Although reversal of sex role and sex identity is shown to be associated with schizophrenia, under situational and social changes rigid sex typing can also be maladaptive (Bem, 1975) and may result in schizophrenic breakdown (H.B.M. Murphy, Chapter 9, this volume). Also, reversal of sex roles and sex identity are not specific to schizophrenia; they are also associated with other disorders, such as neurosis (Kayton and Biller, 1972) and transsexualism.

Heterosexual interest and the presence of affect and delusions in schizophrenic females may suggest less impairment and better prognosis. This suggestion is supported by the finding that schizophrenic males tend to have more process schizophrenia, and schizophrenic females usually have more of the reactive type (Allon, 1971; Lane, 1968). Zigler, Levine, and Zigler (1977) found that paranoid and nonparanoid females obtained higher scores on social competence than their male counterparts. The tendency of schizophrenic females to be more reactive and to have better premorbid adjustment than schizophrenic males may explain their better social and occupational adjustment after hospital discharge (Raskin and Dyson, 1968).

DEPRESSION

In North American and in European countries, there are approximately two depressed females to each depressed male patient. Among depressed males there is a high proportion of severe depression, whereas among depressed females, there is a high proportion of mild depression. Weissman and Klerman (1977) reported that when only manic-depression is considered, the female-male ratio is reduced from 2:1 to 1.2:1. In a community study using a rating scale for depression, Warheit et al. (1973) found that severe depression was much more significantly associated with femaleness than with other variables, such as race and age; the strength of the association was second only to socioeconomic status. Brown and Harris (1978) reported that among females, working-class women have a much higher overall rate of chronic depression in all life stages than middle-class women (Chapter 5, this volume).

Rosenthal (1970) reported that the rate for depression is higher for females than for males between ages 10 and 50, especially from the twenties through the forties. Through the fifties and later, the rate is higher for males, although the difference is not as large as the difference at earlier ages. Admissions to state and county mental hospitals in the United States in 1972 indicate that the pre–World War II trends reported by Rosenthal have partly changed. Guttentag et al. (1977) reported that, between the ages of 18 and 24, the rate of admission is higher for females than for males, but this tendency is reversed between ages 25 and 34. From age 35 on, the rate of admission is consistently higher for females. The greatest sex differences occur between ages 45 and 64, with the rate of admission for females more than double that of males. Rosenthal's report of a high rate of admission during middle age, particularly for females, is confirmed in the 1972 data, although aged women rather than aged men tend to have more depression.

In contrast to hospital admission, community studies using questionnaires (Radloff, 1975) and clinical interviews (Brown et al., 1975) indicate that the peak of depression is during the twenties rather than during middle age. Furthermore, Radloff found that the rate of depression is higher for women than for men in all age groups, with a decline of depression scores after age 25 for both sexes.

The higher rate of depression for females than for males is not universal (Weissman and Klerman, 1977). Sex differences may also be affected, in part, by diagnostic bias (Fleiss et al., 1973).

Radloff (1975) found that among those persons married, divorced, and separated, women had higher mean depression scores than men. Married women were more depressed than married men, irrespective of age, level of education, and income. Furthermore, men in the never-married and widowed categories had higher mean depression scores than did comparable women. Among divorced patients, depressed females were more likely to have been depressed prior to their marital breakdown than depressed males (Briscoe and Smith, 1973).

Hammen and Peters (1978) found a positive relationship between femininity scores and depression. There are also sex differences in the expression of depressive symptoms. Hammen and Padesky (1977) found that depressed men tend to show inability to cry, social withdrawal, somatic preoccupation, a sense of failure, weight loss, and sleep disturbance. Women, on the other hand, were characterized by lack of self-confidence, by self-dislike, and by self-deprecation. Men's attempts to suppress their depressive response and their greater focus on physical and cognitive symptoms may lead them to construe their problems not as depression, but as overwork or physical illness, and thus they may avoid psychiatric treatment.

Sexual Status and Depression

The high rate of depression among women suggests that they are more exposed than men to risk factors leading to depression. It also raises the possibility that both sexes may be equally exposed to risk factors, but women may be more susceptible to them than men. Using 17 scales to rate precipitating factors in depression, Radloff and Rae (1979) found that females scored twice as high as males in the direction associated with depression, which suggests that women are more exposed to situations associated with depressive breakdown. The researchers also found that not all factors equally relate to depression for males and for females. For example, education was more important for married females than for married males, income was more important for males than for females living with spouse but with no children, and getting together with friends and neighbors was more important for females than for males living with no spouse. However, age (the younger the person, the more depressed) and physical illness were similarly associated with depression for both sexes.

Brown et al. (1977) noted that mother loss before the age of 11, rather than loss of the mother after this age or loss of any other relative including the father, increases the risk of depression. Birtchnell (1970) also found that among the severely depressed there is more prior loss of the mother among women than among men.

Radloff and Munroe (1978) reviewed the evidence indicating that helplessness, which is associated with depression, is more prevalent among females than among males. The researchers noted that in female stereotypes, lack of power inside and outside the home and deficient instrumental learning are compatible with the development of helplessness and depression. Radloff and Munroe concluded that breaking away from female characteristics of helplessness should lead to low levels of depression. Their argument is supported by the data, which indicate that women who pursue advanced education, high status career, and high income, or women who remain unmarried, have a relatively low level of depression (Radloff, 1975).

PHOBIAS AND ANXIETIES

Sex Differences in the Rate of Phobias and Anxieties

Kagan (1977) reported that females are more prone than males to fears in infancy. Females become more upset by novel stimuli and are more likely to cry in a strange or an unusual situation (such as the laboratory). Studies of fears of strangers and fears during separation from the mother seem to be inconsistent (Jacklin, Maccoby, and Dick, 1973; Lewis and Brooks, 1974). Among preschool children, boys have more trouble adjusting than girls, and they express more distress during the first week in a play group (Smith, 1974).

When the overall frequency of fears in childhood is investigated, there are no clear-cut sex differences. A study of specific fears in children from age 1½ to age 14 by Macfarlane, Allen, and Honzik (1954) reveals that the frequency of fears is slightly lower in girls than in boys (an average of 25.4 for girls and 33.7 for boys). However, the fears of girls undergo a dramatic increase during adolescence. For example, Macfarlane et al. found that girls have five times more fears than boys at age 13.

Fears among adult females are prevalent in normal persons, in hospitalized patients, and in patients in psychotherapy, regardless of the kind of self-report questionnaires used to rate fear (Hersen, 1973). Among clinical cases, 84% of agoraphobic patients are females, of whom 89% are married (Fodor, 1974). Although rare among adults, animal phobia tends to appear predominantly in women (Marks, 1969). Social phobias and specific phobias tend to be equally distributed among the sexes (Marks, 1969, 1977). Studies of sex differences in the rates of obsessive phobia are inconsistent (Beech, 1974).

Sex Roles and Phobia

Feminine persons tend to score higher than masculine persons on anxiety measures (Cosentino and Heilbrun, 1964). Similarly, data suggest that conformity to the traditional female sex role, such as being a housewife, tends to increase the rates of phobias (Fodor, 1974).

Case studies support the view that the phobic stimulus may trigger a previously learned avoidance-dependent pattern of behavior, which is compatible with sex stereotypes and the early training of women (Radloff and Munroe, 1978). Cases of women who develop agoraphobia just after marriage (Symonds, 1971) suggest that the stimuli that trigger the phobic response are selective and are related to the housewife role (fear of going out in the street, fear of visiting the supermarket and the beauty salon, and fear of harming one's own children).

Brown et al. (1975) observed that the high rate of anxiety and obsessional states among women in North Uist seems to be related to the traditional place of women in the island community. In this rural community, women traditionally are given a meaningful family role, which reduces vulnerability to depression, but also creates conflicts and increases anxiety by forcing women to conform to the housewife role. Similarly, another community study of Australian Aborigines by Cawte (1972) indicated a consistently higher rate of anxiety and fears among women than among men, reflecting the lack of self-sufficiency in women and the exclusion of women from learning those skills needed to master their environment in the aboriginal culture.

Maccoby and Jacklin (1974) suggested that the content of anxiety scales deals with anxieties that affect more females than males. There are, however, only very few items in the scales dealing with boys' specific fears (such as fear of public humiliation or failure and fear of appearing cowardly). Manosevitz and Lanyon (1965) found that women experience more intense fear in situations involving social and interpersonal relationships, whereas men experience more intense fear in situations involving failure. Fear of failure is particularly experienced by men in a competitive achievement situation.

CONVERSION DISORDERS

Historical reports as well as more recent studies indicate that the diagnosis of hysteria is predominantly attached to female patients (Veith, 1965). A survey of studies in Western and non-Western cultures between 1872 and 1972 revealed that epidemic hysteria tends to be almost exclusively a female disturbance, with the exception of hysteria appearing in towns (Sirois, 1974).

It has been suggested that there is a relationship between the adoption of illness behavior and the lack of alternative means of controlling and changing the environment (Bart, 1968; Mechanic, 1974). Because females and persons of low socioeconomic status have less control of their environment (Radloff and Monroe, 1978), they are expected to develop more conversion reactions than other persons. Bart (1968) found that lower-class women with low educational level (or women from rural areas) are more likely to be diagnosed as hysterical. Community studies indicate that members of Class V (lower class) tend to express their problems as somatic symptoms rather than as psychological and interpersonal difficulties, and are thus labeled "hysterical" more often than are members of other social classes (Hollingshead and Redlich, 1958; Myers and Roberts, 1959). Cross-cultural incidence of epidemic hysteria, which mainly afflicts young women, tends to concentrate in the lower socioeconomic groups (Sirois, 1974).

In a physician-patient interaction, the patient may exaggerate or distort his or her health state, but the physician's perspective also determines whether the patient's physical complaints eventuate in the diagnosis of conversion disorder or physical disease. Bart (1968) found that 52% of the psychiatric patients on the neurology service had had a hysterectomy, as compared to only 21% of the patients on the psychiatric service. Psychiatrists who work in general hospitals consistently report conversion symptoms to be common. Their colleagues in the same institutions who have limited specialist experience report fewer conversion symptoms (Mayou, 1975). The preoccupation of physicians (predominantly males) with one particular illness tends to initiate epidemic hysteria in hospital settings among female nurses (McEvedy and Beard, 1970). Weintraub and Aronson (1974) reported that in psychoanalytical practice, the diagnosis of hysteria, which is given over four times more often to women than to men, is made significantly more often by male than by female analysts.

Physicians reinforce the sick role in females more than in males by explaining females' social problems in psychiatric terms and by prescribing psychotropic drugs for these problems (such as loneliness, marital and financial problems, and problems with children). A review of studies on the use of psychotropic drugs by Al-Issa (1980) reveals that in North America and in European countries the ratio of females to males using the drugs is 2:1. Women are more likely than men to take prescribed medication, even when the two sexes report the same symptoms. Furthermore, these sex differences in drug usage disappear when the rates of men and women using over-the-counter drugs are compared, indicating the importance of the role of physicians in overprescribing drugs for women. Weisenberg (1977) pointed out that women receive pain drugs earlier in treatment, whereas men receive them later, on the assumption that men are supposed to tolerate pain. Women are also more likely to be given analgesics on the staff's own initiative, whereas men must first complain about their pain. These sex differences in the use of drugs are not related to sex differences in sensitivity to pain because studies indicate no sex differences in pain threshold.

SUMMARY AND CONCLUSION

Most studies published after World War II have reported that the rates of mental illness are higher for women than for men. This sex differential is particularly evident in studies of neuroses. Women tend to have more depression, fear, phobia, anxiety, and conversion disorders. It is only in the realm of personality disorders that the rates for men are higher than those for women. Data reveal no consistent sex differences in obsessive-compulsive disorders and in schizophrenia in the general population. There are, however, sex differences in the symptoms of schizophrenia, depression, anxiety, and fear; the content of these symptoms seems to be related to sex roles.

Role obligation, stress, the tendency to report symptoms, and social and economic power are factors suggested to explain sex differences in mental illness. However, these factors alone cannot explain the higher rate of personality disorders and antisocial behavior in men throughout the life cycle and across time and space. Animal and human data demonstrating that males are almost consistently more aggressive than females suggest a biological interpretation (Gray, 1971; Maccoby and Jacklin, 1974; Rohner, 1976). From the available evidence, Rohner concluded that there is a biological predisposition for males to behave more aggressively than females, although this differential in readiness to respond aggressively is subject to substantial modification through learning and experience.

A major hypothesis in the study of sex roles and psychopathology is that psychiatric syndromes represent either an exaggeration or a reversal of sex role prescriptions. On the one hand, personality disorders are regarded as an exaggeration of undesirable characteristics associated with the male role. On the other hand, depression, phobia, fears, and conversion disorders are considered an intensification of female characteristics, such as inactivity, helplessness, submissiveness, and dependency.

Developmental studies suggest that many aspects of socialization, particularly those related to sex role, may be involved in either the exaggeration or the reversal of sex roles. One aspect of socialization that has been emphasized by researchers is role discontinuity. It has been suggested that, in a father-absent family in which a boy may acquire a feminine identity in childhood but must shift to a masculine identity in adulthood, compensatory masculinity may develop. Bacon, Child, and Barry (1963) found that both theft and personal crimes, such as assault, rape, and murder, are more common in societies with households that provide the least contact with the father. Similarly, Babl (1979) considered exaggerated masculinity to be a learned method of reducing anxiety by socially validating one's appropriate sex-role identity.

In contrast, Burton and Whiting (1967) investigated cross-culturally the relationship between early socialization experience and sex-role reversal in the male. They found that, in societies where the child's early social interactions are entirely confined to the mother or to another female, the child, both in infancy and childhood, perceives the female status as privileged. Male children will thus covertly practice the female role and may become predisposed to sex-role reversal later in life. One indication of sex-role reversal in societies in which children have exclusive contact with the mother during childhood is the practice of *couvade* among adult males, in which the husband goes to bed and follows the procedure for childbearing during the same time that the wife is in labor (see also Pfeiffer, Chapter 8, this volume).

Because crime and aggression are male rather than female phenomena, most studies of these behaviors have been concerned with the exaggeration of masculine behavior by men. However, a follow-up study by Block (1973) revealed that socialization and femininity levels of both males and females may be involved in the exaggeration or deviation from sex roles. The ideal view of masculinity-femininity in a society and the opportunity available for exposure to learning models (males and females) in childhood are crucial to the adoption of certain sex roles in adulthood.

REFERENCES

Al-Issa, I. 1980. The Psychopathology of Women. Prentice-Hall, Inc., Englewood Cliffs, N. J.

Allon, R. 1971. Sex, race, socioeconomic status, social mobility, and process-reactive ratings of schizophrenics. J. Nerv. Ment. Dis. 153:343–350.

Babl, J. D. 1979. Compensatory masculine responding as a function of sex role. J. Consult. Clin. Psychol. 47:252–257.

Bacon, M. K., Child, I. L., and Barry, H., III. 1963. A cross-cultural study of correlates of crime. J. Abnorm. Soc. Psychol. 66:291–300.

Barry, H., III, Bacon, M. K., and Child, I. L. 1957. A cross-cultural survey of some sex differences in socialization. J. Abnorm. Soc. Psychol. 55:327–332.

Bart, P. B. 1968. Social structure and vocabularies of discomfort: What happened to female hysteria. J. Health Soc. Behav. 9:188–193.

Beech, H. R. 1974. Approaches to understanding obsessional states. In: H. R. Beech (ed.), Obsessional States. Methuen, Inc., London.

Bem, S. L. 1975. Sex role adaptability: One consequence of psychological androgyny. J. Pers. Soc. Psychol. 31:634–643.

Benedict, R. 1938. Continuities and discontinuities in cultural conditioning. Psychiatry 1:161–167.

Birtchnell, J. 1970. Depression in relation to early and recent parent death. Br. J. Psychiatry 116:299–306.

Block, J. H. 1973. Conceptions of sex role: Some cross-cultural and longitudinal perspectives. Am. Psychol. 28:512–526.

Block, J. H. 1976. Issues, problems and pitfalls in assessing sex differences: A critical review of the psychology of sex differences. Merrill-Palmer Q. 22:283–308.

Briscoe, C. W., and Smith, M. D. 1973. Depression and marital turmoil. Arch. Gen. Psychiatry 29:812–817.

Broverman, I. K., Broverman, D. M., Clarkson, F. E., Rosenkrantz, P., and Vogel, S. R. 1970. Sex role stereotypes and clinical judgements of mental health. J. Consult. Clin. Psychol. 34:1–7.

Brown, G. W., and Harris, T. O. 1978. Social Origins of Depression. A Study of Psychiatric Disorders in Women. Tavistock Publications, London.

Brown, G. W., Bhrolchain, M. N., Harris, T. O. 1975. Social class and psychiatric disturbance among women in an urban population. Sociology 9:225–254.

Brown, G. W., Davidson, S., Harris, T. O., Maclean, U., Pollock, S., and Prudo, R. 1977. Psychiatric disorder in London and North Uist. Soc. Sci. Med. 11:366–377.

Burton, R. V., and Whiting, J.W.M. 1967. The absent father and cross-sex identity. Merrill-Palmer Q. 7:85–95.

Busse, E. W., and Pfeiffer, E. 1973. Mental Illness in Later Life. American Psychiatric Association, Washington, D.C.

Cawte, J. 1972. Cruel, Poor, and Brutal Nations. The University Press of Hawaii, Honolulu.

Cheek, F. E. 1964. A serendipitious finding: Sex roles and schizophrenia. J. Abnorm. Soc. Psychol. 69:392–400.

Chesler, P. 1972. Women and Madness. Doubleday & Co., Inc., New York.

Coie, J. D., Pennington, D. F., and Buckley, H. H. 1974. Effects of situational stress and sex roles on attributions of psychological disorders. J. Consult. Clin. Psychol. 42:559–568.

Cosentino, F., and Heilbrun, A. B. 1964. Anxiety correlates of sex-role identity in college students. Psychol. Rep. 14:729–730.

Costrich, N., Feinstein, J., Kidder, L., Marecek, J., and Pascale, L. 1975. When stereotypes hurt: Three studies of penalties for sex-role reversals. J. Exp. Soc. Psychol. 11:520–530.

Darley, S. A. 1976. Big-time careers for the little woman: A dual-role dilemma. J. Soc. Issues 32:85–98.

Dohrenwend, B. P., and Dohrenwend, B. S. 1969. Social Status and Psychological Disorders. John Wiley & Sons, Inc., New York.

Dohrenwend, B. P., and Dohrenwend, B. S. 1974. Social and cultural influences on psychopathology. Annu. Rev.Psychol. 25:417–452.

Dohrenwend, B. P., and Dohrenwend, B. S. 1976. Sex differences in psychiatric disorders. Am. J. Sociol. 81:1447–1471.

Ecker, J., Levine, J., and Zigler, E. 1973. Impaired sex-role identification in schizophrenia expressed in the comprehension of humor stimuli. J. Psychol. 83:67–77.

Farina, A., Felner, R., and Boudreau, L. 1973. Reactions of workers to male and female mental patient job applicants. J. Consult. Clin. Psychol. 41:363–372.

Feld, S. 1963. Feelings of adjustment. In: F. I. Nye and L. W. Hoffman (eds.), The Employed Mother. Rand-McNally, & Co., Chicago.

Fodor, I. G. 1974. The phobic syndrome in women: Implications for treatment. In: V. Franks and M. Burtle (eds.), Women in Therapy. Brunner/Mazel, Inc., New York.

Garnets, L., and Pleck, J. H. 1979. Sex role identity, androgyny, and sex role transcendence. Psychol. Women Q. 3:270–279.

Gove, W. R. 1972. The relationship between sex roles, marital status, and mental illness. Soc. Forces 51:34–44.

Gove, W. R., and Herb, T. R. 1974. Stress and mental illness among the young: A comparison of the sexes. Soc. Forces 53:256–265.

Gove, W. R., and Tudor, J. F. 1973. Adult sex roles and mental illness. Am. J. Sociol. 78:812–835.

Gray, J. A. 1971. Sex differences in emotional behaviour in mammals including man: Endocrine bases. Acta Psychol. 35:29–46.

Guttentag, M., Salasin, S., Legge, W. W., and Bray, H. 1977. Sex differences in the utilization of publicly supported mental health facilities: The puzzle of depression. National Institute of Mental Health report MH 26523–02. Washington, D. C.

Hafner, A. J., Quast, W., and Shea, M. J. 1975. The adult adjustment of one thousand psychiatric and pediatric patients: Initial findings from a twenty-five year follow-up. In: R. D. Wirt, G. Winokur, and M. Roff (eds.), Life History Research in Psychopathology. Vol. 4. University of Minnesota Press, Minneapolis.

Hammen, C. L., and Padesky, C. A. 1977. Sex differences in the expression of depression. Paper presented at the meeting of the American Psychological Association, August 25–30, San Francisco, California.

Hammen, C. L., and Peters, S. D. 1978. Interpersonal consequences of depression: Responses to men and women enacting a depressed role. J. Abnorm. Psychol. 87:322–332.

Hersen, M. 1973. Self-assessment of fear. Behav. Ther. 4:241–257.

Hoffman, M. L. 1977. Personality and social development. Annu. Rev. Psychol. 28:295–321.

Hollingshead, A. B., and Redlich, F. C. 1958. Social Class and Mental Illness. John Wiley & Sons, Inc., New York.

Jacklin, C. N., Maccoby, E. E., and Dick, A. E. 1973. Barrier behavior and toy preference: Sex differences (and their absence) in the year-old child. Child Dev. 44:196–200.

Jones, W. H., Chernovetz, M. E., O'C., and Hansson, R. O. 1978. The enigma of androgyny: Differential implications for males and females? J. Consult. Clin. Psychol. 46:298–313.

Kagan, J. 1977. Psychology of sex differences. In: F. A. Beach (ed.), Human Sexuality in Four Perspectives. John Hopkins Press, Baltimore.

Kayton, R., and Biller, H. B. 1972. Sex-role development and psychopathology in adult males. J. Consult. Clin. Psychol. 38:208–210.

Lane, E. A. 1968. The influence of sex and race on process-reactive ratings of schizophrenics. J. Psychol. 68:15–20.

La Torre, A. 1978. Gender role and psychological adjustment. Arch. Sex. Behav. 7:89–96.

La Torre, R. A., and Piper. 1979. Gender identity and gender role in schizophrenia. J. Abnorm. Psychol. 88:68–72.

Lewis, M., and Brooks, J. 1974. Self, other, and fear: Infants' reactions to people. In: M. Lewis and L. S. Rosenblum (eds.), The Origins of Fear. John Wiley & Sons, Inc., New York.

Linn, E. L. 1961. Agents, timing, and events leading to mental hospitalization. Hum. Organization 20:90–98.

Lucas, C. J., Sainsbury, P., and Collins, G. 1962. A social and clinical study of delusions in schizophrenia. J. Ment. Sci. 108:747–758.

McClelland, D. C., and Watt, N. F. 1968. Sex role alienation in schizophrenia. J. Abnorm. Psychol. 74:226–238.

Maccoby, E. E., and Jacklin, N. J. 1974. The Psychology of Sex Differences. Stanford University Press, Stanford, Calif.

McEvedy, C. P., and Beard, A. W. 1970. Royal free epidemic of 1955: A reconsideration. Br. Med. J. 1:7–11.

Macfarlane, J., Allen L., and Honzik, M. 1954. A Developmental Study of the Behavior Problems of Normal Children. University of California Press, Berkeley.

Manosevitz, M., and Lanyon, R. E. 1965. Fear survey schedule: A normative study. Psychol. Rep. 17:699–703.

Marks, I. M. 1969. Fears and Phobias. Academic Press, Inc., New York.

Marks, I. 1977. Phobias and obsessions: Clinical phenomena in search of laboratory models. In: J. D. Maser and M. E. P. Seligman (eds.), Psychopathology: Experimental Models. W. H. Freeman & Company, San Francisco.

Mayou, R. 1975. The social setting of hysteria. Br. J. Psychiatry 127:466–469.

Mechanic, D. 1974. Politics, Medicine, and Social Science. John Wiley & Sons, Inc., New York.

Murphy, H. B. M. 1977. Male/female differences in psychiatric morbidity; Their use in transcultural studies. Paper presented at IX Congreso Latinamericano di Psiquiatria (APAL), February, La Habana, Cuba.

Myers, J. K., and Roberts, B. H. 1959. Family and Class Dynamics in Mental Illness. John Wiley & Sons, Inc., New York.

Nathanson, C. 1975. Illness and the feminine role: A theoretical review. Soc. Sci. Med. 9:57 62.

Petzel, T. P., and Gynther, M. S. 1969. A comparison of psychiatric diagnosis and behavioral classification as criteria for differentiating psychiatric patients. J. Gen. Psychol. 80:219 227.

Phillips, D. L. 1964. Rejection of the mentally ill: The influence of behavior and sex. Am. Sociol. Rev. 29:679 687.

Phillips, D. L., and Segal, B. E. 1969. Sexual status and psychiatric symptoms. Am. Sociol. Rev. 34:58 72.

Radloff, L. S. 1975. Sex differences in depression. Sex Roles 1:249–265.

Radloff, L. S., and Munroe, M. K. 1978. Sex differences in helplessness—with implications for depression. In: L. S. Hansen and R. S. Rapoza (eds.), Career Development and Counselling of Women. Charles C Thomas, Publisher, Springfield, Ill.

Radloff, L. S., and Rae, D. S. 1979. Susceptibility and precipitating factors in depression: Sex differences and similarities. J. Abnorm. Psychol. 88:174 181.

Raskin, M., and Dyson, W. L. 1968. Treatment problems leading to readmission of schizophrenic patients. Ach. Gen. Psychiatry 19:356–360.

Rogler, L. H , and Hollingshead, A. B. 1965. Trapped: Families and Schizophrenia. John Wiley & Sons, Inc., New York.

Rohner, R. P. 1976. Sex differences in aggression: Phylogenetic and enculturation perspectives. Ethos 4:57 72.

Rosenthal, D. 1970. Genetic Theory and Abnormal Behavior. McGraw-Hill Book Company, New York.

Sarbin, T. R. 1969. The scientific status of the mental illness metaphor. In: S. C. Plog and R. B. Edgerton (eds.), Changing Perspectives of Mental Illness. Holt, Rinehart & Winston, Inc., New York.

Sarbin, T. R., and Juhasz, J. B. 1978. The social psychology of hallucinations. J. Ment. Imagery 2:117 144.

Schwab, M. E. 1977. A study of reported hallucinations in a Southeastern county. Ment. Health Soc. 4:344 354.

Sirois, F. 1974. Epidemic hysteria. Acta Psychiatr. Scand. Supplementum 252.

Smart, C. 1977. Women, Crime, and Criminality: A Feminist Critique. Routledge & Kegan Paul, London.

Smith, K. P. 1974. Social and situational determinants of fear in the play group. In: M. Lewis and L. A. Rosenblum (eds.), The Origins of Fear. John Wiley & Sons, Inc., New York.

Spence, J. T., Helmreich, R., and Stapp, J. 1975. Ratings of self and peers on sex role attributes and their relation to self-esteem and conceptions of masculinity and femininity. J. Pers. Soc. Psychol. 32:29–39.

Swanson, D. W., Bohmert, P. J. , and Smith, J. A. 1970. The Paranoid. Little, Brown & Company, Boston.

Symonds, A. 1971. Phobias after marriage: Women's declaration of dependence. Am. J. Psychoanal. 31:144 152.

Veith, I. 1965. Hysteria: The History of a Disease. University of Chicago Press, Chicago.

Warheit, G. J. , Holzer, C. E., III, and Schwab, J. 1973. An analysis of social class and racial differences in depressive symptomatology: A community study. J. Health Soc. Behav. 14:291–299.

Weinstein, E. A. 1962. Social Aspects of Delusions: Psychiatric study of the Virgin Islands. Free Press, New York.

Weintraub, W., and Aronson, H. 1974. Patients in psychoanalysis: Some findings related to sex and religion. Am. J. Orthopsychiatry 44:102–108.

Weisenberg, M. 1977. Pain and pain control. Psychol. Bull. 84:1008–2044.

Weissman, M. M., and Klerman, G. L. 1977. Sex differences and the epidemiology of depression. Arch. Gen. Psychiatry 34:98–111.

Zigler, E., and Phillips, L. 1960. Social effectiveness and symptomatic behaviors. J. Abnorm. Psychol. 61:231–238.

Zigler, E., Levine, J., and Zigler, B. 1977. Premorbid social competence and paranoid-nonparanoid status in female schizophrenic patients. J. Nerv. Ment. Dis. 164:333–339.

Chapter 8

Culture-Bound Syndromes

Wolfgang M. Pfeiffer

THE RELATION OF CULTURE-BOUND SYNDROMES
TO THE INTERNATIONAL NOSOLOGICAL SYSTEM

It may seem natural to contrast culture-bound syndromes, as clinical pictures of limited distribution, with universally distributed psychiatric diseases. This has, however, proven to be misleading, because culture-bound syndromes are not nosological entities that could be viewed as existing separately alongside the illnesses listed in the psychiatric diagnostic system. Rather, it is a matter of the particular viewpoint adopted, whether a person's being ill is given a conventional psychiatric label or identified as a culture-bound syndrome.

Starting out with a general nosological system like the international diagnostic scheme of the WHO, no essential problems arise in the attempt to fit even patients showing a culture-bound syndrome into one of the conventional psychiatric diagnoses. When we look, however, for critical areas and typical reaction patterns in a certain culture, we meet with more or less culture-specific syndromes, for which there exist local interpretations and terms. If we finally approach patients from the angle of individual life history, which is central to insight-oriented psychotherapy, then both the cultural and the nosological approach retreat in favor of the uniqueness of each human destiny.

Many attempts have been made to integrate culture-specific syndromes into the psychiatric nosological system, but these attempts were doomed to failure, if only because in these two approaches symptoms are perceived and ordered in qualitatively different ways. Admittedly, some

This paper was originally published as *Kulturgebundene Syndrome* in W. M. Pfeiffer and W. Schoene (Eds.), *Psychopathologie im Kulturvergleich* (Ferdinand Enke-Verlag, Stuttgart, 1980). Permission to reproduce this English version is gratefully acknowledged to the original publishers.

terms from the sphere of culture-bound syndromes have found their way into psychiatric classifications. They refer primarily to special forms of hypnoidal alterations of consciousness, phobias, and compulsive syndromes (amok, latah, kayak-angst, purity mania), i.e., well-definable phenomena which, with the aid of each respective concept, can be given a somewhat unequivocal label. This has not, however, succeeded without a corresponding stylization, of which the concept amok offers a good example.

In the Indonesian language, *amok* denotes an aggressive fury and is applicable to an agitated person (regardless of the state of consciousness), to an animal, or to natural forces. With the introduction of European criminal law, however, the necessity arose to differentiate between acts of violence committed in a state of clear consciousness and those carried out in a state of confusion. This led to the adoption and specification of the concept amok (Van Wulfften Palthe, 1948, p. 270), which was thus included among the hypnoidal states that imply legal exemption, without influencing the much more general meaning of the popular linguistic usage to any crucial extent.

Among the diagnoses of the psychiatric nosological system on the one hand, and the designations of the culture-bound syndromes on the other, there are assembled categories of qualitatively so diverse a nature that they cannot be systematically integrated but by distortion. Thus, a psychiatric clinical picture can be interpreted in a number of ways by healers of the same culture. For instance, Indonesian native healers could explain a case of chronic schizophrenia as mental exhaustion, as love sickness, as a bewitched state, or as the result of a confrontation with a ghost or of a curse placed on the family. On the other hand, a culture-bound syndrome involving the idea of sperm loss, common to Asian Indian folk medicine, can represent a variety of medical disturbances, such as malnutrition, chronic pyelitis, bland psychosis, and reaction to conflict (Obeysekere, 1976).

DIFFERENTIAL DIMENSIONS OF THE CULTURAL INFLUENCE ON PATHOGENESIS AND PATHOPLASTY

Even when one views the culture-bound syndromes separately, it is not possible to arrange them according to uniform system. This is because cultural influences contribute differentially to the causation, formation, and interpretation of psychopathological syndromes. Four dimensions can be discerned here:

1. culture-specific areas of stress
2. culture-specific shaping of conduct
3. culture-specific interpretations
4. culture-specific interventions

In relation to all culture-bound syndromes, all four dimensions deserve attention, even though they may carry varying degrees of importance. Thus, the following presentation of culture-bound syndromes is arranged according to these dimensions, as each of them is dominant in the particular case.

Culture-Specific Areas of Stress

A culture can be described according to its areas of conflict arising from typical spheres of demands and denials. Critical stresses are created not only by peculiarities of the family and societal structure, and by ecological conditions, but also by the extreme demands that a society places on many of its members (as in armed confrontations, or because of technical advances).

Family and Societal Structure   The best-known example of pathogenic stress within the intimate sphere is the arranged marriages of the Islamic countries and of India. For the bride, often still a child herself, such a marriage means the first separation from the parental home, and, at the same time, a meeting with an indifferent, often internally opposed partner who becomes the cause of an unprepared for sexual experience, which is often traumatic. Added to this is the foreignness of the situation and the feeling of being delivered up to the husband, and particularly to his family. Reports from North Africa describe nuptial psychoses (Pisztora, 1972; Sutter et al., 1959), in which the patient shows a hypochondriacal, confused, and hysterical character. In India, suicidal acts and possession states are stressed in similar circumstances (Pandey, 1968; Teja, Kanna, and Subrahmanyam, 1970).

The Oedipus complex also has a close connection with the familial structure. Thus, the complex is particularly noticeable in societies that stress paternal authority. It is of special importance to young men, who are facing the problem of their own potency; this leads to other disturbances, such as sperm loss in the Indian sphere or koro in the Chinese sphere (Carstairs, 1956; Rin, 1966). In matriarchal family systems where the father lives outside the family, the Oedipus complex plays a minor role or is totally missing; instead, the authority conflict is directed toward the head of the family, for instance, the mother's older brother, as Malinowski (1927) has noted for the Trobriand Islands. Parallel observations were made by the present author among the Minangkabau of Sumatra.

The Influence of Ecological Conditions   Under extreme ecological conditions people are forced to seek their subsistence in situations that strain the limits of their stress endurance. The kayak-angst of the Eskimos (Gussow, 1963) offers a typical example of this. In western Greenland, the Eskimos go far out to sea in kayaks, little one-man boats, to hunt for seal. When they sit immobile for hours waiting for a seal to surface, many fall victim to an attack of vertigo. They feel dazed and lose awareness of the horizontal position of the boat. In panic-stricken anguish and with violent vegetative reactions they can become so helpless that they have to be guided to land by their companions. The disturbance often takes a progressive course, so that a large number of victims are unable to continue in the kayak hunt. Because the syndrome is tied to the culture-specific situation of the kayak hunt, it is not evident in other cultures, and, in fact, is disappearing now that this form of hunting is generally being given up by the Eskimos.

According to psychiatric diagnostics, kayak-angst is a phobic syndrome that is related to sensory deprivation, which in turn results in an impediment of spatial orientation and perhaps also a decrease in vigilance. It should be noted that kayak-angst is similar to the vertigo at high altitudes commonly experienced in Western cultures.

It is not only extreme natural conditions that bring an individual to the threshold of stress endurance, and thereby typically give rise to syndromes of failing; technical development also causes such states. Thus, phobic anxiety manifestations can occur on planes as well as in elevators. Sensory deprivation with impeded spatial orientation poses a problem in aviation, particularly in space flights. The highway trance of car drivers is caused by a disturbance in alertness brought on by sustained concentration and a monotonous environment.

Culture-Specific Emphasis in Individual Situations   Many situations are given their critical importance through the style and the meaning allocated them by the culture. Thus, the territorial system is a particular source of conflict to individuals at the cultural level of hunter and gatherer. Cawte (1976) in 1968 observed a psychosomatic syndrome among natives of the northern Australian coast. The syndrome is called Malgri and is linked with violations of the territorial system. Malgri afflicts a person only when he has crossed the territorial limits in a twofold manner. First, he must be outside the territory of his group; second, he must leave land and enter the sea without having previously followed the purification rules required at the crossing over from one great natural element to another. In such a case the totem-like guardian of the coastal strip in question, e.g., the spirit of the sea eagle, is thought to be shot like a ball into the abdomen of the careless person, thus leading to violent abdominal pain with nausea and a distended abdomen. Only by the support of the native group engaging in prolonged singing and by the use of a string can the spirit be conducted from the body of the stricken person and into the sea.

In a technical civilization, the educational system should be viewed as such an area of stress. Stress gets critical expression in examination and grade anxiety. Certainly at least our middle classes have managed to attune themselves extensively to these stresses. In countries that have only recently changed over to this competitively oriented educational system, much greater problems arise. First, the young person lacks the appropriate preparation for the novel stresses; second, success is often identified with self-worth to such an extent that failure becomes a catastrophe. Thus, learning disturbances are already evident at the approach of examinations in hypochondriacally colored head-and-eye symptoms (Brain-Fag-Syndrome) (Prince, 1960). In the examination situation proper, phobic reactions with mental blocking and vegetative manifestations are frequent. Finally, the number of suicidal acts after a failed examination is frighteningly high in Japan (De Vos, 1960) and India (Panday, 1968).

Whereas so far we have spoken of the stress character of performance rating and competition, turning to Indonesia we find the prime emphasis on correct behavior. Accordingly, it is primarily situations of embarrassment and disgrace (malu-affect, corresponding to loss of face) that form the basis for abnormal reactions.

Finally, a certain role can become so exaggerated by the culture that it becomes unbearable for some of its members. Thus, among Prairie Indians like the Sioux, the sex role of the male focused on aggressive warfare to such an extent that men again and again chose to assume the sex role of a woman—the so-called berdache (Hassrick, 1964).

Thus, we can discern as the first aspect of culture-bound psychological syndromes specific areas of stress arising from the family and societal structure, from the ecological conditions, and from the particular stress and shape that the culture ascribes to individual situations. Such areas of stress manifest themselves directly in a proliferation of pathological reactions, but only in isolated cases through situationally specific reaction forms, such as kayak-angst and altitude vertigo. To a much greater degree, the respective formation of the abnormal reaction is determined by wider cultural influences (culture-specific shaping of conduct and interpretation) as well as by individual characteristics (such as the readiness to switch into altered states of consciousness).

Culture-Specific Shaping of Conduct

Cultures not only stress certain situations as significant, but they also make available specific patterns of behavior for these situations. Thus, through the ritual of mourning and leave taking, the detachment from the partner is facilitated and the building of new relationships is aided. Furthermore, culture provides freedom in certain situations, so that otherwise prohibited patterns of behavior can be given expression in a set form. For example, there are limited festive seasons that offer the opportunity to get drunk, to express oneself, to be insubordinate, and to have freer sexual contacts. In this way, culture channels conflict-laden needs and thereby carries out a vital mental health function. Beyond that function, culture constantly promotes certain kinds of behavior and suppresses others, according to the position of the individual. Culture also affects abnormal forms of behavior, whether the victim expresses the expected style and pattern of behavior, exaggerates it, or opposes it.

Culturally Approved Patterns of Exceptional Behavior   In most cultures, patterns are given for exceptional behavior, and opportunities are given to enact them. One can find, for example, carnival celebrations in Catholic areas in which the individual is granted otherwise unusual liberties, which at the same time have to be carried out almost in a standardized way. Furthermore, the delegation of otherwise inadmissible behavior to actors is significant, including behavior in ritualized stage presentation.

Such rituals are certainly much more noticeable in foreign cultures. As an institutionalized pattern of aggressive behavior, the insulting contests (*Schimpfduelle*) of the Greenland Eskimos are worth noting. The adversaries in these confrontations present their accusations in song form accompanied by drums (Nansen, 1903, p. 155). Similarly, the natives of the West Australian desert have ritualized forms for conflict within the group. When there is a dispute between certain males, they, encouraged by a circle of onlookers, carry out a duel in which they stab one another with spears against the thighs until both opponents are wounded. A corresponding duel is carried out by women, wherein they hit one another on the head with clubs (Jones, 1971). The mothering in the West African Ndöp ritual constitutes an institutionalized form of regression. The cult leader coats the body of the patient with curdled milk at the same time that the choir of participants sings, "We caress you, we caress you" (Zempleni, 1966).

Besides such uncommon behavior patterns (which are, however, fully incorporated into cultural norms), there are other behaviors that carry the quality of an "approved pattern of misconduct" (Linton, 1956).

A vivid example is offered by the "wild man" behavior in the Highlands of New Guinea (Newman, 1964). In this syndrome, a young man under extreme psychic stress enters a state of motor excitement, assumes a threatening stance, carries out mock attacks, and picks up objects and destroys them. Through skillful intervention, the "wild man" is kept somewhat under control, and, if necessary, is reintegrated into the group through a pampering ritual. This abnormal state provides a cathartic abreaction and also gives the stricken person as well as the group a chance to define their social status anew.

Here one may add acts of aggression against others and against the self, which broadly follow the patterns of societal expectations. In this context, aggressive twilight states of the amok type and of the pseudo-amok type (controlled and therefore less dangerous) must be mentioned, as well as self-mutilations. Instances of the latter include the amputation of a fingerjoint as a grief reaction, as occurs in New Guinea (Burton-Bradley,

1975, p. 49). Societal expectations also affect suicidal actions, for which the culture specifies the situation and the manner in which they might be tolerated (cf. Kiev, 1978).

In the ceremonial walking toward death of the juramentados among the Islamic population in the South Philippines, aggressive and self-aggressive elements are inseparably fused together. The person, feeling weary of life, first obtains his parents' permission, and ultimately also that of the chieftain. Then he has his head shaven clean, takes a bath, dresses in white, and arms himself. Praying all the way, he then goes to some locality where numerous Christians can be found, and throws himself on them while invoking God, the whole time stabbing around himself, until he himself succumbs to his wounds (Ewing, 1955).

Promotion and Suppression of Certain Kinds of Behavior   Exceptional states are distinguished by the fact that, to a greater or lesser extent, they follow prescribed patterns. The more they correspond to these patterns, the sooner they will be perceived as complying with the norms (such as ritual forms of duel or suicide); the more they deviate from such patterns, however, the sooner they will be appraised by the environment as pathological (for example, amok).

However, behavior in abnormal psychic states is influenced not by patterns that are specifically valid for that abnormal state alone; styles of behavior and skills that are encouraged or suppressed in daily life also affect abnormal behavior. Thus, one often finds dancelike features in the motor manifestations of psychotics in Java, although these can hardly ever be observed in Europe. This is compatible with the differential valuation and encouragement of solo dancing in the two cultures. An analogous value orientation regarding pathological behavior is expressed in the comparative observations made by Williams (1950) during the battles in Burma, 1943–1945, concerning British and Indian soldiers. Psychoreactive disturbances appeared among soldiers of both nationalities with equal frequency, but the symptomatology differed fundamentally. Among the British, anxiety manifestations predominated, and the soldiers found it relatively easy to talk about them. For the Indians, however, it was impossible, according to their traditional role orientation, to give their anxieties verbal expression. Instead, they acted out their anxiety and their wish to escape in a hysteriform symptomatology, something which hardly ever happened among the British soldiers.

Another trainable or suppressible ability is the switchover into altered states of consciousness. In central Europe, hypnoidal alterations of consciousness (e.g., hysterical twilight states) were by no means rare as late as the turn of the century; now they have almost disappeared among the indigenous people, although they still appear among foreign workers. This corresponds to the model of most cultures, which puts particular stress on the maintenance of the ego functions and on the alert understanding of the outside world. In contrast, the Bushmen consider hypnoidal states to be necessary for the well-being of the group. As a result of this, about half of the men are able to place themselves in these hypnoidal states at will (Lee, 1966).

It seems that abnormal hypnoidal states (i.e., the ones that appear involuntarily and that deviate from the prescribed pattern) should occur primarily in cultures that also tolerate and encourage such states in the normal sphere. In this context, characteristic differences in symptoms, which are related to the common style of behavior, appear in various people. Thus, amok appears only in men (only men are used to moving about armed) and mostly among illiterates. Latah, on the other hand, is— at least in the Indonesia of today—a disturbance almost wholly limited to women of the lower stratum.

The latah syndrome appears under numerous names in wide areas of Asia and Africa, but has been described particularly for Indonesian areas (Pfeiffer, 1971; Van Wulfften Palthe, 1948; Yap, 1952). The syndrome exhibits a tendency toward altered states of consciousness, mostly of short duration. Two basic forms can be differentiated. In the mimetic form, imitative features, such as echolalia, echopraxia, and automatic obedience, predominate. Apart from fright experiences, a typical triggering factor is a fascinated absorption with external events, such as the gesticulations of a preacher. In the impulsive form, verbal expressions (insults and pornolalia) predominate, and, occasionally, violent aggression also appears. The triggering events are mostly fright experiences, but also include other emotional stresses, such as criticism and ridicule.

Latah syndrome remains harmless and stationary in most cases, something like a personal oddity that amuses onlookers. In isolated cases, however, it manifests itself as progressive and can lead to such a lability of the state of consciousness that the victims become largely helpless and withdraw from the environment. The mimetic form is particularly in accordance with the female model of "the one who receives and obeys," which is valid in the Javanese tradition. The fact that latah has more recently become significantly less frequent can be related to the cultural change that demands from women a greater measure of self-reliance and ability to cope with stressful situations.

Abnormal Behavior as a Contrast to the Cultural Norm   Finally, abnormal behavior can appear as a deliberate rejection of cultural norms— that is, taking a completely negative stance with regard to valid patterns and limits.

Schooler and Caudill (1964) reported that strikingly aggressive behavior was observed among mentally ill Japanese individuals, in contrast to the prevailing life-style. Such an extensive contradiction of social norms is, in general, not compatible with life in a society. The aggression can lead to restrictive measures, often to expulsion or even to physical annihilation (Linton, 1956; Pfeiffer, 1972).

The most thoroughgoing expression of such a contrasting stance to social norms was shown by a syndrome of the Plains Indians, which Wissler (1912) described under the characteristic name "Crazy-Dog-Wishing-to-Die." In such cases, the person concerned showed the opposite of normal behavior on all conceivable points, so that a pattern directly corresponding to a mirror image emerged. Such reversals of normal behavior are also known in the religious sphere. An example is the Hindu Aghoris, "holy beggars," who have chosen the "road of contrariness," which is considered fast but dangerous (Carstairs, 1968, p. 104).

Thus, culture-bound syndromes are formed to a marked extent by the behavioral styles and patterns of each culture, and the individual, even when disturbed, orients himself to the norm, either in a conforming or in a contrasting manner.

Culture-Specific Interpretations

For the full formation of a culture-bound syndrome it is not sufficient that a disturbance is present and that in this state a positive or negative orientation of the behavior to cultural patterns results. Beyond that, it is necessary for the variety of manifestations that the concrete case presents to be structured and interpreted according to traditional conceptions. This procedure is particularly tangible in the naming of the disturbance—the labeling that corresponds to our diagnosis. Thus, the disturbance is raised from the level of individual misfortune to the sphere of the more inclusive scheme of the medical system; this is turn leads to the decision of whether "illness" or some other form of deviance is the case.

Some diagnoses from folk medicine are presented below, and their position in the respective medical system and their influence on the behavior of the patient and his environment are considered.

- *Sperm loss (sukra prameha)* is one of the most frequent symptoms in Asian Indian folk medicine (Carstairs, 1956; Obeyesekere, 1976). The thought of continually losing sperm is particularly anxiety provoking, because sperm is the most important bearer of the power of life according to popular Indian ideology. In this disturbance it is mostly the patient himself who determines the diagnosis, which is already assumed by him through his own observations and complaints. The characteristic symptoms are discharges from the genitalia and a whitish discoloration of the urine. The general condition is compounded by a feeling of weakness and exhaustion. There are often vegetative disturbances and burning sensations on the body surface, as well as joint ailments. Disturbances of concentration and learning and sexual problems frequently bring such patients to a neurologist's office.

Fiery constitution, heated foods, sexual excesses, and the use of intoxicants have been put forward as causative factors. Therapeutically, a "cooling" diet combined with "cooling" medications and baths are often recommended, as well as the use of a tonic that is aimed at an increase of sperm.

Consequently, the diagnosis of sperm loss indicates an illness that, on the whole, is harmless and that can be relieved through medication and an adjustment of diet and life-style. Social effects do arise, insofar as physical rest and sexual restraint are suggested.

• *Koro* (Chinese: *Shuk yang*) is a syndrome originating in Chinese medicine and described in Chinese classical literature (Gwee, 1968). *Yang* refers to the male principle, as well as to the male genitals; *Shuk* denotes withdrawal and dwindling. Thus, *shuk yang* is a dwindling of the male principle of life, expressed by the retraction of the penis into the body, which, in the last analysis, would mean death. The disturbance appears in attacks of heart palpitations and outbursts of sweating and vertigo, and is accompanied by an intense fear of death. These symptoms are similar to those of well-known *sympathicovasal* attack, the only difference being that, in the latter, the heart and not the genitals is the central focus. Disturbances of the Yang-Yin balance are considered causative factors, arising perhaps from previous diseases. To this can be added an acute weakening of the Yang principle, which could come about through excessive sexual strain or through a sudden increase in elements belonging to the Yin principle, particularly as the result of an extreme chill or of cold foods. First, the treatment must counteract the danger of complete penis disappearance, which is considered a life-threatening danger. Prevention is achieved through mechanical means. Second, treatment is aimed at the strengthening of the Yang principle through appropriate diet and suitable medication. In the case of Shuk yang, the diagnosis is usually also made by the patient himself or by others in his environment. Only as a secondary measure is the healing specialist called upon, and he has hardly any other choice than to continue those measures initiated as a kind of first aid by the family of the patient. In addition, the larger environment of his group can get alarmed in view of the assumed threat of the disturbance. This has led, in the case of one Malayan ruler, to the point where his entire people took part in prayers during his Koro attacks (Van Wulfften Palthe, 1948, p. 259).

An unusual variation of Koro appeared in 1967 in Singapore. A rumor had spread in the area that infected pork led to Shuk yang, and therefore hundreds of people sought hospital care with corresponding complaints. With the help of the local doctors and television stations, the health authorities carried out an educational campaign that caused the problem to subside rapidly. The recognized authority succeeded in removing diagnostic labels that had already been attached. In this process, it was helpful that the bond with the traditional medical system was already loosened and that only a few people seeking help had endured a genuine Koro attack, with fearful vegetative symptoms.

• Being labeled a witch and being accused of having killed one's relatives is a situation that a patient often can accept only after fierce resistance. Field (1960) gives vivid examples of this condition at the healing shrines in Ghana, where the confession is forced from patients precisely for the reason that it is seen as a prerequisite to recovery. On the other hand, depressive psychotics would, in a corresponding frame of mind, tend to accuse themselves of witchcraft. The cited examples illustrate how the patient, after being diagnosed, is integrated into a system of conceptions and expectations that deeply influences the clinical picture as well as the course of healing. This process of integration and naming is so important that in many cultures the diagnosis is carried out by specialists and thus is separated from therapy.

Culture-Specific Interventions

A diagnosis is, additionally and particularly, instruction for action. After the interpretation and naming of the clinical picture, therapy follows; then the group establishes its attitude toward the disturbed individual. Opinion can vary from particularly high esteem to indifference, to abandonment, and even to physical annihilation. In any case, the social reaction and the individual therapeutic measures have far-reaching repercussions on the clinical picture, particularly in culture-specific areas of stress, and culture-specific shaping of behavior and interpretation, as will be clarified by some examples.

Responding to the Syndrome as a Road to a Higher Level (Spirit and Power Illness) Among the Salish Indians of the Canadian west coast, the relations to the *power* and the *guardian spirit,* respectively, are central in the traditional rites. When anyone is touched by the power, which happens to some of the young people as winter approaches, this is expressed, as Jilek (1974) describes it, in varied symptoms like depressed states, vegetative symptoms, and behavioral disturbances (for example, alcohol abuse). As long as the condition goes untreated it is viewed as a threat to life.

The therapy consists of bringing the power, which is latent in the patient, to its full manifestation. This takes place through intensive participation by the group in an inititation rite, which symbolizes death and rebirth and ushers in the "life in the power." In the isolation of the cult hut, the initiate discovers his guardian spirit, and at the same time he finds his personal dance and song. In the ceremonial feast of the Winter Dance he then appears with this dance and song in front of the gathered festive audience and receives their recognition.

The disturbance is likely to arise in a crisis situation: the lack of diversion and occupation characteristic of the approaching winter intensifies the expression of the conflicts experienced by the young person standing on the threshold of adulthood. The cultural shaping of the behavior both within the realm of the disturbance and also in the healing ritual, is pronounced (sensory deprivation in the cult hut, with resulting alteration of consciousness, regression, and ecstatic experiences). In accordance with psychiatric nosology, Jilek (1974) speaks of an anomic developmental crisis. He interprets it, however (in contrast with truly pathological changes), as an "institutionalized pathomorphic state" and compares it to the shaman disease, which also can only be overcome through the realization of the power.

Acceptance of the Syndrome as an Individual Peculiarity (Waswās and Other Religious Obsessive-Compulsive Syndromes)   Waswās is an obsessive-compulsive syndrome that is linked with the Islamic ritual of cleansing and prayer. The disturbance was described in Indonesia (Pfeiffer, 1971), but seems also to be widespread in other traditional Islamic areas. The term *Waswās* referred originally to whispered promptings of the devil, but in Indonesia it has taken on the meaning "hesitation" or "doubt." The disturbance arises in a typical area of stress, namely the borderline between the profane and the sacred domain of life. It relates to ritual cleanliness and to the validity of the ritual procedures, which are particularly important in Islam. Thus, the sufferer of Waswās finds it hard to terminate the ablutions because he is afraid that he is not yet clean enough to carry out his prayer in the lawful manner. Similarly, he will repeat the introductory invocations and the raising of the arms more times than is called for, because he feels that his thinking is not yet fully focused on God. Finally, at the end of the prayer he may be beset by doubts about whether he might perhaps have forgotten some words, and so he will start all over again from the beginning.

The disturbance is interpreted according to Islamic tradition. Even as early as 1100 A.D., the mystic Al-Ghazali commented on Waswās in the following manner:

> It is said that the greatest dilemma for the individual undertaking the ablutions is the uncertainty of the heart during the cleansing. . . One may not pour water on oneself more than three times on each occasion . . . and one should not waste water beyond what is necessary, which could happen because of doubt and worry. People, who do it too scrupulously, become at the same time a plaything to the devil, who bears the name Walhan.

The syndrome is thus not conceived as an illness that could be treated. It is instead considered a temptation that is aimed at distracting the person from carrying out his religious duties and that therefore should not be given any undue attention. As a result, the disturbance is integrated into the daily religious life. Certainly it causes some good-natured amusement, but at the same time the victims are respected because of their meticulousness in religious matters. Something of the same nature is true of other religious obsessive syndromes, among which many variants based on Hinduism are known, such as the purity mania (Suci Bhay) described by Chakraborty and Banerji (1975). Typical of this purity mania is the image of an elderly lady who constantly carries under her arm a bottle of Ganges water, which she—dispensing purity—sprinkles around her.

Combating the Syndrome as a Vital Threat to the Individual (Susto)   There is a widespread syndrome in Latin American folk medicine (Rubel, 1964; Sal y Rosas, 1966) that has been called Susto (Spanish: "fright"). It is triggered by a frightening experience, which often leads the victim to fall to the ground. According to the conception of the Kechua-speaking Indians of the Andes, the soul then separates from the body and becomes trapped by the earth. Through looking at the intestines of a guinea pig, the healing expert makes his diagnosis. He then attempts to appease the earth through sacrifices, so that it will return the soul. In both Koro and Malgri, the disturbance is perceived as an acute threat to the stricken person, which leads to supportive action by the healing specialist and the group.

The Syndrome as a Threat to the Group: Annihilation of the Deviant Individual (Windigo Syndrome)   The Windigo syndrome (Teicher, 1960) gets its name from the giant man-eating ice ogre, that even now is a source of panic and anxiety for the Algonquin-speaking Indians of northeastern Canada. The clinical picture concerns a person who gradually feels himself changing into a Windigo and accordingly becomes increasingly preoccupied with the idea of consuming human flesh. The affected person fights this thought desperately, because one such act would mean the final break with human existence. As long as the struggle lasts, others in the environment attempt to free the patient from the demon. Should the obsessional thoughts become overpowering, however, and should cannibalistic acts occur, then the patient would be regarded as fully transformed into a Windigo. He would be slain and burned, in order to render the spirit innocuous. In this case, the loneliness and the food shortage during the winter months should be viewed as a culture-specific area of tension. Such hardships bring cannibalism into the sphere of the thinkable, and at the same time can cause particularly strong defenses to build up against fantasies relating to cannibalism. The behavior is essentially formed by the Indian concept of a person's alliance with a guardian spirit, and, above all, with the myth of the man-eating Windigo.

Although documents are scarce, they do suggest the desperate struggle of the stricken individual against the compulsive idea of being changed into a Windigo. It is imaginable that an individual could be pushed into the position of a negative model so that the group could fight its own tabooed impulses in him and render them harmless. Finally, it can be assumed that particularly depressive psychotics, because of a self-deprecating attitude, would tend to designate themselves as Windigos and strive for self-annihiliation.

In the light of the preceding examples it is clear that the spectrum of social reactions to mental deviations is wide, and that attitudes depend on the interpretation of the symptoms and on the relationship of these symptoms to the cultural value system. On the other hand, the reaction of the social environment also affects the clinical picture, modifies its manifestations, and fundamentally influences its course, which can lead to healing, to the integration of the disturbance, and also to complete derangement and destruction.

SUMMARY NOTES

The study of culture-bound psychological syndromes is particularly appealing because it enables typical conflicts and reaction patterns to come to life with anecdote-like vividness. The number of syndromes is considerable, and adding more exotic names to the list of already-known syndromes poses no problem. Admittedly, the syndromes are only partially conceived as "illnesses." Most likely a patient is considered ill only when he also exhibits physical symptoms, as is the case in sperm loss, koro, and Malgri. Instead, many syndromes are considered individual peculiarities (like latah and Waswās); other disorders have been institutionalized and have thereby become firm components of the culture (for example, possession cults, ritualized forms of aggression, and self-aggression).

As Yap emphasized in 1974 (p. 84), the culture-bound syndromes are based on *biopsychological* forms of reacting, which have a universally human character, i.e., a supracultural character. Correspondingly, the individual case of illness can usually be integrated into the international psychiatric nosological system without any particular problems. In spite of this, the attempt to bring the culture-bound syndromes into a psychiatric diagnostic system is doomed to failure because the symptoms in the two spheres are selected and ordered from qualitatively disparate points of view. It is also impossible to combine the culture-bound syndromes themselves into one separate, integrated system. This is because the shaping and interpretative influence of the culture is effective in different dimensions, four of which are emphasized and clarified in the examples in this chapter.

Culture-Specific Areas of Stress

This section deals with typical areas of conflict, overcharge, and frustrations. They arise from family and societal structure, from extreme ecological conditions, and also from the particular evaluation and shaping of certain life situations (such as territorial boundaries, war, and examinations). Many disturbances derive their specific character from the peculiarity of the area of stress, as, for instance, kayak-angst and highway trance. Such critical areas (for example, a new married woman in her husband's extended family) are mostly characterized only by a generally increased frequency of psychoreactive disturbances. Whether gynecological complaints, possession by a demon, or suicidal attempts arise in this stressful situation is determined by the cultural and individual factors that belong to the following additional dimensions.

Culture-Specific Shaping of Conduct

The cultural tradition offers behavioral patterns not only for critical situations but also for deviant behavior. Beyond such situation-specific patterns, each respective culture encourages certain styles of conduct while suppressing others, a phenomenon that also affects the shaping of the abnormal state. Thus, the tendency toward trances or toward stupor and delusions is linked to certain tendencies generally held by the culture in question (Murphy, 1967; Wittkower and Prince, 1974). Finally, the orientation toward the cultural pattern can also occur in the form of a protest, with the patient exhibiting exactly opposite behavior, like a mirror reflection.

The more closely the stricken person is able to follow a culturally prescribed pattern, the sooner his behavior will be evaluated as conforming to the norm, and the more successful the integration into the societal context will be. A vivid example is the trances that occur in possession cults. When a person succeeds in making his trance conduct conform to the ritual patterns, he can be installed as a medium in the cult. On the contrary, when the person is not suited to the duties of a medium, grave mistakes may provoke very strong countermeasures (Pfeiffer, 1971, p. 105).

Culture-Specific Interpretations

There is undoubtedly a formative power in naming and classifying a disturbance, because the variety of the respective symptoms is seen and interpreted from the viewpoint of this label and thereby is adapted to the typical clinical picture. Naming a disturbance is generally not a momentary procedure, during which the diagnosis is delivered to the passive patient. It is much more likely to be a process extending over considerable time, and one in which the patient and his social environment cooperate actively. This is effected, to some extent, by the choice of a diagnostician, by the selection of information and by attempts made to control the disorder, such as sacrifices (Edgerton, 1969). Should the interpretation of the disorder be unsatisfactory, it is possible to switch to another healer or even to choose a different medical system.

Culture-Specific Interventions

In the reaction of the social environment to disturbed behavior, there is a broad spectrum of responses available that extend far beyond the administration of therapy in the more restricted sense. Responses range from a positive assimilation of the symptoms (such as group cooperation in treating power illness), to amused tolerance (e.g., toward religious compulsive syndromes), to the extreme of panic-stricken terror, which can result in physical annihilation (Windigo). In spite of the close connection between the interpretation of the disturbance and the manner of intervention, the results may vary, because the interventions may be modified through various factors, such as social position and relationship with the family.

A culture-bound syndrome is an expression of complex processes. Undoubtedly, when fully developed, a syndrome can manifest the influence of all four dimensions discussed in this chapter, even though each dimension may have a varying degree of importance. However, it should be stressed again that the concrete illness of the individual can never be fully understood when viewed only from the cultural perspective. Instead, the general aspects of biology and psychology also deserve attention, as well as their pathological variations. Consequently, it is possible, and frequently necessary, even in the presence of a culture-bound syndrome, to make use of scientific-medical methods of diagnosis and therapy. Finally, the personal biography of the stricken individual should be taken into account in culture-bound syndromes, no less than when faced with a diagnosis in modern medical nosology.

The universal spread of technical civilization and of the scientific medicine pertaining to it, has caused the disappearance of well-defined syndromes that are specific to a certain culture. Particularly in the industrial areas of the Western world, where now folk medicine can hardly be separated from the official medicine, it is hard to demonstrate any independent culture-bound syndromes. This does not mean, however, that the dimensions of cultural influence discussed in this chapter have lost their meaning. They have merely become harder to recognize now that the contrast between folk medicine and scientific medicine is missing, and universal diffusion allows local boundaries to disappear.

Therefore, when dealing with clinical pictures in modern medicine (by no means only in psychiatry), one should always ask the question: In what respect and to what extent might cultural influences be at work (in the sense of typical areas of stress, culture-specific forms of behavior, interpretation, and intervention)? Furthermore, it should be asked what impact these cultural factors have on prevention, therapy, and rehabilitation.

REFERENCES

Burton-Bradley,B. G. 1975. Stone-Age Crisis. A Psychiatric Appraisal.Vanderbilt University Press, Nashville.

Carstairs, G. M. 1956. Hinjra and Jiryan:Two derivatives of Hindu attitudes to sexuality. Br. J. Med. Psychol. 29:128–138.

Carstairs, G. M. 1968. The Twice-Born. A Study of a Community of High-Caste Hindus. Hogarth Press, London.

Cawte, J. E. 1976. Malgri, a culture-bound syndrome. In: W. P. Lebra (ed.), Culture Bound Syndromes, Ethnopsychiatry, and Alternate Therapies. University Press of Hawaii, Honolulu.

Chakraborty, A., and Banerji, G. 1975. Ritual, a culture specific neurosis, and obsessional states in Bengali culture. Indian J. Psychiatry 17:211–216.

DeVos, G. 1960. The relation of guilt towards parents to achievement and arranged marriage among the Japanese. Psychiatry 23:287–301.

Edgerton, R. B. 1969. On the "recognition" of mental illness. In: S. C. Plog and R. B. Edgerton (eds.), Changing Perspectives in Mental Illness. Holt, Rinehart & Winston, Inc., New York.

Ewing, J. F. 1955. Juramentado: Institutionalized suicide among the Moros of the Philippines. Anthropol. Q. 28:148–155.

Field, M. J. 1960. Search for Security: An Ethnopsychiatric Study of Rural Ghana. Northwestern University Press, Evanston.

Gussow, Z. 1963. A preliminary report of Kayak-Angst among the Eskimo of West-Greenland. Int. J. Soc. Psychiatry 9:18–26.

Gwee, A. L. 1968. Koro-Its origin and nature as a disease entity. Singapore Med. J. 9:3–6.

Hassrick, R. B. 1964. The Sioux. University of Oklahoma Press, Norman.

Jilek, W. G. 1974. Salish Indian Mental Health and Culture Change. Holt, Rinehart & Winston of Canada, Inc., Toronto.

Jones, I. H. 1971. Stereotyped aggression in a group of Australian Western Desert Aborigines. Br. J. Med. Psychol. 44:259–265.

Kiev, A. 1978. Transcultural perspectives of suicidal behavior. In: L. D. Hankoff (ed.), Suicide: A Comprehensive Handbook. Publishing Sciences Group, Inc., Littleton, Mass.

Lee, R. B. 1966. The sociology of !Kung Bushman trance performances. In: R. Prince (ed.),Trance and Possession States. Bucke Memorial Society, Montreal.

Linton, R. 1956. Culture and Mental Disorder. Charles C Thomas, Publisher, Springfield, Ill.

Malinowski, B. 1927. Sex and Repression in Savage Society, Routledge & Kegan Paul, London.

Murphy, H. B. M. 1967. Cultural aspects of the delusion. Studium Generale 20:684–692.

Nansen, F. 1903. Eskimoleben. Meyer, Leipzig.

Newman, P. L. 1964. "Wild man" behavior in a New Guinea community. Am. Anthropol. 66:1–19.

Obeysekere, G. 1976. The impact of Ayurvedic ideas on the culture and the individual in Ceylon. In: C. Leslie (ed.), Asian Medical Systems: A Comparative Study. University of California Press, Berkeley and Los Angeles.

Pandey, R. E. 1968. The suicide problem in India. Int. J. Soc. Psychiatry 14:193–200.

Pfeiffer, W. M. 1971. Transkulturelle Psychiatrie. Thieme, Stuttgart.

Pfeiffer, W. M. 1972. Die Stellung des psychisch Kranken in aussereuropäischen Kulturen. In: E. Ehrhardt (ed.), Perspektiven der heutigen Psychiatrie. Gerhards, Frankfurt.

Pisztora, F. 1972. Soziokulturelle Einflüsse und Konfliktneurosen bezw. reaktive Psychosen im heutigen Algerien. Psychiatr. Clin. 5:158–173.

Prince, R. 1960. The "Brain Fag" syndrome in Nigerian students. J. Ment. Sci. 106:550–570.

Rin, H. 1966. Two forms of vital deficiency syndrome among male mental patients. Transcult. Psychiatr. Res. 3:19–21.

Rubel, A. J. 1964. The epidemiology of a folk illness: Susto in Hispanic America. Ethnology 3:268–283.

Sal y Rosas, F. 1966. Mitologia médica y prácticas mágicas en el Callejón de Huaylas. Arch. Criminol. Neuropsiquiatr. Disciplinas Conexas 14: 365–387.

Schooler, C., and Caudill, W. 1964. Symptomatology in Japanese and American schizophrenics. Ethnology 3:172–178.

Sutter, J. M., Susini, R., Pélecier, Y., and Pascalis, G. 1959. Quelques observations des psychoses nuptiales chez les musulmans d'Algerie. Ann. Med. Psychol. 117, no. 5.

Teicher, M. I. 1960. Windigo Psychosis. A Study of a Relationship between Belief and Behavior among the Indians of North-eastern Canada. American Ethnological Society, Seattle.

Teja, J. S., Kanna, B. S., and Subrahmanyam, T. B. 1970. "Possession States" in Indian patients. Indian J. Psychiatry 12: 71–87.

Van Wulflen Palthe, P. M. 1948. Neurologie en Psychiatrie. Weltenschappalijke Uitgeverij, Amsterdam.

Williams, A. 1950. A psychiatric study of Indian soldiers in the Arakan. Br. J. Med. Psychol. 23: 130–181.

Wissler, C. 1912. Anthropological Papers of the American Museum of Natural History. 7:32.

Wittkower, E. D., and Prince, R. 1974. A review of transcultural psychiatry. In: S. Arieti (editor-in-chief) and G. Caplan (ed., Vol. 2), American Handbook of Psychiatry. 2nd Ed. Basic Books, Inc., New York.

Yap, P. M. 1952. The Latah reaction: Its pathodynamics and nosological position. J. Ment. Sci. 98:515–564.

Yap, P. M. 1974. Comparative Psychiatry. A Theoretical Framework. University of Toronto Press, Toronto.

Zempleni, A. 1966. La dimension therapeutique du cult des rabs. Ndöp, Tuuru, et Samp. rites de possession chez les Lebou et les Wolof. Psychopathol. Afr. 2:295–440.

IV

CULTURE AND MAJOR PSYCHOPATHOLOGY

Chapter 9

Culture and Schizophrenia

H. B. M. Murphy

Schizophrenia is the mental disorder that imposes the heaviest burden on health services throughout the world, and consequently it is the one that has received the greatest attention from researchers. Despite that attention, however, there is still no clear agreement regarding the criteria for its diagnosis, and research in the 1960s (Cooper et al., 1972) showed that there were marked differences in the ways in which the diagnosis was being employed in New York and in London. (A computer analysis of the data suggested that the British were the more precise and consistent; however, the researchers were all from Britain.) Agreement is easy to obtain on "typical" cases, but in many societies the majority of patients who might receive the diagnosis are not so typical, and it makes a great difference whether that majority is included or excluded when one is looking for connections between the disease and possible cultural factors. To take an extreme example, one psychiatrist working in Uganda concluded that only one out of over 300 patients whom he had seen in the mental hospital deserved to be labeled schizophrenic (Tewfik, 1958), while others working there had placed over 50% of the patients under that diagnosis. For this reason, the great mass of statistical data that exists around the world regarding the frequency and other characteristics of schizophrenia is of little use for cross-cultural comparisons, and the relationship, if any, of culture to schizophrenia has to be sought from a limited number of situations in which uniform criteria have been used or in which the cases are very typical.

The features most characteristic of "typical" schizophrenia have been shown in a large-scale international study (WHO, 1973), using three distinct methods of data analysis, to consist of:

> Lack of insight
> Auditory hallucinations
> Delusions of reference
> Flatness of affect.

However, there is general agreement that one chronic form of schizophrenia, schizophrenia simplex, may occur without the delusions and hallucinations. This complicates cross-cultural studies, because that form, which can easily be confused with mental deficiency if there is not a good history, occurs more commonly in peoples with little formal education, particularly in Asia, than in peoples with advanced education (Murphy et al., 1963). Conversely, if one focuses only on the first three of the four most typical features noted above, as psychiatrists in the United States tend to do, there are a host of other psychotic states that can be drawn in under the schizophrenia label. Other schools of psychiatry tend to call these states acute reactive psychoses, *bouffée délirante*, or paranoid states, and they are particularly common in Third World countries.

In this chapter, the aspect of schizophrenia emphasized is the social rather that the psychological, i.e., the resulting interference with social functioning rather than the presence of delusions and hallucinations. This approach is taken because societies differ greatly in the range of beliefs that they consider normal, and because they can also differ greatly in the degree to which they allow fantasy to project itself on ambiguous experiences and to create what we would call hallucinations. A Philippine anthropologist has described how the people of a particular village there saw or heard fairylike spirits in nearly every tree and pitied him because he was blind to these (Jocano, 1971). A Senegalese psychiatrist has argued that quasi hallucinations are so frequent in his country that they should not be used for diagnostic purposes; he has further pointed out that the cultural traditions there encourage everyone to have ideas of reference (Sow, 1978). However, if we are to explore the possible relationship between culture and schizophrenia, we must have a more precise idea of its nature than simply that it results in poor social functioning. The disorder may be best thought of in terms of defective information processing.

Schizophrenia can be—which is not the same as saying must be—inherited, and a significant percentage of children at high risk of inheriting the disorder exhibit what are called attentional deficits, at an age when the disease itself cannot be detected. Attentional deficits seem to be part of a broader weakness in assembling sensorial inputs (information) in consistent and relevant fashion.[1] When that weakness is sufficiently marked or is overtaxed, the patient makes what seem to be nonsensical inferences from, and reactions to, the information that he is receiving. Patients with other psychoses also seem to be nonsensical, but this mental mechanism is only

---

[1]This is a subject in which research is moving fast, so that references are liable to be out-of-date by the time this book is published. However, the papers included in *The Nature of Schizophrenia* (Wynne, Cromwell, and Matthysse (eds.), 1978) give an overview of the different ideas on the subject at that date.

temporarily or partially upset, whereas in the schizophrenic there is more widespread interference, although one that may be compensated for.

If this distinction is made, there are four main ways in which culture can affect the *risk* of developing schizophrenia:

through the training or mistraining given regarding the processing of
    information
through the complexity of the information to which people are exposed
through the degree to which decisions (acts or responses) are expected of all
    persons given complex or unclear information
through the degree to which schizophrenia-bearing families are discour-
    aged or encouraged to have children.

In addition, culture can be expected to affect the *symptomatology* of the disease, at the very least through the forms that fantasy is encouraged to take. Culture can affect the *course of illness*, most distinctly through the obstacles that it can place in the way of the mentally ill attempting to reassume normal roles. Culture can also affect *response to treatment*, most clearly by promoting trust or distrust of therapists. (The last point is true for all mental disorders.) In this chapter, each of these four aspects of schizophrenia are considered. Attention is given principally to ascertaining the facts, but some consideration is given to how far these facts support or discredit the various hypotheses regarding cultural influence.

INCIDENCE AND PREVALENCE: EXAMPLES OF HIGH RISK

One popular view of the schizophrenic is that he requires admission to a mental hospital at least once in his lifetime. This view is held by many doctors, so that when they refer to the incidence of the disease, they are referring to the rate of first mental hospitalization for patients assigned this diagnosis. When hospital facilities are sufficient, when there is not believed to be any other sound way of treating the disorder, and when this type of care is accepted equally by all sections of the population, then substituting first hospitalizations for true incidence rates constitutes a working compromise. However, in some societies there have never been enough places in the mental hospital; in others there is much more acceptance of such treatment in one section of the population than in another. Also, throughout the Western world there has been, since the mid–1960s, an increasing drive to treat schizophrenics in outpatient clinics, thereby avoiding hospitalization. Accordingly, although hospitalization data can sometimes be used for cross-cultural comparisons, many factors must be considered before these data can be trusted to provide a balanced reflection of the true situation, and there are frequently situations in which they cannot be trusted at all, forcing one to look to other data. Unusually low rates of mental hospitalization are more suspect than unusually high ones, but the latter must not be accepted without scrutiny, and care must be taken to distinguish "first" hospitalization figures from "total" ones.

Excess Schizophrenia in the Irish

The Irish, more specifically the Irish Catholics, have the most striking excess in reported schizophrenia. As Figure 1 illustrates:

1. First admissions in the Republic of Ireland (Eire) are four times those in England and Wales and three times those in the other territories indicated.
2. Rates drop sharply as one crosses from Eire to Northern Ireland, but in the latter territory those for Roman Catholics are almost double the ones for non-Catholics.
3. In Canada, the rates for the Roman Catholics of British origin, who are mainly from Irish culture, are 50% higher than those for other persons of British origin.

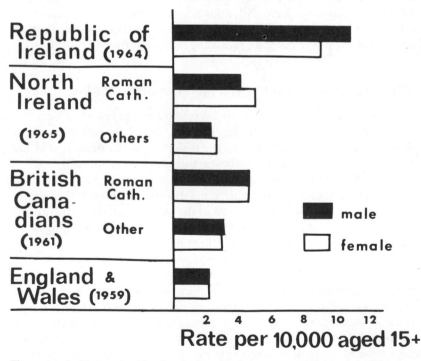

Figure 1. Incidence of schizophrenic first admissions to mental hospital, by sex, age standardized, for various Irish and related populations. (From Murphy, 1975.)

The difference between Eire and England probably goes back to at least the beginning of the century (Murphy, 1968, 1975). The much lower rates in Northern Ireland than in Eire are an exaggeration of a trend within Eire itself, where rates are considerably higher in the southwest than in the northeast (O'Hare and Walsh, undated). The difference between the two Canadian groups, something that cannot be explained on the basis of social class distribution, is an echo of much greater differences among immigrant groups to North America earlier in the century (Murphy, 1975).

Possible explanations for the higher Irish Catholic rates are numerous, but most prove unsatisfactory on closer examination. Thus, differences in diagnostic approach would not explain the Canadian data, and there has been a comparison of diagnostic practices in Eire and in England (Kelleher and Copeland, 1973) that suggests that they are very similar. The theory that the healthy Irish families emigrated, while the sicker families remained, cannot explain how those who arrived in the United States initially had such high schizophrenia rates. The possibility that the hospitals in Eire admitted milder cases than would other hospitals seems belied because the duration of stay was just as long or longer in Eire as in other European countries. Also, reports of numerous, unhospitalized cases were encountered in some rural districts (Scheper-Hughes, 1979). Neurological damage by something like a rare mineral or a slow virus is unlikely, because excessive liability to the disease persists, although in attenuated form, in subsequent generations overseas and does not affect the North Ireland Protestants. An excessive genetic liability in the Celts (for which there is no other evidence) is unlikely, because an unusually high percentage of Irish schizophrenics remain unmarried, because illegitimate births are relatively uncommon, and because the average age of marriage is so late that the disease has usually shown itself before marriage could occur.

The tentative elimination of these various possibilities needed to be undertaken before a cultural explanation for the high rate of schizophrenic hospitalizations could seriously be hypothesized, but now that they have been provisionally eliminated, what reason is there for thinking that culture is involved? There are two factors that could be relevant. The first is the verbal agility and sometimes savage wit that Irish culture encourages; the second is the ambivalence toward individual independence. The verbal agility has made the Irish, for so small a people, disproportionate contributors to the world's literature, and that contribution has been predominantly in two directions—fantasy (Swift and Yeats, for example) and word juggling (Shaw and Joyce). Verbal agility, as one might expect, does not affect just a small elite of writers; it is something that is enjoyed at all levels. The bard was highly respected in earlier ages, the wandering storyteller was still a welcome figure in rural areas at the beginning of this century, with his tales of fairies and other supernatural beings, and today witty attacks or teasing are still a favorite sport. Ireland has been described as the land of the "double-think and double-speak" requiring "a feeling for half-tones and shades and subleties" (Tracy, 1953). An Irish psychiatrist has noted that in the villages, "some individuals, in fact, practice a particularly vicious form of ridicule in which the victim is never sure whether the ridiculer is serious or not. If the victim treats the matter as a joke he or she is insulting the ridiculer who . . . (claims to be) . . . serious; if the victim takes matters seriously he or she . . . (is accused of being) . . . too serious" (Dunne, 1970).

Considering the four main ways listed earlier in which culture could affect the risk of schizophrenia, it is clear that the double-speak increases the complexity and reduces the clarity of information to which people are exposed, while the particular type of ridiculing imposes on the victim a demand that he respond to that unclear information. Furthermore, the other side to the Irish verbal mastery, the use of fantasy, suggests that reality testing may not be highly valued or thoroughly taught in this society, with the result that schizophrenia-prone individuals may have greater difficulty in Irish society than in some other cultures in distinguishing hallucinations and delusions from the testable realities. However, there are other features of Irish schizophrenia that invite a cultural explanation and that relate to dependency. The first such feature of importance in attempting to explain the high rate of schizophrenia is that, although the diagnostic criteria may be the same in Eire as in England and although it is regarded in both places as shameful to have to go to a mental hospital, the so-called schizophrenics whom one finds in Eire seem to be less disturbed than those whom one would find in mental hospitals elsewhere. The anthropologist Scheper-Hughes (1979) has remarked of the inmates of a hospital that she frequently visited in Ireland that there seemed nothing to compel a diagnosis of schizophrenia as opposed to one of 'ontological insecurity' or 'problems of living'." Irish psychiatrists have said that they probably do admit and retain mild cases more readily than do psychiatrists in England, because they prefer to give such individuals shelter rather than to return them to isolated cottages where they would be alone. This need not mean that the "true" incidence of schizophrenia, hospitalized and unhospitalized combined, is less than high, because descriptions by Scheper-Hughes and others indicate that a large number of patients never reach the hospital. Instead, it is more likely that this type of patient seeks a dependency situation and wants to be looked after, not just as a protection against teasing, but because of dependency needs. This dependency relates to another feature of Irish society—the ambivalent relationships between mothers and offspring there.

Writers on Irish alcoholism have linked that disorder to maternal dominance and overprotectiveness (Bales, 1946), and it has been further suggested that such mothers may be schizophrenogenic insofar as they call on some of their offspring (particularly a later-born son) to succeed, while at the same time refusing recognition of whatever success is attained. Clinical studies (Opler and Singer, 1956; Sperling, 1953) suggest that the Irish schizophrenics in the United States (but perhaps other Irish as well) do have unusually prominent problems with mother figures, and Scheper-Hughes (1979) obtained particularly abnormal responses from rural Irish patients to TAT cards featuring such figures. Accordingly, another possible element of Irish culture that may lead borderline schizophrenics to enter the patient role might be the failure of one approved style of mothering to satisfy dependency needs. However, both this hypothesis and the one relating to the complexity of communication must be regarded as unproven, and a wholly different explanation might prove more valid.

Sex Differences in Prevalence of Schizophrenia

On the average, schizophrenia affects both sexes equally among the Irish, although the above hypotheses might lead one to expect an excess of males. [Some male excess is present in many parts of Ireland (O'Hare and Walsh, undated), while an excess of female cases occurs principally among Irish emigrants (Malzberg, 1940).] However, there are some examples in which the disease affects one sex much more than the other. This is of considerable cultural significance, because it is not a finding that would be expected from the various genetic and toxic theories that have been put forward to explain the social variance of the disease. To the author's knowledge, the most dramatic example of a male excess of schizophrenia comes from Sumatra (Indonesia), while the most dramatic example of a female excess is probably that found in some villages in French Canada. However, in each instance the imbalance has been a temporary one, not likely to have lasted more than one or two decades, and arising from exceptional circumstances.

Excess of Male Schizophrenia   The first example is 60 years old and is part of colonial history. At the turn of the century, the Dutch army was continuously engaged in extending colonial rule to new parts of what we now call Indonesia. In some districts, the Dutch were strongly resisted, while in others they were regarded as simply a new group of overlords, perhaps somewhat less punitive than the previous autocrats. One of the peoples from which the resistance was the strongest was the Achinese of Northern Sumatra and, some years after that resistance had finally been crushed, the governor of the district reported that the number of mentally ill persons there seemed unusually high. A competent and sympathetic psychiatrist with some knowledge of local societies was sent to tour the region, and what he found was very striking (van Loon, 1920). First, the active prevalence of psychosis (not just schizophrenia) was high, even by European standards, affecting perhaps 2% of the total Achinese population, and was many, many times higher than the rate in the neighboring, more peaceful Malays. Second, the cases of psychosis among the Achinese were mainly male, even though fewer males than females had survived the war. Figure 2 summarizes the provisional diagnoses that van Loon assigned to the patients, and, although the numbers of male and female mental defectives were about equal, there were five times as many male schizophrenics as female ones. There is no reason to believe that the sex difference here is not genuine, and there *is* reason to think that it developed during the war. Some twenty years earlier, Jacobs, a colonial doctor and anthropologist, wrote a book on the Achinese in which he recorded very little chronic mental illness, but a moderate amount of acute confusional psychosis, affecting mainly the women and not the men (Jacobs, 1894). In this case there is also no reason to believe that the cases were mild or that excessive use was being made of hospital care, because there was no hospital there, and when van Loon went to the villages to see the cases, only the severely abnormal were brought to him.

Our knowledge of the circumstances may help to explain this upsurge of male schizophrenia. The Achinese were a male-dominated society derived partly from the south of India, with strong ideas of caste and of what tasks were proper or improper for a true Achinese male to undertake.

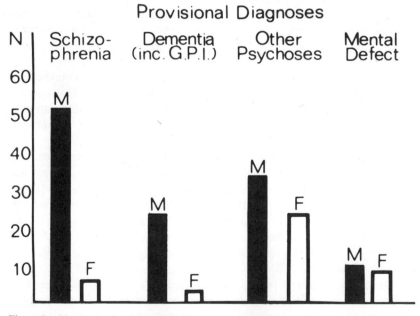

Figure 2.   Numbers of patients with different categories of mental disorder recorded by van Loon during his mental health survey of Achinese communities in northern Sumatra, by sex. M = male; F = female; G.P.I. = syphilitic insanity. (From van Loon, 1920.)

Their economy had been based on overlording conquered peoples, so that warrior status was highly regarded, while women, traders, and agriculturalists were looked down upon (Hurgronje, 1906). During a 20-year war against the Dutch, the Achinese men were occupied almost exclusively with the fighting, while the previously subordinate women began to dominate all that was crucial to community life other than the fighting. When peace was imposed, the men had the alternatives of leaving the real power in the women's hands or of taking over the previously despised roles of farmer and trader. Most of them seemed to have opted, up until the time of van Loon's investigation, for the former, and Dutch administrators described them as lying around listlessly while the women did all the work and seemed to make the key decisions. However, this reversal of roles was not easy for men with such a strong warrior tradition. One gets the impression that the whole male half of the population was sick to some degree, either depressed at their defeat or baffled by the problem of choosing between roles that their culture had formerly despised. There was a fair amount of venereal disease brought in by the conquering forces, but this affected the women as much as or more than it affected the men, so that although syphilitic insanity (G.P.I.) must be considered as a differential diagnosis, it should not have affected the men more than the women.

The most probable explanation for what van Loon found, therefore, is that the role-choice dilemma that faced all Achinese men at the end of the war made some of them schizophrenic. It was not a situation of complex or unclear information in the simple sense, but it was a situation in which individuals were being called upon to choose between alternatives, all of which could be labeled wrong or bad, and in which they were being kept face to face with this choice over a period of years. One can call this a double-bind situation (Bateson et al., 1956), but it was imposed by the culture rather than by parents. It can be blamed on the war, but without that particular cultural background the Achinese would have been able to adjust to peace-time conditions much more easily, as the neighboring Malays had done.

Excess of Female Schizophrenia   The example of a female rate of schizophrenia being significantly higher than the male one also stems from a community survey, and therefore is also independent of social biases toward hospitalizing one sex more than the other. In this survey, 13 Canadian communities were searched for active cases of psychosis, both through local visits to interview key informants and through a record search in all hospitals likely to have admitted patients from that region. The communities were chosen to represent the French, British, Irish, German, and Polish subcultures, and the French-Canadian communities were divided into two categories, three villages being designated traditional, i.e., long-established and stable, and another three being designated new, i.e., more recently established and more exposed to Anglo-Canadian influences (Murphy and Lemieux, 1967). It was in the traditional group that the excess of female schizophrenics was found, this excess occurring in all three of the villages. Figure 3 shows the active prevalence rates in the French-Canadian (FC) group as compared to the rates in the Anglo-Protestant (AP) villages. Despite the relatively small numbers, the difference between the two female rates is highly significant.

The communities were chosen to be similar with respect to economic base, mean income, and distance from large cities, and they were not significantly different with respect to sex ratio and age structure. Thus, cultural background is by far the most important thing that distinguishes the groups. Taking each of the cultures separately, the sex difference within the French-Catholic group is the most striking, and this has been the focus of previous discussions of the data. However, we can also view the data cross-culturally, and can ask what it is about the situations of women in the two types of communities that could produce such a difference in female psychiatric morbidity, while producing no difference in males.

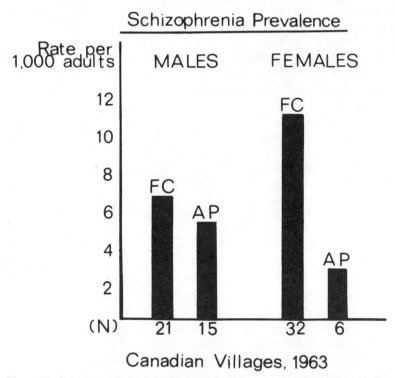

Figure 3.   Prevalence of schizophrenia in Catholic French-Canadian (FC) and in Protestant Anglo-Canadian (AP) villages in Eastern Canada, by sex. (From Murphy and Lemieux, 1967.)

If we look at the roles actually occupied and the functions actually performed by the women in the two sets of communities, little difference is apparent. They are the roles of parent, spouse, farmer's wife, retailer, and shop assistant, as in any agricultural community. Moreover, in both types of community, one can find some farms where the woman is clearly the dominant partner and others where the man is dominant; and in both there had been a tendency for the women of that generation to have stayed longer at school than the men. Thus, the women were a little better educated. With respect to the actual situation, therefore, there seems to be nothing sufficiently different between the women of the two groups of communities to provoke so different a prevalence of schizophrenia, given that the men do not show this difference. However, when we turn from actual roles to ideal ones, that is, to what each culture has held up to its girls as the ideal of womanhood, marked differences appear. In the rural Protestant tradition at that time, the ideals for women were similar to those for men, but somewhat more relaxed. A man was expected to be hard working, honest, moral, independent, responsible, and no less successful than his neighbors; a woman was expected to be hard working, moral, independent, loving, and loyal, but it was acceptable for her to leave the main responsibilities to the man if she so wished, and the concept of success was not so important for her. In the older French-Catholic tradition, a woman was expected to be a good mother, a religious person, a loyal spouse and a hard worker, and she was expected to subordinate herself to her spouse. However, onto that tradition had been grafted, somewhat imperfectly, a more modern doctrine taught by her school teachers, to the effect that she should exploit her superior education and whatever other abilities she possessed—a doctrine that did not easily harmonize with the older idea of subordinate status. In the Protestant communities, the woman was left free to dominate her husband, to be a meek wife, or to pursue an independent career, and there were no real conflicts between the models offered, although there was some conflict on the male side between the theory of all men being equal and the reality of some being better endowed than others. In the French-Catholic communities, there was a definite conflict between the older and the newer ideal models that women were shown, but they pretended that it did not exist.

The conflict of ideal models could, according to the theories advanced earlier, provoke the excess schizophrenia, because there was both an insistence that the women act to fit both sets of ideals and an absence of information as to how that could be done satisfactorily. The smarter women in these traditional villages did manage to satisfy both models by paying lip service to male dominance while at the same time discreetly ruling their husbands. However, that solution was never spoken about openly and each woman had to find it for herself, a task that, although less difficult than that of the Achinese males, was almost equally liable to lead to decisions that the community would label wrong. It can be argued that the excess of female cases might simply be an extreme example of chance variation, and it is certainly true that the explanation suggested here is unproven, but such a cultural hypothesis deserves serious attention.

Other examples of unusually high rates of schizophrenia are to be found in a district of Yugoslavia, among the Singapore Indians, and in certain tribes in Ghana and Liberia. In some of these cases (for instance, among the Singapore), cultural differences have been found between the high-risk group and its lower-risk neighbors that are in line with the arguments offered here; in other cases (for instance, in Liberia), no such differences have been found. Another curious finding, which seems to link schizophrenia to a cultural conflict affecting one sex more than the other, is the fact that in all Canadian subcultures for which comparisons could be made, the rate of schizophrenic first admissions to mental hospital was higher for Roman Catholic males than for non–Roman Catholic males. The most plausible reason for this phenomenon is that Catholic males encounter greater discrepancies between what their church teaches and what the society around them practices than do the males of most other Canadian religious traditions, Protestantism having made the greater accommodation to capitalism. Catholic males are faced with greater difficulties at reconciling these discrepancies, whereas their wives at home are less affected.

INCIDENCE AND PREVALENCE: LOW-RISK EXAMPLES

If there are cultures in which there are unusually high rates of schizophrenia, one would expect that there also are ones in which the rates are unusually low, but we have much less information on the latter, for reasons that were indicated earlier. If one encounters hospitalization statistics indicating a high rate of schizophrenia, these can usually be taken at face value once it has been ascertained that the diagnosis is being made in a customary fashion. If hospitalizations indicate a low rate, however, the most likely explanation is that the patients are not reaching the hospital. They may use private facilities, may seek treatment outside of their own district, or may simply stay at home, and it is therefore only after a field survey that the first impression of a low rate can be trusted. Numerous reports have come from anthropologists in which chronic psychosis is reported to be rare or absent in particular tribes, and it might seem that these reports would be a better source of information than hospital statistics in this matter. However, the reports can rarely be taken at face value, because the size of the population that such anthropologists prefer to study is usually only a few hundred. Therefore, if the average prevalence of schizophrenia is reported as 2–3 per 1,000, it is evident that most anthropological samples are too small for epidemiological purposes. For these reasons, only two main examples of low rates are offered here; both are instances where apparently low rates of hospitalized cases resulted in a field enquiry being undertaken. They concern a North American religious minority, the Hutterites, and some island peoples in the Pacific.

The Hutterite farming colonies of the Canadian and American Middle West had long had a reputation among local doctors and hospitals of good mental health, but it was known that they preferred to look after their own patients, and this reputation therefore invited testing. In the early 1950s, a survey of 19 colonies was carried out by Eaton and Weil (1955), and although the reputation for good mental health proved to be only partly justified, the team found only 8 active cases of schizophrenia in a population of about 8,500. Allowing for age, this is less than one-third the active prevalence rate obtained from the total 13 communities in the Eastern Canada study (see Table 1), and almost exactly one-third of the *hospitalized* prevalence rate for Eire, ignoring the Irish cases not present in hospital on the census day.

What is there in this population that might explain the low rate? One point that must be given consideration is chance genetic selection. In 1950 there were only 15 patronyms in the entire sect, with three names accounting for nearly half of the families, indicating that they stemmed from a very narrow genetic base. Another possibility is social selection, insofar as rules within the sect are strict and persons having difficulty conforming would be inclined to leave. With respect to other cultural influences, one might expect, on the basis of the argument just put forward concerning the Canadian Catholics, that there would be an excess of schizophrenia, because there is still a greater discrepancy between religious teachings and surrounding social norms for the Hutterites than there is for the Catholics. However, on this question there is an important difference to be noted. The Roman Catholic males mix freely and compete individually in the surrounding society; the Hutterites do not, but choose instead to keep themselves separate. As a group, they refuse to share many of the values and norms of the society around them, and they adhere to an interpretation of scripture that is very clear-cut. Moreover, they tend not to make important decisions as individuals, but rather to submit to the decisions of the group or of the colony leaders. Accordingly, it can be argued that as long as a member accepts the Hutterite creed and leadership, he will be considerably sheltered from the need to act on the basis of complex, unclear, or conflicting information.

The frequency of accepting the decisions of leaders or of the group may help explain the South Pacific findings as well. Anthropologists working there had suggested since the 1920s that chronic mental illness was usually (but not always) rare there, and when mental hospitals and psychiatric units spread through the region in the 1960s, the rates of admission were again usually, although not always, very low. In 1977–1978, your author had the opportunity to tour the region as a consultant, a position that permitted me not only to collect official data on such things as hospitalization and suicides, but also to undertake brief field surveys in limited locations (Murphy, 1978). These surveys employed, as far as possible, the same diagnostic criteria and the same basic, key-informant approaches as had been used in the Canadian villages survey. The greater speed with which the visits had to be undertaken was balanced, at least in part, by the greater knowledge that my Pacific informants had of their own communities. Table 1 presents the data from the best-covered communities in this exercise, as well as from the Hutterite survey and from the survey of the 13 Canadian rural communities. (Other Pacific communities yielded lower rates, but on the basis of less information.) The four small Pacific island communities yielded an overall rate practically identical to that of the Hutterites, and less than one-third that of the Canadian villages.

Chance genetic selection could not explain these results, because three racial groups are represented, and exogamy (not practiced among the Hutterites), is practiced in these groups. On Norfolk Island, with a largely European-origin population, conscious selection may have played a part, because the local community has steadily acquired new members from Australia, New Zealand, and other countries, but has also had the custom of putting them on probation for several years and of refusing them the right of further residence if they do not fit in. With the other islands, however, selection is not a factor. What seems more relevant is that these were all communities where a traditional subsistence economy could still operate without too much competition for land or fish, where most key decisions were communal rather than individual, and where there was considerable tolerance for minor deviancy. Because of that tolerance, a possible explanation for the low rate of recognized schizophrenia is that persons who might be judged to have borderline or simple schizophrenia on psychiatric examination might be overlooked by informants because their abnormalities of speech and other functions were ignored. However, the fact remains that the frequency of persons having their daily life disturbed by a schizophreniform illness was apparently low,[2] and transient schizophreniform disorders that were referred for treatment to the medical services also yielded very low treated-incidence rates. The idea that these low rates may be caused by sociocultural conditions is supported by the fact that, in some other South Pacific territories, notably New Caledonia and the Gilbert Islands, the incidence of cases coming into care is considerably higher, and there the local people are either outgrowing their territory

---

[2]A more intensive repeat of this field enquiry is taking place at time of writing.

Table 1.   Active prevalence (during 1 year) of schizophrenia in 4
South Pacific communities, as compared to 19 Hutterite communities and 13 Eastern Canadian communities[a]

Communities	Results		
	Population aged 15+	Cases	Rate
South Pacific			
'Eua (Tonga)	2,000	2	1.0
Aitutaki (Cook Isles)	1,100	3	2.7
Malu'u (Solomons)	1,700	5	2.9
Norfolk Island	1,200	2	1.7
Total	6,000	12	2.0[b]
Hutterite			
(United States and Canada)	4,100	8	1.9
Eastern Canada	18,400	121	6.6

[a] From Murphy (1978) and Eaton and Weil (1955).
[b] Average rate of schizophrenia for South Pacific communities.

and needing to compete for survival (Gilberts) or are being exposed to
unusually drastic social change (New Caledonia).

If one considers only sections of whole societies, then it is possible to
find rates both higher (among the least advantaged) and lower (among the
most advantaged) than those discussed here, because competition undoubtedly leads to schizophrenia-bearing individuals and families being
pushed out of the more advantageous positions. Furthermore, the gap
between the rates of the most and of the least advantaged is necessarily
greater in a highly competitive society (such as that of Texas) than in one
that is much less competitive (such as that of Poland). However, such
selection is unlikely to be relevant to the examples presented here. If one
takes these examples and compares them with other rates for schizophrenia
available in the literature, due allowance being made for type of rate and
diagnostic criteria, another point worthy of comment appears. The average
of other reported rates of schizophrenia seems to be much closer to the level
reported in these low-incidence examples than to that found in the high-
incidence examples. Therefore, it seems likely that there is a certain
minimum risk of schizophrenia, against which culture cannot protect
people, and that although most societies achieve something close to that
minimum, there are a few that, perhaps only over a limited period, manage
to add substantially to that risk.

SYMPTOMATOLOGY

In examining incidence, it has proved most profitable to seek the extremes
of cross-cultural variation and then to try to explain these extremes. The

same approach should theoretically be appropriate for each of the main schizophrenic symptoms, because we might then also be able to distinguish the fundamental symptoms, which are always present, from the pathoplastic symptoms, which can change with circumstance. Unfortunately, in practice that approach will not work, because it is only through its symptoms that we can recognize the disease's presence, and clinicians customarily do not assign the diagnosis of schizophrenia if what they consider to be fundamental symptoms are absent. In place of the approach used with incidence, we have the alternatives of 1) confining our attention to the very small number of studies in which culture-linked differences in symptomatology have been looked for; 2) turning to international comparison studies, which cover a wider range of social groups, but in which cultural influences are ignored; or 3) depending on clinicians' impressions.

The second of these categories of study, international comparisons, has provided the largest amount of seemingly "hard" data, but when looked at more closely, these data prove to have controlled inadequately for such confounding variables as social class, chronicity of illness, and the diagnostic orientations of the usually numerous collaborating clinicians.[3] For this reason, the investigators in these studies have, probably correctly, tended to play down the differences that they find, and your author is inclined to do the same. Regarding the third category, clinicians' impressions, there is also the risk of such confounding variables intervening, but if one collects such impressions from people who are sensitive to sociocultural factors, one can expect a certain correction to have taken place, and if the net is thrown widely enough, one may be able to distinguish broad patterns that can offer a basis for tentative theorizing. Therefore, I first discuss some of these broad patterns, and then deal with research in which cultural differences were specifically looked for and analyzed.

Table 2 summarizes the impressions of 40 psychiatrists in 27 countries, as collected in the early 1960s. These psychiatrists were all interested in transcultural comparisons, they had all worked with patients from more than one culture, and they were specifically asked to compare two or more such groups of patients. They spanned a wide range of views concerning the definition of schizophrenia, and the patients with whom they worked were

---

[3]The International Pilot Study of Schizophrenia has been the most carefully designed research of this type, yielding uniform data in 9 countries on some 1200 patients, over 800 of them diagnosed as schizophrenic. However the study includes exceptional statements, such as in the case of one country in which "19 of the 20 hebephrenics were examined and diagnosed by the same collaborating psychiatrist; the possibility that he was in general more inclined to make this diagnosis than other psychiatrists cannot be excluded" (WHO., 1973, p. 165). Again, looking at the demographic information on the districts from which the patients were drawn, it turns out that in the one supposedly representative of the United States, 20% of the labor force were professionals and only 4% were unskilled workers. Attempts are now being made in a new WHO-sponsored study to overcome some of these limitations.

Table 2. Impressionistic associations between schizophrenic symptoms and cultural groupings

Features of schizophrenia	Sociocultural correlates	Significance (p)
Paranoid type	MOST frequent in urban middle classes	0.05
	LEAST frequent in rural populations	0.05
Catatonic type	LEAST frequent in Euro-Americans	0.05
Hebephrenic type	MOST frequent in Japanese and Okinawans	0.05
Simplex type	MOST frequent in Asians	0.01
Visual hallucinations	MOST frequent in Africa and Near East	0.05
	LEAST frequent in urban Euro-Americans	0.01
Tactile hallucinations	MOST frequent in Africa and Near East	0.10
Delusions of grandeur	MOST frequent in rural populations	0.001
Delusions of destruction	MOST frequent in Christian populations	0.01
Religious delusions	MOST frequent in Christian populations	0.01
	LEAST frequent in Buddhist, Hindu and Shintoist groups	0.01
Delusions of jealousy	MOST frequent in Asian populations	0.05
Depersonalization	LEAST frequent in rural populations	0.01
Flatness of affect	MOST frequent in Japanese and Okinawans	0.01
	HIGH frequency in South American peoples	0.05
Social withdrawal	MOST frequent in Japanese and Okinawans	0.01
Negativism	MOST frequent in India and South America	0.001
Excitement	MOST frequent in Africa and South America	0.05
	LEAST frequent in Anglo-Saxon cultures	0.05
Stereotypic behavior	MOST frequent in East Indians	0.05
	LEAST frequent in Euro-Americans	0.001
Catatonic rigidity	MOST frequent in East Indians	0.01
Suicidal behavior	MOST frequent in Japanese	0.001
Temper outbursts	MOST frequent in Christian populations	0.05

[a]From Murphy et al. (1963).

not necessarily representative of the totality of schizophrenics in the society on which they were reporting. These facts should be borne in mind when interpreting the research results. [In the paper by Murphy et al. (1963), the relationship of some such "observational" factors to the reported distribution of symptoms is also analyzed.]

There are four main categories of variable reflected in the impressions summarized in Table 2: 1) an environmental or situational variable (urban-rural), 2) a religious variable, 3) a variable relating to general, nonschizophrenic traits (suicidal tendencies in the Japanese, for instance), and 4) a variable probably relating to education. In addition, there must be allowance for factors affecting the observing psychiatrist, so that, for instance, many of the features attributed to Euro-American patients may be accounted for by the fact that American psychiatrists (and Latin-American psychiatrists trained in the United States) apply the term *schizophrenia* more broadly than psychiatrists elsewhere.

Regarding the environmental or situational variable, it seems generally true that the paranoid symptoms, notably delusions of reference, are more common in urban than in rural patients. The reason for this is probably that urban people live in a man-made world where everything is expected to have a discernible cause, and the patients therefore seek to assign a cause to their abnormal experiences through their delusions. Rural people, on the other hand, are more accustomed to the unexplainable vagaries of the weather, crop failure, and other natural forces, so that their patients feel less obliged to seek an explanation for every experience. An alternative theory for this urban/rural difference involves the concept of projection, and some psychoanalysts would say that urban populations have developed greater tendencies than rural populations to use projection as a defense. However, there does not seem to be any particular reason for this to happen, and the suggested need for explanation accounts better than the projection theory for the most notable exception to this urban/rural difference, that found in West Africa. West African schizophrenics from rural areas show marked paranoid ideas (Sow, 1978), and the reason seems to be that such ideas are characteristic not of their illness, but of their whole society. Their culture teaches individuals to attribute all misfortune to attacks by other people who are motivated by revenge, envy, or witchcraft needs. It has been claimed that this persecution belief is a projection (Ortigues and Ortigues, 1973), but the argument is not convincing.

The religious variable reflected in the table has its bearing mainly on the content of delusions and illustrates a more general rule—that such content is markedly affected by culture and is a relatively superficial, pathoplastic feature of the disease despite the importance that some clinicians assign to it. Elementary examples of rapid shifts in the content of schizophrenic delusions are found among South American Indians whose move to the cities results in delusions of radio waves and secret police replacing the more traditional delusions about saints, witchcraft, and jungle spirits. Of more interest was a return to delusions about spirit possession in Japan at the end of World War II after the power of the Emperor was so diminished that he ceased to be a satisfactory focus for religious belief. However, when secret police become an important reality in an urban society, delusions about them decline. That Christians should have more delusions of destruction than people of other (mainly Asian) religions, is most probably because of the wrathful character of the Old Testament scriptures, but this calls for special investigation.

Symptoms that seem to be mere exaggerations of general, noncultural traits form the third category of associations in Table 2, schizophrenic, and it could be argued that they should not be thought of as being linked to the disease at all. For instance, during the 1950s the Japanese had one of the highest suicide rates in the world, and few of those taking their own lives were schizophrenic, so that the reference to the association between the Japanese culture and suicidal tendencies as a schizophrenic symptom, which one finds in Table 2, would seem to be an error. However, it would be no less of an error to assume that because a particular characteristic is found in nonschizophrenics, it has nothing to do with a possible relationship between schizophrenia and a given culture. Irish-American schizophrenics exhibit excessive concern about sin and sexual guilt, and a preoccupation with such ideas might contribute to the development of the disease, regardless of the fact that many Irish nonschizophrenics also share this preoccupation. Anglo-Saxons are generally believed to be dull and unexcitable, but is this a sufficient explanation for their schizophrenics having the lowest frequency of catatonic excitement, as Table 2 indicates?

The fourth category, education, poses a similar problem, namely whether it should be regarded as part of culture or as independent of it. It is possible that the relative prominence of depersonalization symptoms among Euro-American patients arises from the fact that their higher average education makes them better able to identify and to communicate these relatively subtle sensations, while the predominance of tactile and visual hallucinations among African patients may relate to the relatively small part that words play in the lives of some of these unschooled peoples. However, one can argue that American culture would not be the same if there were not so high a level of education, and, on the other hand, a higher level of African education, if freely chosen and not imported from the West, might put a much higher value on visual and kinesthetic experiences than European culture does. (The suggestion that the relative predominance of visual and tactile over auditory hallucinations in Africa—a feature also described in other papers—is linked to education is an unproven hypothesis, but it is the author's impression that that same characteristic is much less prominent in African university students who develop the disease.)

Some of the rows in Table 2 relate to a single pair of related cultures, the Japanese and Okinawans, but there are more precise studies of the symptomatology of Japanese and Japanese-American psychiatric patients, and these form a better basis for discussion, leading from what have been mere impressions to something more concrete. The first of the studies, that by Schooler and Caudill (1964), focused on the preadmission symptomatology of patients admitted to a large mental hospital in Tokyo and to a state mental hospital in Maryland, a diagnosis of schizophrenia having been established for the former group by a joint United States–Japanese team in the hope of equalizing criteria. A 50-item symptom and sign checklist was used to abstract uniform data from the case records, but the patients and their families were not directly contacted. The first finding was that there was a 39% more frequent history of assaultiveness among the Japanese than among the American patients, the assaults being made mainly against mother or spouse. Further findings were that the Japanese patients showed significantly more social withdrawal, apathy, and sleep disturbances than the American ones, but also more emotional lability and euphoria, while the Amerian patients showed significantly more hallucinations and bizarre ideas. These findings were in part confirmed and in part contradicted by a later study of Japanese-American and Caucasian patients at Hawaii State Hospital (Katz et al., 1978), because, although the former showed more withdrawal than the latter, they did not, in the hospital, show any greater assaultiveness. That difference could have been caused by the change of setting (Hawaii in place of Tokyo), but further research provided a more probable explanation, one that harmonized with some of the theories of Schooler and Caudill. Although the Japanese-American patients were quiet in the hospital, inquiries to the family indicated that they were considered significantly more negative, violent, and suspicious outside the hospital (Katz et al. 1978).

The Hawaii team has interpreted the difference between reported behavior inside and outside of the hospital as indicating a difference in communal expectations, something that could be true. However, when one takes the two sets of data together, it seems likely that Japanese schizophrenics change their behavior much more than American (Caucasian) ones when moving from home to hospital. Schooler and Caudill (1964), drawing on the clinical experience of a leading Japanese psychiatrist, Takeo Doi, link the aggressiveness of the Japanese patients in their own home and their passivity in the hospital to a type of dependency need (*amaeru*) that the culture fosters and that the patients' families, it is hypothesized, are not believed to be responding to. There is no direct evidence to indicate whether the families are actually deficient in responding to *amaeru* or whether that is a delusion on the patient's part. There is also no evidence to distinguish between that hypothesis and the alternative, but not incompatible one, that the family members are overpossessive. However, there is a striking association between birth rank and schizophrenia among the Japanese (Caudill, 1963), one that varies with social class, and this can be interpreted along the same lines, that is, as resulting from the ways in which economically secure and economically insecure families are able to satisfy the dependency needs of their older and of their younger offspring.

A comparison has also been made in Hawaii between the symptoms of Filipino and Japanese schizophrenics (Enright and Jaeckle, 1963), but most of the other detailed comparisons of schizophrenic symptoms in two or more cultures have taken place on the Atlantic seaboard. There the most notable work was that by Opler and Singer (1956) on Irish- and Italian-Americans, and Parsons's (1960, 1969) comparison of Bostonians and Southern Italians. Other work includes Sperling's thesis (1953) on Irish-, Italian-, and Jewish-American patients; Sanua's (1964) discussion of the family characteristics and symptoms of patients from the same groups, in addition to Protestants; Piedmont's (1962) comparison of German- and Polish-American patients; and Murphy's (1974) work with French- and British-Canadians. Sometimes the comparisons were made only from records, but Opler and Singer showed the value (and perhaps the dangers) of open-ended interviewing, and Parsons used a predominantly anthropological approach in Naples, comparing the family dynamics of the Italian schizophrenic with those in neighboring families as well as with those in North American families. It was found that Irish-American patients showed obsessive thinking about the subjects of sin and sex, relative persistence of delusions, and conflict feelings around mother figures, while Italian-American patients showed significantly more disturbed behavior and rejection of authority (Fantl and Schiro, 1959; and Opler and Singer, 1956). Italian-American patients also shared with Southern Italian patients an only slightly disguised homosexual tendency (Parsons, 1969). German-American schizophrenics seem to be predominantly paranoid, exhibiting suspiciousness, delusions, and hostility, while the Polish-American group were more dependent, manipulative, and somatizing, and showed more catatonic symptoms (Piedmont, 1962).

In all of these studies the differences seem to be genuine, not just a projection of the researcher's expectations. However, many of the results concern only the content of delusions, something that we know is pathoplastic, and it is usually not possible to assess from them to what degree other more supposedly fundamental symptoms of schizophrenia can vary, particularly because there is no real independence of the researcher's observations from his expectations. An exception, however, can be found in the comparison of French- and British-Canadians, because the data were collected by means of a precise, lengthy, and carefully translated interview schedule, and the comparison was repeated in a different part of the country and with depressives. (In nearly all the studies referred to, an effort had been made to match patients with respect to sex, age, chronicity, and social class, and to have the same people interview each group.) Table 3 abstracts from this study some results relating to what is usually considered a fundamental symptom: social withdrawal. As is evident, the French-Canadian schizophrenics retain a high degree of interest in their family and social environment, while the British-Canadian schizophrenics conform more to textbook descriptions, because they have largely lost that interest. (All patients had had the disorder for over one year, but less than five years, and diagnostic criteria were closely similar.) This difference between the two groups reflects a broader cultural difference, because French-Canadians are in general more communally oriented and British-Canadians more individualistic, but the table suggests that the disease does not, as had formerly been thought, destroy an interest in the social milieu. Instead, it seems that social withdrawal is only one more secondary reaction.

CHRONICITY AND COURSE OF ILLNESS

When Kraepelin first made his important differentiation between manic-depressive psychosis and what we now call schizophrenia in 1896, he assigned to the latter the name *dementia praecox*, implying by the use of the term *dementia* that he considered the condition to involve an irreversible

Table 3. Percentage frequency of symptoms of social withdrawal in young male British-Canadian and French-Canadian schizophrenics, matched for chronicity, as recorded with the Mental Status Schedule[a]

| Symptoms | Percentage frequency | | | | |
	BrCan.	Fr.-Can.	Br.-Can.	Fr.-Can.	Significance (p)
Reported on schizophrenics only	Quebec		Ontario		
Complains abundantly of family, friends, and associates	0	65	0	70	0.001
Feels people avoid, reject, or dislike him	12	50	10	70	0.01
Says people know of his guilt, faults, or problems	12	60	10	60	0.01
Reported of both schizophrenics and depressives Feels that he has no friends	Schizophrenia		Depression		
	27	40	20	60	0.02

[a]From Murphy (1974).

loss of thinking power. When Bleuler introduced the term *schizophrenia* in 1911, he did this not only to stress what he considered to be the key feature of the condition, the split personality, but also to correct or protest against Kraepelin's assumption that this is a dementia with irreversible loss. Bleuler's view has prevailed, and it is widely accepted today that schizophrenics can achieve full social recovery. However, there is still some disagreement among psychiatrists concerning how long symptoms should be present before a diagnosis of schizophrenia is made, as opposed to simply a diagnosis of psychosis, and how often chronic deterioration could be expected to occur. Most European psychiatrists in the past saw schizophrenia, in its typical form, as consisting in "a slow, steady deterioration of the entire personality" (Henderson and Gillespie, 1950, p. 295). North American psychiatrists usually had a less gloomy view, but this was linked to the fact that they were applying the diagnosis to what the European would consider to be borderline conditions, perhaps not even psychoses. However, when the European psychiatrists went to work in Africa, Asia, and other developing regions, they frequently found that the cases that they had diagnosed as schizophrenia were recovering more rapidly and completely than their training had led them to expect. Some of these clinicians then decided simply not to apply the term *schizophrenia* to these patients, and one stated that he only found one single true case of schizophrenia in over 300 East African psychotics, most of whom had been labeled schizophrenic by his colleagues (Tewfik, 1958). Others thought that the problem lay not in the diagnosis, but in the prognosis.

The first serious attempt to explore chronicity cross-culturally was made on the island of Mauritius (Figure 4), where the population is partly of Asian and partly of African origin, and where the ratio of psychiatric beds to population at that time was close to European standards. The schizophrenia incidence rate, not counting various forms of reactive psychosis, was almost identical to that in Britain, and the presenting symptoms were very similar to those of British patients. However, 72% of the Mauritian sample had no signs of psychosis and were economically independent at time of follow-up, as compared to 56% and 45% of patients, respectively, in two British follow-up studies—a significant difference. Moreover, 59% of the Mauritian sample had had no reported symptoms since discharge from the mental hospital, as compared to 34% of the British comparison group (Murphy and Raman, 1971).

Murphy and Raman's study, when read in combination with previous psychiatric reports from the tropics, suggests that there might be a general difference between developing and developed countries regarding prognosis in schizophrenia. The large-scale International Pilot Study of Schizophrenia (WHO, 1979) gave support to that hypothesis by revealing clear differences between Nigerian and Indian samples on the one hand, and British, Czechoslovakian, Danish, and American samples on the other.

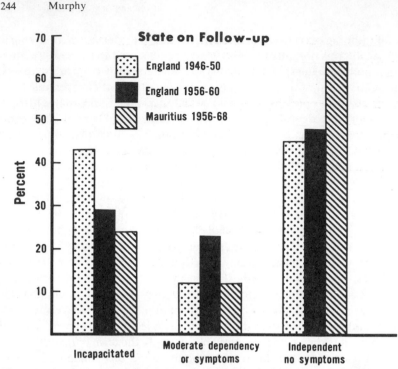

Figure 4.   State of schizophrenic patients in Mauritius and in England at time of follow-up study. (From Murphy and Raman, 1971.)

Since then, a smaller study in Sri Lanka (Waxler, 1979) and a repeat of the Mauritius survey (unpublished) have turned up very similar findings. A follow-up of patients in a different part of India from that used for the WHO study, however, uncovered just as much chronicity as was found in European societies (Kulhara and Wig, 1978).

Even if one disregards the Kulhara and Wig study, which was less complete in its follow-up than the others, it is highly unlikely that so simple a division as that between developing and developed societies would yield a satisfactory explanation for the findings, just as the simple division into chronic and nonchronic proves unsatisfactory as soon as one looks more closely at the data. Between chronic illness and full health, a variety of semichronic states is possible, and there is also a variety of societal types along the developmental continuum. It is too early to draw conclusions from the data we possess on this subject, because, for most of the sources, and certainly for the WHO sources, it is not at all clear that the samples are truly comparable and truly representative. Nevertheless, the evidence indicates that a large number of factors might be operating here, often in conjunction. We can hypothesize that among such factors are:

1.   *Social rejection.*   The more a society rejects and fears the schizophrenic, the greater the difficulty he must overcome in regaining normal roles.

2.   *Rigidity of role ideals.*   The more strictly a society defines what it considers to be the qualities of a "true" man or woman, the more liable schizophrenics are to relapse after they find that they have deviated from these ideals.

3.   *Assignment of responsibility.*   The more patients are expected to be accountable for their own disturbed behavior in the past, the more likely they are to relapse when faced with the task of rationally accounting for that behavior.

4.   *Reality testing.*   The more ambiguously a culture separates what it considers to be real from what it considers to be unreal, the more easily the schizophrenics with impaired reality-testing are able to merge with the masses.

5.   *Sick-role typing.*   The more a society believes that insanity is chronic, the less it will facilitate the patient's efforts to break out of the sick role once he has entered it, even though there may be great tolerance and support for the sick role.

6.   *Acceptance of dependency.*   The more a culture tolerates the idea of dependency, the longer patients are content to remain in the sick role, when the caring agency is seen as benevolent and the external realities are considered harsher.

7.   *Social networks.*   The more interconnected people are in a society, the more aid a patient is likely to find in resisting relapse, assuming that he has retained a place within the society.

Examples could be offered in support of each of these hypothesized factors, but examples could also be offered in contradiction of each of them because they are all present to some degree in every society, and they frequently operate against each other. Thus, the difference between the results from Agra (WHO, 1979) and from Chandigarh (Kulhara and Wig, 1978) in India could be explained on the basis that the latter catchment area is more urban, yields less social support, and is more liable to reject abnormal behavior. However, in a Canadian study it was found that chronicity was less in the more urban than in the more rural parts of a catchment area (Murphy, 1977, footnote 18). A likely explanation for this is that, although the rural population yielded greater support, it also taught a greater acceptance of dependency, and its patients made less effort to regain more normal but more stressful roles. In 1977, the World Health Organization launched a new international study into factors affecting the outcome of major mental illness. The study attempts to disentangle some of these complications, but the task is a difficult one.

RESPONSE TO DRUG TREATMENTS

In comparing outcomes, one might expect treatment to be a major factor for which allowance should be made. However, this is, in fact, rarely done, in part because it has been groups with the more abundant treatments that have had the poorer outcomes, in part because treatment of schizophrenia is seen as alleviating rather than curing the disorder, and in part because the treatments, both organic and social, are so unstandardized that controlling for them would be difficult. However, there seems little doubt that certain drugs do work better in some ethnic groups than in others. The matter is only being touched on here because at the present stage of research we do not know whether the relevant variables are genetic, dietary, sociocultural, or something else, and to discuss the variations under the heading of culture would be presumptuous. Nevertheless, there is some indication that culture might be a factor, and the question certainly should receive further study.

The data that point most strongly to a cultural rather than to an organic factor derive from Djakarta, where patients of different cultural backgrounds, but of the same race, same social setting, and same diet, are treated by the same psychiatric staff. Some drug trials with schizophrenics have taken place there, in which culture (tribe) was recorded but was not initially accorded any attention. When the results of these drug trials were reexamined, taking culture into consideration, it was found that, with the same drug in approximately the same dosage, patients from one Malaysian subculture showed significantly more rapid loss of confusion and irritability, but significantly slower loss of delusions and excitement, than patients of another subculture (Murphy, 1972). Other differences in responses to psychotropic drugs have been found between Europeans and North Americans and between different subcultures in North America. Such differences sometimes apply not only to schizophrenic symptoms but also to the reactions of healthy volunteers. In the Djakarta material, a major cultural difference between the two samples was that one has a matrilineal tradition and the other has a patrilineal tradition, but this seems less potentially relevant than attitude toward authority. Patients from some cultures will consciously or unconsciously fight against, or overreact to, what they feel a drug is doing, while patients from others will cooperate with the treatment.

CONCLUSIONS

From the evidence that has been reviewed in this chapter, it is clear that schizophrenia does vary much more from one culture to another than would be expected from chance. The important question is whether this variance affects the basic schizophrenic process or only the ways in which that process manifests itself. Without better knowledge regarding what that process is, the question cannot be definitely answered. There is, however, an only slightly less important question that can more confidently be answered, namely whether culture affects the degree of disability that the schizophrenic process produces. The answer to this is clearly yes. Sociocultural conditions seem to make a great difference in determining whether patients can regain socially normal functioning after a schizophrenic episode. These conditions can determine whether the symptoms invite acceptance or rejection of the patient by society, and they probably influence whether or not predisposed persons develop the disease. We do not know just how these influences operate, but there are plausible hypotheses available, and the subject could therefore be a profitable one for future research.

REFERENCES

Bales, R. T. 1946. Cultural differences in rates of alcoholism. Q. J. Stud. Alcohol 6:484–496.

Bateson, G., Jackson, D.D., Haley, J., and Weakland, J. 1956. Towards a theory of schizophrenia. Behav. Sci. 1:251–264.

Caudill, W. 1963. Sibling rank and life style among Japanese psychiatric patients. In: H. Alkimoto (ed.), Proceedings of the Joint Meeting of the Japanese Society of Psychiatry and the American Psychiatric Association, 1963. Folia Psychiatr. Neurol. Jpn. 1964, Supplement no. 7.

Cooper, J.E. Kendell, R.E., Gurland, B.J., Sharpe, L., Copeland, J.R.M., and Simon, R. 1972. Psychiatric Diagnosis in New York and London. Oxford University Press, London.

Dunne, D. 1970. Psychiatric problems in County Mayo. Corridor Echo: The Journal of St. Mary's Hospital. (Quoted by A. M. Greely (1972) in: That Most Distressful Nation: The Taming of the American Irish. Quadrangle Books, Chicago.)

Eaton, J.W., and Weil, R.J. 1955. Culture and Mental Disorders. Free Press, Glencoe.

Enright, J. B., and Jaeckle, W.R. 1963. Psychiatric symptoms and diagnosis in two subcultures. Int. J. Soc. Psychiatry 9:12–17.

Fantl, B., and Schiro, J. 1959. Cultural variables in the behavior patterns and symptom formation of 15 Irish and 15 Italian female schizophrenics. Int. J. Soc. Psychiatry 4:245–253.

Henderson, D., and Gillespie, R.D. 1950. A Textbook of Psychiatry for Students and Practitioners. 7th Ed. Oxford University Press, London.

Hurgronje, C.S. 1906. The Achinese. Luzac, London.

Jacobs, J. 1894. Het Familie en Kampongleven op Groot-Atcheh. Brill, Leiden.

Jocano, F.L. 1971. Varieties of supernatural experiences among Filipino peasants: Hallucination or idiom of cultural cognition? Paper presented at the American Psychiatric Association meeting, 1970, Honolulu. Summarized in Transcult. Psychiatr. Res. Rev. 1971, 8:43–45.

Katz, M.M., Sanborn, K.O., Lowery, H.A., and Ching, J. 1978. Ethnic studies in Hawaii: Psychopathology and social deviance. In: L. Wynne, R. L. Cromwell, and S. Matthysse (eds.), The Nature of Schizophrenia, Chapter 51. John Wiley & Sons, Inc., New York.

Kelleher, M.J., and Copeland, J.R.M. 1973. Psychiatric diagnosis in Cork and London: Results of a cross-national pilot study. J. Irish Med. Assoc. 66:553–557.

Kulhara, P., and Wig, N.N. 1978. The chronicity of schizophrenia in North West India: Results of a follow-up study. Br. J. Psychiatry 132:186-190.

Malzberg, B. 1940. Social and Biological Aspects of Mental Disease. New York State Hospitals, Utica.

Murphy, H.B.M. 1968. Cultural factors in the genesis of schizophrenia. In: D. Rosenthal and S.S. Kety (eds.), The Transmission of Schizophrenia. Pergamon Press, Oxford.

Murphy, H.B.M. 1972. Psychopharmacologie et variations ethno-culturelles. Confrontat. Psychiatr. 9:163-185.

Murphy, H.B.M. 1974. Differences between mental disorders in French Canadians and British Canadians. Can. Psychiatr. Assoc. J. 19:247-257.

Murphy, H.B.M. 1975. Alcoholism and schizophrenia in the Irish: A review. Transcult. Psychiatr. Res. Rev. 12:116-139.

Murphy, H.B.M. 1977. Chronicity, community, and culture. In: C. Chiland and P. Bequart (eds.), Long-term Treatments of Psychotic States. Human Sciences Press, New York.

Murphy, H.B.M. 1978. Mental Health Trends in the Pacific Islands. South Pacific Commission, Noumea, New Caledonia.

Murphy, H.B.M., and Lemieux, M. 1967. Quelques considérations sur le taux élevé de schizophrénie dans un type de communauté canadienne-française. Can. Psychiatr. Assoc. J. 12:S72-S81.

Murphy, H.B.M., and Raman, A.C. 1971. The chronicity of schizophrenia in indigenous tropical peoples. Br. J. Psychiatry 118:489-497.

Murphy, H.B.M., Wittkower, E.D., Fried, J. and Ellenberger, H. 1963. A cross-cultural survey of schizophrenic symptomatology. Int. J. Soc. Psychiatry 9:237-249.

O'Hare, A., and Walsh, D. Undated. Activities of Irish Psychiatric Hospitals and Units, 1965-1969. Medico-Social Research Board, Dublin.

Opler, M.K., and Singer, J.L. 1956. Ethnic differences in behavior and psychopathology: Italian and Irish. Int. J.Soc. Psychiatry 2:11-23.

Ortigues, M.C., and Ortigues, E. 1973. Oedipe Africain. Rev. Ed. Plon, Paris.

Parsons, A. 1969. A comparison of Italian and 'Yankee' schizophrenics. Review and newsletter. Transcult. Res. Ment. Health Probl. 9:43-50.

Parsons, A. 1969. Belief, Magic, and Anomie: Essays in Psychosocial Anthropology. Free Press, New York.

Piedmont, E.B. 1962. An Investigation of Ethnic Grouping Differences in the Development of Schizophrenia. Doctoral thesis, University of Buffalo. (Abstracted in Transcult. Psychiatr. Res. Rev. 1966, 3:160-161.)

Sanua, V.D. 1964. A comparative study of schizophrenics of different socio-cultural backgrounds (Protestant, Irish, Catholic, and Jewish). Paper presented at the 1st International Congress of Social Psychiatry, London. (Abstract of related draft in Transcult. Psychiatr. Res. Rev. 1964, 1:63-65.)

Scheper-Hughes, N. 1979. Saints, Scholars, and Schizophrenics: Mental Illness in Rural Ireland. University of California Press, Berkeley.

Schooler, C., and Caudill, W. 1964. Symptomatology in Japanese and American schizophrenics. Ethnology 3:172-178.

Sow, I. 1978. Psychiatrie Dynamique Africaine. Payot, Paris.

Sperling, P.R. 1953. A study of the psychotic within three ethnic groups. Doctoral thesis. Harvard University, Cambridge, Mass.

Tewfik, G.I. 1958. Psychoses in Africa. In: Mental Disorders and Mental Health in Africa South of the Sahara, pp. 127-138. CSA, London.

Tracy, H. 1953. Mind You, I've Said Nothing. Methuen, London.

van Loon, F.H.G. 1920. The problem of lunacy in Acheen. Mededelingen Burger-lijken geneeskundigen Dienst 10:2–49.

Waxler, N.E. 1979. Is outcome for schizophrenia better in nonindustrial societies? The case of Sri Lanka. J. Nerv. Ment. Dis. 167:144–158.

World Health Organization. 1973. Report of the International Pilot Study of Schizophrenia. Vol. 1 WHO, Geneva.

World Health Organization. 1979. Schizophrenia: An International Follow-up Study. John Wiley & Sons, Inc., New York.

Wynne L., Cromwell, R. L., and Matthysse, S. (eds.). 1978. The Nature of Schizophrenia. John Wiley & Sons, Inc., New York.

Chapter 10

Culture and Depression

Frank Engelsmann

Depression is a common experience. Transient episodes of depressive affect are normal, necessary, and universal components of human life. Depressive affect is distinct from depressive illness, which Hippocrates called melancholia, and which Kraepelin, in 1899, labeled manic-depressive insanity. Clinical and biochemical findings on affective disorders indicate that depression is not unitary but a heterogeneous syndrome.

Links between culture and depression do exist, but they are multifaceted and complex and thus are difficult to assess and to interpret. Culture can have an effect on the development and course of depression as well as on response to treatment. Culture can also minimize the development of depressive illness and influence the choice and pattern of depressive phenomena.

In this chapter, cross-cultural approaches to the study of depression as a symptom and as a syndrome are reviewed. The focus is on methods of classification and assessment of depression and its epidemiology in selected cultures. Also evaluated are the social and cultural theories that underlie both the etiology of depression and its conceptualization as a disorder and as an illness in different cultures.

The concept of depression is insufficiently defined. This problem has greatly impeded research and cross-cultural comparison of studies of depression. Introduction of the concept of depressive experience has extended investigations of culture-depression relationships beyond the limits of depression as a clinical syndrome and nosological entity, making the problem larger and more difficult to explore. The description and interpretation of depressive phenomena in their relation to identified ethnocultural characteristics requires a knowledge of cultures and an understanding of culture-sickness relationships, which operate on different levels of complexity. The role of social and cultural components in depressive experience and their interaction with pathology are still poorly

251

understood. Literature on cross-cultural variations of depression continues to yield inconclusive and often controversial results. A better understanding of this problem requires an interdisciplinary approach to biological and anthropological studies, which could provide an account of the cultural meaning of both normal and abnormal behavior.

DEPRESSION AS A HUMAN EXPERIENCE AND AS AN ILLNESS

What do we mean by depression? The concept of depression acquires different meanings under different psychological, social, and cultural circumstances. Depressive manifestations may be transient and appropriate reactions to loneliness, alienation, loss, and other trauma and stress. Depression may be a concomitant or a consequence of acute and chronic physical illness. When does the depressive personality feature, reaction, or phenomenon become a depressive symptom or syndrome? People differ in tolerance and coping capacities. They may attribute depression to a variety of causes, ranging from supernatural powers to the hardships of life. Hutterites, for example, refer to depression as *Anfechtung*, meaning "temptation by the devil" (Eaton and Weil, 1955). There are even cultures that have no concepts representing depression (Borneo, Malaysia, and several African and American Indian cultures). Depression can be expressed somatically and may lack cognitive representation. It should be distinguished, however, from dysphoria and other abnormal behavior. A reasonably valid identification of depressive disorders in terms of symptoms, syndromes, course of illness, and reaction to treatment can be made. Although the concept of depressive illness may be culture bound, it can still be reasonably well defined.

Common signs and symptoms of depression include emotional, physical, behavioral, and cognitive changes. A sad mood, as well as a lack of energy, interest, and enjoyment (anhedonia) belong to the essential clinical features of depression. Emotional changes include sadness, guilt feelings, anger, and anxiety. Physical symptoms involve disturbances of sleep, loss of appetite and weight, and weakness and fatigability. Behavioral changes are manifested in crying spells, withdrawal, and psychomotor retardation or agitation. Cognitive changes are reflected in low and negative self-percept, pessimism, self-blame, and feelings of hopelessness, worthlessness, and uselessness. Suicidal tendencies are often present in depression. Severe depression may be accompanied by delusions of sin and guilt and accusatory and threatening hallucinations. One component of the diagnosis can be derived from the response to medication and treatment, which can be predicted on the basis of genetic history. Response to the treatment of depression has been explored in various ethnic groups.

HISTORICAL VIEW

Links between culture and depression have attracted the attention of clinicians and researchers over the last three decades. It has become increasingly difficult to review the exhaustive literature. Reviews of the literature on depression reveal several central issues, such as the low incidence of depression in non-Western cultures, the lack of guilt feelings and prominent somatization in depressives in some oriental ethnocultural groups, and the lack of universal validity of the concept of depression across cultures. General reviews of cross-cultural studies of depression were published by Benedict and Jacks (1954), Al-Issa (1970), and Kiev (1972). Silverman (1968) prepared one of the first comprehensive reviews of the epidemiology of depression. Pfeiffer (1968) evaluated 40 studies of depression, 22 of which were from non-Western cultures. German (1972) reported on explorations of depression in Sub-Saharan countries and Prince (1968) made a critical review of studies on depression in Africa. Tan (1977) reviewed affective symptoms in non-Western countries, and Yap (1965) reported on the phenomenology of affective disorders in Chinese and other cultures. Fabrega (1974, 1975) and Singer (1975) tried to systematize the social and cultural components associated with depression. Sartorius (1973) stressed the usefulness of cross-cultural approaches for classification and treatment of depressive disorders. Singer (1975), as well as many others, have attempted to find the core symptoms of a universally valid concept of depression, contrary to researchers like Marsella (1978, 1980) and Kleinman (1977), who have stressed the culture-specific influences in the etiology, manifestations, and course of depressive illness and experience. Kleinman (1978, p. 295) argues that depressive disease (a biological disorder of the brain's monoamine neurotransmitters) is universal, but depressive *illness* (the personal and social experience of depressive disease) is culture specific because illness is, by definition, a cultural construct.

Kleinman (1977) criticized Singer for alleged methodological errors and *category fallacies,* which are defined as biased and erroneous interpretations of observed behaviors in foreign cultures. According to Marsella (1978), who studied mainly normal populations (those with no depressive patients), all disorders are a function of culture, because it is impossible to separate an individual from his cultural context. Marsella increased our understanding of the phenomena of depression by exploring indigenous behavior patterns, using sophisticated methodology and applying multivariate statistical techniques to test results.

Many publications have dealt with social, demographic, and other specific variables within cultures. Bagley (1973) reviewed studies of the relationship between depression and social class. Bebbington (1978), in his profound review of the epidemiology of depressive disorders, analyzed the effects of sociodemographic variables on the risk of depression and concluded that such variables do not account for much variance in rates of depression because they are, at best, gross measures. He reviewed different concepts of depression and studies of the life events influencing the occurrence of depression in interaction with other determinants. Fenton (1979) prepared a selective but critical review of studies of affective disorders in different cultures. He pointed out that the diagnosis of depression lacked physiological and biological criteria and remained limited to clinical judgment. Caution is therefore required when evaluating rates of depression in international and cross-cultural comparisons.

NOSOLOGY OF DEPRESSION

The differential diagnosis of depressive illness lacks an integrated unitary base. Depression is an affective disorder characterized by heterogeneity of manifestations and classifications. Although not universally accepted, dichotomous (dualistic) diagnostic classifications have recently become prominent. These involve the primary-secondary distinction (Robins and Guze, 1973), the unipolar-bipolar separation (Leonhard, 1959; Perris, 1966; Winokur et al., 1969), and the endogenous-neurotic classification revised by Kiloh and Garside (1963). Concepts of depression were reviewed by Beck (1967), Lehmann (1974), and Winokur et al. (1969).

Kendell's (1976) paper on classification of depression is subtitled "A Review of Contemporary Confusion." For example, Beck (1967) views the difference between the neurotic and psychotic depressive reaction as quantitative rather than qualitative, while others consider the dimensional approach to be more appropriate and to be superior to the diagnostic labels.

According to the International Classification of Diseases (ICD-9 revision, 1979, in the *Diagnostic and Statistical Manual of Mental Disorders,* 1980), the core depressive syndrome is found in affective psychoses (ICD 296), including the unipolar depression (ICD 296.1) and bipolar affective psychosis (manic-depressive psychosis, circular type, ICD 296.4). Affective psychoses differ from neurotic depression (ICD 300.4) as well as from affective personality disorder (ICD 301.1).

The *Diagnostic and Statistical Manual of Mental Disorders* (DSM-III, 1980) of the American Psychiatric Association uses a different system for the classification of affective disorders, including depression. The essential feature of the affective disorders is a primary disturbance of mood accompanied by related symptoms.

The DSM diagnostic classification reflects a pluralistic view of depressive disorders, and uses a multiaxial diagnostic evaluation represented by a five-digit code. The first three digits indicate the clinical syndrome (similar to the ICD). The fourth digit indicates psychosocial stressors and designates the severity of depression as moderate, marked, severe but not psychotic, psychotic, and depression in partial or full remission. The fifth digit indicates the highest level of adaptive functioning during the past year and thus reflects the recent course of illness in terms of social relations, occupational functioning, and use of leisure time. The DSM manual provides glossaries and detailed criteria for depressive disorders, which exclude signs of schizophrenia, organic mental changes, and simple bereavement. The affective disorders of the DSM are either episodic, chronic, or atypical. The episodic affective disorders, for example, contain the category of a single episode of a major depressive disorder (DSM 296.2x) or a recurrent disorder (DSM 296.3x). The bipolar affective disorder, depressed, has a DSM code 296.5x. The term *major* depressive disorder is used to stress the difference between this and other depressive disorders, such as the *chronic* depressive disorder (depressive personality, DSM code 201.12). One of the systems provided by the DSM manual for identification of major depressive illness is known as the Feighner criteria (Feighner et al., 1972). This system is useful in research and clinical practice for diagnosing serious cases of depression requiring medical attention.

Only a few countries use the DSM and the ICD diagnostic criteria and categories. Although these criteria are not yet securely anchored, they enhance agreement among clinicians and researchers and reduce instances in which a single diagnostic label is used in different ways. The ICD and DSM diagnostic categories are related to the course of illness and outcome of treatment. Although labels may seem to be simple, their simplicity shields them from ambiguity and facilitates communication.

Biochemical data have not been applied in the diagnosis or epidemiology of depression because no reliable and consistent changes in the body's chemistry have been found that distinguish between clinically depressed and nondepressed populations. Many clues have been followed; in particular, the activity of biogenic amine-related enzymes, including monoamine oxidase (MAO), have been measured. Depression has been linked with the depletion of one or more monoamine neurotransmitters and with a more frequent occurrence in women and among older populations (Fenton, 1979).

DIMENSIONS OF DEPRESSION MEASURED ACROSS CULTURES

Cross-cultural studies reveal the importance of objective observation and measurement of depressive phenomena and have stimulated advances in methodology, such as symptom checklists and rating scales for the assessment of depression. These methods are deceptively simple, which accounts for their recent proliferation. They have, however, attained sufficient reliability and validity to have proven useful, within limits, in clinical work and research in cross-cultural epidemiology and theories of psychopathology. An example of depression checklists is Lubin's Depression Adjective Check List (DACL) (Lubin, 1977; Lubin and Levitt, 1979). The DACL is a brief, self-administered measure of state depression that contains 4 equivalent forms of 34 items each and that has been found useful in clinical and cross-cultural studies. Lubin and Levitt (1979) compared samples of black and white males and females in the United States. The blacks obtained higher scores, but the authors reported no significant ethnic differences in patterns of depression as reflected by the DACL.

A simple way to classify depression rating scales is to divide them into unidimensional and multidimensional scales, and into objective (administered by the clinician or researcher) and subjective (based on self-report) rating scales. Representative of the unidimensional depression rating scales are the Hamilton Depression Scale (HAM-D), the Beck Depression Inventory (BDI), and the Zung Self-rating Depression Scale (SDS). Depression rating scales were reviewed by Carroll et al. (1973), Fenton (1976), and Engelsmann (1977).

The 21-item Hamilton Depression Scale (HAM-D) is perhaps the best validated of the unidimensional and objective depression scales. Binitie (1975) compared factorial structures of the HAM-D obtained from Nigerian and English depressed patients. The Nigerian patients presented depressed mood, somatic symptoms, and motor retardation, but feelings of guilt and suicidal ideation were absent. The English, on the other hand, presented the classical symptoms. Although many authors have confirmed the sensitivity of the HAM-D in measurement of the severity of depression and its usefulness in drug trials, the cross-cultural use of the scale has been limited.

In contrast to the unidimensional scales, the multidimensional scales contain subscales that measure depression as well as other diagnostic features reflecting a broad range of manifest psychopathology. Lorr and Klett (1969) compared the symptom profiles of 100 men and 100 women in each of six countries (England, France, Germany, Italy, Japan, and Sweden) on the Inpatient Multidimensional Psychiatric Scale (IMPS). The Japanese patients suffering from anxious depression yielded an IMPS diagnostic profile different from that of the European patients. The Japanese patients had elevated scores on the Somatic Complaints, Paranoid Projection, and Motor Retardation subscales of the IMPS.

The Brief Psychiatric Rating Scale (BPRS), developed by Overall and Gorham in 1962, has become popular because of its brevity and its abstract level of symptom constructs. Only one item, however, measures depressive mood by reflecting the degree of despondency and sadness. Engelsmann et al. (1970) evaluated the BPRS results obtained from experienced psychiatrists in 5 countries (Czechoslovakia, France, Germany, Italy, and the United States) who were asked to describe 12 diagnostic profiles of functional psychoses in terms of the 16 behavior and symptom constructs of the BPRS. The Mahalanobis distance formula D^2 was used to evaluate this international comparison of the BPRS ideal diagnostic patterns. On this formula, the smaller the D^2 value, the closer, or more similar, were the diagnostic profiles. The concepts of psychotic depression showed the smallest distance, that is, the greatest similarity in this international comparison of diagnostic profiles. This study yielded a numerical cross-cultural comparative dictionary of conceptual diagnostic categories of functional psychoses, including several categories of depression. Extension of this diagnostic pattern analysis by means of computers would facilitate the comparisons of psychiatric patient populations across national frontiers (Draguns, 1977).

The best known of the scales based on self-report is the MMPI, which has enjoyed more attention than any other test. The MMPI D scale measures depression, which was the characteristic symptom and psychiatric diagnosis of the patients in the criterion group used for validation. Early factor analyses (Comrey, 1957) revealed that the D scale contained a number of heterogeneous items. As a result, the homogeneity and unitary significance of the D scale was questioned. Butcher and Pancheri (1976) compared factorial structures of MMPI obtained from American, German, and Italian samples. The structures showed impressive similarities and were useful for comparative purposes. Although useful in psychiatry, the MMPI has limited use for the assessment of personality features in studies of the general population. It provides no emically derived items based on indigenous experience and the dichotomous way of answering (yes/no) may lack sensitivity in cultures where people are not used to labeling emotional states.

Currently, the most widely used depression scale based on self-report is the Zung Self-rating Depression Scale (SDS), first published in 1965 and designed to measure severity of depression. In a cross-cultural survey of symptoms of depression in six countries, Zung (1969) provided supportive evidence for the reliability and cross-national validity of the SDS. His study involved 1,043 patients and 364 normal subjects in Japan, Australia, Czechoslovakia, England, Germany, and Switzerland. Patients suffering from depressive disorders had comparable values in the different countries with a mean SDS index of 61.4 points. Patients with primary diagnoses other than depression had a mean index of 53.7 points, while normal subjects had a mean index of 37 points. The Czechoslovakian sample showed the highest SDS scores, followed by the Swedish and German subjects. Zung also validated the SDS in India (Master and Zung, 1977), in the Netherlands, and in Spain. However, repeated factor analysis revealed different factor loadings of the 20 SDS items in the examined groups, suggesting different underlying depressive experience. It is possible that these differences could be assessed by emically derived items, which the SDS lack. Although some groups showed similar symptom frequencies, they may differ in the intensity and duration of the reported difficulties. Marsella (1980) suggests that the SDS may be most valid in societies that share a similar level of westernization.

There have also been criticisms of the SDS. Carroll et al. (1973) could not confirm the discriminative power of the SDS as a measure of severity of depression in defined groups of patients. However, the problem may not be the scale itself, but, instead, a difficulty derived from the self-rating technique. Psychotic, agitated, and regressed patients with impaired perception, judgment, initiation, and coordination are unable to communicate and to report about themselves. The highest scores on self-rating scales are usually produced by patients suffering from depressive and anxiety neuroses. Self-rating of acutely depressed patients is not a reliable estimate of the severity of their symptoms. Self-rating can be useful, however, for monitoring the recovery of depressed patients, for epidemiological purposes, and for case identification both within cultures and cross-culturally. An example of this is the study by Marsella, Kinzie, and Gordon (1973) on Japanese-American, Chinese-American, and Caucasian-American male and female college students who experienced levels of depression corresponding to those found in depressed outpatients. These levels were identified by means of the Zung SDS and a 60-item symptom checklist. The Japanese-Americans showed a strong interpersonal component in the expression of depression. Chinese-Americans showed somatic symptoms (stomach pains and weakness), and the Caucasian-Americans manifested the more traditional existential pattern of depression (despair, loss of purpose, and feelings of emptiness).

Both the objective scales and the depression rating scales based on self-report are useful. They provide relevant data for diagnosis, case identification, and measurement of depressive phenomena in cross-cultural studies, but alone they do not permit classification of subjects into disease categories. Multivariate analysis applied to the scale results revealed new dimensions of depression. The number and nature of dimensions revealed by factor analysis and by other multivariate techniques depend upon the particular populations and upon the basic theory and built-in items of the scale. Translation of scale items requires an understanding of semantics. The multivariate techniques are, however, still in the early stages of development. They are alien to the clinicians' concepts and terminology and yield schematic results. Although their interpretation poses problems for the clinician, multivariate techniques open new avenues for international comparison and for measurement of ethnocultural variations in the diagnosis and experience of depression.

APPROACHES IN DEPRESSION STUDIES ACROSS CULTURES

Opinion Surveys

A simple technique used in the cross-cultural study of depression involves an international canvassing of psychiatrists' views of depressive disorders. Such an opinion survey concerning the essential characteristics (core symptoms) of depression was conducted by Murphy, Wittkower, and Chance (1967), who asked psychiatrists in 30 countries to rate depressive symptoms on a 4-point scale. Such a subjective approach invites improvement and replication. The World Health Organization initiated and coordinated collaborative explorations of depression in hospitalized patients in Switzerland, Japan, Iran, and Canada (Basel, Kyoto, Tokyo, Teheran, and Montreal). Two checklists have been developed for this cross-cultural exploration: a screening form containing agreed upon criteria (core symptoms) of depression, and a schedule for a standardized assessment of patients with depressive disorders (SADD). The schedule was designed for recording and classifying symptoms of nonorganic depression in different parts of the world (Lehmann and Fenton, 1979). Some items were, however, added in different research centers as an optional culture-specific part of the schedule.

The Emic Approach

During the last decade, the emic-etic distinction has become part of the conventional wisdom of cross-cultural psychology. The emic approach studies behavior from within the indigenous system, as compared to the etic approach, in which behavior is studied from a position outside the culture. Kleinman (1977) stressed the emic approach and showed the limits of even such important studies as the International Pilot Study of Schizophrenia (WHO, 1973). Kleinman argues that the International Pilot Study could not examine the impact of cultural factors because its etic methodology had ruled out the main cultural determinants.

Tanaka-Matsumi and Marsella (1976) showed how useful the emic approach is to the problem of culture and depression by using word association and semantic differential methods in an examination of three groups of students: Japanese nationals, Japanese-Americans, and Caucasian-Americans. Factor analysis of the semantic differential yielded different factorial structures revealing different meanings of depression for the three ethnic samples.

The Matched Groups Approach

The matched groups approach involves comparisons of groups of depressed patients matched on demographic variables, diagnosis, or symptom patterns. An example is the work of Kimura (1965), who compared depressed patients in Kyoto and Munich. He found that there was a greater tolerance of depression in Japan, possibly reflected in the fact that *kanashi* ("sad") also connotes "beautiful" and "affectionate." Tonks et al. (1970), who applied the strategy of matched samples to depressed American black and white patients, found only minimal differences. The similarities between black and white depressed patients were more prominent than the differences.

Draguns et al. (1971) have been among the proponents of this matched sample research strategy. In cooperation with other researchers, they compared American patients with Japanese, Argentinian, and Israeli patients. The research was carried out within the framework of the social competence conceptualization of psychopathology, and the groups were compared in terms of differences in role orientation (turning against others, turning against self, and avoidance of others) and sphere of dominance (thought, affect, somatization, and action). In all studies, cultural differences were found in the affective sphere of functioning (quoted from Marsella, 1980).

The Life Event Approach

The life event approach refers to the study of specific change in the social matrix. This approach was described by Paykel (1974) as one of the great issues in twentieth-century psychiatry. It is assumed that persons with depressive disorders are likely to have experienced stressful life events within a defined period preceding the development of depression. The life event approach, however, involves problems of methodology and interpretation. One of these problems concerns the validity of the retrospective reporting assessment, which may be subject to distortion. Prospective studies are necessary. Brown, Harris, and Peto (1973) have suggested that preceding stressful events are not additive in producing depression and that no summation of mild events leads to the onset of depression. However, it has been shown that interaction of life events with other factors could precipitate the onset of depression. The most impressive interactive study is that of Brown and his colleagues (1975, 1977, 1978) carried out in a community sample of Camberwell women. Brown et al. found high rates of depression in working-class women and tried to explain this by a *vulnerability factor*, which consists of the lack of a confiding relationship, the lack of employment, the presence of young children at home, and the loss of mother before the subject was 11 years old. According to Bebbington (1978), the vulnerability model proposed by Brown is subtle, intuitively appealing, and amenable to sophisticated statistical analysis.

COMPARATIVE EPIDEMIOLOGY OF
DEPRESSION IN WESTERN COUNTRIES

Epidemiology is an analysis of morbidity patterns, mainly in terms of incidence and prevalence. Incidence denotes the number of new cases in a given population, most commonly within a year. Prevalence indicates the number of all cases (new and old) in a given population at a given point, period of time, or life span. The epidemiology of depression usually compares samples of a population on the basis of data obtained from hospitals, clinics, and private practice, or from field surveys. One must always consider whether these data are sufficiently representative. In view of the diversity of diagnostic classifications of depression and the change in diagnostic criteria over the course of time, epidemiological data are difficult to compare. The most reliable data for comparative purposes are based on severely depressed patients in hospitals and clinics, although the availability, use, and admission practices of these facilities vary considerably from country to country.

Although exact figures are not available, it seems that 5 out of every 100 adults become significantly depressed at some time in their lives. Many of these people never seek help. Data on prevalence of depression based on hospital admission rates and community surveys indicate the social magnitude of the problem: in 1971, the depressive disorders accounted for 275,555 psychiatric hospital admissions in the United States (Schuyler, 1976). Depressive disorders represented 22.5% of the total psychiatric admissions, second only to schizophrenia (27%), and surpassing those related to alcoholism (15.8%). Silverman (1968), in her comprehensive epidemiological review, selected seven community surveys in Europe and in the United States and found that point prevalence rates for depression ranged widely from 0.2 per 1,000 to 38.4 per 1,000 population. According to Singer (1975), these studies are not comparable because of wide differences in age structure, period of survey, and diagnostic criteria.

Selective reviews of mental hospital data in the 1960s in the United Kingdom (Rawnsley, 1968), in Norway (Oedegard, 1967), in Denmark (Juel-Nielsen and Stromgren, 1963), in the United States (Kramer et al., 1972), and in Canada (Richman, 1966) revealed that the number of hospitalized depressive patients was decreasing, mainly because of the shift to outpatient treatment. The hospital prevalence rates for depression ranged widely from 2.4 per 1,000 to 60 per 1,000 population. The highest rates were reported in Denmark, apparently indicating a more thorough approach in case finding.

In the United States, attention has been focused on the hospital statistics of white and black depressive patients. Although earlier studies had reported lower frequency of depression among the black population as compared to the white population, McGough, Williams, and Blackley (1966) reported that with the better availability of treatment facilities and the introduction of racial integration in the psychiatric hospitals, the pattern of psychiatric illness among blacks in the southern states has changed. The proportion of black patients with psychotic depression and, to a lesser extent, with psychoneurotic depression, has risen to equal, and in some cases even to exceed, that of white patients.

Studies of symptoms rather than of nosological entities yielded high prevalence rates for depression in the general population. However, problems of case finding and identification are prominent and complex. The Stirling County Study (Leighton et al., 1963b) showed a prevalence of depressed neurosis of 7.2%. In the Midtown Manhattan Study (Srole et al., 1962) 236 persons per 1,000 population were classified as depressed. Weissman, Myers, and Harding (1978) used the Schedule for Affective Disorders and Schizophrenia (SADS) (Endicott and Spitzer, 1978) for 511 subjects in one of their New Haven studies. Weissman et al. found that the current rate of major depression was 4.3%, and of minor depression 2.5%, with a combined rate of 6.8%. Similar rates of depression were found by Brown and Harris (1978) and Brown et al. (1975) in community surveys of women in Camberwell, England. The prevalence of depression among these women ranged from 8% to 14.8%. The Present State Examination (Wing, Cooper, and Sartorius, 1974) and the General Health Questionnaire (Goldberg, 1972) were used in these surveys. According to Bebbington (1978, p. 316), these surveys indicate that an element of arbitrariness is still present in the definition of depressive symptoms. Wing et al. (1978) have used the data from these surveys to validate the concept of casehood, using an *index of definition*, which defines levels of disorder corresponding to increasing certainty that the subject is a case of depression.

It is difficult to reach conclusions about the prevalence rates of depression in different Western countries because psychiatrists differ in their diagnostic preferences. The U.S.-U.K. study (Cooper et al., 1972) showed that British-trained psychiatrists diagnosed affective disorders more often than psychiatrists trained in the United States. Cooper et al. (1969) showed that hospital psychiatrists in the United States diagnosed 16.6% of 145 consecutive admissions as depressed, while English hospital staff diagnosed 46.2% of a comparable sample of admissions as depressed. In a broader study, Gurland et al. (1972) reported that American psychiatrists diagnosed only 12.9% of new admissions as depressed, while English psychiatrists gave this diagnosis to 30.9% of new admissions.

A number of sociodemographic variables were specifically related to occurence of depression. Women suffer from depression, mainly from neurotic and unipolar depression, more frequently than men. The male/female ratio is about 1:2 (Weissman and Klerman, 1977) or 1:3 (Scharfetter and Angst, 1978). The bipolar affective psychosis seems to be distributed more evenly between men and women, with a prevalence rate of about 3.5% for both.

Bagley (1973) reviewed the relationships between social class and depression and noted that depression was more frequently reported by persons with higher occupational status. Bagley hypothesized that striving for success is linked with stress and can lead to depression. Other studies, however, reported that the occurrence of depression was evenly distributed among the socioeconomic groups. Brown and his associates (1978) found high occurrence of depression in working-class women in Camberwell, England.

Suicidal behavior is also one of the measures of depression. Data on suicide are difficult to compare because of the different methods of recording and monitoring suicidal behavior. Although suicide was the eleventh leading cause of death in the United States in 1972, with almost 25,000 deaths, this number is probably widely underestimated. Depressive illness has been diagnosed retrospectively in as much as 80% of reported samples of hospital patients who died by suicide (Schuyler, 1976).

SELECTIVE EPIDEMIOLOGY OF DEPRESSION ACROSS CULTURES

A large number of studies of the epidemiology of depression in ethno-cultural groups has dealt with Africa. The studies report a rarity of severe affective illness, as well as relative mildness and short duration of depression, with an absence of guilt feelings and a low suicide rate. Recent studies, however, have suggested that depression is not, in fact, rare, but is masked by somatic and confusional symptoms (Leighton et al., 1963b). Leighton and his associates compared the results of two field surveys of depression using the same procedure in Nigeria and in Canada: depressive symptoms were about four times more common in the Nigerian sample than in the Canadian sample. Depressive disorders have also been found to be common in Senegal, Ethiopia, Sudan, and South Africa. Figures for hospitalized depressive patients ranged as high as 23.5% of the population under study. Differences in the manifestations of depressive states were conspicuous, but seem to be changing. In Senegal depressive patients showed mainly paranoid and somatic symptoms, in Ghana a high frequency of self-accusation of witchcraft was reported, and in Sudan more shame than guilt feelings were found among the depressed patients. However, reports from Ethiopia and Sudan have also indicated that the picture of depression resembled the Western pattern (Singer, 1975).

On the Indian subcontinent, regional differences have been reported in the prevalence of depression based on studies of hospitalized patients as well as on field surveys. Prevalence of depression among the general population in North India ranged from 9 to 16.7 per 1,000 population. Infrequent guilt feelings and prominent somatization were found in southern and western India (Rao, 1973). Ananth (1978) reported a low prevalence of depression in women and related this to the Indian women's fatalistic acceptance of their situation as unalterable. Master and Zung (1977) surveyed symptoms in 430 depressed patients and 97 normal subjects in India, using the Zung SDS. A comparison of the results obtained in India with those previously obtained in the United States, Japan, Czechoslovakia, England, Germany, and Holland showed that depressed patients scored similarly on the SDS in all the countries studied (Zung, 1969).

In Japan, census-type examinations showed a low prevalence rate (2 per 1,000) for affective psychosis. Kimura (1965) found that guilt feelings occurred with equal frequency in Japanese and German depressives, contrary to the previously held belief that they were absent among the Japanese. Kimura also found differences in the direction of guilt feelings. The Japanese felt guilty toward parents, ancestors, and fellow workers; the Germans guilty toward children and God. Yap (1965) studied depressive symptomatology retrospectively in Chinese inpatients in Hong Kong and concluded that the clinical features paralleled those described in the West, but that ideas of guilt were infrequent and mild, and delusions of sin were absent. Yap later modified his position and cast doubts on the validity of the reported differences (Yap, 1971).

Kim (1977) compared depressive symptoms of patients from Korea, England, the United States, and India, as assessed by the Hamilton Depression Scale (HAM–D). The Korean depressives expressed guilt feelings and suicidal wishes in similar proportion to those found in patients in England and in the United States. Guilt feelings among Korean patients were double the percentage of expressed guilt feelings among Indian patients. This finding contrasts with the previous reports that guilt and suicide are seldom found among non-Western cultures. The guilt of the Korean depressives was socially and family oriented, rather than religious. Conforming with previous research, Kim (1977) found high scores reflecting somatic symptoms on the HAM–D in Korean depressive patients.

In Hawaii, Kinzie et al. (1973) studied the point prevalence of depressive symptoms among university students of Japanese, Chinese, and Caucasian ancestry using the Zung SDS. Contrary to previous assumptions, the researchers found that Asians, particularly females, had a significantly higher prevalence of depression than Caucasians. They hypothesized that Asian-American students became more introverted, "turning toward the self," and produced more depressive symptoms under stress. In Indonesia, depression was studied by Pfeiffer (1967, 1971), who found that Indonesian patients display a loss of vitality and somatic symptoms, while the German depressive patients manifest the classical picture of melancholia, with decrease of efficiency, feelings of guilt, and suicidal tendencies.

Cross-cultural studies suggest that non-Western depressives show more somatic complaints, and that the more westernized a culture becomes, the more psychological components are included in the picture of depression. There are, however, many exceptions. Somatic equivalents of depression are often found in patients from Western countries where the condition is labeled "masked depression." There are also specific indigenous disorders, such as koro, latah, amok, and susto, which imply depressive phenomena, dysphoria, and other forms of abnormal behavior. *Susto,* for example, denotes "soul loss" among some Latin American populations. The indigenous equivalent of depression among the Mohave Indians is the *heart-break syndrome,* and the term *totally discouraged* reflects depression in Sioux Indians. Even in the Western diagnostic classifications, which can be traced back to Kraepelin, we can find unique diagnostic categories. An example of this is the concept of *bouffée délirante* used in the French diagnostic classification. This is an acute delusional psychosis that also involves fluctuations of depressive symptoms.

VARIATIONS ACROSS TIME

Reports on depressive illness over the last 20 years, especially among Africans, seem to show a trend toward a Western rate of morbidity and pattern of symptomatology. Prince (1968) has equated the increase in the reported prevalence of depression in Sub-Sahara since 1957 with the gaining of political independence in Africa. In contrast, Lin et al. (1969) compared two census-type studies carried out at an interval of 15 years in three communities in Taiwan and found no significant change in the prevalence of the psychoses, but a significant increase in nonpsychotic disorders, especially in psychoneuroses. Varga (1968) compared case reports on psychotic patients treated in a university psychiatric hospital in Budapest in 1910 with those treated in 1960 and found that the occurrence of depressive symptoms in all psychotic pictures combined had increased in 1960. By contrast, Kramer et al., in 1972, showed that first admissions of affective psychosis to public psychiatric hospitals in the United States had decreased steadily since 1940, while admissions of psychoneuroses and personality disorders had increased.

Murphy (1978) drew attention to shifts in the symptomatology of depression over time. Until the sixteenth century, the number of recorded cases exhibiting exaggerated guilt feelings and self-accusation was very small, and such cases are still rare except among the westernized societies. It is important to examine the conditions under which these feelings became prominent in different societies.

CULTURAL FACTORS AND HYPOTHESES OF DEPRESSION

A series of psychodynamic and psychosocial theories has been developed to explain the onset and manifestations of depression across cultures.

Psychoanalysis

Cultural variations in depression have been explained within the framework of psychoanalytic theory. For example, avoidance of frustration at the oral stage of ego development caused by permissiveness in child rearing could be postulated to account for the alleged rarity of psychotic depression in developing societies. The decline of manic-depressive psychosis in the United States has been attributed to the replacement of the inner determinants, such as feelings of responsibility and guilt, by external support and security (Arieti, 1959). Although sense of responsibility has been positively correlated with depression, there is a lack of empirical and experimental evidence to support such hypotheses.

The concept of guilt has a central role in psychoanalytic theory and is a basic symptom of depressive illness. Studies that show a scarcity of guilt feelings in non-Western cultures may be based on different assumptions and methodology; it seems that the non-Western cultures differ not in frequency, but in content of guilt feelings. Criteria for separating guilt from shame are difficult to establish, and the two feelings have more similarities than differences. Psychoanalytic theories of depression were recently reviewed by Robertson (1979), although he did not deal with their cross-cultural implications.

Language

Emotional states may be differentiated in the lexicon of one country and undifferentiated in another. Cross-cultural differences in this respect are salient. In some African languages, for example, a single word represents both anger and sadness. Leff (1973) explored the links between culture and verbal categories differentiating emotions using the results of the International Pilot Study of Schizophrenia (IPSS) conducted in 9 countries (WHO, 1973). Leff's analysis is based on his work with the Present State Examination (PSE) (Wing et al., 1974) and is concerned with differentiation of anxiety, depression, and irritability as reflected by intercorrelation of their PSE scores. The correlation coefficients were high (thus the differentiation was low) in the developing countries. The countries that showed the highest correlations in all three examined emotional areas were Nigeria and Taiwan, indicating that the patients in these developing countries achieved the lowest degree of emotional differentiation as defined in the study. However, the terms *depression* and *anxiety* were found to be difficult to translate into either Yoruba or Chinese. Leighton encountered similar difficulties in the Yoruba language with the concept of depression. The Yoruba words used in the PSE for depression and anxiety are translated literally as "the heart goes weak" and "the heart is not at rest," revealing somatic connotations. Using the data from the U.S.–U.K. project (Cooper et al., 1972), Leff found a similar lack of differentiation between the examined affective states in American black patients. The blacks, although English speaking, did not use the discriminatory capacity in the same way that the whites did. Results obtained from matched groups of white and black American patients did not permit an explanation of this difference in terms of social class. According to Leff, a factor contributing to the differentiation of emotional states could be the degree of individualism expressed in relationships in different cultures.

Child Rearing and Family Structure

Cultural variations in child rearing and parental attitudes toward independence, training, praise, and punishment were explored in relation to the occurrence of depression. Multiple mothering and permissiveness, for example, can minimize frustration and insecurity during the child's early development and thus can decrease the likelihood that the child will suffer from depression in later life. Emotional deprivation, birth order, and parental age were not found to be etiologically relevant to depression. However, future studies of environmental factors during the early formative years may possibly yield relevant information regarding depression. The effects of cultural change on mental disorders and on depression have been extensively studied, including the effects of urbanization, industrialization, acculturation, and migration. Studies of the relationship between migration and mental illness have been reviewed by Fabrega (1969) and Murphy (1965), but the etiological relationship of migration and depression is complex and the findings are still inconclusive.

The assumption that social cohesiveness is linked with a predisposition to depression has a common-sense appeal. Sharing of values and traditions, the tightly knit family, social ties, and compliance of the individual with group expectations may become distressing and may precipitate or facilitate development of depression. The work of Eaton and Weil (1955) among Hutterites and the opinion survey of Murphy and his associates (1967) about the basic signs of depressive disorders both provide support for the cohesiveness theory of depression. In exploring the cohesiveness theory in relation to the Hutterites, the patriarchal family structure was felt to be a contributory factor in the development of guilt feelings and depression. Similar observations were made by Kimura (1965) about Japanese families. The traditional sense of duty felt by sons toward their parents could account for the high occurrence of guilt feelings toward parents found in Japanese male depressives. Stainbrook (1954) hypothesized that depression is less frequent in those societies with extended family structure. The lack of strict rules and commitments does not lead to resentment of parental authority and to guilt feelings associated with depression. The interaction between social cohesiveness and family structure is complex, and its implications for depression require more examination.

Bereavement

Bereavement behavior was analyzed by Averill (1973) from both the cultural and the biological perspective. Averill distinguished grief from mourning. He considered mourning to be a conventional behavior determined by the customs of society. Grief, on the other hand, is a set of psychological and biological reactions. Mourning rituals and expression of grief can reduce the risk of depression if combined with social support, replacement of the loss, and a new social role. Although grief is considered a normal reaction in many cultures, there is clinical evidence that bereavement has some specific relation to depression.

Religion

Attempts to determine specific links between religion and depression have been inconclusive. A higher prevalence of depression in Jews than in Christians was found in hospital admissions in New York (Malzberg, 1962). However, studies in Israel did not show such a trend. Although European Jews showed consistently higher admission rates for depression than did Oriental Jews (Halevi, 1963), the samples used were not controlled for social class. Fernando (1966) studied differences between Jewish, Catholic, and Protestant outpatient depressives in East London. He found that Jews were significantly less hostile than Catholics and less intropunitive (guilt-ridden) than Protestants. Guilt feelings were rarely found in non-Christian patients (Murphy et al., 1967) as compared to Hutterites, in whom Eaton and Weil (1955) found a high incidence of guilt-ridden depression. The relatively high occurrence of depressive disorders in Hutterites differed from another religious population, a group of parishes in northern Sweden. However, both the reported prevalence and the size of all samples under study was too small to make these findings conclusive.

CONCLUSIONS

The magnitude of the problem created by depression is shown by data from studies in Europe and in the United States. Data indicate that approximately 18% to 23% of females and 8% to 11% of males have, at some time, had a depressive episode. It is estimated that 6% of the females and 3% of the males have had a depressive episode severe enough to require hospitalization (DSM III, 1980). The relationships between depression and the components of culture are complex and are still poorly understood. According to Marsella, there is no universally valid concept of depression, but it is possible to identify core symptoms in depressive disorders. Such criteria of identification have to be validated against outpatient and inpatient depressive populations. Psychiatric categories of depression have been developed within the framework of Western psychiatric theory and practice, but Western societies may tend to internalize experience more than some technically, economically, and educationally deprived societies in which somatic expression of depression is more common. Certainly the prevalence and pathoplasticity of depression is contingent upon the cultural sick role. The sick role may be expressed in somatic terms, as is the case in certain poorer economic groups, or it may be denied, as in some ethnocultural groups in Africa.

Somatic symptoms in depression may also be related to traditional medicinal and healing methods. However, the often-applied dichotomy of Western and non-Western societies involves insufficiently delineated cultural dimensions and is subject to change, similar to the changes that may occur in the distinction between developed and developing countries. Simplified models of depression research may not fit the multilevel culture-illness interactions that are often treated as a linear system of relationships. A refined control of confounding variables, randomization, representativeness of samples, and replication of depression studies would enhance the possibility of generalizing results. Unless there is agreement on the definition of depressive disorders and case identification, cross-cultural and comparative epidemiological studies have limited usefulness. Both emic and etic approaches are helpful in establishing these concepts as well as in determining standard methods for measuring intensity, frequency, and other characteristics of depressive symptoms and syndromes across cultures.

Application of multivariate analysis to scale results may disclose meaningful dimensions and patterns of cross-cultural variations in treated and untreated cases of depression. The use of standard methodologies would facilitate cross-cultural comparison and communication and would encourage an interdisciplinary approach. This would provide an understanding of the cultural meaning of both normal and abnormal behavior, including the experience of depression.

ACKNOWLEDGMENT

I would like to thank Professor H. B. M. Murphy for all of his assistance and advice.

REFERENCES

Al-Issa, I. 1970. Culture and symptoms. In: C. Costello (ed.), Symptoms of Psychopathology: A Handbook. John Wiley & Sons, Inc., New York.

Ananth, J. 1978. Psychopathology in Indian females. Soc. Sci. Med. 12(B):177–178.

Arieti, S. 1959. Manic depressive psychosis. In: S. Arieti (ed.), American Handbook of Psychiatry. Vol. 1. Basic Books, Inc., New York.

Averill, J. R. 1963. Grief: Its nature and significance. Psychol. Bull. 70(6):721–748.

Bagley, C. 1973. Occupational class and symptoms of depression. Soc. Sci. Med. 7:327–340.

Bebbington, P. 1978. The epidemiology of depressive disorder. Cult. Med. Psychiatry 2(4):297–341.

Beck, A. 1967. Depression: Clinical, Experimental and Theoretical Aspects. Hoeber Medical Division, New York.

Benedict, P., and Jacks, I. 1954. Mental illness in primitive societies. Psychiatry 17:377–389.

Binitie, A. 1975. A factor-analytical study of depression across cultures (African and European). Br. J. Psychiatry 127:559–563.

Brown, G. W., and Harris, T. P. 1978. Social Origins of Depression: A Study of Psychiatric Disorders in Women. Tavistock, London.

Brown, G. W., and Harris, T. O., and Copeland, J. R. 1977. Depression and loss. Br. J. Psychiatry 130:1–18.

Brown, G. W., Harris, T. O., and Peto, J. 1973. Life events and psychiatric disorder: Nature of the causal link. Psychol. Med. 3:159–176.

Brown, G. W., Ní Bhrolchain, M., and Harris, T. O. 1975. Social class and psychiatric disturbance among women in an urban population. Sociology 9:225–254.

Butcher, J. N., and Pancheri, P. 1976. A Handbook of Cross-National MMPI Research. University of Minnesota Press, Minneapolis.

Carroll, B. J., Fielding, J. M., and Blashki, T. G. 1973. Depression rating scales. Arch. Gen. Psychiatry 28:361–366.

Comrey, A. L. 1957. A factor analysis of items on the MMPI depression scale. Educ. Psychol. Meas. 28:578–585.

Cooper, J., Kendell, R., Gurland, B., Satorius, N., and Farkas, T. 1969. Cross-national study of diagnoses of the mental disorders: some results from the first comparative investigation. Am. J. Psychiatry Supplement, 125:21.

Cooper, J., Kendell, R., Gurland, B., Sharpe, L., Copeland, J., and Simon, R. 1972. Psychiatric Diagnosis in New York and London: A Comparative Study of Mental Hospital Admissions. Oxford University Press, London.

Diagnostic and Statistical Manual of Mental Disorders. 3rd Ed. 1980. American Psychiatric Association, Washington, D. C.

Draguns, J. G. 1977. Advances in the methodology of cross-cultural psychiatric assessment. Transcult. Psychiatr. Res. Rev. 14:125–144.

Draguns, J., Phillips, L., Broverman, I., Caudill, W., and Nishimae, S. 1971. Symptomatology of hospitalized psychiatric patients in Japan and in the United States: A study of cultural differences. J. Nerv. Ment. Dis. 152:3–16.

Eaton, J., and Weil, R. 1955. Cultural and Mental Disorders: A Comparative Study of the Hutterites and Other Populations. Free Press, Glencoe, Ill.

Endicott, J., Spitzer, R. L. 1978. A diagnostic interview. The schedule for affective disorders and schizophrenia. Arch. Gen. Psychiatry, 35:837–844.

Engelsmann, F. 1977. Rating scales for the assessment of depression. In: J. Ananth and J. Pecknold (eds.), Depression, Prognosis and Prediction of Response. Poulenc, Montreal.

Engelsmann, F., Vinar, O., Pichot, P., Hippius, H., Giberti, F., Rossi, L., and Overall, J. E. 1970. International comparison of diagnostic patterns. Transcult. Psychiatr. Res. Rev. 7:130–137.

Fabrega, H. 1969. Social psychiatric aspects of acculturation and migration: A general statement. Compr. Psychiatry 10:314.

Fabrega, H. 1974. Problems implicit in the cultural and social study of depression. Psychosom. Med. 34:377–398.

Fabrega, H. 1975. Cultural and social factors in depression. In: E. Anthony and T. Benedek (eds.), Depression and Human Existence. Little, Brown & Company, Boston.

Feighner, J., Robins, E., Guze, S., Woodruff, R., Winokur, G., and Munoz, R. 1972. Diagnostic criteria for use in research. Arch. Gen. Psychiatry 26:57–63.

Fenton, F. R. 1976. Rating Scales for Affective Disorders. Montreal. Unpublished manuscript.

Fenton, F. R. 1979. Occurrence and Manifestations of Affective Disorders in Different Cultures: A Selective Review. Montreal. Unpublished manuscript.

Fernando, S. 1966. Depressive illness in Jews and non-Jews. Br. J. Psychiatry 112:991–996.

German, A. 1972. Aspects of clinical psychiatry in Sub-Saharan Africa. Br. J. Psychiatry 121:461–479.

Goldberg, D. P. 1972. The Detection of Psychiatric Illness by Questionnaire. Oxford University Press, London.

Gurland, B., Fleiss, J., Sharpe, L., Simon, R., Barrett, J., Copeland, J., Copper, J., and Kendell, R. 1972. The mislabeling of depressed patients in New York state hospitals. In: J. Zubin and F. Freyhan (eds.), Disorder of Mood. Johns Hopkins Press, Baltimore.

Halevi, H. 1963. Frequency of mental illness among Jews in Israel. Int. J. Soc. Psychiatry 9:268.

Juel-Nielsen, N., and Stromgren, E. 1963. Five years later. A comparison between census studies of patients in psychiatric institution in Denmark in 1957 and 1962. Acta Jutland. Medical Series 13.

Kendell, R. 1976. The classification of depressions: A review of contemporary confusion. Br. J. Psychiatry 129: 15–18.

Kiev, A. 1972. Transcultural Psychiatry. Free Press, New York.

Kiloh, L. G., and Garside, R. F. 1963. The independence of neurotic depression and endogenous depression. Br. J. Psychiatry 109:451–463.

Kim, K. 1977. Clinical study of primary depressive symptom; Part III: A cross cultural comparison. Neuropsychiatry, J. Korean Neuropsychiatr. Assoc. 16: 53–60.

Kimura, B. 1965. Vergleichende Untersuchungen uber depressive Erkrankungen in Japan und in Deutschland. Fortschr. Neurol. Psychiatr. 33:202–215.

Kinzie, J., Ryals, J., Cottington, F., and McDermott, J. 1973. Cross-cultural study of depressive symptoms in Hawaii. Soc. Psychiatry 19:19.

Kleinman, A. M. 1977. Depression, somatization, and the "New cross-cultural psychiatry." J. Soc. Sci. Med. 11: 3–12.

Kleinman, A. M. 1978. Culture & depression (editorial). Cult. Med. Psychiatry 2(4):295–296.

Kramer, M., Pollack, E. S., Redick, R., and Locke, B.Z. 1972. Mental Disorders. Suicide. Harvard University Press, Cambridge, Mass.

Lambo, T. 1960. Further neuropsychiatric observations in Nigeria. Br. Med. J. 2:1966.

Leff, J. 1973. Culture and the differentiation of emotional states. Br. J. Psychiatry 123:299–306.

Lehmann, H.E. 1974. Phenomenology of depression. In: J. Ananth and N.P.V. Nair (eds.), Symposium on Depression. Pfizer, Montreal.

Lehmann, H. E., and Fenton, F. R. 1979. Cross-cultural studies of depression. A preliminary report of a series of studies coordinated by the World Health Organization. Paper presented at the 29th Annual Meeting of the Canadian Psychiatric Association, September 26–28, Vancouver.

Leighton, D.C., Harding, J.S., Macklin, D.B., Hughes, C.C., and Leighton, A.H. 1963a. Psychiatric findings of the Stirling County Study. Am. J. Psychiatry 119:1021–1026.

Leighton, A., Lambo, T., Hughes, C., Leighton, D., Murphy, J., and Macklin, D. 1963b. Psychiatric Disorder Among the Yoruba. Cornell University Press, Ithaca, N.Y.

Leonhard, K. 1959. Aufteilung der Endogen Psychosen. Berlin.

Lin, T., Rin, H., Yeh, E., Hsu, C., and Chu, H. 1969. Mental disorders in Taiwan fifteen years later: A preliminary report. In: W. Caudill and T. Lin (eds.), Mental Health Research in Asia and the Pacific. University Press of Hawaii, Honolulu.

Lorr, M., and Klett, C.J. 1969. Cultural comparisons of psychotic syndromes. J. Abnorm. Psychol. 74:531–545.

Lubin, B. 1977. Bibliography for Depression Adjective Check List: 1966–1977. Edits., San Diego, California.

Lubin, B., and Levitt, E. E. 1979. Norms for the Depression Adjective Check Lists: Age group and sex. J. Consult. Clin. Psychol. 47(1):192.

McGough, W., Williams, E., and Blackley, J. 1966 Changing patterns of psychiatric illness among Negroes of the southern United States. Abstracts Int. Congress Ser. 117:304–305.

Marsella, A. J. 1978. Thoughts on cross-cultural studies on the epidemiology of depression. Cult. Med. Psychiatry 2(4):343–357.

Marsella, A. J. 1980. Depressive experience and disorder across cultures. In: H. Triandis and J. Draguns (eds.), Handbook of Cross-Cultural Psychology. Vol. 6. Psychopathology. Allyn & Bacon, Inc., Boston.

Marsella, A. J., Kinzie, D., and Gordon, P. 1973. Ethnic variations in the expression of depression. J. Cross-Cult. Psychol. 4(4):435–459.

Malzberg, B. 1962. The distribution of mental disease according to religious affiliation in New York state 1949–1951. Ment. Hygiene 46:510.

Master, R. S., and Zung, W. K. 1977. Depressive symptoms in patients and normal subjects in India. Arch. Gen. Psychiatry 34:972–974.

Murphy, H. B. M. 1965. Migration and the major mental disorders: A reappraisal. In: M. Kantor (ed.), Mobility and Health. Charles C Thomas, Publisher, Springfield, Ill.

Murphy, H. B. M., Wittkower, E., and Chance, N. 1967. Cross-cultural inquiry into the symptomatology of depression: A preliminary report. Int. J. Psychiatry 3:6–15.

Murphy, H. B. M. 1978. The advent of guilt feelings as a common depressive symptom: A historical comparison on two continents. Psychiatry 41(3):229–242.

Oedegard, O. 1967. The epidemiology of depressive psychosis. Depression. Acta Psychiatr. Scan. 3:6.

Paykel, E. 1974. Recent life events and clinical depression. In: E. Gunderson and R. Rahe (eds.), Life, Stress, and Illness. Charles C Thomas, Publisher, Springfield, Ill.

Perris, C. 1966. A study of bi-polar (manic-depressive) and unipolar recurrent depressive psychoses. Acta Psychiatr. Scand. Supplement 194:1–188.

Pfeiffer, W. 1967. Psychiatrische Besonderheiten in Indonesia. Aktuel. Frag. Psychiatr. Neurol. 5:102–142.

Pfeiffer, W. 1968. The symptomatology of depression viewed transculturally. Transcult. Psychiatr. Res. Rev. 5:121–123.

Pfeiffer, W. 1971. Transkulturelle Psychiatrie. Thieme, Stuttgart.

Prince, R. 1968. The changing picture of depressive syndromes in Africa: Is it fact or diagnostic fashion? Can. J. Afr. Stud. 1:177–192.

Rao, A. 1973. Depressive illness and guilt in Indian culture. Indian J. Psychiatry 15:231–236.

Rawnsley, K. 1968. Epidemiology of affective disorders. In: A. Coppen and A. Walk (eds.), Recent Developments in Affective Disorders: A Symposium. Ashford, Kent, Headley, London.

Richman, A. 1966. Psychiatric Care in Canada: Extent and Results. Queen's Printer, Ottawa, Canada.

Robins, E., and Guze, S. 1973. Primary and secondary affective disorders. In: F. E. Freyhan (ed.), Disorders of Mood. Karger, New York.

Robertson, B. M. 1979. The psychoanalytic theory of depression. Can. J. Psychiatry 24(4):341–352 and 24(6):557–574.

Sartorius, N. 1973. Culture and the epidemiology of depression. Psychiatr. Neurol. Neurochirug. 76:479–487.

Scharfetter, C., and Angst, J., 1978. Depressionen. Epidemiologie und transkulturelle vergleichende psychiatrie. Dtsch. Med. Wochenschr. 103:913–918.

Schuyler, D. 1976. Treatment of depressive disorders. In: B. Wolman (ed.), The Therapist's Handbook, Treatment of Mental Disorders. Van Norstrand Reinhold Company, New York.

Silverman, C. 1968. The Epidemiology of Depression. Johns Hopkins Press, Baltimore.

Singer, K. 1975. Depressive disorders from a transcultural perspective. Soc. Sci. Med. 9:289–301.

Srole, L., Langner, T., Michael, S., Opler, M., and Rennie, T. 1962. Mental Health in the Metropolis: The Midtown Manhattan Study. McGraw-Hill Book Company, New York.

Stainbrook, E. 1954. A cross cultural evaluation of depressive reactions. In: P. Hoch and J. Zubin (eds.), Depression. Grune & Stratton, New York.

Tan, E. S. 1977. The presentation of affective symptoms in non-western countries. In: G. D. Burrows (ed.), Handbook of Studies on Depression. Elsevier North Holland, New York.

Tanaka-Matsumi, J., and Marsella, A. 1976. Ethno-cultural variations in the subjective experience of depression: Word association. J. Cross-Cult. Psychol. 7:379–397.

Tonks, C., Paykel, E., and Klerman, G. 1970. Clinical depression among Negroes. Am. J. Psychiatry 127:329–335.

Varga, E. 1968. Changes in the symptomatology of psychotic patterns. Transcult. Psychiatr. Res. Rev. 5:93.

Weissman, M. M., and Klerman, G. L. 1977. Sex differences and the epidemiology of depression. Arch. Gen. Psychiatry 34(1):98–111.

Weissman, M. M., Myers, J. K., and Harding, P. 1978. Psychiatric disorders in a United States urban community. Am. J. Psychiatry 135:459–462.

Wing, J. K., Cooper, J. E., and Sartorius, N. 1974. Present state examination. In: The Measurement and Classification of Psychiatric Symptoms. Harvard University Press, Cambridge, Mass.

Wing, J. K., Mann, S. A., Leff, J. P., and Nixon, J. M. 1978. The concept of a case in psychiatric population surveys. Psychol. Med. 8:203–218.

Winokur, G., Clayton, P., and Reich, T. 1969. Manic Depressive Illness. C. V. Mosby Company, St. Louis, Mo.

World Health Organization. 1973. The International Pilot Study of Schizophrenia. World Health Organization, Geneva.

Yap, P. 1965. Phenomenology of affective disorder in Chinese and other cultures. In: A. deReuck and R. Porter (eds.), Transcultural Psychiatry. Little, Brown, & Company, Boston.

Yap, P. 1971. Guilt and shame, depression and culture; A psychiatric cliché re-examined. Community Contemp. Psychiatry 1:35.

Zung, W. K. 1969. A cross-cultural survey of symptoms in depression. Am. J. Psychiatry 126(1):154–159.

V

CULTURE AND
PERSONALITY DISORDERS

Chapter 11

Culture and Personality Abnormalities

H. J. Eysenck and S. B. G. Eysenck

INADEQUACIES OF THE DIAGNOSTIC APPROACH

Most discussions about psychiatric abnormalities, personality disorders, and behavioral dysfunction use nosological terms derived from a system of psychiatric diagnosis. There are many reasons for believing that this procedure, far from making factual agreement easier, makes it more difficult, and may, in fact, make the scientific study of mental abnormality impossible. It is well known that the reliability of psychiatric diagnoses is very low; so low, indeed, that the amount of "true" variance may not be higher than 10% (Eysenck, 1973). Judgments having such low reliabilities generally cannot have any high degree of validity.

Even if psychiatric diagnoses were reliable, it is doubtful that much scientific meaning would attach to them in view of the fact that the system in use is purely descriptive, is largely arbitrary, and is not based on any causal principles demonstrated along experimental lines. Worst of all, the system assumes that diagnostic labels refer to categorical distinctions between different disorders, whereas the evidence is very strong that we are dealing with dimensions rather than categories (Eysenck, 1970b). The evidence regarding the superiority of the dimensional over the categorical point of view has been reviewed in the publications mentioned above; if this criticism can be justified, it accounts largely for the low reliability of categorical diagnoses, and demonstrates the inappropriateness of these diagnoses to the fundamental characteristics of the field.

These difficulties are inherent in comparisons carried out within any particular country; they become much more serious when cultural comparisons are intended. It cannot be assumed, as it has often been assumed, that a diagnostic label like schizophrenia carries the same meaning for psychiatrists brought up in different cultures. Even when comparing very closely related groups, such as English and American psychiatrists, the meaning attached to the term *schizophrenia* may be entirely different. Cooper et al. (1972) have reported a thorough attempt to compare the diagnostic labels attached to groups of patients by English and American psychiatrists, and found that identical patients were five times more likely to be diagnosed as schizophrenic by American than by British psychiatrists! Thus, the nationality of the psychiatrist may be much more important than the symptoms presented by the patient as far as the diagnosis is concerned.

Similarly, there are absurdly large differences in diagnostic frequency between the United States and England. It has been found that the mental hospital first admission rate for England and Wales for manic-depressive psychosis in the age group 54-64 years was about 20 times the corresponding American rate (Kramer, 1969). Smaller, but still striking differences in admission rates for schizophrenia between the two countries are discussed by Cooper et al. (1972). As a result of their investigations, Cooper and his colleagues developed a diagram illustrating the difference between American and British concepts of schizophrenia, which appears in Figure 1. The figure shows how hopeless it would be to compare simple incidence rates between the two countries as indicative of any real differences in the occurrence of psychiatric disorders.

Copeland et al. (1971) have shown that there is relatively little variation in diagnostic usage from one region to another within the British Isles, but within America there is evidence to suggest that usage is much less uniform. Thus, first admission rates for schizophrenia per 100,000 population, age adjusted to the 1960 United States population, was over three times larger in New York State than in North Carolina, California, or Illinois. This might suggest that the differences between English and American diagnostic habits found by Cooper et al. (1972) might be because of peculiarities of New York psychiatrists, but Anglo-American videotape comparisons based on the diagnoses of psychiatrists from other parts of the United States (Katz, Cole, and Lowery, 1969; Sandifer et al., 1968) disprove this hypothesis.

Would using more behavior-related terms produce greater agreement than using all-inclusive diagnostic labels? This is very doubtful. To give one example: the subject of one videotaped interview was rated by 67% of a group of 133 American psychiatrists as having delusions, by 63% as having passivity feelings, and by 58% as having thought disorder. The corresponding percentages for an audience of 194 British psychiatrists shown the same videotape were 12% for delusions, 8% for passivity feelings, and 5% for thought disorder. As Cooper et al. (1972) point out, the finding "strongly suggests that an important conceptual element is present on top of the perceptual difference; it suggests, in other words, that the two groups

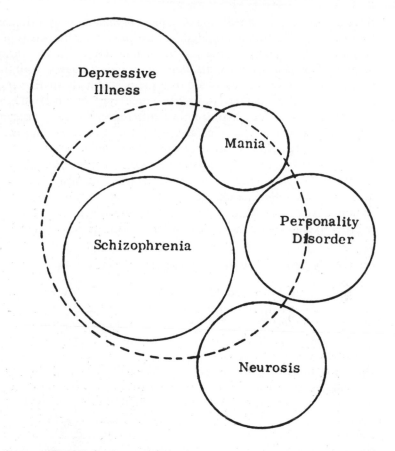

_____ **British Concepts**

_ _ _ _ _ **New York Concept of Schizophrenia**

Figure 1.   British and New York concepts of schizophrenia compared. From Cooper et al., 1972. Reprinted by permission.

mean different things by thought disorder and passivity feelings as well as perceiving or recognising different deviations from normal behavior to begin with." It is clear that even the use of apparently more behavior-related terms than those involved in all-inclusive diagnostic labels would not seriously redress the balance.

Cooper et al. (1972) conclude that "in spite of the fact that most of the differences between American and British mental hospital admission rates have now been shown to be spurious, it is still possible . . . that community-based comparisons will reveal genuine differences in prevalence of some types of mental illness." This possibility exists, but

there are difficulties in realizing it. Unless psychiatrists in different countries can be given training in identical procedures of diagnosis, it will be
very difficult to compare the results of their efforts in any meaningful
manner. This is a pervasive problem that renders nugatory all the comparisons that have been carried out in the past. An alternative approach,
discussed in this chapter, is to use some type of questionnaire thus
obviating the cultural and training differences between psychiatrists.
However, such efforts, particularly when they are based on instruments
whose meaning derives from a categorical psychiatric system (such as the
MMPI) must also run into similar difficulties of definition and concept. To
illustrate the prevalence of these difficulties, we also discuss clinical
diagnoses, although the chapter is predominantly concerned with personality inventories. Recognizing the difficulties encountered is important
in order to understand the results obtained using questionnaires.

CROSS-NATIONAL MMPI RESEARCH

In its intent, the Minnesota Multiphasic Personality Inventory (MMPI) is
closest to the usual psychiatric diagnostic techniques. This test, consisting
of some 550 questions, culled from traditional treatises in psychiatry on
characteristic symptoms of patients suffering from mental disorders, was
constructed on the basis of a criterion-oriented analysis. Using groups of
clinically diagnosed schizophrenics, hysterics, psychopaths, and other
patients, the makers of the inventory constructed scales on the basis of the
discriminant properties of individual items, thus maximizing the ability of
the scales to discriminate between different diagnostic groups. The MMPI
is a direct derivative of psychiatric diagnostic practice and, as such, must
share the same weaknesses and difficulties.

If there are large differences between groups of psychiatrists in the use
of terms like *schizophrenia*, and if these differences occur not only between
countries but also within countries, then the selection of a criterion group is
to some extent arbitrary and dependent on the particular judges chosen.
The same is true of all the other groups on which the MMPI was validated,
and the scales are therefore doubly subjective and idiosyncratic. First, they
mirror general psychiatric practices that have no formal, experimental, or
theoretical basis. Second, they focus rather narrowly on particular psychiatric practices at a given time and place, which cannot be generalized to
other times and to other places. The wide use the scales have received tends
to obscure these difficulties in the minds of practitioners, but the problems
are very real and should not be disregarded.

With these considerations in mind, we discuss the evidence presented
by Butcher and Pancheri (1976) in their *Handbook of Cross-National
MMPI Research*. The authors state that "determining the predictive
effectiveness of the MMPI for psychiatric patients from different cultures

is probably the most important problem in cross-cultural MMPI research" (p. 123). The authors further recognize that "when the study . . . involves a cross-cultural comparison, the problems become even more complicated, because factors such as different nosological classification systems and culturally conditioned diagnostic styles are likely to affect the results of any empirical cross-cultural study." How do Butcher and Pancheri attempt to overcome these problems?

In several chapters of their handbook, Butcher and Pancheri discuss the translation and adaptation of the MMPI to different nationalities and cultures. The authors also analyze the internal structure of the MMPI, and compare item characteristics across seven national groups and the United States sample. The samples used were normal American subjects and normal subjects from Israel (Hebrew), Pakistan (Urdu), Mexico and Costa Rica (Spanish), Italy (Italian), Switzerland (German), and Japan (Japanese). The authors intend to show "that the result will demonstrate that the MMPI item pool has a higher degree of translanguage *generality* for normal populations" (p. 98). In the first analysis reported in the book, average MMPI scale scores for the various national groups were compared with the Minnesota normals to present a general picture of the MMPI scale differences between national groups used in the study. Figure 2 shows the mean profiles for national groups for male normal subjects; the size of the differences found is similar for females, for whom a figure is also given in Butcher and Pancheri's book. The authors conclude that the differences indicate that, for most of the mean validity in clinical scales, "the scores are within one half a standard deviation of the original Minnesota normal group." The most extreme elevation differences seem to occur in the sample of Japanese subjects, although the Japanese females show less extreme deviation than the males. Butcher and Pancheri seem to regard the differences as trifling, but differences of half a standard deviation between large groups would normally be regarded as large and certainly significant. For most of the groups, most of the scores lie in the "normal" band, between 50 and 70, but that is a wide band, and in normal populations one would not expect an endorsement of many of the very unconventional items that characterize the abnormal aspects of the spectrum.

Butcher and Pancheri then discuss their investigation of the comparability of MMPI factor structure across nationalities. The importance of factor analytic comparisons for the purpose of cross-cultural study has been noted by several authors (Cattell and Warburton, 1961; Irvine, 1969; Kikuchi and Gordon, 1970; Triandis, Vassiliou, and Nassiakou, 1968). More recently, Brislin, Lonner, and Thorndike (1973) have devoted a whole chapter of their book on cross-cultural research methods to factor analytic methodology, in recognition of the importance of this method.

The reasons for the importance of factor analytic study in the cross-culture medium are evident. Factor analysis defines the concepts in terms

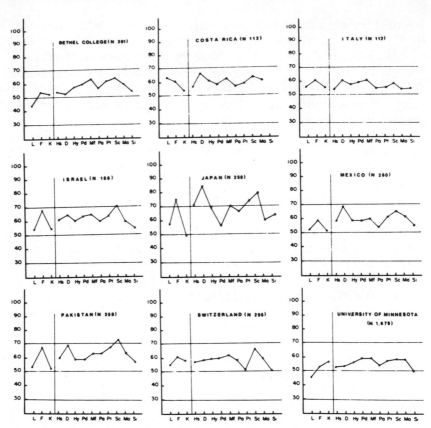

Figure 2.   Mean profiles on the MMPI for national groups of male normal subjects. From Butcher and Pancheri, *A Handbook of Cross-National MMPI Research*. University of Minnesota Press, Minneapolis. Copyright © 1976 by the University of Minnesota.

of which experimental work can be undertaken and which explanations are sought. If these concepts differ from one culture to another, the differences are indicated by the emergence of different factor patterns, and this is a clear indication that no cross-cultural comparisons are possible. If, on the other hand, similar or identical patterns emerge, then a comparative study can be done. The hope underlying such studies was expressed by Comrey and Nencini (1961) when they stated that, "if a well-substantiated factor structure of personality can be worked out for American subjects, it probably will apply reasonably well to Italian and perhaps other Western Europeans." Evidence from the factor analytic study of the Cattell 16PF scales does not substantiate such a hope. Investigators in different countries, such as England, Germany, and Canada have failed to discover a structure similar to that found by Cattell in the United States; even other investigators in the United States have been unable to replicate Cattell's original findings (Eysenck and Eysenck, 1969; Greif, 1970; Howarth, 1972; Howarth and Browne, 1971; Saville and Blinkhorn, 1976; Timm, 1968).

There are large numbers of factor analytic studies of the MMPI; recent reviews of the literature have been done by Block (1965), Horn, Wanberg, and Appel (1973), Overall, Hunter, and Butcher (1973), and Stein (1968). There are many difficulties involved with this type of work, particularly when scales are intercorrelated and factor analyzed. Many scales share identical items, which should strictly rule out the calculation of correlations and the factor analysis of the resulting matrices. The analysis of item intercorrelations is preferable, but this has been done less frequently. Usually when the clinical scales of the MMPI are factored, two major strong factors emerge—the first identified with general pathology and the second identified with something like extraversion-introversion.

Prior to the Butcher and Pancheri study, there were only a few studies of the factor structure of the MMPI available in foreign language translation; Comrey (1960), Comrey and Nencini (1961), Hobi (1972), and Pancheri and Stracca (1972) are the exceptions. Comparisons were made between American, German, and Italian samples, and the resulting factors showed reasonable similarities.

The Butcher and Pancheri (1976) study used the non-K corrected scores for the 3 validity scales, and the 10 clinical scales for 14 national samples of normal males and females (7 each). A principal components analysis was followed by normal Varimax rotation; communalities were obtained by placing unity in the diagonals. Four factors were extracted in each analysis, following the Scree criterion. There are certain reservations about the method of rotation adopted. Varimax rotation forces factors into orthogonality; it would have been better had an oblique rotation been adopted, thus allowing factors to find their natural correlation with each other. From the data given, it is impossible to say to what extent this feature has affected the results in any given sample, or how different the oblique structures would have been from sample to sample.

Butcher and Pancheri conclude that "the overall similarity of the factor structure across national groups for both male and female normals is quite impressive." They also conclude that "the four factors that were extracted in each national group are clearly interpretable." These four factors are psychoticism (with high loading on scales F, Hs, Pd, Pa, Pt, Sc, and Ma), overcontrol (the highest loadings on scales L, K, Hy, and negatively on Ma), social introversion (with loadings on D, Pt, Sc, and particularly on Si), and masculinity-femininity (with loadings only on Mf); because only one scale loads on masculinity-femininity, it may for practical purposes be disregarded.

The tables given by Butcher and Pancheri that show the loadings on the various factors for the various samples indicate the degree of similarity of factor structures. It would have been better had Butcher and Pancheri calculated indices of factor comparisons to give an accurate indication of the degree of similarity. Simple inspection cannot make up for proper statistical investigation of such important matters. However, in the study there is an overall similarity of factor loadings that is very impressive.

Butcher and Pancheri also discuss item endorsements and the differences observed between different nations. They raise an interesting question: "How . . . does the investigator know whether an obtained item difference represents an interesting cultural difference or simply a translation problem? The answer, of course, is that you do not at first know and the discrepant finding must be followed up." The question is much more complex than that, as is the appropriate answer. The Eysenck studies indicate that the only proper answer is a factor analytic study of item intercorrelations, and that by failing to carry out such an analysis, Butcher and Pancheri have made it impossible to give a proper answer to the question they raise. As a consequence of this failure, it is difficult to know how to interpret the correlations of true item endorsements between the national groups and the United States reference sample, which the authors present in their book (p. 116). These correlations range from 0.95 for the American group to 0.61 for the Japanese group, with a majority of correlations in the range of low 0.80. The results seem to suggest marked differences between cultures, but the method of analysis used does not make any clear decision possible. Butcher and Pancheri agree that "there appear to be sufficient differences between Western and non-Western subjects in endorsement patterns of scales that measure psychopathology to caution against blind acceptance of MMPI scale scores and to suggest a need for additional research to verify the generality of the concept."

Butcher and Pancheri next discuss the cross-national validity of the MMPI. The groups studied were American, Italian, and Swiss, but unfortunately the groups were not homogeneous with respect to severity of pathology and diagnostic composition. Factor analyses of inter-correlations of scales for the three pathological samples "showed a basically similar structure across several different national groups." The factors found were similar to those already discussed.

Of greater interest was a discriminant function study, carried out "to determine if the MMPI could discriminate diagnostic groups despite linguistic and cultural differences." Too many of these studies have been done to discuss them in detail, but the result of one such study is illustrated in Figure 3. In this particular study, there are three national groups and three different groups in pathology, i.e., normals, depressives, and psychopaths. There are two major canonical variates. The first variable is interpretable as representing normality versus abnormality, with the normal groups having low scores and the abnormal groups having high scores, and the second variable is identified as contributing a differentia-

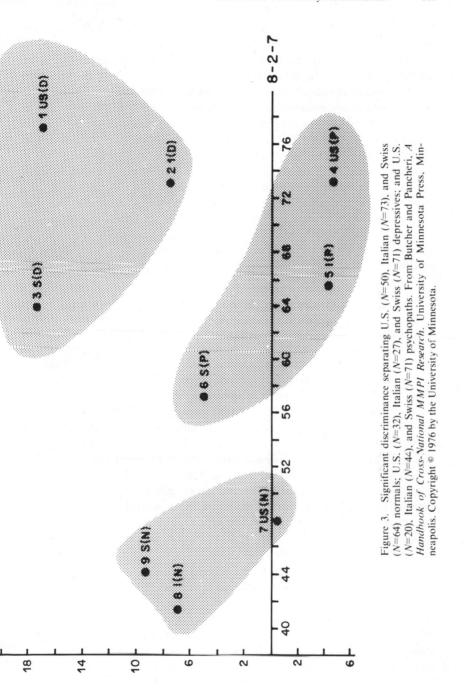

Figure 3. Significant discriminance separating U.S. (N=50), Italian (N=73), and Swiss (N=64) normals; U.S. (N=32), Italian (N=27), and Swiss (N=71) depressives; and U.S. (N=20), Italian (N=44), and Swiss (N=71) psychopaths. From Butcher and Pancheri, *A Handbook of Cross-National MMPI Research*. University of Minnesota Press, Minneapolis. Copyright © 1976 by the University of Minnesota.

tion between different types of abnormality. The results indicate reasonable cross-cultural validity for the scales.

The studies reviewed here are impressive with respect to the large numbers employed, the care taken with translation and with the selection of samples, and the statistical ingenuity shown. There are also weaknesses, most of which are recognized by the authors. The MMPI item pool is oriented toward psychiatric symptomatology, and thus makes it impossible to draw more general conclusions about aspects of personality not covered. The populations studied have been fairly narrow samples of normal subjects or psychiatric patients and cannot be regarded as truly representative of the countries under investigation. Furthermore, we believe that certain technical points make the solutions adopted by Butcher and Pancheri nonoptimal. In spite of this, these researchers have succeeded in demonstrating the possibility of transcending national and cultural boundaries, and of arriving at conclusions that have greater generality than would be possible for studies carried out in a single country.

CROSS-CULTURAL STUDIES OF TRAIT AND STATE ANXIETY

The authors of the MMPI use psychiatric classification and nosology as their basis, but, in their book *Cross-Cultural Anxiety*, Spielberger and Diaz Guerrero (1976) concentrate on one crucial aspect of abnormal behavior—namely anxiety. Spielberger (1966, 1972) has critically discussed the theory and measurement of anxiety and has elaborated in detail the fundamental concepts of state and trait anxiety originally introduced by Cattell and Scheier (1961). He has also developed brief, reliable, and validated scales of state and trait anxiety both for adults (Spielberger, Gorsuch, and Lushene, 1970) and for children (Spielberger, 1973). The principles underlying these tests are well known. In brief, trait anxiety refers to an underlying general tendency in people to respond with high or low degrees of anxiety to various stressful situations; state anxiety refers to the actual responses experienced at a given time and in a given situation. Usually the two are highly correlated, but not highly enough to conclude that they measure exactly the same thing.

The book by Spielberger and Diaz-Guerrero covers in detail the nature and measurement of anxiety and the problems arising in its cross-cultural measurement. The authors also discuss the adaptations of the scales in Portugal, France, Turkey, and Spain. Clearly, great trouble was taken over the translation of the items, and reliabilities in the various countries are not dissimilar from the American ones. Some studies are also available to show construct validity of the scales. Some of the studies in the book make use of other instruments, such as Kelly's Personal Construct

Grid, and some report on state and trait anxiety in cardiac and dermatological patients in Italy. None of these studies is more than marginally relevant to culture and personality abnormalities.

A different position is taken in a study on test anxiety and general anxiety in Mexican and American school children. The instrument used here was the Test Anxiety Scale for Children (TASC), developed by Sarason et al. (1960). The TASC is a 30-item questionnaire that was specifically designed to measure test anxiety in children. Also given were a Lie Scale (LSC) and a Defensiveness Scale (DSC). These scales were given to a total of 392 children, half of them Mexican and half of them American; all were in the first, fourth, or seventh grade when the study began. The Mexican and American children were precisely paired by sex, socioeconomic level, and school grade at the time they were initially tested. Taking the results for all age and SES groups combined, it was found that the Mexican subjects scored higher than the American children on all three TASC scales, the difference being largest for the TASC and relatively small but still significant for the DSC. Interpretation of this study is difficult because no evidence is presented to indicate that the meaning of the terms or situations is identical for the two groups; at best the results can be interpreted as furnishing us with testable hypotheses for further research.

Another study in Spielberger and Diaz-Guerrero's book is concerned with a cross-cultural study of Canadian and Swedish college students. The authors of this study (Endler and Magnusson) make the point that, in examining the relationship between A-trait and A-state, it is necessary to consider the nature of the evocative situations in the context of possible person-by-situation interactions. Endler and Magnusson also suggest that it is possible in some situations to arouse one aspect of A-state (such as autonomic and physiological responses) but not others (such as avoidance responses), which suggests that A-state may be multidimensional. Finally, the researchers suggest that A-trait might also be multidimensional, particularly in contrasting interpersonal ego threat situations with ambiguous threats of physical danger situations. This study was, in part, devoted to an analysis of these complexities in the context of a cross-cultural study.

Two self-report trait anxiety inventories were used by Endler and Magnusson, as well as two self-report measures of state anxiety. Factor analyses of intercorrelations between individual items were carried out, as well as analyses with respect to total scores across items. The results of the analyses showed considerable similarities between the two cultures. Factor analyses of the trait anxiety situation scales yielded two main factors for both the Swedish and the Canadian male and female samples: interpersonal ego threat and physical danger (shame anxiety and harm anxiety).

Analysis of the state anxiety measures indicated the existence of at least three factors for both the Swedish and Canadian samples, with different factor patterns for the two groups.

Endler and Magnusson found that "the correlations and factor analyses of the state and trait anxiety scales do not *empirically* support the conceptual distinction between trait and state anxiety; both state and trait anxiety scales used in the study were found to be multi-dimensional" (p. 131). With respect to cultural differences, Swedish males and females combined reported more physical danger and ambiguous (novel) trait anxiety and less general trait anxiety than Canadian males and females combined. The conclusion most pertinent to culture and personality was that "there is a remarkable similarity between Swedish and Canadian college students with respect to anxiety reactions in different kinds of situations" (p. 133).

The last study mentioned in Spielberger and Diaz-Guerrero's book is the only one that really attempts to tackle the fundamental question of identity of concepts and responses in different cultures; it seems to reach a conclusion equally as cautious and optimistic as that of the MMPI investigators. The two cultures being compared (Canada and Sweden) have many similarities, and it is not surprising to find similar reaction patterns. Furthermore, the samples are highly selected and constitute only a very small proportion of the population in both countries. Nevertheless, the results are promising and show that future work in this field may be of considerable psychological importance. The actual differences in anxiety that were found cannot be generalized. They may be specific to the particular populations tested, but it would be inappropriate to generalize them to all Swedish and Canadian students, let alone to Canadians and Swedes as a whole.

PERSONALITY AND NATIONAL CHARACTER

The work of Lynn (1971) is also concerned with national differences in anxiety, but he attacks the topic from a different point of view. Lynn, in his highly original book, suggests using demographic and epidemiological data for the purpose of making deductions about national character. This view is based on the fact that there are known personality correlates of data such as those relating to cigarette and alcohol consumption, suicide, psychosis, ulcer deaths, murders, celibacy, coronary deaths, and hypertension. The evidence behind the suggestion that these factors are correlated with personality within certain national groups is given in Lynn's book. Lynn suggests that many of these statistics are related to anxiety, and this leads him to the suggestion that it might be interesting to intercorrelate these statistics to discover whether a general factor might be found in their intercorrelations, to which the designation anxiety might usefully be given. Lynn's analysis is based on the following variables: suicide, mental illness, calorie intake, alcoholism, coronary heart disease and arteriosclerosis, vehicle accident deaths, cigarette consumption, ulcers, hypertension, celibacy, and murder. Values for these variables were ascertained for 18 different countries and then intercorrelated using the 18 countries as subjects. A very strong general factor was found, loading on all but the last four of the items mentioned. Thus, anxiety is defined by objective and reasonably accurate demographic and epidemiological data, and by combining them suitably, it is possible to rank the countries involved in order of anxiety states. The 18 countries obtained the following ranks, from high to low, in anxiety: Japan, Germany, Austria, Italy, France, Belgium, Netherlands, Norway, Finland, Denmark, Switzerland, Sweden, Australia, Canada, the United States, New Zealand, the United Kingdom, and Ireland.

Does this anxiety factor have any objective correlates outside the demographic and epidemiological data included in the analysis? Lynn has shown that there is a remarkable correlation of 0.67, significant at the 1% level, between anxiety rank and economic growth of the different countries concerned between 1950 and 1965.

Thus, a country's rate of economic growth, i.e., the rate at which its total national wealth increases, is correlated with the amount of anxiety evidenced in this country by the different variables already mentioned. The evidence of the correlation itself does not enable us to say in which direction the causal arrow points. Is it that anxious people work harder and consequently contribute more economic growth, or does economic growth produce conditions of life that are conducive to anxiety? No answer to this problem is possible on the basis of the data.

Is it possible to replicate this model? There is only one set of nations available, so, on the national scale, a replication cannot be carried out. However, Lynn attempted to carry out a duplication of his own study, using the different states that comprise the United States of America. Some of the epidemiological and demographic data do not exist for the individual states, but there were data for a sufficient number of the variables to make an examination of the intercorrelations worthwhile. The 49 mainland states in the year 1956 were used as "subjects," the variables were again intercorrelated, and the resulting matrix factor was analyzed as before.

The analysis discovered several factors in addition to the anxiety factor, such as an age factor and a percentage of Negroes factor. However, the main finding was that in Lynn's study, "the anxiety factor has been replicated among the States of the United States of America." This is an important replication that supports the rather original methods used by Lynn.

Nevertheless, the psychological meaningfulness of equating a demographic-epidemiological factor with a psychological concept like anxiety is still doubtful. Direct evidence seems to be required in order to make this connection.

Such direct evidence is provided in a study by Hofstede (1976), who tabulated stress scores for many different nations. These stress scores were derived from answers to the question: "How often do you feel nervous or tense at work?" Table 1 shows the resulting stress scores and the anxiety factor scores, according to Lynn's analysis. There is a surprisingly high correlation—0.72 (Spearman rank correlation)—between the two sets of data. This finding provides convincing evidence that the interpretation of data given by Lynn is meaningful.

Lynn (1971) also examines possible causal factors, such as climatic effects and race. After a detailed examination of the evidence, he gives his view as follows:

> . . . it cannot be claimed that the territories surveyed in this chapter provide a conclusive answer to the possibility that some climatic factor is involved in national anxiety differences. Nevertheless, there does seem quite a considerable amount of evidence to suggest that some climatic influence may be present. . . . Storminess is perhaps the most promising, since this is a climatic variable with the highest correlation with national anxiety levels. Even if storminess is a crucial factor, what element in storminess is important—the increase of electromagnetic long waves, or of ozone, or of some more esoteric factor–cannot for the moment be determined [p. 198].

Regarding race, Lynn develops the provisional hypothesis that "the Nordic race is less anxious than the Alpine and Mediterranean." These causal hypotheses are offered very tentatively, and readers are advised to look at the original monograph for the supporting evidence.

Two other papers by Lynn and Hampson (1975, 1977) are important and relevant. Anxiety is only one dimension of personality. In Eysenck's (1970a) system, extraversion is as important as anxiety (or neuroticism, as Eysenck prefers to call it). Using Eysenck's demographic, epidemiological method, Lynn and Hampson (1975) tried to discover whether it would be possible to discover evidence for a two-dimensional system corresponding to Eysenck's N and E model among nations. The results of a study using 12 such variables and 18 countries, factor analyzing the intercorrelations, gives the result shown in Figure 4. Lynn and Hampson's description of the model follows:

> The strategy adopted has been to set up a model of the relationship of twelve behaviour variables (suicide, crime, etc.) to extraversion and neuroticism, and then to test the model by an examination of the relationship

Table 1. Anxiety factor scores, according to
Lynn's analysis, and questionnaire stress scores for
various countries

Country	Anxiety factor scores, according to Lynn	Stress scores
Austria	3.73	78
Japan	2.95	145
France	2.37	98
Germany	2.11	86
Italy	1.05	101
Finland	0.61	78
Switzerland	0.28	92
United States	0.18	69
Belgium	0.15	126
Canada	−0.29	79
Denmark	−0.55	32
Australia	−0.75	69
Norway	−0.86	52
Sweden	−0.86	50
Netherlands	−1.52	77
New Zealand	−1.61	66
Great Britain	−2.41	67
Ireland	−4.58	68

of these variables among nations. The success of this enterprise will be judged
by the degree to which the national data meet the model. . . . The comparison
shows that all the variables except one fall approximately into the places
described by the model. . . . In general it is probably reasonable to conclude
that the factor structure among the set of 12 demographic and epidemiological
variables accords fairly closely with the model set up in the first part of this
paper. It would appear therefore that a two factor personality theory is capable
of extension into the field of national differences and can predict and explain
relationships between a number of national demographic and epidemiological
variables that have not hitherto been known [1975, p. 230.]

   If the factor scores on N and E are then used to characterize a nation, a
diagram can be made like that presented in Figure 5. In addition to closely
replicating the anxiety factor as N, the figure shows the United States to be
the most extraverted nation and Japan to be the most introverted.

   Lynn and Hampson (1977) attempted to sort out some of the environmental variables that might affect national differences in neuroticism
and extraversion, because they were not content with the climatic and
racial causes. Using the methods of their first paper, they measured the
national levels of neuroticism and extraversion in 18 advanced Western

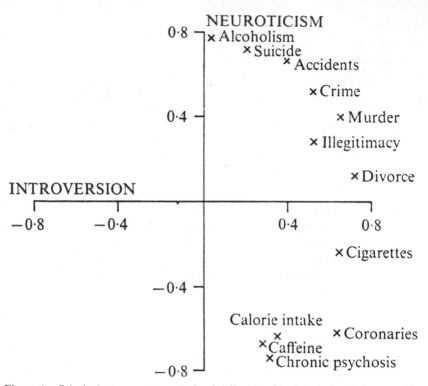

Figure 4. Principal components analysis of different epidemiological and demographic data. From Lynn and Hampson, 1975.

nations at intervals from 1935 to 1970. The researchers showed that levels of neuroticism rose significantly in the nations that suffered military defeat and occupation in World War II, and then declined during the 1950s to prewar levels. National levels of extraversion, they found, had been generally rising over this period.

Lynn and Hampson also noted that in five of the six years under investigation, national per capita income significantly correlated with extraversion. A final correlation of +0.60 was derived from treating each nation in each year as an independent subject. The correlation expresses the magnitude of the association between national levels of extraversion and per capita income over the 35-year period. The authors conclude:

> These correlations indicate that a population's mean level of extraversion is substantially associated with its per capita income both between nations at various points in time and within nations over time. The consistency of the association between extraversion and affluence suggests that the two are causally related but the nature of the causal connection must remain a matter for speculation. [p. 136]

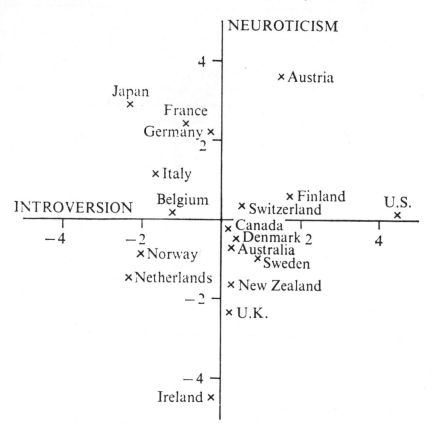

Figure 5.   Standing of different nations with respect to personality factors derived from demographic and epidemiological data.

The originality of Lynn's method of analysis and the very positive outcome of his researches suggest that it would be useful to extend this method further and to compare the results achieved with those obtained by the use of questionnaires and clinical diagnoses. Each of the methods used in cross-cultural comparison has obvious advantages and disadvantages, and a great deal can be learned by looking at the amount of agreement found in the results of different methods.

DIMENSIONS OF PERSONALITY AND CULTURAL DIFFERENCES

The work of H. J. and S.B.G. Eysenck differs from other studies both in the theories investigated and in the methods and aims of the studies carried out. The major concern of the Eysenck studies has been to isolate the major dimensions of personality, particularly as these are concerned with abnormal behavior, to construct measuring instruments for these dimensions, to investigate the genetic and other causal factors involved in producing the differences observed (particularly physiological causes underlying behavior), and thus to construct "a model for personality" (Eysenck, 1980). Cultural studies fit naturally into this scheme, because if the major dimensions investigated are as fundamental as Eysenck believes, then it would seem to follow that identical dimensions should be found in other countries, nations, and cultures; if this were not so, then the universality of the model would be called in question.

The model contains three major dimensions: extraversion-introversion (E), neuroticism-stability (N), and psychoticism-superego control (P). In addition, the latest scale for the measurement of these personality variables also includes a Lie scale (L), which was originally intended to measure dissimulation but has also been found to measure what may be another personality dimension, namely conformity. Much relevant material concerning the construction and validation of the scales can be found in Eysenck and Eysenck (1969, 1976).

The personality dimensions in this system are indicative of personality differences that *underlie* the development of neurotic or psychotic disorder; they are not to be identified with these disorders. Thus, we do not believe that mental disorders show categorical differences from each other or from normality. Our theory is that the disorders involve *continua* of which the fully blown neurosis or psychosis is merely an extreme. It follows that the underlying dimensions cannot be measured by the use of such instruments as the MMPI, which concentrates on symptoms indicative of the extreme stage, although one system can, in theory, be mapped into the other (Wakefield et al., 1974). Figure 6 illustrates the conceptual placement of 9 MMPI scales in Eysenck's three-dimensional personality theory; Wakefield et al. (1974) give empirical support for this analysis in their work.

Given that most studies have used normal subjects in cross-cultural comparisons, it seems better to use scales concerned with normal behavior, such as the Eysenck Personality Inventory or the Eysenck Personality Questionnaire, rather than the MMPI, which is regarded by most people as unusual and inappropriate, because it asks about symptoms that are extremely rare or even nonexistent in normal populations.

Some of the early studies using the Eysenck questionnaires have simply translated them into different languages as needed, and have then compared scores of the various populations with those given by the original standardization groups (Hekmat, Khajari, and Mehryar, 1974; Honess and Kline, 1974; Hosseini, Mehryar, and Razavied, 1973; Irfani, 1977; Irfani, in press; Kline, 1967; Mehryar, Hekmat, and Khajari, 1975; Orpen, 1972; and Westhoff and Sorembe, in press). Psychometric scores can be obtained readily enough, but the meaning of these scores is not always apparent, and

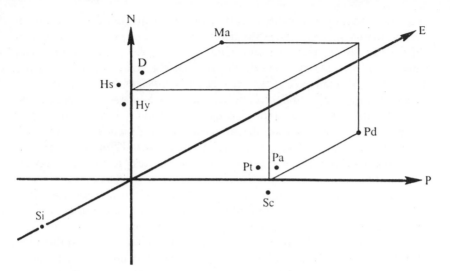

Figure 6. Conceptual placement of nine MMPI scales in Eysenck's three-dimensional personality theory. From Wakefield et al., 1974. Reprinted with permission.

any straightforward interpretation of results is of doubtful psychological value (Eysenck, Adelaja, and Eysenck, 1977; Iwawaki, Eysenck, and Eysenck, 1977). The method advocated by Eysenck and Eysenck combines some of the features used in work on the MMPI and on the Spielberger anxiety scales and adds some new ideas. Ultimately, the Eysencks' approach is based on an extension of the psychometric method used to provide internal validation for trait or type questionnaires within a given culture. Consider the methodology used for the construction of measures of extraversion, neuroticism, and psychoticism (Eysenck and Eysenck, 1969, 1976). Given the hypothesis that a given type or trait concept may, with advantage, be postulated, items are written that express the putative nature of the trait/type as expressed in a variety of situations. Questionnaires containing numbers of such items are then administered to suitable populations, the item answers are correlated, and a factor analysis is carried out. Depending on the results of such an analysis, the postulated factor may be rejected as nonexistent (or at least impossible to measure and to determine by means of the chosen items), or it may be concluded that something similar to the postulated factor emerges from the data, but that it is not as clearly defined as one might wish. Psychometrically "bad" items are then excluded, new ones are written, and the whole process is repeated as many times as is necessary to achieve a satisfactory scale.

This method may be used with advantage in trying to ascertain whether certain personality factors can be measured meaningfully in a different country or culture. What is required is the application of the scale in question to residents in the country of origin (in our case England) and in the country to be compared. Provided that suitable populations have been chosen for testing (selected for items like age, sex, social status, and education), the rule can be established that the scores on the tests are comparable *if, and only if, the correlation matrices between items are identical (or closely similar) between the two countries.* A related test would be to compare the factor loadings of the items, perhaps using factor comparison techniques like those discussed in Eysenck and Eysenck (1969). Coefficients of factor comparisons of above 0.95, or, ideally, above 0.98, might be required in order to accept the test results as properly comparable.

Three possible outcomes of such a study might be expected. There might be almost perfect comparability, there might be complete lack of comparability, or there might be a fair degree of comparability, but with distinct exception. The first of these (almost perfect comparability) has been found by the authors in several published and unpublished studies comparing English and foreign groups, in which the foreign groups were culturally very close to the English, for example, in New Zealand, or even not as close, as in Yugoslavia. Complete lack of comparability has never been found by the authors. Identical factors, clearly recognizable and with high factor comparison indices, have never failed to appear, even in unlikely samples (such as Nigeria and Japan).

Most frequent were results showing good agreement, but there were definite exceptions; some items failed to show even reasonably similar factor loadings on what were clearly identical factors. (See Dimitriou and Eysenck, 1978; Eysenck and Eysenck, in press; Eysenck and Seisdedos, 1978; Eysenck, Gupta, and Eysenck, in press; Eysenck et al., 1980; Lojk, Eysenck, and Eysenck, 1979; Saklofske and Eysenck, 1978; and Tarrier, Eysenck, and Eysenck, in press.) The existence of such items, provided they were capable of some rational explanation, might advance our understanding of national differences and similarities in personality; a special effort has been made to discover such explanations. Collaboration with native psychologists and psychiatrists in these countries furnished convincing explanations in almost every case. Two examples may suffice to illustrate these comparisons. In Nigeria, items on the P scale relating to cruelty to animals lost their loading completely. This was clearly related to the different values accorded to animals in an almost entirely agricultural and rather primitive economy, as compared to those in a largely urban and industrial society. In Greece, items relating to insurance lost their high loadings on the P factor. This was because insurance is very uncommon in Greece, and also because recent insurance scandals, in which some of the few big firms engaging in insurance went broke, effectively sapped confidence in this method of safeguarding one's self against risk. Alternative items were also proposed by our local collaborators, and will be tested in the next round of data gathering and factor analyses.

In comparing two national or cultural groups, it is clearly unsatisfactory to use a scale in which one or more items are inapplicable in one of the comparison groups, even though the indices of factor comparison might be very high. A better method would be to construct new questionnaires including only those items on which identical items have very similar factor loadings in the two countries. These (truncated) scales would obviously be shorter than the original ones, and therefore would have slightly lower reliability, but they would be valid for comparisons between the two countries. In the study of Greece, for instance, it was found that on the original P scale the Greeks had significantly higher scores than the English. When the revised scales were used for the comparison, the two countries showed little in the way of differences! Thus, even the inclusion of one or two items that do not fit into the picture may give rise to erroneous conclusions. It seems that testing each item in the questionnaire for validity is an absolutely vital step in the methodology, and if this is not done, then comparisons cease to have any psychological meaning.

A possible source of validation that has been used in a number of cases is the use of extraneous criteria. For instance, in England, males have higher E and P scores, and females have higher N and L scores. It is usually found that these relations also obtain in other countries, and this may serve as a validation criterion. Similarly, in the original work it was found that neurotics have high N and low E scores, that psychotics have high P and high L scores, that criminals and psychopaths have high P, E, and N scores and low L scores, and that drug takers have high P and N scores. Samples of neurotics, psychotics, criminals, and drug takers have been tested in various countries (for example, criminals in Hungary and drug takers and psychotics in Nigeria) with positive results that confirm experience with English samples (Eysenck, 1977c).

We now consider the indices of factor comparison actually discovered in some of the nations surveyed (Table 2 gives the specific figures). To aid in the understanding of these indices of factor comparison, data is provided comparing indices of factor comparison derived from the standardization group, totaling several thousand men and women, with results obtained in a Gallup Poll quota sample of 600 English males and 598 English females (Eysenck, 1979). In these comparisons both groups are English, but one is a quota sample of the population, while the other is made up of different groups that happen to be included in the standardization sample. Table 2 shows the indices of factor comparison; none of them are effectively below 0.99, thus indicating that identical factors are found in different male and female populations within the same country. It was also found that means and standard deviations showed very similar results for the two

Table 2.   Indices of factor comparisons between English and various other groups. P = psychoticism-superego control; E = extraversion-introversion; N = neuroticism; L = lie scale

Compared groups	Factor indices			
	P	E	N	L
English standardization males v. English quota sample males	0.99	1.00	1.00	1.00
English standardization females v. English quota sample females	0.99	1.00	1.00	1.00
English males v. Yugoslav males	0.97	0.97	1.00	0.98
English females v. Yugoslav females	0.97	0.99	1.00	0.99
English males v. French males	0.98	1.00	1.00	1.00
English females v. French females	0.97	1.00	1.00	0.98
English males v. Indian males	0.97	0.99	0.99	0.96
English females v. Indian females	0.95	0.99	0.99	0.98
English males v. Greek males	0.94	0.99	0.98	0.98
English females v. Greek females	0.89	1.00	0.96	1.00
English males v. Nigerian males	0.98	0.99	0.99	0.98
English females v. Nigerian females	0.66	0.91	0.92	0.93
English males v. Portuguese males	1.00	0.99	1.00	1.00
English females v. Portuguese females	0.99	0.98	1.00	0.99
English males v. Australian males	0.93	1.00	0.99	0.99
English females v. Australian females	1.00	1.00	0.99	0.99
English males v. Iranian males	0.98	0.99	0.99	1.00
English females v. Iranian females	0.94	1.00	0.98	0.99
English males v. Brazilian males	1.00	0.99	1.00	1.00
English females v. Brazilian females	0.99	0.98	1.00	0.99
English schoolboys v. Japanese boys	0.96	0.99	0.99	0.89
English schoolgirls v. Japanese girls	0.97	1.00	0.94	0.98
English boys v. New Zealand boys	0.99	1.00	1.00	1.00
English girls v. New Zealand girls	0.99	0.98	1.00	1.00
English boys v. Spanish boys	0.97	0.98	0.99	0.99
English girls v. Spanish girls	0.92	0.98	0.99	0.99

samples. We may conclude that slight departures from random sampling procedures are not likely to vitiate results in any intended cultural comparison.

With very occasional exceptions, all the indices between different cultural groups in Table 2 are very high. The great majority are in excess of 0.98, and only occasionally do they drop below that level. The general impression is that these dimensions of personality have transcultural validity and can be used to characterize both normal and abnormal personality anywhere in the world (unless, of course, it can be shown that some cultural groups not studied differ from those included in these surveys). A fundamental demonstration of worldwide validity is necesary in order to make any comparisons meaningful, but even this is not enough. It is necessary, in each individual comparison, to study all the items in each scale in order to eliminate the small number of items nonapplicable to a particular culture. Only when both of these steps are successfully undertaken—when there is a very high index of factor similarity and when nonmatching items have been removed from the scales—can we proceed to the last step in the procedure and compare the actual mean scores of people participating in the studies.

Even these precautions may not be enough. It is also necessary to compare the reliabilities of the scales in the different countries as well as the intercorrelations for the different countries of the scales and the factors. The hypothesis of cultural comparability demands that these correlations should be of a similar order and in a similar direction. In our own studies, this has always been the case; therefore, it seems that we are justified in carrying out cross-cultural comparisons along these lines.

CULTURAL DIFFERENCES: GENETIC OR ENVIRONMENTAL?

An important question already mentioned in connection with Lynn's study is what causal factors are involved in cultural differences in personality and abnormality, as may be discovered between different national, cultural, or racial groups. Lynn has suggested both genetic (racial) and cultural determinants and has given evidence for the importance of these factors, as well as of factors that do not fall easily under either category, such as climatic conditions. There is also the question of how to separate and investigate genetic causes and environmental causes. Because very little work has been done in this field, much of our review must be speculative, but because the problem is an important one, we suggest ways and means of overcoming some of these difficulties.

As far as the major dimensions of personality are concerned, there is strong evidence to suggest the paramount importance of genetic causes (Eysenck, 1975, 1976). The same is true of psychiatric conditions of mental abnormality (Fieve, Rosenthal, and Brill, 1975). An excellent summary of the evidence can be found in Shields (1973).

Detailed studies of the inheritance of extraversion (Eaves and Eysenck, 1975), neuroticism (Eaves and Eysenck, 1976a, 1976b), and psychoticism (Eaves and Eysenck, 1977) have also been done. These analyses were carried out on very large samples of MZ and DZ twins, using the most recent methods of biometrical genetical analysis as pioneered by Mather and Jinks (1971). The major results that were found, in connection with all the major personality dimensions, are as follows:

1. Genetic factors determine between 60% and 80% of the reliable variance of the scores on all three variables; this is similar to the amount of variance accounted for in the intelligence field. Thus, there is no question that genetic factors are predominant in causing differences in personality between individuals within a given culture.

2. The genetic factors involved are almost entirely of the additive kind; there is no evidence for either assortative mating or dominance. In this case, personality differs from intelligence, in which both assortative mating and dominance play an important part.

3. Of the two types of environmental influences, within-family (E_1) and between-family (E_2), the evidence suggests that the latter play a very limited part, if any, in causing individual differences in personality. This finding rules out theories concerning the development of personality that implicate parental influences, such as those suggested by Freud, Laing, and others. This finding also suggests that it is difficult to discover environmental causes related to between-family determinants like socioeconomic status and schooling.

4. The major personality factors show very little, if any, direct correlation with social factors, such as socioeconomic status and schooling; again, they differ considerably from intelligence where correlations with such factors are very high.

Given the very strong determination by genetic factors of differences in personality, it would be tempting to conclude that difference between groups (nations, races, etc.) would also be determined by genetic factors. However, this does not follow logically. As Eysenck (1971a) has pointed out in connection with the race and intelligence controversy, there is a gap involved between the study of individual differences and the study of groups, which cannot readily be bridged. Eysenck asks the question:

> Can we . . . argue that genetic studies of the kind discussed . . . give *direct* support to the hereditarian position? The answer must, I think, be in the negative. The two populations involved (black and white) are separate populations, and none of the studies carried out on whites alone, such as twin studies, are feasible. . . . The direct argument is weakened even more by the fact that no proper twin studies, or other genetic studies of a similar kind, have been done with negro subjects; practically all our evidence comes from whites. [pp. 117, 118]

Eysenck continues the argument, pointing out another consideration: "Critics are perfectly right in saying that the genetic evidence existing at the moment is not conclusive. However, it constitutes presumptive evidence which is quite strong, and cannot be disregarded" (p. 118). Is there no way in which we could get over this hurdle and could establish by more direct means the importance of genetic factors in causing differences in personality between nations, races, or cultural groups? An attempt to do this has been made by Eysenck (1977b). He begins his argument with the observation that there is good evidence that the Japanese score significantly higher than British groups on the personality dimensions of introversion and neuroticism. This conclusion is supported both by analysis of demographic data (Lynn, 1971; Lynn and Hampson, 1975) and by questionnaire studies (Iwawaki, Eysenck, and Eysenck, 1977, 1980). In order to discover whether these differences are caused by genetic factors, at least to some degree, we may begin with the finding of Angst and Maurer-Groeli (1974) that there are significant differences in the frequency of blood groups found among European extraverts and introverts, and between highly emotional and unemotional persons. Introversion is significantly more frequent among persons having the AB blood group. Emotionality (neuroticism) is significantly more frequent in persons having blood group B than in persons having blood group A. If we can interpret these findings as evidence for some pleiotropic mechanism linking blood groups and personality, then it becomes possible to put forward testable hypotheses relating to national and racial comparisons in the personality field. In particular, it may be predicted that the Japanese would have a significantly higher proportion of persons with the AB blood group, and also that they would have a significantly smaller proportion of persons with blood group A than with blood group B. We have used the ratio A/B to test this hypothesis.

Relevant figures for blood groups can be found in Mourant, Kopek, and Domaniewska-Sobezak's book (1976) for very large and variegated samples of both English and Japanese groups. Regarding the percentage of persons with blood group AB, the proportions are 3.01 in England and 8.98 in Japan—a very sizable difference in the predicted direction. There are some variations in different samples and in different parts of the countries in question; the extreme values for large samples are 1.63 and 4.11 in England, and 6.63 and 12.88 in Japan. There is no overlap.

The ratio A/B is, as predicted, larger in England than in Japan; the mean values are 4.54 and 1.64 respectively. Considering the variability within each country, in large samples extreme values are 2.0 and 7.33 in England, and 1.32 and 1.95 in Japan—again there is no overlap. There seems to be little doubt that with such large samples (the total British samples amounted to 616,106 persons, the total Japanese samples amounted to 421,151 persons) the predicted differences are significant statistically. These data would seem to support the hypothesis that there are genetic factors predisposing the Japanese to be more introverted and more neurotic than the British. To confirm the issue, it would seem desirable to investigate a Japanese sample to ascertain whether the relationship between blood group and personality were actually similar to that found by Angst and Mauer-Groeli.

The data quoted above are not decisive in answering the question of genetic determination of racial and national differences. They are only offered as a suggestion for the possible use of blood groups (and perhaps other polymorphisms) in answering questions that as yet have not been considered in this connection. There seem to be pleiotropic relationships between personality and blood groups that have not yet been utilized to any degree. In addition to neuoticism and extraversion, there is some evidence that psychoticism may also be so related (Elston, Kringlen, and Nambrodini, 1973; Eysenck and Eysenck, 1976). It seems possible that the connection of blood groups with personality factors, and possibly with mental disorders (Mauer-Groeli, 1974a, 1974b), may lead us into the investigation of genetic factors as determinants of national and cultural differences in personality and mental abnormality. They may also help to explain the maintenance of a balanced polymorphism of the ABO system.

SUMMARY AND CONCLUSIONS

Different people working in the field of personality disorders have had different purposes, and it is important to keep their objectives separate. Thus, people working with the MMPI have been concerned primarily with demonstrating the possibility of using the scale in different cultural contexts and with transplanting into these contexts the psychiatric model in the terms in which the MMPI was constructed and validated. If, as we believe, this model itself is subject to very damaging criticism, then the relative success with which the MMPI can be adapted to different cultures is not necessarily an advantage. It would be better to construct a better model and better measuring instruments for that model, and only then to begin to export the particular measuring instrument that finally emerges (Eysenck, 1971b).

In contrast to the aim of the MMPI researchers, the Eysencks' major purpose in carrying out cross-cultural comparisons was to validate a fundamental theory of human nature involving the definition and measurement of the major dimensions of personality. The Eysencks' purpose is very different, and hence the methods used also are rather different from those used by investigators concerned with the MMPI, although certain similarities remain. The main point of contrast between the two approaches is that the users of the MMPI accept without question the American system of psychiatric nosology, in spite of the fact that it is not based on any properly scientific theories or investigations, whereas the

Eysencks are primarily concerned with *constructing* a scientific basis for future use. The fact that one model can, to some extent, be mapped into the other is of considerable interest, and suggests that if certain fundamental concepts in the MMPI system could be changed (for instance, transforming categorical concepts like schizophrenia into dimensional concepts like psychoticism), then the findings of the one system could be translated into findings of the other.

Spielberger and his colleagues utilize another very different approach. They are concerned primarily with the adaptation of a particular measuring instrument, namely the anxiety trait and state scales, into foreign languages and cultures. They are not concerned either with a psychiatric system of nosology (as are the MMPI authors) or with a fundamental system of personality description (as are the Eysencks). The aim of Spielberger and his colleagues is a relatively simple one. Success cannot be gainsaid, although from the point of view of transcultural comparison of mean values, the evidence is not sufficient to enable us to attribute much meaning to such comparisons.

Lynn's approach is again different. His research is concerned primarily with the elaboration of a new method for comparing personality patterns in different cultures through the use of demographic and epidemiological statistics. Although at first it might have seemed unlikely that this approach would provide much fruitful evidence in this field, the success of the method has been truly astonishing, and comparisons with questionnaire studies have cross-validated it in a totally unexpected manner. Particularly interesting is the agreement of the factor analytic studies carried out by Lynn on his data with the differently based work of H.J. and S.B.G. Eysenck. This agreement cross-validates both approaches, and suggests that underlying the cross-cultural differences observed are some truly biological factors, measured, in part, by the Eysenck scales.

Given the meaningfulness of cross-cultural differences, we have noted the difficulty of attributing these differences to genetic or to environmental causes and of specifying these causes, although some attempt has been made to do so. The complexities are awesome, but further work in the manner suggested by Lynn and Eysenck might be worthwhile. At the present time we have only suggestions as to the likely causes of the differences observed in the different studies summarized here.

Regarding the substantive element, many specific differences emerge, and it should be noted that many of these differences appear and reappear in the different studies. Thus, the extreme reactions of Japanese subjects on various scales come out on the work of the MMPI group, of Lynn, and of Eysenck; other similarities between different studies are also apparent. The differences that appear are not so large that they could not just be temporary effects of causes like those suggested by Lynn, e.g., winning or losing a particular war. What is almost more impressive than the consistency of the differences observed by different authors is the relatively slight extent of these differences. Butcher and Pancheri suggest a difference not exceeding half a standard deviation, and, indeed, few of the differences observed by other authors exceed that limit. In terms of the IQ coefficient, the mean differences would not exceed 7 or 8 points, which is much less than what is observed in relation to intelligence, in which whites exceed blacks, Chinese exceed Malays, and Hungarians exceed Gypsies (by approximately 15 or 16 points). Possibly, the failure to achieve better differentiation is because personality scales are less reliable and less valid than intelligence tests, but there may be additional explanations. Perhaps different groups are really more similar with respect to personality than with respect to intelligence. At the moment, the evidence is not available that would enable us to answer such a question.

We may conclude that the dimensions of personality seem to be very much the same in all the different nations, countries, and cultures where they have been studied, and that differences in position on these dimensions exist, but are not large, even though they are consistent from time to time and from study to study. Positions apparently can be changed by such social factors as winning or losing a war. They may also be influenced by climatic conditions, and, to some degree, they may be innate. Our major conclusion is that mental abnormalities show such great variation *within* countries that *between* countries comparisons must inevitably result in the discovery of rather small and relatively unimportant differences. However, the fact that the dimensions of variation are identical from country to country makes it possible and interesting to study causal influences and to compare them between countries. This seems to be an important research project that has not previously received much attention.

The study of culture and personality abnormalities is a very difficult discipline that has not hitherto attracted much notice; in this area, comparatively little work has been done. This chapter was written in the hope of attracting more attention to this field and of suggesting ways and means to investigate the rather intractible problems encountered in studying cross-cultural disorders.

REFERENCES

Angst, J., and Maurer-Groeli, Y.A. 1974. Blutgruppen and Persönlichkeit. Archiv Psychiatr. Nervenkr. 218:291–300.
Block, J. 1965. Challenges of Response Sets. Appleton-Century-Crofts, New York.
Brislin, R. W., Lonner, W. J., and Thorndike, R. M. 1973. Cross-Cultural Research Methods. John Wiley & Sons, Inc., Interscience Division, New York.
Butcher, J. N., and Pancheri, P. 1976. A Handbook of Cross-National MMPI Research. University of Minnesota Press, Minneapolis.

Cattell, R. B., and Scheier, I. H. 1961. The Meaning and Measurement of Neuroticism and Anxiety. Ronald Press Co., New York.

Cattell, R. B., and Warburton, F. W. 1961. A cross-cultural comparison of patterns of extraversion and anxiety. Br. J. Psychol. 52:3–15.

Comrey, A. L. 1960. Comparison of certain personality variables in American and Italian groups. Educ. Psychol. Meas. 20:541–550.

Comrey, A. L., and Nencini, R. 1961. Factors in MMPI responses of Italian students. Educ. Psychol. Meas. 21:657–662.

Cooper, J. E., Kendell, R. E., Gurland, B. J., Sharpe, L., Copeland, J.R.M., and Simon, R. 1972. Psychiatric Diagnosis in New York and London. Oxford University Press, London.

Copeland, J. R. M., Cooper, J. G., Kendell, R. E., and Gourlay, A. J. 1971. Differences in usage of diagnostic labels amongst psychiatrists in the British Isles. Br. J. Psychiatry 118:629–640.

Dimitriou, E. C., and Eysenck, S. B. G. 1978. National differences in personality: Greece and England. Int. J. Intercult. Relat. 2:266–282.

Eaves, L., and Eysenck, H. J. 1975. The nature of extraversion: A genetical analysis. J. Pers. Soc. Psychol. 32:102–112.

Eaves, L., and Eysenck, H. J. 1976a. Genetic and environmental components of inconsistency and unrepeatability in twins' responses to a neuroticism questionnaire. Behav. Genet. 6:145–160.

Eaves, L., and Eysenck, H. J. 1976b. Genotype x age interaction for neuroticism. Behav. Genet. 6:359–362.

Eaves, L. J., and Eysenck, H. J. 1977. Genotype-environmental model for psychoticism. Adv. Behav. Res. Ther. 1:5–26.

Elston, R. C., Kringlen, E., and Nambrodini, K. 1973. Possible linkage relationships between certain blood groups and schizophrenia and other psychoses. Behav. Genet. 3:101–106.

Eysenck, H. J. 1970a. The Structure of Human Personality. 3rd Ed. Methuen, Inc., London.

Eysenck, H. J. 1970b. A dimensional system of psychodiagnostics. In: A. R. Mahrer (ed.), New Approaches to Personality Classification. Columbia University Press, New York.

Eysenck, H. J. 1971a. Race, Intelligence, and Education. Temple Smith, London.

Eysenck, H. J. 1971b. On the choice of personality tests for research and prediction. J. Behav. Sci. 1:85–89.

Eysenck, H. J. (ed.). 1973. Handbook of Abnormal Psychology. 2nd Ed. Pitman, London.

Eysenck, H. J. 1975. A genetic model of anxiety. In: C. D. Spielberger and I. G. Sarason (eds.), Stress and Anxiety. Hemisphere Publishing Corporation, Washington, D. C.

Eysenck, H. J. 1976. Genetic factors in personality development. In: A. R. Kaplan (ed.), Human Behavior Genetics. Charles C Thomas, Publisher, Springfield, Ill.

Eysenck, H. J. 1977b. National differences in personality as related to ABO blood group polymorphism. Psychol. Rep. 41:1257–1258.

Eysenck, H. J. 1977c. Crime and Personality. 3rd Ed. Routledge and Kegan Paul, London.

Eysenck, H. J. 1979. Personality factors in a random sample of the population. Psychol. Rep. 44:1023–1027.

Eysenck, H. J. 1980. A Model for Personality. Springer-Verlag, New York.

Eysenck, H. J., and Eysenck, S. B. G. 1969. Personality Structure and Measurement. Knapp Edits, San Diego, Calif.

Eysenck, H. J., and Eysenck, S. B. G. 1976. Psychoticism as a Dimension of Personality. Hodder & Stoughton, London.

Eysenck, H. J., Gupta, B. S., and Eysenck, S. B. G. National differences in personality: India and England. Indian J. Psychol. In press.

Eysenck, H. J., Eysenck, S. B. G., Gauquelin, M., Gauquelin, F., Pascal, C., and Pascal, D. 1980. La Structure de la personalité chez les français confrontée a celle des anglais: Comparaison "cross-culturelle." La Personalité 1–2:7–29.

Eysenck, S. B. G., and Seisdedos, N. 1978. Un estudio inter-naciones de la personalidad. Rev. Psicol. 33:271–281.

Eysenck, S. B. G., Adelaja, O., and Eysenck, H. J. 1977. A comparative study of personality in Nigerian and English subjects. J. Soc. Psychol. 102:171–178.

Fieve, R. R., Rosenthal, D., and Brill, H. 1975. Genetic Research: Psychiatry. Johns Hopkins Press, London.

Greif, S. 1970. Untersuchungen zur deutschen Übersetzung des 16PF Fragebogens. Psychol. Beiträge 12:186–213.

Hekmat, H., Khajari, F., and Mehryar, A. H. 1974. Psychoticism, neuroticism, and extraversion: The personality determinants of empathy. J. Clin. Psychol. 30:559–561.

Hobi, V. 1972. Ein Beitrag zur Faktorenstruktur des MMPI. Schweiz. Z. Psychol. 31:298–305.

Hofstede, G. 1976. Nationality and Organisational Stress. European Institute for Advanced Studies in Management, Brussels.

Honess, T., and Kline, P. 1974. The use of EPI and J.EPI with a student population in Uganda. Br. J. Soc. Clin. Psychol. 13:96–98.

Horn, J. L., Wanberg, K. W., and Appel, M. 1973. On the internal structure of the MMPI. Multivar. Behav. Res. 8:131–171.

Hosseini, A. A., Mehryar, A. H., and Razavied, A. A. 1973. Extraversion, neuroticism, and psychoticism as measured by Eysenck's inventory in Iran. J. Genet. Psychol. 122:197–205.

Howarth, E. 1972. A factor analysis of selected markers for objective personality factors. Multivar. Behav. Res. 7:451–476.

Howarth, E., and Browne, J. A. 1971. An item-factor-analysis of the 16PF. Personality 2:117–139.

Irfani, S. 1977. Eysenck's extraversion, neuroticism, and psychoticism inventory in Turkey. Psychol. Rep. 41:1231–1234.

Irfani, S. Extraversion, neuroticism, and psychoticism among highschool and university students in Iran. Psychol. Rep. In press.

Irvine, S. H. 1969. Factor analysis of African abilities and attainments: Constructs across cultures. Psychol. Bull. 71:20–32.

Iwawaki, S., Eysenck, S. B. G., and Eysenck, H. J. 1977. Differences in personality between Japanese and English. J. Soc. Psychol. 102:27–33.

Iwawaki, S., Eysenck, S. B. G., and Eysenck, H. J. 1980. The universality of typology: A comparison between English and Japanese schoolchildren. J. Soc. Psychol. 112:3–9.

Katz, M., Cole, J. O., and Lowery, H. A. 1969. Studies of the diagnostic process: The influence of symptom perception, past experience, and ethnic background on diagnostic decisions. Am. J. Psychiatry. 125:937–947.

Kikuchi, A., and Gordon, L. 1970. Japanese and American personal values: Some cross-cultural findings. Int. J. Psychol. 5:183–187.

Kline, P. 1967. Extraversion, neuroticism, and academic performance among Ghanian University students. Br. J. Educ. Psychol. 36:93–94.

Kramer, M. 1969. Cross-national study of diagnosis of the mental disorders: Origin of the problem. Am. J. Psychiatry 125, Supplements 1–11.

Lojk, L., Eysenck, S. B. G., and Eysenck, H. J. 1979. National differences in personality: Yugoslavia and England. Br. J. Psychol. 70:381–387.

Lynn, R. 1971. Personality and National Character. Pergamon Press, London.

Lynn, R., and Hampson, S. L. 1975. National differences in extraversion and neuroticism. Br. J. Soc. Clin. Psychol. 14:223–240.

Lynn, R., and Hampson, S. L. 1977. Fluctuations in national levels of neuroticism and extraversion, 1935–1970. Br. J. Soc. Clin. Psychol. 10:131–137.

Mather, K., and Jinks, J. L. 1971. Biometrical Genetics. Chapman and Hall, London.

Maurer-Groeli, Y. A. 1974a. Blutgruppen und Krankheiten. Arch. Psychiatr. Nervenkr. 218:301–318.

Maurer-Groeli, Y. A. 1974b. Blutgruppen, Persönlichkeit, und Schulabschluss. Schweiz. Z. Psychol. 33:407–410.

Mehryar, A. H. 1970. Some data on Persian translation of E.P.I. Br. J. Soc. Clin. Psychol. 9:257–263.

Mehryar, A. H., Hekmat, H., and Khajari, F. 1975. Comparison of Eysenck's PEN and Lanyan's Psychological Screening Inventory in a group of American students. J. Consult. Clin. Psychol. 43:9–12.

Mourant, A. E., Kopec, S. C., and Domaniewska-Sobezak, K. 1976. The distribution of Human Blood Groups. Oxford University Press, London.

Orpen, L. 1972. The cross-cultural validity of Eysenck's Personality Inventory: A test in Afrikaans-speaking South Africa. Br. J. Soc. Clin. Psychol. 11:244–248.

Overall, J. E., Hunter, S., and Butcher, J. N. 1973. Factor structure of the MMPI-168 in a psychiatric population. J. Consult. Psychol. 41:284–286.

Pancheri, P., and Stracca, M. 1972. Studio di dati emersi in una populazione psichiatrica mediante l'analisi fattoriale del MMPI. Riv. Psichiatr. 7:112–128.

Saklofske, D. W., and Eysenck, S. B. G. 1978. Cross-cultural comparisons of personality: New Zealand children and English children. Psychol. Rep. 42:1111–1116.

Sandifer, M. G., Hordern, A., Timbury, G. C., and Green, L. M. 1968. Psychiatric diagnosis: A comparative study in North Carolina, London, and Glasgow. Br. J. Psychiatry 114:1–9.

Sarason, S. B., Davidson, K. S., Lighthall, F., Waite, R. R., and Ruebuch, B. K. 1960. Anxiety in elementary school children. John Wiley & Sons, Inc., New York.

Saville, P., and Blinkhorn, S. 1976. Undergraduate Personality by Factored Scales. NFER Publishing Co., London.

Shields, J. 1973. Heredity and psychological abnormality. In: H. J. Eysenck (ed.), Handbook of Abnormal Psychology. 2nd Ed. Pitman, London.

Spielberger, C. D. 1966. Theory and research in anxiety. In: C. D. Spielberger (ed.), Anxiety and Behavior. Academic Press, Inc., New York.

Spielberger, C. D. 1972. Anxiety as an emotional state. In: C. D. Spielberger (ed.), Anxiety: Current Trends in Theory and Research. Academic Press, Inc., New York.

Spielberger, C. D. 1973. Manual for the State-Trait Anxiety Inventory for children. Consulting Psychologist Press, Palo Alto, Calif.

Spielberger, C., and Diaz-Guerrero, R. 1976. Cross-Cultural Anxiety. John Wiley & Sons, Inc., London.

Spielberger, C. D., Gorsuch, R. L., and Lushene, R. G. 1970. Manual for the State-Trait Anxiety Inventory. Consulting Psychologist Press, Palo Alto, Calif.

Stein, K. B. 1968. Cluster analysis of the MMPI. In: P. McReynolds (ed.), Advances in Psychological Assessment. Science & Behavior Books, Inc., Palo Alto, Calif.

Tarrier, N, Eysenck, S. B. G., and Eysenck, H. J. National differences in personality: Brazil and England. In press.

Timm, U. 1968. Reliabilität und Faktorenstruktur von Cattell's 16PF Test bei einer deutschen Stichprobe. Z. Exp. Angew. Psychol. 15:354–373.

Triandis, H., Vassiliou, V., and Nassiakou, M. 1968. Three cross-cultural studies of subjective culture. J. Pers. Soc. Psychol. 8:1–42.

Wakefield, J. A., Yom, B. L., Bradley, P. E., Doughtie, E. B., and Cox, J. A. 1974. Eysenck's personality dimensions: A model for the MMPI. Br. J. Soc. Clin. Psychol. 13:413–420.

Westhoff, K., and Sorembe, V. Zur Brauchbarkeit des Eysenck-Persönlichkeits-Inventars (Form A) als Individuadiagnostikum. Diagnostica. In press.

Chapter 12

Cultural Variations in Alcohol Abuse

Herbert Barry, III

Alcohol and culture are closely linked with each other. Alcoholic beverages constitute important and highly valued components of the social life in many cultures. Drinking generally occurs in a social context. Cultural customs influence the drinking practices, the attitudes toward drinking and drunkenness, and the effects of alcohol intoxication.

The principal purpose of this chapter is to analyze the cultural conditions associated with pathological effects of alcohol. Descriptions of adaptive, beneficial use of alcoholic beverages are included for two reasons. First, effective cultural restraints on drinking can be contrasted with cultural patterns of excessive, destructive drinking. Second, any custom that exists has been selected for survival by a stringent process of cultural evolution. The most destructive practices may have beneficial effects on the society, although there may be no benefits for the individuals who are afflicted.

The principal source of information for this chapter consists of a series of cross-cultural studies, beginning with Horton (1943), in which measures of insobriety or drunkenness were correlated with diverse other cultural customs in samples of preliterate societies. Further useful information is available in detailed observations and interpretations of drinking customs in individual cultures, ethnic groups, and nations. Snyder (1958) analyzed the rarity of drunkenness among Jews. Accounts of various other cultural influences on drinking are included in a book edited by Marshall (1979).

Heath (1975, 1976a, 1976b) has surveyed the extensive literature on cultural variations in drinking customs. Abstracts of publications are printed in the *Journal of Studies on Alcohol* and are available from the National Clearinghouse for Alcohol Information, a service of the National Institute on Alcohol Abuse and Alcoholism. The *Social Sciences Citation*

Index (Garfield, 1977) enables the user to identify pertinent articles in a particular year, either by a combination of two key words in its title (such as Alcohol and Culture) or by its citation of one or more key references (such as Horton, 1943, or Snyder, 1958).

Other types of resources are available for cross-cultural research. Barry (1980a) explains how to locate and use the ethnographic information on the numerous societies included in the Human Relations Area Files. Barry and Schlegel (1980) have compiled information on many aspects of culture in a carefully selected world sample of 186 societies. Many of these societies were included by Horton (1943) and also were considered in subsequent cross-cultural studies of drinking. The Ethnographic Atlas (Murdock, 1967; Barry, 1980b) provides selected information on a world sample of more than 1,000 societies.

PSYCHOPHYSIOLOGY OF ALCOHOL

Cultural drinking customs must adjust to the physical and behavioral changes caused by alcohol. Pharmacological and psychological studies of this psychoactive drug have contributed knowledge that helps us to understand the social functions of drinking. Such studies have been extensively summarized in a two-volume review by Wallgren and Barry (1970). A brief, subsequent summary appears in a chapter by Barry (1977a).

The principal physiological effect of alcohol intoxication is its disruption of the functions of the central nervous system. The drug slows and partially blocks transmission of messages among the neurons of the brain. Accordingly, alcohol is pharmacologically classified as a general depressant. Sufficiently high doses cause stupor or loss of consciousness. The alcohol effect is lethal if the respiratory control center in the brain is depressed sufficiently to prevent breathing.

Because of the detrimental effects of alcohol, the cultural use of this drug is generally associated with recreational or festival occasions rather than with working, fighting, or learning. Even at doses that cause no noticeable incapacities, some types of mental functions are impaired. Low doses of alcohol can impair performance that requires divided attention because alcohol impairs the ability to give concurrent attention to different tasks. An example of a task requiring divided attention is the job of a sentry who watches for intruders while talking with a companion or planning the dinner menu. Alcohol causes the person to concentrate on one of the tasks, while neglecting the others. Automobile driving may involve many types of divided attention, such as steering the car, planning the route, watching other traffic, talking with a passenger, listening to the radio, observing the scenery, and fantasizing. Alcohol effects are dangerous for drivers, especially for youths who have learned to drive recently, because they have not yet integrated the diverse activities of driving into a well-established habit pattern.

Some conspicuous effects of high doses of alcohol are walking with a staggering gait and speaking with slurred enunciation. There is also a large increase of swaying while trying to stand still. The affected person may be unable to do tasks that require precise sensorimotor coordination. Sensory functions are more resistant to the drug effect, so that doses close to the anesthetic level are required to cause noticeable impairment of visual or auditory acuity.

Because of the dangerous effects of alcohol intoxication, cultural customs generally establish standard quantities of a single unit or serving of alcoholic beverages. The drinker can thereby monitor intake in terms of number of drinks. For example, in the United States, one serving of beer is generally a can, a bottle, or a glass of 12 ounces (360 milliliters), containing approximately 5% alcohol by volume. The volume of absolute alcohol is 18 milliliters, weighing 15 grams. In a person weighing 132 pounds (60 kilograms), 15 grams constitute a dose of 0.25 grams alcohol per kilogram body weight. Therefore, four servings of beer result in a strongly intoxicating dose of 1.0 gram alcohol per kilogram body weight.

Beverages with a higher percentage of alcohol are served in smaller volumes so that each serving contains a similar amount of absolute alcohol. Wine has approximately 15% alcohol by volume, three times as much as beer, and the typical serving is 2.5 ounces (75 milliliters) in a glass, one-fifth as much as beer. Therefore, the absolute alcohol is slightly less (37.5%) in each serving of wine than of beer. Distilled spirits (such as vodka, gin, whiskey, and brandy) have approximately 50% alcohol by volume, ten times as much as beer, and the typical serving is 1.5 ounces (45 milliliters) in a shot glass, one-eighth as much as beer. Therefore, the absolute alcohol is slightly more (25%) in each serving of spirits than of beer.

Approximately 30 minutes are required for most of one serving of alcohol to be absorbed from the stomach and intestines. Rapid consumption would allow intake of anesthetic or even lethal quantities before the drinker experiences substantial intoxicating effects. Therefore, drinking customs generally require slow consumption or an appreciable interval between successive servings. The rate of intake necessarily becomes much slower after the intoxication reaches its peak. The drug is metabolized by the liver at a slow, steady rate of approximately 0.01% (10 mg%) per hour. Therefore, an interval of two hours between servings is required to avoid increasing the alcohol consumption in the body.

If 1.0 gram alcohol per kilogram body weight is drunk within one hour, the peak alcohol concentration in the blood and brain is approximately 0.1%. This figure, one part in a thousand, corresponds to the ratio of alcohol (one gram) to the body weight (one kilogram). A common alternative term for 0.1% concentration is 100 mg % (one thousand times the percentage). This concentration is generally defined as intoxicating and thereby impairs the ability to drive an automobile.

If alcohol were equally distributed in all body tissues, the peak concentration after 1.0 gram alcohol per kilogram body weight would be less than 0.1% because of the metabolism of part of the drug before all of it is absorbed. An opposite influence also occurs because alcohol is not absorbed by the body fat. Therefore, the concentration is higher in body water, which predominates in the blood and brain.

The blood and brain alcohol concentration resulting from the same amount of absolute alcohol intake is influenced by the weight and sex of the drinker. Four typical servings of beer (1.0 gram absolute alcohol), which result in 0.10% maximum blood alcohol in a drinker who weighs 132 pounds (60 kilograms), results in 0.15% blood alcohol (50% more) in a drinker who weighs 88 pounds (40 kilograms) and 0.067% blood alcohol (33% less) in a drinker who weighs 198 pounds (90 kilograms). Because of individual variations in weight, cultural customs usually do not require the drinkers to consume the same number of servings. The same amount of alcohol intake results in higher blood concentrations in women than in men, not only because of the smaller average body size of women, but also because women have a higher proportion of body fat. Accordingly, in most societies women drink less than men, and childen drink little or no alcohol.

Most of the studies on psychophysiology of alcohol have attempted to generalize the drug effects to all humans or to all animals of the species that is tested. Cultural variations in drinking practices are thereby attributed to variations in other aspects of culture, requiring different adjustments to the same pharmacological influence. Some of the cultural variations, however, might be attributable to genetically controlled differences in sensitivity to alcohol.

A conspicuous racial difference in response to alcohol is indicated by findings of intense facial flushing and other physiological effects in Mongoloids but not in Caucasoids. Cultural groups of Mongoloids tested were Japanese, Taiwanese, and Koreans (Wolff, 1972), the Eastern Cree tribe of North American Indians (Wolff, 1973), Chinese (Zeiner, Paredes, and Christensen, 1979), and Japanese (Mizoi et al., 1979). The intense reaction to alcohol in these groups is accompanied by a large increase in heart rate and the activation of the sympathetic nervous system (Mizoi et al., 1979; Zeiner et al., 1979). The reaction occurs only in some Mongoloids and thus is not a universal attribute of this large racial category. The effect seems attributable to elevated levels of the metabolic product of alcohol—acetaldehyde (Mizoi et al., 1979; Zeiner et al., 1979). Because of the rapid metabolism of acetaldehyde to acetate, a pharmacologically inactive substance, acetaldehyde is normally limited to small amounts and is present only in combination with alcohol. Large amounts of acetaldehyde are extremely toxic, indicated by the severe reaction after alcohol consumption when the acetaldehyde metabolism is blocked by pretreatment with disulfiram (Antabuse). In the studies by Zeiner et al. (1979) and Mizoi et al. (1979), the acetaldehyde levels were low, but were much higher in the flushing than in the nonflushing individuals.

The physiological sensitivity to alcohol might contribute to the absence of alcohol consumption aboriginally among most tribes in North America and Oceania and to the rarity of heavy drinking by the Chinese. Heavy drinking characterizes many Mongoloid people, however, such as Japanese, some East Asian groups, South American Indian tribes, and North American Indians after the introduction of distilled spirits by the Europeans. A speculative possibility is that the intense physiological reaction, which is a deterrent to drinking, also enhances the pleasurable effects of alcohol. The adverse reactions might disappear after repeated drinking occasions because of the development of tolerance to this portion of the alcohol effects.

Evidence has been reported that alcohol metabolism is faster in Mongoloid than in Caucasoid drinkers (Farris and Jones, 1978; Hanna, 1978). This difference implies a capability for larger amount of chronic alcohol intake and thus a greater risk of alcoholism among Mongoloids.

PLEASURES AND PERILS OF INTOXICATION

The word *intoxication* has two contrary sets of meanings. One set of meaning includes excitement, delirium, elation, and enthusiasm. These emotions are pleasurable, accounting for the widespread popularity of alcohol intoxication. The other set of meaning refers to toxic, poisonous, and adverse effects associated with the impairment of functions, or even with incapacitation caused by high doses of alcohol. The combination of pleasure with toxicity results in the severe problems that develop from chronic alcohol consumption.

Drinking customs in preliterate societies (Child, Bacon, and Barry, 1965) and in contemporary nations (Marshall, 1979) demonstrate the powerfully pleasurable effect of alcohol intoxication. Production or procurement of alcoholic beverages consumes a large proportion of the economic resources. Drinking is a highly valued activity in most cultures.

The pleasurable effects of alcohol involve contrasting responses to the drug. One response is sedation, attributable to the generalized depressant action of alcohol. Subjective reports include feelings of calmness and relaxation. Another response is stimulation, indicated by subjective reports of feelings of excitement and exhilaration. This combination of pleasurable effects may be especially effective in social settings, because the sedation relieves the anxieties and avoidance involved in social interactions, while the stimulation facilitates social behavior. Accordingly, drinking is a social rather than a solitary activity in most cultures.

An intense, compulsive need for the pleasurable effects of alcohol is necessary to account for the repeated occasions of heavy drinking that constitute the prevalent behavior in many cultures, despite the severely adverse effects. Several different theories have elaborated on the pleasurable sedative and stimulating effects of alcohol.

Horton (1943) suggested that the sedative effects of insobriety provide an escape from the chronic anxiety aroused by subsistence insecurity. A drug that relieves severe, prolonged anxiety will be felt and manifested as a stimulant agent, even if its pharmacological action is purely depressant. An extension of this theory is that alcohol relieves the conflict caused by expressing contradictory emotions. For example, alcohol intoxication may simultaneously gratify wishes for feelings of both masculinity and femininity. In men, drunkenness may arouse masculine expressions of power (McClelland et al., 1972), self-assertion, and self-reliance, while in women, drunkenness may gratify the traditionally contrary feminine wishes by allowing submission to the powerful pharmacological actions and by necessitating dependence on other people for protection. Wilsnack (1974) has reported that alcohol arouses expression of femininity in women, but drinking is generally regarded as a masculine activity. The mental impairment caused by alcohol enables the drinker to ignore the logical inconsistency of expressing both masculine and feminine attributes.

Disinhibitory effects of alcohol may be sufficient to explain the pleasurable, exhilarated feelings caused by this depressant drug (Barry, 1977a). Normal, sober behavior is regulated by strong inhibitory functions, and these are more vulnerable than excitatory functions to alcohol and to most other toxic agents. Disinhibition can account for louder speech, expansive gestures, and impulsive, assertive behavior during intoxication. Disinhibitory effects of alcohol also can account for an increase in aggressiveness. This is evident in the association of drunkenness with homicide and with other crimes of violence and in observations of drinking behavior in many cultures. This increased aggression has been demonstrated in well-controlled laboratory experiments (Zeichner and Pihl, 1979, 1980). Researchers found that alcohol intoxication increased aggressive behavior in young men who believed they were giving painful electric shocks to another person. A further effect of the alcohol was to make the men less sensitive to what they believed were the effects of the strength of the electrical shock punishment that they had chosen to inflict.

A physiological mechanism for disinhibitory effects of alcohol has been demonstrated by Mendelson, Mello, and Ellingboe (1977). The drug suppresses testosterone production peripherally (in testicular tissues), but the low testosterone levels prevent the normal inhibitory effect on secretion of luteinizing hormone centrally (in the brain), which stimulates testosterone production. The elevated levels of luteinizing hormone might contribute to sexual and emotional arousal during alcohol intoxication.

Stimulant effects of alcohol might be attributable to acetaldehyde, which is formed as the metabolic product of alcohol (Truitt and Walsh, 1971). High doses of acetaldehyde have unpleasant effects, but under normal conditions the stimulant effects might be pleasurable, while the adverse effects are minimized by the low acetaldehyde concentrations and are counteracted by the concurrent sedative effect of alcohol. The important role of acetaldehyde is suggested by evidence that relatives of alcoholics have an unusually high level of acetaldehyde in their system after a test dose of alcohol (Schuckit and Rayses, 1979). Relatives of alcoholics also show weaker behavioral effects after a test dose of alcohol (Schuckit, 1980), but this may be because a higher dose of alcohol is required to produce any pleasurable effects rather than a smaller dose producing a lesser degree of pleasurable effects of alcohol intoxication.

The pleasurable effects of alcohol may indicate benefits for the drinker. Pleasure is normally nature's way to identify and to repeat beneficial conditions. Drinking relaxes tensions, relieves anxiety, and facilitates social behavior. The differential behavior under the drug condition may establish new habits and may expand the scope of behavior (Barry, 1977a).

Several types of evidence suggest that moderate drinking increases longevity and decreases risk of coronary heart disease. Comparisons among several countries and changes during several decades in the United States indicate an inverse relationship between amount of alcohol consumption and death rate from atherosclerotic heart disease (La Porte, Cresanta, and Kuller, 1980).

The pleasures of drinking are accompanied by perils caused by the powerful effects of the drug. Intoxicated behavior may be violent and destructive. Even moderate doses cause loss of self-critical facilities, indicated by a prevalent tendency for people to believe they are performing well under the influence of alcohol doses, even though the alcohol clearly has a detrimental effect. In addition to this cognitive deficit, the sedative effects of alcohol diminish caution, resulting in greater boldness or rashness. The intoxicated automobile driver becomes willing to make riskier maneuvers, and, at the same time, the impairment in capability caused by alcohol results in a higher degree of objective hazard from the decision to accept a particular level of subjective risk.

Further perils result from repeated drinking. The pleasurable effects of alcohol tend to be sought too often. The development of tolerance results in the need for increasing amounts of the drug to attain the desired effects. Physical dependence and withdrawal illness induce the victim to continue drinking excessively (Barry, 1979b). Chronic consumption of large amounts of alcohol can lead to dangerous medical conditions, including dietary deficiency, liver cirrhosis, and brain damage.

Chronic, excessive drinking behavior is often described by the terms *alcohol abuse* or *drug abuse* or *substance abuse*. The distinction between *use* and *abuse* is helpful, especially when applied to alcohol, because the drug is also used with apparent benefit by many individuals and societies. It is inaccurate, however, to refer to abuse of alcohol. The drug is the agent but the abuse is self-inflicted by the drinker. Therefore, self-abuse with alcohol conveys more accurately the intended meaning.

The most reliabale indication of self-abuse with alcohol is the continuation of drinking even after the occurrence of severe social or physical damage because of alcohol. The persistence of self-destructive behavior indicates the presence of self-destructive motives (Barry, 1974, 1977b). The pleasure obtained by relief from conflicts and anxieties can explain the first few episodes of intoxication, but is insufficient to account for chronically excessive drinking while the social and physical punishments for drinking become increasingly severe.

Comparison with social norms is an important element in identifying and defining alcoholics. A simple definition of alcoholism is any drinking that exceeds the amount tolerated by the society. Cultural customs specify the range of approved drinking behaviors and also the punishments for deviation. Drinking behavior that is condemned in one culture may be approved in another culture.

Chronic, excessive consumption is limited to a minority of drinkers. A culture could not survive for long if self-abuse with alcohol were the typical behavior. The occurrence of this pathology in a substantial proportion of the people requires the presence of each of three conditions. The first condition is the motivation to drink, causing people to crave severe intoxication (Barry, 1974, 1977b). The second need is cultural permission and the encouragement of alcohol intoxication. In societies where heavy drinking is forbidden or discouraged, people who crave the effects of alcohol intoxication choose other forms of self-destructive behavior, such as self-abuse with other drugs, gambling, social withdrawal, violence, or suicide. The third condition is availability of sufficient alcohol. Barry (1968) identified several societies in which chronic alcoholism was reported to be limited to chieftains, who had special access to alcohol.

The presence of alcoholics may provide benefits for the other members of the culture, thereby helping to explain why this pathological behavior by some individuals persists in many societies. The existence of any form of deviant behavior indicates a cultural tolerance for individual freedom of choice. This cultural attribute encourages diversity of behavior, which enhances the ability of the culture to adapt to new conditions. The opposite cultural attributes of rigid controls and uniform behavior may effectively prevent alcoholism at the cost of more severe cultural disadvantages.

In addition to the general advantage of indicating permission for deviant behavior, the presence of alcoholics may serve specific social functions. The self-destructive behavior of alcoholics serves as a reminder to others to restrain their drinking. Social solidarity may be increased by the need to protect and to help alcoholics. In this way, the expression of dependency needs by the alcoholic may satisfy cultural needs for nurturant activities. Useful expression of hidden desires and sentiments may be provided by the impulsive, unrestrained behavior of alcoholics. An ethnographic account of a Mexican community (Dennis, 1975) gives several examples of this adaptive role of drunken members, divulging general attitudes toward other members and toward outside authority figures.

In some societies, extreme drunkenness constitutes the prevalent and approved behavior during drinking occasions rather than indicating an expression of deviance by some individuals. Horton (1943) identified numerous societies with high insobriety and summarized the ethnographic accounts of their drinking customs. Child, Bacon, and Barry (1965) included a summary of the ethnographic information indicating an extremely high rating in their category, Frequency of Drunkenness, by the San Blas Cuna of Panama. Naroll (1969) identified 19 societies with the extreme behavior of drunken brawling.

In all these societies, the episodes of drunkenness are separated by days of abstinence. The alternations between intoxication and sobriety may have beneficial effects for the society as well as for the individual. The conflicts and anxieties of social behavior are temporarily relieved by alcohol intoxication. The drinking occasions express sociability and may enhance feelings of solidarity, removing barriers of age and status. Several ethnographic reports reprinted by Marshall (1979) describe these functions of drinking.

CULTURAL COMPARISONS

The functions of alcohol intoxication may be studied by identifying characteristics of societies where drunkenness is frequent, compared to societies where drunkenness is absent or rare. Cross-cultural research enables use of the large number of societies and the wide diversity of cultural customs that have been described in ethnographic accounts. Several studies have used this method to make inferences about the adaptive functions of alcohol intoxication.

Horton (1943) found that in a sample of 57 societies, most of those with high insobriety obtain food by hunting, fishing, or gathering rather than by agriculture. He concluded that the motivation for alcohol intoxication is to relieve the anxiety that he assumed is higher for individuals whose food depends on daily collecting rather than on agriculture. This conclusion was contradicted by Field (1962), who related Horton's measure of insobriety with classifications of economy and social organization in Murdock's World Ethnographic Sample and with ratings of child training (Barry, Bacon, and Child, 1967). High insobriety characterizes most societies with egalitarian social structure or with scope for different individual choices. Variables associated with high insobriety include bilateral descent, neolocal residence, and absence of class stratification. The findings suggest that insobriety is prevented by hierarchical and rigid social structures, indicated by unilinear descent, patrilocal residence, and hierarchical status groups.

Bacon, Barry, and Child (1965) tested relationships of various cultural attributes with Frequency of Drunkenness in a larger sample of 139 societies. Quantitative ratings of the drinking measure can be used to divide the societies approximately equally into those that are low and those that are high in Frequency of Drunkenness. Table 1 shows that several cultural attributes associated with a high rating in Horton's category of Insobriety (Field, 1962; Horton, 1943) are likewise associated with high Frequency of Drunkenness.

The types of economy and rules of descent, shown in Table 1, are based on codes in the Ethnographic Atlas (Murdock, 1967; Barry, 1980b). The proportion of societies with high Frequency of Drunkenness is low where food is obtained by intensive agriculture (use of plow, fertilizers, or irrigation) and high where food is collected (hunting, fishing, or gathering).

Table 1.   Number of societies in which the rated Frequency of Drunkenness is low (2–8) or high (9–14), and percentage of societies rated high, as related to the designated categories of type of economy, rule of descent, and geographical region

Variable	Category	Frequency of Drunkenness		
		Low (N)	High (N)	High (%)
Type of economy	Intensive agriculture	13	4	24
	Extensive agriculture	17	11	39
	Animal husbandry	3	3	50
	Food collecting	13	23	64
Rule of descent	Patrilineal	22	12	35
	Other	13	11	46
	Bilateral	11	18	62
Geographical region	Africa	18	4	18
	East Eurasia	7	7	50
	Insular Pacific	5	3	38
	North America	14	12	46
	South America	2	14	88

High Frequency of Drunkenness also is associated with presence of bilateral rather than patrilineal descent. Other forms of descent (matrilineal, both patrilineal and matrilineal, quasilineal, and ambilineal) are intermediate. These attributes are consistent with Field's (1962) conclusion that hierarchical and rigid social relationships are associated with low Insobriety. They are also consistent with Horton's (1943) suggestion that high anxiety is associated with high Insobriety if individual anxiety is diminished by conditions that restrict freedom of choice and mobility of status.

Barry et al. (1965) reported a high positive correlation ($r = 0.68$, $N = 48$) between Frequency of Drunkenness and Horton's measure of Insobriety. Both alcohol measures showed similar relationships with measures of subsistence economy, unilineal kin groups, and patrilineal exogamy.

Table 1 also shows large differences among geographical regions in percentage of societies with high Frequency of Drunkenness. One additional region, Circum-Mediterranean, is represented in this sample by only one society, which has high Frequency of Drunkenness. The regional variations in this alcohol measure can be explained largely by corresponding regional variations in other attributes shown in Table 1 (Barry, 1968). Agriculture and patrilineal descent characterize most of the African societies, whereas food collecting and bilateral descent characterize most of the South American societies.

Table 2 shows relationships of Frequency of Drunkenness with several measures that pertain to individual behavior. Instrumental Dependence is one of a series of ratings of adult motivational satisfactions summarized by Bacon, Barry, and Child (1965). High satisfaction of this motive is to some degree a consequence of hierarchical, rigid social structure, which is

Table 2.   Number of societies in which the rated Frequency of Drunkenness is low (2–8) or high (9–14), and percentage of societies rated high, as related to the designated categories of adult behavior, inheritance, and status of adolescent boys

Variable	Category	Frequency of Drunkenness		
		Low (N)	High (N)	High (%)
Satisfaction of instrumental	High (18–27)	19	7	27
dependence in men	Low (10–17)	5	14	74
Inheritance of land	Patrilineal	20	7	26
	Matrilineal	3	2	40
	None	9	15	63
	Children	1	6	86
Inheritance of	Unequal	16	5	24
movable property	Equal	17	21	55
Segregation of	Present	19	8	30
adolescent boys	Absent	19	27	59

associated with low Frequency of Drunkenness. Importance of the adult motivational variable as an influence on drinking behavior is suggested by the remarkably high inverse relationship of satisfaction of Instrumental Dependence in adult men with Frequency of Drunkenness shown in Table 2. The product moment correlation is −0.48, reported by Bacon, Barry, and Child (1965).

The other variables in Table 2 were obtained from Murdock's Ethnographic Atlas (Barry, 1980b). Patrilineal descent is expressed by patrilineal inheritance of land, associated with low Frequency of Drunkenness, whereas bilateral descent is expressed by bequeathing land to children, associated with high Frequency of Drunkenness. The association of drunkenness with equal distribution of movable property among heirs is consistent with Field's (1962) conclusion that egalitarian status charaterizes most societies with high Insobriety. Segregation of adolescent boys, which is associated with low Frequency of Drunkenness, is often a concomitant of patrilineal descent and indicates severe restriction of the activities of young men.

Bacon, Barry, and Child (1965) reported that high Frequency of Drunkenness was related to several other cultural variables, including intense training of children to achieve, exclusive role of the mother as the nurturant agent for infants, and absence of communal eating. They concluded that high Frequency of Drunkenness is associated with cultural customs that frustrate or deny desires to be dependent on other people. This conclusion is compatible with the relationships reported by Horton (1943) and Field (1962), but includes additional findings.

Ambiguous relationships have been reported between drunkenness and measures of indulgence toward infants or children. Field (1962) found a tendency for high infancy and childhood indulgence in societies with high Insobriety. Bacon, Barry, and Child (1965) found no relationship between the same measures of indulgence and the new measure of Frequency of Drunkenness. Barry (1976) found that a new measure of infancy indulgence was negatively correlated with Frequency of Drunkenness.

These divergent findings probably reflect opposing tendencies. Indulgence may be impaired by the individualism and social isolation associated with high Frequency of Drunkenness, but also by the rigid and hierarchical social structure associated with low Frequency of Drunkenness.

In societies with high Frequency of Drunkenness, the tendency for exclusive care by the mother (Bacon, Barry, and Child, 1965) limits the amount of attention feasible. In societies with high Frequency of Drunkenness, infants also tend to have low duration of bodily contact with the caregiver, and to receive low amounts of ceremonialism and of magical protectiveness (Barry, 1976).

Contrary to these relationships, Rohner (1975) has shown that high indulgence of children (parental acceptance) characterizes most societies with the type of subsistence economy (hunting, fishing, or gathering) that is related to high Frequency of Drunkenness. In addition, extreme emotional deprivation during infancy seems to develop adult traits incompatible with drunkenness. Barry (1969) identified three societies with extremely low indulgence of infants (Alorese, Marquesans, and Trukese). The adult social relationships are highly suspicious and fearful. The disinhibitory effect of alcohol might be dangerous for these people. In each of these societies, alcohol was not drunk aboriginally and there was no subsequent development of frequent drunkenness.

In many societies, intense drunkenness persists as a social norm because the adverse consequences are limited by restrictions on availability of alcohol. The raters of Frequency of Drunkenness were instructed to "estimate what the overall drunkenness would be if an unlimited supply of alcohol were available year around" (Bacon, Barry, Child, and Snyder, 1965). In an effort to measure pathological drinking patterns, Barry (1979a) identified ten societies that were high in both categories of Quantity and Frequency of drinking. Most of them had severe problems with drinking. Other predominant characteristics were weak display of affection toward infants, strong encouragement of adult self-reliance, and an economy based on hunting, fishing, or gathering. Bilateral descent, which is associated with high Frequency of Drunkenness, characterizes most of the 11 societies identified as high in quantity of drinking, but low in frequency of drinking. The abstract by Barry (1979a) erroneously reversed the designation of rules of descent (bilateral, unilineal).

Further correlates of drinking have been studied by content analysis of folklore themes in 44 societies (McClelland et al., 1972). The Drinking measure combined the ratings of Frequency of Drunkenness and General Consumption (Bacon, Barry, Child, and Snyder, 1965), thereby taking into account the amount of absolute alcohol actually consumed, in addition to the intensity of intoxication on the typical drinking occasions. The societies high in Drinking tend to have folktales in which collateral kinship terms *(aunt, uncle, niece, nephew)* are more frequent than parent-child terms *(father, mother, son, daughter, child)*. Other folktale terms associated with low or high Drinking were factor analyzed by Wanner (1972). High Drinking is associated with folktale terms that are high in a Power factor and low in an Inhibition factor. Wanner (1972) concluded that people whose folktales manifest impulsive power concern drink heavily because alcohol intoxication enhances the drinker's sense of potency.

High Drinking is also associated with various cultural attributes. McClelland et al. (1972) reported a strong inverse relationship with male solidarity (ritualization of male activity or presence of men's housing). This finding is consistent with measures shown in Table 2. McClelland and his colleagues also reported that high Drinking is correlated with high frequency of achievement responses and also with high frequency of obedience responses in childhood. The authors suggested that a conflict over assertive behavior contributes to the motivation for high Drinking. This is similar to the association of high Frequency of Drunkenness with a conflict over dependency (Bacon, Barry, and Child, 1965).

Wanner (1972) used factor analysis to identify two groups of cultural attributes associated with the high Drinking. One of these groups indicates socioeconomic simplicity. The other group indicates absence of male institutions. The authors suggested that in societies with these two characteristics, individuals are required to be continually assertive and successful but are also prevented from gaining permanent prestige. High Drinking may function as a means of gaining temporary feelings of power.

Wanner (1972) also reported that a cold, dry climate is associated both with high Drinking and with absence of male institutions. The relationship of Drinking with male institutions seems to persist, although attenuated, when controlling for climate. Drinking is strongly related to climate, even when controlling for male institutions. Africa exemplifies a region with a predominantly warm, wet climate, the presence of male institutions, and low Drinking (Table 1). A speculative explanation for the role of climate is that cold, dry weather constitutes a type of harsh environment that enhances both the need for individualistic effort and the motivation for the physical and emotional warmth provided by contacts with other people. Conflict over dependency is thereby intensified. Alcohol intoxication relieves this conflict and also produces physical feelings of warmth caused by dilation of peripheral blood vessels.

In a study of 58 "mostly primitive societies," Naroll (1969) classified Drunken Brawling as present in 19 societies and absent in 8, with no data on this trait in the other 31. Drunken Brawling showed high positive correlations with Defiant Homicide Cases and Warfare Frequency, a low positive correlation with Suicide Wordage, and little or no positive correlations with Men's Divorce Freedom, Witchcraft Accusations, Wife Beating, and Marriage Restrictiveness. The drinking measure was thus related selectively rather than in general with other presumed measures of cultural pathology.

Schaefer (1976) rated Drunken Brawling and Extreme Male Insobriety in a sample of 57 societies. Both alcohol measures were associated with several measures of socioeconomic simplicity, with belief in malicious, capricious spirits, and with a less intense relationship between father and son than between husband and wife. These findings support Field's (1962) association of insobriety with a loose, egalitarian social structure but contradict Field and support Horton (1943) in showing evidence for individual anxiety (malicious, capricious spirits) in societies with Drunken Brawling or Extreme Male Insobriety.

Drinking shows generally consistent patterns of relationships with other variables in several studies that include independent alcohol measures and a wide variety of other cultural variables. Societies with high insobriety or drunkenness or drinking tend to consist of small, loosely structured communities with food collecting rather than food producing as the principal mode of subsistence. Severe conflict and individualistic, assertive, uninhibited behavior are indicated by child-training practices, folktales, family structure, and supernatural beliefs. The proposed explanations for the drinking include relief from anxiety or conflict (Bacon, Barry, and Child, 1965; Horton, 1943; Schaefer, 1976), pleasurable feelings of power (Wanner, 1972), and opportunity provided by the social structure (Field, 1962). These different explanations may be compatible with each other and may constitute different aspects of the incentives for drinking.

These studies are mostly limited to preliterate societies in which the availability of alcohol is limited. The findings may not apply directly to the United States or to other societies in which large amounts of alcohol are continuously accessible. Variations among the preliterate societies may be mainly caused by motivational factors, while variations in the United States may be mainly caused by social controls and self-restraint. The studies of preliterate societies have an important advantage, however, because they provide a wide variation among cultures in normal, approved drinking practices. A large number of independent societies is available for testing relationships between alcohol measures and other cultural attributes.

DIFFERENCES AMONG NATIONS AND THEIR COMPONENTS

The political and technological developments that lead to the formation of large nations enable the production of as much alcohol as people are physically capable of drinking. This potential for excessive alcohol consumption is counteracted by social controls that effectively limit drinking by most people. Extreme drunkenness occurs as a prevalent custom in some countries, but only at infrequent intervals. Frequent drunkenness is limited to a minority of deviant individuals.

Europe is a region of heavy alcohol consumption. Sulkunen (1976) stated that, at the end of the 1960s, the people of Europe, making up less than 15% of the world population, consumed about half the alcohol. High alcohol consumption also characterizes six other countries that have been derived from, or influenced by, European culture (Argentina, New Zealand, Chile, Canada, the United States, and Japan). These six countries plus Europe together comprise less than 20% of the world population, but these people consumed 80% of the alcohol. Statistics on measures of alcohol consumption in individual countries are available in deLint (1975), Lynn (1971), Noble (1979), and Sulkunen (1976). These lists include a sample of European countries and some or all of the six additional countries that have been named. Three lists include Australia, which also shows heavy alcohol consumption. One list (Noble, 1979) includes Israel, which has the smallest amount of alcohol consumption.

The largest amount of alcohol consumption per capita is in France. DeLint (1975) estimated a mean of 24 liters absolute alcohol annually by people 15 years and older in 1970. This corresponds to 53 grams alcohol daily, approximately 1.0 gram per kilogram body weight for women and 0.7 grams per kilogram body weight for men if the total intake were evenly divided between the two sexes. These amounts, distributed during the day, are not sufficient to cause severe intoxication or physical damage. Some individuals, however, drink consistently more than the mean. Anderson (1968) reported a French government estimate that among the men, 15% are alcoholics and 30% endanger their health by drinking. Sadoun, Lolli, and Silverman (1965) systematically studied French drinking in the years 1956-1957. The mean daily alcohol consumption was approximately 55 grams by men, 20 grams by women. The mean daily alcohol intake by a sample of alcoholics was approximately 270 grams (4 grams per kilogram body weight by men).

Most French adults drink every day, in the form of wine with lunch and dinner. Severe intoxication and drinking between meals are additional drinking patterns, which occur infrequently in most adults, but chronically in a large minority. French drinking has been compared with Italian drinking by Sadoun et al. (1965) and by many other commentators. The typical pattern in both countries is to drink wine every day with lunch and dinner, but in Italy this is very rarely supplemented by severe intoxication or by drinking between meals. The per capita annual consumption of absolute alcohol by Italians 15 years old and older in 1970 (deLint, 1975) was 21 liters—12% less than the 24 liters consumed by the French.

The per capita alcohol consumption is much lower in most of the other countries. DeLint (1975) showed an annual amount of 10 liters consumed in the United States. The lowest consumption amount on the list was 4 liters in Norway. In the majority of countries, alcohol is drunk predominantly in the form of beer or distilled spirits rather than wine (Sulkunen, 1976), and most people do not drink every day.

Differences among nations in the number of deaths caused by liver cirrhosis correspond closely to differences in per capita alcohol consumption. Noble (1979) reported a correlation of 0.85 between these two measures in 17 countries. Cirrhosis mortality is highest in France, whereas Italy, with 12% less consumption, has 28% less cirrhosis mortality. The greater severity of drinking problems in France is thereby indicated more accurately by the difference in cirrhosis mortality than by the difference in the amount of alcohol consumption. These two countries exceed all the others in both measures, with the exception of Austria, which, compared to Italy, has 38% less alcohol consumption, but 14% more cirrhosis mortality.

Lynn (1971) reported that in 18 countries, cirrhosis and alcoholism deaths (1966) were negatively correlated with rates of mental illness ($r = -0.49$) and coronary deaths ($r = -0.49$), and were positively correlated with suicide rates ($r = 0.37$). These correlations, together with a pattern of several weaker relationships, were interpreted as showing that a high rate of cirrhosis and alcoholism deaths indicated a high level of anxiety among the citizens. In support of his conclusion, cirrhosis and alcoholism deaths showed a rank order correlation of $+0.59$, with a measure of anxiety obtained from questionnaires given to students in 11 of the countries.

The same conclusion was made by Horton (1943) from a sample of preliterate societies. The sample of nations (Lynn, 1971) is much smaller and has a more limited range of cultural attributes, although it has a wide range in per capita alcohol consumption. An alternative possible interpretation is that high per capita alcohol consumption is tolerable and becomes established only in countries with a stable social tradition and a high degree of self-control by most individuals. The price per liter of ethanol consumed is lowest in Italy and France (Noble, 1979). These attributes might account for the inverse correlations with frequency of hospitalization for mental illness and with deaths from coronary heart disease. The student's transitional and socially mobile status might arouse high anxiety, and the high frequencies of deaths caused by suicide, liver cirrhosis, and alcoholism might be direct consequences of many years of persistent drinking.

The frequency of drinking may be limited more stringently in nations where many individuals have a stronger desire to experience severe intoxication. For example, in comparison to Italy, the per capita alcohol consumption is much less in Poland, but the frequency of drunkenness (blood alcohol above 0.1%) is more than twice as high (Sulkunen, 1976). Several measures of problems with drunkenness (Noble, 1979) reveal that the most severe problems occur in countries with low alcohol consumption rates.

The rate of hospital admissions for alcoholism or for alcoholic psychosis is highest in Finland. Episodes of extreme intoxication are traditional in that country, where national prohibition coincided with the same drastic attempt to control the drinking problem in the United States. The frequency of pedestrians and drivers adjudged to be under the influence of alcohol per vehicle kilometer is highest in Australia. The number of drunk or impaired driving charges per vehicle kilometer is highest in Japan, with the United States a close second (only 1% less). In each of these nations, the severe problems with drunkenness indicate intense motivations to escape conflicts by extreme intoxication, while strict social controls or severe disapproval limit this behavior to rare occasions or to a small minority of the population. Blane (1977) and Jessor et al. (1970) contrast the intense ambivalence toward alcohol in the United States with the casual, accepting attitude in Italy.

Another measure of intensity of desire for alcohol is the percentage of national private consumption expended on alcoholic beverages (Noble, 1979). Ireland is highest (11.1%) among 11 nations included in this measure; the United States is lowest (1.3%). The important role of alcohol in Irish culture is described by Bales (1946), Stivers (1976), and Walsh (1972).

Descriptions of drinking patterns show occurrence of severe drunkenness in Japan (Sargent, 1967; Yamamuro, 1954). Drinking is also a severe social problem in the Soviet Union, in spite of low mean per capita consumption (Connor, 1971). A good ethnographic description of drinking customs in a village in Austria has been done by Honigmann (1963). Strong pressures toward heavy drinking in taverns (*Gasthäuser*) are counteracted by effective social controls. Drinking in Greek villages (Blum and Blum, 1964) occurs predominantly during festivals, with more emphasis on moderation as the norm.

Light drinking is the norm and severe intoxication is rare in some nations outside Europe. Alcohol consumption is low in Israel (Noble, 1979), and alcoholism is very rare among Jews (Keller, 1970; Snyder, 1958) and also among Chinese (Barry, 1968; Singer, 1972). Long traditions of strong social attachments in Jewish and Chinese communities provide effective social controls and presumably alleviate the feelings that impel drunkenness.

Measures of mean alcohol consumption and drinking problems in a nation are composites of variations in many attributes, including occupation, ethnic heritage, and region. Cahalan and Room (1974) have summarized and evaluated variations in the United States. The higher rate of alcohol consumption and of drinking problems in cities rather than on farms may be attributable to the fact that social relationships and occupations are generally more mobile and insecure in cities. Occupational differences have been reviewed by Cosper (1979). Carstairs (1954) reported a striking contrast between two Hindu castes in India. The Brahmans (priestly caste) abstain from alcohol. The Rajput (ruling and warrior caste) have episodes of intoxication, but they approve of, and, in many cases, practice moderation in drinking. Inheritance among the Rajput is patrilineal; much less is given to a younger son than to the first son. These customs are associated with low Frequency of Drunkenness in preliterate societies (Table 2).

Drinking problems among Americans with various ethnic heritages and religious affiliations have been compared by Cahalan and Room (1974). They found the highest frequency of problems among Latin Americans (Catholics). There was a high frequency also among blacks (conservative Protestants), especially in comparison to the low frequencies among other conservative Protestant groups (British, Irish, and German). Among Catholic groups, the frequency of problems was high for the Irish and lowest for the Italians. The Jewish group was the one with the lowest frequency of problems.

Regional variations in a nation may provide useful tests of relationships between alcohol measures and other attributes in the same sample of regions. The disadvantage of less range of variation within the same nation than among nations is compensated by holding constant the national self-consciousness and other attributes that are shared by all residents of the same country.

Data on 16 regions of France in 1959 (Sadoun et al., 1965, page 40) show an inverse relationship between absolute alcohol consumed and death rates from alcoholism and cirrhosis of the liver ($r = -0.69$). Two areas in the north (Normandy plus Brittany and Alsace) had the highest death rates and the lowest consumption. Four areas in the south had the lowest death rates and above average consumption. The high positive correlation of alcoholism deaths with per capita consumption among nations (Noble, 1979) thus is not always found within the same nation. Southern France resembles more closely the neighboring country of Italy with respect to lower death rate than does northern France.

Lynn (1971, page 111) reported a positive correlation ($r = 0.41$) between consumption of alcohol in 1873 and suicides 1878–1887 for the departments of France. Smart (1977) found that for the 50 states of the United States plus the District of Columbia, the rate of alcoholism in 1970 was positively correlated with per capita income in 1972 ($r = +0.59$) and with percentage of population in urban areas in 1970 ($r = +0.53$). Lynn (1971) reported that in 49 states of the United States (omitting Hawaii and the District of Columbia) in 1956, alcoholism and cirrhosis deaths showed high positive correlations with psychosis rate ($r = 0.68$) and with ulcer deaths ($r = 0.61$). These relationships suggest a positive association between alcoholism and anxiety. The same interpretation by Lynn (1971) was based on additional measures that showed lower correlations with the alcoholism measure.

CONCOMITANTS OF CULTURAL CHANGE

Relationships between drinking practices and other cultural customs in a sample of societies are interpreted with the assumption that these customs have changed as a result of interactions with each other to form a coherent pattern that contributes to cultural survival. This process of cultural evolution can be observed directly by identifying and by quantitatively measuring cultural customs that change concurrently with changes in drinking practices. The customs that remain unchanged are thereby held constant and omitted as possible causes or consequences of the changes in the alcohol measure.

Introduction of alcohol by an alien culture constitutes a drastic change. Most of the societies in North American and the Insular Pacific (Table 1) had no alcoholic beverages until the advent of European explorers and traders within the last few centuries. The contact with aggressive and technologically advanced European civilization resulted in many societal changes, of which drinking was only one. Nevertheless, the pleasurable and disinhibitory effects of alcohol seem to have caused special difficulties in adjusting to the powerful intruders.

Leland (1976) and MacAndrew and Edgerton (1969) have described episodes of extreme drunkenness and violence by American Indians. Some individuals and even communities were thereby destroyed, but many of the people and tribes survived the disruptive effects of liquor and other problems inflicted by the Europeans. A prevalent Indian custom is to share alcohol with all companions and to rapidly finish any available supply of liquor. This custom establishes an approved norm of excessive drinking, but has the adaptive functions of enhancing social solidarity and emphasizing cultural group identification.

A large proportion of contemporary Indians suffer drinking problems, but the majority drink moderately or not at all (Noble, 1979). Some influences on successful adaptation to liquor may be indicated by comparisons among tribes. Stratton, Zeiner, and Paredes (1978), in a comparison among several tribes in Oklahoma, found that problems with alcoholism were generally more severe in tribes with aboriginal subsistence economy in the form of food collecting (hunting, fishing, and gathering) than in tribes subsisting on agriculture. Kunitz et al. (1971) found a higher rate of liver cirrhosis deaths among the Hopi than among the Navahos. The Hopi drinker is ostracized and thus tends to drink alone without effective social restraints. Navaho drinking is predominantly a group activity of young men, many of whom became abstainers at an older age.

The advent of alcohol use seems to have had a less severely destructive effect on societies of the Insular Pacific. The more rigid social stratification prevalent in this area may have counteracted the disinhibitory and disorganizing effects of alcohol intoxication. Lemert (1964) compared three patterns of drinking behavior (festive, ritualized, and deviant) in Polynesian societies. The deviant pattern, characteristic of the Samoans, occurs infrequently and only in a small minority of individuals. Similarly, in Melanesia, on the island of Etal near Truk, drinking was found to be limited to young men on infrequent occasions, and extreme intoxication occurred only in a minority of deviant individuals (Nason, 1975).

Among the sample of preliterate societies (Bacon, Barry, Child, and Snyder, 1965), Frequency of Drunkenness does not depend on whether the alcohol was drunk aboriginally or whether it was introduced by an alien culture. Alcohol was introduced by an alien culture in most of the societies in the Insular Pacific and North America, and Table 1 shows that the societies in these regions are divided between low and high Frequency of Drunkenness. Barry (1968) demonstrated that the relationship of Frequency of Drunkenness with Instrumental Dependence in Adulthood is similar, whether alcohol was drunk aboriginally or was introduced by an alien culture. Some drinking practices differ, however, depending upon whether alcohol has been drunk aboriginally. In most societies where alcohol has been introduced recently, drinking is not ceremonial or ritualized (Bacon, Barry, and Child, 1965), and there is no sex difference in frequency or amount of drinking (Child, Barry, and Bacon, 1965). Therefore, integration of drinking into a ceremonial or religious context and less drinking by women than by men seem to be gradual cultural adaptations.

Alcohol was drunk aboriginally by most of the societies in Africa and South America. The advent of a powerful, alien culture nevertheless affected drinking practices in addition to other features of culture in these regions. The introduction of distilled spirits, the availability of increased amounts of alcohol from traders, and the concomitant culture disintegration contributed to a prevalence of excessive drinking in Central and South America. Table 1 shows that most of the societies in South America are classified as high in Frequency of Drunkenness, and in some societies, an aboriginal custom of heavy drinking was intensified. Taylor (1979) has summarized reports of excessive drinking following the Spanish conquest of the Aztec empire. Paredes (1977) described the moderate, strictly controlled Aztec drinking customs prior to that conquest.

In Africa, most of the societies are classifed as low in Frequency of Drunkenness (Table 1). The associated cultural attributes (Tables 1 and 2) seem to have made these societies resistant to the disruptive effects of European intrusion. Hutchinson (1961) described excessive drinking and social disorganization among the Bantu tribes of Southern Africa, but these occurrences were limited and their onset was in the middle of the nineteenth century, about two centuries after the first settlement by Europeans in that region. Netting (1964) has described a more typical contemporary pattern of restrained and socially controlled drinking by the Kofyar of northern Nigeria, although beer is very highly valued and has recently become more plentiful. Robbins (1977) reported that among the Ganda of Uganda, the traditional beer remains the predominant beverage in spite of the availability of distilled liquor.

The transition from one cultural tradition to another involves conflicts and alienation. These conditions cause many individuals to drink excessively. Madsen (1964) described this behavior by Agringados in southern Texas, in their attempt to shift from the Latin to the Anglo culture. Madsen and Madsen (1969) described similar but less severe behavior by *mestizos* in Mexico, who were shifting from Indian to Spanish culture. This problem contributes to the high alcoholism rate among many ethnic groups in the United States, such as Indians, Spanish-speaking persons, and blacks (Noble, 1979). A higher rate of liver cirrhosis was found among Hopi Indians who live off the reservation (Kunitz et al., 1971). According to a description of the Tarahumara Indians of northern Mexico (West, 1972), alcoholism occurs only among those who have become significantly acculturated, such as by intermarriage with *mestizos*. Snyder (1958) reported that drinking problems are very rare among Orthodox Jews and progressively more frequent among Conservative, Reform, and Secular Jews. Midgley (1971), in a study of a Muslim community in Cape Town, South Africa, found that 13% of the members violated the religious prohibition of drinking. Most of the drinkers lived in a predominantly Christian neighborhood and did not attend mosque regularly.

Conflict and alienation may develop from transition in occupation or status, even without change in ethnic affiliation. Transition in sex role may account for a much higher alcoholism rate found among women in nontraditional rather than in traditional roles (Noble, 1979).

Among people who are vulnerable to alcoholism because of culture conflict or alienation, an increase in opportunity may result in drinking problems. Doughty (1971) described a Peruvian community in which a large hydroelectric construction project led to a sudden increase in income and thereby to an increase in consumption of alcoholic beverages. Some of the workers lost their jobs because of drinking too much. Maccoby (1972), who studied a Mexican *mestizo* village, found alcoholism in a higher percentage of small landowners (*ejiditarios*), who were not required to work every day, than in landless day laborers (*non-ejiditarios*). Greater ability to purchase liquor might account for a high correlation between alcoholism deaths and mean income measured by variations among the states of the United States (Smart, 1977).

Historical surveys indicate that when increased availability or lower prices have stimulated alcohol consumption, the ensuing increase in drinking problems has led to strong temperance movements and to stricter social controls. The result has been fluctuations in drinking.

Glatt (1977) has summarized the history of drinking in England. The introduction of inexpensive distilled spirits in the late seventeenth century resulted in widespread drunkenness, especially in the years 1720–1750. Restrictive legislation and an increase in price caused the drinking problem to recede, but a new upsurge of drunkenness began in 1830 with legislation that permitted the opening of many new alehouses. This phase was counteracted by the rise of the temperance movement, by the 1872 Licensing Act, and by restrictive legislation at the outbreak of World War I in 1914. A new upsurge in drinking has occurred since 1950. Statistics reported by deLint (1975) show an increase of 22% in per capita alcohol consumption in Great Britain from 1960 to 1970. An important contributing factor may be a decrease in price of liquor relative to most other products because inflation has caused a rise in most prices without a comparable increase in taxes on alcoholic beverages.

Similar changes in alcohol consumption occurred in other European countries. Sulkunen (1976) reported a stable amount of alcohol consumption in the years 1871–1900 for the United Kingdom and for other European countries, followed by a progressive, and, in most countries, a large decline up to 1937. DeLint (1975) showed a large increase in most countries from 1960 to 1970.

In Ireland, a pattern of heavy drinking by young men developed in the middle of the nineteenth century during a time of increase in average age of marriage and in proportion of unmarried adults, following overpopulation and famine (Stivers, 1976). Subsequent alleviation of difficult social conditions and stimulation of the temperance movement in Ireland have resulted in a low per capita alcohol consumption, although an unusually high proportion of personal income is spent on alcoholic beverages (Noble, 1979). Heavier drinking and a high rate of alcoholism occurred among the Irish and their descendants who emigrated to the United States. The national tradition of drunkenness apparently aggravated the effects of initially alien status, cultural transition, and predominantly urban environment among the emigrants. There was a high rate of alcoholism among Irish-American women, whereas in Ireland heavy drinking was limited to men (Stivers, 1976).

The early New England settlers in the seventeenth century continued the contemporary English custom of heavy drinking, and many instances of drunkenness were reported (Lender, 1973). The religious orientation of the colonists probably enhanced social disapproval and inhibited the deviant behavior, but not to a drastic degree. Rorabaugh (1976, 1979) has summarized available records on alcohol consumption in the English colonies in America and the United States in the years 1710–1975. Per capita consumption, at a stable, high level in the years 1710–1790, increased by about 20% to a peak in 1830, concurrent with a sharp decrease in the price of whiskey. The rise of the temperance movement and increased controls led to a sharp decrease by 1850 to about one-fourth the rate of consumption in 1830. The consumption remained stable for the next 30 years (1850-1880). A rise of about 20% in the years 1885-1915 was followed by national prohibition in 1920-1933. Consumption increased to the level of the period 1850-1880 by 1945 and to the level of 1915 by 1970, but it remained less than half the average for the years 1710-1790.

The history of drinking customs in Japan was summarized by Yamamuro (1954). Numerous episodes of national prohibition, beginning in 646 A.D., have alternated with phases of apparently high consumption, although the national religion during much of the time was Buddhist, which prohibits "strong drink." Statistics reported by Sargent (1967) indicate a drastic decrease in alcohol consumption in Japan during and shortly after World War II (1942-1947) followed by a rapid increase above the prewar level by 1960.

In contrast to the large fluctuations in alcohol consumption in England, in the United States, and in Japan, a tradition of moderate, ceremonial drinking has persisted in the Jewish culture since the return from exile in Babylon and the formation of a theocratic society in 537 B.C. Thus, the drinking customs have remained stable throughout two and a half millennia. The strong religious tradition has apparently been a more important influence than the drastic and often traumatic changes in political, environmental, and economic circumstances. It is probable that many of the preliterate societies, studied at only one time period, likewise have maintained the same drinking customs for many centuries.

CONCLUSIONS

Pleasurable and beneficial effects of alcohol for many individuals are indicated by the known physiological effects of the drug and by the frequent behavior of drinking observable in many healthy, well-adjusted people. Beneficial effects of drinking customs in many societies can be inferred from the high valuation of alcoholic beverages and the persistence of their use in the majority of societies.

Any beneficial and pleasurable behavior tends to develop excessively. This danger is especially severe in the case of a powerful pharmacological agent, such as alcohol. Pathological effects of excessive drinking have been observed in many individuals and societies. In some societies, however, adaptive social functions are fulfilled by permitting self-destructive drinking in a minority of deviant members.

The numerous preliterate societies, which have developed diverse customs in a high degree of isolation from each other, constitute useful material for analyzing the cultural conditions that accompany different drinking customs. Several independent studies have yielded a substantial amount of correlational information. Frequent drunkenness tends to occur in societies that are not technologically advanced, that have heavy reliance on food collecting (hunting, fishing, and gathering), that maintain an egalitarian social structure, and that permit little elaboration of political authority. Frustration of dependency motives, and training children to be assertive rather than compliant are other characteristics of these societies. Several researchers have offered different interpretations of the same data, depending on whether they regarded the social organization or the motivational concomitants as the principal causative agents for high frequency of drunkenness. A further factor may be that in food-collecting societies without technological advancement or high levels of political integration, limitations in the ability to produce large amounts of alcohol may minimize the need for social controls and may thereby permit expressions of extreme drunkenness on the infrequent occasions when enough alcohol is available.

A few correlational studies have been done on contemporary nations, which are technologically advanced, with high degrees of political integration. Their agricultural economic base can produce as much alcohol as the population is physiologically capable of consuming. Accordingly, the differences in drinking customs among nations seem to be influenced more by variations in social control than by motivations of the individuals. Amount of alcohol consumption per capita is a readily available, accurate, and convenient measure, but it does not seem to be a valid measure of the tendency for excessive drinking, because high consumption per capita is permitted only in countries where controlled, steady drinking without severe intoxication is well established as the social norm. Rate of deaths from liver cirrhosis is closely related to per capita consumption.

A more valid measure of the tendency for excessive drinking in nations seems to be the frequency of problems associated with alcohol, such as hospitalizations for alcoholism, arrests for drunkenness, and traffic accidents with alcohol involvement. These problems are limited to a deviant minority of individuals, and generally are found only in nations where the per capital alcohol consumption is low. These correlates with drinking problems indicate the development of stringent social controls to counteract the predilection for drunkenness.

Correlations among nations provide useful information, but the number of nations is limited, and most of them influence each other by trade and by other communications. A valuable research technique might be the analysis of variations within the same nation, such as regions of France and states of the United States. Such studies would be especially useful if comparable measures and correlations could be obtained from regions of several different nations.

Changes within the same society may also provide important information. Specific economic, social, and behavioral changes may be related to concurrent changes in drinking practices, thereby holding constant the many cultural attributes that remain unchanged. More extensive and systematic studies are needed, obtaining comparable measures of changes from one generation to the next in samples of several societies or nations. Comments on cultural change thus far have focused on the drastic changes over the span of several generations after alcohol or distilled spirits were introduced by a powerful, alien culture. Severely disruptive effects of alcohol have been reported under these conditions, but most individuals and societies have survived this experience in spite of many horror stories.

The long history of alcohol use in Europe, in the United States, and in Japan shows cyclical fluctuations in drinking. Excessive drinking develops when liquor becomes cheaper or less stringently controlled; this stage is followed by a phase of strict controls, strong temperance sentiment, and sometimes national prohibition; and then a repetition of the phase of excessive drinking occurs. Such a cyclical pattern may be characteristic of technologically advanced nations in which the social organization and the individual motivations result in a tendency toward excessive drinking. A contrast is the stable pattern of moderate drinking, limited to ritual, ceremonial contexts, which has been maintained in the Jewish culture for two and a half millennia. It is also probable that many preliterate societies have maintained the same drinking customs for many centuries.

REFERENCES[1]

*Anderson, B. G. 1968. How French children learn to drink. Trans-Action 5(7): 20-22. (Marshall: pp. 429-432.)

Bacon, M. K., Barry, H., III, and Child, I. L. 1965. A cross-cultural study of drinking: II. Relations to other features of culture. Q. J. Stud. Alcohol Supplement no. 3, pp. 29-48.

Bacon, M. K., Barry, H., III, Child, I. L., and Snyder, C. R. 1965. A cross-cultural study of drinking: V. Detailed definitions and data. Q. J. Stud. Alcohol Supplement no. 3, pp. 78-111.

Bales, R. F. 1946. Cultural difference in rates of alcoholism. Q. J. Stud. Alcohol 6:480-499.

Barry, H., III. 1968. Sociocultural aspects of alcohol addiction. In: A. Wikler (ed.), The Addictive States. Res. Pub. Assoc. Nerv. Ment Dis. 46:455-471.

Barry, H., III. 1969. Cultural variations in the development of mental illness. In: S. C. Plog and R. B. Edgerton (eds.), Changing Perspectives in Mental Illness, pp. 128-155. Holt, Rinehart & Winston, Inc., New York.

Barry, H., III. 1974. Psychological factors in alcoholism. In: B. Kissin and H.

---

[1]Those references marked by an asterisk (*) can also be found reprinted in M. Marshall (ed.), 1979, Beliefs, Behaviors, & Alcoholic Beverages; A Cross-Cultural Survey. University of Michigan Press, Ann Arbor.

Begleiter (eds.), The Biology of Alcoholism. Vol. 3. Clinical Pathology, pp. 53 107. Plenum Publishing Corp., New York.

Barry, H., III. 1976. Cross-cultural evidence that dependency conflict motivates drunkenness. In: M. W. Everett, J. O. Waddell, and D. B. Heath (eds.), Cross-Cultural Approaches to the Study of Alcohol; An Interdisciplinary Perspective, pp. 249 263. Mouton, The Hague.

Barry, H., III. 1977a. Alcohol. In: S. N. Pradhan and S. N. Dutta (eds.), Drug Abuse: Clinical and Basic Aspects, pp. 78–101. C. V. Mosby Company, St. Louis, Mo.

Barry, H., III. 1977b. The correlation between personality and the risk of alcoholism. In: C. M. Idestrom (ed.), Recent Advances in the Study of Alcoholism, pp. 56 68. Proceedings of the First International Magnus Huss Symposium. Excerpta Medica, Amsterdam.

Barry, H., III. 1979a. Quantity-frequency drinking categories for comparing preliterate societies. Alcoholism: Clinical and Experimental Research. Abstract, 3:168.

Barry, H., III. 1979b. Behavioral manifestations of ethanol intoxication and physical dependence. In: E. Majchrowicz and E. P. Noble, (eds.), Behavioral Pharmacology of Ethanol. Vol. 2, pp. 511–531. Plenum Publishing Corp., New York.

Barry, H., III. 1980a. Description and uses of the Human Relations Area Files. In: H. C. Triandis (ed.), Handbook of Cross-Cultural Psychology. Vol. 2. H. C. Triandis and J. W. Berry (eds.), Methodology, pp. 445–478. Allyn & Bacon, Inc., Boston.

Barry, H., III. 1980b. Ethnographic Atlas XXVIII, Part 2. Ethnology 19:367–385.

Barry, H., III, and Schlegel, A. (eds.). 1980. Cross-Cultural Samples and Codes. University of Pittsburgh Press, Pittsburgh.

Barry, H., III, Bacon, M. K., and Child, I. L. 1967. Definitions, ratings, and bibliographic sources for child training practices of 110 cultures. In: C. S. Ford (ed.), Cross-Cultural Approaches, pp. 293–331. HRAF Press, New Haven.

Barry, H., III, Buchwald, C., Child, I. L., and Bacon, M. K. 1965. A cross-cultural study of drinking: IV. Comparison with Horton ratings. Q. J. Stud. Alcohol Supplement no. 3, pp. 62 77.

Blane H. T. 1977. Acculturation and drinking in an Italian American community. J. Stud. Alcohol 38:1324 1346.

Blum, R. H., and Blum, E. M. 1964. Drinking practices and controls in rural Greece. Br. J. Addict. 60:93 108.

Cahalan, D., and Room, R. 1974. Problem Drinking among American Men. Monograph no. 7. Rutgers Center of Alcohol Studies, New Brunswick, N. J.

*Carstairs, G. M. 1954. Daru and Bhang: Cultural factors in the choice of intoxicant. Q. J. Stud. Alcohol 15:220–237. (Marshall: pp. 297–312.)

Child, I. L., Bacon, M. K., and Barry, H., III. 1965. A cross-cultural study of drinking: I. Descriptive measurements of drinking customs. Q. J. Stud. Alcohol Supplement no. 3, pp. 1 28.

Child, I. L., Barry, H., III, and Bacon, M. K. 1965. A cross-cultural study of drinking: III. Sex differences. Q. J. Stud. Alcohol Supplement no. 3, pp. 49–61.

*Connor, W. D. 1971. Alcohol and Soviet society. Slavic Rev. 30:570–588. (Marshall: pp. 433–449.)

Cosper, R. 1979. Drinking as conformity; A critique of sociological literature on occupational differences in drinking. J. Stud. Alcohol 40:868–891.

DeLint, J. 1975. Current trends in the prevalence of excessive alcohol use and alcohol-related health damage. Br. J. Addict. 70:3–13.

*Dennis, P. A. 1975. The role of the drunk in a Oaxacan village. Am. Anthropol. 77:856–863. (Marshall: pp. 54–64.)

*Doughty, P. L. 1971. The social uses of alcoholic beverages in a Peruvian community. Hum. Organizat. 30:187–197. (Marshall: pp. 64–81.)

Farris, J. J., and Jones, B. M. 1978. Ethanol metabolism in male American Indians and Whites. Alcoholism 2:77–81.

Field, P. B. 1962. A new cross-cultural study of drunkenness. In: D. J. Pittman and C. R. Snyder (eds.), Society, Culture, and Drinking Patterns, pp. 48–74. John Wiley & Sons, Inc., New York.

Garfield, E. 1977. Essays of an Information Scientist. Vols. 1 and 2. ISI Press, Philadelphia.

Glatt, M. M. 1977. The English drink problem through the ages. Proc. R. Soc. Med. 70:202–206.

Hanna, J. M. 1978. Metabolic responses of Chinese, Japanese, and Europeans to alcohol. Alcoholism 2:89–92.

Heath, D. B. 1975. A critical review of ethnographic studies of alcohol use. In: R. J. Gibbins et al. (eds.), Research Advances in Alcohol and Drug Problems. Vol. 2, pp. 1–92. John Wiley & Sons, Inc., New York.

Heath, D. B. 1976a. Anthropological perspectives on alcohol: An historical review. In: M. W. Everett, J. O. Waddell, and D. B. Heath (eds.), Cross-Cultural Approaches to the Study of Alcohol; An Interdisciplinary Perspective, pp. 41–101. Mouton, The Hague.

Heath, D. B. 1976b. Anthropological perspectives on the social biology of alcohol: An introduction to the literature. In: B. Kissin and H. Begleiter (eds.), The Biology of Alcoholism. Vol. 5. Social Aspects of Alcoholism, pp. 37–76. Plenum Publishing Corp., New York.

*Honigmann, J. J. 1963. Dynamics of drinking in an Austrian village. Ethnology 2:157–169. (Marshall: pp. 414–428.)

Horton, D. 1943. The functions of alcohol in primitive societies: A cross-cultural study. Q. J. Stud. Alcohol 4:199–320.

*Hutchinson, B. 1961. Alcohol as a contributing factor in social organization: The South African Bantu in the nineteenth century. Rev. Anthropol. 9:1–13. (Marshall: pp. 328–341.)

Jessor, R., Young, H., Young, E., and Tesi, G. 1970. Perceived opportunity, alienation, and drinking behavior among Italian and American youth. J. Pers. Soc. Psychol. 15:215–222.

*Keller, M. 1970. The great Jewish drink mystery. Br. J. Addic. 64:287–296. (Marshall: pp. 404–414.)

*Kunitz, S. J., Levy, J. E., Odoroff, C. L., and Bollinger, J. 1971. The epidemiology of alcoholic cirrhosis in two southwestern Indian tribes. Q. J. Stud. Alcohol 32:706–720. (Marshall: pp. 145–158.)

La Porte, R. E., Cresanta, J. L., and Kuller, L. H. 1980. The relationship of alcohol consumption to atherosclerotic heart disease. Prev. Med. 9:22–40.

Leland, J. 1976. Firewater Myths; North American Indian Drinking and Alcohol Addiction. Monograph no. 11. Rutgers Center of Alcohol Studies, New Brunswick, N. J.

*Lemert, E. M. 1964. Forms and pathology of drinking in three Polynesian societies. Am. Anthropol. 66:361–374. (Marshall: pp. 192–208.)

Lender, M. 1973. Drunkenness as an offence in early New England; A study of "Puritan" attitudes. Q. J. Stud. Alcohol 34:353–366.

Lynn, R. 1971. Personality and National Character. Pergamon Press, Inc., Oxford.

MacAndrew, C., and Edgerton, R. B. 1969. Drunken Comportment; A Social Explanation. Aldine Publishing Company, Chicago.

McClelland, D. C., Davis, W., Wanner, E., and Kalin, R. 1972. A cross-cultural study of folk-tale content and drinking. In: D. C. McClelland, W. N. Davis, R. Kalin, and E. Wanner (eds.), The Drinking Man, pp. 48–72. Free Press, New York.

Maccoby, M. 1972. Alcoholism in a Mexican village. In: D. C. McClelland, W. N. Davis, R. Kalin, and E. Wanner (eds.), The Drinking Man, pp. 232–260. Free Press, New York.

Madsen, W. 1964. The alcoholic agringado. Am. Anthropol. 66:355–361.

* Madsen, W., and Madsen, C. 1969. The cultural structure of Mexican drinking behavior. Q. J. Stud. Alcohol 30:701–718. (Marshall: pp. 38–54.)

Marshall, M. (ed.). 1979. Beliefs, Behaviors, & Alcoholic Beverages; A Cross-Cultural Survey. University of Michigan Press, Ann Arbor.

Mendelson, J. H., Mello, N. K., and Ellingboe, J. 1977. Effects of acute alcohol intake on pituitary-gonadal hormones in normal human males. J. Pharmacol. Exp. Ther. 202:676–682.

* Midgley, J. 1971. Drinking and attitudes toward drinking in a Muslim community. Q. J. Stud. Alcohol 32:148–158. (Marshall: pp. 341–351.)

Mizoi, Y., Ijiri, I., Tatsuno, Y., Kijima, T., Fujiwara, S., and Adachi, J. 1979. Relationship between facial flushing and blood acetaldehyde levels after alcohol intake. Pharmacol. Biochem. Behav. 10:303–311.

Murdock, G. P. 1967. Ethnographic Atlas. University of Pittsburgh Press, Pittsburgh. (See also Ethnology, 1967, 6:109–236.)

Naroll, R. 1969. Cultural determinants and the concept of the sick society. In: S. C. Plog and R. B. Edgerton (eds.), Changing Perspectives in Mental Illness, pp. 128–155. Holt, Rinehart & Winston, Inc., New York.

* Nason, J. D. 1975. Sardines and other fried fish: The consumption of alcoholic beverages on a Micronesian island. J. Stud. Alcohol 36:611–625. (Marshall. pp. 237–251.)

* Netting, R. M. 1964. Beer as a locus of value among the West African Kofyar. Am. Anthropol. 66:375–384. (Marshall: pp. 351–362.)

Noble, E. P. (ed.). 1979. Alcohol and Health; Technical Support Document. Third Special Report to the U. S. Congress. DHEW Publication no. (ADM) 79–832. U. S. Government Printing Office, Washington, D. C.

Paredes, A. 1977. Social control of drinking among the Aztec Indians of Mesoamerica. J. Stud. Alcohol 36:1139–1153.

* Robbins, M. C. 1977. Problem-drinking and the integration of alcohol in rural Buganda. Med. Anthropol. 1(3):1–24. (Marshall: pp. 362–379.)

Rohner, R. P. 1975. They Love Me, They Love Me Not. HRAF Press, New Haven.

Rorabaugh, W. J. 1976. Estimated U.S. alcoholic beverage consumption, 1790–1860. J. Stud. Alcohol 37:357–364.

Rorabaugh, W. J. 1979. The Alcoholic Republic: An American Tradition. Oxford University Press, New York.

Sadoun, R., Lolli, G., and Silverman, M. 1965. Drinking in French Culture. Rutgers Center of Alcohol Studies, New Brunswick, N. J.

* Sargent, M. J. 1967. Changes in Japanese drinking patterns. Q. J. Stud. Alcohol 28:709–722. (Marshall: pp. 278–288.)

Schaefer, J. .M. 1976. Drunkenness and culture stress: A holocultural test. In: M. W. Everett, J. O. Waddell, and D. B. Heath (eds.), Cross-Cultural Approaches to the Study of Alcohol; An Interdisciplinary Perspective, pp. 287–321. Mouton, The Hague.

Schuckit, M. A. 1980. Self-rating of alcohol intoxication by young men with and without family histories of alcoholism. J. Stud. Alcohol 41:242–249.

Schuckit, M. A., and Rayses, V. 1979. Ethanol ingestion: Differences in blood acetaldehyde concentrations in relatives of alcoholics and controls. Science 203:54–55.

*Singer, K. 1972. Drinking patterns and alcoholism in the Chinese. Br. J. Addict. 67:3–14. (Marshall: pp. 313–326.)

Smart, R. G. 1977. The relationship of availability of alcoholic beverages to per capita consumption and alcoholism rates. J. Stud. Alcohol 38:891–896.

Snyder, C. R. 1958. Alcohol and the Jews. Free Press, Glencoe, Ill.

Stivers, R. 1976. A Hair of the Dog; Irish Drinking and American Stereotype. The Pennsylvania State University Press, University Park.

Stratton, R. , Zeiner, R., and Paredes, A. 1978. Tribal affiliation and prevalence of alcohol problems J. Stud. Alcohol 39:1166–1177.

Sulkunen, P. 1976. Drinking patterns and the level of alcohol consumption: An international overview. In: R. J. Gibbins et al. (eds.), Research Advances in Alcohol and Drug Problems. Vol. 3, pp. 223–281. John Wiley & Sons, Inc., New York.

Taylor, W. B. 1979. Drinking, Homicide & Rebellion in Colonial Mexican Villages. Stanford University Press, Stanford, Calif.

Truitt, E. B., and Walsh, M. J. 1971. The role of acetaldehyde in the actions of alcohol. In: B. Kissin and H. Begleiter (eds.), The Biology of Alcoholism. Vol. 1. Biochemistry, pp. 161–195. Plenum Publishing Corp., New York.

Wallgren, H., and Barry, H., III. 1970. Actions of Alcohol. Vol. 1. Biochemical, Physiological, and Psychological Aspects. Vol. 2. Chronic and Clinical Aspects. Elsevier, Amsterdam.

*Walsh, D. 1972. Alcoholism and the Irish. J. Alcohol. 7:40–47. (Marshall: pp. 394–404.)

Wanner, E. 1972. Power and inhibition: A revision of the magical potency theory. In: D. C. McClelland, W. N. Davis, E. Wanner, and R. Kalin (eds.), The Drinking Man, pp. 73–98. Free Press, New York.

West, L. J. 1972. A cross-cultural approach to alcoholism. Ann. N. Y. Acad. Sci. 197:214–216.

Wilsnack, S. C. 1974. The effects of social drinking on women's fantasy. J. Pers. 42:43–61.

Wolff, P. H. 1972. Ethnic differences in alcohol sensitivity. Science 175:449–450.

Wolff, P. H. 1973. Vasomotor sensitivity to alcohol in diverse Mongoloid populations. Am. J. Hum. Genet. 25:193–199.

*Yamamuro, B. 1954. Notes on drinking in Japan. Q. J. Stud. Alcohol 15:491–498. (Marshall: pp. 270–277.)

Zeichner, A., and Pihl, R. O. 1979. Effects of alcohol and behavior contingencies on human aggression. J. Abnorm. Psychol. 88:153–160.

Zeichner, A., and Pihl, R. O. 1980. Effects of alcohol and instigator intent on human aggression. J. Stud. Alcohol 41:265–276.

Zeiner, A. R., Paredes, A., and Christensen, H. D. 1979. The role of acetaldehyde in mediating reactivity to an acute dose of ethanol among different racial groups. Alcoholism 3:11–18.

Chapter 13

Culture and Sexual Deviation

Stewart Meikle

CULTURE AND SEXUAL DEVIATION

Most of our ideas regarding what constitutes normal and abnormal sexual behavior remain culture bound. Although lip service is paid to the importance of cross-cultural data, the vast quantity of published material on the subject still draws on Western, and in particular, on North American sources. Although such information is valuable, it is limited in terms of the populations to which it can be applied, and in order to find more generalizable answers to questions concerning the nature and causes of sexual deviations, a greater account of cross-cultural data must be taken. Although much of the research that is required to answer these questions has yet to be carried out, there is a considerable body of information already published to which psychologists should have more ready access. One of the principal aims of this chapter is to summarize some of this material. More adequate explanations are required, not only of deviant sexual behavior, but also of normal human sexuality. The assumption that we already have clear knowledge about what motivates normal sexual activity needs to be further questioned.

The decision to describe some aspects of human behavior as deviant may seem arbitrary to some people. However, the term is used here in its statistical rather than in its moralistic sense. For the vast majority of the human race, heterosexual activity still remains the norm. Suggested alternatives to the term *deviation*, such as "difficulties of sexual preference and expression" (Allman and Jaffe, 1978), or "alternative sexual behaviour" (Haas, 1979), are not only clumsy, but are still unfamiliar to most readers. Somewhat similar objections can be leveled at the DSM–III diagnostic scheme (American Psychiatric Association, 1980), in which the bulk of what were previously called sexual deviations appears under the minor heading of Paraphilias. Aside from the questionable need to generate another Greek hybrid word, this scheme has the additional disadvantage of excluding homosexuality, concerning which considerable cross-cultural data exists. Accordingly, this chapter follows a deviance framework purely as a matter of convenience, with full recognition of the limitations of the term. Space limitations necessitated careful selection of topics, and voyeurism and fetishism were excluded from consideration because they are generally a Western phenomenon about which the cross-cultural data have little to say.

In their earlier survey of sexual behavior, Ford and Beach (1951) specifically excluded historical cross-temporal data from consideration on the grounds that 1) historical cultures had not been studied firsthand by trained investigators; 2) only fragmentary records have come down to us from the past, and it is difficult to estimate how reliable and representative these are; and 3) most of the writers of historical material were probably drawn from a cultural elite whose views on sexual behavior may not have reflected the opinions of the culture at large. Although these problems surely exist, it seems not only presumptuous, but also rash to dismiss the accumulated record of human history on the grounds that professionals, trained in objective recording methods, did not make the original observations. Although historical information varies widely in quality, there seems little doubt that some very acute observers recorded what they saw with just as much accuracy, and perhaps more insight, than many of today's professionals. Greater reliance can be placed on historical material when its conclusions are based on several sources, rather than just a single source. Thus, Dover's (1977) findings on Greek homosexuality are based on mutually supportive evidence drawn from written records, rock graffiti, wall paintings, and research on then-current Greek institutions. Given these considerations, this chapter draws on both recent and remote cross-cultural material.

HOMOSEXUALITY

An adequate definition of the term *homosexuality* requires both agreed behavioral and motivational referents. The significance of such behavior differs, depending upon whether it is engaged in for lust or for money. At a behavioral level, considerable disagreement exists as to what constitutes homosexuality, a term that covers both male and female same-sex activity. The problem partly relates to the distinction between homosexuality and homosexual behavior. In the former case, the individual probably believes himself to be a homosexual, and both his sexual desires and his overt behavior are consistent with this. In the case of homosexual behavior, however, an individual may indulge in homosexuality on one or two occasions during adolescence, but thereafter consider himself exclusively heterosexual. In order to make some distinctions in this area, Kinsey, Pomeroy, and Martin (1948) developed a seven-point scale for assessing degree of homosexuality, ranging from a score of one, which reflects exclusive heterosexuality, to a score of seven, which corresponds to exclusive homosexuality. Kinsey's ratings were made on the basis of both subjective responsiveness and objective behavior. Thus, an individual who thought about homosexuality a great deal, but who never engaged in it, might obtain the same rating as one who was an active participant. On the whole, it would seem desirable that fantasy and behavior be evaluated separately. On a more general level, it is likely that our understanding of all human sexual activities, including homosexuality, would be enhanced if investigators, in addition to examining overt behavior, would also routinely evaluate more basic structures, such as sex role identity, sex role preference, and sex role adoption, as described by Constantinople (1973). However, at present little attempt has been made to do this on a cross-cultural basis.

Historical data regarding deviant sexual behavior are hard to obtain prior to the time of the Greeks. Some information is available, however, from translated cuneiform tablets, although many of these writings may have been censored by prudish translators to such a degree that it is often unclear what form of sexual behavior is being referred to (Bullough, 1976). During the Sumerian period of Mesopotamian history (approximately 3,000 B.C.), homosexuality apparently existed, and may, in fact, have become institutionalized in the form of religious male prostitution. Later, during the Assyrian period (about 1,100 to 600 B.C.), open homosexuality between free men had become less socially acceptable, although it continued to be practiced. By the time of the Persian ascendancy (about 600 to 550 B.C.), severe penalties were being exacted for homosexual behavior; persons found guilty could legitimately be killed by anyone. In general, the social structure during this period was one where women and marriage were valued mainly as a means of producing children, thus perpetuating the race, but they were rarely considered important for companionship.

Historical Views on Homosexuality

Homosexuality has long been known to have played a significant role in classical Greek society, but the recent scholarly work of Dover (1977) presents the available material in a particularly clear fashion. Male citizens, as distinct from slaves, apparently were basically bisexual. Among this class, it was generally accepted that homosexual and heterosexual interests could alternate in the same individual. It was not believed that such changes either produced, or were the result of, psychological problems. The open expression of homosexual interest was also allowable, and the subject itself was treated uninhibitedly in both literature and art. There is no reliable historical data to indicate how this bisexuality of the Greeks arose, although certain of their social institutions created a favorable climate for its maintenance. For example, the philosophy of hedonism was consistent with the view that it was legitimate for humans to seek experiences that made them happy. Because sexual enjoyment was one such activity, it was easy to accommodate homosexual pleasure within that principle. In addition, the Greek fascination with beauty, and especially with the ideal that male perfection consisted of being "beautiful in body and soul," meant that physical beauty in males became highly valued. In addition, Greek city states depended for their survival on the development of a warrior class capable of providing defense. The gymnasia were initially developed as exercise arenas to ensure that young males would be physically fit for this purpose. In time, these settings also became social foci for older males, who were then subject to simultaneous intellectual and sexual stimulation. Finally, Greek women of the citizen class were effectively segregated from potential young male partners until marriage, and even after this they would mainly be confined to their homes. As a result, during the time when sexual interest among the males could be expected to be at its peak, access to female partners was minimal. However, homosexuality in Greece cannot be attributed solely to the nonavailability of women, because prostitution was also widespread. Also, many males continued homosexual practices after marriage. Although the views of Greek women on this matter are not generally known, suggestions that male bisexuality may have been resented can be gleaned from a remark attributed to an unknown Greek comedian: "I do not care for a man who himself wants one" (Licht, 1932). Licht (1932) also suggests that Greek males did not feel that having an affair with a youth constituted unfaithfulness to a wife.

The Greeks apparently distinguished "honorable" homosexual activity, involving the sexual attraction of an older mentor to a younger male, from the homosexual activity used to demonstrate the power of one male over another. In a case in which power was an important factor, the passive partner would adopt a "female" role, involving a bent or lowered position, would permit either anal or oral penetration, and would accept money for services rendered. Although a citizen could acceptably assume either the older or the younger role, taking the passive position was considered humiliating and unworthy. The psychological significance of the inserter and insertee roles has been played down in the Anglo-American literature in the last few years, on the grounds that homosexual partners generally engage in both activities. However, the recent report of Carrier (1977), involving samples of Mexican, Brazilian, Turkish, Greek, lower-class American, and Chicano cultures, suggests that the equation of inserter with dominant masculine roles, and of insertee with passive feminine roles may be the more common view. To the extent that this argument is valid, homosexual activity may then be utilized to demonstrate the power of one individual over another.

In general, the evidence from Greek history indicates that a society can tolerate a considerable degree of bisexuality, in the male at least, and can remain vigorous intellectually, artistically, and militarily. The common fear that widespread acceptance of such behavior must lead to social decadence is not supported by the evidence from Greece.

Although there is considerable reference to homosexuality among the Roman poets, including Catullus, Virgil, Horace, Ovid, Petronius, Martial, and Juvenal, there does not seem to have been the same general enthusiasm for homosexuality among the Romans that existed among the Greeks. Slaves were considered fair game, and it was very common for young Roman males to have sexual relations with handsome male slaves (Kiefer, 1934). On the whole, however, the Romans were perhaps more distinguished for their cruelty than for their sexual peccadilloes.

The Christian attitude toward homosexuality stems from the Old Testament story of Sodom and Gomorrah. Allegedly these cities were destroyed by God as a punishment for the high incidence of homosexual practices there. Although this is apparently an inaccurate New Testament distortion of the original form of the story, it is this version that has guided followers of Christianity in their general condemnation of homosexual practices. Despite this disapproval, homosexuality has continued to attract many prominent followers. Extensive lists of important homosexuals, complete with short biographies, are available in Garde (1969) and Rowse (1977).

Recent Cross-Cultural Data on Homosexuality

When attention is directed from the historical to the more recent cross-cultural data on homosexuality, problems of both classification and motivation emerge. For example, a rich source of cross-cultural data can be found in the Human Relations Area Files. However, it is not always clear from the original sources contained in these files whether the behavior being discussed is homosexuality, hermaphroditism, transvestism, transsexualism, or pedophilia. In addition, the motives, and therefore the significance, of these behaviors vary from culture to culture. Despite this, it is possible to simplify the task of defining the behavior by limiting consideration to examples of fairly clear-cut homosexuality. When this method is adopted, several different motives for homosexual behavior can be detected.

First, a number of societies view homosexuality as a desirable preparatory experience for adult sexuality. Often these activities are expected to terminate at maturity. Thus, the Telegu (Dube, 1955) follow a "practice makes perfect" philosophy, in which older and more experienced youths convey to younger ones that the penis grows longer through masturbation, that maturity is arrived at earlier in this way, and that boys who do not indulge in the activity are not tough and can be considered half girls. Small groups of boys may then progress, through mutual masturbation, to the point at which an older boy may persuade a younger one to lie down with him and imitate the coital act. Usually the activity involved is limited to rubbing the penis against the anus, and no penetration occurs. A similar reason for engaging in homosexual behavior is ascribed to the Mongo people by Hulstaert (1938). In this culture, boys assume the positions of husbands and wives, with one saying to the other, "This is what I do with your sister." Hulstaert concludes that, although the action is homosexual, the feeling behind it is heterosexual. In this sense, then, such behavior can be viewed as preparation for adult heterosexual activity.

Wilson's (1951) report on the Ngonde people contains evidence that such early homosexual activities are often without lasting effect. Homosexual practices among the Ngonde were reportedly very common in the boy's villages. The behavior began between 10 and 14 years of age and continued until marriage, at which point homosexual relations were firmly relinquished. These few examples and several others contained in Money and Ehrhardt (1972) combine to suggest that homosexuality, in some cultures at least, is viewed mainly as a precursory activity in the development of full heterosexual maturity, and that no permanent distortion of sexual orientation need be expected as a result, despite a fairly vigorous and early homosexual exposure.

A second, fairly obvious theme emerging from the cross-cultural data on homosexuality relates to the nonavailability of the opposite sex. Many males who seem to be essentially heterosexual turn to homosexuality as a substitute outlet. Cipriani (1966), in discussing the Onge people of the Andaman Islands, states: "All the Onges have homosexual tendencies. I became aware of this on one of my longer expeditions, when I had taken only men with me, and on subsequent occasions I therefore allowed the men to bring their wives" (p. 557). Religious orders that include celibacy as a condition of membership also sometimes unwittingly create conditions likely to result in homosexuality. Thus, Peter (1963) reports that "the monasteries in Tibet proper have, however, a very strong reputation for male homosexuality, and jokes about master-novice relations are often made along these lines" (p. 458). In some societies that are formally heterosexual, the limited contact between the sexes constitutes a de facto segregation. Thus, Hausen (1961), commenting on the Kurdish people, points out that the only males still involved in the women's world are boys of less than five or six years of age. The separation of the two sexes during the day means that the men inhabit a world devoid of women. Therefore their emotional needs are usually met by other men. The result is that it is common to see men walking together with arms around each others's waists or with interlaced fingers, behavior they would never contemplate exhibiting in public with a female.

A third theme emerging from the cross-cultural data on homosexuality is the economic aspect. Engaging in homosexual activity for money is very common in North America. Reiss (1961), in his discussion of homosexual prostitutes, states that most of them do not consider themselves as homosexual at all, and that their motive is primarily financial, with little pleasure involved. A similar state of affairs exists among the Kanuri people, where a man of little means may advance socially by making himself available sexually to a homosexual member of the upper classes (Cohen, 1960).

Although these examples describe societies that either approve of, or at least tolerate, homosexual behavior under some circumstances, it should be recognized that not all communities that have been studied reflect this degree of acceptance. Although Ford and Beach (1951) reported that 64% of the societies they examined considered homosexuality normal and acceptable to some degree, they also found that in 36% of the communities it was absent or rare. In some cases this is because it is thought to be unnecessary. For example, among the Kikuyu "the freedom of intercourse allowed between young people of the opposite sex makes it unnecessary" (Kenyatta, 1953, p. 162). Some societies feel that homosexuality is so unnatural that it could only be committed by someone who is abnormal. Thus, with reference to the Lepchea people, Gorer (1938) states: "Sodomy is strongly anti-social—it is called nam-toak, an act producing a year of disaster . . . a sodomite who brings, or risks bringing, a year of disaster on the community is not responsible for his acts. No disgust is shown" (p. 102). Similar views are reported for the Dogan people (Pauline, 1940) and for the Meau (Bernatzik, 1947).

In summary, historical societies' attitudes toward homosexuality vary from considerable acceptance among the Greeks to strong disapproval among the Hebrews, with the Romans' attitude falling somewhere in between. The general pervasiveness of Christianity in the West has meant that most societies influenced by this doctrine have also disapproved of homosexuality. Nevertheless, even where extensive pressures have been brought to bear to discourage it, homosexuality has never been eradicated. The more recent cross-cultural data suggests the existence of a wide variety of attitudes, with the majority of societies showing some acceptance of homosexuality and about one-third rejecting it. However, even among those societies in which homosexual behavior is accepted, the endorsement is by no means unconditional in the manner aspired to by various Western homophile associations. In many instances, the approval applies to a limited period of time, such as in childhood or adolescence. In other cases, homosexuality is only acceptable in restricted circumstances, as, for example, when females are not available. The fact that many societies actively encourage childhood and adolescent homosexuality, yet later successfully foster exclusive heterosexual behavior, is of significance to our ideas concerning etiology. Early exposure is not, in itself, sufficient to explain later homosexuality. Although predisposition may account for some cases of homosexuality, particularly in which an element of effeminacy is involved, it is probable that the social meaning attached to early homosexual experience is also important. Thus, in instances in which the individual interprets early homosexual activity as either preparatory or substitutive for heterosexual acts, no lasting impairment of heterosexual interest is likely. However, where the individual believes that such early experience automatically means that he is homosexual, then the chance of later transferring to heterosexual partners is significantly reduced. The tendency to discuss homosexuality in dichotomous either/or categories may foster such interpretations. In addition, certain types of individuals may be especially prone to make these distinct interpretations, particularly those persons with close-binding mothers, distant, nonsignificant fathers, and a history involving childhood rejection of stereotyped sex-role activities (Bieber et al., 1962; Evans, 1969).

Transvestism/Transsexualism

Stoller (1971) has pointed out that, although the central defining characteristic of transvestism is cross-dressing, this behavior also occurs in transsexualism and in effeminate homosexuality. The difference is that, while the transvestite is usually a heterosexual male who wishes to remain so and who merely cross-dresses to achieve sexual arousal (a mild fetish), the transsexual suffers from a gender identity confusion in which the individual's feeling of being a male or a female is in conflict with his or her genital anatomy. Surgical resolutions are frequently sought by transsexuals. On the other hand, the effeminate homosexual, who may occasionally cross-dress, is distinguished from the other two types in that he knows and accepts that he is male, but is sexually attracted to members of his own sex. However, the effeminate homosexual has no desire to change sex and is satisfied with his present sexual organs. Further complications arise in the cross-cultural literature because some authors apparently utilize the term *hermaphrodite* for what is probably either *homosexuality* or *transsexualism*. Because of these confusions, this section deals with the phenomenon of cross-dressing, examines some of the cross-temporal and cultural literature relating to it, and only then attempts to assign causes.

Historical Instances of Cross-Dressing

The Western attitude toward cross-dressing is often traced to the biblical passage in Deuteronomy (22:5): "The women shall not wear that which pertaineth unto man, neither shall a man put on a woman's garment; for all that do so are an abomination unto the Lord thy God." Several of the Christian saints are reported to have cross-dressed, and despite the above passage, the church's attitude toward them seems to have been surprisingly tolerant. The fact that the majority of these cases were females suggests a relatively greater acceptance of female, as opposed to male cross-dressing. Nevertheless, exceptions existed and in the old morality plays, female parts were usually taken by male actors, most of whom were recruited from the ranks of the priesthood (Bullough, 1976). The somewhat greater tolerance for female cross-dressing may have been related to the medieval view regarding the relative worth of males and females. According to this way of thinking, it was understandable, and therefore forgivable, for the occasional (inferior) female to attempt to improve her lot in life by emulating the (superior) male. However, the notion that a male would voluntarily elect to pass as a female was much less comprehensible to the medieval mind and so was more compellingly considered deviant. In several recorded instances in which females attempted to pass themselves off as monks, the motivation seems to have initially arisen as a response to some life crisis. Pelagia did so to escape from her past, which included prostitution. Margarita Pelagius, in order to avoid the horrors of the nuptial couch, hurriedly escaped in male dress, cut her hair, and took refuge in a monastery under the name of Pelagius, where eventually she was elected Prior. Similar stories exist concerning Marina, Perpetua, Athanasia, Wilgefortis, and Pope John (Joan). Among the twelve articles of accusation against Joan of Arc, two dealt with her so-called transvestism (Bullough, 1976).

Green (1969b), in reviewing the medieval French literature on transsexualism, records that Henry III of France wished to be viewed as a woman, dressed accordingly, and insisted on being addressed as "Sa Majesté." Somewhat later in the seventeenth century, the Abbé de Choisy, after a childhood upbringing that included being dressed in girl's clothing, reported that he eventually came to believe that he was female and derived the maximum pleasure from being treated as such. Transsexual abbés seem to have been prominent in France at this period, as reflected in the case of the Abbé d'Entragues who attempted to make his face paler, and thus more feminine, through facial bleedings. In eighteenth century Britain it was not uncommon to find females passing as male soldiers or sailors. In most such cases the motivation behind the cross-dressing seems to have involved escaping from impending punishment or from intolerable social or economic conditions. In other cases, the behavior arose simply from the desire to be with a sweetheart who was already in the military, which can hardly be viewed as a sexual deviation.

Recent Data on Cross-Dressing

A link between causes for cross-dressing noted in the historical period and causes noted in more recent cross-cultural data is provided by Green's reference to the Abbé de Choisy having been raised as a girl by his mother. Several more recent references indicate this type of background as one source of cross-dressing behavior. Thus, Hrdlicka (1975), in commenting on the nineteenth-century Koniag, a Southern Alaska Eskimo people, mentions the custom of raising some male children as women. In some cases this was done because a boy child appeared to look girlish to the parents and was simply brought up accordingly. In other instances, parents who were eagerly awaiting the birth of a girl, in their disappointment at receiving a boy, reacted by bringing up the latter as a female. Such individuals often later became the homosexual partners of chiefs. Similar practices occurred among the early nineteenth-century Alut. In this society, if boys happened to be handsome, they were often brought up as girls, were taught the arts of women, and had their beards plucked, their skins tattooed, and their hair braided like women's. Many of these individuals eventually became concubines (Langsdorff, 1817). Instances of reverse training are also on record. Nahane couples who had too many female children and who desired a son would deliberately select a daughter "to be like a man." The girl would be raised as a boy, would be dressed in masculine clothes, and would be trained to perform male tasks. Often these females evolved considerable strength and hunting skills. Many of them eventually extended into homosexual relationships (Honigmann, 1954). Although caution should always be exercised in making cross-cultural comparisons, these examples seem to correspond most closely to Western transsexualism, rather than to transvestism. Not only was cross-dressing apparently permanent in these cultures, but there also seems to have been a considerable degree of gender identity change. These reports provide evidence that, given sufficient environmental pressure, major changes in sexual identity can result.

Some cultures maintain distinctions between the various categories of cross-dresser that are very similar to Stoller's (1971) scheme, involving transvestism, transsexualism, and effeminate homosexuality. Thus, Linton (1933), in referring to the Bara people, an African tribe, states that, although they distinguish between hermaphrodites, homosexuals, and cross-dressers, they view all three cases as responses to impotence. The hermaphrodites were believed to adopt the female role at birth, whereas the other two types only developed the behavior at puberty or later. An example of an individual adopting the female role in response to impotence involves the case of a man of 60 who had led a normal heterosexual life until his early fifties. At that point, a long illness left him impotent and unfit for heavy work. He declared he was no longer a man, adopted women's dress, and learned to weave, eventually making his living in this manner. No adverse criticism followed this dramatic change. The Navaho also recognized and accepted individuals who cross-dressed. A distinction was made between those who adopted a female role for a limited period and those who were permanently feminized. Apparently some individuals would dress up as females for the first 18 to 20 years of life and then would adopt a male role. Others began cross-dressing early in life and remained feminine in dress and behavior throughout their lives. No criticism was leveled against such individuals, who were viewed as a valuable asset to a family because they were thought to bring good fortune (Hill, 1935).

In some societies, cross-dressing was not only accepted but it was also felt to bring with it special powers. Among many North American Indian tribes these individuals were called berdaches. Commonly, such persons, in response to a dream, became convinced that they should adopt a female role. Will and Spinden (1906), in discussing the Mandan people, state: "There are a number of men who dressed and acted like women and were treated in every way as such. These men claimed to follow this life by an order from the spirits given to them in a dream." Similar motives for adopting a female existence are reported for the Arapaho (Kroeber, 1902), for the Winnebago (Lurie, 1953), for the Ojibwa (Kinietz, 1947), and for several other North American Indian tribes. Sometimes the decision to cross-dress seems to have been based on a dream that misfired. Fletcher and La Flesche (1911) indicate that "the young men who go to fast sometimes remain out for many days. This is done to secure dreams or visions which will support them in manly enterprises . . . but sometimes it happens that a young man has dreams or visions which make him imagine that he is a woman. From that time on he takes upon himself the dress and occupations of a woman" (p. 132). Another motive for adopting the transsexual role could be an irresistible command conveyed through a dream. Some of these dreams may have involved wish fulfillment, but others seem to have occurred despite the dreamers' stated wishes.

In the cross-cultural literature on cross-dressing, there is an almost complete absence of reports on what might be considered transvestism. The reason for this lack may be that those who conducted investigations outside of Western culture were not psychologists, and therefore failed to elicit the appropriate information. However, this seems unlikely because these same reporters provided extensive information on other deviant sexual behavior, including homosexuality and transsexualism. Transvestism is usually conducted in secret, and thus is less vulnerable to direct observation, but the same is true in the West, where it is generally widely recognized. At the very least, transvestism seems to be a relatively uncommon deviation outside of Western society.

Aside from those cases in which cross-dressing was simply a consciously adopted disguise donned to avoid other difficulties, the bulk of the cross-cultural literature deals with either transsexualism or with effeminate homosexuality, using Stoller's (1971) terminology. In the case of transsexualism, which seems to be the more common phenomenon, many societies recognize such individuals at an early stage and permit them to assume the opposite sex role fairly permissively. Such individuals show cross-gender behavior characteristic of Western transsexuals, as described by Green (1969a), among others. In other instances of what seems to be transsexualism, the impetus comes from the parents rather than from the children themselves. In some ways, this corresponds to the arbitrary parental decisions reported by Money and Ehrhardt (1972), in which a variety of gender anomalous children were deliberately and successfully raised to be either male or female. The sudden conversion of a male to a female through the medium of a dream apparently has no Western equivalent, unless one chooses to equate it with a psychotic delusion. However, this seems far-fetched, and at present such changes are probably better viewed as having no cultural parallel in the West. The fact that transsexuals carried considerable prestige in some societies may have compensated for the status lost through the change from the male to the female role.

The effeminate homosexual category referred to by Stoller (1971) is not well represented in the cross-cultural literature, although the distinction between this category and transsexualism is difficult to make, given the lack of discriminating information in much of the data. The Kashmiri minstrels, studied by Gervis (1954), with their exaggerated feminine movements, and waist-long hair, and seductive smiles, may fit into this category, as may the late nineteenth-century fellahin male dancers in Egypt, described by Klunzinger (1878).

EXHIBITIONISM

Although homosexuality and transsexualism occur in many cultures throughout the world, exhibitionism does not, although it is much more common among Western societies than elsewhere. Exhibitionism alone probably accounts for about one-third of all reported sexual offenses in the United States, Canada, and Anglo-Saxon Europe (Rooth, 1974). Rooth (1973) suggests (from an examination of Index Medicus references relating to exhibitionism) that the frequency of exhibitionism may be less among the Latin (French and Italian) than among the Anglo-Saxon (German and

English) European countries. However, at present this hypothesis must be viewed as extremely tentative because of variations in the reporting procedures used by different countries.

As yet no major historical review has been attempted regarding the incidence and circumstances under which exhibitionism occurred in the historical past, nor is there much information in the currently available cross-cultural literature to draw upon. Rooth (1973) attempted to assess the relative incidence of exhibitionism in 40 Asian, African, and South American countries by contacting physicians living in these areas and by obtaining their estimates. Replies were obtained from 24 countries (a 64% return rate). It was concluded that, although exhibitionism existed on the statute books as a legal offense and was theoretically punishable in all cases, in practice prosecution was rarely carried out. Prior investigators have suggested that the discrepancies in reported incidence of exhibitionism between the West and other areas may have been caused by the rapid industrialization in the Western part of the world. However, Rooth points out that Japan, which is heavily industrialized, has a very low frequency of reported incidents. Other non-Western countries with low frequencies include India and Burma. Hong Kong, however, another industrialized Eastern area, has an incidence of exhibitionism that closely matches that of Western countries. Until some standardization is brought into the reporting methods, there seems no sure way of resolving these discrepancies. Rooth suggests a number of points that might explain these differing frequencies. One cause might be the limited amount of childhood and adolescent heterosexual exploratory behavior available in most Western cultures, and the lengthy interval between sexual maturity and the establishment of regular heterosexual coitus. This in turn leads to a relatively high frequency of masturbation as a substitute, with the possibility of sexual arousal becoming more readily conditioned to anonymous, passive, fantasized females. In addition, Rooth also implicates ignorance as a factor in exhibitionism, on the grounds that a substantial number of Western males wrongly believe that females are excited by the type of direct genital display to which they themselves respond.

The generally low frequencies of reported exhibitionism in non-Western countries described by Rooth are certainly confirmed in the other readily available cross-cultural literature. An examination of the Human Relations Area Files by the author revealed very few such references, and some of these simply reported the lack of such activity among a particular people. Nevertheless, a few positive reports do appear. Gutierrez de Pineda (1950), in an account of Goajiro people of South America, states that exhibitionism is considered a punishable act because it offends against the modesty of those present. In this society, the gravity of the offence is judged in relation to the social standing of those offended against, so that a great fine is levied if the victim is of a high as opposed to a low social status. It is interesting that exhibitionism would be recognized as an offense among a people who are not otherwise bothered by nudity, because both sexes undress in public for bathing purposes. However, under bathing circumstances the women take care to cross their legs, and the men hold the penis in such a way as to avoid giving offense to bystanders. This practice suggests that, although many primitive societies are scantily clothed, they have fairly subtle social rules designed to discriminate between acceptable and nonacceptable nudity. Other reports of relatively isolated incidents of exhibitionism in tribal societies appear in Krige and Krige (1943), in Elwin (1947), and in Oakes (1951).

The most common explanations of Western exhibitionism have drawn on either learning theory (McGuire, Carlisle, and Young, 1965) or on psychoanalysis (Fenichel, 1945). According to learning theory, young males, caught by females in the act of urinating, were thought to have had sexual excitement conditioned to exposing behavior. However, such chance events presumably also occur with females, and yet the incidence figures suggest that no such similar conditioning occurs. In the case of psychoanalysis, exhibiting behavior is generally considered to be a reassurance against castration anxiety. Although this explanation has the advantage of accounting for the sex differences in exhibitionism, it is framed within a theoretical approach that many find difficult to accept. Recently Jones and Frei (1979) have made an attempt to explain the sex differential in exhibiting behavior in terms of an archaic but innate male predisposition toward penile display. Their evidence is drawn from work with the squirrel monkey, in which males are found to display the erect penis under conditions of aggression and social greeting as well as of courtship. The authors report similar behavior among the Asmat and Anyu males of New Guinea, where a penile display dance is initiated in response to fear, elation, or surprise. Jones and Frei suggest that a common element in these examples is the use of the penis to express hostility as well as sexuality. Innate predisposition is then used to explain why one chance exposure, as expressed in the history of many exhibitionists, results in such persistent and driven behavior. Although this proposal may offer an explanation for the rapid acquisition of this form of deviance, it does not seem to account for the wide cultural discrepancies in its frequency, particularly because many of the cultures where it is virtually nonexistent are the ones where chance exposure would be most likely to occur. In fact, the apparent one-trial learning in the history of some exhibitionists may be misleading, because the one event can easily be followed by endless cognitive repetitions that effectively constitute many trials. On the whole, it is more likely that social factors, specific to Western culture, constitute the controlling variables behind the relatively high incidence figures. What these variables are needs to be clarified, although some leads have been proposed, including the eroticizing of nudity (Chesser, 1971) and the general discouragement of sexual activity with accompanying feelings of sexual inadequacy and guilt, both of which remain common in Western societies (Witzig, 1968).

ZOOPHILIA

From the review of Kinsey et al. (1953) on zoophilia, it is clear that historical accounts of sexual contacts between animals and humans have existed for a long time. Both legal and religious injunctions against the sexual involvement of males with animals existed in the Hittite Code, in the Old Testament, and in the Talmud, presumably with the aim of curbing existing offenses. Only in the Talmud, however, was there a specific injunction aimed at female contact with animals. However, both Greek and Roman mythology contain numerous examples of gods appearing in various animal guises to visit their favor upon females. Similar themes appear in art and literature. According to the view of Kinsey et al. (1953), much of this interest in contacts between animals and females represented males' wishful thinking, and that females generally are not attracted to this type of sexual activity, either in fantasy or in reality. Kinsey's data suggest that for both sexes zoophilia is a low-frequency activity. The statistics indicate that 1.5% of the preadolescent females and up to 3% of the preadolescent males, and 3.6% of the adult females and 8% of the adult males admitted to animal sexual contacts. Most of the female contacts were with household pets, such as dogs or cats. In the males, a wider range of animals had been employed. Subgroup differences in frequency were also apparent; between 40% and 50% of boys reared on farms had had some sexual involvement with animals, 17% to the point of orgasm. To these males, observing farm animals engaging in sexual action was often found to be personally stimulating, and, with the effective nonavailability of human females, the result was sexual experimentation with animals.

In Western culture, the general reaction to zoophilia has been determined by biblical injunction. Other societies have also taken a strict stance against the behavior. Among the Rwala, although bestiality was reportedly rare, it was punished by death to both participants (Musil, 1928). Similar strong reactions have been reported among the Balinese (Covarrubias, 1937), who viewed bestiality as a heinous offence that threatened the spiritual health of the community and that was likely to result in disasters for all, including such adversity as epidemics and loss of crops. At the time Covarrubias was collecting his data in the early 1930s, bestiality was so horrifying to the Balinese that they could only explain it by indicating that the perpetrator was bewitched into believing that the animal appeared as a beautiful woman.

Some societies, although they disapprove of zoophilia, react in a milder manner. Thus, among the Yanomamö, a South American tribe, a man known to have copulated with a dog is simply treated with contempt by everyone in his group (Chagnon, 1977). Several peoples, aware of the temptations to which males who spend much of their time with animals are exposed, take steps to reduce these risks. La Barre (1948), in commenting on the high incidence of bestiality amongst the Aymara llama drivers, notes that under the Incas severe laws were enacted against bestiality. Even after the Spanish conquest, an old law had to be enforced that did not permit llama drivers to start their journeys unless accompanied by their wives: ". . . this regulation was understood to be intended as a safeguard against such abuses." In other instances, social reaction to bestiality is either mild or nonexistent. In discussing the Caucasian people of southwest Russia, Luzbetak (1951) states that the penalty for bestiality with horses is either trivial or does not exist at all. A similar reaction is reported by Landy (1959) with reference to the Vall Cana, a Caribbean tribe. Reichel-Dolmatoff (1951) indicates that, among the Cagaba of South America, contact with animals forms an important part of the sexual experience of almost every individual. A relatively unique rationalization in support of this form of sexual deviation is mentioned by Blanguernon (1955). In commenting on the Tuareg, he states that although bestiality is rare, it is practiced as a remedy for venereal disease.

The overall impression obtained from the cross-cultural literature on zoophilia is that it generally is one of the less common forms of deviation, although the incidence varies widely. Its frequency is influenced by a number of factors, including the proximity of animals and the availability of females. Social reaction to zoophilia ranges from horrified disgust, associated with severe punishment, to complete acceptance, without social penalties.

CONCLUSION

Despite the unevenness in quality of the cross-cultural literature on sexual deviations, several themes emerge that are significant to our understanding of this area. It is evident, for example, that widespread homosexuality can exist in a society without major disruption of the social fabric. In the case of Greece, homosexual preferences coincided with a highly innovative artistic and intellectual life. Whether the converse applies, that is, whether the same sort of cultural enrichment can exist in societies that harshly proscribe homosexuality, is not so apparent, although many communities have certainly attempted such suppression. Against societal pressures, however, homosexuality has remained stubbornly resistant and has often simply gone underground. Somewhat paradoxically, several examples exist in which a tolerant attitude toward youthful homosexuality is followed by the expectation that such behavior will be replaced by exclusive heterosexual interests in due time. This belief seems to run counter to the current Western view of homosexuality, where it is generally held that early and extensive exposure is likely to alter sexual orientation permanently. One explanation of this paradox may relate to the way the participants in homosexual activities construe their behavior. When homosexuality is viewed as a preparatory or substitutive heterosexual activity, the risks of permanent orientation changes may be reduced or eliminated. However, this also implies that greater emphasis needs to be given to cognitive explanatory factors. The question of predisposition essentially remains unresolved.

The available data suggest that true transvestism remains largely a Western phenomenon. It is clear that cross-dressing is a recognized behavior in many different cultures, but most often it occurs within the context of transsexualism, or, less commonly, in effeminate homosexuality. The individual who dons female clothing as a means of achieving sexual gratification is cross-culturally rare. The available information suggests several means by which transsexualism develops. In some instances, external agencies, such as parents, arbitrarily decide to masculinize or feminize a child. This seems to correspond roughly to the parental treatment administered to hermaphrodite children, as referred to by Money and Ehrhardt (1972), and perhaps therefore has a Western equivalent. In several cultures, the push toward transsexualism seems to have been internal, in that existing effeminacy in the child was simply accepted by the parents, and opposite-sex training was then prescribed. The sudden change to transsexualism in response to a dream seems to have no Western equivalent. However, the fact that many societies provide specific roles for transsexuals suggests that it is a widespread phenomenon that exists despite major differences in cultural environment.

Exhibitionism is generally uncommon outside of the industrialized West. To what extent this should be attributed to industrialization and to what extent other aspects of Western culture are to blame is not clear. Certainly in societies where clothing is relatively skimpy, exhibitionism is virtually nonexistent. Nonavailability of heterosexual partners, together with the Western habit of directing masturbatory activity at anonymous, passive, female figures may be of importance in understanding the acquisition of exhibitionistic behavior.

Zoophilia is probably best understood within the rubric of heterosexual deprivation, and, as such, can be considered an alternative sexual outlet that is readily available in rural communities, where, for one reason or another, heterosexual access is denied.

REFERENCES

Allman, L. R., and Jaffe, D. T. 1978. Abnormal Psychology in the Life Cycle. Harper & Row Pubs., Inc., New York.

American Psychiatric Association. 1980. Diagnostic & Statistical Manual of Mental Disorders. 3rd Ed. American Psychiatric Association, Washington, D.C.

Bernatzik, H. A. 1947. Akha und Meau, Probleme der Angewandten. Vökerkunde in Hinterindien. Kommissionsverlag Wagner'sche, Universitäts-Buchdruckerei, Innsbruck.

Bieber, I., Dain, H. J., Dince, B. R., Drellich, N. G., Grand, H. C., Gundlach, R. H., Kremer, M. W., Rifkin, A. H., Wilbur, C. B., and Bieber, T. B. 1962. Homosexuality: A Psychoanalytical Study. Random House, New York.

Blanguernon, C. 1955. Le Hoggar. Arthaud, Grenoble, France.

Bullough, V. L. 1976. Sex in History: A Virgin Field. Science History Publications, New York.

Carrier, J. M. 1977. "Sex-role preference" as an explanatory variable in homosexual behavior. Arch. Sex. Behav. Vol.6, no. 1.

Chagnon, N. A. 1977. Yanomamö, the Fierce People. Holt, Rinehart & Winston, Inc., New York.

Chesser, E. 1971. Strange Loves: The Human Aspects of Sexual Deviation. William Morrow & Co., Inc., New York.

Cipriani, L. 1961. Hygiene and medical practices among the Onge (Little Andaman). Anthropos 56:557.

Cohen, R. 1960. The structure of Kanuri society. Dissertation in Anthropology, University of Wisconsin. University Microfilms Publications, no. 60–986, Ann Arbor, Mich.

Constantinople, A. 1973. Masculinity-femininity: An exception to a famous dictum? Psychol. Bull. 80(5):389–407.

Covarrubias, M. 1937. Island of Bali. Alfred A. Knopf, Inc., New York.

Dover, K. J. 1977. Greek Homosexuality. Duckworth, London.

Dube, S.C. 1955. Indian Village. Cornell University Press, Ithaca.

Elwin, V. 1947. The Muria and their Ghotul. Oxford University Press, Bombay.

Evans, R. B. 1969. Childhood parental relationships of homosexual men. J. Consult. Clin. Psychol. 33:129–135.

Fenichel, O. 1945. The Psychoanalytic Theory of Neuroses. W. W. Norton & Company, Inc., New York.

Fletcher, A. C. and La Flesche, F. 1911. The Omaha Tribe. U. S. Bureau of American Ethnology. Twenty-seventh annual report, 1905/06. Washington, D.C.

Ford, C. S., and Beach, F. A. 1951. Patterns of Sexual Response. Harper & Row Pubs., Inc., New York.

Garde, N. I. 1969. Jonathan to Gide. Nosbooks, New York.

Gervis, P. 1954. This is Kashmir. Cassell, London.

Gorer, G. 1938. Himalayan Village: An Account of the Lepchas of Sikkim, p. 102. Michael Joseph, London.

Green, R. 1969a. Childhood cross-gender identification. In: R. Green and J. Money (eds.), Transexualism and Sex Reassignment. Johns Hopkins Press, Baltimore.

Green, R. 1969b. Mythological, Historical, & Cross Cultural Aspects of Transsexualism. In: R. Green and J. Money (eds.), Transexualism and Sex Reassignment. Johns Hopkins Press, Baltimore.

Gutierrez de Pineda, V. 1950. Organizacion social en la Guarjira. Instituto etnológica nacional. Vols. III, XV. Bogotá.

Haas, K. 1979. Abnormal Psychology. D. Van Nostrand Company, New York.

Hausen, B. H.1961. The Kurdish Woman's Life: Field Research in a Muslim Society, Iraq. Nationalmusset, Copenhagen.

Hill, W. W. 1935. The hand trembling ceremony of the Navaho. El Palacio 38.

Honigmann, J. J. 1954. The Kaska Indians: An Ethnographic Reconstruction. Yale University Press, New Haven.

Hrdlicka, A. 1975. The Anthropology of Kodiak Island. AMS Press, New York.

Hulstaert, G-E. 1938. Le Marriage des Knundo. G. van Campenhout, Brussels.

Jones, I. H., and Frei, D. 1979. Exhibitionism—A biological hypothesis. Br. J. Med. Psychol. 52:63–70.

Kenyatta, J. 1953. Facing Mount Kenya: The Tribal Life of the Gikuyu. Secker and Warburg, London.

Kiefer, G. H. 1934. Sexual Life in Ancient Rome. Abbey Library, London.

Kinietz, W. V. 1947. Chippewa Village: The Story of Katikitegow. Cranbrook Press, Bloomfield Hills, Mich.

Kinsey, A. C., Pomeroy, W. B., and Martin, C. E. 1948. Sexual Behavior in the Human Male. W. B. Saunders Company, Philadelphia.

Kinsey, A. C., Pomeroy, W. B., Martin, C. E., and Gebhard, D. H. 1953. Sexual Behaviour in the Human Female. W. B. Saunders Company, Philadelphia.

Klunzinger, C. B. 1977. Upper Egypt: Its People and Its Products. AMS Press, New York. (Reprint of 1878 edition.)

Krige, E. J., and Krige, J. D. 1943. The Realm of a Rain Queen: A Study of the Pattern of Lovedu Society. Oxford University Press, London.

Kroeber, A. L. 1902. The Arapaho. Am. Mus. Nat. Hist. Bull. 18:1–229, 279–454.

La Barre, W. 1948. The Aymare Indians of the Lake Titicaca Plateau, Bolivia. American Anthropological Association, Menasha, Wisconsin.

Landy, D. 1959. Tropical Childhood: Cultural Transmission and Learning in a Rural Puerto Rican Village University of North Carolina Press, Chapel Hill.

Langsdorff, G. H. 1817. Voyages and Travels in Various Parts of the World During the Years 1803, 1804, 1805, 1806, and 1807. George Philips, Carlisle, Pa.

Licht, H. 1932. Sexual Life in Ancient Greece. George Routledge & Sons, London.

Linton, R. 1933. The Tanala: A Hill Tribe of Madagascar. Field Museum of National History, Chicago.

Lurie, N. O. 1953. Winnebago berdache. Am. Anthropol. 55:708–712.

Luzbetak, L. J. 1951. Marriage and the Family in Caucasia: A Contribution to the Study of North Caucasian Ethnology and Customary Law. St. Gabriel's Mission Press, Vienna-Mödling.

McGuire, R. J., Carlisle, J. H., and Young, B. G. 1965. Sexual deviations as conditioned behaviour: A hypothesis: Behav. Res. Ther. 2:185–190.

Money, J., and Ehrhardt, A. A. 1972. Man & Woman, Boy & Girl; The Differentiation and Dimorphism of Gender Identity from Conception to Maturity. Johns Hopkins Press, Baltimore.

Musil, A. 1928. The Manners and Customs of the Rwala Bedouins. American Geographical Society, New York.

Oakes, M. von C. 1951. Beyond the Windy Place: Life in the Guatemalan Highlands. Farrar, Straus & Young, New York.

Pauline, D. 1940. Organisation Sociale des Dogan. Editions Domat— Montchrestien, F. Loviton et Cie, Paris.

Peter, Prince George of Greece and Denmark. 1963. A Study of Polyandry. Mouton, The Hague.

Reichel-Dolmatoff, G. 1951. Los Kogi: Una Tribu de la Sierra Nevada de Santa Marta, Columbia. Tomo II. Editorial Iqueima, Bogotá.

Reiss, A. J., Jr. 1961. The social integration of queers and peers. Soc. Probl. 9:102–120.

Rooth, G. 1973. Exhibitionism outside Europe and America. Arch. Sex. Behav. 2:351–363.

Rooth, G. 1974. Exhibitionists around the world. Hum. Behav. 3:61.

Rowse, A. L. 1977. Homosexuals in History: A Study of Ambivalence in Society, Literature, and Arts. Weidenfeld & Nicolson, London.

Stoller, R. J. 1971. The term "transvestism." Arch. Gen. Psychiatry 24:230–237.

Will, G. F., and Spinden, H. J. 1906. The Mandans: A Study of Their Culture, Archaeology, and Language. Harvard University Press, Cambridge.

Wilson, M. H. 1951. Good Company: A Study of Nyakyusa Age-villages. Oxford University Press, London.

Witzig, J. J. 1968. The group treatment of male exhibitionists. Am. J. Psychiatry 125:75–81.

VI

CULTURE, PSYCHE, AND SOMA

Chapter 14

Brain, Culture, and Neuropsychiatric Illness

Horacio Fabrega, Jr.

INTRODUCTION

The manifestations and symptoms of psychiatric disorders are frequent topics of investigation in anthropology, psychology, and psychiatry. In studies of this type, the researcher contends that cultural factors might be operative in the way a person who is ill behaves and in the way he or she is dealt with in a group. Within this perspective in psychiatry, and within its counterpart perspective in anthropology, culture, and personality theory, behavior is examined from a psychological and social point of view. Emphasis is placed on such things as thought content and progression, perceptions, emotional expression, social relations, and conventions about deviance; these kinds of phenomena are typically approached using the perspectives of the social sciences. Culture, ordinarily defined as a people's system of social symbols and their meanings, is a variable traditionally linked to the methods of these sciences (Geertz, 1973).

The influences of culture may also be approached from a neurobiological point of view (Fabrega, 1977). From this standpoint, behavior is considered to be the output of an organ consisting of neurological routines, which are a product of evolution, but which require an experiential base that is culturally conditioned (Fabrega, 1979). The assumption is made that a people's view of the world and their guidelines for operating in it play a key role in the development and maturation of the individual and influence the way in which the whole nervous system comes to be organized and the way in which it functions. For example, according to the neurobiological view, cultural factors are believed to influence the way that sensory stimuli are built into perceptions; the way that these stimuli influence basic motor schemata and general programs of action; the way that conventions about time, space, and motor expression get encoded neurologically and enter into the formation of key concepts, such as object, person, self, other, and ecologic setting; the way that internal visceral or "emotional" responses come to be structured and linked to culturally specific mental experiences about the world and about both social and physical activity; and the way in which language plays a role in contextualizing this whole system of meaning.

This chapter provides a general perspective for conceptualizing the role of culture in psychiatric illness in terms of brain-behavior relationships. The first section contains a neurobiological analysis of culture and behavior. Next, the question of cultural influences on the manifestations of psychiatric illness is considered, using functional and organic illnesses as test cases. An analysis of this question leads to a general discussion of the nature of psychiatric disorders. The importance of distinguishing between the neurobiologic and sociocultural aspects of these disorders is stressed. Finally, a way of conceptualizing and explaining the gap between the neurobiological and the sociocultural is presented.

CULTURE AND BRAIN FUNCTION

Types of Brain-Behavior Relationships in Man

One can propose at least three ways in which to look at the problem of brain-behavior relationships in man. The following is a brief summary of ways in which different types of scientists conceptualize brain-behavior relations and the relevance this has for psychiatry and the social sciences.

Intra-Social or Personality Domain   When they are ill because of a specific disease, persons of any city of any well-demarcated age and social group will display different behavioral changes and will be preoccupied with different types of concerns. They will seem to share basic premises about reality, and their way of thinking, perceiving, and remembering could be said to be roughly similar. Despite this, however, one could point to differences in behavior. These differences are caused by personality or psychosocial factors. Insofar as behavior is the output of a brain, one can properly speak of personality or psychosocial programming of the brain. This programming can be described in different ways, for example, in terms of psychoanalysis and behavior reinforcing principles. Most neuroscientists refer to this particular type of brain-behavior relationship when they speak of the mind-body problem. A recent exposition or theory of this problem has been presented by Mountcastle and Edelman (1978).

Cultural-Linguistic Domain   Consider two highly different societies, which we will call society A and society B. Members of A are literate, school educated, and speak an Indo-European language. Members of B live in the highlands of a remote continent, are not literate or school educated, and speak a non–Indo-European language whose lexicon and grammar differ substantially from the language spoken by the members of A. The life-styles of the two groups are sharply different. In choosing to distinguish the groups on the basis of literateness, formal education, and language structure (as well as according to the life-style differences that go with these), one has maximized the likelihood of the existence of what anthropologists, linguists, and psychologists speak of as cultural differences. In certain respects, members of A and B can be said to differ in their behavior; one could say that differences *seem to exist* in such areas as memory, thinking, and use of color terminology. Members of both groups all perceive, remember, and think; furthermore, behavioral variation exists among members of group A as well as among members of B. However, superimposed upon intrasocietal differences are group differences. If there are behavior differences across these two groups in the areas noted, then in some way the organization and functioning of the brains of the members of the two groups must differ. When psychiatrically or neurologically ill, members of A and B might be expected to show different patterns of symptoms. This type of brain-behavior relation serves as the subject of this chapter.

    Phylogenetic Domain   Work in primatology reveals a high degree of social organization in infrahuman primates. Individual members of a foraging group engage in any number of behavioral activities. The cognitive abilities of chimpanzees and baboons are well known, and include sense of self, ability to orient spatially, ability to represent the world and to make discriminations about it, and ability to communicate emotionally and through symbols (Fabrega, 1977). Although there is great controversy about the nature of the differences in the cognitive activities of infrahuman primates versus those of man (i.e., whether these differences are qualitative or quantitative), the existence of some form of difference is accepted and includes speech, elaborate propositional thinking, and the capacity to remove oneself from the now and project oneself forward or backward in time. Intuitively, one believes that these behavioral differences between man and infrahuman primates are associated with differences in brain organization and function. Thus, the differences reflect a phylogenetic type of brain-behavior difference (Fabrega, 1977).

The Neurological Representation of Culture

In considering culture, one thinks of symbols, rules, and/or conventions about such things as the world, others, the self, and work. A review of the literature on cultural practices indicates uniformities underlying much of the behavior studied by anthropologists (Fabrega, in press). Moreover, even when cultural differences are singled out, culture as a symbol system influences and patterns behavior, provided that the behavior is examined in symbolic, or cultural, terms. Although a tautology of symbolic forms is often reflected in the way culture and behavior are conceptualized, so-called symbolic behaviors are the outcome of (are produced by) brain programs or routines of some sort. How is one to understand cultural differences in terms of neural substrates?

Neuropsychologists speak of the engram as the physical brain substrate of memory. Although it is not often mentioned explicitly, it is very likely that social scientists' ideas of culture and symbols can be equated with the engrams of the semantic memory system. As described by Tulving (1972) and illustrated by Warrington (1975), it is this system that presumably embodies the repository of knowledge and beliefs that an individual acquires as he learns his culture. Information of the semantic memory system may embrace such overlearned things as role prescriptions, attitudes, and values, as well as beliefs—all of which constitute the data of social scientists. In summary, one brain analogue of culture could involve protein changes that influence conduction properties of synapses and populations of neurons and that serve as substrates for the posited semantic memory system. Molecular changes of this type may also be equated with the modules of Mountcastle and Edelman (1978). Understanding how these molecular changes operate is, at present, beyond the reach of neuroscientists.

Another brain analogue of culture (not explicitly mentioned as such in the literature) can be equated with what neuroscientists call motor programs (Deuel, 1977; Heilman, Schwartz and Geschwind, 1975; Miles and Evarts, 1979; Rosenbaum, 1977; and Turvey, 1975). Motor programs are physical changes (involving molecular arrangements, patterns of synaptic transmission, and neural nets) in the brain that mediate and/or serve to organize sequences of coordinated skeletal and visceral muscle movements. Motor programs account for the execution of organized human action, including neuromuscular activity, nonverbal communication, and the expression of affect, emotion, and speech—all of which are linked to internal bodily states. Speech is an excellent example of a form of human motor activity that is dominated and coordinated by thought processes. Complex motor actions like those involving speech are generally thought of as being coordinated by hierarchical structures. The uppermost or executive structure has little or no direct control over actual motor output. The executives in charge of speech are defined as sensorimotor ideas or concepts (McNeill, 1979). These are outgrowths of sensorimotor action schemas, which serve to generate movement in infants and which constitute the earliest forms of cognitive activity. Thus, at an early stage of development, sensorimotor ideas are considered to be simultaneously part of action and part of meaning, serving as the basis of sensorimotor behavior and cognition. It is believed that these ideas and schemata are the earliest templates for speech and that they provide a motor basis for thought and awareness.

There is a suggestion in the neurological literature that motor programs for speech may partially embody knowledge, although the information discussed here as semantic memory is best thought of as being represented in a physically separate manner (Geschwind, Quadfasel, and Segarra, 1968). The location, the neural organization, and the mode of operation of these motor programs in relation to memorial, cognitive, and visceral systems are beyond understanding at present. Nevertheless, motor programs in the brain can also be thought of as constituting neurologic substrates of culture, although neuroscientists handle these programs as if they were universal, disregarding the question of cultural specificity and differences.

A selective review of the literature indicates that when neurologically oriented researchers explicitly invoke cultural factors, they refer to such things as patterns of cerebral asymmetry and/or relative amounts of brain tissue of a certain type, which might be required (for cultural reasons) to carry out specific psychologic functions (Fabrega, in press). A basic assumption is that the brain is like a vector, the entries of which are neural centers, and each of which is organized and functions in a uniform way across the species. This vector is judged as a potential that social experiences can draw on. Cultural influences are equated with the way entries in this vector are used, i.e., overemphasized or underemphasized. Neurologically, then, culture is linked to special emphases to which brain regions are put and to the overall pattern and arrangement that results from such differential emphases. However, there is a tendency to view much of the behavior linked to culture as a reflection of universals in the underlying "hardware" of the brain (Fabrega, in press).

Ways in which Culture Affects Brain-Behavior Relations

Three ways in which culture may affect brain-behavior relations are suggested here. First, cultural rules involving behavior and child rearing may, in a purely mechanical sense, regulate which physical environmental stimuli impinge on the newborn and on the developing infant (and to what degree). In this model, any cultural meaning that the stimulations may have is not considered important. Physical environmental agents typically are studied by neural scientists, and, to varying degrees, each (given sufficient under- or overload conditions) can be expected to affect neural development and function, and also, by implication, can affect behavior. The extent to which such stimuli must be controlled in order to produce discernible effects on adult animal behavior is variable. Whether human infants are ordinarily subject to analogous levels of under- or overstimulation is questionable, and the possibility that culture (which is viewed by many as an adaptive system) could adversely (maladaptively) program physical stimuli that are required for "normal" brain maturation raises philosophical questions. Nonetheless, on logical grounds alone, one should allow for this possibility.

Complementing this more or less mechanical view of cultural influences, is a dynamic view, in which the rationale behind cultural conventions in child-rearing practices plays an influential role. Parental influences reflect a code, which is internalized by the infant, and which then helps to regulate which level and/or pattern of stimuli is attended to, selected, processed, and integrated in the higher levels of the nervous system. This influence might take place, not in primary sensory areas, but rather in secondary association areas, where intermodal integrations and transformations are believed to take place. Initially, speech may be learned verbally from the caregivers, nonverbally (emotively, through such activities as cooing, touching, fondling, and directing) and later through the acquisition of actual language and speech. Stimuli from the environment may be considered "packaged," or ordered in a meaningful way for the infant. Much brain maturation takes place under the influence of social stimulations, the cultural meanings of which are not yet evident to the infant. Moreover, there are obvious limits to the extent to which neural representations of social symbols can filter physical stimuli and tune the nervous system. This effect of culture on brain functioning is clearly evident in the language that the infant eventually learns, and, as Condon and Sander (1974) have suggested in the prelinguistic stage as well. Moreover, culture and language together influence the way that a person comes to recognize and like music, the way that he shows emotion, and, to some extent, the way that he construes space and orients himself spatially. It may be that, in an analogous way, language and cultural conventions regulate the way other brain capacities come to be realized, such as those for taste, emotion, pain, and other bodily states that are given cultural significance. So-called higher cortical capacities (such as those underlying language) govern not only abstract (semantic) meaning, but also hedonic meaning (the affective, or emotional), which implicates subcortical structures. In contemporary interpretations of human brain organization, emphasis is given to the various brains (for example, protomammalian and limbic) that are seen as somehow fused together. In these accounts, emphasis is given to the role that language, and therefore culture, plays in modifying the functions of the ancestral brain (MacLean, 1973).

A final model of how cultural influences might affect the organization of the brain and behavior is suggested by an adult who migrates to a new social group and who comes to adopt its social practices. Such an individual would no doubt learn a great deal (nonverbally) simply by observation and imitation, although his native language system would play an influential role in the process (through verbal introspection, rehearsal, and training). A better understanding of the conventions of the group would follow from learning its language. In both instances, neurolinguistic substrates play a critical mediating role. How and to what extent other structures and levels of the nervous system participate in this type of enculturation is not known. The literature dealing with recovery from aphasia among polyglots also contains suggestions that emotion and language performance are linked together in complex ways (Albert and Obler, 1978; Paradis, 1976).

Cultural Programming of Brain-Behavior Relations

One way of conceptualizing the gap between brain organization and other cultural conventions and symbols is provided by McNeill (1979), who draws heavily on the developmental ideas of Piaget (Flavell, 1963; Piaget, 1959). McNeill focuses on speech (not on culture or language), defining it as a form of motor activity that is dominated and coordinated by thought processes. He posits that the executives in charge of speech are *sensorimotor* ideas or concepts that are representable as sensorimotor action schemata.

As articulated by Piaget, human infants are endowed naturally with a basic capacity for cognition and for language. These capacities, although innate, lie dormant during the early months of development when elementary sensorimotor actions are prominent. During the sensorimotor period of development, cognitive functioning in a child is one means for organizing motor action. Action schemata, or neurologic templates for motor action, are, in essence, the source of meaning to the child for events that involve him and the world. Sensorimotor ideas thus constitute *units of meaning* that emerge ontogenetically from action schemata involving the child's own sensorimotor behavior. As illustrated by McNeill, ideas that can be represented as sensorimotor action schemata include such things as event, location, action, entity, and person.

During the first year of life, there is an elaboration of sensorimotor schemata. New schemata are developed and coordination between these is established. At this stage, the speech of the child includes single word utterances. During the second year, sensorimotor action schemata are said to be interiorized. Thus, although the schema remains in close contact with the action structurally, the actual motor performances associated with the action schemata become less and less important. In essence, the schema is differentiated from the overt action, resulting in an imitation or image of the action. Actions are then said to be mentally representable. Children produce utterances containing more than one word upon transition from the sensorimotor period to the representation period, when schemata are interiorized.

The emergence of patterned speech in a child thus coincides with the process of interiorization and indicates that the child can now represent actions in speech and in thought. At the end of the sensorimotor period there is a natural basis for the evolution of minimal units of speech production that are based on meaning; that is, units of meaning that are pronounced physically as wholes. The child at this time acquires the ability to motorically produce sensorimotor action schemata for cognition, which in turn organize the action schema for speech production. In this manner, speech, a form of motor activity that is innate and that develops during a critical period of development, is linked, on the one hand, with the earlier semantics of sensorimotor actions, and, on the other, with the later semantics of cognition.

Sensorimotor ideas can be detected in the speech of adults. Conversely, the semantic arrangements detectable in adult speech utterances are evident in the speech of children. The similarities in the semantics of child and adult speech imply an isomorphism between adult language structures and children's cognitions. As an example, the sentence "I place my trust in my doctor's ability" refers to an abstract idea, yet, at the same time, contains the sensorimotor idea of location (i.e., the "thing," trust, is placed in the "place," called ability). Sensorimotor ideas like location are thought by McNeill (1979) to play a key role in speech production, because they control articulatory movements and serve as elements of thought. During the phase of development following the sensorimotor period, the child gradually acquires the ability to extend the meaning of sensorimotor ideas so that they come to represent increasingly abstract ideas. The process whereby sensorimotor ideas are extended to meanings that are no longer strictly sensorimotor is termed by McNeill as *semiotic extension.* The following three sentences illustrate levels of abstraction that depict the process of semiotic extension:

1. The doctor felt my pulse. [an idea of an event]
2. The lab results arrived. [no personal causation but still a physical event (minimal abstraction)]
3. I will place my trust in my doctor's ability. [an abstract event that still conveys the idea of an event]

The process of semiotic extension is gradually set up as a child's cognitive growth proceeds. During ontogenesis, new linguistic abilities emerge to provide the basis for the semiotic extension, which, in essence, is set up by the process of cognitive growth. According to this view, linguistic abilities are developed and used in response to the growth of cognition, and this developmental process constitutes *cognitive determinism.*

McNeill claims that during the development of higher cerebral functions, such as language and thought (and during the execution of these same functions in adults), there exists both a linguistic and a cognitive determinism. *Cognitive determinism* refers to the process by which cognitive abilities develop and elaborate and come to influence and make use of language. The same process takes place during the production of adult speech, which is produced in response to cognition. On the other hand, *linguistic determinism* refers to the process by which the language structure, through constraints of word order and syntax, "forces" a distinctive conceptual orientation on the speaker during speech production. In a sense, during the production of a speech segment, semiotic extension takes place whenever the literal meaning of the speech segment is not entirely representable at a sensorimotor level. The kind of extension of meaning that takes place is influenced by the types of linguistic devices available to the speaker. In essence, the structure and also the semantics of a person's language set up a distinctive type of mental attitude or state in the speaker.

McNeill illustrates linguistic determinism by comparing the way in which the English and Japanese languages handle the description of events. In using English, a speaker adopts what is termed an *operative conceptual orientation* when he chooses the direct object of a verb. This active form of expression is natural in English. The same idea can be expressed in the passive form, but requires the use of special syntactic devices. When the passive form is used for expression, the speaker's conceptual orientation is receptive. In Japanese, an opposite state of affairs exists. In this case, if the speaker uses what is termed the *neutral* form of expression, his or her conceptual orientation is receptive. Thus, neutral object verb relations "force" a receptive orientation on the Japanese speaker. A Japanese speaker can use the special syntactic device of nominalization to express events from an operative orientation. In summary, a typical contemplative or interpretive attitude is generated in the mind of a speaker during the flow of language, which bears a relation to preferred patterns of expression natural to that language. Thus, in the English speaker, the operative orientation of the verb-object relation is natural and creates the idea in the mind that *actions* have logical priority over objects. In the Japanese speaker, the receptive orientation is more natural and seems to generate the idea that *objects* are logically prior to actions.

CULTURE AND THE MANIFESTATIONS OF PSYCHIATRIC ILLNESS

Culture-Bound or Culture-Specific Disorders

For well over the last half century, first anthropologists and then psychiatrists have been interested in the nature of certain behavior disturbances that have been observed in specific societies or regions of the world. Most of these disturbances (variously called culture-bound syndromes or disorders) are familiar, and they include bena bena, amok, koro, susto, Windigo psychosis, and Arctic hysteria. Some of the properties of these syndromes include 1) abrupt onset, 2) relatively short duration (days, but seldom weeks, although information here is notoriously weak), and 3) absence of what psychiatrists term a *formal thought disturbance*. In some instances, persons afflicted show unusual mental changes and hyperactivity. Although the behavior can seem bizarre, it must be judged as reasonably organized. In other words, the behavior in question makes sense to the group. In fact, it is the coherence and pattern inherent in the manifestations of these disturbances that renders them interesting and important. Some of the disturbances are characterized by mental symptoms, the content of which is highly specific (for example, Koro—the fear of the penis disappearing) and in some instances symbolic (Windigo—possession by a mythologically important spirit, leading to a craving for human flesh, and eventually to cannibalism).

One dominant opinion about the culture-bound syndromes is that they are in some way reactive to sociocultural circumstances, and that they are atypical variations of psychogenic disturbances, which are believed to have a very wide distribution in human populations anyway (Yap, 1974). The words *reactive* and *psychogenic* raise problems for anyone trying to formulate an understanding of psychiatric illness in neurobiologic terms; the words, as it were, block out the nervous system. That the nervous system is grossly affected in some varieties and instances of culture-bound disturbances is very clear, because persons afflicted sometimes show features of a toxic or confusional psychosis with an impairment in the level of consciousness that is followed by amnesia. In other instances, a phobic or obsessive hyperalerted state without impaired consciousness is found. Little more can be said about the neuropsychiatric aspects of culture-bound syndromes. There is a poverty of information about phenomenology and behavioral manifestations of the culture-bound disturbances; relatively few firsthand, in-depth, and clinically relevant descriptions of the culture-bound syndromes exist. Moreover, discussions about neurologic substrates are almost totally lacking. A recent critical review of the literature dealing with the concept, supporting evidence for, and validity of, the so-called atypical psychoses concludes that problems of methodology, sampling, and diagnosis preclude drawing firm generalizations about the nature of these psychoses. The reviewer includes in his analysis so-called culture-bound syndromes (Manschreck and Petri, 1978; Pfeiffer, Chapter 8, this volume).

In general, culture-bound syndromes raise basic questions about the nature of psychiatric disease and illness. Because the disturbances are so radically different in manifestations, their mere existence underlines the important role of culture in providing content and organization to behavior disturbances. The specificity of the content of the culture-bound syndromes has had the effect of drawing attention to social and psychodynamic influences. Conversely, the neurobiological basis of them has been all but neglected. Yet, insofar as one finds reference to manifestations like level of consciousness, confusion, amnesia, and attention in some instances, one is forced to look into the matter of brain-behavior relations and cultural programming. In reflecting on the culture-bound syndromes, two classes of phenomena that cannot be adequately bridged in contemporary behavioral neurology or in neuropsychiatry are evident: a range of culturally interpretable behaviors varying in degree of organization and an altered state of brain function (which varies as to visibility).

Major Psychiatric Disorders

Schizophrenia There is a large literature in anthropology and psychiatry that deals with the role of culture in the manifestations of the major psychiatric disorders (Al-Issa, 1977; Gharagozlou and Behin, 1979; Katz et al., 1978; Odejide, 1979; Waxler, 1974). One traditional perspective is that behaviors that are viewed as pathological in one culture may be viewed as entirely normal in another culture. This perspective seems to totally deny the possibility that psychiatric disorders possess any universal aspects. A related perspective is that cultural factors can mask the manifestations of psychosis and can even protect certain individuals (such as Shamans) who suffer from specific psychiatric disorders. Although this perspective does not deny possible universal aspects of psychosis, it argues for a relativistic emphasis regarding their meaning. In recent years these old relativistic perspectives have been severely undermined. Two lines of attack have been prominent: one stems from an increasing appreciation of the neurobiological aspects of psychosis (for example, schizophrenia) and the other stems from a scrutiny of data from cross-cultural field studies dealing with the social interpretations of psychiatric disorders (J. M. Murphy, 1976; Stevens, 1973).

Murphy's article (1976) in particular seems to suggest that the neurobiologic changes of schizophrenia produce changes in behavior that will inevitably be judged as illness (not as deviance, or shamanism, or eccentricity). It is important to keep in mind that the argument of Murphy is directed at the extremist claims of a few labeling theorists (who use phrases like "specious," "fictive," and "culture boundedness" to describe schizophrenia). Moreover, the material reviewed in Murphy's article is based largely on judgments about severe, chronic, and deteriorated forms of schizophrenia. In brief, as Edgerton (1969) has implied, it is in no way inconsistent to believe that schizophrenia has a neurobiological basis, that severe and chronic forms of schizophrenia (and other forms of insanity-madness) are consistently judged as illness across societies and historical epochs, and that sociocultural factors are critically important in affecting both the manifestations of psychiatric disorders and the social responses to them.

To illustrate the importance of language and cultural factors in schizophrenia, one can use as an example the so-called first-rank symptoms, which many believe constitute sufficient conditions that enable one to diagnose the disease in Western nations. These symptoms include having audible thoughts; experiencing that one's thoughts are being withdrawn or inserted into one's mind by others; experiencing the diffusion or broadcasting of thoughts; experiencing one's feelings, impulses, or actual actions as somehow alien or externally controlled; and having a delusional mood and/or a delusional perception. These psychological experiences, it is claimed, constitute the fundamental symptoms of schizophrenia. Level of social functioning is not an explicit component of these symptoms, although it is implied that this is likely to be impaired. Koehler (1979) has recently discussed first-rank symptoms as embracing three types of continua. Specifically, he posits a delusional continuum, a passivity continuum, and a sense deception continuum. Rather than constituting basic indicators of schizophrenia per se, the phenomena described by Koehler can be viewed as implicating basic Western assumptions about human action and social reality. It may be the case that, among Western people, the neurobiologic changes of schizophrenia produce manifestations that include, phenomenologically, the eroding or blurring of these particular assumptions.

A working assumption can be that the first-rank symptoms of schizophrenia are partly based on cultural conventions about the self. These symptoms imply that, to a large extent, persons are independent beings whose bodies and minds are separated from each other and function autonomously. In particular, the symptoms imply that, under ordinary conditions, external influences do not operate on and influence an individual. Thoughts are recurring inner happenings that the self "has"; thoughts, feelings, and actions are separable things that, together, account for self-identity; thoughts and feelings are silent and exquisitely private; one's body is independent of what one feels or thinks; and one's body, feelings, and impulses have a purely naturalistic basis and cannot be modified by outside supernatural agents. In brief, contemporary Western psychology articulates a highly differentiated mentalistic self that is highly individuated and that looks out on an objective, impersonal, and naturalistic world. It is based on this psychology (the Western cultural perspective) that schizophrenic symptoms are articulated.

All of the assumptions that underlie the first-rank symptoms—which together provide a rationale for their pathological nature—seem linked to

Western notions about human psychology and causality. Any careful ethnography of the way that simpler people explain phenomena, account for human action, and delineate personal identity indicates ethnocentric components in these assumptions. Many such simpler people believe in the constant interconnection between the natural and the preternatural, between the bodily and the mental, and between the various dimensions and contents of human awareness that are arbitrarily set apart in Western psychology. If, in fact, people already believe themselves to be affected by external influences, and if they sense and experience these influences constantly and accommodate themselves in various ways to the necessary connection that they believe exists between feeling, thinking, bodily activity, and external control, then how will the "basic lesion" of schizophrenia show itself behaviorally? In short, which of the behavioral descriptors of schizophrenia is one not likely to see, and which ones is one likely to see different versions of, in the event that the assumptive world of the person who has the basic lesion rests on highly different premises about self, behavior, and causality? It should be clear that the claim here is not that unusual psychological experiences or social behaviors are not part of schizophrenia, but rather that the form and meaning that the experiences and behaviors take in modern European culture (reviewed by Koehler, 1979) are partly an outcome of the ways in which the self is constructed there.

Depression   A recent review of the literature on the manifestations of depression (Engelsmann, Chapter 10, this volume; Marsella, 1980) points to cultural differences, a finding consistent with the writings of other culturally oriented psychiatrists. The review encompasses literature involving clinical observations, culture-specific disorders, symptoms among patients matched by diagnosis and sample, international surveys, and factor analytic studies. Of special importance is the finding that psychological aspects of depression (such as depressed mood, guilt, feelings of self-deprecation, and purposelessness) seen in the Western world are often absent in non-Western societies. Somatic aspects were noted frequently in the reviewed research, regardless of the culture studied. Often it was only when non-Westerns become westernized that the anticipated psychological aspects of depression were found to emerge. Depressed somatic functioning—*vegetative depression*—thus did not seem to have the corresponding depressed mental experience that was observed in the West. Whether a depression in the operation of psychological processes was found was not reported. If the consequences and implications of depression for an individual are affected by the quality of mental experiences correlated with the depression, different types of social behaviors can be anticipated.

One could use the conclusions of these reviews of empirical studies (that is, the similarity in vegetative phenomena) to argue that a uniform set of changes in depression affects subcortical structures of the brain. On the other hand, differences in the psychological and social manifestations of depression imply differences in the organization and function of the cortical substrates that more generally subserve language, thought, experience, and social behavior.

The study by Leff (1973, 1977) is related to this question of the character of psychosocial behavior changes in depressive illness in different cultures. He used reliable information collected (by means of the Present State Examination) on patients hospitalized in different psychiatric centers. Psychiatrists' ratings of patients' verbal reports and social behavior thus constituted the data base. Scores on three emotion variables were correlated: anxiety and depression, depression and irritability, and anxiety and irritability. Leff compared the correlations of emotions across a number of sociocultural groups of patients, which he classified as belonging to developed and developing nations. In using correlations between emotion scores, Leff posited that a correlation of +1.0 between two emotions represented the least possible discrimination between the two emotions. On the other hand, a correlation of –1.0 represented the greatest possible discrimination between the two emotions. One could, of course, say that both types of emotions could be present, but implicit in Leff's reasoning is that a similar level of overlap of symptoms probably exists in these centers, and that the size of the correlations reflects the degree of discrimination of the patients. His results show an interesting pattern of differences. As an example, China and Nigeria subjects showed the highest intercorrelations. As predicted, patients from developing countries showed significantly higher correlations in all three pairs of emotions when compared to patients from developed countries. Leff concluded that groups (societies) differ in ease of differentiation between emotional states, and that this is because of relative availability of linguistic categories for the description of subjective states.

Explanation of the appearance of depression is facilitated if one distinguishes between emotion as a basic category of human experience, and emotion as a symbolic domain that is lexically coded, which languages capture in a direct and explicit way. The indications are that emotions are probably universal and that the structure of affective experience also has universal features (Ekman, 1972). However, the prevalence of linguistic labels for emotions may vary in frequency across societies. By means of lexically encoded emotional terms, one is able to speak and think more precisely and elaborately about internal subjective states. In a fundamental way, the domain of emotion and the domain of the self have impact on each other semantically. Besides serving as a means for qualifying the state of the self, emotion words can also be used to qualify other types of phenomena. In Western culture social situations and bodily states are often qualified by using emotional terms.

If a semantic domain is richly encoded (if words of a particular category are prominent) in a group's language, one can assume that the domain is important in a social and cultural sense. The domain, in other words, not only has been clearly demarcated from related domains, but it has been differentiated as well. This seems to be the case with emotion in Western culture, with the effect that social relations, bodily experience, and the self are linked semantically and in an elaborate way through emotion and related mentalistic terms.

These points illustrate the connectedness that exists between things described as biological as opposed to things described as cultural. In Western populations, neurobiologic correlates of depression and conditions of social disarticulation produce behaviors elaborated along mentalistic and emotional lines. It is very likely that this is partly a consequence of what anthropologists term the *psychic unity* of man. This is to say that all people, regardless of culture, are likely to feel down and bad when things go awry for them, either socially or physically. However, to a certain extent, the similarity between depression and social disarticulation is partly a consequence of the fact that the psychic sphere, considered as a semantic domain, is richly encoded and symbolically important in Western cultures. The fact that our (lay, cultural) concepts about the self draw heavily on emotion and related mentalistic premises serves to make the appearance of these conditions more ambiguous.

A review of the literature suggests cultural differences in the manifestations of depression. Psychological and mental symptoms seem to be less prominent (and/or less differentiated) in certain simpler societies. One way of explaining these differences is to point to the influence of the (culturally dominant) psychologic perspective, which is heavily mentalistic and which elaborates semantically on emotion as a descriptor of the self. According to this view, it is not strictly correct to say that depression is different in other cultures; one could also say that depression is different in *Western* culture. When considering the major psychiatric illnesses (like schizophrenia and depression) one needs to keep in mind that at issue are psychological and social (illness) behaviors that necessarily are colored by cultural factors. This means that our view of these illnesses is, to an indeterminate extent, ethnocentric.

Theoretical Possibilities

It seems that a number of neuropsychiatric syndromes or diseases would serve as useful objects of study for someone hoping to clarify the kind of influences culture might have on brain-behavior relations. One neuropsychiatric problem that may serve as an illustration involves so-called temporal lobe epilepsy (Blumer, 1975).

A basic orientation of research is that, in one sense, temporal lobe epilepsy involves relatively specific neuronal excitations in certain areas of the brain. However, in these specific areas are encoded basic routines that carry the experiential base of a people's way of life, and neuronal activation in them is likely to elicit behaviors that reflect this experience. It is very likely that much of the ictal behavior of the person with temporal lobe epilepsy will display characteristics that are culturally invariant. Thus, one anticipates little cross-cultural variability in things like automatisms of the face and mouth, confused and dazed wanderings, epigastric and abdominal sensations, and unformed hallucinations—all of which are typically described as accompaniments of seizures. Such phenomena are thought of as reflexive and unmotivated, and stereotyped and elementary in a visceral and sensorimotor sense.

Phenomena that reflect higher forms of cortical activation, such as formed hallucinations, illusions, dyscognitive states, and affective experiences, seem to present intriguing material for the culturally oriented neurobiologist. In a trivial sense, cultural differences are likely to be manifest in the content of such mental phenomena; for example, what an individual hears, sees, or misperceives. Cultural differences are also likely to be manifest in the general interpretations that are given to those experiences, both by the person and by co-members of the group. Cultural differences are likely in these instances because content and interpretations are obviously based on native categories of meaning or world views. On the other hand, cultural differences may also be manifest in more subtle ways. Thus, the structure or form of these mental experiences is likely to contain interesting clues. For example, in Western culture, formed auditory hallucinations are often heard as voices speaking about the self; these hallucinations reflect themes of general cultural significance (such as sex and violence); and they often appear in the first or third person and may involve the actual name of the person. If similar types of formed auditory hallucinations occur cross-culturally, questions arise, such as in which grammatical form do they appear, where are they actually heard, what dimension of experience and self do they draw on, and do they involve actual naming? More generally, how are formed auditory hallucinations structured among peoples who speak languages that are sharply different in a grammatical sense and among whom conceptions of personhood are also sharply different? A key point is that, in one sense, a hallucination of this type represents a limbic seizure spread, but, in another sense, it represents a reading of the way the brain codes experience structurally. In other words, self, other, and a symbolic view of the world are fused in the hallucination. Assessments of how hallucinations are interpreted give a surface view of culture, whereas structural analysis of many such hallucinations provides deeper views. Such analysis might reveal both the kinds of coordinates of experience that, in an elementary sense, are represented neurologically and the types of emotions associated with them. In a similar fashion inquiries could be made about the uniformities versus the differences in structure of formed visual hallucinations and in distortions of the sense of time (for example, déjà vu and jamais vu), which are frequently seen during ictal states. Are the form and content of these disturbances universal or might they differ among people who have different conventions about time and space?

Electrical stimulation of the human hippocampal formation and of the amygdala is known to evoke emotional phenomena. However, the category of phenomena seems to be independent of the exact site stimulated, and instead seems to be related to who was being stimulated (Halgren et al., 1978). It is thus reasonable to state that the type of emotional reactions (such as anxiety versus pleasure versus anger) found during ictal states may bear a relation to the modal patterns of emotional regulation and expression that are prevalent in a group. Of course, what is found to be pleasurable, frightening, or irritating will differ cross-culturally. However, one must inquire whether the manner in which these emotional experiences are structured and enacted also differs (for example, the psychophysiology of the emotion, or the way in which self or others are incorporated in the emotion). Whatever emotion "is" involves a subjective experience of some type that includes sensations about the body, a linguistic reading of the experience, and an enacted routine (emotional expression). Emotions bear the impact of the specific types of situations and relations that a person has been involved in, and the categories of experience that a group conventionally endorses as appropriate to situations and relations are thus also important in how emotions are construed. The study of emotion cross-culturally is beset by methodological problems linked to the differential ways in which language and cognitive categories relate to subjective phenomena and bodily sensations (Leff, 1973, 1977). The comparative study of ictal emotional states may provide a way of better articulating the influence of these categories. Finally, an assumption in the study of emotion is that both pancultural and culture-specific influences play a role in the nonverbal expression of emotion (Ekman, 1972). Cross-cultural studies of emotional expression during ictal states might also reveal clues as to how these two influences are neurologically encoded.

Of equal if not greater interest to the culturally oriented neurobiologist are the kinds of changes in interictal behavior that are observed in patients with temporal lobe epilepsy. Patients with this disorder are said to show personality and social behavioral traits that may very well be a consequence of repeated and more or less random limbic system activation (Bear and Fedio, 1977; Penry and Daly, 1976; Waxman and Geschwind, 1975). For example, temporal lobe epilepsy patients have been described as showing religiosity, hypergraphia, deepened affects, hypermoralism, changes in sexual interest and activity, and a humorless sobriety. Such behavior changes may be judged as the long-term (sociopsychological) effects of limbic system stimulation in brains whose functions already bear the influences of Western cultural conventions about emotion, thinking, action, bodily experience, and worldly–other worldly governance. Such clinical descriptions inform one about the disorder and about the organization, mode of functioning, and transformation of the brains in which the disorder occurs. It is thus reasonable to inquire about the kinds of personality and behavior changes that might be observed among persons with temporal lobe foci who operate in terms of different religious and moral conventions, whose patterns of discourse differ, who verbally and cognitively code emotions differently, who place altogether different values on self and aggression, and who are unable to record in writing their unusual experiences. In this context, a personality change should be viewed as a shorthand way of describing the cultural logic that behavior takes on when basic affective states underlying approach and avoidance are activated randomly over a protracted period of time. It is no doubt the case that the amygdala and the related limbic structures emotionally tone and contextualize complex environmental stimuli that arise in conjunction with social relations and actions of various types (Gloor, 1978). However, the rationale, significance, and possibly the organization of the resulting experiences will more than likely bear the influence of cultural conventions. Continued random stimulation of these areas can be expected to produce culturally specific emotional experiences, which may in time come to transform (in an equally specific way) the behaviors and interests of the persons. The nature of this transformation should inform one about basic elements of emotional experience and about their social consequences; specifically, it should indicate what profiles of emotions are encoded and the significance accorded to them, how emotions affect conceptions of self-other and social relations, and how culture normalizes and/or molds the expression of emotional experience over time.

NEUROBIOLOGIC AND SOCIOCULTURAL ASPECTS OF PSYCHIATRIC DISORDERS

Areas of Concern to Neuroscientists versus Social Scientists

A review of the literature in cross-cultural psychology suggests that universals exist in cognition and in perception (Fabrega, in press). Neuropsychological differences linked to bilingualism and writings systems in the Japanese as well as differences involving bodily states are tantalizing and suggestive, but they imply mainly quantitative differences in the way specific brain regions function and are used by culture, and they need to be viewed in the context of pervasive uniformities in function (Sasanuma, 1975; Shapiro and Watanabe, 1972; Weisenberg, 1977; Yamadori, 1975). Overriding universals in brain-behavior relations seem to be inconsistent with the material reviewed dealing with culture-bound syndromes that suggests differences in manifestations of major psychiatric illnesses. How is one to resolve, or at least to explain, such an apparent inconsistency between universals and cultural differences?

A consideration of the basic aims and modes of inquiry of a neurobiologically as opposed to a culturally oriented psychiatrist can provide the beginnings of an explanation. A neuroscientist intent on demonstrating cultural influences on brain-behavior relations needs first to show that an association exists between a culturally relevant situation or stimulus and a brain event, and/or that an association exists between a stimulus or situation and a behavior known to be an outcome of a specific brain event. Each of the three classes of phenomena (stimulus, brain event, and behavior) needs to be clearly specified and measured. Given this prerequisite, it is necessary for the neuroscientist to show that there are differences on the relevant measures across groups of individuals who belong to different language and cultural communities. The behavior involved would probably include a motor response of some sort, with the researcher manipulating an expectancy based on the culture of the individual. In this experimental context, the subject would be required to attend and/or to make a decision of some sort. To show associations between culture and brain-behavior relations, the neuroscientist is forced to reduce observations to very discrete phenomena.

This type of logic is essentially also applicable to the cognitive psychologist intent on demonstrating that cultural groups differ in ways of perceiving, making decisions, remembering, discriminating, or problem solving. The psychologist is required to make his text understandable and appropriate to the subject so that it motivates and engages equivalent cognitive processes. Moreover, he must ensure that responses of his subjects are discrete and unambiguous so that they can be reliably measured. When the neuroscientist evaluates behavior, he or she, too, will be guided by these restrictions. Key elements in the strategy of the neuroscientist or of the cognitive psychologist are thus *abstraction* and *specificity*. Claims about cultural differences in neurologic or psychologic processes involve physical measures and/or behaviors that are highly discrete and isolated out of a social context.

A neurologically oriented psychiatrist who is pursuing the question of possible cultural differences in psychiatric illness can adopt the strategy of the neuroscientist or cognitive psychologist and concentrate on highly discrete phenomena. If he or she found differences on measures of psychiatric illness that could be related to brain events or functions, this would allow the claim to be made that the brains of the persons with the disease-illness were different across cultural groups and/or that the disease-illness itself was different in the groups.

Phenomena ordinarily studied by culturally oriented psychiatrists are at a far different level of abstraction than those studied by neurologically oriented ones. Thus, mental symptoms (such as delusions and hallucinations), social adjustment changes, rate of onset and/or duration of psychotic disorganization are far removed from the discrete and abstract items that engage the neural scientist and/or cognitive psychologist. In fact, culturally oriented psychiatrists tend to be interested in demonstrating differences in the configuration of psychiatric illness as a whole. That is, it is the logic or psychosocial rationale inherent in illness, viewed as an experiential and whole behavioral structure, that seems to claim the interests of the researcher. Such a psychiatrist seeks to demonstrate that the illness, viewed either in terms of the ill person or in terms of group co-members, makes sense only when semantic aspects (its context or meaning) are taken into consideration. In other words, it is the symbolic dimension of social and psychological behaviors that claims principal interest in this instance. A useful way to capture these differences in orientation is to say that culturally oriented psychiatrists are drawn to features of illness (to the symbolic dimension of psychosocial behavior changes), whereas neuro-scientifically oriented psychiatrists are drawn to features of disease (to the physical changes in the brain).

Conceptualizing the Gap Between Disease (Brain Changes) and Illness (Behavior Changes)

The manifestations of psychiatric illness (PI) are the outcome of physical disturbances in the functioning of brain structures. These structures regulate arousal, attention, sensory inhibition, motivation, and mood, and disturbances in them produce widespread behavioral effects that include activation of the motor programs for speech cognition. Because these programs are culturally contextualized (e.g., via the semantic memory system), brain changes underlying psychiatric illness are associated with experiences and actions (such as moods, attitudes, thoughts, and behavioral dispositions) that bear the imprint of language and culture. A number of factors need to be dealt with separately in order to explain the way that disease changes in the central nervous system lead to the psychosocial behavior changes of psychiatric illness.

In semiotic theory, a sign is a physical part of, or something integral to, that to which it refers. *Signs of disease* can thus mean phenomena that physically indicate disease. In the case of general medical diseases, this would include such things as swellings, discolorations, lumps, and emanations from body orifices. Many signs of disease are not visible to the naked eye, such as those just mentioned, but rather are hidden from view and are observed or measured by the use of instruments that, in effect, extend one's power of observation. However, the phenomena observed and recorded are equally physical and also constitute signs of disease (such as EEG changes).

Signs of neuropsychiatric diseases include changes in level and sense of awareness and in sensorimotor behaviors. Sense of awareness and well-being include general cognitive functions (mental clarity, discrimination, and alertness). The word *sensorimotor* is used here to refer to behaviors involving reflexes, postural changes, muscular tone, involuntary movements, coordinated muscular contraction, changes in sensation, and covert (hidden) vegetative responses involving the viscera, blood vessels, and organs. The behavior changes observed in cases of aphasia, apraxia, agnosia, amnestic disorders, and the disconnection syndromes, can be thought of as sensorimotor in nature. That is, the behaviors follow directly from a physical disorder in the brain, and the symbolic aspects are relatively unimportant. Many psychiatrists think of the behavioral changes of depression (psychomotor retardation and sleep disturbance) and of schizophrenia (first-rank symptoms) as sensorimotor in nature. Thus, sensorimotor behaviors would also be considered as signs of disease.

Bodily perceptions are private, subjective experiences that the individual links to his or her body and that are reported through language. All languages provide users with a means of describing bodily perception; the data for this description are changes in the peripheral and central nervous system (a product of pancultural uniformities in the way the body is structured anatomically and neurologically). Lexical universals have been demonstrated regarding body part terminologies, with the body viewed as a concrete object in space, but little comparative data exist about description of internal body states.

The language used to describe body changes relates somehow to beliefs about illness and about the self that are acquired by the individual from his social group. Beliefs and orientations of an individual must conform to uniformities in the perceptual system and to the organization that exists in nature, but they also bear the mark of cultural conventions. Beliefs, orientations, and cognitive processes more generally serve to pattern, order, and regulate the way that persons view their physical and social environment and the way that they behave socially.

Beliefs and orientations about illness and the self are influenced by the theories about illness that a group endorses and also by their theory of personhood; each of these theories draws on, and is complementary to, the other. Both types of theories can be viewed as systems of meaning that are grounded in symbolic conventions. They are thus products of the individual's culture and social experiences. Persons from different cultures are assumed to endorse different theories about self and about illness; these theories influence how individuals interpret disease changes and how they behave and act while ill.

Medically relevant environmental happenings also have impact on illness-related experiences of a person. These happenings are proximal or distal in time, they are linked either to the physical or to the social environment, and their importance is partly dictated by the native theories of illness and personhood. In other words, what is happening to a person currently and what has happened to him in the past both can play a role in how a person behaves while ill, and can affect what he thinks of the illness, what he worries about, and how he will respond. How a person interprets social happenings is influenced by his culture, by his social position, and by his education, among other things—the same kinds of factors that influence his theory of illness and of personhood.

In summary, the term *illness* refers to the totality of social and psychologic behavior changes (including any signs or physical effects of disease), which, on conventional grounds, are judged to have medical significance in a particular society (for instance, the behavior is disvalued or requires corrective action). A society identifies many different types of illnesses. From a biomedical standpoint, the structure and content of any one type of illness result from biophysiologic as well as from sociocultural factors, some of which have been enumerated. With this material as background, one can say that the structure and content of a psychiatric illness (such as depression or schizophrenia) may be explained as an outcome of distinctive kinds of disease processes (perhaps involving neurotransmitter changes in subcortical centers or asymmetries in hemispheric control mechanisms) that physically alter the regulation and control of (sensorimotor) behaviors subserving affect and/or attention. However, from a social and psychologic point of view, the content and structure of this behavior is an outcome of cultural factors (involving such things as symbolic conventions about the self, the body, cosmology, and illness happenings in the world). The factors involving symbolic conventions account for the manifestations or social appearance of psychiatric illness.

According to this formulation of psychiatric illness, the substantive nature of illness will vary to the same extent that a people's theory of self, of illness, and of environmental happenings varies. Such a view of illness draws attention to the social and cultural embeddedness of illness. Rather than being something abstracted out of a social context—a characterization appropriate to disease and to signs of disease—psychiatric illness encompasses attitudes, expectations, and beliefs of others about persons who are psychiatrically ill. To the extent that cultural conventions about (psychiatric) illness encourage support and acceptance of the ill person and promote expectations of recovery, and to the extent that they discourage rejection, stigmatization, and expectations of permanent deficit, to that extent may such conventions be expected to promote continued social functioning and participation of the ill person.

Accordingly, a view of psychiatric illness that draws attention to its psychosocial (behavioral) manifestations and to the centrality of cultural conventions in programming these manifestations necessarily includes in its purview the long-range consequences of illness. In such a view, issues such as the labeling of responses to psychiatric illness (which are typically thought of as social and outside the confines of what illness "really is"), governed by the same types of conventions that govern the programming of the manifestations. Intrinsic to the postulate that culture affects the expression of psychiatric illness is that it also affects social responses, and, with these, the duration and course of the illness.

REFERENCES

Albert, M. L., and Obler, L. K. 1978. The Bilingual Brain. Academic Press, Inc., New York.

Al-Issa, I. 1977. Social and cultural aspects of hallucinations. Psychol. Bull. 84:570–587.

Bear, D. M., and Fedio, P. 1977. Quantitative analysis of interictal behavior in lobe epilepsy. Arch. Neurol. 34:454–467.

Blumer, D. 1975. Temporal lobe epilepsy and its psychiatric significance. In: D. F. Benson and D. Blumer (eds.), Psychiatric Aspects of Neurologic Disease. Grune & Stratton, New York.

Condon, W. S., and Sander, L. W. 1974. Neonate movement is synchronized with adult speech: Interactional participation and language acquisition. Science 183:99–101.

Deuel, R. K. 1977. Loss of motor habits after cortical lesions. Neuropsychologia 15:205–215.

Edgerton, R. B. 1969. On the "recognition" of mental illness. In: S. C. Plog and R. B. Edgerton (eds.), Changing Perspectives in Mental Illness. Holt, Rinehart & Winston, Inc., New York.

Ekman, P. 1972. Universals and cultural differences in facial expressions of emotions. In: J. K. Cole (ed.), Nebraska Symposium on Motivation, 1971. University of Nebraska Press, Lincoln.

Fabrega, H., Jr. 1977. Culture, behavior, and the nervous system. Annu. Rev. Anthropol. 6:419–55.

Fabrega, H., Jr. 1979. Phylogenetic precursors of psychiatric illness: A theoretical inquiry. Compr. Psychiatry 20:275–288.

Fabrega, H., Jr. Cultural programming of brain behavior relations: A neuropsychiatric emphasis. In: J. Merikangas (ed.), Brain Behavior Relations. In press.

Flavell, J. H. 1963. The Developmental Psychology of Jean Piaget. D. Van Nostrand Company, Princeton, N. J.

Geertz, C. 1973. The Interpretation of Cultures. Basic Books, Inc., New York.

Geschwind, N., Quadfasel, F. A., and Segarra, J. M. 1968. Isolation of the speech area. Neuropsychologia 6:327–340.

Gharagozlou, H., and Behin, M. T. 1979. Diagnostic evaluation of Schneider first rank symptoms of schizophrenia among 3 groups of Iranians. Compr. Psychiatry 20:242–245.

Gloor, P. 1978. Inputs and outputs of the amygdala: What the amygdala is trying to tell the rest of the brain. In: K. D. Livingston and O. Hornykiewicz (eds.), Limbic Mechanisms, pp. 189–210. Plenum Publishing Corp., New York.

Halgren, E., Walter, R. D., Cherlow, D. G., and Crandall, H. 1978. Mental phenomena evoked by the human hippocampal formation and amygdala. Brain 101:83–118.

Heilman, K. M., Schwartz, H. D., and Geschwind, N. 1975. Defective motor learning in ideomotor apraxia. Neurology 25:1018–1020.

Katz, M. M., Sanborn, K. O., Lowery, H. A., and Ching, J. 1978. Ethnic studies in Hawaii: On psychopathology and social deviance. In: L. Wynne et al. (eds.), The Nature of Schizophrenia, pp. 572–585. John Wiley & Sons, Inc., New York.

Kleinman, A. M. 1977. Depression, somatization, and the "new cross-cultural psychiatry." Soc. Sci. Med. 11:3–9.

Koehler, K. 1979. First rank symptoms of schizophrenia: Questions concerning clinical boundaries. Br. J. Psychiatry 134:236–248.

Leff, J. P. 1973. Culture and the differentiation of emotional states. Br. J. Psychiatry 123:299–306.

Leff, J. P. 1977. The cross-cultural study of emotions. Cult. Med. Psych. 1:317–350.

MacLean, P. D. 1973. A triune concept of the brain and behavior. In: T. J. Foag and D. Campbell (eds.), A Triune Concept of the Brain and Behavior. University of Toronto Press, Toronto.

McNeill, D. 1979. The Conceptual Basis of Language. Erlbaum Publishing Company, Hillsdale, N.J.

Manschreck, T. C., and Petri, M. 1978. Cult. Med. Psychiatry 2:233–268.

Marsella, A. J. 1980. Depressive experience and disorder across cultures. In: H. Triandis and J. Draguns (eds.), Handbook of Cross-Cultural Psychology. Vol. 5. Psychopathology. Allyn & Bacon, Inc., Boston.

Miles, F. A., and Evarts, E. V. 1979. Concepts of motor organization. Annu. Rev. Psychol. 30:327–362.

Mountcastle, V. B., and Edelman, G. M. 1978. The Mindful Brain. MIT Press, Cambridge, Mass.

Murphy, J. M. 1976. Psychiatric labeling in cross-cultural perspective. Science 191:1019–1028.

Odejide, A. O. 1979. Cross-cultural psychiatry: A myth or reality. Compr. Psychiatry 20:103–109.

Paradis, M. 1976. Bilingualism and aphasia. In: H. Whitaker and H. Whitaker (eds.), Studies in Neurolinguistics. Academic Press, Inc., New York.

Penry, J. K., and Daly, D. D. (eds.), 1976. Complex Partial Seizures and their Treatment. American Elsevier Publishing Company, New York.

Piaget, J. 1959. The Language and Thought of the Child. Routledge & Kegan Paul, Ltd., London.

Prince, R. 1968. The changing picture of depressive syndromes in Africa: Is it fact or diagnostic fashion? Can. J. Afr. Stud. 1:177–192.

Rosenbaum, D. A. 1977. Selective adaptation of "command neurons" in the human motor system. Neuropsychologia 15:81–91.

Sasanuma, S. 1975. Kana & Kanji processing in Japanese aphasics. Brain Lang. 2:369–383.

Shapiro, D., and Watanabe, T. 1972. Reinforcement of spontaneous electrodermal activity: A cross-cultural study in Japan. Psychophysiology 9:340–344.

Stevens, J. R. 1973. An anatomy of schizophrenia. Arch. Gen. Psychiatry 29:177–89.

Tulving, E. 1972. Episodic and semantic memory. In: E. Tulving and W. Donaldson (eds.), Organization of Memory. Academic Press, Inc., New York.

Turvey, M. T. 1975. Preliminaries to a theory of action with reference to vision. Status Report on Speech Research SR-41. Haskins Laboratories.

Warrington, E. K. 1975. The selective impairment of semantic memory. Q. J. Exp. Psychol. 27:634–657.

Waxler, N. E. 1974. Culture and mental illness—A social labeling perspective. J. Nerv. Ment. Dis. 159:379–395.

Waxman, S. C., and Geschwind, N. 1975. The interictal behavior syndrome of temporal lobe epilepsy. Arch. Gen. Psychiatry 32:1580–1586.

Weisenberg, M. 1977. Pain and pain control. Psychol. Bull. 84:1008–1044.

Williams, J. M. 1976. Synaesthetic adjectives: A possible law of semantic change. Language 52:460–479.

Witkowski, S. R., and Brown, C. H. 1978. Lexical universals. Annu. Rev. Anthropol. 7:427–451.

Yamadori, A. 1975. Ideogram reading in alexia. Brain 98:231–238.

Yap, P. M. 1974. Comparative Psychiatry: A Theoretical Framework. University of Toronto Press, Toronto.

Chapter 15

Culture and Psychosomatics

Hector Warnes and Eric D. Wittkower

It is generally agreed that the linear relationship between mind and body suggested by the term *psychosomatic* is invalid and that the so-called psychosomatic disorders are multifactorial in origin. Outstanding among nonpsychological etiological factors are hereditary constitution and harmful events, both prenatal and postnatal. The position taken by the observer concerning psychological etiological factors depends on his orientation. Halliday (1948) views psychosomatic disease against the background of a sick society. Ruesch and Bateson (1951) emphasize disturbances of communication as etiological agents. H. G. Wolff (1950a,b) focuses his attention on disturbing life situations. Dunbar (1946) correlates personality profiles with psychosomatic disorders. Alexander and French (1948) demonstrate the relationship between conflict constellation and vegetative dysfunction. Garma (1950) concentrates on the reactivation of early object relationships combined with physiological regression, while Marty, de M'Uzan, and David (1963) emphasize the importance of deficiency in fantasy life in psychosomatic patients.

Attempts have been made to establish systematic relationships between conflict constellations, personality profiles, behavioral patterns, attitudes, life events, and various psychosomatic disorders. Mead (1947) and Henry (1949) related differences in psychosomatic patterns to variations in mother-child relations and to variations in the mother-child socialization within a variety of nonliterate societies and within different family structures in Western society.

Interaction between the organism and the cultural system determines various patterns of characterological defenses, coping styles, illness behavior, response to therapy, and differential susceptibility to illness. To provide a comprehensive view of the complexity and multicausality of psychosomatic disorders, the cultural component must be included in the multitude of etiological factors.

The study of the distribution, prevalence, and frequency of disease throughout the world is the object of epidemiology. Although M. Pflanz (1971) has presented some evidence that the frequency and prevalence of illnesses vary in relation to dwelling place (city or country), social class, and occupational group, he has been skeptical about linking these differences to sociocultural factors alone and has focused mainly on methodological problems. Other investigators have given tentative and cautious interpretations of epidemiological data (Cooper, 1964; Kessel and Munro, 1964; Susser and Watson, 1971). Some investigators, such as Scotch and Geiger (1963) and Henry and Cassel (1969) have clearly underscored the importance of sociocultural factors in the etiology of essential hypertension. Groen (1970, 1971a,b) speculated on the influence of social changes on psychosomatic illnesses, which he believed were culturally induced. The data he presented were derived from transcultural experience and from observations (in Holland and in concentration camps) during World War II (Groen, 1970, 1971a,b; Eitinger, 1971).

This chapter is confined to the cultural interpretation of the epidemiological data on various psychosomatic disorders. A thorough presentation on the incidence of psychosomatic disorders according to class, age, occupation, sex, and particular social changes, such as social stress, emigration, migration to the cities, industrialization, war, disaster, and alienation are beyond the scope of this chapter.

Several cardiovascular, gastrointestinal, and respiratory cross-cultural epidemiological studies are surveyed, and tentative sociocultural and psychosomatic explanations for some of the findings are offered.

INVESTIGATIVE DIFFICULTIES

Research in investigative difficulties is scarce because of these same investigative difficulties:

1. A thorough knowledge of the cultures in which the study is to be carried out is required. Because there are few psychiatrists or anthropologists who can work competently in both fields, team cooperation, which is costly and is not easy, becomes a necessity.
2. Hospitalized patients suffering from psychosomatic disorders constitute a self-selected sample.
3. Patients suffering from psychosomatic disorders are usually admitted to medical wards and therefore are not easily accessible to psychiatrists.
4. Language difficulties may constitute a barrier to communication.
5. Psychological tests (projective tests and intelligence tests) are, to some extent, culture-bound.

6. In many developing countries, x-ray equipment and laboratory facilities for adequate physical investigation are lacking, and infectious diseases and worm infestations, which obscure the clinical picture, are rampant.
7. The small number of available psychiatrists in developing countries are not always qualified to deal with the underlying psychodynamics in psychosomatic patients.

APPROACHES, OBJECTIVES, AND METHODOLOGIES

There are two major approaches to cultural and transcultural psychosomatics: the investigator may either ask himself why, in sociocultural terms, certain psychosomatic variants occur, or, starting with sociocultural features, he may ask himself what effect these variants have on the frequency of psychosomatic disorders and on the nature of their manifestations.

The objectives of research of this kind are, among others, the determination of the total frequency of psychosomatic disorders in relation to cultural stress and of the predominance of some psychosomatic disorders in relation to established conflict constellations reinforced by prevailing value orientations. The methodology of transcultural psychosomatic research consists in the application of the same investigative technique to persons and to situations in contrasting cultures or subcultures. The investigative tools used include interviews, postmortem findings, field surveys, hospital records, psychological tests, and questionnaires. Uniformity of methodological approach is essential to ensure comparability of contrasting situations.

PROBLEMS

Problems that present themselves in research on psychosomatic disorders include the following:

1. Do psychosomatic disorders occur everywhere in the world?
2. Is their *total* frequency higher in some cultural areas than in others?
3. Is the frequency of *some* psychosomatic disorders higher in some cultural areas than in others?
4. To what extent do differences in value orientations, such as differences in family structure, role, and status of women influence the frequency of psychosomatic disorders?
5. To what extent does culture change, e.g., industrialization and urbanization, increase the frequency of psychosomatic disorders?
6. Does migration influence the rate of psychosomatic disorders?
7. Are the psychodynamics of the psychosomatic disorders that are

explored and described in patients in Europe and America equally operative in other parts of the world, such as in developing countries?

8. Which methods of treatment for psychosomatic disorders are employed in different parts of the world and what is their efficacy?

9. Which cultural strategies are likely to prevent psychosomatic disorders?

DATA OBTAINED

What data have been obtained on psychosomatic disorders? It is generally agreed that one's cultural environment has a predisposing or preventive effect on mental illness. Cultural stress factors described by Dubreuil and Wittkower (1976) pertain 1) to cultural content, such as excessive amount and intensity of taboos, value saturation, cultural polymorphism, role deprivation, cultural systems of sentiments, and basic personality structure; 2) to the broad category of social organization, namely, anomie, social rigidity, and minority status; and 3) to different types of sociocultural changes. Conversely, cultures and subcultures offer protective shelter against social anarchy and psychological isolation. Cultures provide mechanisms that alleviate the negative effects of tensions arising from the constraints imposed on individuals by social rules and inequalities— mechanisms that serve as emotional outlets—and they provide appropriate techniques and specialists for curing, isolating, or punishing individuals perceived as sick, marginal, or guilty. Consequently, one should expect that the rate of mental disorders is subject to cultural variations in relation to the presence or absence of powerful cultural stress factors. Actually, a few concrete data to this effect are available.

If it is difficult to give a correct estimate of the comparative frequency of *mental disorders* in contrasting cultures, it is even more difficult, for the reasons given, to compare the total frequency of *psychosomatic disorders* in contrasting cultures, especially if developing countries are considered. Although such differences probably exist, as postulated by Halliday for Scotland, by Ammar for Tunisia, and by Groen on a global scale, there is little evidence to prove that sociocultural factors, such as loosening of family structure, emancipation of women and children, and detribalization, can account for an increase in psychosomatic disorders. Nor is there any convincing evidence to confirm the assumption that the rate of psychosomatic disorders has increased in response to a decrease of other psychological disorders, such as conversion hysteria. The general impression is that in the big cities, for instance those of Africa, psychosomatic disorders are just as common as they are in the cities of America or Europe, but that significant differences exist in the *total* frequency of psychosomatic disorders between urban and rural areas.

We are on much firmer ground if we confine ourselves to cultural differences in specific psychosomatic disorders, and especially in those disorders whose presence can be verified by postmortem examination. Examples of cardiovascular, gastrointestinal, and respiratory disorders are given in this chapter.

CARDIOVASCULAR DISORDERS

In Jenkins' review (1977) of recent epidemiological studies of the psychosomatic aspects of coronary heart disease (CHD), "psychological and social variables and various aspects of behavioral style were clearly associated with the risk of developing arteriosclerotic and coronary heart disease." A wide range of rates of CHD incidence, prevalence, and mortality in different parts of the world was reported by Keys (1970). For the seven countries studied, the highest CHD rates in all age groups were found in Finland and in the United States, while the lowest rates were consistently found in Greece, Yugoslavia, and Japan. Even lower rates seem to prevail in Nigeria, where a series of 8,000 necropsies revealed only six myocardial infarctions involving arteriosclerosis (Jenkins, 1977). Garcia-Palmieri et al. (1972), comparing prevalence of coronary disease in Honolulu, Puerto Rico, and Framingham, Massachusetts, found that when the Framingham risk factor equation was applied to Honolulu or to Puerto Rico, twice as many CHD cases were predicted to occur as were observed.

Medalie et al. (1973) followed the cases of 10,000 Israeli government employees for five years, documenting the occurrence of myocardial infarction (MI) in immigrants from different countries. The lowest rates of MI were found among persons born in Middle Eastern countries outside Israel. The highest rates of MI occurred among immigrants from Europe. Appels (1973) has shown an overall positive correlation between the need for achievement as a cultural index and the mortality rate of arteriosclerotic and degenerative heart disease; however, he found no correlation between CHD and a nation's level of need for affiliation and power.

Death rates from cardiovascular disease, and in particular from arteriosclerotic and degenerative heart disease, in the locally born and principal immigrant groups in Australia have been calculated for both sexes in age groups of a 10-year spread. Upon arrival in Australia, immigrants from England, Wales, and Italy have much lower rates than those prevailing in people already in Australia. The longer their period of residence in Australia, however, the greater the immigrants' death rate from cardiovascular disease becomes, until it significantly exceeds the rate existing in their countries of origin (Stenhouse and McCall, 1970). The psychosomatic point of view is defensible on the grounds that about half of the patients with CHD show the traditional risk factors.

Two other important variables, alone or in combination with traditional risk factors, have been considered in an impressive body of research pertaining to psychosocial stress and to a certain personality type—the type A behavior pattern (Glass, 1977). The major classes of interacting variables as identified by Kasl (1977) are: 1) the traditional biological risk factors; 2) the behavioral risk factors (such as smoking and diet); 3) the social-ecological variables (social change, work setting, and social support); 4) the personality dimensions and psychological reactions (such as anxiety-tension, vulnerability to exhaustion and to the "Sisyphus reaction," and pre-disposition to type A behaviors) and 5) the sociodemographic and background factors.

Prevalence rates of coronary heart disease (CHD) were compared between different cultural groups in various parts of the world as shown in Table 1 (based on postmortem findings). CHD rates in the white population of the United States or in the Union of South Africa are higher than in the white population of the British Isles. The CHD rate in the Indian population in Johannesburg is just as high as that of the white population in Johannesburg, whereas that of Euro-Africans in Johannesburg is considerably lower, and that of the Bantu population is very low indeed (1.0% to 3.6%) (Walker, 1963). CHD is very uncommon among Chinese in South Africa, with prevalence equal to that of Chinese in China.

There is general agreement that CHD is exceedingly rare in African Negroes. Out of 1,384 admissions to the University College Hospital in Ibadan, Nigeria, Lauckner, Rankin, and Adi (1961) found only two cases

Table 1.   Percentages of total deaths from coronary heart disease in populations of various countries

Country	Male and female death rates (up to 74 years of age)	
	Percentage males	Percentage females
United States		
(total population)	33.0	22.1
New York	38.1	31.0
England and Wales	19.3	11.8
Scotland		
Edinburgh	27.8	26.7
South Africa (Johannesburg)		
white population	37.0	24.1
Euro-African population	11.0 to 16.0	7.2 to 15.3
Indian population	38.5 to 40.5	15.8 to 28.9
Bantu population	1.0 to 3.6	1.3 to 2.1

of CHD, both males over 70 years of age. Ammar (1967) reported that coronary and cerebral thrombosis are equally common in urban and rural populations in Tunisia. He agreed with the findings of Parhad (1965) from Kuwait that individuals of an aggressive personality are most frequently affected by coronary disease.

Yano and Ueda (1963) compared rates of patients hospitalized for CHD in Japan and in the United States (in Hiroshima and in Framingham, Massachusetts). As Table 2 shows, the rates of CHD were four times higher in the United States than in Japan, and the differences were particularly striking in the younger age groups. Their studies confirm the relatively infrequent occurrence of CHD in the Japanese. Autopsy studies in Singapore indicate a low prevalence of CHD among Chinese versus a relatively high prevalence among Indians (Danaraj et al., 1959). CHD constituted 50% of all heart disease in Indian males above the age of 20, whereas among male Chinese it constituted between 10% and 20%. Muir (1960) reported on 552 autopsies in Singapore, and found major differences in the frequency of CHD between Indian, Chinese, and Malay peoples. The Indian Moslem was found to be 20 times more liable, and the Indian Hindu ten times more liable to die from coronary heart disease than the Chinese and the Malay. If hospital admission practices and selection of patients were responsible for the differences noted, one would expect other acute and subacute cardiovascular disorders to have exhibited a corresponding differential, which did not occur.

The effect of culture change on CHD was demonstrated by a study of Yemenite Jews in Israel (Birnbaum, Groen, and Kallner, 1960). In this study, in contrast to the previously reported studies, race, diagnosis, and availability of medical services were constant. These Yemenites had emigrated from segregated communities in Arabia to Israel. Among the early immigrants who had been exposed to a Western way of life for over twenty years, the death rate in middle-aged men for degenerative heart disease, mainly CHD, was 3.3 per thousand, whereas for recent immigrants the rate was only 0.49 per thousand.

Cassel's studies (1974) have shown that populations living in small cohesive societies insulated from the changes that are occurring in modern technological countries have low *blood pressures,* which do not differ in the

Table 2.   Large-scale epidemiological studies on prevalence of coronary heart disease in Japan and in the United States (Hiroshima and Framingham, Massachusetts)

		Prevalence (ages 30–59)	
Location	Time period	Percentage males	Percentage females
Hiroshima (Japan)	1958–1960	6	3
Framingham (United States)	1949–1952	22	11

young and the aged, and these people rarely suffer from major cardiovascular diseases (CHD and strokes). Studies have shown that people who have left such societies (for instance, migration from the Tokelaus to New Zealand) and who have had prolonged contact with Western culture have higher blood pressures and exhibit the familiar relationship between older age and higher blood pressure found in most studies of Western populations.

Henry and Cassel (1969) studied several factors in the etiology of hypertension and demonstrated that perception of threatening events in the social environment is the crucial factor. In over 30% of a victorious battalion, Graham (Henry and Cassel, 1969) found blood pressures of over 180 mm Hg. Miasnikov observed a similar epidemic of high blood pressure during the siege and bombardment of Leningrad. When the stress was lifted in both groups, their blood pressure returned to normal. The differences in the rate of rise of blood pressure with aging in various cultural groups throughout the world has been linked, by Scotch and Geiger (1963) and by others, to psychosocial stress factors. Lowenstein (1961) studied the blood pressures of two tribes of Indians in Brazil. One tribe exhibited a rise of blood pressure with age and the other did not. The tribe that did show a rise of blood pressure had accepted some of the culture of Catholic Brazil and was in the process of acculturation. The elderly Navaho in the United States who elected to stay in their homeland and to continue their traditional culture, the Samburu in Northern Kenya related to the Masai living in an isolated ecological niche (Mann, 1965), farmers in a small village on the northern coast of Japan who had retained much of their traditional culture, and villagers in the countryside near New Delhi were all found to live without a major increase of blood pressure with age (Henry and Cassel, 1969).

Significant differences in blood pressure between rural and urban Zulus have been noted (Table 3). Comparison of mean systolic blood pressures in representative samples of urban Zulus and Americans showed

Table 3.   Large-scale blood pressure studies in black populations

Location	Mean systolic blood pressures (all ages)	
	Male	Female
Zulu (urban)	131	130
Zulu (rural)	123	121
Liberia	125	119
Nassau	143.5	150.5
United States	150.6	158.2

that urban Zulus have higher blood pressures than white Americans, yet not as high as American Negroes (Scotch, 1960; Scotch and Geiger, 1963).

Rosen (Baasher, 1964) compared blood pressure levels of apparently healthy American adults with members of the Maban tribe in Sudan (650 miles southeast of Khartoum). He found that among the Maban the blood pressure remains unelevated from childhood to old age, whereas in the American population, after the fourth decade the blood pressure increases progressively with advancing age. Pflanz (1966) reported that in India and in Ghana the population with higher education tends to have higher blood pressure.

Donnison (1938) noted that, among 1,800 hospital admissions on the shores of Lake Victoria in Kenya, he could find no case of essential hypertension. In his book *Civilization and Disease,* Donnison advocates that successful childhood integration of inborn drives into socially accceptable patterns is the critical factor in creating a stable nonhypertensive society. Scotch and Geiger (1963), studying the urban and rural Zulus in the Union of South Africa, reached the conclusion that hypertension resulted from a failure of the individual to develop adaptive behavior to meet the demands of the environment. According to Ammar (1967), reporting from Tunisia, hypertension is rare among African tribal populations who have not yet experienced acculturative changes, although it is commonly seen among urban Africans. Cruz-Coke, Etcheverry, and Nagel (1964), studying the migration of Eastern Islanders to Chile, introduced the term *ecological niche* to explain the consistently low blood pressure of groups living in isolated regions and enjoying an unchanging and unchallenged tradition handed down over generations. When the niche is breached and there is a change of culture, some prove less adaptable than others.

Essential hypertension is rare or absent in technologically undeveloped population groups (Maddocks, 1961). Chavez (1942) reported a prevalence of essential hypertension of only 2.6% among Mexican Indians as compared to 36.9% among whites in Mexico and 57% among Negroes in the United States. Essential hypertension is uncommon among Eskimos, in the interior of Senegal (Collomb, 1964), in certain areas of New Guinea, and among the Cook Island Maoris.

In a comparative study of 4,252 white and 5,936 Negro patients in the United States by Schultze and Schwab (1936), the incidence of hypertensive cardiovascular disease for Negroes was found to be 12.5%, and the incidence for white patients was 4.9%. Furthermore, the highest incidence of hypertensive heart disease in the Negroes occurs in the fourth decade, whereas in whites, the peak is reached in the fifth decade. According to Schultze and Schwab (1936), the high incidence of hypertension in the American Negro is probably caused by his inability to cope with a complex environment. External locus of control was also put forward as an explanation, which refers to the black person's feeling that no means are available for achieving any long-range goal and his sense of powerlessness in influencing his fate. The blacks in America have been subjected to much social discrimination, humiliation, and unequal opportunity. Sociocultural etiology is also suggested as a factor in hypertension, because the American Negro's genetic pool is derived largely from Eastern Senegal and Liberia, where the incidence of hypertension is extremely low.

GASTROINTESTINAL DISORDERS

The prevalence of *peptic ulcer* differs in different geographic areas of the world and in different areas of the same country. Eagle and Gilman (Raper, 1958) found that only 0.4% of 1,144 autopsies in South African Bantus showed peptic ulcers. In the United States, blacks are less prone to peptic ulcer than whites. Pisot et al. (Bonne et al., 1938) claimed that the Chinese in Indonesia suffered from peptic ulcer 14 times more often than did the surrounding population. In Uganda, the symptoms and the diagnosis of peptic ulcer are rarely encountered among Africans, but, at necropsy, the scars of peptic ulcer are no less common than they are among the British (Raper, 1958).

Among 675 Negroes in equatorial Africa, 121 duodenal ulcers were found by Payet et al. (1962). Near Dakar, among 280 Negroes, 57 gastroduodenal ulcers were found. Duodenal ulcer, which is essentially an urban disorder, has been noted in Senegal, Algeria, and Tunisia. The personality type of ulcer patients in Senegal was reported by Payet et al. (1962) to be anxiety ridden, and in almost half of the cases there was a traumatic experience prior to onset of illness. Payet et al. postulated that the psychodynamic constellation for the development of ulcer in Africa is not different from that found in Europe.

Tables 4 and 5 present postmortem findings and hospital admission percentages regarding gastroduodenal ulcerations in various cultural settings. The statistics obtained are somewhat puzzling. They show, as might be expected, low rates of gastroduodenal ulcerations in Bantus as compared to those in Europeans, but there are also some surprisingly high rates of these disorders in some African groups, especially in South Indians (Vellore). Prevalence of peptic ulcer was found to be higher in Hindus than in members of the Moslem or Christian faith. In Indonesia, ulcer of the stomach and of the duodenum was found to be much more prevalent among Chinese than among Javanese workers who worked under the same circumstances on a large plantation (M. Pflanz, 1971). In another study from Java, Bonne et al. (1938) found a higher frequency of major gastric lesions (cancer and ulcer) in Chinese than in Malays. Indian women from a Pacific northwest coastal tribe were found to have a high prevalence of

Table 4. Prevalence of duodenal ulcer, of peptic ulcer, and of scars in various populations, according to postmortem statistics

Country	Sex	Prevalence[a]	Disorder
Great Britain	M	4.6	Duodenal ulcers
	F	1.4	and scars
Scotland	M,F	9.3	Duodenal ulcers and scars
Germany	M,F	9.0	Peptic ulcers and scars
Iceland	M	0.43	Duodenal ulcers
	F	0.35	
Uganda	M,F	14.5	Peptic ulcers and scars
South Africa (Bantu population)	M	0.7	Duodenal scars
	F	0.03	

[a]Expressed as percent.

duodenal ulcer, about four times greater than that for non-Indian women, and above the rate of occurrence in southwestern Indians. The high rate was explained by Shore and Stone (1973) in the light of cultural heritage and current acculturation stresses, namely, the role of northwestern Indian women in a martriarchal culture and the pressure on the Indian woman who lives in a minority-group–poverty-level community.

According to Groen (1970), *ulcerative colitis* is a disease of Western culture, very rarely found in the developing countries of Asia and Africa. Observations to this effect have been reported from India (Gupta, 1956) and from Uganda (Walker, 1963). In Uganda, Billinghurst and Welchman

Table 5. Proportion of patients with duodenal ulcers among all patients in hospitals in various countries

Country	Sex	Rate of cases per 10,000 inpatients
Italy	M,F	130
Greece	M,F	120
Netherlands	M	140
	F	35
India (Madras)	M	140
India (Vellore)	M,F	170
Singapore	M,F	26
Senegal (Africans)	M	95
	F	43
Sierra Leone	M	6
	F	4
South Africa (Bantu)	M,F	1.5

(1966) reported on four Africans of the Buganda tribe who were admitted to the Mulago Hospital in Kampala with a typical confirmed diagnosis of idiopathic ulcerative colitis. Three of them showed some of the personality traits known to be associated with this disorder, and in one the onset of the illness was related to psychological stress. Wigley and MacLaurin (1962) recorded rarity of hospitalization for ulcerative colitis in Maoris after making adjustments for differences in admission rates between Maoris and patients of European descent. Only two definite cases were found in Maoris, the difference in incidence being much greater than could occur by chance, and no Maori deaths were recorded that were caused by this illness. Among 1,384 patients admitted to the University Hospital in Ibadan, Nigeria, Lauckner et al. (1961) found only three cases of nonspecific colitis. Ulcerative colitis is said to be common in Jews (Acheson, 1960). Birnbaum et al. (1960) report from Israel that the disease is more common in Occidental than in Oriental Jewish immigrants. A very low incidence of nonspecific colitis was found among Indian villagers by Gupta (1956).

ASTHMA

Epidemiological observations regarding bronchial *asthma,* apart from national, cultural, and local differences in reporting symptoms, which equally apply to most psychosomatic disorders, is complicated by differences in exposure to allergens (Leigh and Marley, 1967).

Nathanson and Rhyne (1970) ascribed the difference in prevalence rate seen in asthmatics to: 1) differential reporting of symptoms from culture to culture, 2) different exposure to air pollution or to risk of infection in different cultures or social groups, and 3) differences between subgroups in both the quality and the quantity of psychosocial stress that they generate for their members.

It has been shown that allergic and psychological factors are interrelated in the etiology of bronchial asthma. Psychological stresses of all sorts may precipitate asthmatic attacks in the presence of an allergic diathesis. Alexander and French (1948) noted that asthmatics are unduly attached to their mothers, that asthmatic attacks are frequently triggered by the loss of the mother's affection or by a fear of losing it, and that the asthmatic attack symbolically represents a repressed cry. The association of bronchial asthma and exposure to allergens in certain geographical areas has been noted (for example, the presence of grain products, of castor bean dust, or of industrial air pollution in Yokohama and New Orleans [Carroll, 1968]). The psychological factors in allergic disorders have been elaborated by Abramson (1954), Wittkower and Engels (1967), and Freeman et al. (1964).

The global picture as presented in a study of the world literature on asthma is confusing and often contradictory (see Table 6). Collomb (1964) observed that asthma is rarely seen in Senegalese children. Only a few cases have been seen in a Dakar pediatric service out of a total of 3,000 sick children. By contrast, Chuang (1967) found that the rate of asthmatic children in Libyan pediatric wards is exceptionally high. In Israel, asthma is more frequent among Jewish immigrants from Iraq than among other groups of the population. In a community study of 1,350 inhabitants of a village near Cairo, El Mehairy et al. (1965) found 6.07% of the population to be afflicted with allergic disorders. The frequency was higher in the male population, because males were more likely to be exposed to allergies during work. There were 47 cases of bronchial asthma, either alone or in combination with allergic rhinitis, urticaria, and conjunctivitis.

In North Greenland, Ehrstrom (1951) found four cases of allergic disease, including one asthma, in a population of 1,500. All four cases had acquired the style and customs of the West. Trowell and Jellife (Carothers, 1953) state that in South India the picture of chronic asthma with more or less perpetual disability is very rarely seen among children. Lask (1966) writes that asthma is preeminently a disease of civilization and perhaps of education. Roughly 2% of the University students in Britain have active asthma and 4% have a history of asthma, as compared to 1% of active asthma in the general population.

Table 6. Prevalence of asthma in various countries

Country	Prevalence[a]	Type of population tested
Isle of Wight (Graham, 1967)	2.3	school children
Baltimore Survey, State of Maryland (Nathanson and Rhyne, 1970)[b]	9.9 to 13.9[c]	school children
Sweden (Kraepelin, 1954)	0.73 to 1.4	school children
Finland (Eriksson-Lihr, 1955)	0.6 to 0.7	school children
United States (Harris and Shure, 1956)	2	school children
Taiwan (Hsu and Lin, 1965)	2.7	geriatric patients
Tristan Islanders (Citron and Pepys, 1964)	49	adults and children
Libya (Chuang, 1966)	11	pediatric wards
United Arab Republic (El Mehairy et al., 1965)	2.3	population sample

[a] Expressed as percent.

[b] Asthmatic symptoms by social class, religion, household size, and index of emotional support.

[c] Higher in boys and in classes III and IV of Protestant families.

The Isle of Wight study by Graham et al. (1967), conducted among 9-11 year-old children, gives an asthma prevalence rate of 2.3%. It showed that asthma is overrepresented in social classes I and II (upper classes) and underrepresented in the lower social classes. Nathanson and Rhyne (1970) found highest rates among Protestant middle-class boys from small families in a study of 4,100 children aged 6-11 in the State of Maryland (Table 6). These families characteristically encouraged dependency and imposed pressures on their sons for achievement and independence. There is consensus that the ratio male: female is about 3:1, but there are discrepancies in the annual prevalence of asthma in children of roughly comparable age. Prevalence rates range from 0.73% in Sweden to 2.8% in the United States. A somewhat higher prevalence rate was also observed in urban than in rural areas. In Nathanson and Rhyne's study (1970) there was no significant difference in the proportion of asthmatic symptoms between white and Negro children.

Different Jewish ethnic groups in Israel differ in their predisposition to asthma (Glazer, 1969). The Tokelau Island Migrant study has shown that asthma is extremely uncommon in those Polynesian people living in their home islands (Prior, 1971, 1977). This observation was attributed to the absence of industrial pollutants and chemicals and the extremely limited availability of dairy products. The picture changes among the migrants moving to New Zealand. The relative risk of asthma is 18.7 times greater in Tokelau males and 4.4 times greater in Tokelau females migrating to New Zealand as compared to the risk for those people living in the Tokelau Islands (Stanhope, 1977).

DISCUSSION

Various authors have speculated on the meaning of these various findings, which show that, in cross-cultural comparison, striking differences in the rates of some psychosomatic disorders exist. The differences are almost certainly influenced by: 1) the sick role, 2) illness behavior, perception of symptoms, and medical care seeking, 3) the health belief model of that population, 4) the population's definition of normality, 5) the role of the family, 6) adherence to medical regimen, and 7) case reporting and case finding. It would be cautious to postulate, along with Mechanic (1974), that "the important issues in understanding how life events (or for that matter socio-cultural stress) interact with social, psychological, biological, and intrapsychic variables require specification of what events influence what illnesses under what conditions through what processes?" The evidence obtained suggests that both cardiovascular and gastrointestinal psychosomatic disorders are more frequent in the urban populations of developing countries and in the cities of Europe and of America than in the rural populations. The situation is less clear regarding bronchial asthma, and there are gross inconsistencies in reported data. How can these differences and inconsistencies be accounted for? Probably not a single factor, but a combination of factors is involved in the explanation.

Race and Migration

Many writers on the subject of race and migration are inclined to attribute the differences noted to differences between races. This view is hardly tenable because 1) despite identity of race, gross differences in rates of essential hypertension and coronary disease exist between American and African Negroes; 2) Maoris in New Zealand have much higher rates of these cardiovascular disorders than those living on Pacific atolls (Prior, 1971, 1977), and 3) the rate of degenerative heart disease, mainly CHD, in Yemenites living in Israel for over twenty years was found to be considerably higher than that of recent immigrants.

As a test of the hypothesis that migration and westernization are associated with an increased prevalence of a variety of diseases among adult Chamorros, 200 Chamorro natives from the Mariana Islands were examined by Reed, Labarthe, and Stallones (1970). These individuals, although similar in genetic background, had different sociocultural experiences by virtue of their residence in Rota, Guam, and California. A 24-hour dietary survey was completed for a subsample in each area, and 10-year mortality data were obtained in Guam and California. The frequency of specific measures of disease, except for those related to coronary heart disease, were similar in all three areas. Higher mortality rates from CHD for the Chamorros living in California, as compared to those living in Guam, were found. Analysis of sociocultural and illness variables, independent of geographic area, failed to show association of any disease variable with any measure of mobility or sociocultural orientation. In Palau, the same research team found that blood pressure followed a gradient from the least urban to the most urban environment. Even the relatively high values in the Palau population were low in comparison to the United States population (Labarthe et al., 1973; Reed, 1973). These gradients were found to support a relationship between modernization and risk of cardiovascular disorders among adult Palauans.

In another study, Prior (1977) compared people who subsequently migrated to those people who remained on the Tokelau Islands. The younger male premigrants were taller, heavier, had higher blood pressures, and more urinary sodium excretions than their nonmigrating counterparts. The authors speculate that the younger, more athletic males migrate actively and that the women and older men acquiesce to this decision to move. Prior underscores the need for longitudinal studies that define the characteristics of the migrant prior to migration.

Life Expectancy

Differences in life expectancy in different parts of the world must be taken into account. If, in some countries, the expected span of life is short, the expected rate of coronary disease is certain to be low. However, the differences in the rates observed are so enormous that this can hardly be the only explanation. Moreover, it has been shown by Walker (1963) that, despite roughly equal mortalities from cerebral vascular disease in whites and in Bantus, the death rate from coronary vascular disease is high in whites and very low in Bantus.

Diet, Eating Habits, and Alcohol Consumption

Another factor to be taken into consideration concerns diet, eating habits, and alcohol consumption. Unsaturated fat intake varies considerably cross-culturally, and it is higher in technologically developed countries where coronary heart disease is common. Osfeld and D'Atri (1977) presented data showing that the Guatemalan highlanders, urban Chinese living in Taiwan, the disintegrating Washo tribe, forced to leave its ancestral homeland, Japanese farmers, and Indian villagers all exhibited some evidence that rapid culture and social change leading to conflict are correlated positively with blood pressure levels and possibly with higher rates of rise of pressure with age. However, current research has generally failed to control for the effects of diet changes on weight gain, which has placed the significance of the role of stressful social changes in a different light. For example, the study on Japanese Americans by Marmot (1977) and Syme (1970) showed that those who had maintained traditional Japanese culture had the lowest prevalence of coronary heart disease—a finding that is, in part, explained by the dietary hypothesis. Preference for modern food was associated in Reed's Micronesian studies (1973) with high blood pressure, high cholesterol, obesity, and high symptom score. Equally significant is that consumption of gastric acid stimulants, such as spices, coffee, and alcohol, is higher is some countries than in others, and the custom of serving and eating hot food may predispose to gastric ulceration.

Gastrointestinal Infections and Worm Infestations

One would imagine that ulcerative colitis would be common in countries in which gastrointestinal infections, such as amoebic dysentery and worm infestations, are rampant. As has been demonstrated, this is not the case as far as can be established in the absence of rectoscopic facilities.

Psychosocial Stress

Stress is the nonspecific response of the body to any demand made upon it (Selye, 1956). In Selye's view, the agent or situation acting as stressor might be pleasant or unpleasant; what really matters is the intensity of the demand for readjustment or adaptation. The same degree of stress, induced by the same meaningful psychosocial stimuli or agent may produce different lesions or disorders in different individuals. In the interpersonal field there are three broad defense reactions, which Selye (1974) calls: 1) the syntoxic, which involves denial of the threat and adjustment; 2) the catatoxic, which results in fight against the threat; and 3) flight. At the cellular level, a similar mechanism exists in reaction to stress. The coping process in reaction to stress depends on the perception and meaning of the threat and the sense of competence (or self-fulfillment) of the individual. Selye suggests that individuals able to perform effective coping responses develop fewer somatic reactions than helpless individuals. There are three coping strategies: cognitive, affective, and behavioral coping styles (Kiely, 1972). Whether there is a loss or a threat of loss, an injury or a threat of injury, or a sustained frustration of biological drives, the ultimate outcome will depend on the cultural measures designed to absorb or circumvent stress factors in intra-individual coping strategies, on disease related factors and on the prevalent life setting. The latter refers to the particular effects of bereavement on mortality and morbidity and to the increased psychosocial stress associated with aging, which, according to Scotch (1960), can be related to increased incidence of hypertension with increased age in different cultures. The increase of mortality and psychiatric morbidity following bereavement (Young, Benjamin, and Wallis, 1963), the increased incidence of peptic ulcer in a certain population following heavy air raids, and the association of various disorders with a period of increased stress, as exemplified by the studies of Rahe, Meyer, and Smith (1964) regarding coronary thrombosis, leave no doubt that stress factors are paramount in precipitating somatic disorders. Scotch (1960) explained the difference in blood pressure found between rural and urban Zulus as being caused by the continual stress associated with city life. Scotch noted that the Zulus in the city, in contrast to those on the reserve, are subjected to overt acts of humiliation by whites, are faced with widespread unemployment, and have their authority as household heads threatened by female dominance. Daily frustrations in relations with whites are displaced onto the Zulus' wives, with a correspondingly high rate of alcoholism and hypertension in urban Zulu women.

Hinkle and H. G. Wolff (1961) concerned themselves with the adverse effect of psychosocial stress on physical health in various ethnic groups residing in New York—native Americans, Chinese, and Hungarians. The researchers noted considerable differences in the illness rates in comparing the groups studied. In particular, Hinkle and Wolff found that the Chinese group had a much greater tolerance for change and disruption than did an equivalent group of Yankees. They concluded that this apparent tolerance for change, which is actually concealed stress, may account for the higher rates of hypertension among Chinese than among Yankees in New York. The authors emphasize that all diseases seem to occur more frequently in people who perceive their life situations as demanding, threatening, and frustrating.

The Impact of Civilization

Studies have also been made on the impact of civilization on psychosomatic disorders. Prior (1971, 1977) and his team studied 2,700 Maoris living in various stages of exposure to Western influence, culture, and dietary habits. Three Maori communities were investigated: the Pukapuka, on an isolated island in the Pacific, where life, work, and dietary habits have changed little in the past century; the Rarotonga, on Cook's Island, a halfway station between the simple life and more developed society; and the New Zealand Maoris, who must deal with the complicated Europeanized life of New Zealand. Differences in the blood pressure pattern between the Pukupukans, Tokelauans, Rarotongans, and the New Zealand Maoris, all Polynesians and of the same broad ethnic family, support the hypothesis that the differences in disease patterns are basically caused by environmental factors rather than by genetic factors. In Prior's 1960 mortality survey (1971) (age adjusted), the New Zealand Maoris developed hypertension and coronary heart disease four to five times more frequently than women of the same age and ethnic group living on atolls in the central Pacific. This observation prompted a prospective epidemiological study by both the Medical Research Council of New Zealand and by the World Health Organization.

The Pukupukans lead an unsophisticated communal life with virtually no time urgency. They have plenty of physical labor and a subsistence, not a money, economy. Their diet consists of fish, coconuts, vegetables, and rice. In Rarotonga, the Maoris consume more salt, are obese, and grow up in a society where the social structure, achievement goals, economy, and life-style are in between the simplicity of the Pukapukans and the complexity of the New Zealand Maoris. Prior's studies showed that the further the Pacific natives move from the quiet, carefree life of their ancestors, the closer they come to gout, diabetes, arteriosclerosis, obesity, and hypertension. The authors believe that diet, physical activity, and the way of life are responsible for this gradual shift. From these considerations, one may conclude that there is a price to pay for civilization.

Basic Personality

Stress response is closely related to basic personality, that is, to the cultural stereotype of personality characterized by core values transmitted from generation to generation by child-rearing practices. It seems more than likely that if values in one's personality system are not reinforced by values in one's cultural system, conflicts or conflict constellations may arise or may be intensified, which, according to classical psychosomatic theory, are typical of certain psychosomatic disorders. For instance, the high rates of essential hypertension and of coronary disease in American Negroes as compared to the rates in rural Africans may be related to the restraints imposed by American society on expression of aggressive impulses against the white majority. Similarly, the conflict between infantile receptive strivings and the adult ego, pride, and aspiration for independence, accomplishments, and self-sufficiency is regarded as typical of peptic ulcer patients and is more a feature of Western society than of rural Africa. Some of the apparent inconsistencies in the ulcer statistics presented may be explained on this basis. For instance, the high rate of gastroduodenal ulcerations in Indians may be accounted for by the recent culture change in India where, with the recession of the caste system, striving for status has been rife. Much research in this area, both by anthropologists and by psychiatrists, is needed. Comparison of members of subcultures suffering from the same disorder in the same country seems especially promising. Up until now it has been little known whether the psychodynamics of patients suffering from cardiovascular and gastrointestinal disorders in developing countries correspond to those of patients suffering from those disorders in developed countries.

Culture Change

Cultures in transition or change are beset with conflicting values, evolving or vanishing myths, and maladjustment reactions to new stimuli. Le Guerinel (1971) has suggested that the psychosomatic patient loses his cultural framework and thus is unable to transform his traditional myths into fantasies. The individual who has lost his roots becomes prey to his own somatic mirroring and enters into an identificatory conflict with his group and with his culture. The split that occurs between his social and his psychological structure widens his isolation from the group and fosters projection onto his fantasied body image. Lehmann (1972) expressed Levi-Strauss's concept succinctly:

> Les mythes traditionnels n'en disent plus assez et ce qu'ils disent encore structurent des relations sociales devenues trop oppressives; quant aux mythes importés ils n'en disent pas encore suffisamment pour construire un avenir et entrainer à l'action . . . Le déficit de signifié dépasse la limite du supportable.

Defense mechanisms in the African Negro remain fluid and unstructured in comparison to other cultures. Their ego defenses are collective and cannot be separated from the family and tribal group. These characteristics facilitate identification with the healer, which in turn enhances the therapeutic effectiveness of culturally prescribed methods. Groen (1971a, 1971b) is of the opinion that in primitive subcultures the social taboos against the acting out of aggression are less rigid, which facilitates open conflicts and expression of fear and anger.

The hypothesis of failure to adapt to transitional strain was given support by the field studies of Scotch and Geiger on the impact of sociocultural stress among Zulus in the process of acculturation to European culture.

Henry and Cassel (1969), in their study of changes in blood pressure with age in different cultural groups, concluded that blood pressure is lower where the culture is stable, where traditional forms are honored, and where the group members are secure in their roles and are adapted to them by early experiences.

Ammar (1967) is of the opinion that traditional African cultures provide a mirror for psychosomatic phenomena inasmuch as they tend to translate psychological and sociocultural stresses into physical manifestations. Acculturative changes bring with them added stresses that are translated into psychosomatic disorders. The frequency of psychosomatic disorders among individuals in this category exceeds the incidence in Europe and America. The situation is aggravated by the fact that individuals experiencing rapid acculturation no longer draw support from the traditional treatment techniques. Mead (1947) wrote lucidly: "As periods of cultural change inevitably carry with them a greater degree of heterogeneity, in the history of any culture or subculture, periods will be found in which adequate social forms for the expression of points of strain and tension in the personality will be lacking, and the individual will be forced back upon his own body for symbolic expression."

Each of the factors discussed above need not be mutually exclusive. Syme's work on cultural mobility, Marmot's studies on Japanese Americans, and Prior's long-term research on the Tokelau Island Migrant Population all seem to support Cassel's three hypotheses:

1. Migrants who do not receive any feedback or evidence that their actions are leading to desirable or anticipated consequences have increased susceptibility to disease.
2. Not all members of a population are equally susceptible to the effects of social pressures. The higher levels of blood pressure and hypertensive disease in the blacks in the United States compared to the whites could be cited as an example of a group of people who are often in the subordinate position and who have a particular risk of social and family disorganization.
3. Protective factors in a given culture may neutralize or cushion the individual from the physiological or psychological consequences of stressful social pressures.

Prior (1977) cautiously stated:

It could be argued that the changes related to the experience of migration itself, the social uprooting, culture conflict, and lack of feedback, would have a more important effect that would lessen with adaptation compared with environmental factors such as diet change, salt use, and weight gain. This needs to be tested in further long term migrant studies, including information concerning migrant status prior to migration. The concept of protective factors, both social and biological, is an important one and properly developed may allow for more effective intervention than attempts to reduce "stressor situations."

Other factors not included in this chapter have been considered by Paulley (1950, 1975) to be of importance, such as strict religious sects versus less strict ones in the prevalence of ulcerative colitis and differences and changes in the sex incidence of ulcerative colitis; duodenal ulcer may also be included, in terms of altered male versus female roles. "Oral tensions," the "rat race," and "work addiction" are other personality factors deeply rooted in culture that may influence the prevalence of psychosomatic illnesses.

PREVENTIVE MEASURES

Preventive measures should consider the relative weight of every factor discussed. Singer (1975) has cogently summarized various hypotheses to account for cultural differences in psychosomatic disorders in terms of cultural shaping of the mother-child relationship and cultural shaping of psychodynamic defense mechanisms. For instance, it has been postulated that restraint of expression of aggression accounts for the high rates of essential hypertension in American Negroes and in the Japanese, that male dependency accounts for the allegedly high frequency of gastrointestinal and cardiovascular complaints among Arab men, and that sustained libidinal cathexis of the body caused by prolonged skin contact between mother and child accounts for a supposedly high prevalence of somatization among Africans. The dominance-submission strivings and conflicts between infantile needs and adult ego demands and aspirations that are rampant in Western society are believed to facilitate the development of psychosomatic illnesses. Japanese group cohesiveness, with its emphasis on group welfare and group consensus, in contrast to Western individualism and autonomy, is thought to account for the lower rate of coronary heart disease in the Japanese. Loss of cultural identity consequent to westernization is thought to have had an unfavorable impact on the prevalence of psychosomatic disorders in Japan after World War II (Ikemi et al., 1974). In Howard's overview of Polynesian-Micronesian populations (1979), he offers the hypothesis that these populations are being pressured to accommodate to urbanized life while lacking appropriate psychodynamic defenses. This pressure leads to a continual triggering of the autonomic nervous system, which then sets off an alarm response and induces stress.

S. Wolf (1969) noted a remarkably low death rate from myocardial infarction (less than half that of the neighboring communities) in Roseto, an Italian-American community of 17,000 in Pennsylvania. This low rate of coronary disease in Roseto was all the more remarkable because of the great prevalence of high-risk factors in this community, such as obesity, hypertension, diabetes, large consumption of animal fat, cigarette smoking, little muscular exercise, and a pattern of behavior characterized by "tireless striving and doing things the hard way without commensurate satisfactions." In Roseto, throughout the 12 years of the study, there was only one death from myocardial infarction under age 47, and most of the deaths occurred in men and women in their seventies and eighties. For the Rosetans, the family was the focus of life and the men were found to be the unchallenged heads of their households.

The small number of Rosetans who had myocardial infarction had become alienated from the mainstream of their culture. Equally significant is the finding that Italian laborers working in Switzerland are known to have a higher rate of coronary disease than comparable age groups in Italy. A similar finding was quoted among Yemenite Jews and Ceylonese (S. Wolf, 1969). S. Wolf therefore postulates that a cohesive, mutually supportive social group with strong family and community ties reduces the risk of coronary disease.

There is growing evidence that certain types of psychosomatic illness are associated with a society's whole way of life and with social and economic development. Psychosomatic medicine, in a cultural frame, would be relevant to preventive medicine in "developing compensating cultural forms which will relieve the somatic strain, or dignifying, for example, hypertension as a way of dying, or altering some of our cultural emphases so that the individual organisms will not pay the particular prices which they now pay for being socialized" (Mead, 1947). Intimate knowledge of different cultures and human groups "will help promote positive changes in families, communities and societies at large" (Dubreuil and Wittkower, 1976). The positive functions of culture are those "cathartic strategies" described by Dubreuil and Wittkower (1973, 1976) in their paper on primary prevention. These strategies include trance and possession, rituals, periodic carnivals, dance, and the various ways of displacing and handling aggression through magic, symbolism, and overt conflict. However, sociocultural stress has had a more overriding influence on the onset of disease than the positive sociocultural factors have had in preventing it.

Bereavement, retirement, and social isolation are major crises that are dealt with in various ways by different cultures. Western society has not learned to cope effectively with these crises nor does it pay more than lip service to the growing support for the view that certain illnesses are more likely to occur at a time when a patient must adapt to a life crisis.

Apart from altering a distress-inducing life-style and learning more effective techniques of decreasing the psychosomatic impact of major crises, the whole area of child-rearing methods and mother-child relations are directly relevant to primary prevention in the field of psychosomatic medicine. The role of diet, exercise, autogenic training, yoga, and other methods that lead to improved psychophysiological homeostasis cannot be underestimated.

Regarding the prevention of psychosomatic disorders, the World Health Organization's thirteenth report cogently stated: "Rapid social change, industrialization, automation, disintegration, and cultural change, to name a few, are the context and are factors in benign and noxious family situations and in other benign and noxious life experiences. The medical profession is a part of the world's changing society and cannot maintain a withdrawn or passive position" (WHO, 1964).

REFERENCES

Abramson, H. A. 1954. Evaluation of maternal rejection theory in allergy. Ann. Allergy 12 (2):129–140.

Acheson, E. C. 1960. Distribution of ulcerative colitis and regional enteritis in United States veterans with particular reference to Jewish religion. Gut. 1:291–293.

Alexander, F., and French, T. M. (eds.). 1948. Studies in Psychosomatic Medicine: An Approach to the Cause and Treatment of Vegetative Disturbances. Ronald Press Co., New York.

Ammar, S 1967 Médecine psychosomatique en Afrique. Méd. Hyg. 8 fevr. 25 (766):142–145.

Appels, A. 1973. Coronary heart disease as a cultural disease. Psychother. Psychosom. 22:320–324.

Baasher, T. A. 1964. Treatment and prevention of psychosomatic disorders in East Africa. Am. J. Psychiatry 121:1095–1102.

Billinghurst, J. R., and Welchman, J. M. 1966. Idiopathic ulcerative colitis in the African: A report of four cases. Br. Med. J. 1:211–213.

Birnbaum, D., Groen, J. J., and Kallner, G. 1960. Ulcerative colitis among the ethnic groups in Israel. Arch. Intern. Med. 105:843–848.

Bonne, C., Hartz, P., and Klerks, J. V., et al. 1938. Morphology of the stomach and gastric secretion in Malays and Chinese and the different incidents of gastric ulcer and cancer in these races. Am. J. Cancer 33:265–279.

Carothers, J. C. 1953. The African mind—in health and disease. Monograph, series 1–17. World Health Organization, Geneva.

Carroll, R. E. 1968. Epidemiology of New Orleans. Epidemic Asthma. Am. J. Public Health 58 (9):1677–1683.

Cassel, J. 1974. Hypertension and cardiovascular disease in migrants: A potential source of clues? Int. J. Epidemiol. 3 (3):204–206.

Chavez, I. 1942. Incidence of heart disease in Mexico; Study of 2,400 cases of organic heart disease. Am. Heart J. 24:88–98.

Chuang, C. Y. 1967. A clinical investigation of asthmatics in the Misurata area, Libya, North Africa. J. Formosan Med. Assoc. 28 May. 66:256–271.

Citron, K. M., and Pepys, J. 1964. An investigation of asthma among the Tristan da Cunha Islanders. Br. J. Dis. Chest 58:119–23.

Collomb, H. 1964. Psychosomatic conditions in Africa. Transcult. Psychiatr. Res. Rev. 1:130–134.

Cooper, B. 1964. The epidemiological approach to psychosomatic medicine. J. Psychosom. Res. 8:9–15.

Cruz-Coke, R., Etcheverry, R., and Nagel, R. 1964. Influence of migration on the blood pressure of Eastern Islanders. Lancet 1:697–699.

Danaraj, T. J., et al. 1959. Ethnic group differences in coronary heart disease in Singapore—An analysis of necropsy records. Am. Heart J. 58:516–526.

Donnison, C. P. 1938. Civilization and Disease. William Wood & Co., Baltimore.

Dubreuil, G., and Wittkower, E. D. 1976. Primary prevention. A combined psychiatric-anthropological appraisal. In: J. Westermeyer (ed.), Anthropology and Mental Health: Setting a New Course. Mouton Publishers, The Hague.

Dunbar, F. 1946. Emotions and Bodily Changes. Columbia University Press, New York.

Ehrstrom, M. C. 1951. Medical studies in North Greenland 1948–1949; Allergic diseases and pulmonary emphysema. Acta. Med. Scand. 140:317–323.

Eitinger, L. 1971. Acute and chronic psychiatric and psychosomatic reactions in concentration camp survivors in society. In: L. Levi (ed.), Stress and Disease. Vol. 1. Oxford University Press, Oxford.

El Mehairy, M. M., and El Tarabishy, N., et al. 1965. Observations on the incidence of allergic disorders in a village in the United Arab Republic. Ann. Allergy 23:93–99.

Eriksson-Lihr, Z. 1955. Special features in allergy in children. Acta Allergol. 8:289.

Freeman, E. H., Feingold, B. F., and Schlesinger, K., et al. 1964. Psychological variables in allergic disorders: A review. Psychosom. Med. 26:543–574.

Garcia-Palmieri, M., Costas, R., and Gordon, T., et al. 1972. Differences in coronary heart disease in Honolulu, Puerto Rico, and Framingham. Paper presented at the 45th Scientific Session of American Heart Association, Dallas.

Garma, A. 1950. Gastric neurosis. Int. J. Psychoanal. 31:53.

Glass, D. C. 1977. Behavior Patterns, Stress, and Coronary Disease. Halsted Press, New York.

Glazer, I. 1969. Etiologic factors of bronchial asthma in Israel. Int. Arch. Allergy Appl. Immunol. 36:172–179.

Graham, P. J., Rutter, M. L., and Yule, W., et al. 1967. Childhood asthma: A psychosomatic disorder? Some epidemiological considerations. Br. J. Prevent. Soc. Med. 21:78–85.

Groen, J. 1970. Influence of social and cultural patterns on psychosomatic diseases. Psychother. Psychosom. 18:189–215.

Groen, J. 1971a. Psychosocial influences in bronchial asthma in society. In: L. Levi (ed.), Stress and Disease. Vol. 1. Oxford University Press, Oxford.

Groen, J. 1971b. Social change and psychosomatic disease in society. In: L. Levi (ed.), Stress and Disease. Vol. 1. Oxford University Press, Oxford.

Gupta, N. N. 1956. Influence of Hindu culture and social customs on psychosomatic disease in India. Psychosom. Med. 18(6):506–510.

Halliday, J. 1948. Psychosocial Medicine. W. W. Norton & Company, Inc., New York.

Harris, M. C., and Shure, N. 1956. Study of behavior patterns in asthmatic children. J. Allergy 27:312–323.

Henry, J. 1949. Anthropology and Psychosomatics. Psychosom. Med. 11:216–222.

Henry, J. P., and Cassel, J. C. 1969. Psychosocial factors in essential hypertension. Recent epidemiologic and animal experimental evidence. Am. J. Epidemiol. Sept. 90:171–200.

Hinkle, L. E., Jr., and Wolff, H. G. 1961. The Role of Emotional and Environmental Factors in Essential Hypertension. Proceedings of the Symposium on Pathogenesis of Essential Hypertension, p. 129. State Medical Publishing House, Prague.

Howard, A. 1979. Polynesia and Micronesia in psychiatric perspective. Transcult. Psychiatr. Res. Rev. Oct. 16.

Hsu, C. J., and Lin, T. C. 1965. Observation on the geriatric patients. Comprehensive study of 1,695 in-patients over 61-years-old in the department of internal medicine, N.T.U.H., between 1956–1962. J. Formosan Med. Assoc. 28 Aug. 64:426–439.

Ikemi, H., Ago, Y., and Nakagawa, S., et al. 1974. Psychosomatic mechanism under social changes in Japan. J. Psychosom. Res. Feb. 18:15–24.

Jenkins, C. D. 1977. Epidemiological studies of the psychosomatic aspects of coronary heart disease: A review Adv. Psychosom. Med. 9:1–19.

Kasl, S. V. 1977. Contributions of social epidemiology to studies in psychosomatic medicine. Adv. Psychosom. Med. 9:160–223.

Kessel, N., and Munro, A. 1964. Epidemiological studies in psychosomatic medicine. J. Psychosom. Res. 8:67–81.

Keys, A. 1970. Coronary heart disease in seven countries. Circulation (Supplement 1) 41:1–211.

Kiely, W. F., 1972. Coping styles. Adv. Psychosom. Med. 8:109–114.

Kraepelin, S. 1954. The frequency of bronchial asthma in Swedish school children. Acta Paediatr. Supplement 100, 43:149.

Labarthe, D., Reed, D., and Brody, J., et al. 1973. Health effects of modernization in Palau. Am. J. Epidemiol. 98:161–174.

Lask, A. 1966. Asthma, Attitude, and Milieu. J. B. Lippincott Company, Philadelphia.

Lauckner, J. R., Rankin, A. M., and Adi, F. C. 1961. Analysis of medical admissions to University College Hospital, Ibadan, 1958. West Afr. Med. J. 10:3–32.

Le Guerinel, N. 1971. Le language du corps chez l'Africain. Psychopathol. Afr. 7 (1):13–56.

Lehmann, J. P. 1972. Le vécu corporel et ses interprétations en pathologie africaine. A propso des inhibitions intellectuelles en milieu scolaire. Rev. Méd. Psychosom. 14:43–67.

Leigh, G., and Marley, E. 1967. Bronchial Asthma—A Genetic, Population, and Psychiatric Study. Pergamon Press, Oxford.

Leighton, A. H., Lambo, T. A., and Hughes, D. C., et al. 1963. Psychiatric Disorder Among the Yoruba. Cornell University Press, Ithaca, N.Y.

Lowenstein, F. W. 1961. Blood pressure in relation to age and sex in the tropics and subtropics. Lancet 1:389–392.

Maddocks, I., 1961. Possible absence of essential hypertension in two complete Pacific Island populations. Lancet 2:396–399.

Mann, G. V., Shaffer, R. D., and Rich, A., et al. 1965. Physical fitness and immunity to heart-disease in Masai. Lancet 2:1308–1310.

Marmot, M. 1977. Social and cultural factors in coronary heart disease in Japanese

Americans. Stanhope Proceedings of a Seminar: Migration and Health, pp. 57–77. Wellington, New Zealand.

Marty, P., de M'Uzan, M., and David, C. 1963. L'investigation Psychosomatique. Presses Universitaires de France, Paris.

Mead, M. 1947. Concept of culture and psychosomatic approach. Psychiatry 10:57–76.

Mechanic, D. 1974. Discussion of research programs on relations between stressful life events and episodes of physical illness. In: B. S. Dohrenwend and B. P. Dohrenwend (eds.), Stressful Life Events: Their Nature and Effects, pp. 87–97. John Wiley & Sons, Inc., New York.

Medalie, J. H., Kahn, H. A., and Neufeld, H. N., et al. 1973. Myocardial infarction over a five-year period. I. Prevalence, incidence, and mortality experience. J. Chronic Dis. 26:63–84.

Muir, C. S., 1960. Coronary heart disease in seven racial groups in Singapore. Br. Heart J. 22:45–53.

Nathanson, C. A., and Rhyne, M. B. 1970. Social and cultural factors associated with asthmatic symptoms in children. Soc. Sci. Med. 4:293–306.

Osfeld, A. M., and D'Atri, D. A. 1977. Rapid sociocultural change and high blood pressure. Adv. Psychosom. Med. 9:20–37.

Parhad, L. 1965. The cultural-social conditions of treatment in a psychiatric out-patient department in Kuwait. Int. J. Soc. Psychiatry. 11:14–19.

Paulley, J. W. 1950. Ulcerative colitis: Study of 173 cases. Gastroenterology 16:566–576.

Paulley, J. W. 1975. Cultural influences on the incidence and pattern of disease. Psychother. Psychosom. 26 (1):2–11.

Payet, M., Sankale, M., Pene, P., Bao, O., Moulanier, M., Sow, A. M., and Seck, I. 1962. Le contexte psychosomatique de l'ulcère chez le Noir Africain (à propos de 50 cas observés a Dakar). Bull. Soc. Méd. Afr. Noire langue Fr. 7:444–450.

Pflanz, M. 1971. Epidemiological and sociocultural factors in the etiology of duodenal ulcer. Adv. Psychosom. Med. 6:121–151.

Pflanz, M. P. 1966. Soziale and epidemiologische aspekte der psychosomatischen medizin. Proceedings of the 4th World Congress of Psychiatry, pp. 566–569. Madrid.

Prior, I. A. M. 1971. The price of civilization. Nutr. Today 6 (4):2–11.

Prior, I. A. M. 1977. Migration and physical illness. Adv. Psychosom. Med. 9:105–131.

Rahe, R. H., Meyer, M., and Smith, M. 1964. Social stress and illness onset. J. Psychosom. Res. 8:35–44.

Raper, A. B. 1958. The incidence of peptic ulceration in some African tribal groups. Trans. R. Soc. Trop. Med. Hyg. 52 (6):535–546.

Reed, D. 1973. Health effects of modernization in Micronesia. In: R. W. Force and B. Bishop (eds.), The Impact of Urban Centers in the Pacific. Pacific Science Association, Honolulu.

Reed, D., Labarthe, D., and Stallones, R. 1970. Health effects of Westernization and migration among Chamorros. Am. J. Epidemiol. 92 (2):94–112.

Ruesch, J., and Bateson, G. 1951. Communication: The Social Matrix of Psychiatry. W. W. Norton & Company, Inc., New York.

Schultze, V. E., and Schwab, E. H., 1936. Arteriolar hypertension in American negro. Am. Heart J. 11:66–74.

Scotch, N. A. 1960. A preliminary report on the relation of sociocultural factors to hypertension among the Zulus. Ann. N. Y. Acad. Sci. 84:1000–1009.

Scotch, N. A., and Geiger, H. J. 1963. The epidemiology of essential hypertension.

11. Psychologic and sociocultural factors in etiology. J. Chronic Dis. 16:1183–1213.

Selye, H. 1956. The Stress of Life. McGraw-Hill Book Company, New York.

Selye, H. 1974. Stress Without Distress. J. B. Lippincott Company, Philadelphia.

Shore, J. H., and Stone, D. L. 1973. Duodenal ulcer among northwest coastal Indian women. Am. J. Psychiatry 130 (7):774–777.

Singer, K. 1975. The role of culture in psychosomatic disorders. Psychother. Psychosom. 26 (5):257–264.

Stanhope, M. 1977. The Tokelau Island migrant study. Prevalence of common conditions in atoll and New Zealand dwellers compared. Stanhope Proceedings of a Seminar, pp. 99–109. Wellington, New Zealand.

Stenhouse, N. S., and McCall, M. G. 1970. Differential mortality from cardiovascular disease in migrants from England and Wales, Scotland, and Italy, and native born Australians. J. Chronic Dis. 23:423–431.

Susser, M. W., and Watson, W. 1971. Sociology in Medicine 2nd Ed. Oxford University Press, London.

Syme, L. 1970. Cultural mobility. FEJFAR WHO report on cardiovascular epidemiology in the Pacific, p. 51. World Health Organization.

Walker, A. R. 1963. Mortality from coronary heart disease and from cerebral vascular disease in the different racial populations in South Africa. South Afr. Med. J. 37:1155–1159.

Wigley, R. D., and MacLaurin, B. P. 1962. A study of ulcerative colitis in New Zealand, showing a low incidence in Maoris. Br. Med. J. 2:228–231.

Wittkower, E. D., and Dubreuil, G. 1973. Psychocultural stress in relation to mental illness. Soc. Sci. Med. 7 (9): 691–704.

Wittkower, E. D., and Engels, W. D. 1967. Psychophysiological allergic and skin disorders. In: A. M. Freedman, H. I. Kaplan, and B. J. Saddock (eds.), Comprehensive Textbook of Psychiatry. Vol. 2, 1685–1695. Williams & Wilkins Company, Baltimore.

Wolf, S. 1969. Psychosocial forces in myocardial infarction and sudden death. Circulation Nov. Supplements IV, XXIX, and XL, pp. 74–81.

Wolff, H. G. 1950a. Life stress and bodily disease; Formulation. Assoc. Res. Nerv. Ment. Dis. Proc. (1949). 29:1059–1094.

Wolff, H. G. 1950b. Life stress and cardiovascular disorders (Henry Jackson lecture). Circulation 1:187–203.

World Health Organization. 1964. Technical Report Series: 275 Psychosomatic disorders. Thirteenth Report of the WHO Expert Committee on Mental Health.

Yano, K., and Ueda, S. 1963. Coronary heart disease in Hiroshima, Japan: Analysis of the data at the initial examination, 1958–1960. Yale J. Biol. Med. 35:504–522.

Young, M., Benjamin, B., and Wallis, C. 1963. The mortality of widowers. Lancet 2:454–456.

Chapter 16

Cultural and Ethnic Factors in Reaction to Pain

Matisyohu Weisenberg

A cart passes by, upon which swings a man attached to a pole. Two large steel hooks have been inserted under the man's skin and muscles on both sides of his back. The man is hanging by ropes attached to the pole, which in turn is attached to the special cart. At first glance it might seem that this man is undergoing yet another form of punishment and torture. Further observation, however, indicates that the hanging man was specially honored by being chosen. His task, as practiced in certain parts of India, is to bless the children and crops throughout a series of villages. He is therefore transported by cart from place to place. What is amazing is that the chosen person does not seem to be suffering pain, even when he swings freely, hanging only by the hooks in his back; instead, he seems to be in a "state of exaltation." Even more amazing is what happens when the hooks are removed. The wounds heal rapidly, practically without any medical treatment. After approximately two weeks, the marks on his back are just about gone (*Kosambi* as described in Melzack, 1973).

The mother-to-be is busily working in the fields. Her child is about to be born. She stops working briefly to give birth. The mother does not seem to be in distress. Her husband, however, has gone to bed and is groaning and moaning as if he were in great pain. The husband remains in bed with the baby to recover from the birth while the mother goes back to work in the fields (description of the *Couvade* by Kroeber, 1948, as mentioned by Melzack, 1973).

A Papago Indian in the southwestern United States is admitted to the hospital with severe second- and third-degree burns. It seems that this condition has existed for at least several days, because the area is already infected. Burns cause extreme pain, which is not only caused by the original wound. Treatment itself is usually described as excruciatingly painful, and the required daily change of dressing takes at least an hour. Yet, with only a medium dosage of medication, the Papago Indian's reaction consists of only an occasional increase of pressure applied to his bed (Christopherson, Swartz, and Miller, 1966).

Upon entering the hospital ward, an Italian patient is groaning, moaning, and complaining to the nurse about the great deal of pain he is suffering. He seems to be almost in tears. When reminded that he still has to undergo several tests to determine the cause of his pain, the patient says that he does not care. He would like something to relieve the pain even before the diagnosis is known (Zborowski, 1969).

In turn, several beds away is a Jewish patient who is also complaining of pain. However, he refuses medication as long as the doctor has not yet identified what is wrong with him. He does not want simply to mask the pain. The Anglo-Saxon patient agrees with the need to be concerned about the meaning of the pain. However, the Anglo-Saxon patient feels there is no need to scream or cry about the pain. Besides, it really does not help anyway. When asked about pain, his Irish neighbor seems to deny that he has any at all (Zborowski, 1969).

The individuals described above are reacting to what are usually considered painful situations. Each individual responds in a different way. All are members of different ethnic and cultural groups. Their response or lack of response in the face of clearly painful stimuli, along with other puzzling findings, have had an important influence on our understanding and conceptualization of pain phenomena. These newer concepts have important implications for the daily practice of health care, and they also help to dispel a variety of well-entrenched stereotypes. A greater understanding of cultural and ethnic differences and their implications for pain perception and reactions can thus be achieved. This chapter first defines special terms used in light of current theoretical views of pain phenomena and then deals with cultural differences in pain perception and reaction (Weisenberg, 1975, 1977).

SOME DEFINITIONS

Zborowski (1969) has used the Kluckhohn (1944) definition of culture as the total way of life of a people, as the social legacy that the individual acquires from his group. Kroeber and Kluckhohn (1952, as quoted by DeVos and Hippler, 1969) refer to culture as consisting of historically derived and selected ideas and, especially, their attached values. In this chapter, terms like *culture*, *race*, and *ethnic* or *social grouping* are used as concepts referring to the influence of different social environments on behavior. Biological processes are also subject to social influences. People satisfy their biological needs, such as eating, drinking, and reproducing, according to a set of social norms. Similarly, pain as a biological process is also regulated by social norms. Some behaviors are sanctioned and approved; others are not.

To appreciate how social influence can regulate reactions to pain requires an understanding of pain as a concept. The International Association for the Study of Pain (IASP) Subcommittee on Taxonomy has defined pain as "an unpleasant sensory and emotional experience associated with actual or potential tissue damage, or described in terms of such damage" (1979, p. 250). The IASP group has emphasized that pain is always subjective. Each person learns what pain is on the basis of his own experiences. Pain is a sensation. However, it is also an unpleasant emotional experience. Pain may or may not be associated with tissue damage. There is no way to reliably distinguish tissue damage pain from pain not resulting from tissue damage, based upon subjective report. Although pain most often has a physical cause, nociceptive (harm-producing) stimulation is not synonymous with pain perception. Pain perception is always a psychological state.

THEORETICAL VIEWS OF PAIN

Theoretically, there have been many approaches to understanding the many puzzling aspects of pain phenomena. One of the most important recent approaches is the gate-control theory of pain (Melzack and Wall, 1965, 1970). Although the gating mechanism proposed by the theory is still a point of controversy, the basic conceptual approach has gained wide acceptance. According to the theory, pain has a sensory component similar to other sensory processes. It is discriminable in time, space, and intensity. However, pain also has an essential aversive, cognitive, motivational, and emotional component that leads to behavior designed to escape or to avoid the stimulus. Different neurophysiological mechanisms have been described for each system. Higher cortical areas are involved in both discriminative and motivational systems influencing reactions on the basis of cognitive evaluation and past experience.

More than any other theoretical approach, gate-control theory emphasizes the tremendous role of psychological variables and their effect on the reaction to pain. Especially with chronic pain, successful pain control often involves changing the motivational component while the sensory component remains intact. Hypnosis, anxiety reduction, desensitization, attention-distraction, alleviation of depression, and other behavioral approaches can be effective alternatives and supplements to pharmacology and surgery in the control of pain; their effects are felt mostly on the motivational component of pain.

In a more recent statement on gate-control theory, Melzack and Dennis (1978) emphasized differences between chronic and acute pain. With acute pain, there is usually a well-defined cause and a characteristic time course whereby the pain disappears after the occurrence of healing. The rapid onset of pain is referred to as the *phasic* component. The more lasting persistent phase is referred to as the *tonic* component. The tonic component serves as a means of fostering rest, care, and protection to the damaged area so as to promote healing.

However, with chronic pain, the tonic component may continue even after healing has occurred. It can be affected by memories of past experience that cause it to produce abnormal nerve firing patterns. Thus, once the pain is under way, the role of neuromas, nerve injury, or other physical damage begins to be of lesser importance. Therapy is required to affect abnormal nerve firing patterns. Once the person is free from the influence of these patterns, even temporarily, he can begin to maintain normal activity. Normal activity, in turn, fosters patterns of activity that inhibit abnormal firing. These abnormal firing mechanisms can be affected by multiple inputs that include antidepressant drugs, electrical stimulation, anesthetic blocks, and the establishment of realistic goals for the patient to achieve to make life worth living.

Recently, an endogenous pain control system has been discovered in the brain (Cannon, Liebeskind, and Frenk, 1978). Among the other mechanisms, it seems that the body produces its own group of endogenous morphinelike substances called endorphins (Simon, Hiller, and Edelman, 1975; Hughes et al., 1975). However, a great deal is still unknown about these substances. Studies dealing with the endogenous pain control system provide a neurohumoral basis for the behavioral and psychological control of pain, perhaps even providing a basic mechanism for explaining cultural differences.

Behavioral approaches have stressed the consequences of pain as they are exhibited in the activities of the individual with pain (Fordyce, 1976, 1978). Much of the behavioral conceptualization of pain has developed as a result of dealing with chronic pain patients. These conceptualizations do not directly contradict neurophysiological or neurohumoral formulations. Instead, behavioral approaches mostly view pain phenomena from a different level of analysis.

According to Fordyce (1976, 1978), if there were no resulting pain behaviors, then there would be no pain problem. Pain behavior does not need to occur as a direct consequence of nociceptive stimulation. A person can perceive an experience ordinarily associated with nociceptive stimulation even without there being a nociceptive stimulus. In turn, the presence of a nociceptive stimulus does not necessarily lead to pain behavior. Suffering that occurs as a result of emotional distress can be mislabeled as pain. Pain behaviors may then occur. These behaviors are erroneously attributed to nociceptive stimulation.

Fordyce greatly stresses the distinction between acute and chronic pain. Acute, time-limited pain does lead to a variety of pain behaviors, e.g., grimacing, moaning, and limping. Acute pain expression is subject to learning and conditioning. However, because of its short time duration it is more readily tied to its nociceptive stimulus. Acute pain may require some temporary life-style changes; however, it usually does not lead to a lasting change in life-style.

Chronic pain, however, persists for an extended period of time. Symptom behaviors continue to occur and are therefore more readily subject to learning and conditioning, independent of the nociceptive stimuli that led to their original occurrence. In addition, the chronicity often leads to major, lasting changes in life-style, activities, and social relationships. Over time there is more and more rehearsal of sick behavior and less of well behavior. Once disability ceases, return to well behavior may become a formidable task.

One important behavioral concept that must be singled out is modeling. According to Bandura (1971), most of our learning takes place through a process of modeling, that is, observing how others react to circumstances in their environment and what the consequences are. Modeling applies to pain and to pain perception as well. Individuals can learn which actions lead to painful experiences, which behaviors are appropriate under such circumstances, and how others in a similar circumstance and with a similar background are capable of coping with the painful situation.

In the laboratory, Craig and Weiss (1971, 1972) and Craig and Neidermayer (1974) have demonstrated that pain tolerance is subject to the social influence of models in a laboratory situation. In one study (1971), subjects rated the intensity of incremental shocks following the rating of a confederate model. In one condition, the model tolerated a great deal of shock before labeling it as painful, while in a second condition he tolerated a great deal less before calling it painful. The high-tolerance group of subjects rated as painful shock a mean intensity of 8.65 milliamperes. The low-tolerance group rated a mean of 2.50 milliamperes as painful, which is about 70% less intense. Furthermore, Craig and Neidermayer (1974) were not able to demonstrate any heart rate or skin conductance differences between high- and low-tolerance groups, which shows that the subjects were not merely masking subjective discomfort.

Another study (Craig and Weiss, 1972) complemented the first by using a constant nonaversive shock. Each one of a group of subjects was paired with a model who rated the nonaversive shocks as increasingly painful. Compared to a control group, the model-paired subjects reported as painful those levels of shocks usually judged as nonaversive.

In the pain literature, modeling effects have been demonstrated as significant in clinical preparation for surgery (Melamed, 1977), in reducing the pain of treatment of burn patients (Fagerhaugh, 1974), and in a variety of other clinical and laboratory settings (Craig, 1978). In short, modeling processes can be an effective part of pain expression and control. It is even possible that modeling can affect sensory as well as motivational aspects of pain (Craig, 1978).

Modeling and social norms effectively can influence pain expression and control, even under the most excruciatingly painful circumstances, as demonstrated in studies of the burn-control unit. Strauss, Fagerhaugh, and Glaser (1974) and Fagerhaugh (1974) analyzed the effect of social interaction and modeling on pain expression in a burn unit. A burn unit characteristically has critically ill patients who are in open view of staff and of each other for an extended period of time from weeks to months. Burn patients suffer excruciating pain from the treatment process as well as from the original tissue damage. One patient stated: "I never imagined anything could be so painful. I thought the pain would never end. I don't know how I tolerated the pain. I always thought of myself as strong about tolerating pain. I was a dentist's delight, but this pain is indescribably terrible" (Fagerhaugh, 1974, p. 645).

A social modeling control system with strict norms is observable in the way patients may or may not express pain. Constant crying and complaints of pain are viewed as demoralizing to other patients as well as to staff. Patients learn to lean on each other for support and for pain control techniques.

These study descriptions show how effective modeling phenomena can be. Modeling processes probably operate in a similar manner among social-cultural groups. Members learn that some sensations are to be tolerated, while others are not. Similarly, some sensations are labeled as painful, while others are not. The modeling process is a shorthand, vicarious means of teaching a person the consequences of a behavior without necessitating trial and error experience.

Communication is an important function of pain that has been stressed, especially by psychiatry. Psychiatrically oriented approaches have been written mainly to account for reactions to chronic pain that have been refractory to routine medical/dental treatment.

Szasz (1955) speaks of pain as a mode of communication. Pain arises as a consequence of threatened loss of, or damage to, the body. The communication aspects of the pain are extremely important in understanding reactions to pain. At the first level are the straightforward facts, which the clinician requires to evaluate the physical symptom. The second level involves use of the pain complaint as a cry for help, and it is tied to the first level. At the third level of communication, pain can be viewed as a symbol of rejection in a situation in which the request for help has been frustrated. Pain complaints can become a form of aggression and a means of atoning for guilt.

Importantly, pain reactions often convey a great deal more than a signal that tissue damage is occurring. As Szasz (1955), Plainfield and Adler (1962), Zborowski (1969), and others have pointed out in discussing human reactions to pain, communication aspects are frequently over-looked. Pain reactions can mean "Don't hurt me," "Help me," "It's legitimate for me to get out of my daily responsibilities," "Look, I'm being punished," or "Hey, look, I am a real man."

Recent statements on pain have emphasized that pain is a complex phenomenon. It is not synonymous with tissue damage, although it certainly is related to it. Pain perception involves a basic sensory component as well as motivational components. Reactions to pain are subject to learning and conditioning. They are also subject to social influence. Most psychological and behavioral controls involve the motivational aspects of pain. It is very likely that cultural differences are also related to the motivational components of pain. In the following section these differences are discussed in light of the recent theoretical statements on pain.

UNDERSTANDING CULTURAL AND ETHNIC DIFFERENCES

Given that there are both motivational and sensory components of pain, it is likely that the motivational aspects are more important in producing cultural and ethnic differences in pain perception.

Behaviorally, the differing effects of motivational and sensory systems have been demonstrated in the study of the cultural reactions to pain by Sternbach and Tursky (1965). Yankee, Irish, Jewish, and Italian women were asked to respond in two different ways to electric shock stimulation. On one task (involving motivational aspects), they were asked to specify several points by means of the method of limits. The lower threshold was referred to as the point when the subject became aware of the stimulus, and the upper threshold was referred to as the point when "you tell us you don't want any more." Some subjects were coaxed to accept a higher level of shock. No ethnic group differences were obtained for the lower threshold level, but significant group differences were obtained for both upper thresholds. The Italians tolerated the least amount of shock and differed significantly from Yankee and Jewish subjects. The Irish were at the low end of the tolerance scale and did not significantly differ from other groups.

Subjects were then presented with a magnitude estimation task, involving sensory aspects requiring them to discriminate the differences in shock intensity by assigning appropriate numbers to a series of nine different stimuli compared to a standard shock, labeled as ten. No ethnic group differences were obtained. That is, the results obtained could not demonstrate differences in the sensory discrimination of pain stimuli. However, results were obtained to show differences in willingness to tolerate pain stimuli (motivational aspects).

Weisenberg et al. (1975) studied the reactions of black, white, and Puerto Rican patients awaiting dental treatment. Over three-fourths of the group were then experiencing pain, while almost an equivalent number expected their dental treatment to be painful. Dependent variables included measures of anxiety, attitudes toward pain, and palmar sweat prints obtained in the waiting room and in the dental chair. No physiological differences were obtained between the different cultural and ethnic groups. Differences between cultural and ethnic groups were obtained on trait anxiety (Spielberger, Gorsuch, and Lushene, 1970) and dental anxiety (Corah, 1969). Attitude differences were also obtained, reflecting relative willingness either to deny or to avoid dealing with the pain, or to get rid of the pain. This is shown by the responses given to items such as "The best way to handle pain is to ignore it," or "It is a sign of weakness to give in to pain," or "When I am sick I want the doctor to get rid of the pain even before he finds out what the trouble is." Puerto Rican patients showed the strongest endorsement of these items, the white showed the weakest, and blacks were in between. In general, Puerto Rican patients seemed to be the most anxious about pain. The white patients were at the opposite extreme, while the black patients were in between, except for the dental anxiety measure on which blacks yielded the lowest score. The two anxiety and two attitudinal measures were accurate enough to permit correct groupings of 18 out of 24 Puerto Ricans, 12 out of 25 blacks, and 16 out of 24 whites. Once more, motivational aspects stand out as important elements in accounting for cultural and ethnic differences.

Wolff and Langley (1968), in reviewing cultural factors in pain reactions, also emphasize the importance of attitudes: "It appears to be quite clear from the studies by Lambert, Libman, and Poser (1960), Poser (1963), and Sternbach and Tursky (1965) that cultural factors in terms of attitudinal variables, whether explicit or implicit, do indeed exert significant influences on pain perception" (p. 498).

The Lambert et al. study (1960) and the Poser studies (1963) indicated that differences between religious groups in the reaction to pain can be demonstrated when subjects are challenged by statements like "Jews (Christians) cannot tolerate pain as well as Christians (Jews)."

Buss and Portnoy (1967) have shown that challenge and group identification are not limited to religious groups. The investigators have demonstrated that the stronger the identification a person has with his group, the more willing he is to tolerate pain of electric shock to conform to his group norm under challenge. Subjects in an electric shock experiment first rated groups for strength of identification. After a baseline shock pain tolerance series, subjects were given false norms for tolerance regarding their reference group, such as "Russians have a greater tolerance for pain than Americans" (page 107). The greater the subject's identification with Americans, the greater was the increase in pain tolerance.

Although no cultural differences have been demonstrated showing that the basic underlying physiological mechanisms differ, this does not mean that physiological functioning does not differ. Attitudes can also affect physiological processes. Attitudes have been shown to affect autonomic functioning, as demonstrated by Tursky and Sternbach (1967) and Sternbach and Tursky (1965) in their study of reactions to the pain of electric shock. Yankees, defined as Protestants of British descent who have a phlegmatic, matter-of-fact orientation toward pain, showed the fastest rate of adaptation to electric shock of diphasic palmar skin potentials. Irish subjects, described as inhibiting their expression of suffering and concern for pain, consistently showed a lower palmar skin resistance. The orientation of the Italian subject toward the present was found in the positive correlation between upper pain threshold and heart rate (those with the highest threshold had the highest heart rate). The opposite was seen in Jewish subjects, who were future oriented in the clinic but not in the laboratory. Jews showed a negative correlation between upper threshold and heart rate (those with the highest upper threshold had the lowest heart rates).

Cultural differences have been shown to affect basic perceptual processes. Perception seems to be independent of physiological differences between groups. Identical sets of stimuli are perceived as similar within one social-cultural group and different within another (Tajfel, 1969). In a number of perceptual areas it is possible to specify and even control the variables that affect the perception and its resistance to change once formed. For example, Wrightsman (1960) was able to manipulate the amount of fear subjects felt while they waited for an injection. A subject's degree of anxiety seemed to correspond with the anxiety felt by other members of the subject's group, even if verbal communication between subjects was not allowed.

Pollis (1965) found that initial judgments made concerning an ambiguous pulse rate produced by an audiogenerator were more resistant to influence when made with a friend than when made either alone or with a stranger. In cases of emotional arousal, existing stereotypes are strengthened. Secord, Bevan, and Katz (1956) found more of an exaggeration of the differences between blacks and whites among prejudiced subjects. Similarly, in our society many social groups view the dentist as a person who inflicts pain. With the emotional arousal that occurs in the dental operatory, this stereotype may also become exaggerated. As a result, pain might seem greater for those holding this attitude toward dentists.

Undoubtedly, perception of pain is also affected by the groups to which a person belongs. Such differences in reactions to pain are not at all unexpected from the view of a theory of social comparisons (Festinger, 1950, 1954). Basically, the theory states that there exists a drive to test the validity of a person's judgment and opinions of the outside world. When outside sensory means for evaluation are reduced, the individual turns toward his social environment for validation of his judgments. Because pain is a private ambiguous situation, comparison with others helps to determine what reactions are appropriate. Is it permissible to cry? Does one have to "grin and bear it"? When is it permissible to ask for help? When is it appropriate to mask the pain with analgesics?

People learn to express their own reactions by observing the reactions of others. The models chosen are those who are similar to oneself, while those too divergent are rejected (Bandura and Whalen, 1966).

The first important source of comparison is the family, in which cultural norms are transmitted to the children. As Shoben and Borland (1954) have shown in their study of dental fears, the experiences and attitudes of the family toward dental care are the most important factors determining whether the person will react with anxiety to dental treatment, will avoid it for a long time, or will be uncooperative in the chair. Johnson and Baldwin (1968) also found that children whose mothers had high anxiety scores showed more negative behavior during an extraction than children of mothers with low anxiety scores.

Thus, cultural differences seem to involve some form of social comparison processes that undoubtedly include modeling and other social influence processes. Some aspects of pain expression are reinforced; others are not. Although perceptual processes are affected, most of the influence can be seen in attitudes and other motivational aspects of pain. No basic physiological differences per se have yet been demonstrated, although they may exist.

THE CURRENT STATE OF KNOWLEDGE
OF SOCIAL-CULTURAL REACTIONS TO PAIN

Several cultural and ethnic groups have been studied for reaction to pain under a variety of conditions, including both clinical and laboratory settings. These studies include Italians, Irish, Jews and Yankees (Sternbach and Tursky, 1965; Zborowski, 1969; Zola, 1966), blacks (Chapman and Jones, 1944; Merskey and Spear, 1964; Weisenberg et al., 1975; Woodrow et al., 1972), Eskimos and Indians (Meehan, Stoll, and Hardy, 1954), Puerto Ricans (Weisenberg et al., 1975), Papago Indians and Mexican Americans (Christopherson et al., 1966), and an assortment of other anthropological studies of groups around the world (Wolff and Langley, 1968). The recent interest in acupuncture has also led to a number of reports concerning oriental reactions to pain (Chapman, 1975).

Major differences between these groups seem to be related to what are commonly referred to as the tolerance or motivational components of pain, rather than as the discrimination of the pain sensation. Wolff and Langley (1968) have pointed out that these studies vary in quality. In general, there is a paucity of studies, and well-controlled studies are even less available.

In making generalizations from the available studies, it is important to view cultural differences in their entire context. For example, in a recent clinical study of whites, blacks, and orientals using a deep pain tolerance test (Woodrow et al., 1972), it was found that whites tolerated the greatest amount of pain, orientals the least, and blacks an in-between amount. This seems most surprising, considering the well-known stereotype of the stoic oriental. However, it is necessary to consider the conditions of testing and the influence of the tester on the outcome. Would the same results have been obtained with an oriental tester? Would the same results be obtained in the orient? Does tolerating more pain imply that less anesthetic will be used in later medical procedures?

In a similar vein, it is not at all clear how far the influence extends when cultural and ethnic variables are identified. Does influence affect the first generation only or does it carry through to several generations? At this stage of our knowledge we cannot say.

From the clinical standpoint, an easily used, standardized, independent measure of pain is badly needed. In recent years, a number of attempts have been made to construct verbal scales using a variety of pain descriptors (Melzack, 1975). What is not clear from these important efforts is how much these verbal scales are culture bound. Can a scale that is constructed in Montreal, Canada, be applied in Tel-Aviv, Israel? Wolff (1978) has claimed that these verbal scales are not easy to use with a population possessing a lower educational level. It is likely that a similar problem would exist when crossing cultures in which terms are different or unavailable. (For example, in Hebrew there is no separate term for the word *ache*.)

ADDITIONAL IMPLICATIONS OF CULTURAL DIFFERENCES

The implications of cultural differences go beyond basic knowledge of perceptual processes or pain measurement per se (Weisenberg, 1974).

Diagnosis of Disease

Pain is a private experience upon which the diagnosis of disease is frequently dependent. Routine clinical diagnosis relies heavily upon the patient's description of the degree of pain, its location, and the localization or diffuseness. For instance, in the diagnosis of temporomandibular joint disease, the patient's verbal report is vital. Often there is little radiographic evidence upon which to base a conclusion. Furthermore, even if joint destruction is apparent on x-rays, it is not really possible to say that a given amount of joint destruction will result in a given amount of pain. The patient is still the main source of information on the amount and type of pain he is experiencing. Such patient description is appropriate if it can be trusted to be reliable.

However, Zola's findings (1966) should also be considered. He contrasted Irish and Italian patients who came to an eye, ear, nose, and throat clinic. The Irishman was likely to confine his chief complaint to the eye, ear, nose, or throat while the Italian, even with a diagnosed eye or ear disorder, chose another part of the body. The Irishman more often than the Italian denied the presence of pain. The Irishman stated: "It was more a throbbing than a pain . . . not really pain, it feels more like sand in my eye" (page 623). The Irishman also tended to localize his problem. The Italian tended to speak of a diffuse difficulty. In the diagnosis of *otitis externa* for example, in answer to the question "Is there any pain?" the Irishman said, "There's a congestion . . . but it's a pressure, not really pain." The Italian answered, "Yes . . . if I rub it, it disappears. . . . I had a pain from my shoulder up to my neck and thought it might be a cold."

It thus becomes important for diagnosticians to realize that pain is communicated in many different ways. Knowledge of a patient's social and cultural background can help in understanding the communication.

Judging the "Correct" Response of the Patient

Practitioners frequently expect patients to behave in a certain prescribed manner. Patients who do not follow these expected patterns of behavior are often labeled as "crocks." Attempts are sometimes made to pass the patient on to someone else. By observing cultural and ethnic differences in the reaction to pain, the practitioner can learn that there is no one correct way to react to pain. Knowing these differences can, in turn, help to avoid prejudiced reactions to patients.

Pilowsky and Bond (1969) studied 21 females and 15 males suffering from malignant disease. The researchers recorded the number of times the patient asked for pain relief and the number of times the staff offered it on their own. Female patients were more likely than male patients to be provided with drugs to reduce pain on staff initiative, when these patients were very concerned about their pain or illness. Older patients were not given powerful analgesics as frequently and were not treated by the nursing staff on the staff's own initiative. Thus, relief from pain was more related to staff definition of what was appropriate than to degree of illness. Treatment in this case was determined by social characteristics of patients.

Treatment to Reduce Pain

There are a variety of treatment techniques available for producing relief from pain, which include chemical means, reassurance, relaxation, hypnosis, distraction, and acupuncture. There does not seem to be one best method despite the popularity of certain procedures, such as administering drugs. Knowledge of the patient's social-cultural background can increase the likelihood of suiting the treatment to the patient. For example, Zborowski (1969) found that Jewish patients resisted pain-masking analgesics given before determination of the diagnosis and future prognosis; by contrast, Italian patients were interested in immediate pain relief. Thus, reassurance regarding prognosis prior to treatment seems more important in treating the Jewish patient, while activities to relieve pain seem to be indicated first for the Italian patient.

Under conditions of high anxiety and pain, Beecher (1959) found that the pain relief obtained from morphine and from a placebo were closely matched (52% of patients relieved with morphine, 40% of patients relieved with placebos). Under conditions of lower anxiety, morphine was substantially more effective in relieving pain (89% of patients with morphine, 26% of patients with placebos). In general, Beecher determines the effectiveness of relief by placebos to be 35% of patients. We must thus be concerned not simply with relieving pain, but also with reducing anxiety. Anxiety relief not only makes the patient more comfortable, but also enhances the effectiveness of an anesthetic; this has been shown in presurgical studies (Egbert et al., 1963; Egbert et al., 1964).

In the study of black, white, and Puerto Rican patients coming for treatment to a dental emergency clinic (Weisenberg et al., 1975), Puerto Rican females displayed the highest level of anxiety. It would be likely, therefore, that they would receive the most pain relief from reassurance, placebos, or other means that would reduce their anxiety.

Dispelling Stereotypes

The study of cultural reactions to pain can affect stereotypes based on lack of research or poor methodology. For instance, Chapman and Jones (1944) conducted a study in which "a majority of the group were of Northern European stock; the remainder included 25 Southern Negroes, 15 Ukrainians, and 30 of Jewish and other Mediterranean races" (page 81). All subjects were tested for pain perception and pain reaction threshold using radiant heat. Eighteen of the 25 Negroes and a corresponding number of "Northern Europeans" were compared. Negroes perceived pain at a lower level and had tolerance levels closer to pain perception level than the Northern Europeans. The "Mediterranean races" were closer to the level of Negroes in pain perception and reaction, although they were more apt to protest being subjected to so intense a stimulus.

These findings, or "myths" as Zborowski (1969) calls them, seem to have persisted for many years despite the obvious overgeneralizations made on the basis of "25 Southern Negroes" and an unspecified but small number of "Mediterranean races." Current knowledge of the reactions of blacks tested by white examiners, for example, would have predicted low pain tolerance for the southern blacks (Katz, 1964).

More recent studies show different results. Merskey and Spear (1964) found no difference in pain reactions of 28 white and 11 Afro-Asian male medical students using the pressure algometer. Winsburg and Greenlick

(1968) found no difference in rated pain reaction between black and white obstetrical patients.

EVALUATIVE AND CONCLUDING COMMENT

Cultural and ethnic differences in the reaction to pain have been well documented. Evidence has been presented from a variety of different sources and disciplines. The research quality of the data varies greatly. In some cases the data are anecdotal (Christopherson, Swartz, and Miller, 1966), while in other instances the data are based upon laboratory study (Sternbach and Tursky, 1965). The most widely quoted study used a descriptive method of inquiry commonly found in anthropological studies (Zborowski, 1969).

Most studies have not been well controlled, nor have enough social-cultural groups been studied to expand theory and to achieve some of the desirable applications of this knowledge. The study of Chapman and Jones (1944) has been widely quoted. It is based upon "25 Southern Negroes, 15 Ukrainians, and 30 of Jewish and other Mediterranean races." Chapman and Jones (1944) used a small number of subjects from whom conclusions were drawn for several entire cultural and racial groups. The same criticism can be made of Zborowski (1969), in which a small number (146 for all four groups) of Veteran's Administration Hospital males has become the prototype of all Irish, Jewish, Italian, and Anglo-Saxon males.

Theoretically, pain is currently viewed as a complex phenomenon that includes both sensory and motivational components. Suffering is mostly associated with the motivational component of pain (Weisenberg, 1977). Most evidence today supports the association of cultural differences with the motivational components of pain. Specifically, the major findings obtained relate to differences in attitude toward pain. Attitude change, however, can represent a significant ingredient in the treatment of chronic pain (Fordyce, 1976).

The present state of cultural studies, however, has left a number of questions unanswered. It is not at all clear from these studies just what the developmental sequence of pain attitudes is. Are there stages of learning in which children acquire the pain response? The lack of information reflects the general state of few studies of pain reactions in children. Methodologically, it is also difficult to obtain a "pure" measure reflecting pain that is not based upon verbal report. Verbal report itself is difficult to use with pain, because it is a private, subjective reply. Just what does the child mean when he says it hurts?

Another unknown at this time is the effect of the mixing of cultures. When Zborowski (1969) describes the Irish, Italian, and Jewish reactions to pain, are these invariable? What are the effects of a dominant culture on these reactions? How many generations does it take to change the cultural influence? How do changes of environments and social groups affect the expression of pain?

The current state of research does permit a number of theoretical processes to be described in the acquisition and transference of cultural reactions to pain. Important mechanisms include social comparison processes (Festinger, 1950, 1954) and modeling (Craig, 1978). However, up to now, aside from a few laboratory studies, most of the work has been descriptive and *post hoc*. Very little attempt has been made to take the descriptive data and apply their conclusions in predictive studies. Predictive studies should deal with pathological, disease-related pain as found in the clinic and not simply with laboratory-induced pain. Beecher (1959) has argued that pain in the laboratory and pain in the clinic may not be the same. The implications of the pain itself also differ. However, for stimulus control, the laboratory is still desirable. The ideal studies would utilize both settings.

Although there is still much to be done, studies of cultural and ethnic differences as well as other variables have helped to change current concepts of pain and pain control. There are a number of important implications arising from cultural and ethnic differences in the reactions to pain, such as the need to study cultural and ethnic differences to assess pain properly. Such assessment is necessary for correct diagnosis and optimal treatment of pain. Diller (1980), for example, has shown how cultures differ in the language and concepts used to report pain. Proper knowledge of pain semantics is a necessity for accurate diagnosis within a given culture.

Knowledge of cultural differences also becomes important in dispelling stereotypes and prejudice. There is no one, correct way of reacting to pain. Thus, the study of cultural and ethnic differences in pain perception has both theoretical and practical application.

REFERENCES

Bandura, A. 1971. Analysis of modeling processes. In: A Bandura (ed.), Psychological Modeling. Atherton, Chicago, Ill.

Bandura, A., and Whalen, C. K. 1966. The influence of antecedent reinforcement and divergent modeling cues on patterns of self-reward. J. Pers. Soc. Psychol. 3:373–382.

Beecher, H. K. 1959. Measurement of Subjective Responses: Quantitative Effect of Drugs. Oxford University Press, New York.

Buss, A. H., and Portnoy, N. W. 1967. Pain tolerance and group identification. J. Pers. Soc. Psychol. 6:106–108.

Chapman, C. R. 1975. The management of chronic pain in the United States and Japan: A cross cultural comparison. Clin. Med. 82:39–47.

Chapman, W. P., and Jones, C. M. 1944. Variations in cutaneous and visceral pain sensitivity in normal subjects. J. Clin. Invest. 23:81–91.

Cannon, J. T., Liebeskind, J. C., and Frenk, H. 1978. Neural and neurochemical mechanisms of pain inhibition. In: R. A. Sternbach (ed.), The Psychology of Pain. Raven Press, New York.

Christopherson, V. A., Swartz, F. M., and Miller, B. H. 1966. Socio-cultural Correlates of Pain Response. University of Arizona, Tucson.

Corah, N. L. 1969. Development of a dental anxiety scale. J. Dent. Res. 48:596.

Craig, K. D. 1978. Social modeling influences on pain. In: R. A. Sternbach (ed.), The Psychology of Pain. Raven Press, New York.

Craig, K. D., and Neidermayer, H. 1974. Autonomic correlates of pain thresholds influenced by social modeling. J. Pers. Soc. Psychol. 29:246–252.

Craig, K. D., and Weiss, S. M. 1971. Vicarious influences on pain-threshold determinations. J. Pers. Soc. Psychol. 19:53–59.

Craig, K. D., and Weiss, S. M. 1972. Verbal reports of pain without noxious stimulation. Percept. Mot. Skills 34:943–948.

DeVos, G. A., and Hippler, A. E. 1969. Cultural psychology: Comparative studies of human behavior. In: G. Lindzey and E. Aronson (eds.), The Handbook of Social Psychology. Vol. 4. Addison-Wesley Publishing Company, Inc., Reading, Mass.

Diller, A. 1980. Cross-cultural pain semantics. Pain 9:9–26.

Egbert, L. D., Battit, G. E., Turndorf, H., and Beecher, H. K. 1963. The value of the preoperative visit by an anesthetist. JAMA 18:553–555.

Egbert, L. D., Battit, G. E., Welch, C. E., and Bartlett, M. D. 1964. Reduction of postoperative pain by encouragement and instruction of patients. N. Engl. J. Med. 270:825–827.

Fagerhaugh, S. Y. 1974. Pain expression and control on a burn care unit. Nurs. Outlook 22:645–650.

Festinger, L. 1950. Informal social communication. Psychol. Rev. 57:271–282.

Festinger, L. 1954. A theory of social comparison processes. Hum. Relat. 7:117–140.

Fordyce, W. E. 1976. Behavioral Methods for Chronic Pain and Illness. C. V. Mosby Company, St. Louis, Mo.

Fordyce, W. E. 1978. Learning processes in pain. In: R. A. Sternbach (ed.), The Psychology of Pain. Raven Press, New York.

Hughes, J., Smith, T. W., Kosterlitz, H. W., Fothergill, L. A., Morgan, B. A., and Morris, H. R. 1975. Identification of two related pentapeptides from the brain with potent opiate agonist activity. Nature 258:577–579.

International Association for the Study of Pain, Subcommittee on Taxonomy. 1979. Pain terms: A list with definitions and notes on usage. Pain 6:249–252.

Johnson, R., and Baldwin, D. C., Jr. 1968. Relationship of maternal anxiety to the behavior of young children undergoing dental extraction. J. Dent. Res. 47:801–805.

Katz, I. 1964. Review of evidence relating to effects of desegregation on the intellectual performance of Negroes. Am. Psychol. 19:381–399.

Kluckhohn, C. 1944. Mirror for Man: A Survey of Human Behavior and Social Attitudes. McGraw-Hill Book Company, New York.

Kroeber, A. L., and Kluckhorn, C. 1952. Culture: A critical review of concepts and definitions. Papers Peabody Museum 47, no. 1.

Lambert, W. E., Libman, E., and Poser, E. G. 1960. The effect of increased salience of a membership group on pain tolerance. J. Pers. 38:350–357.

Meehan, J. P., Stoll, A. M., and Hardy, J. D. 1954. Cutaneous pain threshold in native Alaskan Indian and Eskimo. J. Appl. Psychol. 6:297–400.

Melamed, B. G. 1977. Psychological preparation for hospitalization. In: S. Rachman (ed.), Contributions to Medical Psychology. Vol. 1. Pergamon Press, Oxford, England.

Melzack, R. 1973. The Puzzle of Pain. Basic Books, Inc., New York.

Melzack, R. 1975. The McGill pain questionnaire: Major properties and scoring methods. Pain 1:277–299.

Melzack, R., and Dennis, S. G. 1978. Neurophysiological foundations of pain. In: R. A. Sternbach (ed.), The Psychology of Pain. Raven Press, New York.

Melzack, R., and Wall, P. D. 1965. Pain mechanisms: A new theory. Science 150:971–979.

Melzack, R., and Wall, P. D. 1970. Psychophysiology of pain. Int. Anesthesiol. Clin. 8:3–34.

Merskey, H., and Spear, F. G. 1964. The reliability of the pressure algometer. Br. J. Soc. Clin. Psychol. 3:130–136.

Pilowsky, I., and Bond, M. R. 1969. Pain and its management in malignant disease. Psychosom. Med. 31:400–404.

Plainfield, S., and Adler, N. 1962. The meaning of pain. Dent. Clin. North Am. Nov., pp. 659–668.

Pollis, N. 1965. Relative stability of reference scales formed under individual togetherness and group situations. In: C. W. Sherif, M. Sherif, and R. E. Nebergall (eds.), Attitude and Attitude Change: The Social Judgment-Involvement Approach, pp. 207–211. W. B. Saunders Company, Philadelphia.

Poser, E. G. 1963. Some psychosocial determinants of pain tolerance. Paper presented at the 16th International Congress of Psychology, Washington, D. C.

Secord, P. F., Bevan, W. and Katz, B. 1956. The Negro stereotype and perceptual accentuation. J. Abnorm. Soc. Psychol. 53:78–83.

Shoben, E. J., and Borland, L. 1954. An empirical study of the etiology of dental fears. J. Clin. Psychol. 10:171–174.

Simon, E. J., Hiller, J. M., and Edelman, I. 1975. Solubilization of a stereo-specific opiate-macromolecular complex from rat brain. Science 190:389–390.

Spielberger, C. D., Gorsuch, R. L., and Lushene, R. F. 1970. Manual for the State-Trait Anxiety Inventory. Consulting Psychologists Press, Palo Alto, Calif.

Sternbach, R. A., and Tursky, B. 1965. Ethnic differences among housewives in psychophysical and skin potential responses to electric shock. Psychophysiology 1:241–246.

Strauss, A., Fagerhaugh, S. Y., and Glaser, B. 1974. Pain: An organizational-work-interactional perspective. Nurs. Outlook 22:560–566.

Szasz, T. S. 1955. The nature of pain. Arch. Neurol. Psychiatry 74:174–181.

Tajfel, H. 1969. Social and cultural factors in perception. In: G. Lindzey and E. Aronson (eds.), The Handbook of Social Psychology. Vol. 3. Addison-Wesley Publishing Company, Inc., Reading, Mass.

Tursky, B., and Sternbach, R. A. 1967. Further physiological correlates of ethnic differences in responses to shock. Psychophysiology 4:67–74.

Weisenberg, M. 1974. Cultural and racial reactions to pain. Paper presented at the American Association for the Advancement of Science Symposium on the Control of Pain, San Francisco, Calif.

Weisenberg, M. (ed.). 1975. Pain: Clinical and Experimental Perspectives. C. V. Mosby Company, St. Louis, Mo.

Weisenberg, M. 1977. Pain and pain control. Psychol. Bull. 84: 1008–1044.

Weisenberg, M., Kreindler, M. L., Schachat, R., and Werboff, J. 1975. Pain: Anxiety and attitudes in black, white, and Puerto Rican patients. Psychosom. Med. 37:123–135.

Winsburg, B., and Greenlick, M. 1968. Pain responses in Negro and White obstetrical patients. J. Health Soc. Behav. 9: 222–227.

Wolff, B. B. 1978. Behavioural measurement of human pain. In: R. A. Sternbach (ed.), The Psychology of Pain. Raven Press, New York.

Wolff, B. B., and Langley, S. 1968. Cultural factors and the response to pain: A review. Am. Anthropol. 70:494–501.

Woodrow, K. M., Friedman, G. D., Siegelaub, A. B., and Collen, M. F. 1972. Pain tolerance: Differences according to age, sex, and race. Psychosom. Med. 34:548–556.

Wrightsman, L. S. 1960. Effects of waiting with others on changes in level of felt anxiety. J. Abnorm. Soc. Psychol. 61:216–222.

Zborowski, M. 1969. People in Pain. Jossey-Bass, Inc., San Francisco.

Zola, J. K. 1966. Culture and symptoms: An analysis of patients' presenting complaints. Am. Sociol. Rev. 31:615–630.

INDEX

Acetaldehyde
  metabolism, 312–313
  stimulant effects, 315
Aesculapian authority, 73–74, 80
Affective disorders, *see also specific disorder*
  atypical, 255
  chronic, 255
  episodic, 255
  measurement, 129–130
  and past social status, 145–147
  provoking agents, 141–144
  and social class, 125–156
    research instruments, 126–129
  vulnerability factors, 144–145, 260–261
Affective psychoses, 254
  bipolar, sex difference in, 263
Africa, *see also specific African country*
  depression in, 43
    increased prevalence of, 265
  drinking habits in, 318, 329
  North, nuptial psychoses reported in, 203
  West
    Ndöp ritual, 206
    rural populations, paranoid schizophrenia among, 238
Africans, schizophrenic symptoms among, 237, 239
Age, and rates of mental illness, 182
Aggression
  abnormal expression of, among Japanese, 208–209
  and alcohol, 314
  patterns, correlated to societal expectations, 206–207
  restraint of, and psychosomatics, 407
  sex differences in, 195
Aging, stress associated with, 403
Agoraphobia, 192
Agringados, excessive drinking, 330
Alcohol
  beneficial effects, 315–317
  blood and brain concentration, 312
  correlated to suicide, 327
  and driving, 310, 312, 315, 325
  high doses, 311
  intoxication, 313–317

adaptive functions of, cultural comparisons, 317–323
  definition, 313
  disinhibitory effects, 314–315
  perils, 315–316
  pleasurable effects, 313–317
  sedative effects, 314
  stimulant effects, 315
  low doses, effects, 310–311
  metabolism, 311–312
  psychophysiology, 310–313
  response to, racial differences in, 312–313
  use
    correlated with climate, 322
    correlated with folklore themes, 321
    related to cultural change, 327–332
Alcohol abuse, 309–338
  cultural variation in, 11–12
  motivation for, 11
  prevalence, 11–12
Alcoholism
  and anxiety, 327
  definition, 316
  among Irish, 226
  prevalence, in U.S., 261
Algeria, prevalence of ulcers in, 396
Algonquin Indians, Windigo syndrome, 213–214, 370
Allergic disorder, psychological factors in, 398
Aluts, transvestism among, 348
Amae, 36
Amaeru, *see* Japanese, dependency need
Amok, 202, 208, 265
Androgyny, 185
Anti-psychiatry, 97–98
Antisocial behavior, 195
Anxiety
  association with alcoholism, 327
  biological function, 19
  caused by educational system, 204–205
  national differences in, 288–290
  and pain, 421–422
  relief, 427
  self-report of, study using,